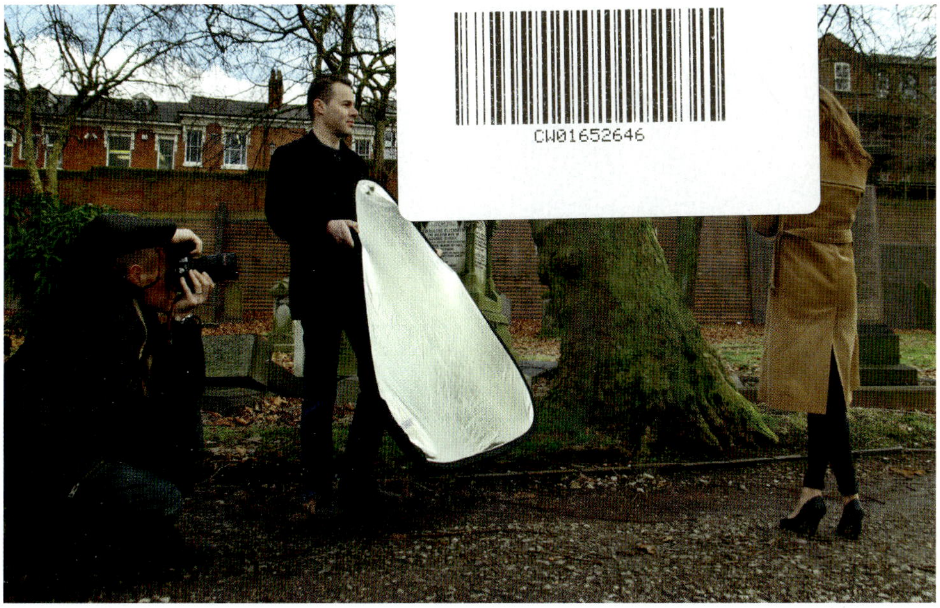

Welcome...

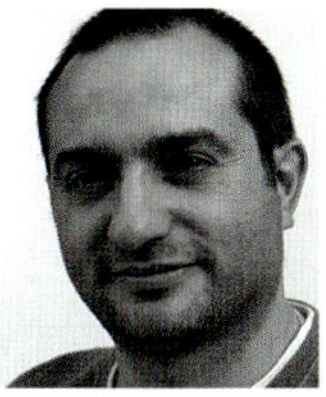

"If you've recently started using a digital SLR or Compact System Camera, you have taken a major step towards shooting better pictures. Boasting an incredible level of versatility, delivering superb image quality and forming the heart of a system that can be expanded with lenses, flashguns and various other accessories, these interchangeable-lens cameras has led to a revolution in photography. While these digital cameras are relatively easy to use for simple 'snapshot' photography, the truth is that getting the very best from your camera kit and, more importantly, developing the creative side of your photography, requires some time and dedication to learning new techniques and skills. The good news is that *Getting Started in Digital Photography*, produced by the experts at *Digital SLR Photography* magazine, is packed with information, advice and techniques that will help you become a better photographer. If you've ever looked at images from the professionals and wondered how they managed to get such great results, then this guide is for you. We've covered all the basics of photography and provided tried and tested practical techniques for shooting stunning images, along with expert advice to choosing the best gear and pages of inspiring images to get your creative juices flowing. Good luck with your photography. All the best!"

DANIEL LEZANO, EDITOR

Meet our digital photography experts

All our experts are team members or regular contributors to *Digital SLR Photography* magazine. For more expert advice and inspiration, pick up the latest issue, available on the second Tuesday of every month. For further information, visit the magazine's website at www.digitalslrphoto.com

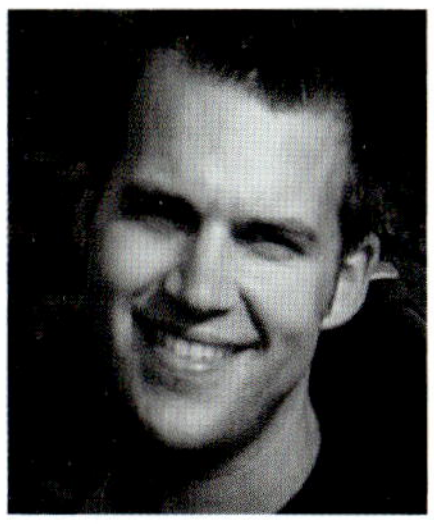

ROSS HODDINOTT
A regular contributor to *Digital SLR Photography*, Ross is an award-winning nature photographer, specialising in natural history and macro photography.

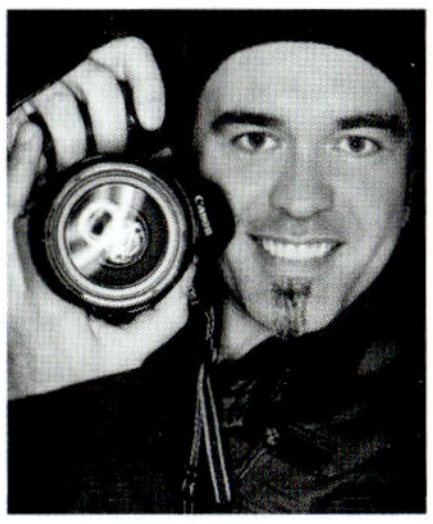

BRETT HARKNESS
Brett is one of the UK's leading portrait and social photographers and runs regular photo workshops. For further details, visit: www.bretttharkness.com

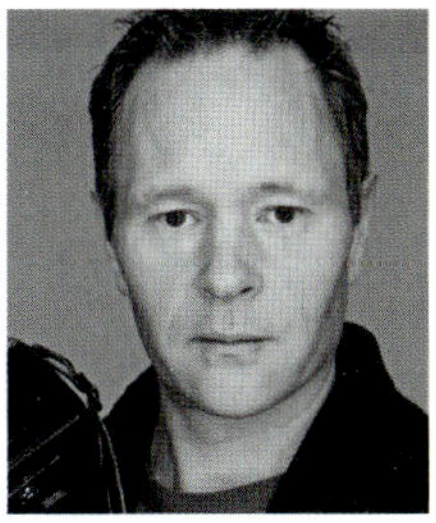

PAUL WARD
Paul is a professional photographer who regularly contributes to *Digital SLR Photography*. He's expert in all types of photography from portraits to landscapes.

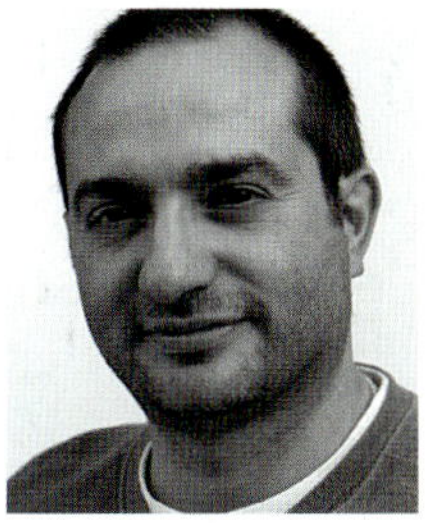

DANIEL LEZANO
Editor Lezano is passionate about photography and has been taking pictures for over 25 years. He is especially keen on shooting portraits with natural light and in the studio.

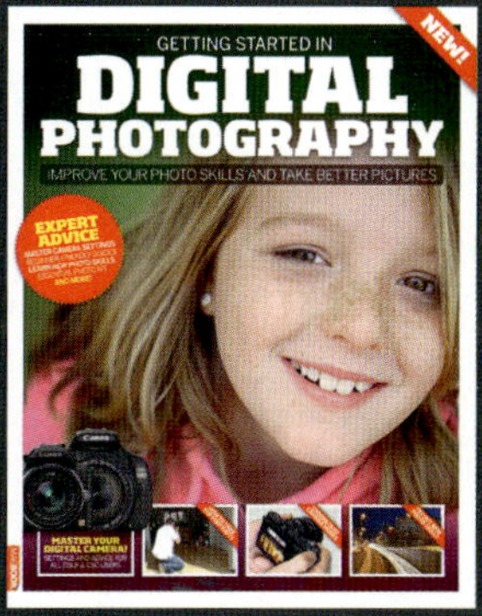

COVER IMAGE: LEE FROST

Produced by *Digital SLR Photography* at:
6 Swan Court, Cygnet Park,
Peterborough, Cambs PE7 8GX
Phone: 01733 567401. Fax 01733 352650
Email: enquiries@digitalslrphoto.com
Online: www.digitalslrphoto.com

Editorial

To contact editorial phone: 01733 567401

Editor **Daniel Lezano**
daniel_lezano@dennis.co.uk

Art Editor **Luke Marsh**
luke_marsh@dennis.co.uk

Features Editor **Caroline Wilkinson**
caroline_wilkinson@dennis.co.uk

Designer **Luke Medler**
luke_medler@dennis.co.uk

Editorial Co-ordinator **Jo Lezano**
jo_lezano@dennis.co.uk

Editorial contributors: Brett Harkness, Ross Hoddinott, Lee Frost, Bjorn Thomassen, Paul Ward & Donna Willingham

Advertising & Production

Display & Classifield Sales: 0207 907 6651

Advertising Sales **Guy Scott-Wilson**
guy_scott-wilson@dennis.co.uk

Sales Executive **Joshua Rouse**
joshua_rouse@dennis.co.uk

Production Controller **Dan Stark**
dan_stark@dennis.co.uk

Publishing & Marketing

NICKY BAKER DIGITAL PRODUCTION MANAGER
DHARMESH MISTRY BOOKAZINE MANAGER
ROBIN RYAN PRODUCTION DIRECTOR
JULIAN LLOYD-EVANS MD OF ADVERTISING
DAVID BARKER NEWSTRADE DIRECTOR
BRETT REYNOLDS CHIEF OPERATING OFFICER
IAN LEGGETT GROUP FINANCE DIRECTOR
JAMES TYE CHIEF EXECUTIVE
FELIX DENNIS CHAIRMAN

Getting Started in Digital Photography ISBN 1-907779-47-7
Printed by Benham Goodhead Print (BGP)

CONTENTS

Understand your camera

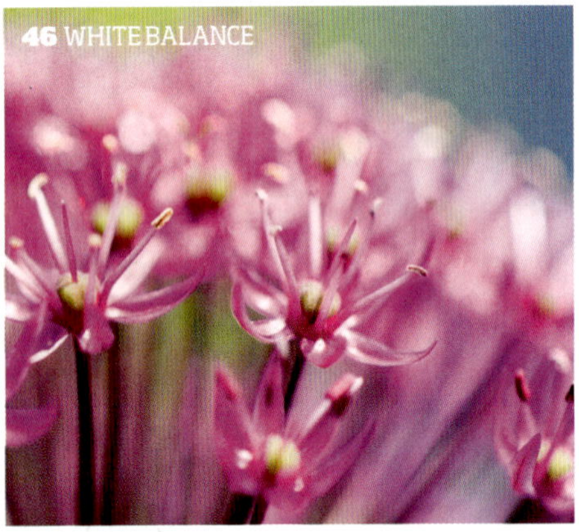
46 WHITE BALANCE

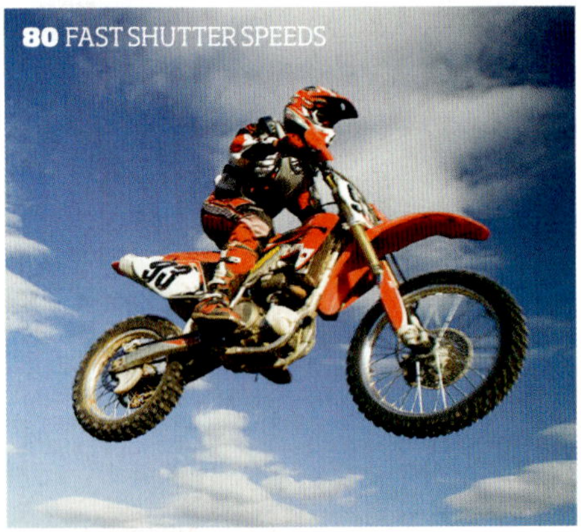
80 FAST SHUTTER SPEEDS

TURN TO PAGE 122 TO FIND OUT ABOUT OUR FANTASTIC SUBSCRIPTION OFFERS

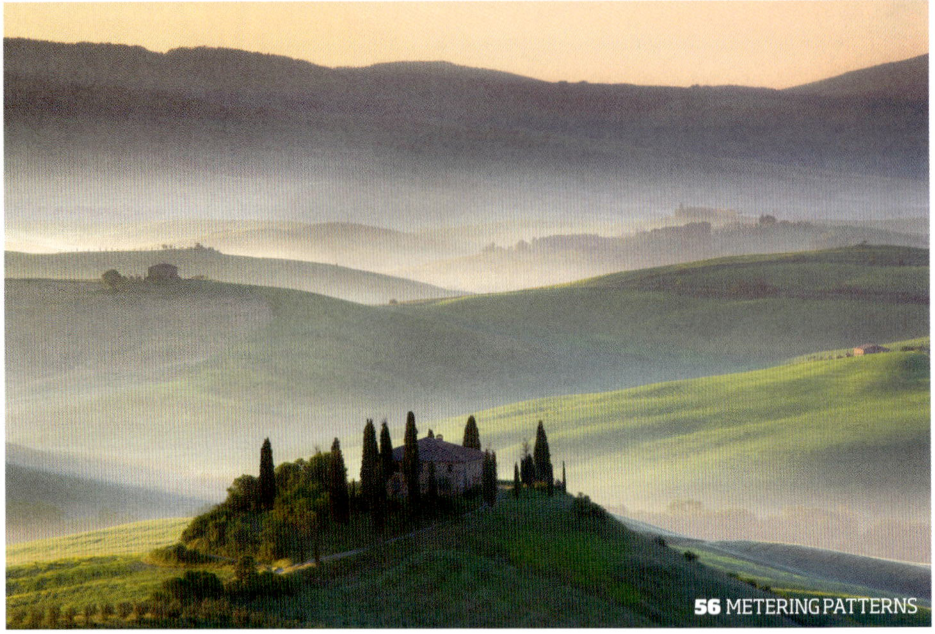
56 METERING PATTERNS

Photo technique

Choosing & using kit

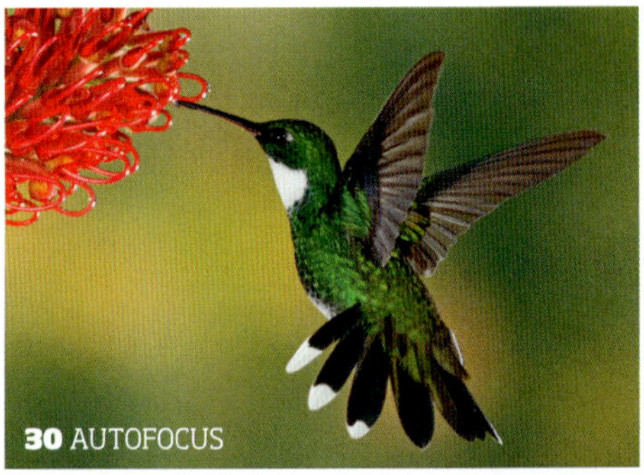
30 AUTOFOCUS

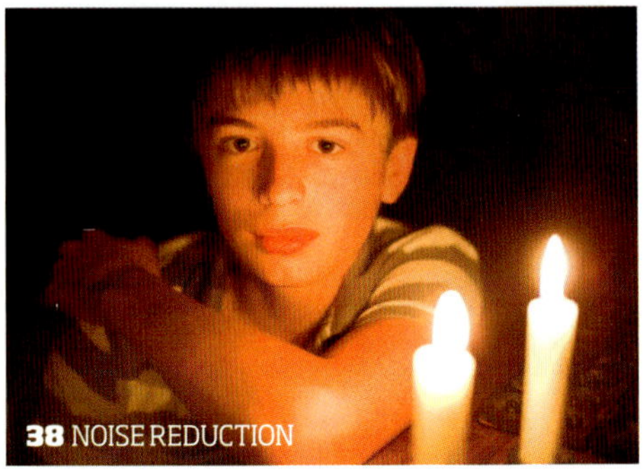
38 NOISE REDUCTION

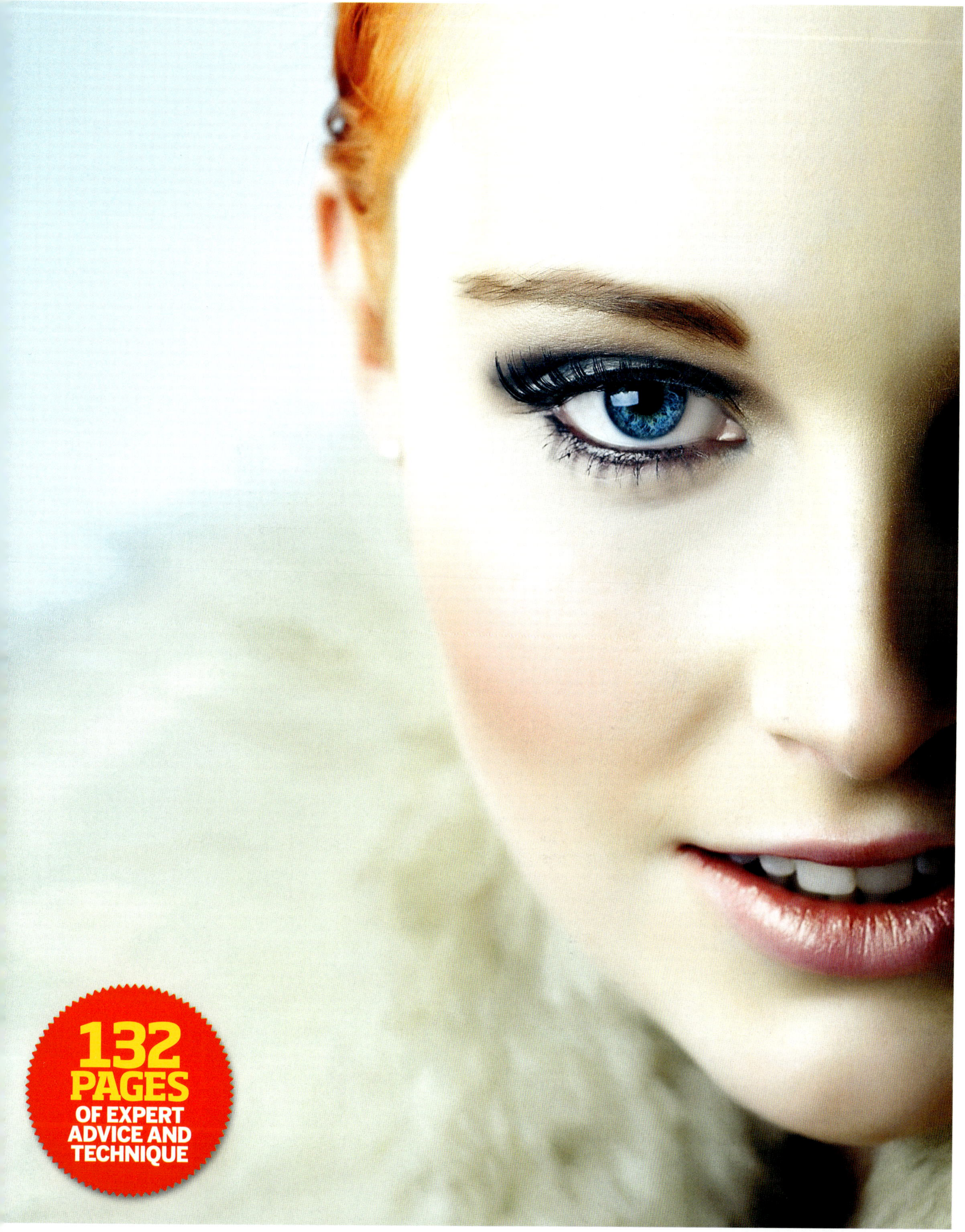
132
PAGES
OF EXPERT
ADVICE AND
TECHNIQUE

Interchangeable-lens cameras

Understanding how your camera works is key to getting the best from it. We take a look at the main features you'll find on digital SLRs and Compact System Cameras

UNTIL VERY RECENTLY, if you wanted a digital camera with interchangeable lenses, then your choice was easy: most of us would opt for a 35mm-based digital SLR, (while a minority of pros chose a medium-format DSLR costing tens of thousands of pounds). However, in the last couple of years, Compact System Cameras (CSCs), also known as 'hybrids', have come on to the scene, offering an alternative option.

This latest generation has many similarities to DSLRs, offering virtually identical specifications and operating in a similar manner, albeit with one or two major differences. The handling, features and performance of digital SLRs have been refined and improved over the years so that users find them as simple as possible to operate. It makes sense then, since most manufacturers of CSCs also produce digital SLRs, that CSCs feature similar operating systems to their SLR counterparts. Not only does this mean CSCs have the potential to be great performers as its technology is already quite advanced, but it makes the crossover from one camera type to another fairly easy for those who want to make the transition.

In this section of the guide, we'll be looking at all the key features of your digital camera, explaining what they do and how you should use them to improve the quality of your images. We'll also be comparing and contrasting the two main interchangeable-lens camera systems. As you'll discover, both share many common areas and only a few practical differences. In this month's issue, we provide a general overview of a camera's main functions and look in detail at the heart of every digital camera: the image sensor.

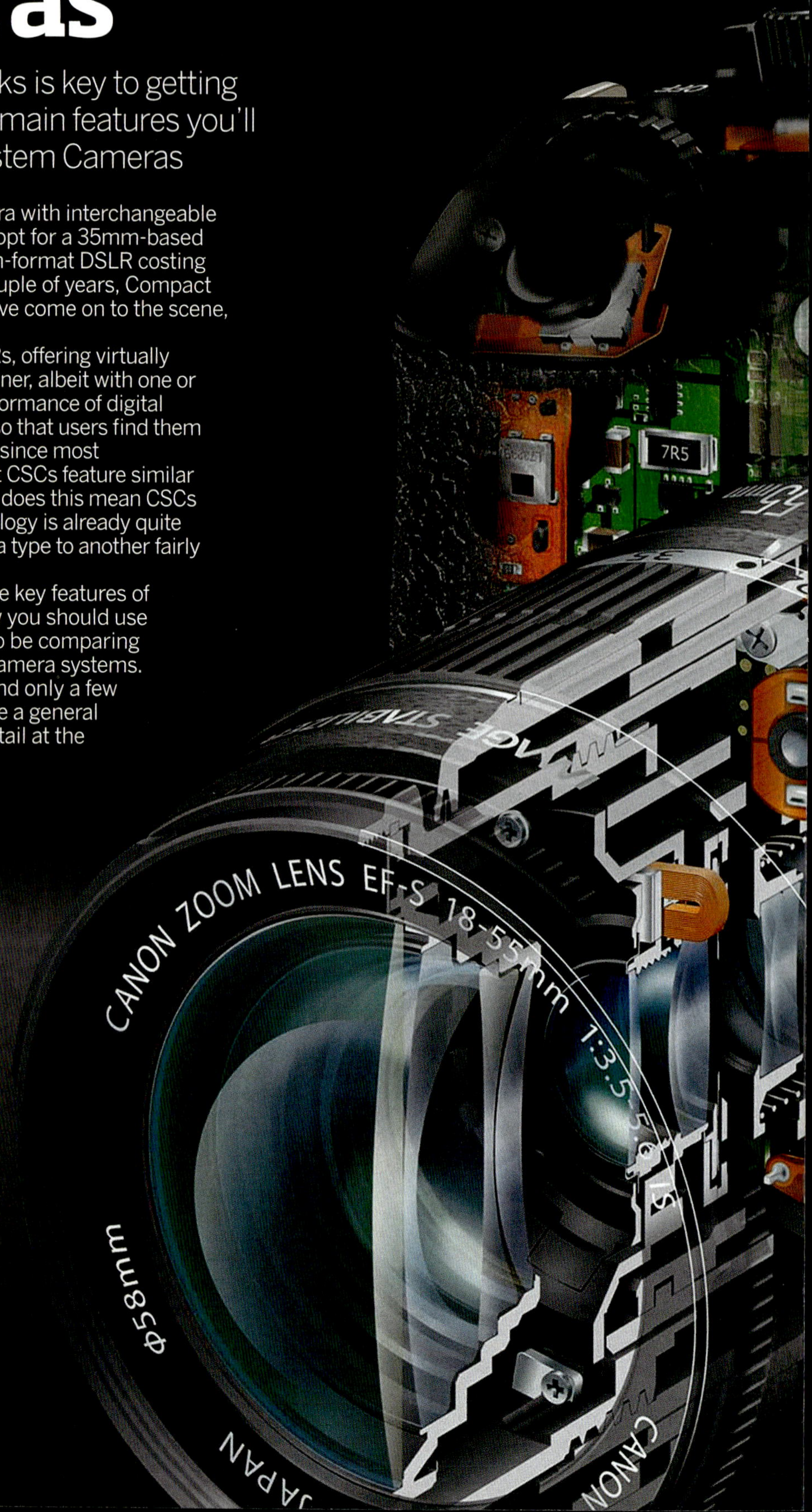

Know your camera inside & out!
Digital cameras boast an incredible amount of technology. Our guide aims to explain all the key features and reveal a few secrets, too.

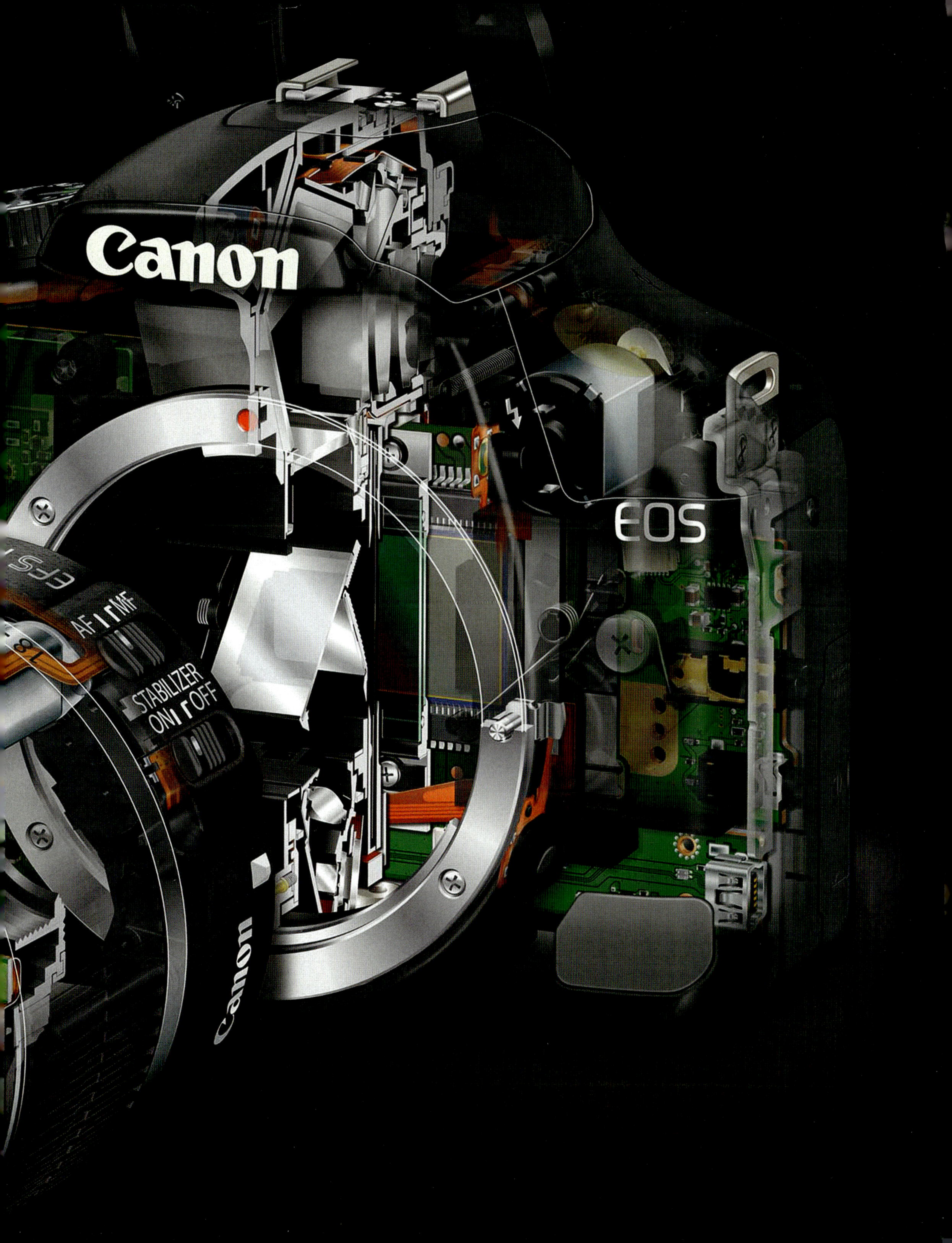
Canon
EOS
AF MF
STABILIZER
ON OFF
Canon

Anatomy of an interchangeable-lens camera

Find your way around your digital camera with our annotated guide. As you'll discover, there are more similarities than differences between a DSLR and a CSC!

REGARDLESS OF WHETHER you're using a digital SLR (DSLR) or a Compact System Camera (CSC), you have in your possession an incredibly impressive piece of equipment. Your camera is packed with cutting-edge technology designed to deliver perfect images for the vast majority of shooting situations, as well as, more recently, HD video. Despite all these features, the cameras are also designed to be as easy to use as possible, with some models managing to be simpler to use than others. That said, with so much on offer, it's easy to get confused as to the purpose of some functions, or to totally overlook useful facilities that could make your life easier. No problem: we're here to help. Our informative guide covers everything you need to know to get the most from your camera and, more importantly, help you take better pictures.

DID YOU KNOW?
With your camera set to single-shot AF and single frame advance, once you have pressed the shutter release to take the initial image, releasing it only to the halfway stage locks the AF and exposure settings for the next shot.

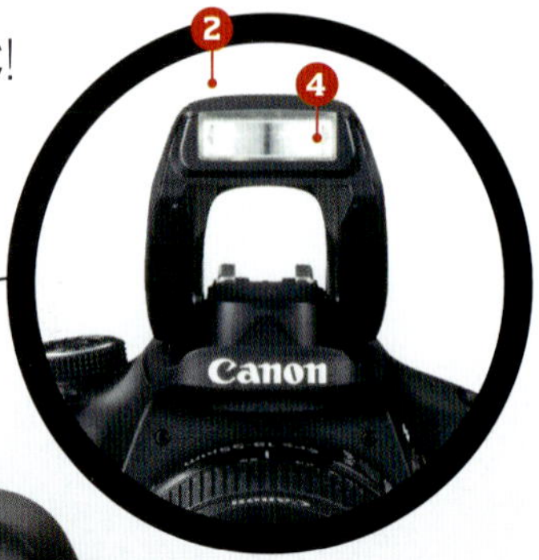

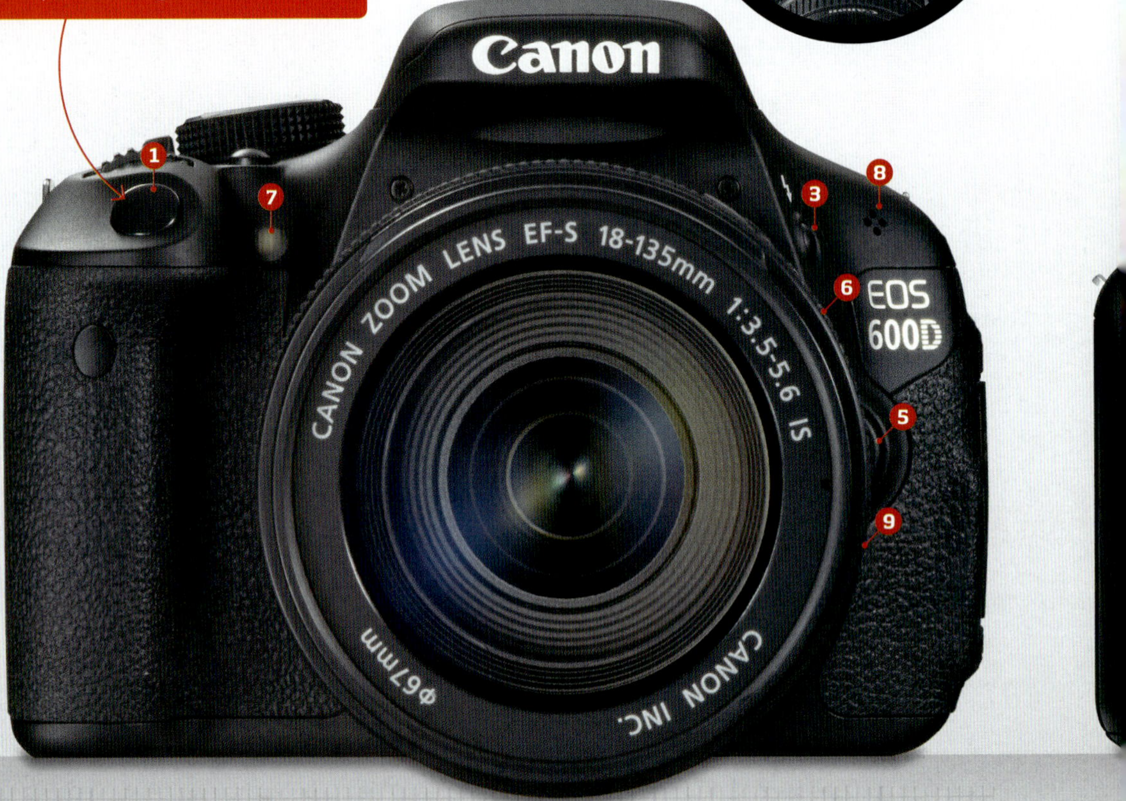

Key features and controls found on DSLRs & CSCs

1) Shutter release button: The shutter button has a two-stage action – press halfway to activate the AF and metering systems and fully depress it to take the exposure.

Did you know? If you've left your camera switched on for a few minutes and it's entered standby mode to preserve battery power, tap the shutter release gently to switch it back on. Also worth noting is that many cameras have a custom function that can set whether the shutter release locks AF, exposure or both.

2) Integral flash: Found on the vast majority of cameras. However, a few top-end DSLRs and some CSCs lack this facility, catering for flash via the hotshoe mount only. Many CSCs lacking an integral flash have a small clip-on unit supplied along with the camera. Flash coverage is usually good enough for a moderate wide-angle lens and subjects within a couple of metres away. All offer a choice of flash modes. The auto mode is fine for capturing standard low-light portraits, but there are a number of flash modes on offer that allow for far more creativity, including slow-sync and rear-curtain sync.

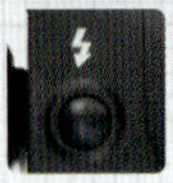

3) Flash-up button: Press to pop up the integral flash (if your camera has one). While some cameras automatically raise the flash when required in certain fully-automatic modes, all require you to activate it manually should you wish to use it in a semi-auto or manual exposure mode.

Did you know? With some cameras, you can press and hold the Flash-up button to access additional flash modes, rather than needing to use the menu system to do this. With most models, a separate flash mode button on the four-way control is used to do this.

4) AF illuminator lamp: In low light, your camera can struggle to focus. The AF lamp, housed in the integral flash or on the front of the camera body, fires a flash burst or a patterned beam of light to aid the AF lock on the subject.

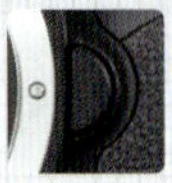

5) Lens release button: Press this button to allow the lens to be removed.

Did you know? Nikon's lenses are removed in the opposite direction to most other brands.

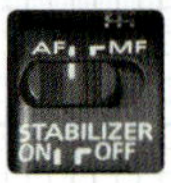

6) AF/M: This switch, found on the lens or the camera body, is used to set the focusing to manual or autofocus.

7) Self-timer lamp: Visually indicates the self-timer countdown.

8) Microphone: Used to record audio when shooting movies. Can also be used on some cameras to 'write' audio notes to images.

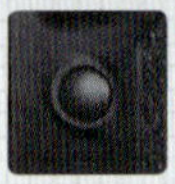

9) Depth-of-field preview: Once popular on film SLRs, this is now less common. Using it closes the lens iris to the selected aperture, allowing you to preview the extent of depth-of-field in the viewfinder. However, this darkens the viewfinder image, making it tricky to use, especially with small apertures. Cameras with electronic viewfinders boost the brightness when using depth-of-field preview, which is an advantage over optical viewfinders.

Did you know? Canon users can use this function with LiveView, allowing depth-of-field to be more easily assessed on the LCD monitor than is possible with the viewfinder.

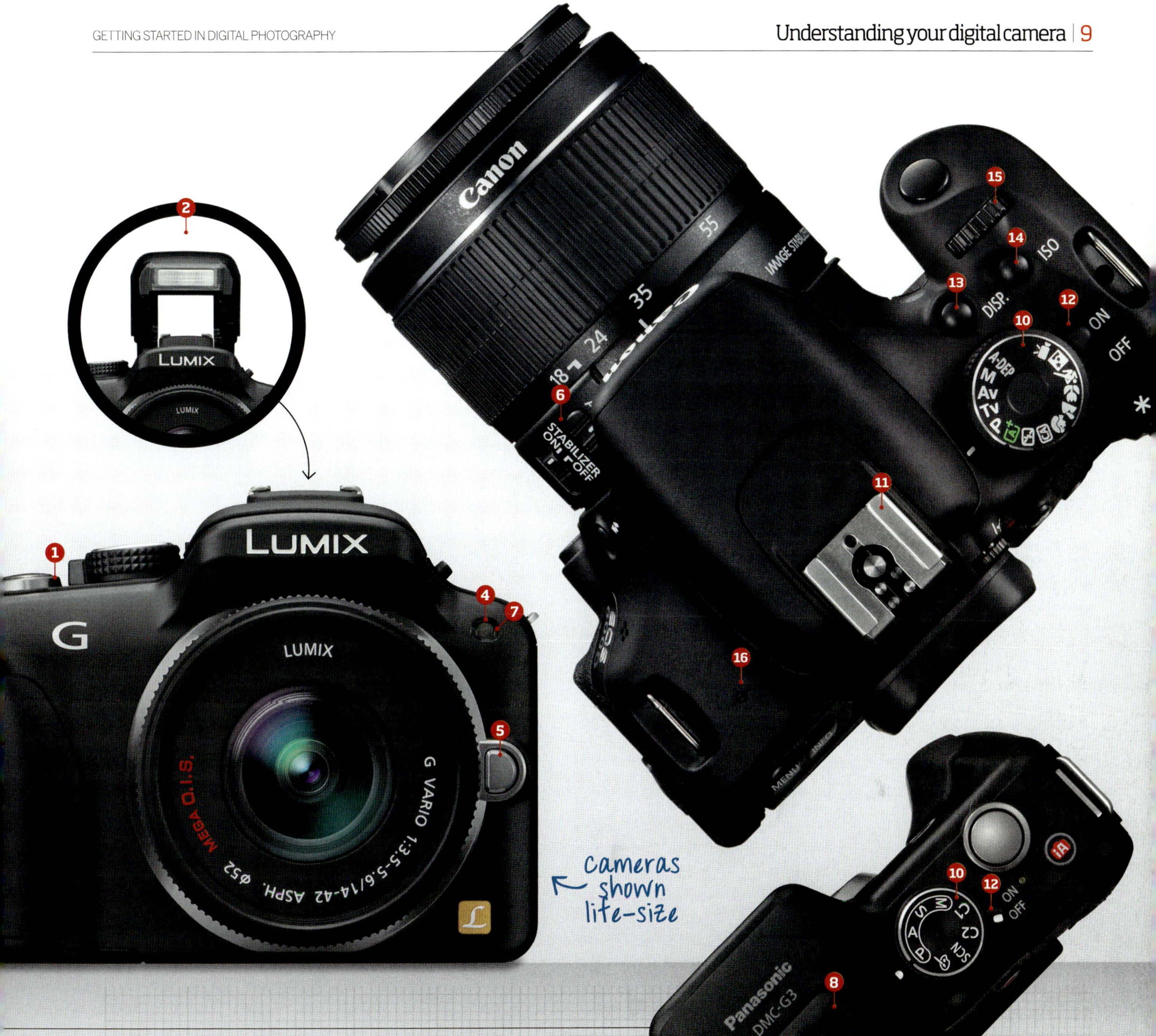

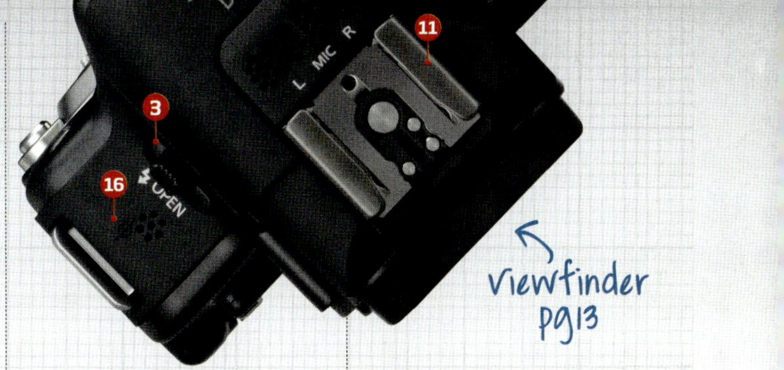

10) Main dial: This is arguably the most important control on your camera as it is used to set the exposure mode. Some have a central locking system, but most haven't, so before shooting, be sure it hasn't been nudged to a mode you don't wish to use.

Did you know? Many semi-pro/pro DSLRs use a button rather than a dial to set the exposure mode.

11) Hotshoe: Also known as an accessory shoe, this allows you to fit a flashgun to your camera. These flashguns provide additional power and features and give you far greater scope with your flash photos. As well as a flashgun, you can attach other accessories, such as a control unit for syncing multiple flash set-ups and remote triggers. The central contact fires the flash, the others are used to transfer information.

Did you know? The unconventional design of the Sony hotshoe is based on the Minolta Dynax hotshoe, introduced in 1988.

12) On/off switch: Turn the camera on or off with this switch. If you leave it to the On position accidentally, the camera will normally switch off the power after five minutes if unused. Press the shutter release gently to switch the camera back on.

13) Display: Your camera uses a default exposure display on its monitor. Pressing the display button changes the format: bringing up the histogram, changing the colour of the screen display or switching it off.

14) ISO: The ISO rating determines the 'sensitivity' of your sensor to light, much like different film speeds in the past. A low ISO rating has less sensitivity, but delivers better image quality. Once you increase the ISO rating, the amount of signal 'noise' increases, leading to a loss in quality (mainly in terms of colour reproduction and sharpness), which is most apparent at speeds of around ISO 800 and above. Recent models offer better noise handling than older models.

15) Input dial: This is usually placed close to the shutter release or by the thumbrest on the rear. It's an important dial that is used to change variables such as the shutter speed or aperture.

16) Sensor plane marker: This marking provides a visual marker as to where the sensor plane is.

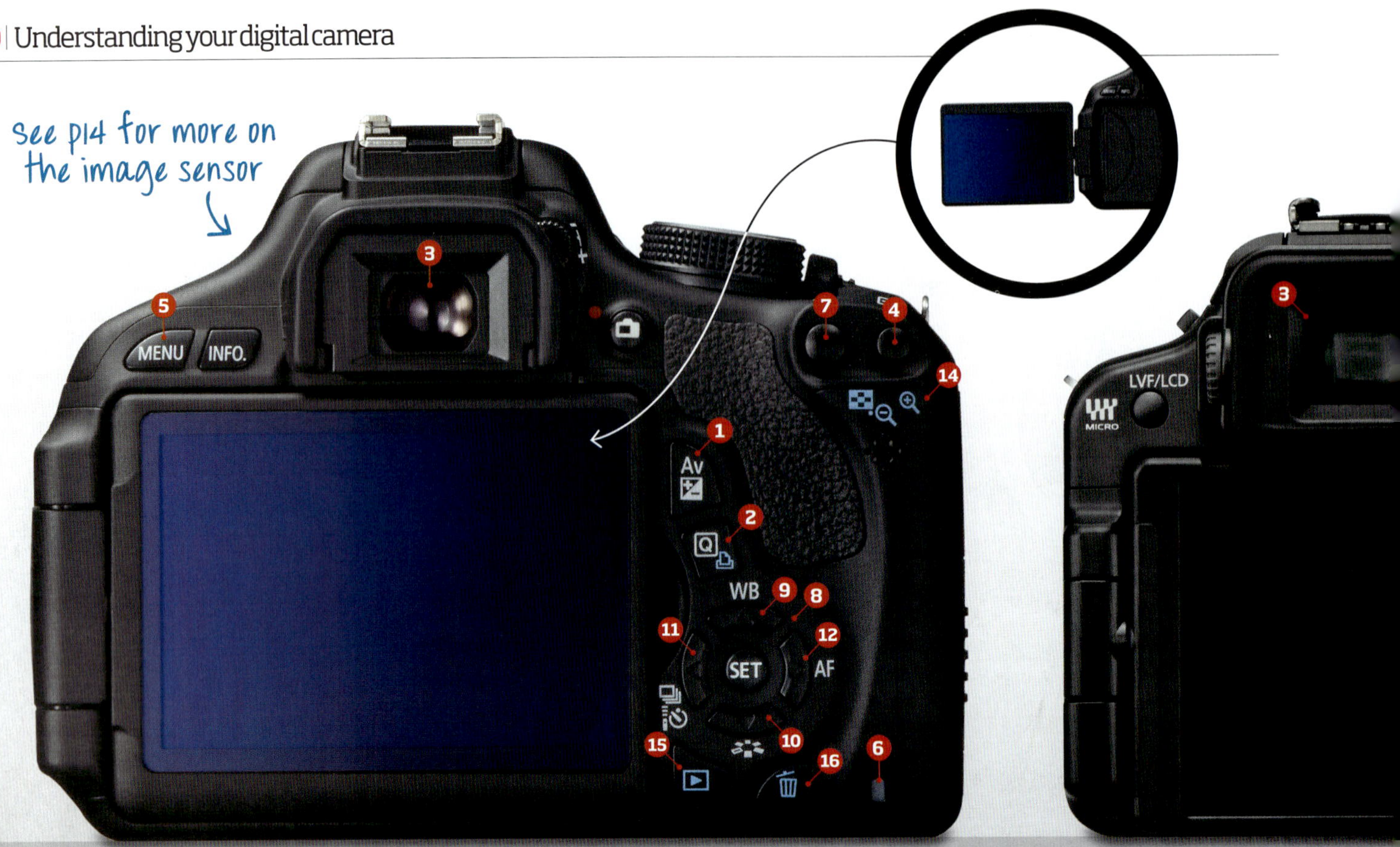

Key features and controls found on DSLRs & CSCs

1) Exposure compensation: This is the most commonly used exposure override and increases or decreases the indicated exposure by a set amount, usually in 1/3 or ½-stop increments. With experience, you'll discover how its use suits certain scenes, such as adding +2 stops when shooting snow or setting a negative value (-2 to -3 stops) when using flash to darken the background for added mood. When shooting in manual mode, pressing this button allows the aperture to be changed.

Did you know? Most cameras have a custom function that lets you set whether changes are made in ½, 1/3 or full-stop increments.

2) Shortcut button: 'Shortcut' buttons are becoming increasingly common, giving fast access to key features via the LCD monitor and four-way control. For instance, press Canon's Q (Quick) button and you can quickly access the aperture/shutter speed, ISO rating, Picture Style, White Balance and exposure compensation, to name but a few. On some cameras, such as the Pentax K-x, a similar function is performed by the Info button, while other brands, such as Sony, offer a Fn (function button) that allows for shortcuts.

3) Viewfinder: Digital SLRs offer Through The Lens (TTL) viewing, so what you see in the viewfinder is an image coming directly through the lens. Sony's Alpha DSLTs (eg the A33, A35 and A55) have an electronic finder, as do CSCs that sport a viewfinder. We cover viewfinders in more detail on p13.

4) AF point selection: Multi-point AF is found on all cameras, helping with focus on off-centre subjects. This button lets you switch between multi-point AF or switch to single-point AF. Choosing one point only is useful in situations when you need precise control of the focus, such as with portraits when you need to be certain to focus on the subject's eye. The central AF point normally boasts the most precise AF sensor, making it the best choice.

5) Menu: Press this to access all of the camera's functions. It's worth navigating the menu system and learning its set-up when you first get the camera. As you'll discover, all use a series of sub-menus/tabs split into various categories to make your life easier.

6) Image processing lamp: This lights up when images are being transferred from the camera to the memory card.

7) AE-Lock: This popular override is particularly useful when you need to work quickly as it's fast to set. Use it to take and lock a meter reading from a mid-tone when shooting in tricky lighting situations. It's particularly useful when shooting a backlit subject.

Did you know? You can use AE-Lock with any metering pattern, but it's best to switch to the spot/partial or centre-weighted average pattern, rather than using it with multi-zone metering.

8) Four-way control: Virtually every new DSLR and CSC boasts a four-way control system on its rear, as it offers a fast and versatile form of setting key functions. Each button has its own primary function, but the four-way set-up allows the same buttons to be used with the menu display to scroll through the navigation system.

9) White Balance: As well as the default Auto White Balance (AWB) setting, your camera has a number of presets for different lighting conditions. Setting the best matched preset will ensure more accurate colours. You can also set a custom White Balance yourself using a grey card. With experience you'll discover how setting an incorrect WB setting can lead to creative results.

10) Picture Styles: As well as the standard setting, your camera has a number of picture settings that are optimised for certain types of subject, such as portraits, landscapes and so on. You can also customise some settings to suit your own preferences.

11) Frame advance: The standard setting for your camera is to shoot a single frame with every press of the shutter button. However, it can be set to shoot sequences when set to continuous. You can also delay the exposure being taken by setting the ten/12-second self-timer, which is ideal when you want to be in the picture yourself. The two-second self-timer is used to reduce the risk of shake when using a long exposure. You can also use this button when you want to shoot using a remote release.

12) AF button: Your camera offers at least two main autofocus modes: single-shot AF for static subjects and servo/continuous AF for moving subjects. Many also have an AI Servo/Auto-AF mode, which works like single-shot until subject movement is detected, when it switches automatically to continuous focus.

13) Movie mode: Fancy shooting video rather than taking 'stills'? That's no problem for the latest DSLRs and CSCs, that shoot high quality movies, many in Full HD. A variety of formats and settings are available to suit amateur and professional use.

14) Image magnification: The magnifying glass symbols are found on virtually every camera. They highlight the buttons that are used to zoom in to images to check sharpness when reviewing images or using LiveView. Once zoomed in, the four-way control is used to move around the magnified image.

15) Playback: Use this to review images on your memory card.

16) Delete: Press this while in Playback mode to delete the currently displayed image.

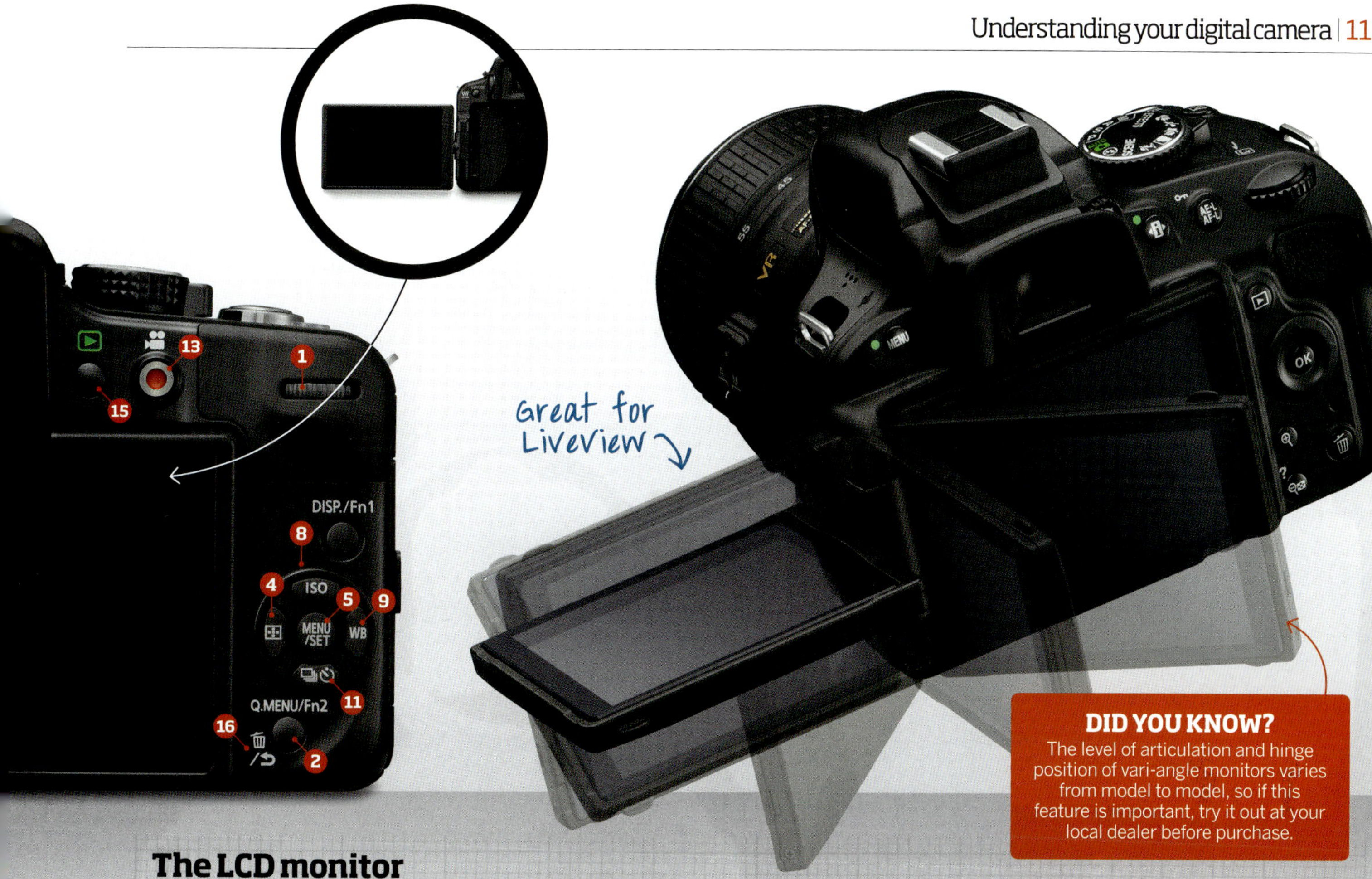

DID YOU KNOW?
The level of articulation and hinge position of vari-angle monitors varies from model to model, so if this feature is important, try it out at your local dealer before purchase.

The LCD monitor

With a number of key roles, the importance of the LCD monitor should not be underestimated, as you'll be using it on a regular basis, Here are the essential facts to consider.

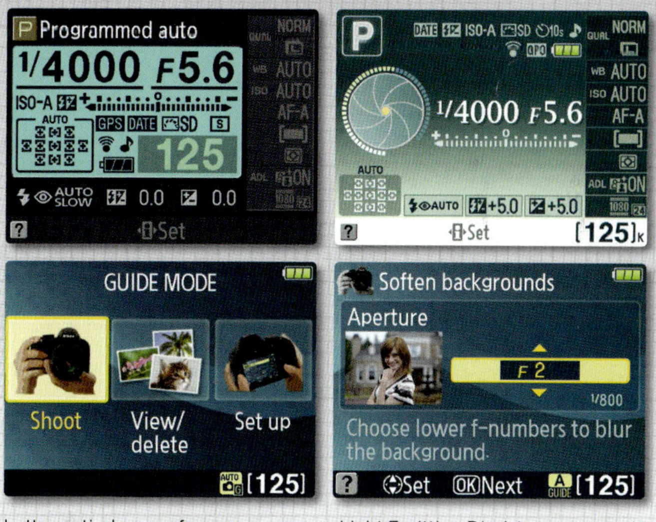

Screen size: Most current cameras have a screen size of at least 2.7in, with many boasting a 3in screen. The larger the screen the better, as it makes it quicker to navigate the menu system and easy to review images or use LiveView.

Screen resolution: The resolution, stated in dots, is important as the higher it is, the sharper the display. Most monitors have a 460,000-dot screen, which is very good, but way short of the sharpness and clarity of screens that boast 920,000 or more dots.

Vari-angle monitors: While most screens are fixed, articulated monitors are becoming increasing common due to their usefulness when using LiveView or when shooting movies.

Menu system: The many control buttons on your camera allow you to quickly select most key modes and functions, but it's the camera's menu system that allows you access to every feature on the camera. Every menu has sub-divisions or 'tabs' for the various types of functions they control, making it easier and quicker to access the function you want. Canon and Nikon are generally regarded as having the best-designed menus but all are easy to use once you've played with them for a little while.

Exposure information: The default setting for the monitor is to show the key exposure information on the screen. You can usually customise the layout and colours to your liking, so check your camera's instruction manual or explore the menu system a little to see what options are available.

Screen brightness: Many users aren't aware that their camera's menu system offers an option that allows the brightness of the display to be adjusted. Set it to your liking – most people boost brightness when shooting in bright conditions, reduce it in low light and use a mid-setting in studio conditions or when checking exposure accuracy.

Touchscreen functionality: A feature of a small number of CSCs that allows you to select modes, focus and fire the shutter by pressing the appropriate icons on the monitor screen.

Quick Guides: A feature that is becoming increasing common is the Quick Guide. Found predominantly on entry-level models, it provides illustrated instructions for various picture-taking skills.

Monitor hood: Bright daylight makes it difficult to view the monitor, even with more recent models that boast displays with better anti-glare performance. A simple and inexpensive way to improve your viewing of the screen is to attach a monitor hood, which shields direct light from reaching the screen. With some CSCs lacking a viewfinder and having the monitor as the only method for composing images, using a hood can make a major difference.

Screen construction: The vast majority of monitors use a Liquid Crystal Display (LCD) but a number use different materials that are claimed to offer brighter colours and better anti-glare performance. These include Samsung's AMOLED (Active Matrix Organic Light Emitting Diode) and the OLED (Organic Light Emitting Diode) screen used on some Olympus CSC models.

LiveView: This facility lets you use the monitor to frame the scene. With some cameras, when critical focusing is needed, part of the image can be magnified to allow for 'fine-tuning' of the focus. While the AF performance of LiveView in the past was poor, more recent cameras have shown a marked improvement. Sony Alpha's LiveView system, along with the latest Olympus and Panasonic CSCs, boasts excellent LiveView AF. However, while monitors are sharp and offer good contrast, they are still difficult to use in bright lighting conditions, so we'd recommend using an LCD shade.

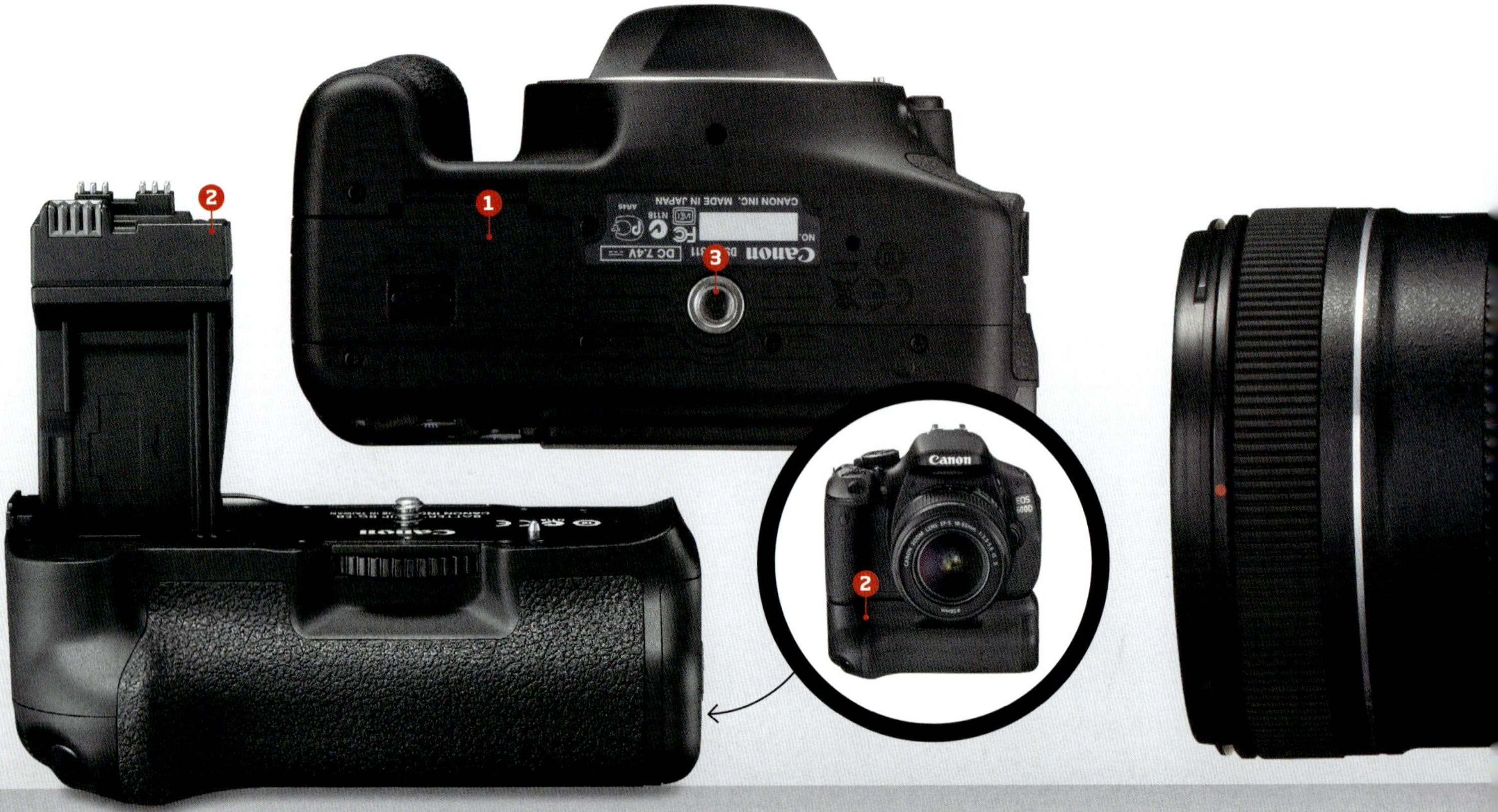

Compartments & connections

1) Battery: A few cameras use AA batteries, but the vast majority use lithium-ion batteries. These are rechargeable and last for several hundred frames, but have the disadvantage of being more expensive should you need a spare.

Did you know? Independent brands like Hahnel, Delkin and Hama produce compatible lithium batteries considerably cheaper than branded batteries.

2) Accessory grip: It's worth noting that many cameras allow optional grips to be attached. These offer a number of advantages as follows:

Handling: The additional grip provides a more solid hold, which is particularly useful when using the camera in portrait format. Bear in mind, however, that it also means you've a larger and heavier outfit to carry.

Additional function buttons: The grip has a secondary set of buttons that duplicate those on the body and again help when shooting in portrait format. These are usually made up of the following: shutter release, input dial, exposure compensation, AF point selection and AE-Lock.

Additional power: The grip holds additional batteries, which allows for extended shooting. With many grips, as well as allowing the use of lithium-ion batteries, an adapter allows AA batteries to be used, too.

3) Tripod bush: A ¼in thread bush is located on the bottom of every camera and is a standard size for use with tripods, monopods and other camera supports.

Card slot: Most cameras feature a card slot, protected by a hinged door, on the right side of the camera. Better-specified models have a twist-lock security switch to prevent it accidentally opening. Placing the card slot in the battery compartment on the base of the camera is becoming increasingly common, but we're not so keen on this position as it causes problems with access when your camera is tripod-mounted. Some cameras offer two slots rather than one, boosting capacity and allowing you to set up the camera to transfer video to one slot and still images to the other, or do a similar thing with Raw and JPEG files.

4) Camera connections: The following are the most popular connection sockets:

HDMI: Plug your camera directly into your HDTV and view images and movies on the big screen.

Remote: Connect a corded remote and shoot night exposures with less risk of camera shake.

USB: Connect your camera directly to a computer or a compatible inkjet printer.

Mic: When shooting video, plug in an external microphone to greatly improve audio quality.

PC socket: Found on the front of many enthusiast and pro-spec cameras, this accepts the standard sync lead for use with studioflash.

How size and weight relates to build quality

All cameras are made to a very high standard, but some are made to a higher standard than others, so it's worth noting how build quality varies as you spend more.

Budget 'entry-level' models are made to be as small and light as possible, hence they have a mainly polycarbonate body that feels somewhat plasticky compared to rivals.

Mid-range cameras are designed for heavier use and so are more sturdy, often having an alloy chassis to improve strength. Some have enhanced weatherproofing, too.

Pro models use a steel or magnesium alloy chassis and shell for maximum protection. All areas of the camera, from the reinforced shutter system to the weatherproof seals around the buttons and dials, are made as durable as possible. The outcome of this is that the cameras are bigger and heavier.

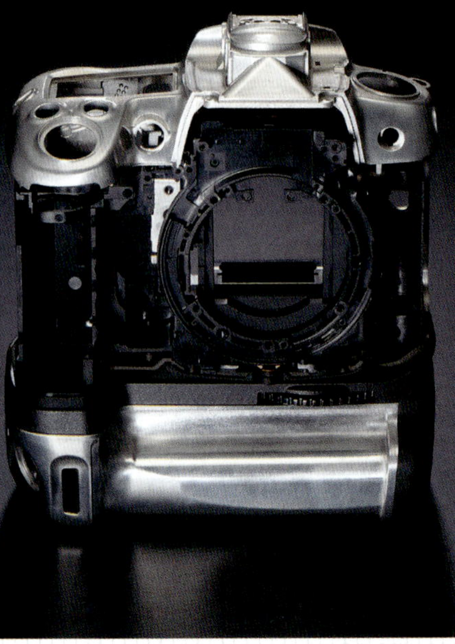

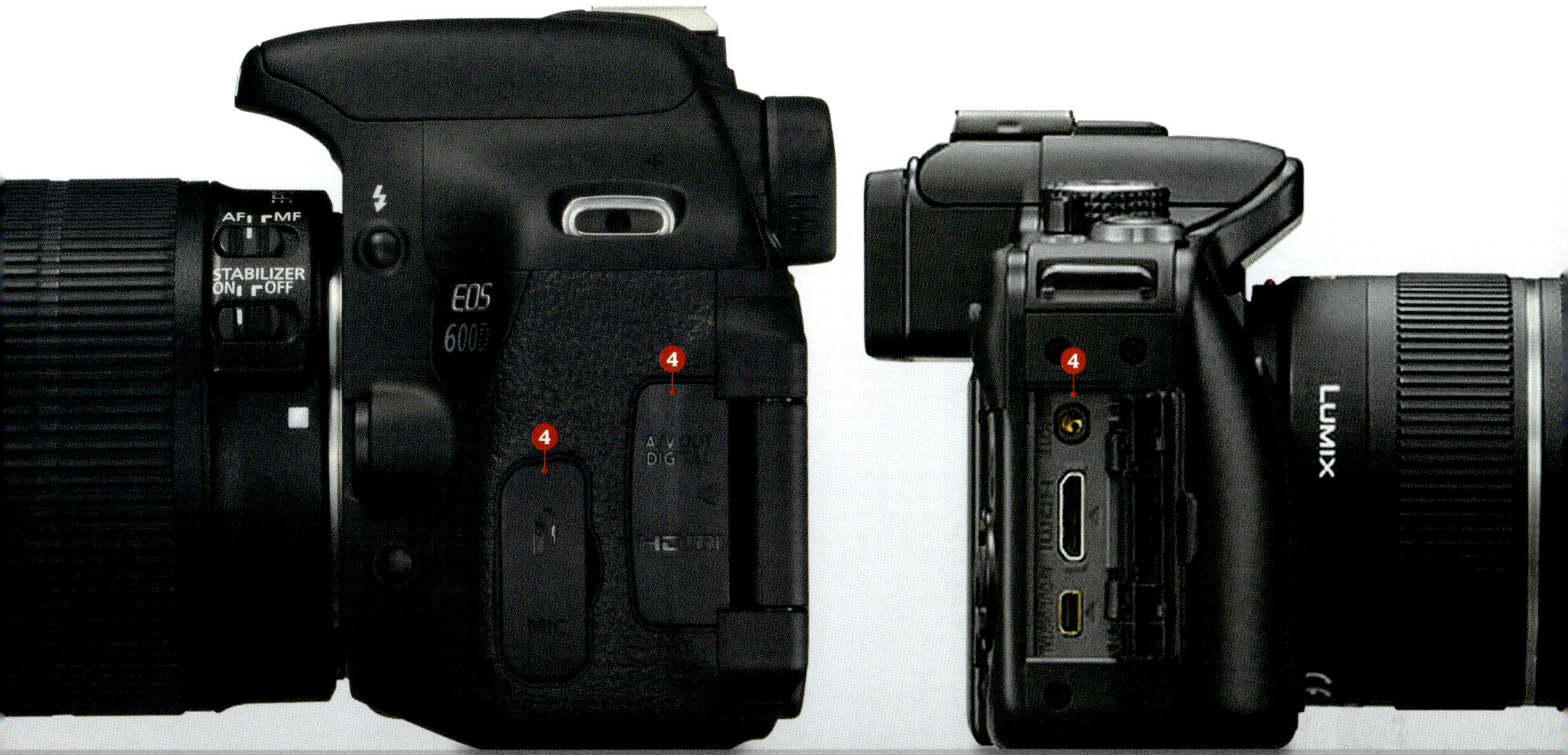

The viewfinder

The viewfinder is important as, for most photographers, it's how the image is framed. Its size and clarity improves as you spend more on your DSLR. Entry-level models have relatively small but clear viewfinders, mid-range DSLRs see an improvement, with viewfinders being larger and brighter. Full-frame DSLRs have the best viewfinders, providing a large, very sharp and clear image.

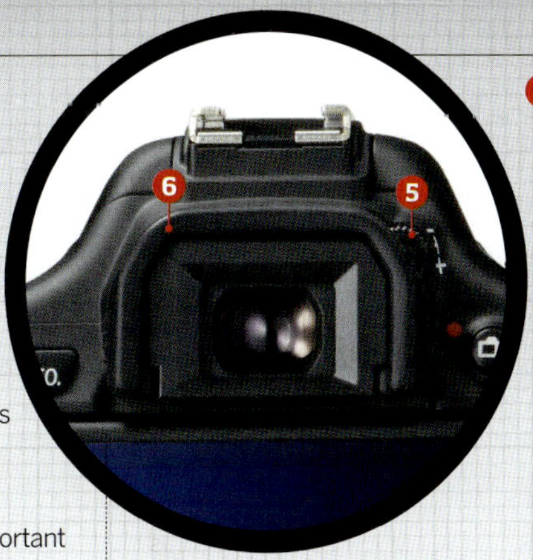

5) Dioptric correction: Spectacle wearers can use a dial or switch to sharpen the viewfinder image for use without wearing their glasses. Most cameras offer a range of around +2 to -1 dioptres.

6) Viewfinder hood: Provide a comfortable rest and prevent stray light entering the viewfinder. Most are detachable, allowing for viewfinder accessories to be fitted. These include a viewfinder extender, which provides more comfortable viewing, and an angle-finder that aids low-level viewing.

7) Viewfinder screen: Most show the position of the focusing points while some show the central spot/partial metering zone. Most screens have LEDs on the AF points that light up red when activated. Exposure information is usually shown along the bottom in green, although some have it running along the right side.

Did you know? A small number of mid-range and semi-pro/pro models boast interchangeable viewfinder screens to suit specialist uses, such as macro or architectural photography. Some cameras allow you to superimpose gridlines on the screen via a custom function, meaning you don't have to buy an extra screen.

Viewfinder blind: It's important to cover the viewfinder when taking pictures as stray light penetrating the viewfinder housing can reach the metering sensor, leading to poor exposures. Some top-end cameras have an integral blind, but for most consumer-level DSLRs, an eyepiece cover is provided with the camera either as a standalone accessory or attached to the supplied camera strap.

Eye sensor: This handy little feature saves battery power by deactivating the LCD monitor when it senses that the photographer's eye is looking through the viewfinder.

Frame coverage: While the semi-pro and professional models boast a 100% coverage, most models only provide a 95% coverage of the image frame. This means that, when composing the image, the final result will include slightly more of the scene at its edges than is evident through the viewfinder.

Magnification: The higher the magnification of the viewfinder, the better, as it means a clearer, larger image that places less strain on the eye. Most cameras offer a similar performance in this respect to similarly priced rivals.

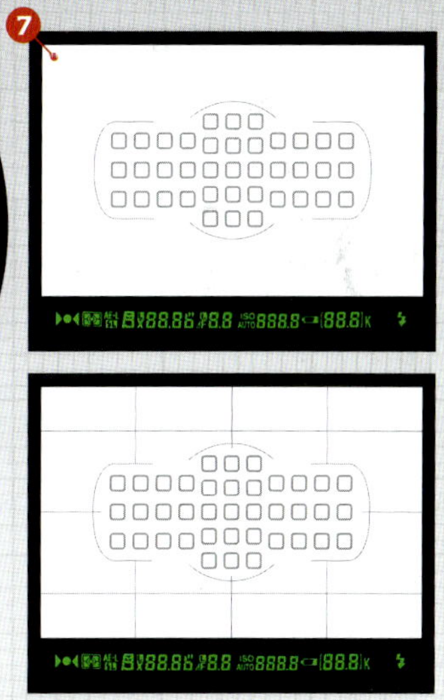

ABOVE: Some cameras have a Custom Function to add gridlines.

Electronic viewfinders

CSCs, as well as Sony's translucent-mirror DSLTs (Alpha A33, A35 and A55), use an electronic colour finder as opposed to the traditional optical type found in DSLRs. These have the advantage of providing 100% coverage and their live display is useful to judge exposure and White Balance. They also allow for plenty of exposure information to be displayed. However, they're not without their problems, particularly when used in low light, as they don't provide as clear an image as conventional viewfinders. The latest electronic finders are better than previous generations in this respect, but traditional viewfinders still hold the edge in terms of clarity and brightness.

Did You know? Some CSCs lack an integral viewfinder altogether, with users using the LCD monitor to compose the scene. This is usually to keep down the cost of the camera or to reduce its size.

Remove the lens and it's easy to tell a digital SLR from a CSC. The sensor on a DSLR is obscured by the reflex mirror (and also the shutter curtain behind it), while the sensor of the CSC is fully exposed.

1) Lens mount: The lens mount has electronic pins to transfer information used by the autofocus and exposure systems between the camera and lens. Different brands have different lens mounts, although Olympus PEN and Panasonic Lumix CSCs share the Micro Four-Thirds 'open' lens mount system.

2) DSLR: Reflex mirror Digital SLRs have a reflex mirror that reflects light upwards where a prism directs it towards the viewfinder. When you fire the shutter release button, the mirror raises out of the light path and a shutter curtain behind it opens to allow the exposure to reach the sensor. It's a tried and tested system, but adds to manufacturing costs and size of the camera when compared to CSCs.

3) CSC: Missing a mirror While digital SLRs and CSCs share many similarities, the biggest difference is that CSCs lack a reflex mirror. This allows them to be smaller and slimmer than a DSLR. The lack of a mirror means CSCs use an electronic finder and/or LCD monitor to compose images, with the image coming directly from the sensor, which is clearly visible when the lens is removed.

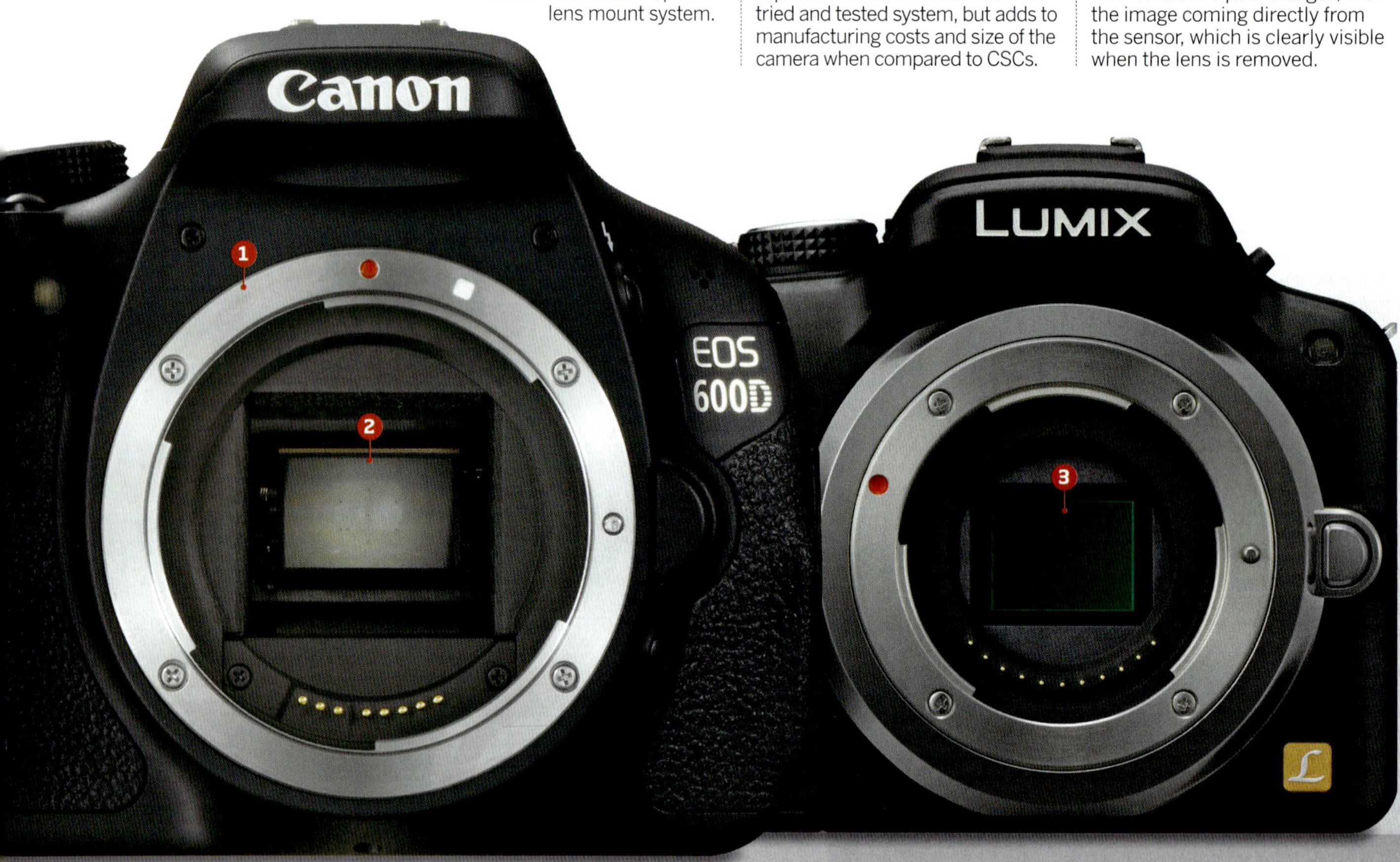

Image sensor

THE SENSOR AT THE HEART OF THE CAMERA PLAYS A FUNDAMENTAL ROLE IN DIGITAL PHOTOGRAPHY. UNDERSTAND ITS KEY CHARACTERISTICS TO GET THE MOST FROM YOUR CAMERA

Sensor size

Image sensors are produced in a number of sizes, with the full-frame sensor being the same size as a 35mm film frame. It's vital that you understand the importance of sensor sizes for a number of reasons, as follows:

1) The size of the sensor determines the effective focal length of lenses used with the camera (see panel).

2) In general, larger sensors can produce better quality images because the pixels are larger, produce less noise and aren't so tightly cramped together.

3) Larger sensors are more expensive to produce, so cameras are more expensive, too.

4) A camera with a larger sensor also has a bigger, brighter viewfinder.

5) All else being equal, larger sensors give slightly shallower depth-of-field compared to smaller sensors.

Full-frame sensors are found in semi-pro and pro models, and have the same dimensions as a 35mm film frame. Their size allows for extremely high-resolutions: Canon's EOS-1Ds MkIII has 21.1 million pixels, Sony's Alpha 900 has 24.6 megapixels, while the Nikon D3x has 24.5 million pixels.

The APS-H sensor is used in the EOS-1D series and is aimed predominantly at sports and wildlife photographers who prefer the extra boost the slightly smaller sensor provides.

APS-C is the most popular sensor size, found in the vast majority of DSLRs, as well as the Sony and Samsung CSCs.

The Four-Thirds sensor was the smallest of the four main types until the release of the Nikon 1 System and Pentax Q.

Full-frame: 36x24mm
APS-H: 28.7x19.1mm
APS-C: 23.6x15.5mm *(Nikon, Pentax, Sony)*
APS-C: 22.3x14.9mm *(Canon)*
Four-Thirds: 17.3x13mm
Nikon CX-format: 13.2x8.8mm
Pentax Q: 6.17x4.55mm

DID YOU KNOW?
The two main sensor types are CMOS (Complementary Metal-Oxide-Semiconductor) and CCD (Charged Coupled Device). The former is the most commonly used.

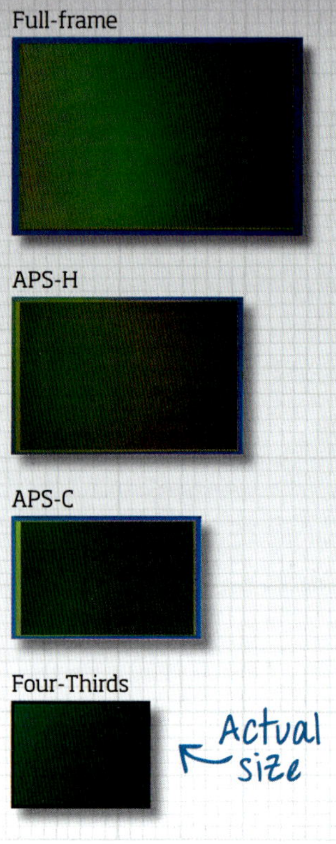

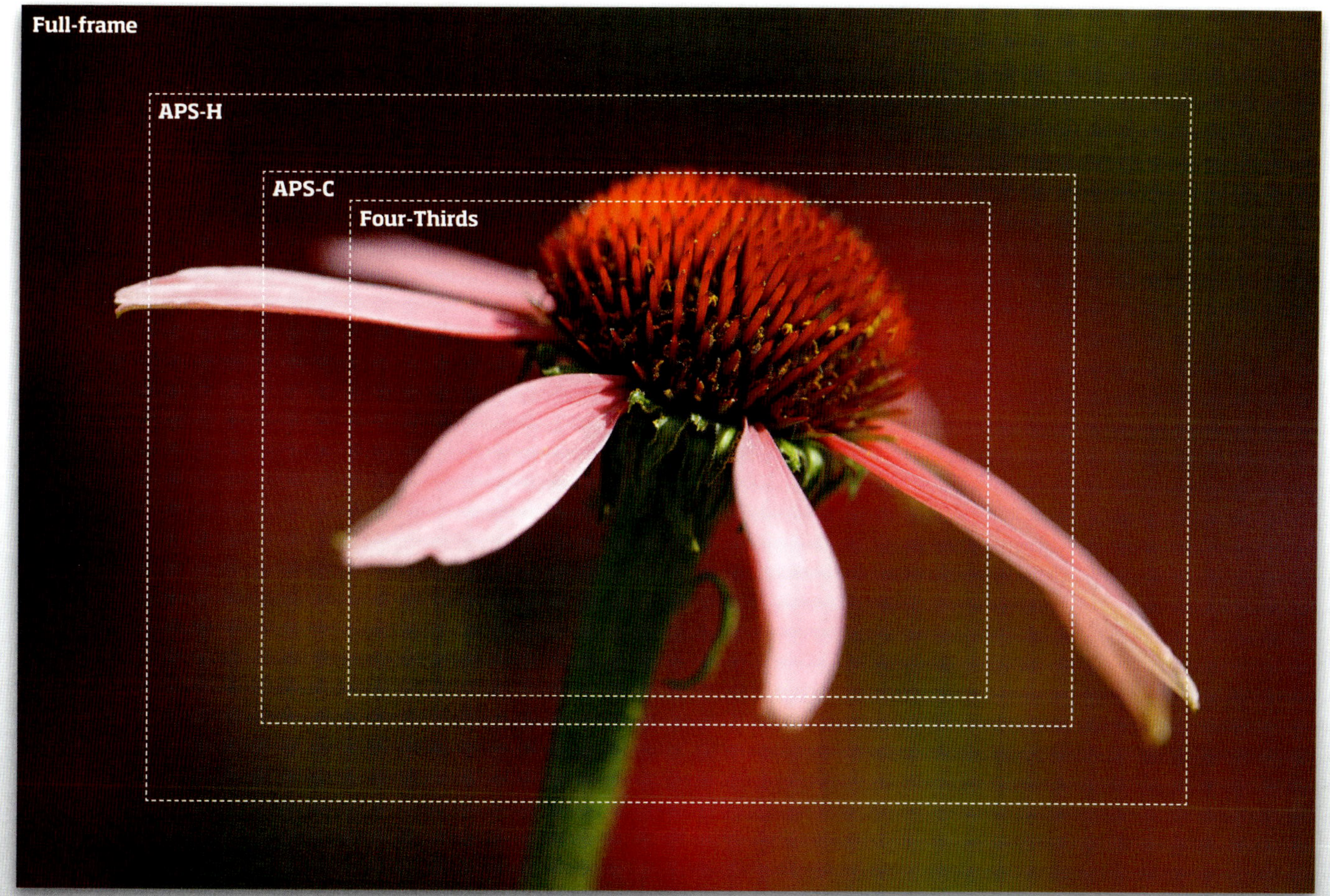

DID YOU KNOW? A small number of image sensors do not follow the standard design. These include Fuji's Super CCD and Sigma's Foveon sensor.

Sensitivity

Back in the 'analogue' days, film sensitivity was stated as an ISO (International Standards Organisation) rating. This system is also used with imaging sensors. The lower the ISO rating, the less sensitive the sensor is to light. As you increase the ISO rating, the signal output of the sensor is increased to boost its sensitivity, but this has the effect of increasing noise, too, which is undesirable. The sensitivity range varies from sensor to sensor, but most offer ISO 100-6400. Top-end models offer a low ISO 50 rating, while some cameras have a top ISO of 102,400, which is sensitive enough to capture images at night. Most cameras offer some form of noise reduction as an option.

Image resolution

An image sensor is made up of millions of light-receptive photosites, best known as pixels. The more pixels a sensor has, the higher its resolution. The general term for a million pixels is 'megapixels', hence a sensor with 12-million pixels is commonly referred to as having a 12-megapixel resolution.

While it's easy to assume that sensors with a higher resolution deliver better image quality than those with less pixels, that is not always the case. The size of the sensor plays a part: as mentioned earlier, the larger pixels on bigger sensors generally deliver superior quality. Also important is the image processor, which uses the raw information provided by the sensor to produce the images. It's important to remember that the optical quality of the lens used on the camera has a major influence on overall quality, too.

Sensors & lenses

The relationship between the image sensor and the lenses used with your camera can seem confusing at first, but you'll get used to it with a little experience. It all relates to how the coverage provided by a lens changes depending on the sensor size.

If you take two identical lenses and fit one to a camera with a full-frame sensor and the other to a camera with an APS-C sensor, you'll find that the latter provides a magnified version of the scene. This is because the smaller sensor uses a smaller area of the 'circle of illumination', which refers to the light passing through the lens. In effect, the smaller sensor 'crops' the image, using only a central portion, and is said to have increased the effective focal length of the lens. This is usually stated as an equivalent to the 35mm film format or full-frame sensor.

Each sensor has a crop factor, which must be multiplied with the focal length to give the effective focal length. For instance, APS-C sensors have a crop factor of 1.5x (1.6x with Canon), and Four-Thirds sensors have a crop factor of 2x. So, for example, a 50mm lens used on a Four-Thirds sensor is stated as providing the equivalent focal length as a 100mm lens. The image it produces has the same field of view as a 100mm lens used on a 35mm film/full-frame sensor.

The importance of this increase in effective focal length is that lenses used with smaller sensors effectively have more pulling power than when used on larger sensors. So a 100-300mm used on a Nikon DSLR with an APS-C sensor has an effective focal length of 150-450mm. That's great news if you shoot a distant subject as you can fill more of the frame with it. The downside is apparent when using wide-angles: its coverage is restricted as it no longer has such a wide field-of-view. The crop factor of the main sensor sizes are:

Full-frame: 1x
APS-H: 1.3x
APS-C: 1.5x *(Nikon, Pentax, Sony)*
APS-C: 1.6x *(Canon)*
Four-Thirds: 2x
Nikon CX-format: 2.7x
Pentax Q: 5.5x

Digital-only lenses

The popularity of the APS-C sensor has led to various manufacturers making lenses suitable only for DSLRs with this size of sensor. These digital-only lenses are usually more compact than mainstream lenses and cannot be used on DSLRs with full-frame sensors as they will cause gross vignetting. These digital-only lenses are designated by the main brands as follows:

Canon EF-S; Nikon DX, Sigma DC and Tamron Di II.

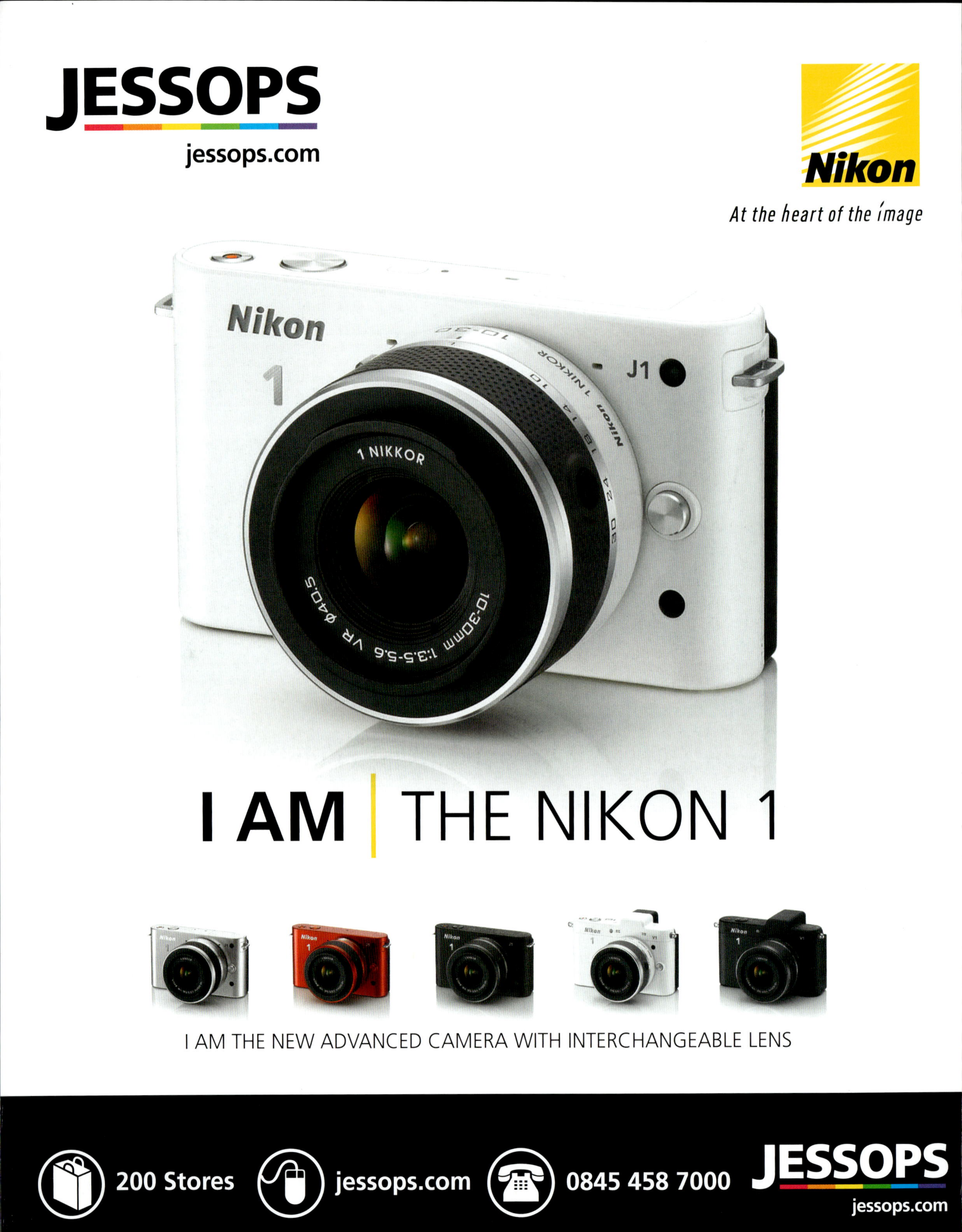
JESSOPS
jessops.com
Nikon
At the heart of the image
I AM THE NIKON 1
I AM THE NEW ADVANCED CAMERA WITH INTERCHANGEABLE LENS
200 Stores
jessops.com
0845 458 7000
JESSOPS
jessops.com

Understanding exposure modes

Want to take better shots? Then learn how to use each mode to its best advantage to improve your images…

DIGITAL CAMERAS ARE complicated instruments, seemingly with more features and functions these days than the control room of a nuclear submarine. Of course, if you press the wrong button on your camera, the worst that's going to happen is you'll ruin a potentially great shot, rather than start a world war! Nevertheless, if you want to realise your full potential as a photographer, it's important that you can find your way around the very thing you use to take photographs.

High on the list of essential features you need to understand are exposure modes, simply because you need to use one of them every time you press the shutter.

The basic job of an exposure mode is to ensure that just the right amount of light reaches the image sensor to record a 'correctly' exposed image using a suitable aperture and shutter speed combination. DSLRs and CSCs typically have four main exposure modes – program, aperture-priority, shutter-priority and manual – plus a range of specialist program modes, biased to specific subjects, such as sport, landscape, portraits and close-ups.

All the modes are designed to give the correct exposure, but where they differ is in how they influence the final result, the amount of control you have over the aperture and shutter speed selected, and also how quick and easy they are to use.

Chances are you have a favourite exposure mode that you use all the time. Whether or not it's the best mode for you is another matter, as many photographers tend to settle on a way of working and stick with it without considering the alternatives. To help you find out, this detailed guide to exposure modes explains what each one does so that you can pick and choose different modes for different subjects, and start making the most of your camera.

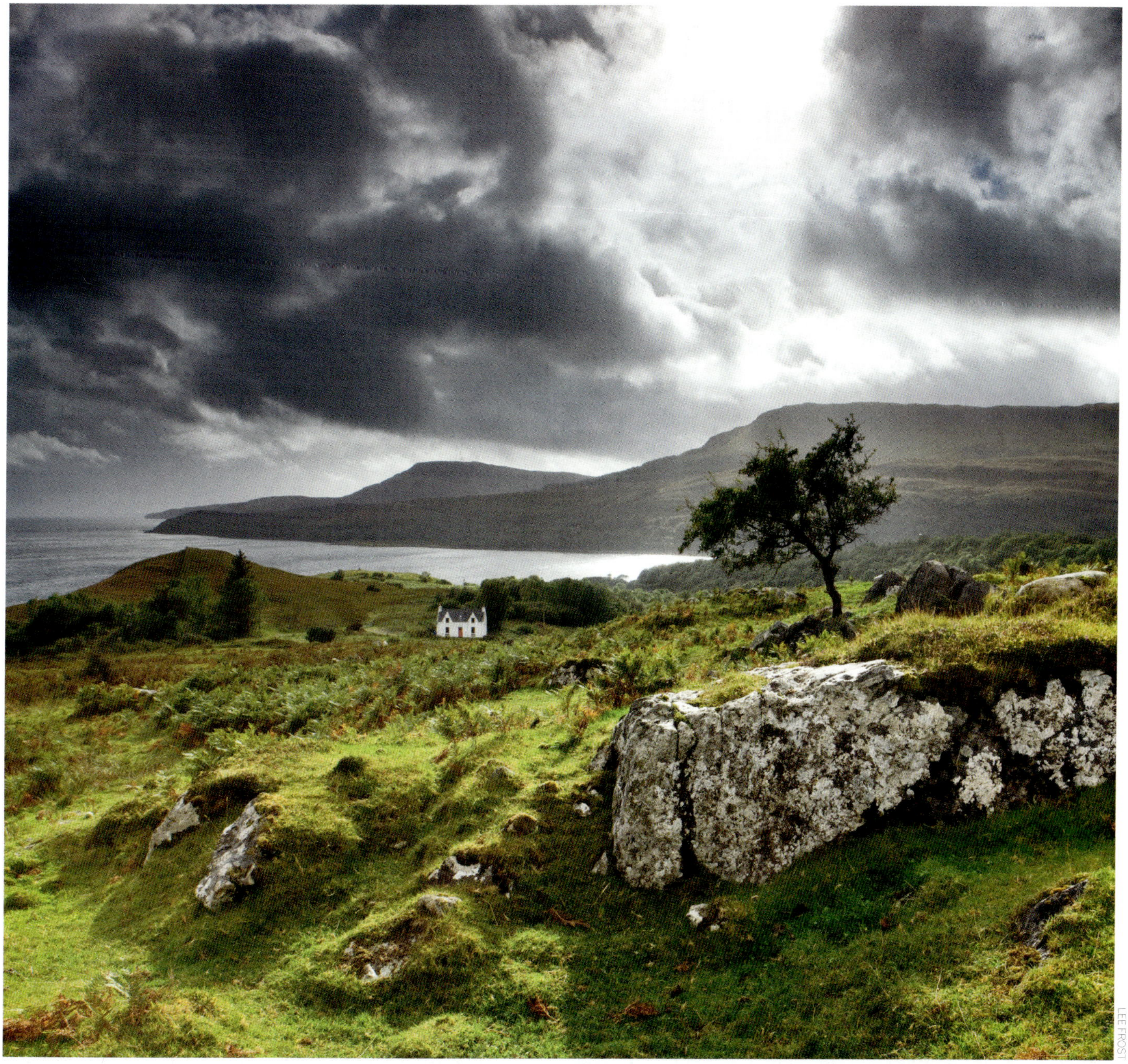

LEE FROST

Understanding exposure modes

Read the instructions!
Every camera has program modes that work slightly differently, so it's worth spending a few minutes reading the instructions to see how yours works

If taking better pictures is your goal, then you need to understand exposure modes. Don't worry, it's not as difficult as you might think…

THE EXPOSURE MODE you select will play a major role in how your camera captures the scene, so it's essential you learn how each works and the influence they have on the final result. Your camera offers you a wide choice of options, but they can be divided into two main types: basic and creative. The basic modes include the Full-Auto and Scene modes: in other words, the fully-automatic modes that only give you very basic control over how the picture is taken. These modes are meant for beginners to photography who have yet to learn the fundamentals, such as how apertures and shutter speeds work.

The creative modes, which we also like to term the core four, are program, aperture-priority, shutter-priority and manual mode. These provide you with creative control of your photography and because they are the four modes we'd recommend you learn, we'll cover them in detail in this guide. These four modes all work in very different ways: for instance, in program mode, the camera takes care of the shutter speed and aperture, but gives you scope to adjust virtually every other setting on the camera. Aperture- and shutter-priority modes are semi-automatic: you take care of either the aperture or shutter speed, with the camera taking care of the other. Manual, as you'd expect, is where you have control of both. With experience, you'll come to have your favourite – for most people, that's aperture-priority mode, but there are times when you may count on some of the other modes, too. By following our expert advice, you'll be able to choose the appropriate mode every time, which will help you to take better pictures.

How to set exposure modes

As the exposure mode is a primary function of the camera, it should be simple to set. Virtually all DSLRs have an exposure mode dial on the top-plate, which allows the mode to be set easily and quickly. Pro DSLRs normally negate the dial in favour of a mode button, used in conjunction with the input dial. Some CSCs have a mode dial similar to a DSLR, located on the top-plate or on the rear, or a touchscreen option. Many – in particular, those at the budget end – lack a dial and instead use the menu screen and four-way control.

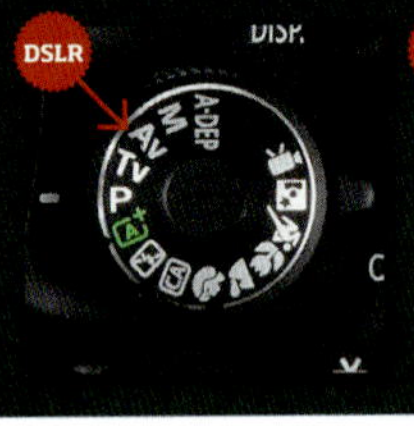

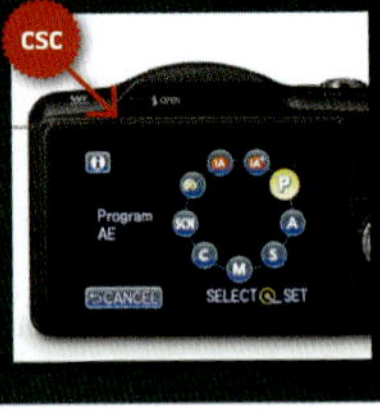

– Scene modes (also known as subject-biased programs)

Scene modes represent (in principle, at least) the perfect way for beginners to take brilliant pictures of different types of subjects. It all seems so easy: a novice shooting their loved one needs only choose portrait mode and snap away; while a walker on Snowdonia sets Landscape mode and, hey presto, a stunning scenic is recorded. The truth is a little less photo-utopia than this. While the camera will take a sharp, well-exposed image, it won't be anywhere near as good as if you use a creative mode and select the camera settings yourself. Ultimately, Scene modes give high-quality snaps that you could take with a decent compact – your DSLR or CSC can give you so much more, so only use them if taking images of scenes where you're unsure what to do.

Every Scene mode is designed to bias the camera for the subject you're shooting: to do this, it removes control of the camera's key features. We're not just talking about just the shutter speed and aperture either – metering, AF, exposure overrides, drive mode, built-in flash and White Balance, as well as the ISO, are all taken out of your hands. From a beginner's point of view, that's a lot of potential problems taken care of by the camera, but from a creative photographer's point of view, that's a major loss of control. Our reference table shows the most popular Scene modes and the key functions the camera takes care of or allows you to control. It's applicable to most, but not all cameras, so check your instructions for a more detailed guide. As you'll see, you've much less influence on the result as using program or a creative mode, which is why the camera will never replace the photographer – it simply does not know what type of image you're trying to capture. The other key weakness of Scene modes is that they'll always play it safe with exposure settings – in particular, using a shutter speed to avoid shake (the camera generally presumes you're shooting hand-held). It will rarely go to extremes either, so if you're shooting a portrait in bright light and want very shallow depth-of-field, you're unlikely to find the aperture wide open, but rather at a more safe setting of f/5.6.

	Functions	Full Auto	Portrait	Landscapes	Close-up	Action	Program
General settings	Aperture & shutter speed	●	●	●	●	●	○*
	ISO rating	●	●	●	●	●	○
	White Balance	●	●	●	●	●	○
Focusing	One-Shot AF	-	●	●	●	-	○
	Continuous AF	-	-	-	-	●	○
	AI-Focus	●	-	-	-	-	○
	AF point selection	●	●	●	●	●	○
Exposure	Multi-zone	●	●	●	●	●	○
	Spot/Partial	-	-	-	-	-	○
	Centre-weighted	-	-	-	-	-	○
	Exposure compensation	-	-	-	-	-	○
	AEB & AE-Lock	-	-	-	-	-	○
Drive	Single frame	○	○	○	○	-	○
	Continuous	-	-	-	-	-	○
	Self-timer	○	○	○	○	○	○
Built-in flash	Auto-flash	●	●	-	●	-	○
	Forced-on	-	-	-	-	-	○
	Flash-off	-	-	●	-	●	○

Table key: ● Set automatically ○ User-selectable - Not available * Program Shift

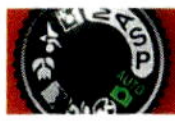 – Program mode (P)

Set your camera to 'P' and it becomes a fully automated machine. Point it towards a subject or scene you want to photograph and not only will it measure light levels to determine the correct exposure, but it will then go ahead and set both the aperture and shutter speed for you to achieve that exposure.

Whether or not you see this as an advantage or a hindrance depends how much experience you have behind a camera. Beginners like program mode because it's quick and easy – all you do is point, focus and shoot, with the minimum of things to think about, and therefore less chance (or so it seems) of making a mistake. Experienced hands are less enthusiastic about program mode for the very same reason: they feel it's too automated and prefer to take control of the camera, rather than feeling that the camera has taken control of them. This is achieved by opting for a semi-automatic or manual mode.

For snapshots at parties or when you're on holiday and so on, program mode is ideal as it will deliver good photographs time after time. It can also work well if you're wandering around, shooting a variety of different subjects, or if you need to act fast when taking photographs at, say, carnivals and festivals, and are more interested in getting decent shots rather than trying to create works of art.

The main drawback with program mode is that the combination of aperture and shutter speed seems almost to be chosen at random by the camera, so you may find when you point it at your subject in readiness to take a shot that it sets a wide aperture and fast shutter speed when you really need a smaller aperture to increase depth-of-field or a slower shutter speed to blur movement. The camera doesn't know this because it can't read your mind (technicians are working on that one!), but it does go some way towards this by offering program shift (see panel on the right).

You can also increase or reduce the exposure to correct errors for creative effect by using the camera's exposure compensation facility. This makes program mode much more versatile and, in experienced hands, it can work well as a quick and easy all-rounder. Nevertheless, it still tends to be the choice of beginners who don't yet understand things like depth-of-field and just want to take sharp, well exposed photographs. And once they do have a better understanding, they then tend to progress on to less automated exposure modes that offer increased control.

Program shift

Program shift lets you change the combination of aperture and shutter speed by rotating the input dial until you get your preferred choice. Use it to quickly change the aperture to a wider or smaller one, letting the camera change the shutter speed to maintain correct exposure, or select a faster or slower shutter speed, and watch the aperture change automatically. If you're shooting landscapes, for example, where you want more depth-of-field, you just need to 'shift' towards a smaller aperture, whereas if you're shooting action, 'shift' towards a faster shutter speed.

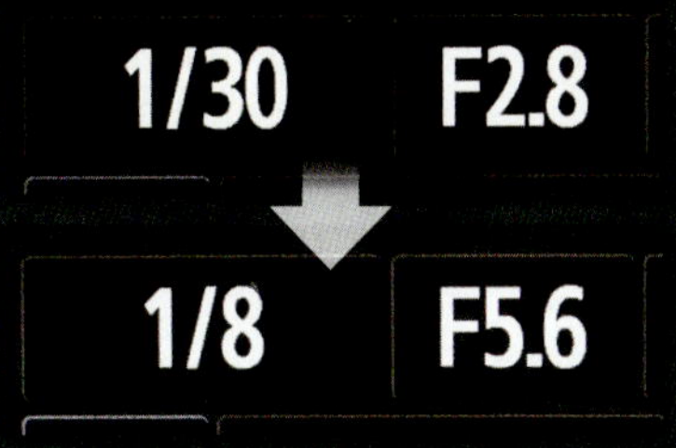

Shooting situations when it's best to use program mode

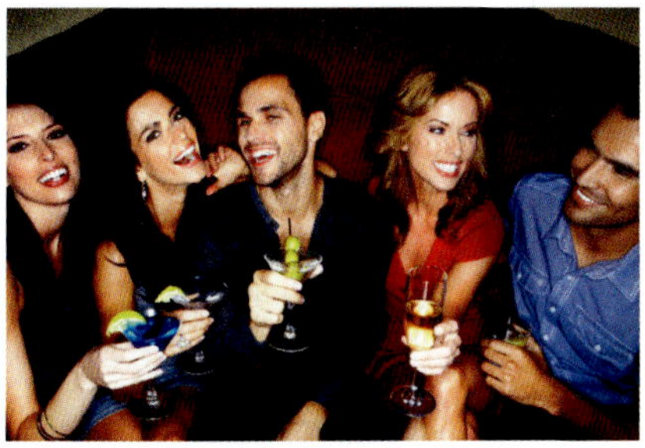

1) Indoor 'informal' shots
If you're taking informal pictures of family and friends, select P, pop up the flash if needed and fire away. You could also use Full-Auto, but this usually results in the flash being used, which often gives a less pleasing result.

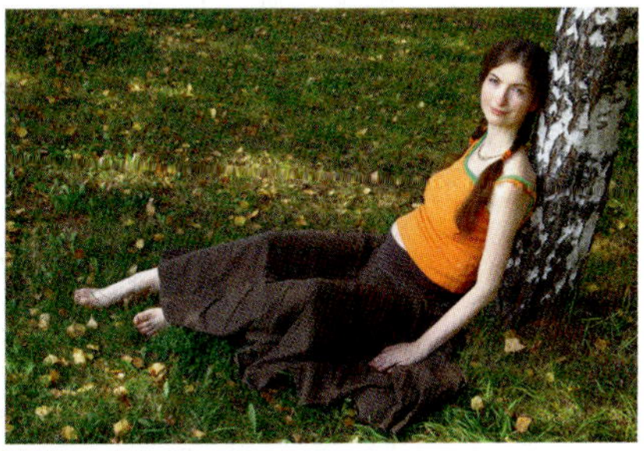

2) Fill-in flash exposures
Program is a good choice when you want to add a touch of fill-in flash to outdoor portraits. Just pop up the flash (or switch on a hotshoe-mounted flashgun) and let the camera take care of the exposure for you.

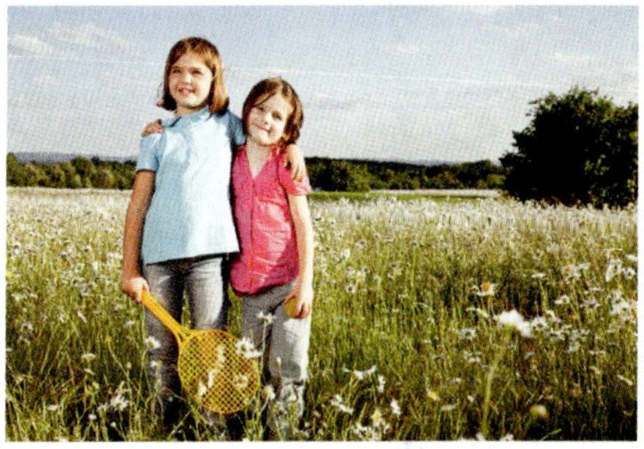

3) 'Fuss-free' general photography
When you simply want to quickly grab a scene and haven't time to change settings, select program, fire off a couple of shots, then if you have time, use program shift to alter settings a little more to your liking. Perfect for candids.

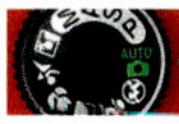 – Full-Auto & program

As well as the standard program mode (P), most cameras offer another fully automatic mode, commonly known as the 'green square', 'Green Auto' mode or 'Full-Auto' mode. At first sight, this may seem identical to the program mode, but they have their differences. Your camera's instruction book can give more details, but the key difference is that with program mode, only the aperture and shutter speed are set automatically by the camera: all the other functions, such as AF or metering patterns, can be set by you. This also includes the flash. In program, the camera indicates when flash is required (by flashing the lightning symbol), but requires you to pop up the integral flash before it will fire. With full-auto mode, the camera will automatically fire the flash if required. This is because the Full-Auto mode assumes the user has minimal photo knowledge: in other words, that they are an absolute beginner. Many cameras now boast an intelligent auto (iAuto or A+) mode, which acts much like the Full-Auto mode, but allows the user more control.

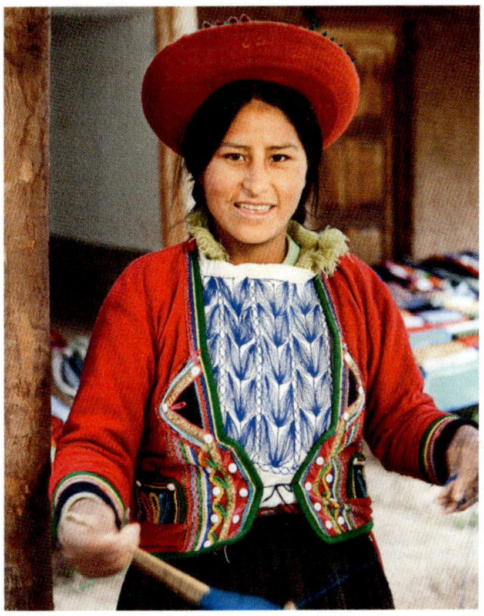

Program mode and flash

When light levels fall, the lightning symbol flashes as a visual indication for you to pop up the flash. If you don't, the camera will still take the picture, but if you're hand-holding, you risk shake. If you pop up the flash, the camera sets the shutter speed to the flash sync speed and usually leaves the aperture wide open to extend the flash range. The camera is only concerned with correctly exposing the subject, so the background will normally appear very dark – if you want to reveal detail in the backdrop, you need to use another mode.

Flashing shutter speeds

Your camera will do its best to give a winning combination of shutter speed and aperture, but in extremely bright or dark shooting situations (ie very rare situations), this may prove impossible. In very bright conditions, if the maximum shutter speed and smallest aperture are flashing, it indicates a risk of overexposure, so lower the ISO rating and, if the problem persists, use an ND filter. In dark situations, if the slowest shutter speed and maximum aperture blink, it means you risk underexposure, so raise the ISO rating.

– Aperture-priority mode (A or Av)

As the name implies, if you set your camera to this exposure mode, priority is given to the aperture selected. In fact, you decide which aperture (f/number) to set, and once you've done that (by using the input dial or appropriate buttons), the camera instantly chooses and sets a shutter speed to achieve correct exposure, based on the light reading taken by the metering system. The aperture and shutter speed set will be displayed in the camera's viewfinder, top-plate LCD and/or rear LCD monitor so you're fully aware of both, even though you've only chosen the aperture.

Aperture-priority is an ideal exposure mode to use when you need to control depth-of-field (how much of the scene appears sharply focused). If you're shooting landscapes and architecture where front-to-back sharpness is required, all you do is select a small aperture, such as f/11 or f/16 or f/22. At the other extreme, if you need to minimise depth-of-field so only a shallow zone of sharp focus is achieved – when shooting portraits, for example – you can set a wide aperture (small number), such as f/4 or f/2.8.

Because the camera instantly responds to any change of aperture by adjusting the shutter speed so correct exposure is maintained, you can work quickly – shooting at a small aperture (and slower shutter speed) one minute, then switching to a wider aperture (and faster shutter speed) the next. This also makes aperture-priority the best exposure mode for general shooting situations, and it's perhaps the most widely used mode among serious and experienced photographers.

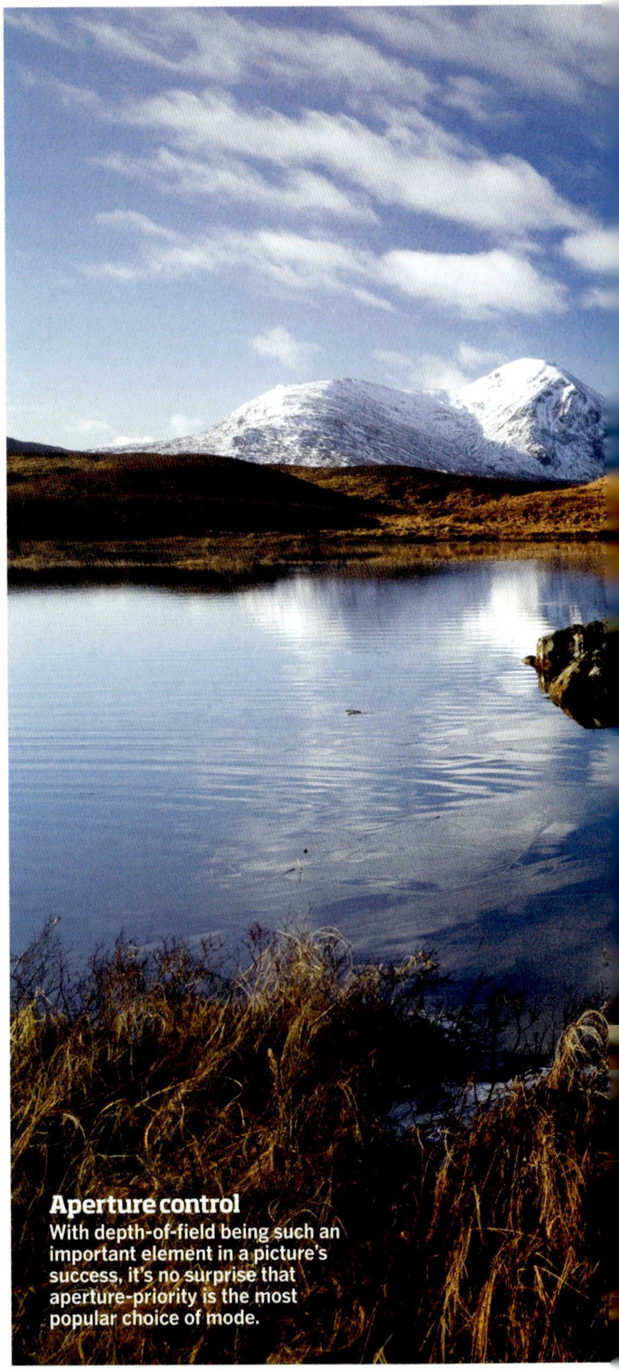

Aperture control
With depth-of-field being such an important element in a picture's success, it's no surprise that aperture-priority is the most popular choice of mode.

Shooting situations when it's best to use aperture-priority

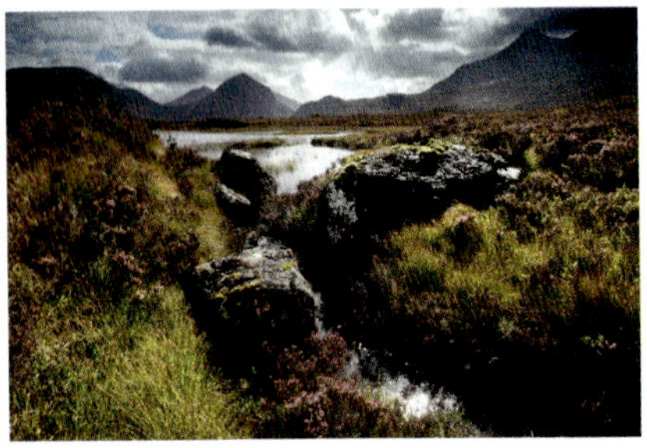

1) Landscapes: maximise depth-of-field
By changing the aperture, you're in full control of depth-of-field and how much of the scene appears sharp. Most landscape photographers use aperture-priority for this reason.

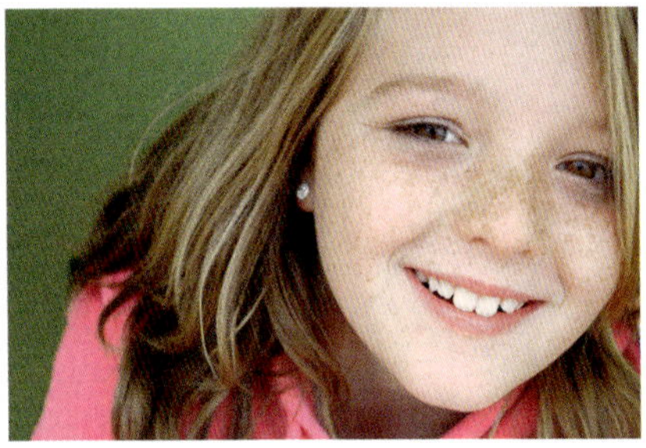

2) Portraits: background out of focus
Most portraits aim for the subject to stand out from the background so as to grab the viewer's gaze. Nothing does this better than focusing on the eye and choosing a wide aperture.

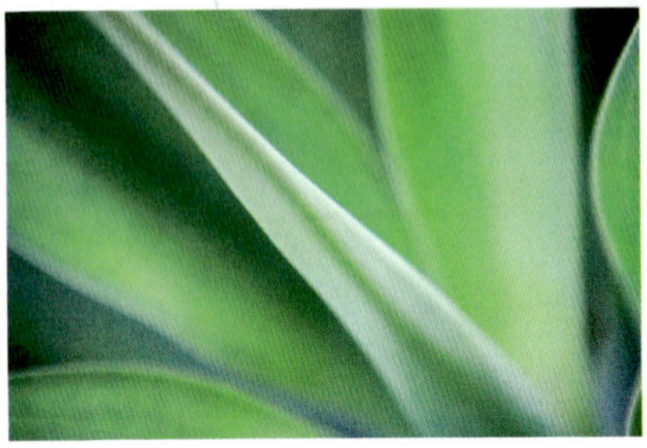

3) Macro photography
When you're working at very close distances, depth-of-field is minimal, so critical focusing, along with being able to use the optimum aperture, is essential for sharp results.

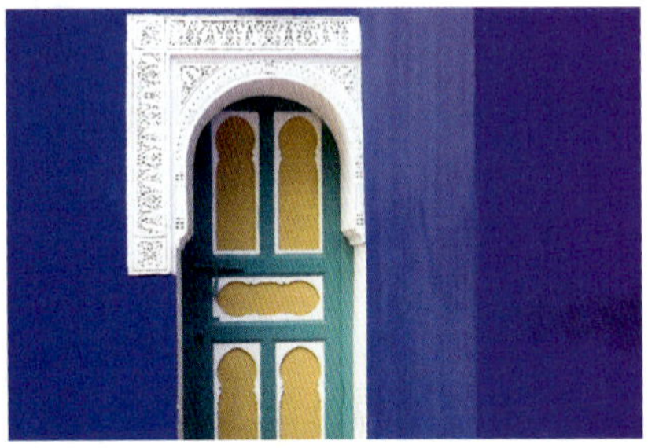

4) Optimal sharpness from your lens
Every lens has an aperture that gives the sharpest results – usually between f/8 and f/13. So if ultimate sharpness is your aim, set aperture-priority and shoot at these settings.

Aperture-priority & slow shutter speeds

The main thing to be aware of when using aperture-priority is that as you choose a smaller aperture, the corresponding shutter speed set by the camera will become slower and slower, so the risk of camera shake increases. It's easy to forget this when you're busy shooting, especially in low light, or if you decide to use a polarising filter, which loses two stops of light, as you're giving priority to the aperture and depth-of-field. But it's also important to keep an eye on the shutter speed being set by the camera so you don't end up with blurred images! Once the shutter speed drops below a level that you can safely hand-hold, you've three options:

1) Set a wider aperture so the shutter speed increases. For example, if the shutter speed at f/11 is 1/15sec, at f/8 it will be 1/30sec, at f/5.6 it is 1/60sec and at f/4 it will be 1/125sec. This option won't work if you need a small aperture to give lots of depth-of-field, but photographers often stop their lens down too far, so you may be able to use a wider aperture without compromising depth-of-field.

2) If you can't sacrifice depth-of-field by using a wider aperture to increase the shutter speed, mount your camera on a tripod or some other support so that it's not going to move. That way, it doesn't matter if the shutter speed is really slow. This is the best option for static subjects, such as landscapes, architecture and still life.

3) The final option is to increase the ISO setting so a faster shutter speed can be used. For example, if shooting at ISO 100 at 1/30sec at f/16, increasing the ISO to 200 will allow you to use a shutter speed of 1/60sec at f/11, raise it to 400 and the shutter speed will be 1/125sec at f/11, and so on.

If you're on the ball, you can combine the above options. Increasing a stop lets you maintain your chosen aperture and use a faster shutter speed without much compromise on image quality. If that doesn't do the trick, you can also open up the aperture a stop without losing too much depth-of-field.

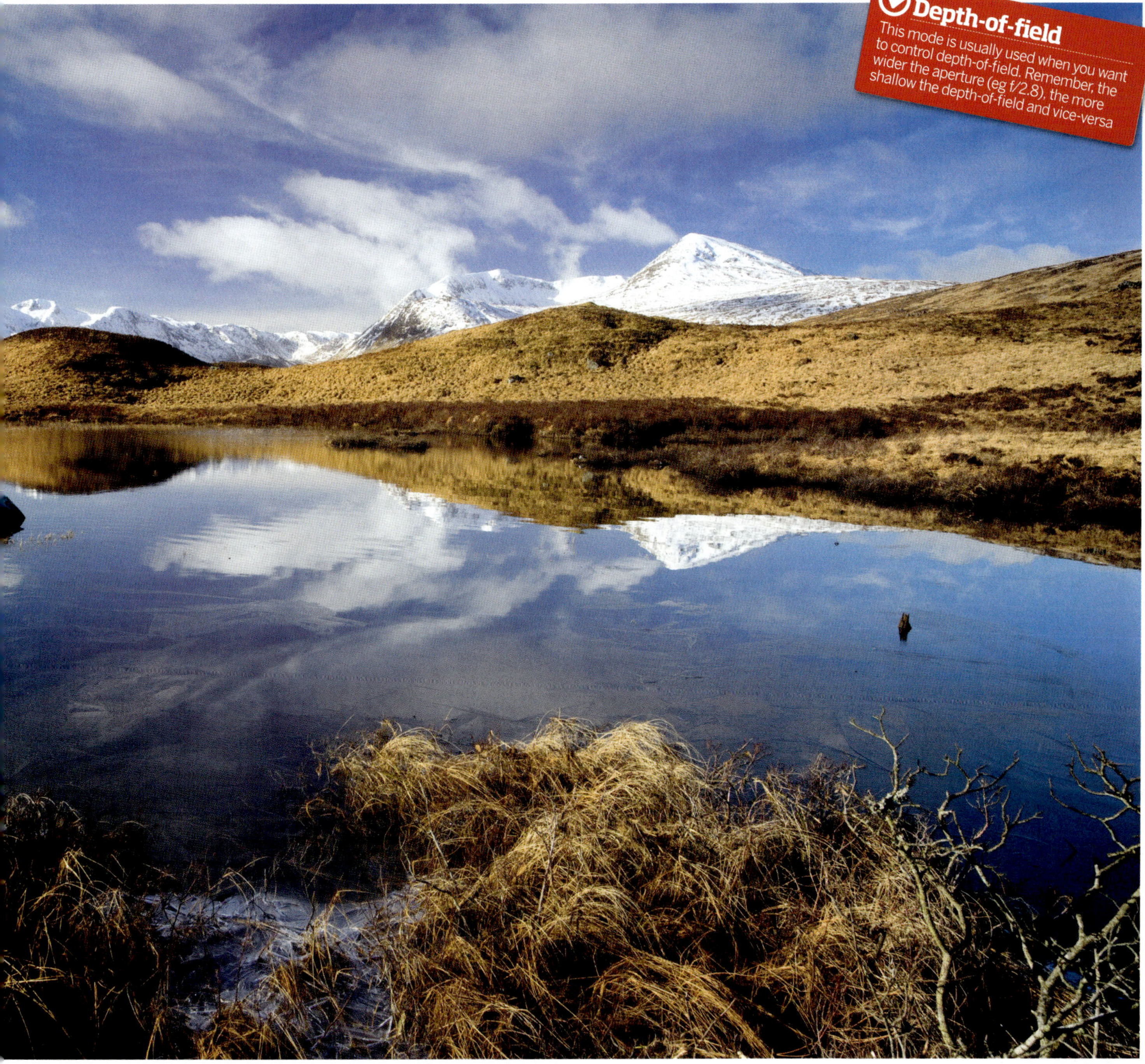

ALL IMAGES: LEE FROST

Depth-of-field

This mode is usually used when you want to control depth-of-field. Remember, the wider the aperture (eg f/2.8), the more shallow the depth-of-field and vice-versa

Aperture-priority and flash

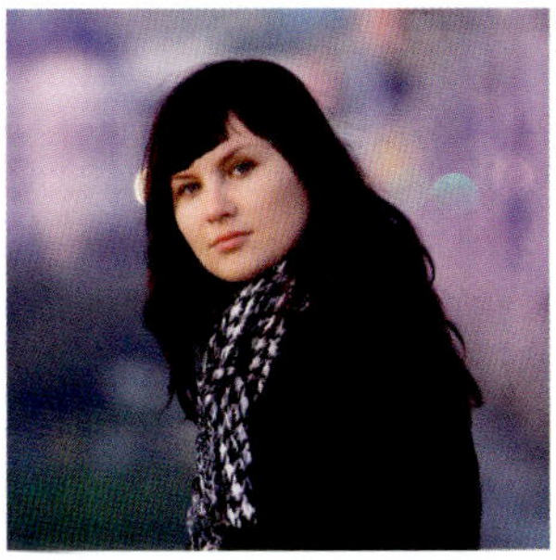

ISTOCK PHOTO

How aperture-priority works with flash varies on the brand and model of camera you have. For instance, with most Canon and Pentax models, once you select the aperture, the camera chooses a shutter speed to correctly expose the background, so in low light, the camera needs to be tripod-mounted to avoid shake. In effect, the camera is automatically applying slow-sync flash. With Nikon, Sony and Olympus, the shutter speed is limited to prevent shake, unless the slow-sync flash mode is selected. Check the instruction manual to see how aperture-priority works with flash and experiment with results.

Warning! Flashing shutter speed

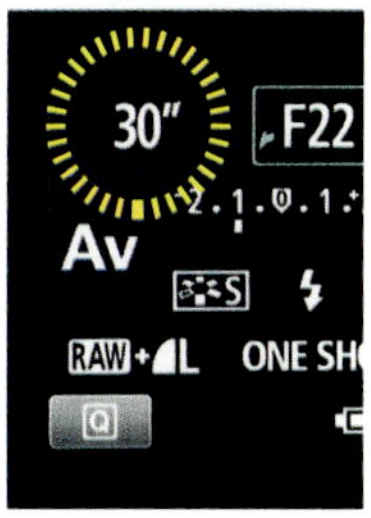

When selecting the aperture, you may get to a point where the shutter speed starts flashing. This indicates that the camera is unable to provide a corresponding shutter speed, which will lead to poor exposures. This could be because you're shooting in very bright light and have selected too fast an aperture or, alternatively, have set too small an aperture in low light. With the former situation, lower the ISO rating and consider using an ND filter. With the latter, raise the ISO rating. If this doesn't solve the problem, you'll need to change the aperture setting until the shutter speed stops flashing.

Exposure compensation and aperture-priority

If you apply exposure compensation in aperture-priority mode, the shutter speed is adjusted to change the exposure and the aperture stays the same, as you are giving it priority. For example, if you're shooting at 1/250sec at f/4 and you dial in +1EV (one stop) of exposure compensation, the camera will change the shutter speed to 1/125sec, but leave the aperture unchanged at f/4.

– Shutter-priority mode (S or Tv)

This is the second semi-automatic exposure mode that you'll find on all DSLRs and CSCs, and, as the name suggests, it gives priority to the shutter speed. Shutter-priority allows you to choose the one you want to use while the camera sets the aperture automatically to achieve correct exposure – in other words, it's the opposite to aperture-priority.

Shutter-priority is the ideal exposure mode to use when you're shooting subjects that require careful choice of shutter speed to control motion. Sport and action are top of the list as you generally want to freeze movement by choosing a shutter speed that matches the subject: the faster the movement, the faster the shutter speed needed to freeze it, and vice versa. Common sense, really. Nature photographers often use shutter-priority, too, when photographing birds in flight, say, or animals on the move. While everyday action subjects, such as your kids running around in the park or the family dog shaking its wet coat after a dip in the sea, may also benefit from the use of shutter-priority mode.

Of course, shutter-priority isn't reserved only for freezing movement: sometimes you will also want to intentionally blur it to capture a sense of grace and motion in your images. Sport and action subjects can be photographed using a slow shutter speed by panning the camera, so the subject comes out relatively sharp while the background is blurred. Or you may simply decide to keep the camera still and let moving subjects record as colourful streaks. Moving water in rivers, waterfalls and the sea is also often photographed using a slow shutter speed, so it records as a milky blur. In each case, there is usually an optimum shutter speed to help you achieve the best result, and shutter-priority mode will allow you to set it.

You may be one step ahead of us here and thinking, 'But surely I can set the shutter speed I want in aperture-priority mode just by changing the aperture until the camera sets the shutter speed I want, or in program mode by changing the aperture and shutter speed combination?' If so, you're correct. However, the benefit of using shutter-priority mode when you need to shoot at a certain shutter speed is that, once it's set, it won't change if the light levels fluctuate or you change camera position. If the exposure needs to be adjusted in shutter-priority mode, it's the aperture that changes, so that the shutter speed remains constant (the opposite happens in aperture-priority). The same applies if you use your camera's exposure compensation to increase or reduce the exposure – in shutter-priority mode, the aperture is increased or reduced and the shutter speed remains unchanged.

If prevailing light levels are too low to allow you to use a fast enough shutter speed, even with the lens at its widest aperture, all is not lost – simply increase the ISO. For example, if the fastest shutter speed you can manage at ISO 100 is 1/125sec, at ISO 200 it will increase to 1/250sec, at ISO 400 it will be 1/500sec, and so on, giving you additional control so you can set the shutter speed you need.

At the other extreme, if you need to set a slow shutter speed to blur movement, when light levels are high you may find that the slowest you can manage isn't slow enough. Again, reducing the ISO may do the trick. Some cameras have a 'Low' ISO setting that's half the speed of the default ISO, so if you select it, the slowest shutter speed you can use will halve – from 1/15sec to 1/8sec, for example. If that doesn't work, you'll need to resort to using filters. A polariser loses two stops of light, so if you pop one on your lens, ¼sec becomes one second. Alternatively, use a Neutral Density (ND) filter to increase the exposure – a 0.6ND will have the same effect as a polariser, a 0.9ND requires a three-stop exposure increase and a 1.2ND requires a four-stop exposure increase. For general shooting, you won't need filters for slower shutter speeds, but once you start experimenting with the creative use of blur, they are useful and allow you to make full use of your camera's shutter speed range.

Avoid camera shake with the reciprocal rule

There is an easy method to determine when you risk your images suffering from camera shake. Ensure the shutter speed you use is the reciprocal of the focal length. So if you use a 55-200mm, set a shutter speed of at least 1/200sec; with a 70-300mm, use at least 1/300sec, and so on. Obviously lenses boasting an image stabiliser allow you to get away with slightly slower speeds than the reciprocal rule suggests, but it remains a good guideline to follow.

Shooting situations when it's best to use shutter-priority

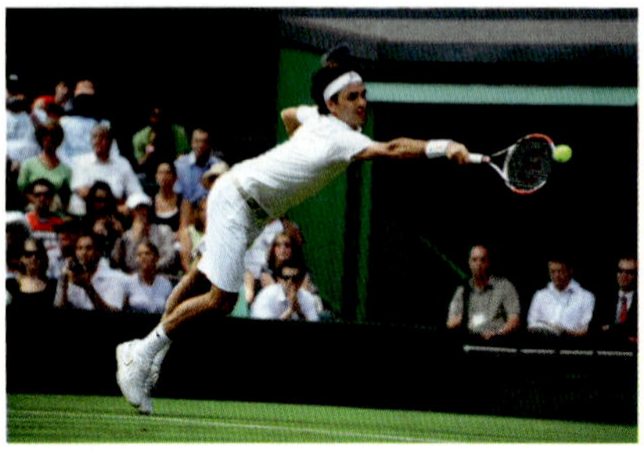

RICHARD PELHAM

1) Sports & wildlife: freezing action

When shooting fast-moving subjects with the aim to freeze their movement, you need to set a fast shutter speed. Using shutter-priority lets you set the exact speed you want to use.

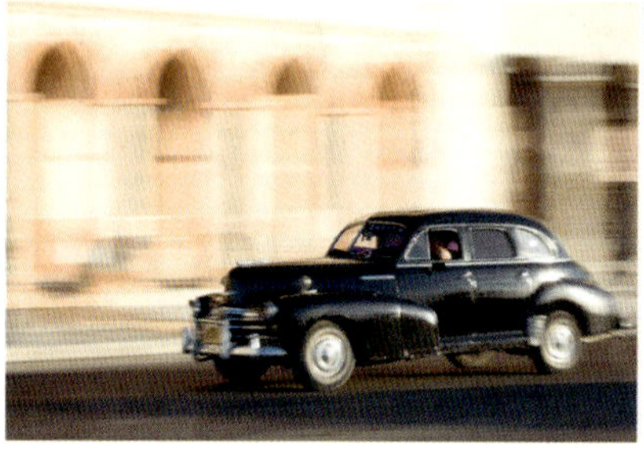

LEE FROST

2) Moving subject: emphasise motion

If you want to get a little more creative with your images of moving subjects, try using a slower shutter speed to blur their movements. It's also the ideal mode for panning too.

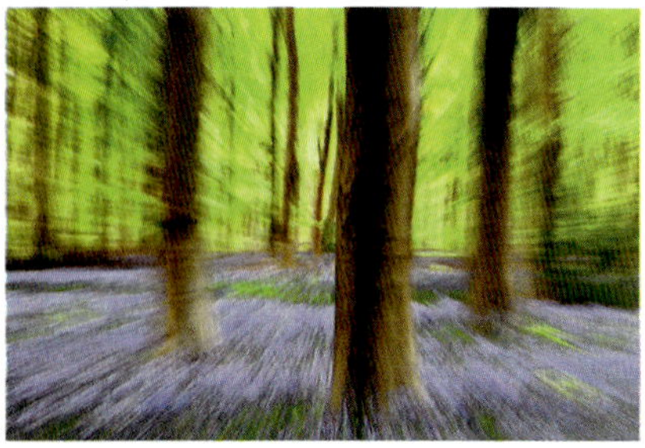

HELEN DIXON

3) Zoom bursts

This creative technique involves zooming the lens during a relatively slow exposure. Using shutter-priority lets you determine which shutter speed is best for the zoom you're using.

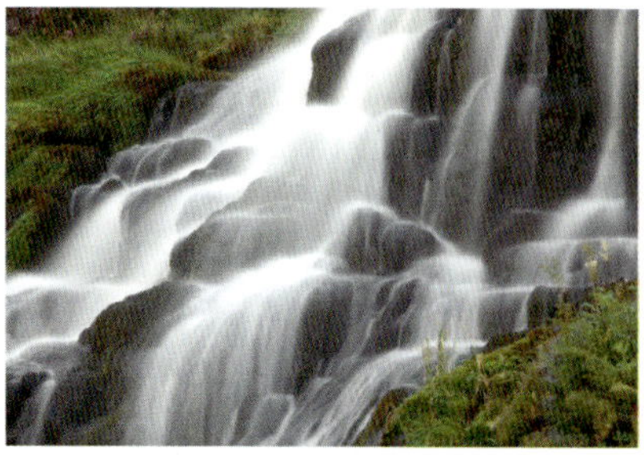

LEE FROST

4) Landscapes: blurring water

The shutter speed has a dramatic effect on how water is recorded. Using shutter-priority, use a fast shutter speed to freeze its motion, or a very slow speed to turn it into a milky blur.

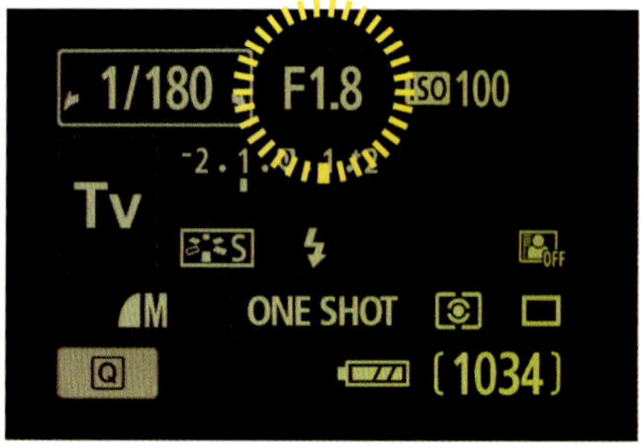

Warning! Flashing aperture

When choosing a shutter speed, the aperture value may start to blink, indicating that the camera is unable to provide a corresponding aperture setting speed, which may lead to poor exposures. This could be because you have selected too fast or too slow a shutter speed for the lighting conditions. If this is the case, change the ISO rating until the aperture no longer blinks, or if shooting in very bright conditions, use an ND filter.

Exposure compensation and shutter-priority

If you apply exposure compensation in shutter-priority mode, the aperture is changed and the shutter speed stays the same. So if you have an exposure of 1/250sec at f/5.6 and apply +1EV, it will change to 1/250sec at f/4.

Shutter-priority with flash

Virtually all cameras handle flash exposures in shutter-priority the same way. You choose the shutter speed you want to use and the camera selects an aperture that will allow the scene to be correctly exposed by the ambient light, with the flash output exposing the subject correctly.

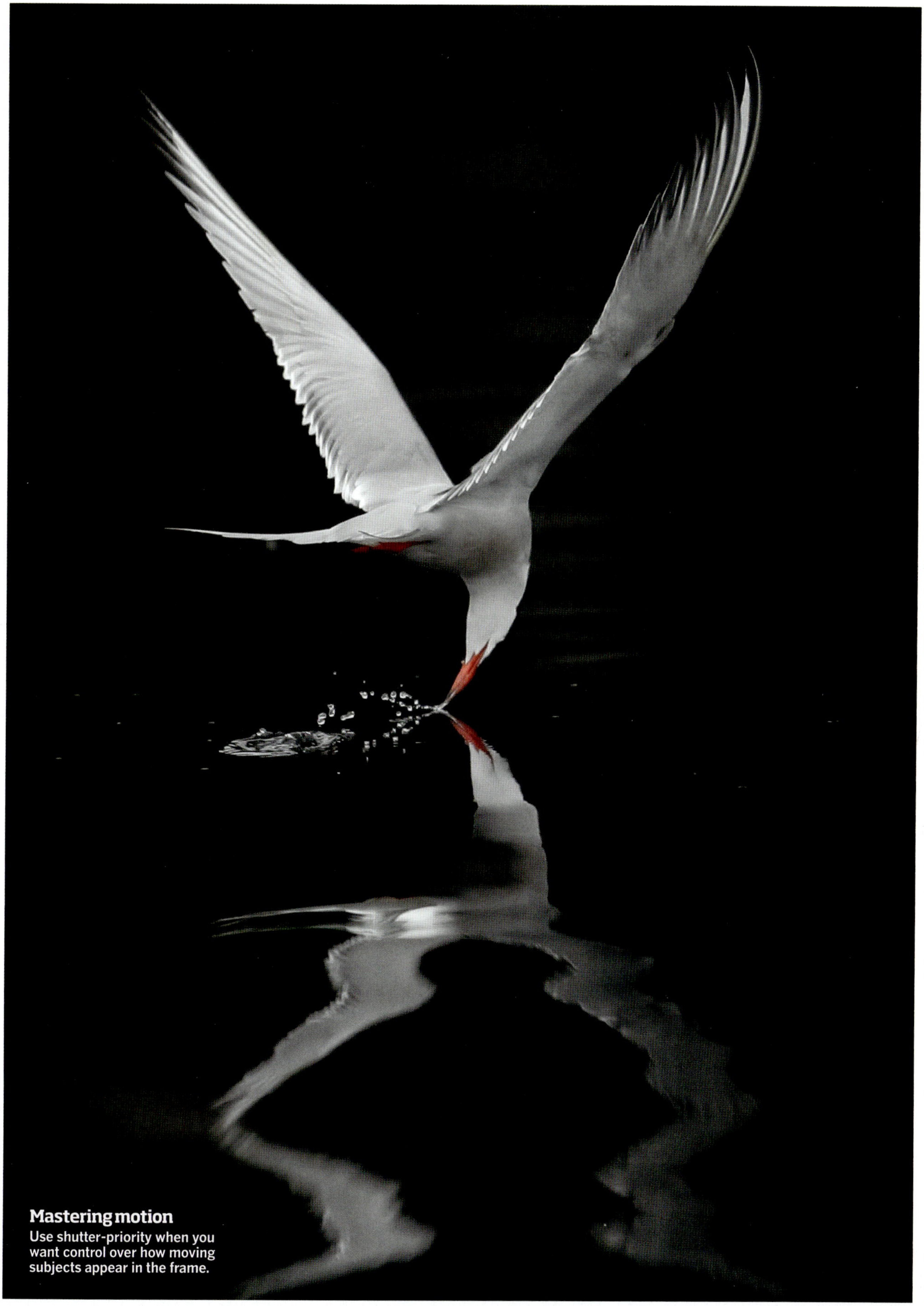

MIGUEL LASSA

Mastering motion
Use shutter-priority when you want control over how moving subjects appear in the frame.

– Manual (M)

Manual exposure mode is called manual because you have to do all the work. Whereas with other modes the camera sets the aperture and shutter speed for you – or one or the other – in manual, you set both. An indicator in the viewfinder, top-plate LCD and/or rear screen tells you when the combination you've chosen has achieved correct exposure, or how far over or under the 'correct' exposure you are. Because of this, it's the slowest exposure mode to use and, consequently, the least used.

Some photographers swear by manual mode because they foolishly believe that the camera's metering system is more accurate in that mode than any other. However, there is absolutely no truth in this. The only way you can change how your camera measures light to determine the correct exposure is by selecting a different metering pattern. But if you leave the metering pattern alone (most of us prefer to use whichever multi-zone pattern our camera offers, such as Evaluative with Canon and Matrix with Nikon), it will measure light in exactly the same way, no matter which exposure mode you use. Anyone favouring manual exposure mode over, say, aperture-priority for this reason is therefore making life more difficult for the sake of it, with no gain.

So, is there a use for manual exposure mode in this modern, automated digital age? Absolutely. If you're shooting with studioflash, for example, you need to set manual mode so that you can set the aperture needed to give the correct flash exposure, along with the camera's flash sync speed. If you use studioflash with aperture-priority mode, you can still select the aperture, but the camera will automatically set a shutter speed to correctly expose the ambient light levels, not the flash. If you do a lot of low-light photography and regularly need to use the Bulb (B) setting so the shutter can be left open to record traffic trails, fireworks, star trails etc, you may also need to set the camera to manual exposure mode to access the Bulb setting. Some DSLRs have Bulb as a self-contained setting, but on many, it's simply at the end of the shutter speed range in manual exposure mode.

Another benefit of manual exposure mode is that once you've set the exposure on the camera, it won't change, even if you move the camera or light levels go up or down. If you're shooting in tricky or changeable light, but need to maintain a fixed exposure, it's easier to do that in manual mode than using exposure compensation, or the exposure lock in conjunction with a different exposure mode.

Of course, this can be a curse as much as a blessing because if light levels change and you need to change the exposure, but forget to when shooting in manual mode, you'll end up with a badly exposed image. This doesn't happen with the other exposure modes because either the aperture, shutter speed or both are set by the camera, so if light levels change, the exposure will also change automatically to maintain correct exposure.

There are some photographers who prefer manual mode to other exposure modes, simply because they feel more in control of the camera, and that's perfectly fine. If you've only started shooting seriously in recent years, you may find this idea rather daft, but for photographers who spent years or decades shooting with manual-only cameras, old habits die hard and it just feels more familiar.

Setting apertures & shutter speeds in manual

This varies from camera to camera, but the majority of models use the following method: with the camera in manual mode, use the input dial to change the shutter speed. To change the aperture, press and hold the exposure compensation button and use the input dial to select the aperture. With some CSCs, the process is a little more fiddly, requiring you to use the four-way control and ring surrounding it to access the aperture and shutter speed.

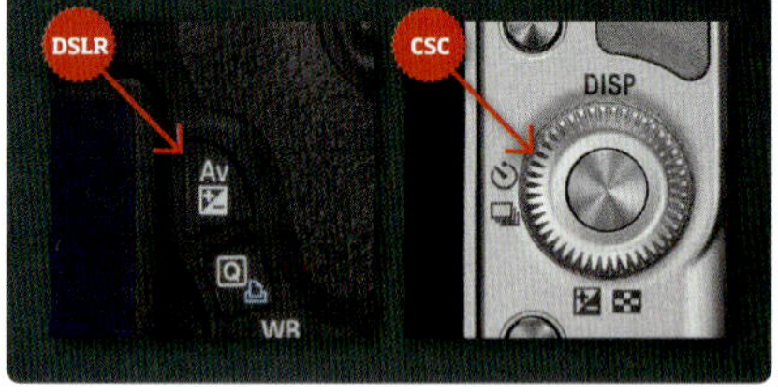

In experienced hands, manual mode can also be quick and reliable because it keeps you more in touch with both the aperture and shutter speed, and if the exposure needs to be overridden to correct error, you can do it by changing one, the other or both, instead of having to rely on using the camera's exposure compensation facility.

It's a case of one man's meat being another man's poison. Manual is slower and slightly more fiddly than other modes, but some of us just prefer it that way!

Shooting situations when it's best to use manual mode

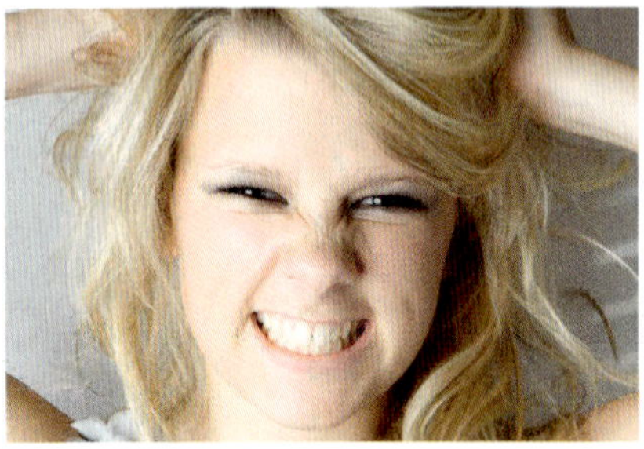

1) Studioflash photography

You need to use manual mode when using studioflash. The shutter speed must be set at the flash sync speed (or lower), while the exposure is determined by the aperture.

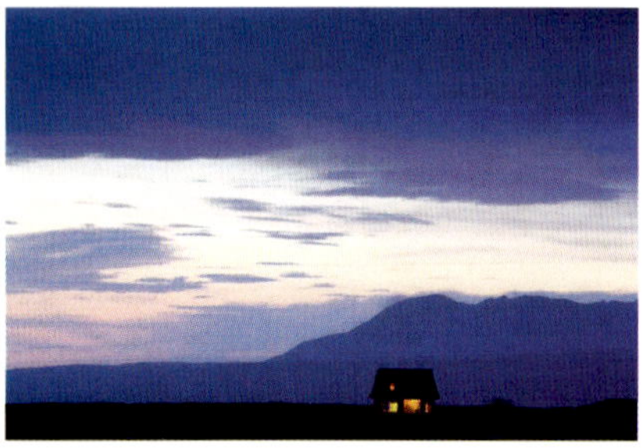

2) Night photography

While you could use either of the semi-auto modes for night shots, manual mode is the fastest way to make changes to the exposure, making it best for speed and convenience.

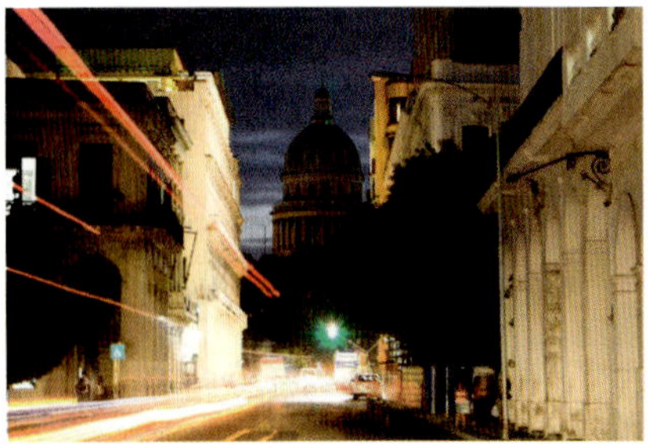

3) Bulb exposures

The vast majority of cameras need to be set to manual mode to allow for the selection of the Bulb setting. This allows for creative long exposures that can last for up to an hour.

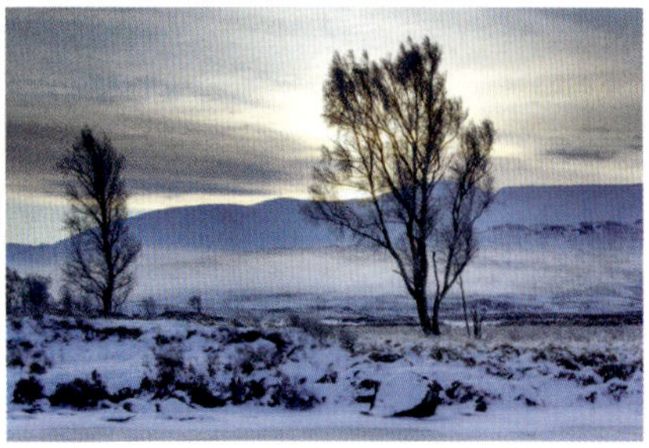

4) Exposure bracketing

Those new to bracketing often use aperture-priority with exposure compensation, but a faster way is to make adjustments to the aperture and shutter speed in manual.

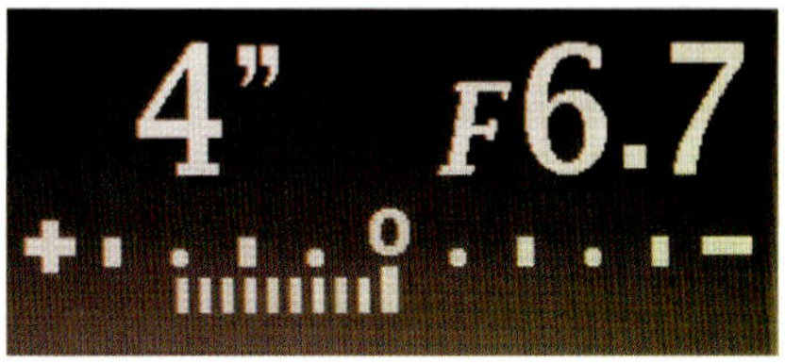

Using the exposure scale

Achieving the correct exposure in manual mode is easier than you may think. When changing the aperture and camera settings, all you need to do is use the exposure scale as a guide to whether your current settings will lead to over- or underexposure. Change the aperture and/or shutter speed until the exposure level mark sits on the '0', which indicates correct exposure. There is no exposure compensation facility in manual mode, but you can effectively over- or underexpose the scene deliberately by moving the level mark from '0' to a positive or negative value.

Manual mode with flash

Many people believe that because the camera is in manual, the flash functions in manual mode, too. In fact, that's not the case. In manual mode, you select an aperture and shutter speed to illuminate the background, with the flash concentrating only on correctly exposing the subject. Even though the camera is in manual mode, the flash still uses TTL (Through The Lens) flash metering to give an accurate flash exposure. With more sophisticated flashguns, a distance scale appears on the rear LCD monitor so that you're given an indication of the distance the flash can cover.

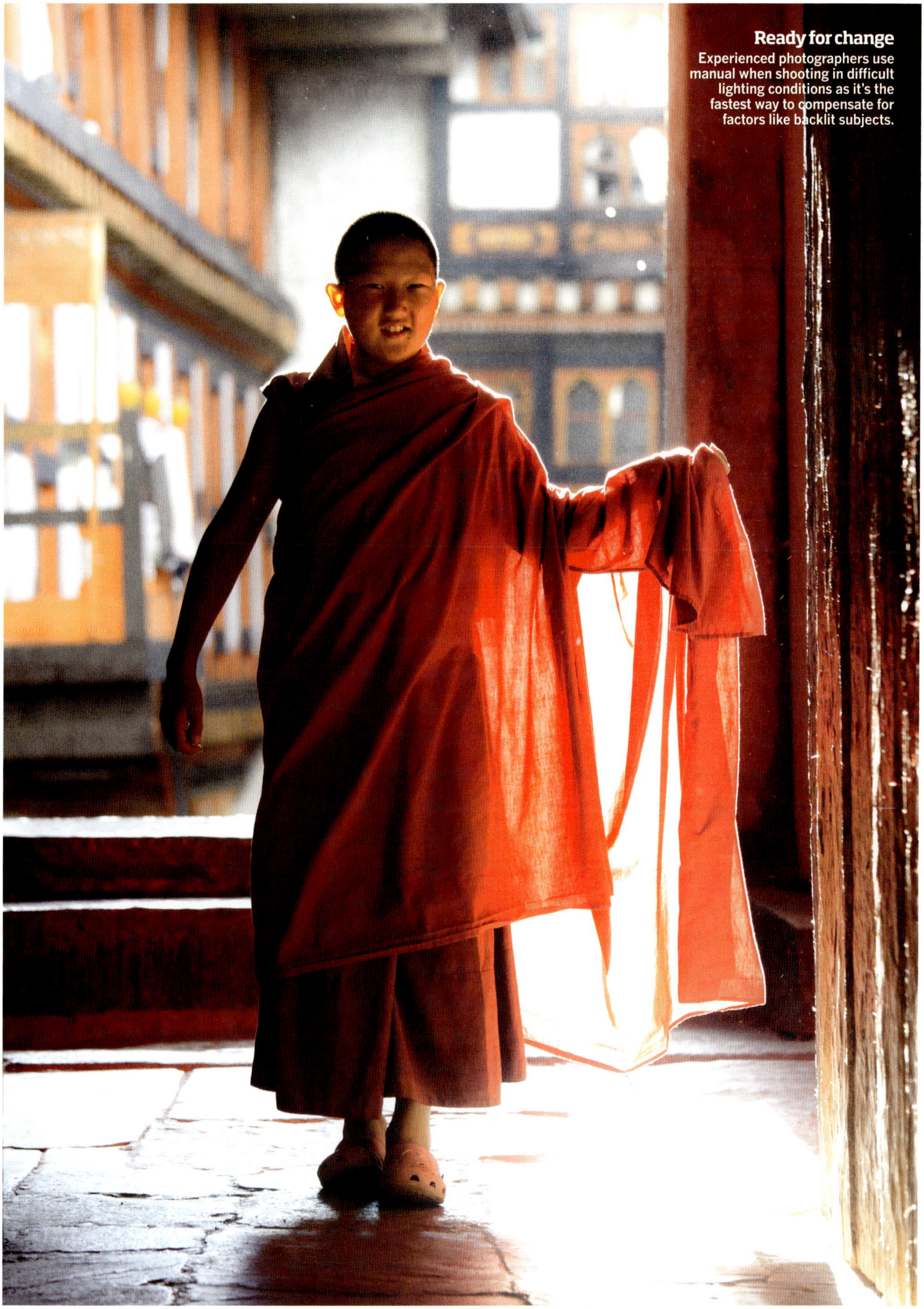

Ready for change
Experienced photographers use manual when shooting in difficult lighting conditions as it's the fastest way to compensate for factors like backlit subjects.

Autofocus: Understanding the fundamentals of how AF works

Your camera offers a variety of autofocus options to help ensure you capture sharp results and it's important that you know how they work

THE TECHNOLOGY BUILT into even entry-level DSLRs these days is phenomenal when you think about it; all that computer wizardry processing information in milliseconds to give us high quality images at the touch of a button. The trouble is, because today's digital cameras are so good, we tend to rely on them too much, expecting perfect photographs every time, and when we don't get what we want, we blame the camera!

This is especially true when it comes to focusing. Wind the clock back 25 years and focusing was a manual affair. Some of you may remember those halcyon days spent twiddling thumb and forefinger while trying to get two images to merge at the centre of the focusing screen so that sharp focus was achieved, but for most your only experience of focusing will be pointing the camera at your chosen subject, pressing the shutter release and assuming a sharply focused image will result.

More often than not it does, especially when shooting static subjects that dominate the composition. But in some situations you will need to take control – either by choosing settings to suit certain subjects and conditions, or by taking over completely and focusing manually. We'll be taking a look at those scenarios shortly, but first a quick rundown on how autofocus actually works, so you hopefully have a better understanding of why the camera doesn't always do what you want it to do!

Basically, when light passes into your camera through the lens, most of it is bounced up off the reflex mirror into the viewfinder so you can see an image, but some is also reflected down onto a sub-mirror, which then bounces that light onto the AF sensor. On top of the AF sensor is a set of optics that splits the light into two beams. The sensor analyses these beams to determine how far out-of-focus the image is and whether focus is in front of or behind the focal plane, then adjusts focus accordingly. This happens so quickly that your camera can continually adjust focus as you track a moving subject, making successful action photography easier than ever before.

The system, known as Phase-Detection, uses the AF sensors to determine where to focus. The number of sensors varies from model to model but generally, the more expensive the camera, the more sensors there are – the Canon EOS 550D has 9, for example, while the Nikon D3s has 51. You can either activate them all, then leave the camera to decide which ones to use, or select a specific sensor or sensors so you have more control over what the lens focuses on. Phase-Detection AF isn't foolproof and even the best systems can struggle when used in low light or if you try to focus on a plain area.

If you use LiveView mode, the AF system switches from Phase-Detection to Contrast-Detection, as the system can only work when the reflex mirror in the camera is in the 'down' position for viewing. When you use LiveView the mirror flips up so light entering the lens goes straight to the camera's sensor. Contrast-Detection works on the principle that the contrast in an image is at its highest when that image is sharply focused so the AF system adjusts focus stage by stage and analyses contrast, often going past the critical point so it knows where it is then adjusting back and locking focus. Contrast -Detection can focus on any part of the image area, which is why compact cameras have features such as Face-Detection. In the past, it proved slower than Phase Detection, so wasn't suitable for focus tracking on moving subjects, and struggled in low light. However, notable exceptions are the Sony Alpha's LiveView, which uses a unique system, and the latest generation of Compact System Cameras.

AF sensors

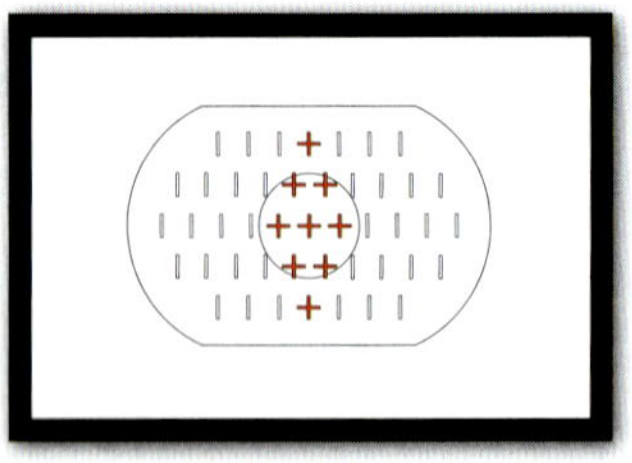

There are two types of AF sensor used in DSLRs – cross-type and line or linear. DSLRs have a mixture of both, with the cross-type being clustered more around the central area of the viewfinder and linear sensors towards the edges. Cross-type sensors comprise of two linear sensors crossing at 90°, hence the name. They're more accurate than linear sensors as they can detect both vertical and horizontal light patterns whereas linear sensors can only work in one dimension. Therefore, cross-type sensors are more effective. That said, on high-end DSLRs that have lots of cross-type AF sensors, some of these sensors only work as cross-type when used with 'fast' lenses that have a maximum aperture of f/2.8 or wider, so if you're using zooms with a maximum aperture of f/4 or f/5.6, some of the cross-type sensors will only work like linear sensors.

Focus and metering

In more recent DSLRs – such as the Nikon D7000 – the AF is linked to the metering system to increase the chance of correct exposure. So, if you're using single point AF, the exposure set will be biased towards the brightness/tonality of whatever is behind the selected AF point whereas if you're using a wide area AF where a number or AF points are active, the exposure will be influenced by whatever is behind the selected area (which gets bigger as the number of AF points increases). Nikon's Scene Recognition System broke new ground by linking the autofocus metering and White Balance systems, while more recently Canon has incorporated iFCL (Focus, Colour and Luminance), a system using autofocus colour and luminance information.

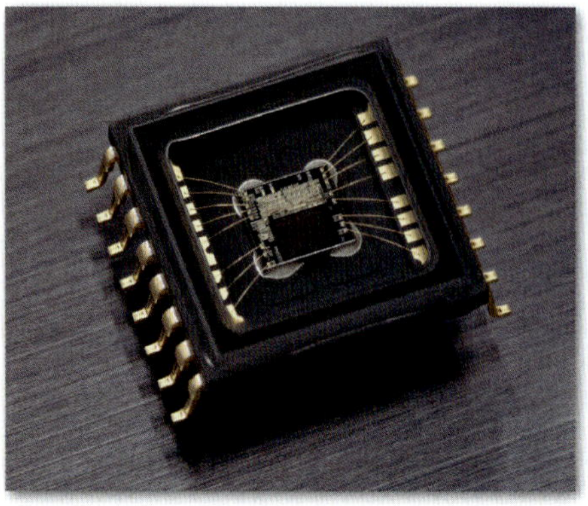

Critical focus

Learning more about your camera's AF modes will help ensure you focus on the correct area of the image.

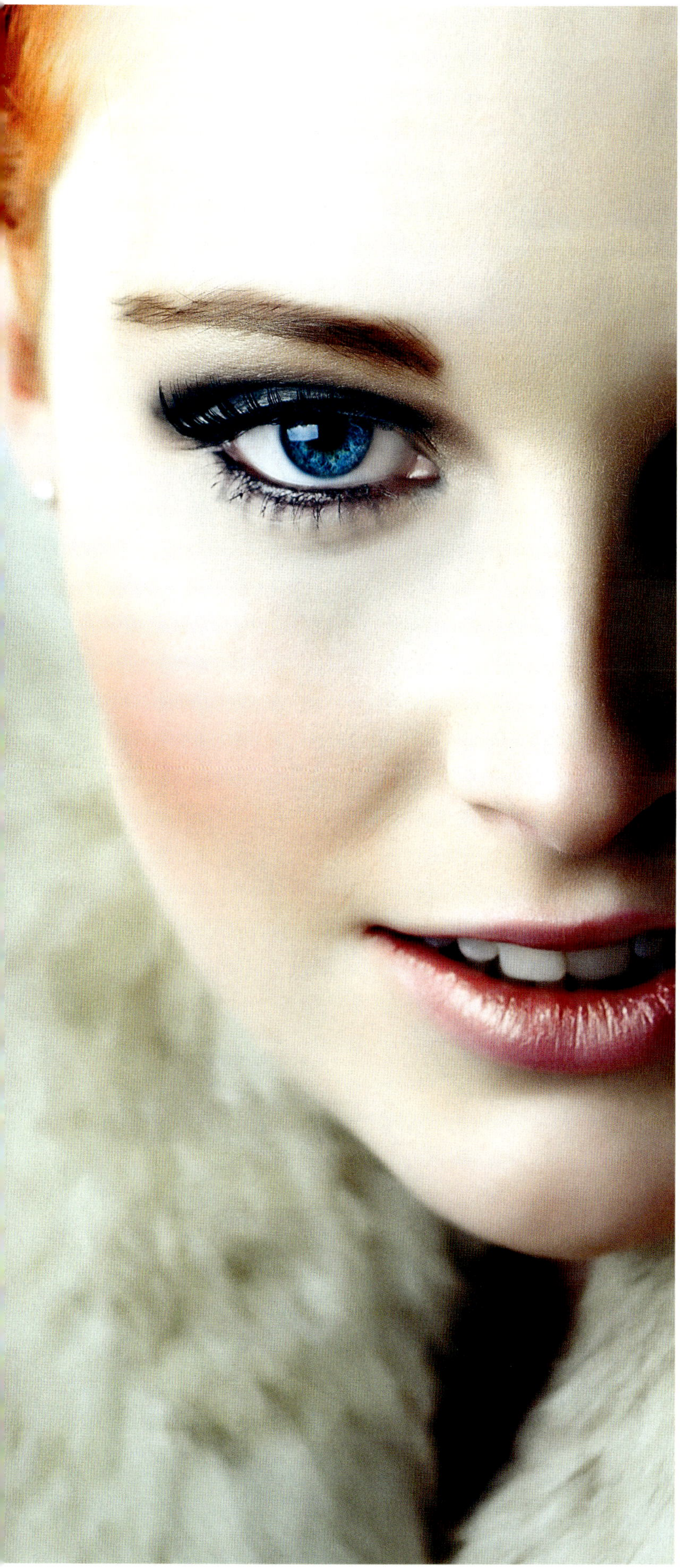

KARL SHAW

A range of focusing options

Digital SLRs and Compact System Cameras now offer several ways in which you can focus on your subject. Here are the most common types.offer a modes. Here we show how to set it on five popular DSLRs from the leading

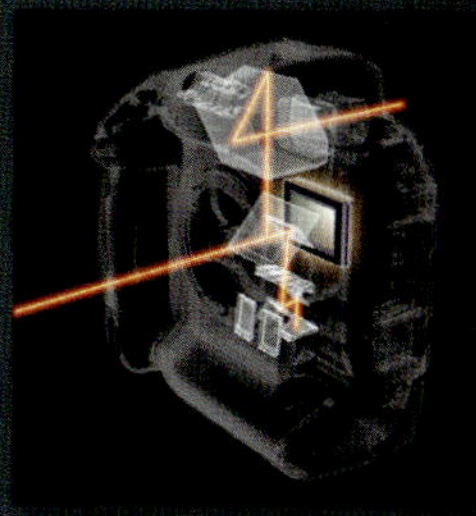

Phase Detection: This method is the system that has been traditionally used by film and digital SLRs and remains the primary method used for focusing in these cameras. Its main advantage is that it is incredibly quick and accurate, regardless of whether the subject is close by or at a distance. The system works by using a beam splitter within the camera that directs light on to a sensor – this measures what is known as the phase difference to calculate the subject distance. Phase detection struggles when there is a lack of contrast in the scene, such as in low light – we cover these problems and their solutions on page 32. Up until the last year or two, it was undeniably the fastest, most accurate form of autofocus in cameras, but the latest generation of Compact System Cameras offer contrast-AF systems that rival the performance of passive AF.

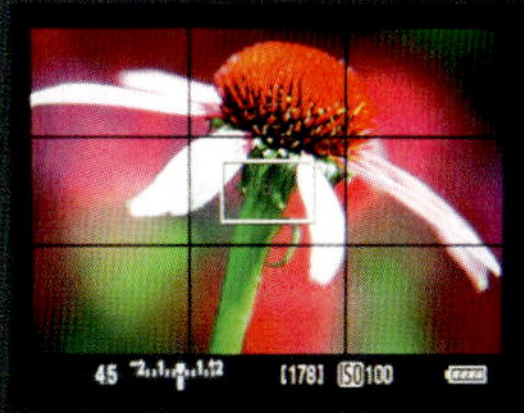

Contrast-AF: The vast majority of Compact System cameras, as well as the LiveView system used on many DSLRs, focus on subjects using contrast rather than distance to achieve accurate results. In the past this system has proven to be slower and less accurate than the phase-detection method, but recent generations of DSLRs and CSCs have show major improvements in performance. In fact the latest CSCs boast contrast-AF systems as fast – if not quicker – than most DSLRs. While the contrast-AF used in most DSLR's LiveView systems lag behind phase-detection AF, the Sony Alpha's LiveView is on a par with the best contrast-AF and phase detection systems.

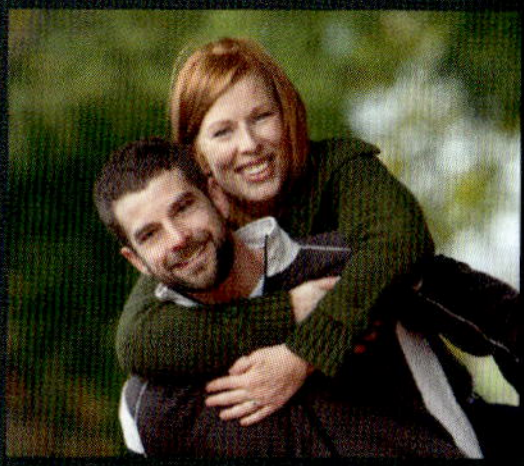

Face-priority AF: This system first appeared on digital compacts but has since been included on many CSCs as well as a small number of DSLRs. It is designed to make it very easy for photographers to capture sharply-focused portraits – in particular with two or more people in the frame. The camera does this by 'detecting' faces anywhere in the frame and focusing on it. This is a useful focus mode for beginners who are still getting used to multi-point AF.

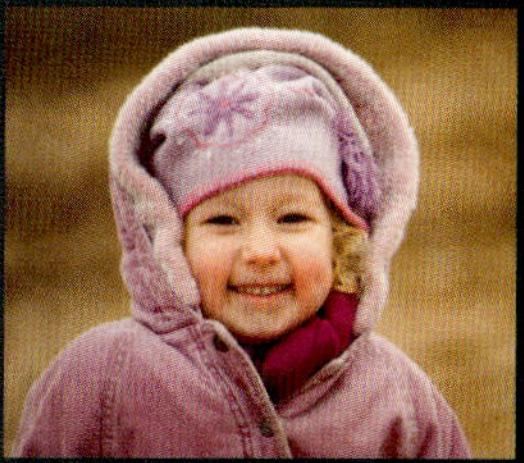

Smile detection AF: This facility takes face-priority AF a step further, with the camera firing the shutter once it detects the subject in the frame smiling. While this might seem like a bit of a gimmick, it's useful when you're shooting a self-portrait, as the camera won't fire until you smile. It's also handy when shooting groups. Shout out 'Smile!' and the camera as well as the subjects will respond to your request!

Touchscreen focus: A growing number of CSCs now boast touchscreen LCD monitors, that allow you to change modes and functions by touching the relevant icons on the screen. This includes focusing – by using your finger to press the screen where your subject is positioned, you're able to instantly activate the AF system to lock focus on it.

Trap focus: A small number of cameras offer a feature that allows you to set the focus to a particular distance, then leave the camera to fire the shutter once the subject reaches this distance. It's particularly useful when photographing fast moving subjects that are difficult to track using alternative focusing systems.

Autofocus: Your choice of modes

Your camera's AF system has two user-selectable functions: the AF mode and the AF point selection. Knowing how to each for different shooting situations will help ensure your subject is correctly focused

Autofocus modes: These allow you to either lock on the subject or continuously adjust AF to track it

Single-shot AF

AF-S

In AF-S mode, the focus locks on the subject when you partially depress the shutter release and stays focused on the same distance for as long as the shutter is held down. A focus confirmation indicator in the viewfinder lights when the lens has locked focus, and an audible 'beep' can be heard. You then press the shutter button all the way down to take a shot. AF-S is ideal for static subjects – however, if either you or the subject moves once focus has locked, your subject may well end up out of focus as the focus will remain on the original point. To avoid that, you have to press the shutter release again to refocus on the subject in its new position. If the camera struggles to lock focus – say, because the area you're trying to focus on is closer than the minimum focus distance – the shutter won't fire. You can use AF-S with focus lock to focus on off-centre subjects. To do this, select single AF point (most people choose the central point), adjust the composition of the shot so the focus point falls over the area you want to focus on and partially depress the shutter button to lock focus. Providing you keep the shutter button held down, the focus won't shift, so you can recompose, then press the shutter button down fully to take the shot.

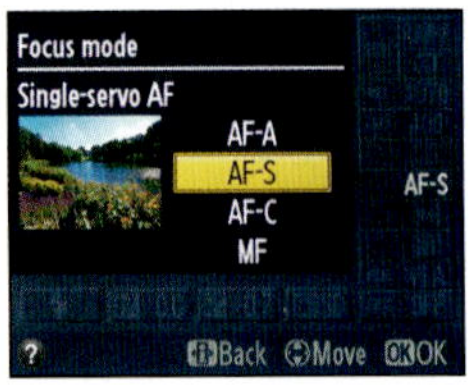

Perfect for...

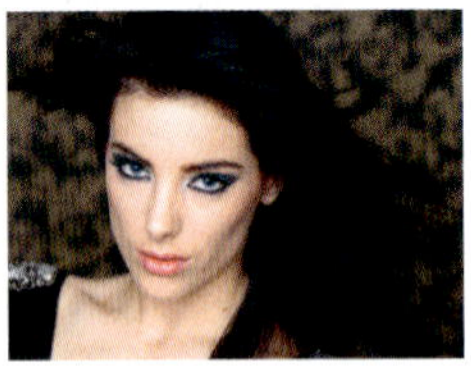
PAUL WARD

Portraits: Use one AF sensor to focus on the eye and capture perfect portraits.

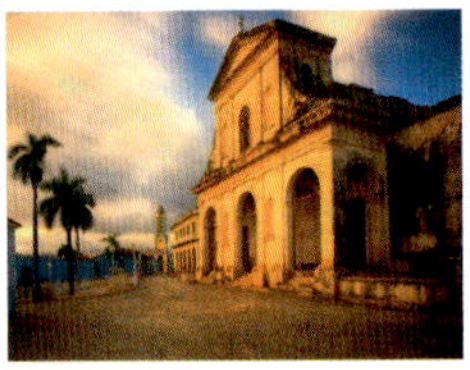
LEE FROST

Architecture: Single-shot AF is ideal for static subjects, like buildings and bridges.

Continuous AF

AF-C

Also known as Servo-AF, in this mode, the autofocus will continually adjust to keep your subject in sharp focus if it's moving or you're moving – or both! To use AF-C, make sure an active AF point is positioned over your subject then partially depress the shutter button to lock focus. Providing you keep the shutter release partially depressed, and an active AF point over your subject, it should remain in sharp focus until you're ready to press the shutter button down fully to take a shot. If you have the camera set to continuous drive mode, you can also shoot rapid sequences of images by keeping the shutter button pressed down, and each frame should be in focus. That said, unlike AF-S, in AF-C mode the shutter will fire and take a shot even if the lens hasn't locked focus, or focus has strayed onto something other than your main subject, and when this happens you need to be careful that you don't end up with lots of out of focus images. Using Focus Assist points or Dynamic/Extended area AF will help, as it means that if the subject falls outside the main AF point you're using to track it, other AF points will keep it in sharp focus. This is handy for tricky subjects, such as birds in flight.

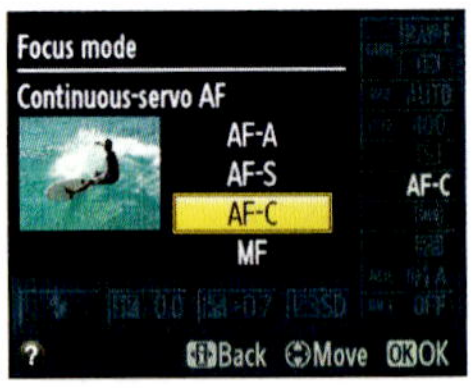

Perfect for...

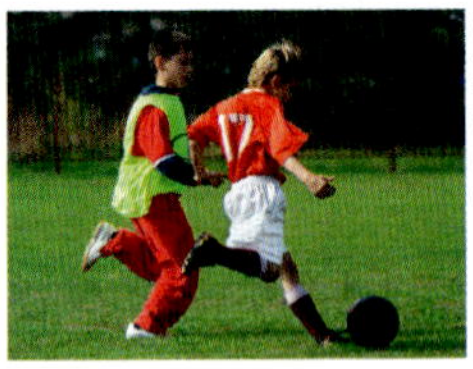
ISTOCK PHOTO

Sport: Your first attempts at fast-moving subjects should be with AF-C mode.

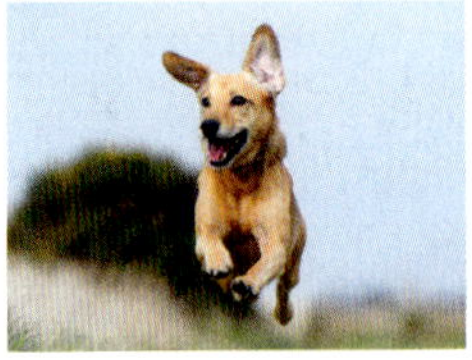
ISTOCK PHOTO

Animals: Try continuous AF on wildlife to ensure you take sharp wildlife images.

Automatic AF

AF-A

This is an 'intelligent' AF mode found in some of the latest DSLRs and CSCs where the camera automatically switches between AF-S and AF-C, depending on the subject. If the camera detects that the subject is stationary then it will set AF-S mode to get it in focus, whereas if it detects that the subject you're shooting is moving, it will set AF-C to increase the chance of you getting the image pin-sharp. It's a handy mode to use if you're shooting a variety of different subjects in quick succession, some moving, some not, such as street photography and reportage. However, experienced photographers tend to stick with a specific AF mode so they know how the camera might react.

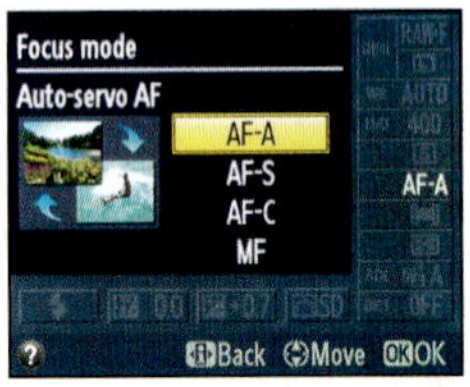

Perfect for...

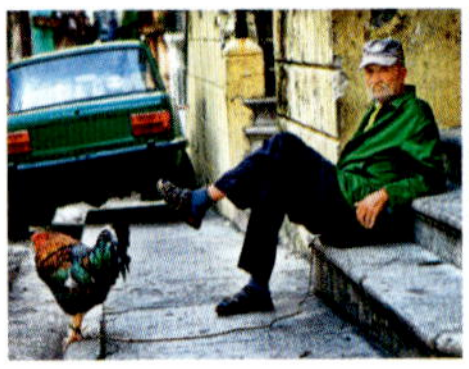
BRETT HARKNESS

Candids: If you're focusing on a subject without looking through the viewfinder.

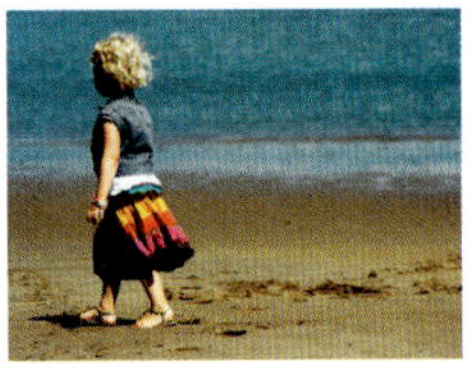
BRETT HARKNESS

Children: AF-A focus locks on a child, then tracks them should they start moving.

Know your modes

While most cameras offer all these AF modes, each have a slightly different designation, as follows:

	AF-S	AF-C	AF-A
CANON	One Shot	AI Servo	AI Focus
NIKON	AF-S	AF-C	AF-A
OLYMPUS	S-AF	C-AF	–
PENTAX	AF.S	AF.C	AF.A
SONY	AF-S	AF-C	AF-A

Manual focus

M

Although the latest AF systems are fast, accurate and reliable, there is still a case for using good old manual focus. If you've been a photographer for a long time, you may simply prefer it – old habits die hard and all that – but for some static subjects, being able to choose exactly where the lens focuses can be of benefit. With landscapes, for example, you usually want to record the whole scene in focus. To do that you need to be able to control how far into the scene the lens is focusing (ideally on the hyperfocal distance), and it's much easier to do that if you focus manually. Once you've focused the lens manually, you can also leave the camera in position while you wait for the light to improve, say, and be ready to shoot. It's also useful in low light or low contrast scenes where AF may struggle and macro is another area where manual focus can be handy. Depth-of-field can be so shallow that only the point you actually focus on will come out sharp, so it's preferable if you can choose that point and be able to adjust it as required, without relying on AF points and focus lock. Manual focus isn't so useful for moving subjects – AF-C is quicker and more reliable – but for static subjects, it's definitely worth trying.

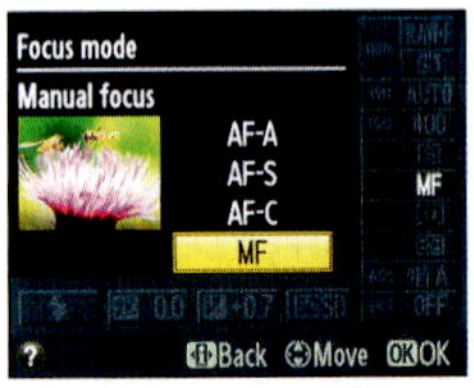

Perfect for...

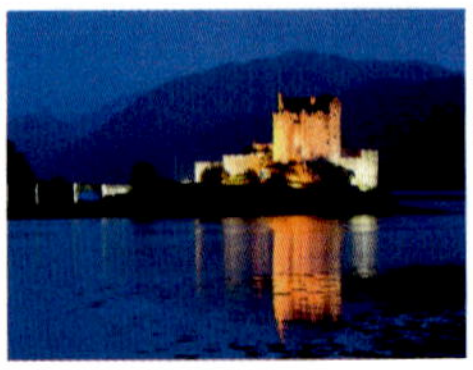
LEE FROST

Low light: Your AF may have trouble locking on a subject, so focus manually.

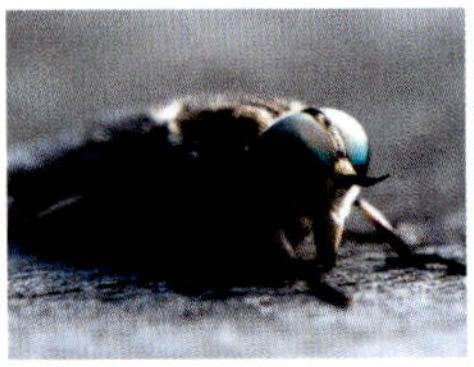
ROSS HODDINOTT

Macro: With very shallow depth-of-field, it ensures the correct area appears sharp.

Focus point selection: Have all AF sensors active to cover a large area or focus using a single AF point

Single-point AF

Serious photographers tend to use single-point AF all the time as it allows you to choose exactly what the lens focuses on, rather than leaving it to the camera and risking it making a bad decision. There are two ways to do this. The first is to select the central AF point, as it's the most sensitive point your camera has. If the area you want to focus on is off-centre, all you do is place the central AF point over that area, half-press the shutter release to lock focus, recompose the shot and fire. This may sound fiddly, but if you do it all the time, it becomes second nature. The second method is to select a single off-centre AF point and use that. If you're taking lots of shots of an off-centre subject, especially if that subject is moving, this works better than using the central AF point as you don't need to recompose after locking focus. It's also preferable when shooting at really wide apertures and depth-of-field is shallow. Locking focus with the central AF point then recomposing may mean that the point you focused on is no longer in focus, whereas this won't be the case if you select an AF point that allows you to compose the shot then focus on the desired spot, such as a person's eye, without moving the camera.

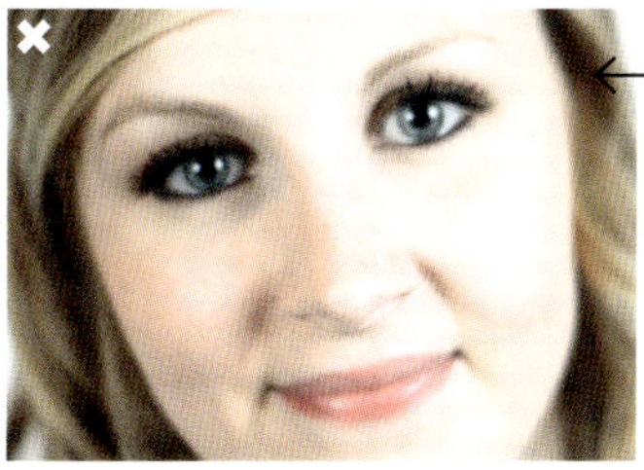

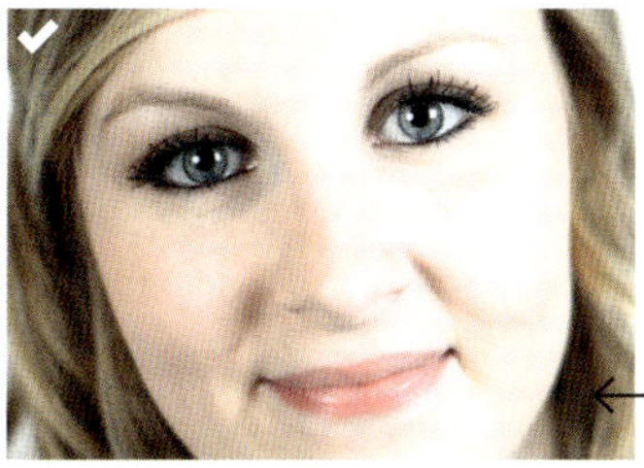

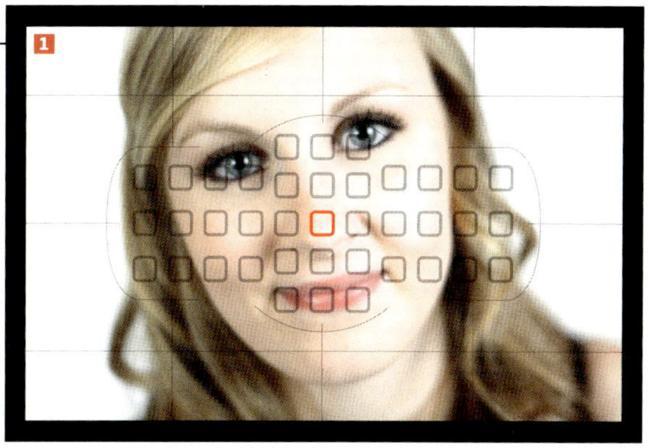

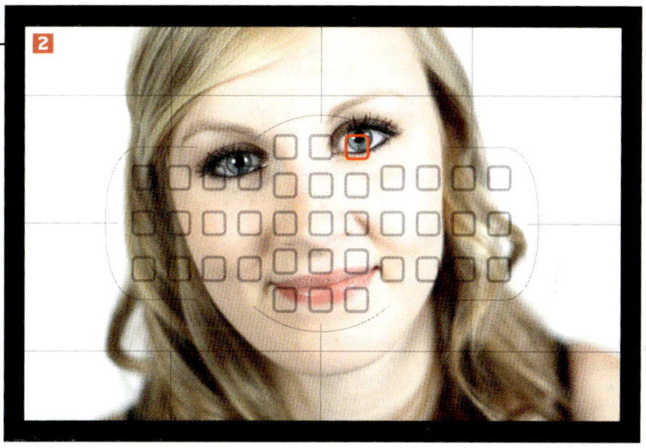

USING SINGLE-POINT AF: 1) With multi-point AF selected, the camera has focused on the nose and due to the very shallow depth-of-field, the face is out of focus. 2) Select single-point AF and choose the sensor that falls over the subject's eye to ensure the subject is focused correctly. The final image now has the subject's eyes in sharp focus.

Multi-point AF

In multi-point AF mode, all the focus points, or a number selected by you, are active at the same time and when you partially press the shutter button, the points that are activated (in other words, are focusing on the subject) will flash red. Preference tends to be given to whatever is closest to the camera. If you're an absolute beginner, multi-point AF can be handy, as it gives you one less thing to think about. If you're taking general shots with your lens set to a smallish aperture (f/8, f/11, f/16), multi-point AF can also work fine because you want everything in focus and no one element in the scene needs to take centre stage. However, because you have little control over what the lens focuses on, in situations where you do need to focus on something specific, such as a person's eye, it's best avoided as focus error is likely, especially when you're shooting at a wide aperture and depth-of-field is limited. The main exception on some cameras is where you can select a main focus point, then nominate others around it as focus 'assist' points so that if your subject strays beyond the main focus point, the others will still keep it in focus. If a moving subject is travelling across the frame, and remains at roughly the same distance from you, multi-point AF can also work because as the subject moves to an area covered by another AF point, that sensor becomes active and keeps the subject in sharp focus.

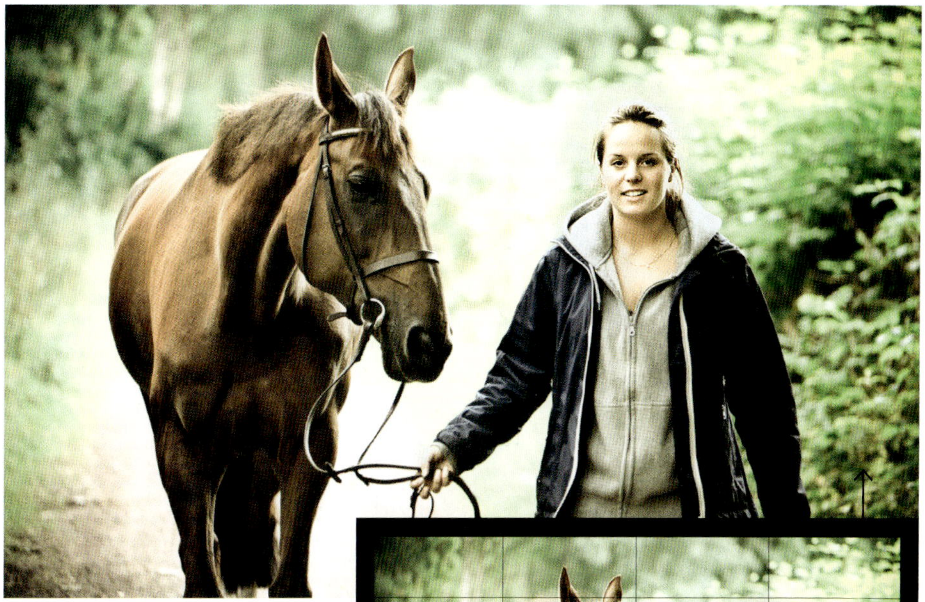

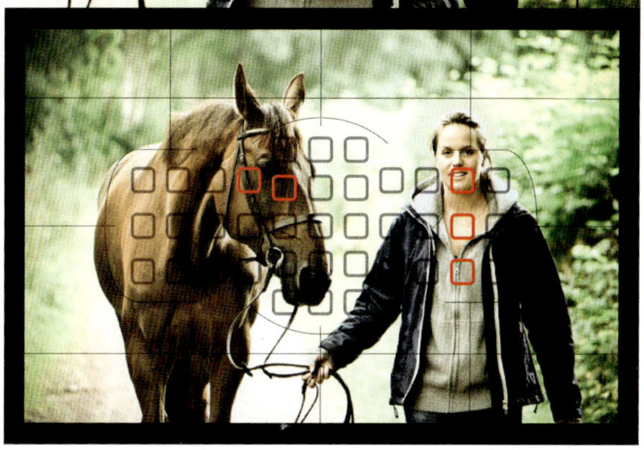

USING MULTI-POINT AF: When in multi-point AF mode, and having partially depressed the shutter button, the focus points select areas closest to the camera. When focus is locked, the points turn red. If you want to select different focus points, release and re-press the shutter.

How to focus on a moving subject

Your camera's continuous AF system will do its best to track a moving subject, but it isn't always perfect. There are skills you can learn, however, to improve your chances of taking some impressive pictures

ANIMALS RUNNING AT TOP speed, birds in flight, race cars topping 200mph… Experienced sport and nature photographers make it look easy to produce pin-sharp, well composed and perfectly timed images of subjects that are moving so fast it's hard for the eye to keep up, never mind a camera. But it isn't easy, and when you consider that long, heavy telephoto lenses are usually required, which means depth-of-field is severely limited, the level of skill required becomes even greater because there's so little room for error.

If you started photography when there was only manual focus, you'll know that autofocus systems are a dream: they make the task of capturing moving subjects easier than ever before because they're so accurate and responsive. They're not totally foolproof, though, so you still need to have your wits about you.

Small subjects moving at high speed are especially tricky because in order to keep them in sharp focus when using AF, you must make sure an active AF point falls over them – if you fail to do that, the focusing is likely to start 'hunting' for something else to lock onto and your main subject may well be thrown out of focus. In the case of birds in flight, where the background is usually plain sky, this can be disastrous because the lens will struggle to focus on the sky and throw the main subject out of focus. And you'll probably struggle to get it back in focus before the opportunity has gone. Sports subjects, such as football and rugby, also pose problems because another player crossing the path of the one you're tracking may cause the lens to shift focus – usually at the critical moment you're about to shoot! Put that match under floodlighting or murky conditions and it gets even harder as AF systems are less effective in low light.

The more you practise, the better you'll become. You need to get used to how your camera's focusing system works, its weaknesses and how to change AF points quickly with the camera at your eye so you never lose sight of your subject. It will also help for you to know how to optimise the performance of the AF system using features such as Assist Points, Dynamic Area AF and others specific to particular cameras. The technology is there to help you – so let it! The focusing technique you use is also governed by the type of moving subject you're shooting. We explain the best two focusing techniques to try.

Pre-focusing

When moving subjects follow a predictable route, they're easier to photograph because you can lay and wait for them by focusing on a specific point. If you watch motor racing, for example, you'll see that the drivers all take the same racing line around the track, so you can pre-focus your lens on a point, then fire away whenever a car reaches it. In effect, you let the race come to you, rather than chasing the action. The same applies with any sporting event or subject that follows a predictable route – athletics, motocross, cycling and so on.

To pre focus-use AF, select single-shot (AF-S) and single-point AF. The focus point activated can be the central one, but if you use it, you may have to focus, lock focus by keeping the shutter button partially depressed, then recompose and wait for your subject before firing. It's easier to select a focus point that falls on the area your subject will pass so you don't have to recompose. The alternative is manual focus. A benefit of this is that once the lens is focused on a point, it stays focused even when you take your finger off the shutter button, so if there's a chance you can take several shots in fairly quick succession, it may work better than using AF, where the lens will need to refocus each time you press the shutter release.

Finally, don't wait until your subject reaches the point you've focused on before firing the shutter, as the slight delay between you deciding to fire and your finger actually depressing the button may be long enough for the subject to have passed the critical point before the shutter opens. Instead, fire just before it reaches the point you've focused on and you should end up with a perfect shot.

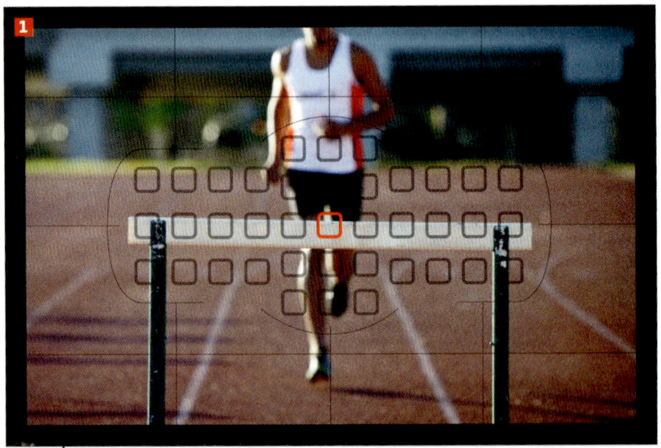

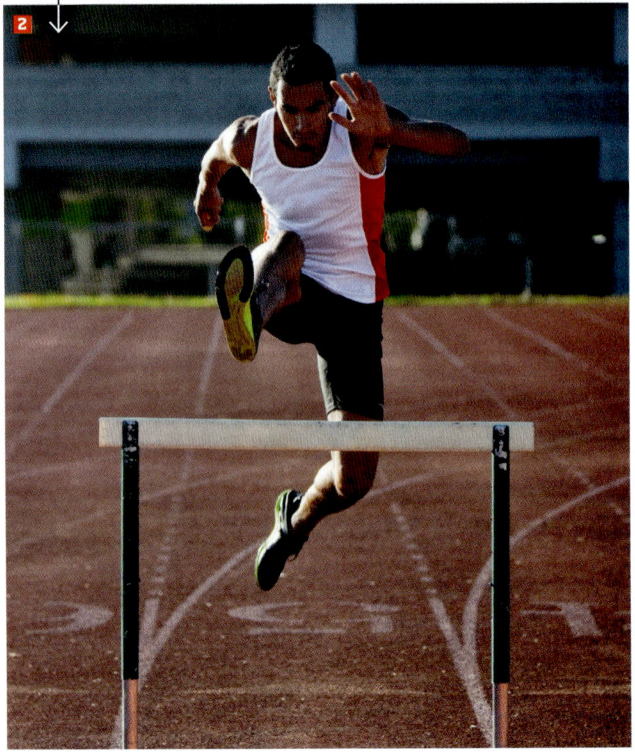

USING PRE-FOCUSING: This set of images provides an ideal scenario for using the pre-focus technique to ensure the subject is recorded in sharp focus. 1) With the camera set to single-point AF and with AF-S selected, half-depress the shutter button and lock focus on the hurdle. 2) Wait until the athlete approaches and as he reaches the hurdle, fire the shutter. Easy!

Use it for...

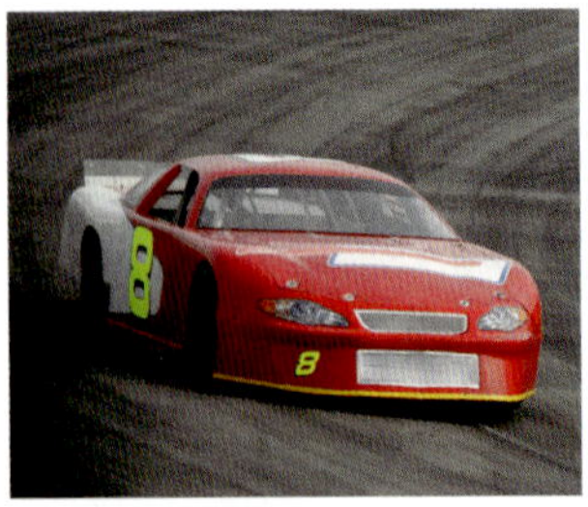
ISTOCK PHOTO

MOTOR RACING: As all the cars follow the optimum racing line, you should pre-focus on a part of track you know the cars will pass and press the shutter as they reach it.

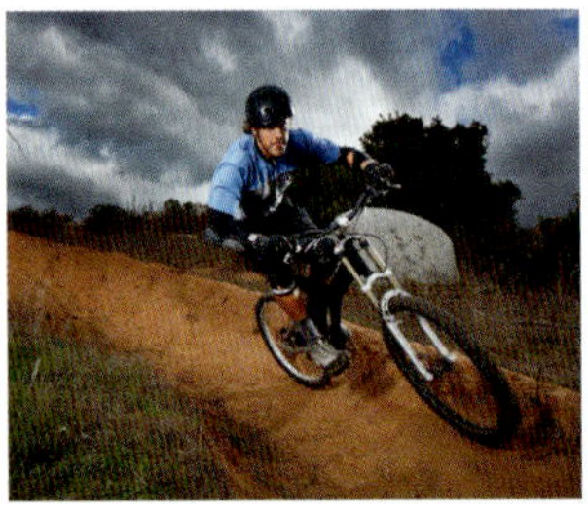
ISTOCK PHOTO

CYCLING: Pre-focus on a specific part of the track or, if you're shooting the end of a race, focus on the finishing line and press the shutter as the cyclists approach it.

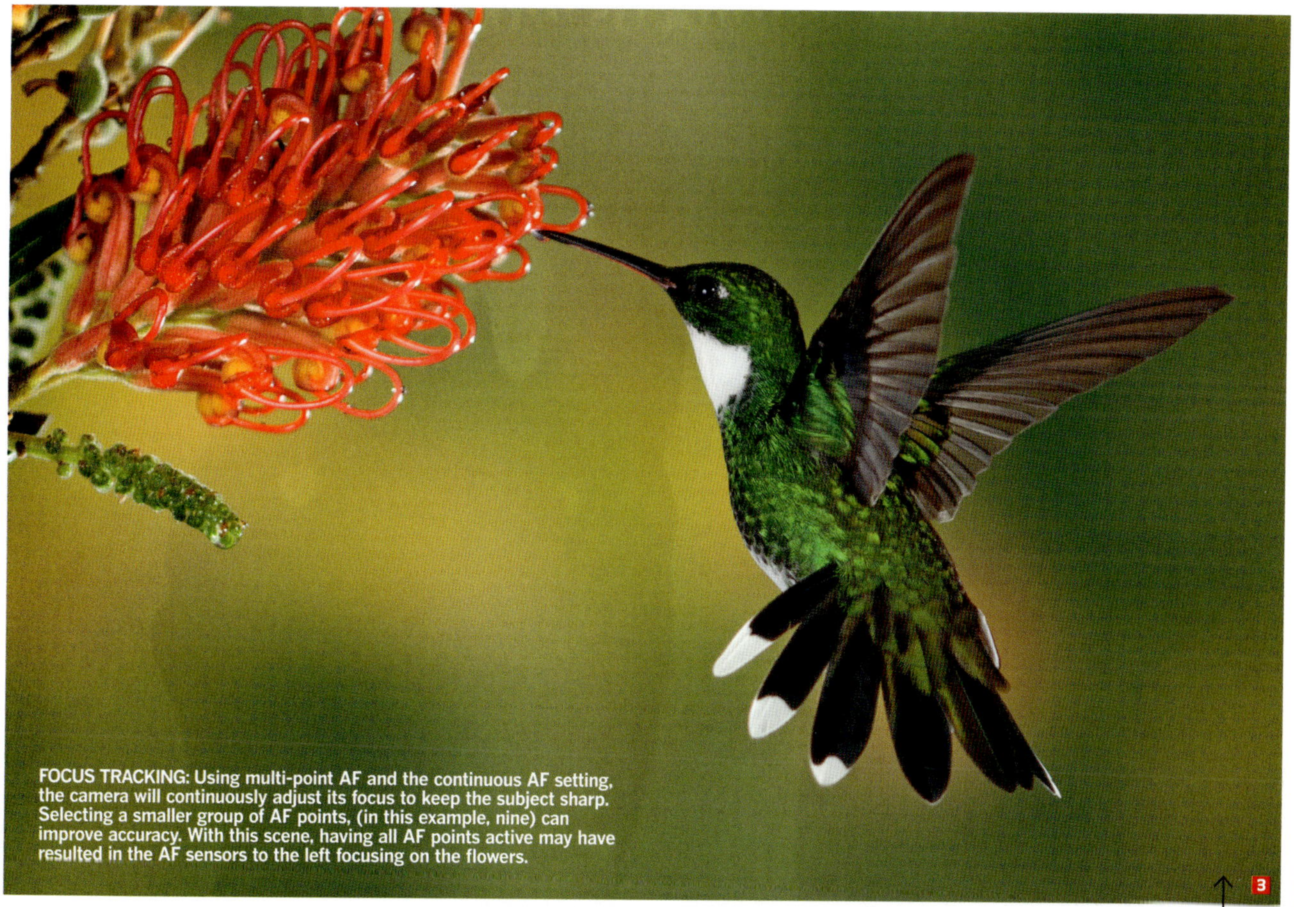

ISTOCK PHOTO

FOCUS TRACKING: Using multi-point AF and the continuous AF setting, the camera will continuously adjust its focus to keep the subject sharp. Selecting a smaller group of AF points, (in this example, nine) can improve accuracy. With this scene, having all AF points active may have resulted in the AF sensors to the left focusing on the flowers.

Focus tracking

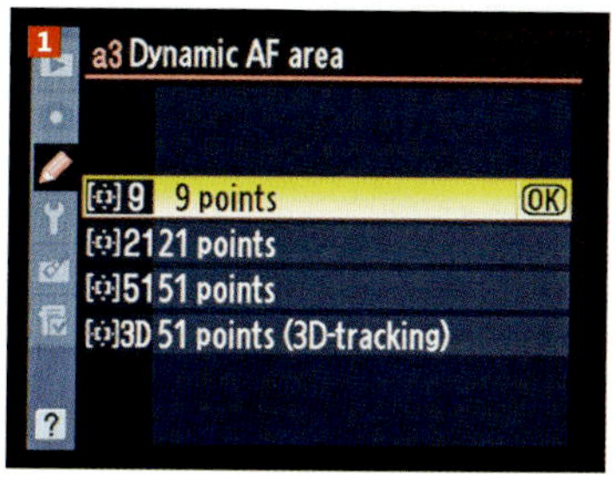

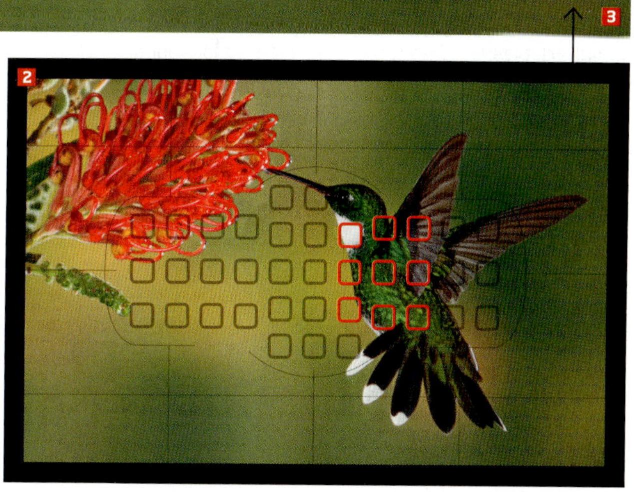

If your subject doesn't follow a predetermined route, such as a football player, a bird in flight or a wild animal chasing its prey, you need to track it with your camera until you're ready to take a shot. In pre-digital days this involved a technique known as 'follow-focusing' where you manually adjusted focus as you followed your subject – a skill that took years to master. Thankfully, autofocus now does it for you, so even relative beginners can take pin-sharp shots of fast-moving action.

First, you need to set continuous AF mode so it automatically adjusts focus as camera-to-subject distance changes, providing an active AF target falls over the subject. Next, choose a focus point setting that increases your chance of keeping that subject sharp. Having all the AF points active doesn't always work well because the AF will be confused as to what it should focus on, especially when subjects occupy a small part of the frame. Using one AF point makes it hard to keep your subject sharp at all times. However, there are other AF settings, such as Focus Assist points or Dynamic Area AF, that allow you to select one AF point but have others around it that act as back-up, so that if your subject strays from the main AF point, the others will keep it sharply focused. Alternatively, some cameras allow you to use a small group of AF points (usually five, seven, nine or 11) in the central area of the frame.

Once the camera is set and ready, all you do is pick your subject in the viewfinder, lock focus by partially depressing the shutter button, then follow your subject while keeping the shutter button down. The focus automatically shifts to keep the subject sharp and you can fire at will. Whether or not you also set the camera to continuous drive mode is up to you. It's handy being able to shoot rapid sequences of images, but stick to short, steady bursts – remember, the camera's buffer will fill up quickly with continuous firing, and you don't want that to happen just as the action peaks!

Use it for...

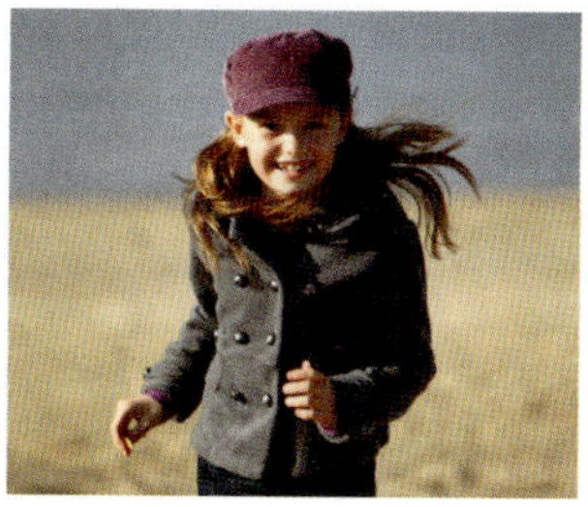

DANIEL LEZANO

CHILDREN AT PLAY: The erratic movement of children will test your camera's AF tracking to the limit. Shoot in bright light to improve your rate of success.

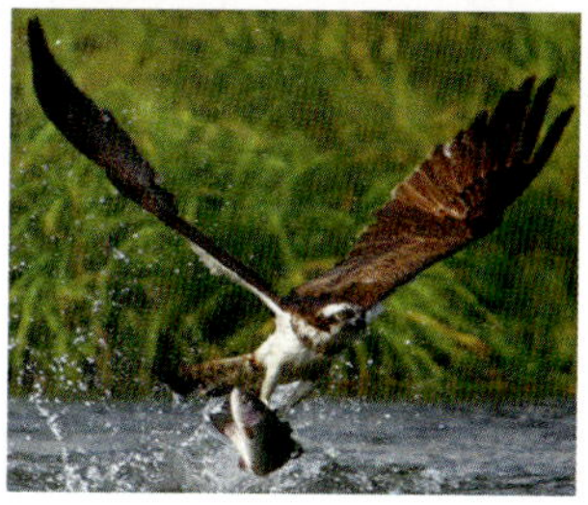

MIGUEL LASA

WILDLIFE: Focus tracking is ideal for following the movement of animals, such as birds flying or deer running, and is an ideal technique to try with a telezoom.

How to help your autofocus when it struggles

Your camera's autofocus system is responsive and accurate in most shooting situations, but not all. Across the next two pages, we'll cover situations where AF might struggle and provide advice on the techniques you need to help you achieve the perfect focus with minimal effort

Shooting low-light or low-contrast subjects

As light levels fall, AF is less effective. The phase-detection system in your DSLR or CSC is better than the contrast-detection AF found in digital compacts, but it's not totally foolproof. Outdoors, shooting urban scenes with man-made illumination, you shouldn't have any problems using AF (single-point and AF-S is recommended), as there will be bright areas and plenty of contrast, but if you're shooting landscapes by moonlight or the night sky, or indoors in low light, the AF may struggle to lock onto your subject. Some DSLRs and CSCs have a Focus Assist illuminator, which is basically a light that shines when low lighting is detected, to increase contrast in the subject so that the lens can focus. Many flashguns also have infrared illuminators that do the same job. If you don't have either, shining a torch on your subject will allow you to focus. Alternatively, try using single-point AF with the central AF point selected – as it's the most sensitive – and focus on something the same distance from you as your subject that the lens can lock onto, hold the shutter button down, recompose and take the shot. If that fails, focus yourself by switching from AF to manual – always a good last resort.

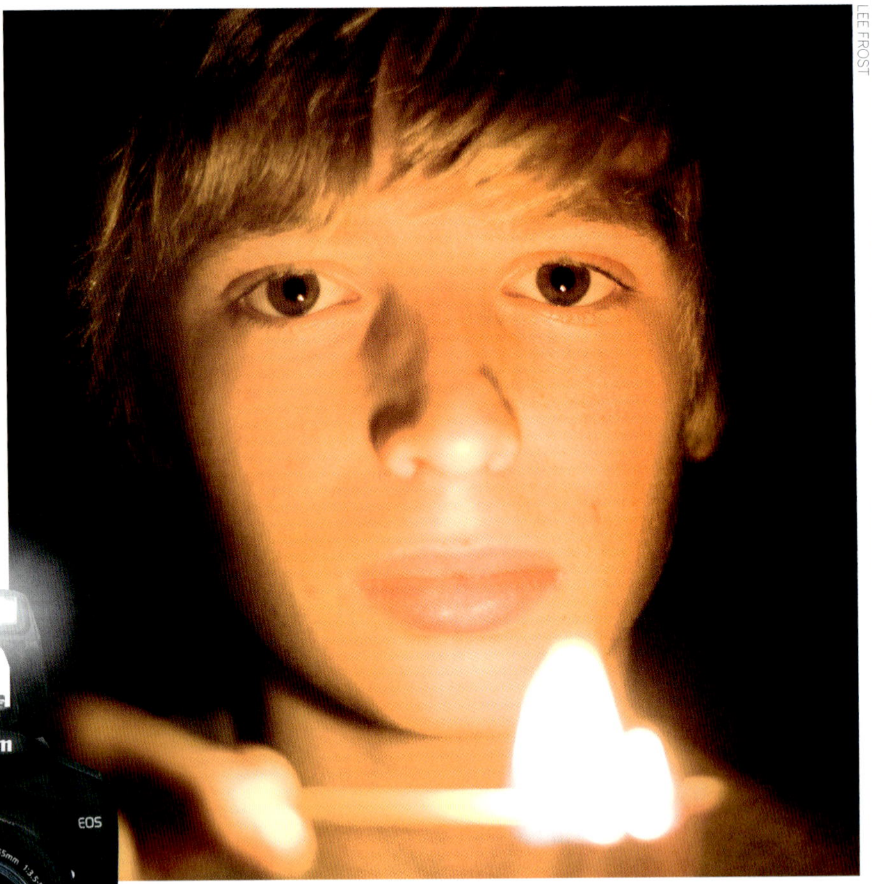
LEE FROST

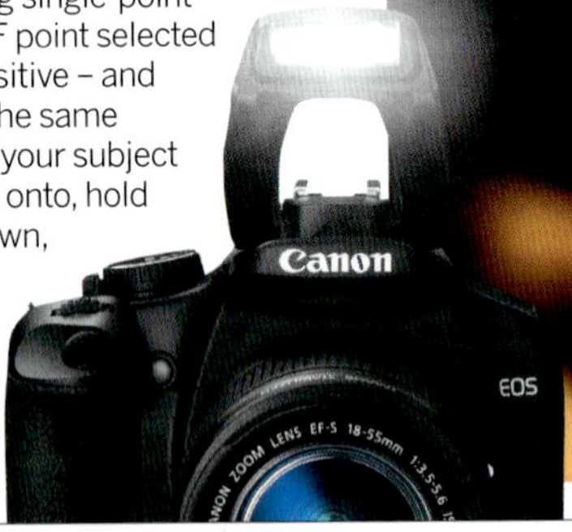

Three tricky focusing scenarios: Problems & solutions

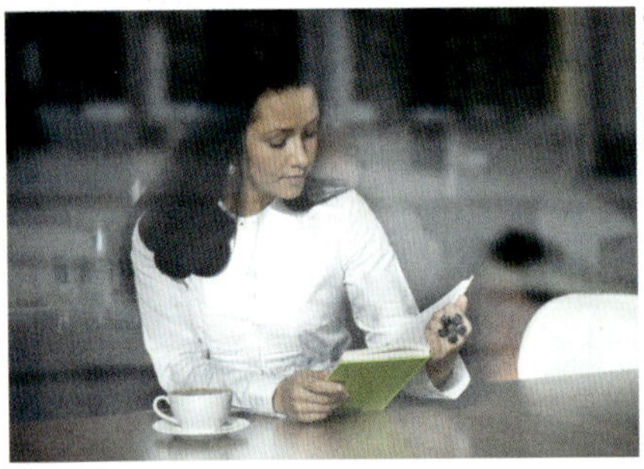
ISTOCK PHOTO

1) Shooting through glass

If you try to shoot through a window using autofocus, you may find that your lens either hunts around and fails to focus on anything, or locks focus on the glass itself, rather than the scene beyond it. This is especially true if the glass is dirty or scratched, as your camera will detect contrast and assume that's what you want to focus on. Try using single-point AF. If that doesn't work, switch to manual focus so you can focus the lens where you want it.

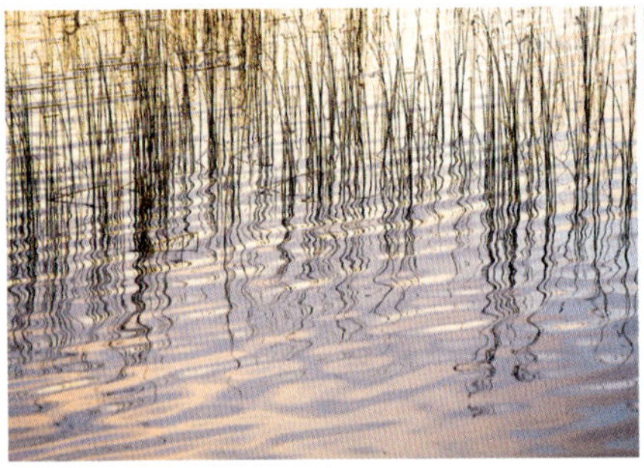
LEE FROST

2) Shooting reflections

The key with shooting reflections in water, glass and metal is not to focus on the reflective surface, but on the reflection itself, so you know that the reflection will be in sharp focus. This is particularly important if you're shooting with a telephoto lens or at a wide aperture, as depth-of-field is reduced. If you try to do this using autofocus, your lens may focus on the reflective surface. If that happens, switch to manual focus and refocus on the reflection.

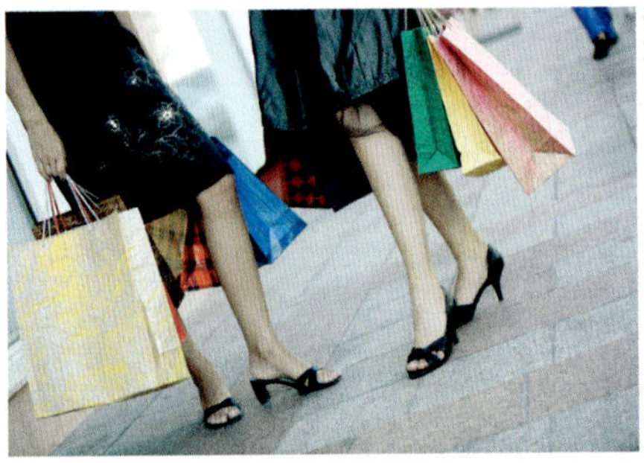
ISTOCK PHOTO

3) Shooting from the hip

This is a hit-and-miss technique as you can't actually see what you're shooting, but it can produce fantastic results. The best method is to set manual focus and pre-focus the lens on a certain point. Use a mid-aperture like f/8 or f/11 to get decent depth-of-field, especially when using wide-angle lenses, which give you lots of depth-of-field at small apertures. Also try multi-point AF – you may find it works well as long as your main subject is the closest to you.

Shooting animals in zoos

The key to photographing zoo animals is to try to exclude any signs of captivity so the shots could just as easily have been taken in the wild. A good starting point is to set your lens to its maximum aperture, so depth-of-field is reduced and you can throw the background out of focus. Another reason for doing this is that if you have to shoot through wire mesh fencing or cage bars that are closely spaced, the lack of depth-of-field should throw them so far out of focus that you can't see them. For the best results, place the lens as close to the mesh/bars as you can. AF should work fine – single-shot and single-point AF being the best settings – though if the lens struggles to focus on your subject, you can always use focus lock to focus, recompose and shoot. If you're shooting through the glass panel of an aquarium, fit a rubber lens hood to your lens and rest that against the glass to cut out glare and reflections. The lens should focus through the glass without any problems using AF – though using manual focus is an option if necessary.

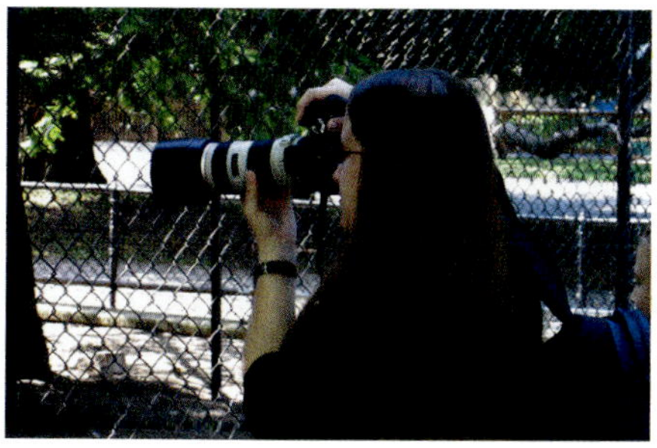

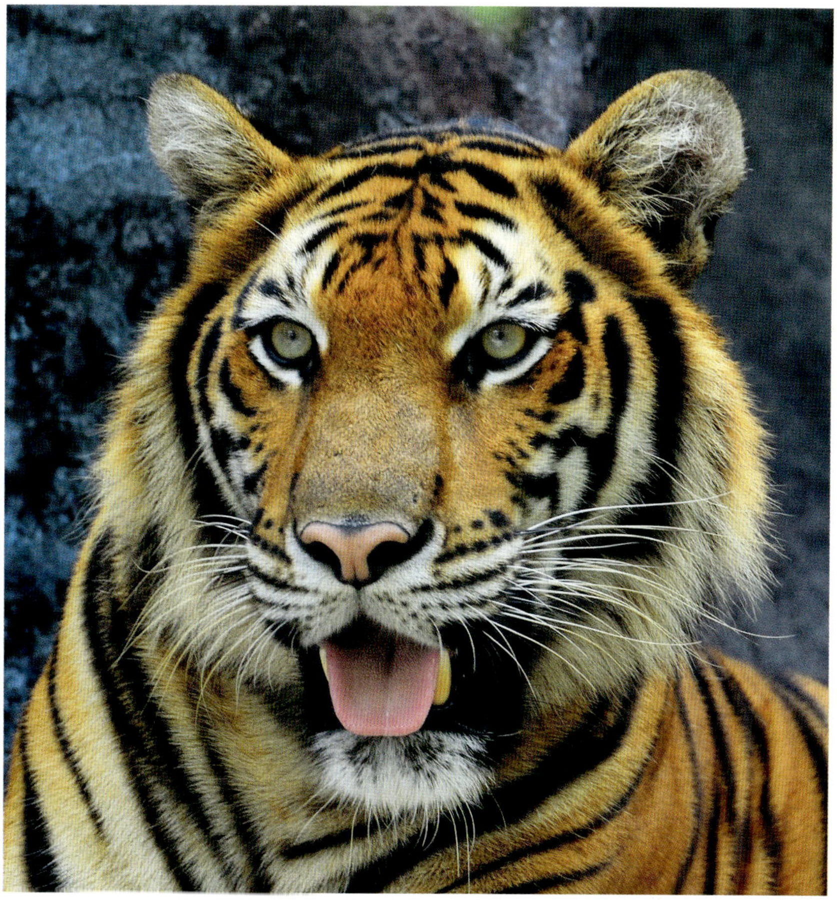

BOTH: ISTOCK PHOTO

Hyperfocal focusing: For front-to-back sharpness

A scene that is sharp throughout is usually the goal when shooting landscapes and unless you have a creative reason to do so, it looks odd if the foreground or most distant areas of the scene are out of focus. To ensure that doesn't happen, you need to be able to control depth-of-field to ensure the whole scene comes out sharp. The most effective way is by using a technique known as hyperfocal focusing, which is based on the idea that depth-of-field is maximised for any given focal length and aperture setting if you focus the lens on a specific distance – the hyperfocal distance. The charts below show the hyperfocal distances for common focal lengths. As you can see, the distances are quite specific. Focusing on those distances using AF is possible – all you do is position an active AF point over an area in the scene that you think is the correct distance away, half-depress the shutter button to lock focus, recompose, then take the shot. However, this is fiddly to do with the camera on a tripod and you'll have to repeat it for each frame. Another option is to compose the shot as you want to take it, choose a point in the scene you feel represents the hyperfocal distance, then set an AF point that covers that area and focus using AF-S mode. A much easier solution is to use manual focus, compose the shot and focus on the hyperfocal distance by eye. That way, once focus is set, it stays set, so you wait until the light's just right before shooting.

Hyperfocal distance: APS-C sensors

Focal length	12mm	15mm	17mm	20mm	24mm	28mm	35mm	50mm	70mm	100mm	135mm
Aperture f/8	3.2ft	5ft	6.4ft	8.9ft	12.6ft	17ft	27ft	55ft	105ft	218ft	395ft
f/11	2.3ft	3.5ft	4.5ft	6.2ft	9ft	12ft	19ft	39ft	75ft	155ft	280ft
f/16	1.7ft	2.5ft	3.3ft	4.4ft	6.4ft	8.6ft	14.5ft	27ft	54ft	110ft	198ft
f/22	1.2ft	0.9ft	2.3ft	3.2ft	4.5ft	6ft	9.5ft	19.2ft	38ft	77ft	140ft

Hyperfocal distance: Full-frame sensors

Focal length	16mm	20mm	24mm	28mm	35mm	50mm	70mm	100mm	135mm
Aperture f/8	3.8ft	5.6ft	8.0ft	11ft	17ft	35ft	68ft	138ft	250ft
f/11	2.6ft	3.9ft	5.8ft	7.8ft	12ft	25ft	48ft	98ft	178ft
f/16	1.9ft	2.9ft	4.0ft	5.5ft	8.5ft	17.5ft	34ft	70ft	125ft
f/22	0.4ft	2.0ft	2.9ft	3.9ft	6ft	12.5ft	24ft	49ft	89ft

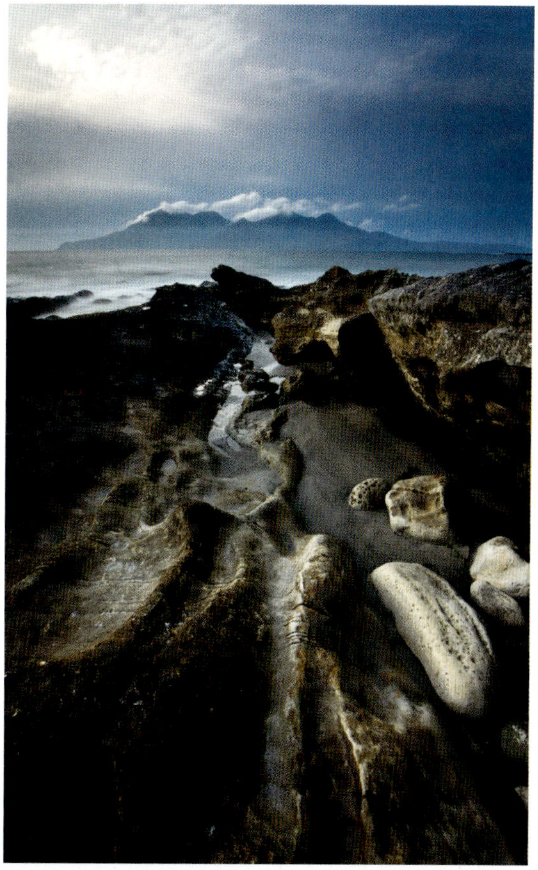

LEE FROST

Image quality

Your camera offers a number of image settings, based around shooting in Raw or JPEG, which have a major effect on the quality of your images. We explain what they are and when you should use them

WHEN YOU TAKE A PICTURE, your camera sends the information from the image sensor via the processor to the memory card. You have control, via the Image Quality settings, over how the image data from the sensor is processed before reaching the memory card. You can set it to record the highest image quality, to compress the image information at varying degrees, or to shoot at a lower resolution to fit more on the card and speed up processing. The choice is yours and it's worth understanding the options available to ensure your images best suit your requirements.

Main file formats: Raw & JPEG

There are two main file formats a digital camera can save your images as: Raw and JPEG. Raw format is, as its name suggests, an unprocessed file that contains all the original data captured by the image sensor. It's used when maximum image quality and flexibility is desired, but the resultant large file size means that speed and the number of files that can be stored on a memory card are reduced. Shooting in JPEG has a number of advantages, which is why many amateur photographers favour it. Images captured as a JPEG are processed more quickly than a Raw file and require less space on a memory card, so you can store considerably more images. As images are compressed to reduce the file size, there is some loss in quality, but for most uses, when minimum compression is used, this is negligible. And for those of you wondering, JPEG stands for Joint Photographic Experts Group.

Most cameras allow you to select Raw+JPEG, which provides you with a JPEG image for fast image review and selection, and the Raw files to edit for best quality.

Raw formats

The following are the Raw file extensions for major brands

Canon: .CR2/.CRW
Nikon: .NEF
Olympus: .ORF
Panasonic: .RW2
Pentax: .PEF/DNG
Samsung: .SRW/DNG
Sony: .ARW

Image quality and memory card capacity

The following table is a quick guide to the approximate number of full resolution images that fit on a 4GB and 8GB card at different image settings. As you can see, each brand compresses to different levels, so the figures aren't always as you'd expect them to be. Cameras used for this table were the Panasonic Lumix GF3, Samsung NX11, Nikon D7000 and Canon EOS 550D.

CAMERA RESOLUTION (MEGAPIXELS)	RAW		RAW + JPEG (Max)		JPEG (Max quality)		JPEG (Min Quality)	
	4GB	8GB	4GB	8GB	4GB	8GB	4GB	8GB
12	280	540	180	370	600	1,180	1200	2,350
14.6	140	280	102	200	550	1,120	1,700	3,350
16	116	225	82	160	280	550	1,100	2,100
18	150	300	118	230	555	1,080	1,100	2,150

JPEG: Image compression

As mentioned earlier, shooting in JPEG is a compromise between image quality and file size. JPEG is what's known as a 'lossy' format in that some information is lost to be able to compress the image. The more the image is compressed, the higher the amount of information that is lost and hence the image quality will be worse. When selecting JPEG as your file format, you can set the level of compression and therefore determine the amount of data loss.

Most cameras provide a choice of three settings, allowing minimal, medium and maximum amounts of compression. If you choose the minimal compression, you'll reduce file size but limit the amount of information lost, and because the best-quality JPEGs look virtually indistinguishable in general use to Raw files, this is the most popular choice of setting with many photographers.

Once you compress image files further, you begin to lose increasing amounts of data that degrade the image, reducing the level of detail and introducing what is commonly termed artefacts: most notably blockiness and added noise, noticeable in areas of the image with even tones. The problem of JPEG compression isn't as clear to see with images that are reproduced at a small size, but if you crop areas of an image or print A4 or larger, it's far easier to spot compression-related problems. We've magnified a portion of an image to show the difference of saving at high, medium or maximum compression.

One final point to note is that you lose a little extra data every time you resave an image. So save the same JPEG file ten or 20 times and it will have lost a significant amount of information that may be apparent when viewed at high magnification.

Raw to JPEG

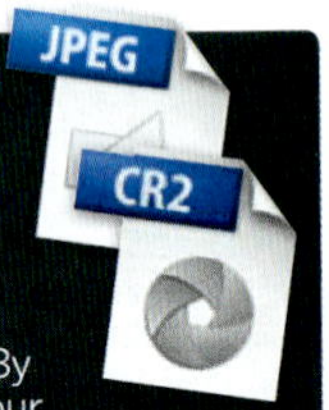

One major advantage of shooting in Raw that's rarely mentioned, is the benefits of converting to a JPEG in post-production. By converting a Raw file on your computer, the resulting image will normally retain slightly more detail than a JPEG processed in-camera. The difference is small, but for the very best JPEG, convert from Raw.

Where to find Image Quality settings on your camera

This is a major function, so you should find it is one of your first options. Here's where to locate it on most popular brands of camera.

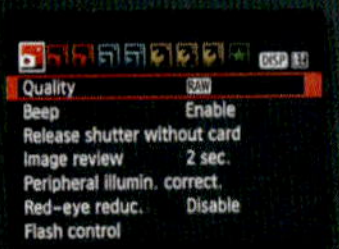

Canon
The Quality option is very easy to find: it's on the first line of the first tab.

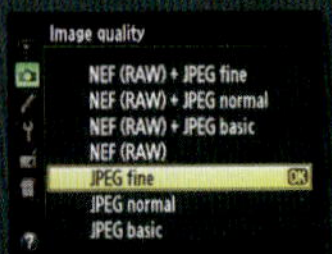

Nikon
Found on the Shooting Menu or accessed via a Quality button.

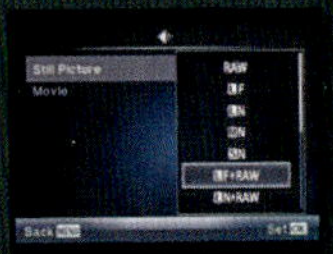

Olympus
Look for the symbol, located on the Shooting Menu 1.

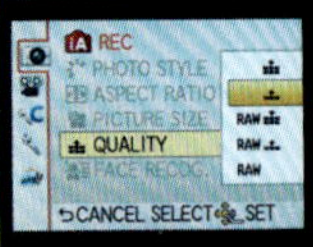

Panasonic
Press MENU and choose Rec or add Quality option to your Q MENU.

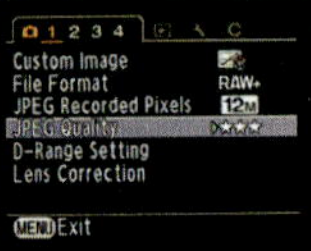

Pentax
Press the MENU button and Image Quality is on camera menu 1.

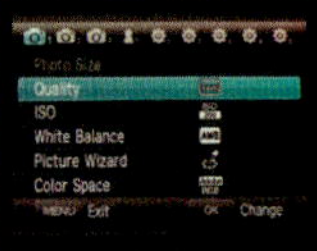

Samsung
Press the MENU button and Image Quality is on Shooting Menu 1.

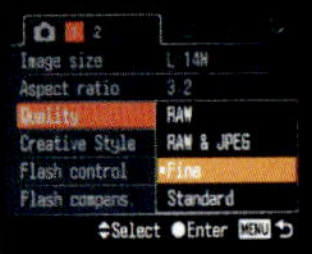

Sony
Press the MENU button and you'll find Quality on Shooting Menu 1.

IMAGES: LEE FROST

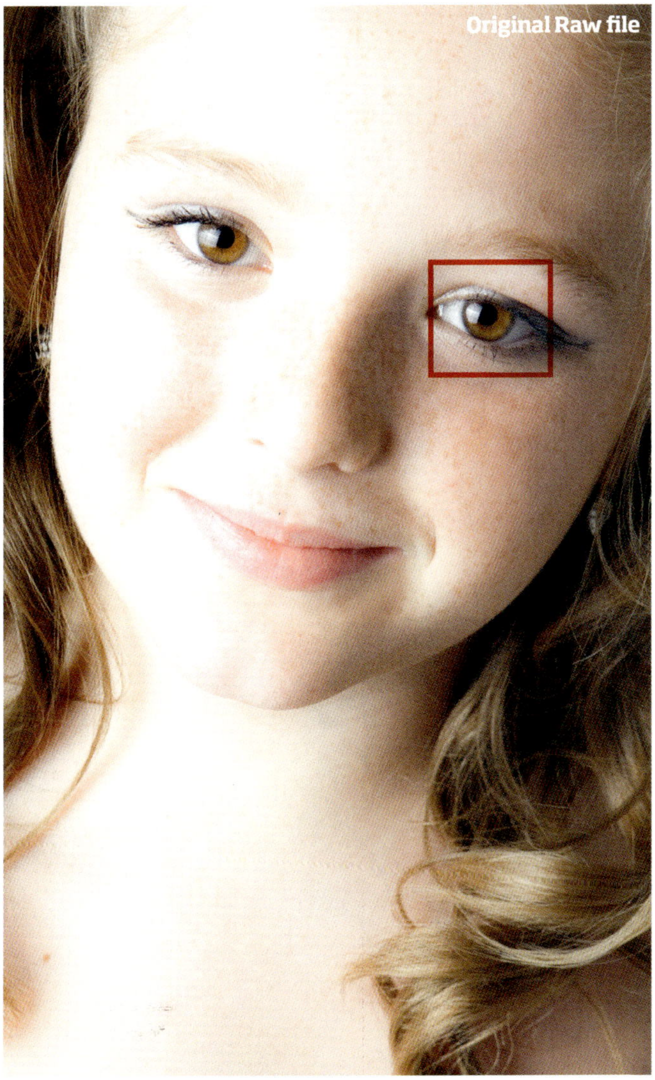

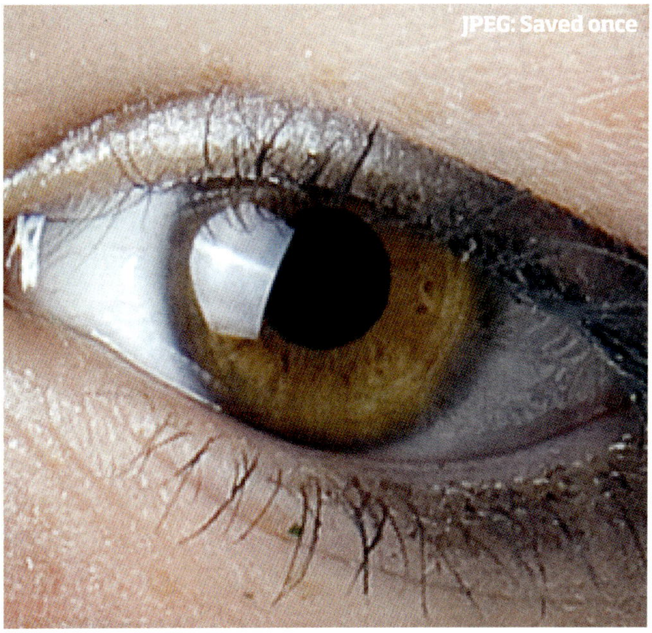

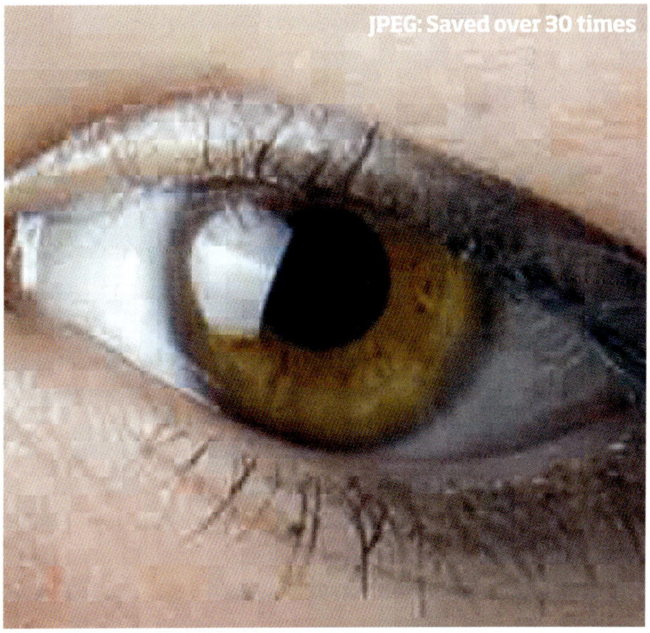

Above: JPEG quality comparison JPEGs use a 'lossy' compression system, which means with every save, a little bit of image information is lost. Resave a file too many times and it will adversely affect image quality.

Image size

As well as taking pictures at maximum resolution, you can set your camera to shoot at lower resolutions, too. The most common use for this is when taking images for web use, when memory card capacity is at a premium or when shooting items to sell on eBay. You'll need to refer to your camera's instruction manual to see what each setting relates to in terms of resolution, but, in general, the middle setting shoots at slightly higher than mid-resolution, while the lowest setting is around two- to four-megapixels. Here's how the image sizes are stated on popular brands (note some older models may vary).

Brand	Maximum resolution	Medium resolution	Lowest resolution
Canon	L	M	S
Nikon	L	M	S
Olympus (older)	SHQ	HQ	SQ
Olympus (newer)	L	M	S
Panasonic	L	M	S
Pentax (K-x)	12M	10M or 6M	2M
Samsung (NX11)	14M	10M or 6M	2M
Sony	L	M	S

JPEG compression

JPEG compression is displayed differently, depending on your brand of camera, as follows. Remember, select minimum compression for the best quality and maximum compression when you need to maximise space on your card at the cost of image quality.

Brand	Least Compression	Medium Compression	Most Compression
Canon	◢	▟	-
Nikon	Fine	Normal	Basic
Olympus (older)	SHQ	HQ	SQ
Olympus (newer)	F	N	-
Panasonic	===	---	-
Pentax*	☆☆☆	☆☆	☆
Samsung	Super Fine	Fine	Normal
Sony	Fine	Standard	-

* Some newer Pentax models offer four levels of compression

ISO rating

By changing the ISO rating, you're able to affect the sensor's sensitivity to light and your ability to capture great images in all lighting conditions

THE ISO (International Standards Organisation) rating was originally created to indicate the sensitivity of film emulsion, but has carried on through to the digital age, where it now provides a standard measure of an image sensor's sensitivity to light. The lower the ISO rating, the less sensitive the sensor is to light; the higher the ISO rating, the more sensitive it is. The ISO rating, along with the aperture and shutter speed, plays an integral part in the exposure of an image. Low ISO ratings are sometimes described as 'slow', as using it usually results in a slow shutter speed being required; while high ISO ratings are occasionally termed 'fast' because they allow for fast shutter speeds to be used. However, the most common terms for ISO ratings are low (ISO 200 and below), medium (ISO 250-640), fast (ISO 800-1600) and very fast (ISO 3200 and above).

ISO 'sensitivity' and noise

The image sensor is receptive to light and has an electronic current, or signal, passing through it, which feeds the image information through to the processor before the data is transferred to the memory card. As you change the ISO rating, you're actually not increasing the sensor's sensitivity to light, but rather adjusting the strength of the signal passing through it. Increasing the signal has the unwanted side effect of increasing signal noise, which becomes more visible in images taken with fast ISO ratings. The higher the ISO, the stronger the signal and therefore the greater the amount of noise present in images.

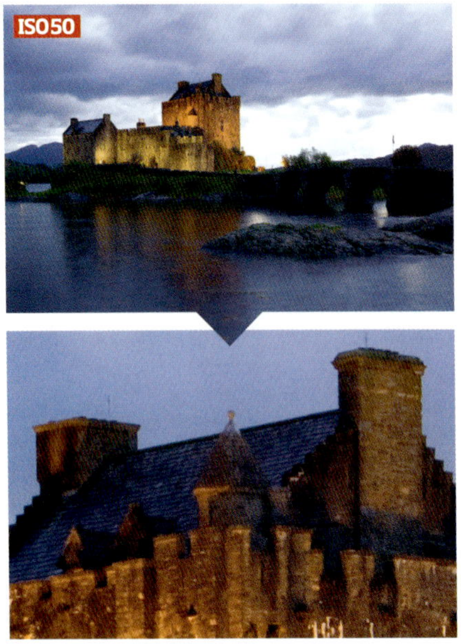

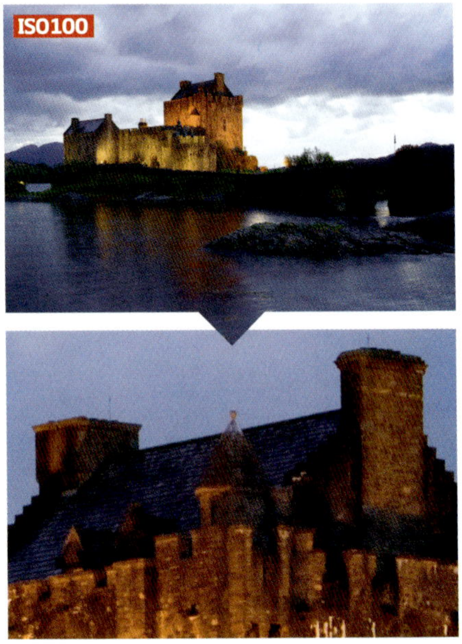

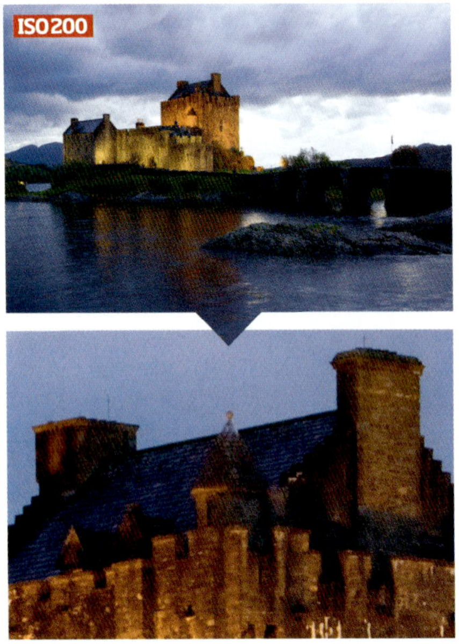

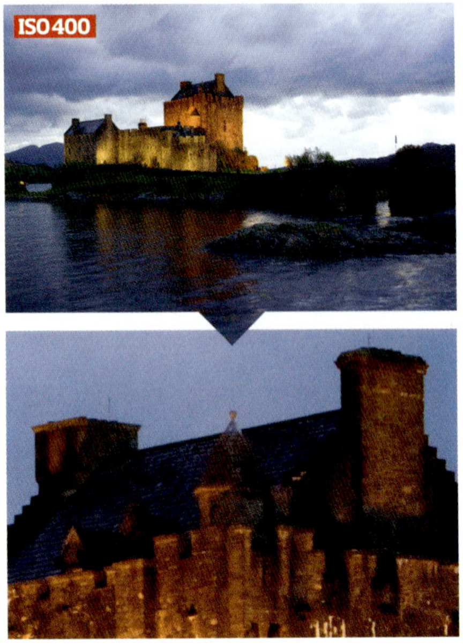

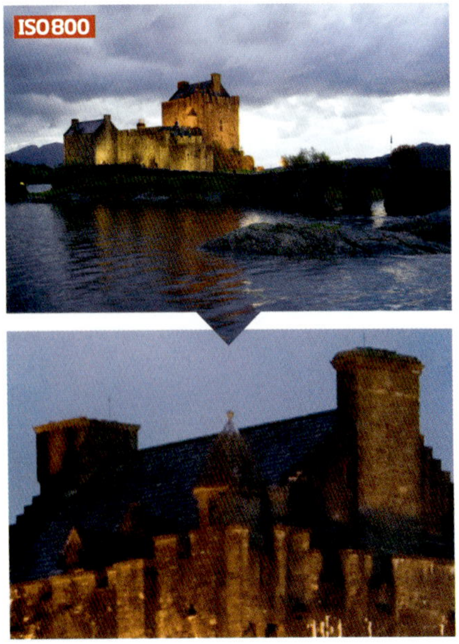

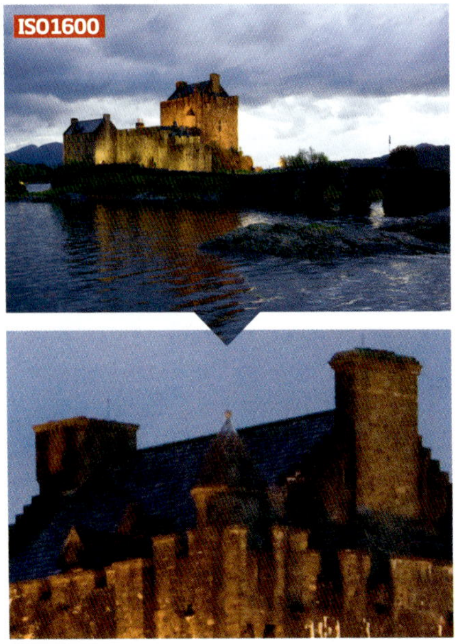

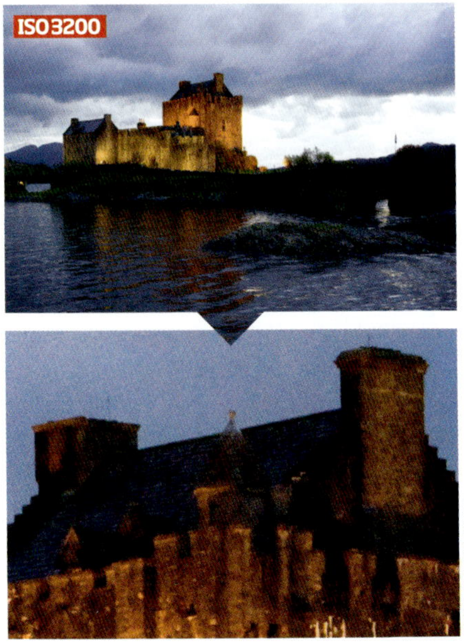

IMAGES: LEE FROST

Using ISO ratings

Most cameras cover the ISO range of 100-3200, a few go as low as ISO 50, while many go as high as ISO 6400. There are a few models with even higher ISO ratings, such as the Nikon D3s, which has a maximum ISO of 102,400! As with apertures and shutter speeds, ISOs are changed in full stops or fractions of a stop. All you need to do is press the ISO button and select the rating you wish to use, based on the shooting conditions and the effect you're trying to capture. As with the other two exposure variables, ISO can be used creatively, so getting to understand how ISO works can really benefit your photography. Remember that your choice of ISO has an effect on how your scene is captured, especially if it includes any moving elements. A low ISO limits the choice of shutter speeds, so may result in moving subjects being blurred, whereas a fast ISO gives you more choice at the expense of noise.

As well as being able to set ISO manually, there is an Auto setting that lets the camera choose the ISO for you. This is particularly useful when shooting in low light as it helps balance ambient light with flash, but we'd suggest you avoid the ISO Auto setting when shooting creatively. For instance, there is no point tripod-mounting your camera to shoot dusk and setting a high ISO of 1000 to avoid shake, as it will only add substantial noise.

Knowing what ISO rating is best to use comes with experience, in much the same way as learning which shutter speed or aperture is best. However, there are some general guidelines as to when you should select a low, medium or high ISO rating, as follows…

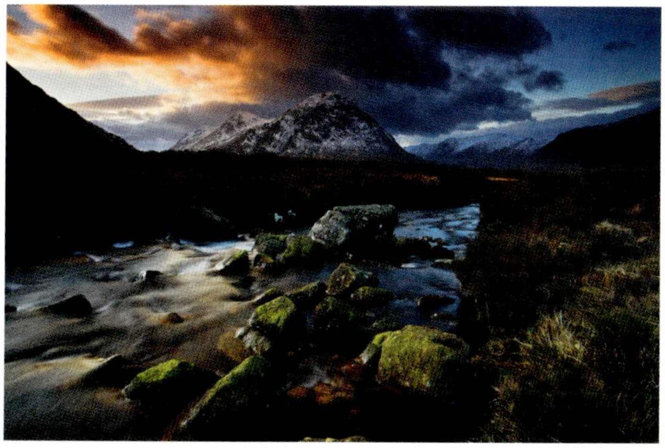

ADAM BURTON

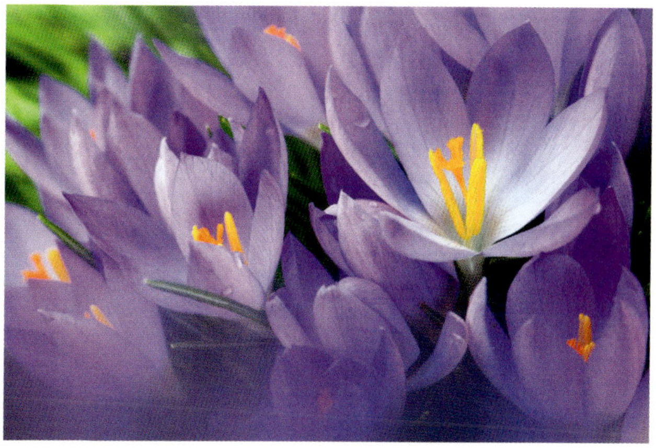

HELEN DIXON

When to use Low ISOs (ISO 50-200)

For the best possible image quality, use a low ISO. Colours are at their most accurate, tones exhibit smooth gradation, noise is minimal, while sharpness and detail is at its highest. A low ISO means the sensor has low sensitivity to light and limits your choice of shutter speeds, so even at a wide aperture, take care to avoid camera shake by using a tripod or image stabilisation. Most enthusiast and pro landscape photographers shoot with a low ISO and their camera on a support. Studio-based photographers using flash heads use a low ISO, too, as the powerful studioflash heads provide enough light to shoot handheld. Avoid using a low ISO if you're shooting hand-held, except in the brightest conditions. Even then, take care if using a mid-to-small aperture with a telezoom.

When to use medium ISOs (ISO 250-640)

We'd suggest you make ISO 400 your default setting. It gives a two-stop advantage over ISO 100, which provides far more flexibility in your choice of exposure settings. Despite this increase in speed, all but the most discernible eye will see any difference in quality compared to an ISO 100 image. Those regularly using the integral flash will note an increase in flash range: ideal when shooting portraits indoors. So, what are the drawbacks? Well, there aren't really any of significance. You could argue that colours aren't as natural, noise is higher and sharpness lower, but, in truth, the differences are hard to spot. So, for general use, leave your camera at ISO 400 unless shooting in low light and need a faster speed, or want to use a low ISO for the ultimate quality.

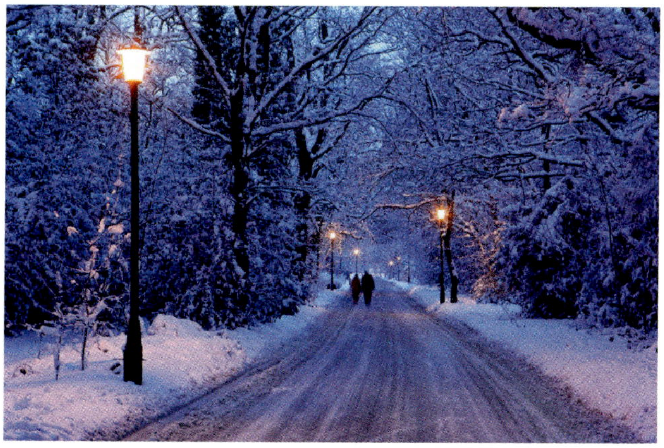

HELEN DIXON

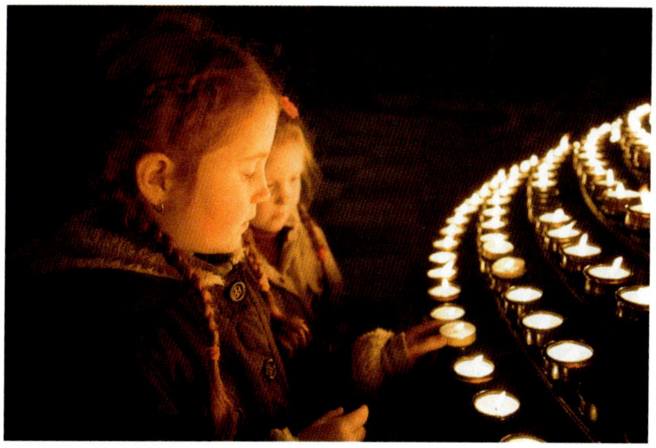

ISTOCK PHOTO

When to use fast ISOs (ISO 800-1600)

Selecting a fast ISO rating should be the result of necessity. A higher ISO results in images having more noise and less sharpness, especially if using Noise Reduction (covered later). That said, the most recent cameras have seen a marked improvement in the quality of their high-ISO images. The most obvious time to use a high ISO is when taking hand-held pictures in low light, such as outdoors in the evening or indoors. A high ISO allows you to select a fast enough shutter speed to avoid shake, with the use of an image stabiliser helping matters further. Many use a low ISO and risk images being blurred by camera movement, but we suggest using a fast ISO: it's better to have a sharp, noisy image taken at ISO 1000 than a blurry image taken at ISO 400.

When to use very fast ISOs (ISO 3200+)

Digital cameras already perform better at fast ISOs than film managed, especially models like Nikon's D3x, which produces unbelievable quality at high ISOs. Images taken at ISO 3200 are characterised by increased noise, less than accurate colours and reduced sharpness, with all these inherent problems getting worse as the ISO rating is increased. Some models, like the Canon EOS-1D MkIV and Nikon D3s, boast a top rating of ISO 102,400 – fast enough to capture images by moonlight, making it ideal for surveillance, but for most forms of photography, this speed is excessive. Therefore, only use it if you really have to. If you're out at night and spot a yeti or a UFO hovering overhead, by all means select ISO 12,800 or above and capture the evidence. Otherwise, use a lower ISO.

Noise Reduction

On the previous pages, we see how noise increases as you use higher ISO ratings. It's also the case that long exposures can increase noise, too. Here we cover the two Noise Reduction systems found on your camera

BEFORE LOOKING AT Noise Reduction, it's worth noting that there are two main types of noise: Luminance noise and Chrominance noise. Luminance noise is the dark grey or black noise (often called grain) present in all images. As subject detail is linked to this type of noise, removing this noise will lead to a loss in detail. Chrominance noise is the coloured speckled noise, more readily seen in darker areas of the frame. It isn't linked to detail and so its removal has less effect on image sharpness.

In-camera Noise Reduction

Most cameras boast both modes of in-camera NR. Long exposure Noise Reduction is used to reduce noise from long exposures of several seconds or minutes, while High ISO Noise Reduction reduces noise from images captured using a high ISO rating.

The High ISO NR targets Chrominance noise, with the aim of minimising loss in detail. With High ISO NR, most models offer a simple On/Off choice, while others offer a choice of Low, Standard or Strong settings. In our limited tests, we've found Strong has an unwanted impact on Luminance noise, so we'd avoid using it and stick to using Low or Standard settings, or switching it to Off and using post-processing software.

The Long Exposure NR shoots a 'Dark Frame' along with the actual exposure, and then uses the noise data from the dark frame to subtract noise from the actual image. It's a system that works well in most cases, but exposure times are doubled, as the Dark Frame lasts as long as the actual exposure.

The success of both these types of NR varies from camera to camera, so it's worth running a series of tests with your camera and comparing results with and without NR. Please note that Raw files are excluded from in-camera Noise Reduction, so its effect will only be seen on JPEGs.

Noise Reduction software

There are a number of third-party software packages that can be used to reduce image noise and here we provide an outline of the most popular three packages. It's worth noting that all offer the option of a free 30-day trial, so have a try and see which you find easiest to use and most effective.

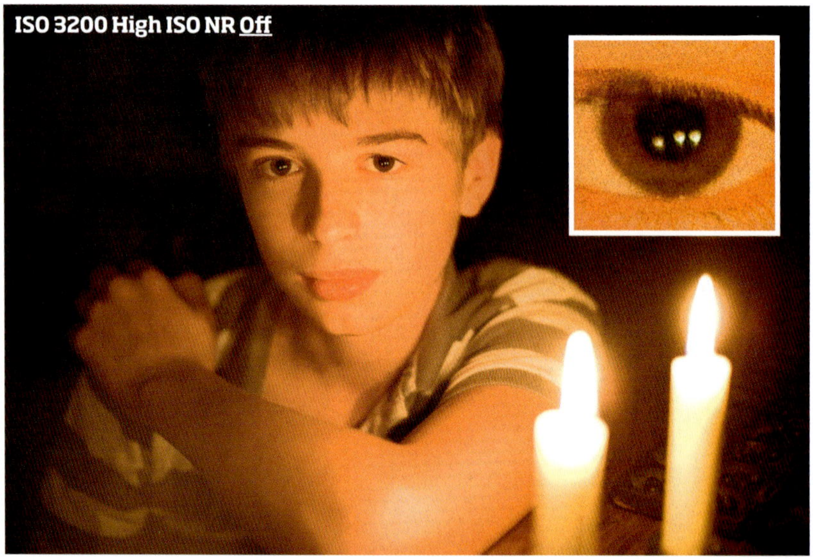

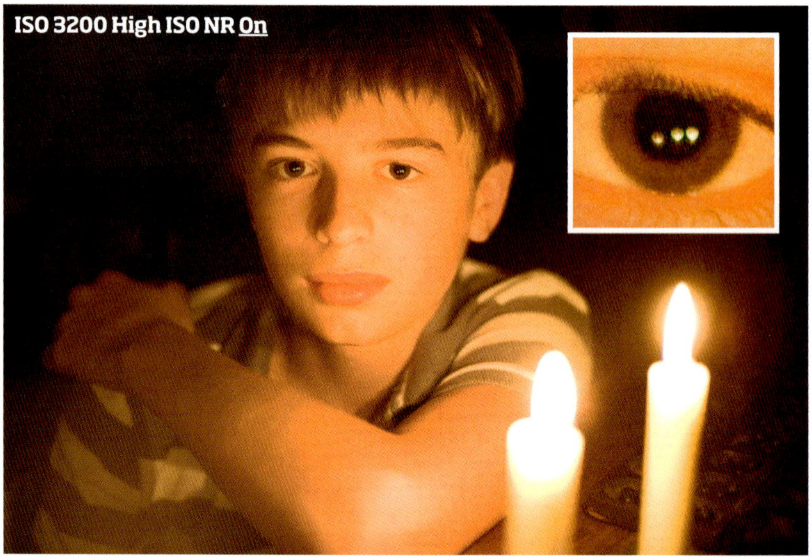

ISO Noise Reduction comparison Taken at ISO 3200, noise is evident, as expected with Noise Reduction off. Using NR reduces the problem, but with a small loss in sharpness.

The best software packages for noise reduction

Photoshop CS5 £650 Elements 10 £80

www.adobe.com

You'd expect the world's leading image-editing package to offer a decent Noise Reduction facility, and you're not wrong. JPEG users can access noise via Filter>Noise> Reduce Noise and get very good results. However, for even better performance, we'd recommend you apply noise reduction to your Raw files, along with any other edits you need to make, before converting to JPEG or TIFF.

Noise Ninja $35-$80

www.picturecode.com

A favourite with many professionals, as well as amateur photographers, Noise Ninja is also used by various newspaper and photo agencies around the world. If it's good enough for them, it's more than likely good enough for you! Various options are available, from a standalone version to one that works through Photoshop Elements, Photoshop CS, Lightroom and Apple Aperture. Well worth trying out.

Adobe Lightroom 3 £238

www.adobe.com

This brilliant package added a Noise Reduction facility that combines ease of use and speed with superb results. Using Luminance and Color sliders, applying Noise Reduction is simple and fast. If you already own Lightroom 3, there's little need to look elsewhere, as it's very capable. If you don't, this facility, along with its Raw converter and various other editing benefits, make it a worthwhile buy.

Noiseware 4.0 $50-$70

www.imagenomic.com

This Photoshop plug-in is gaining an increasing reputation for offering a wide range of features and excellent performance. Its DetailGuard mode allows you to alter luminance and colour noise, while also protecting detail and colour accuracy. With a range of manual and automatic functions, it has plenty of depth. It's not as easy to use as Noise Ninja (its main rival), but it offers plenty, so it's worth a look via its free trial.

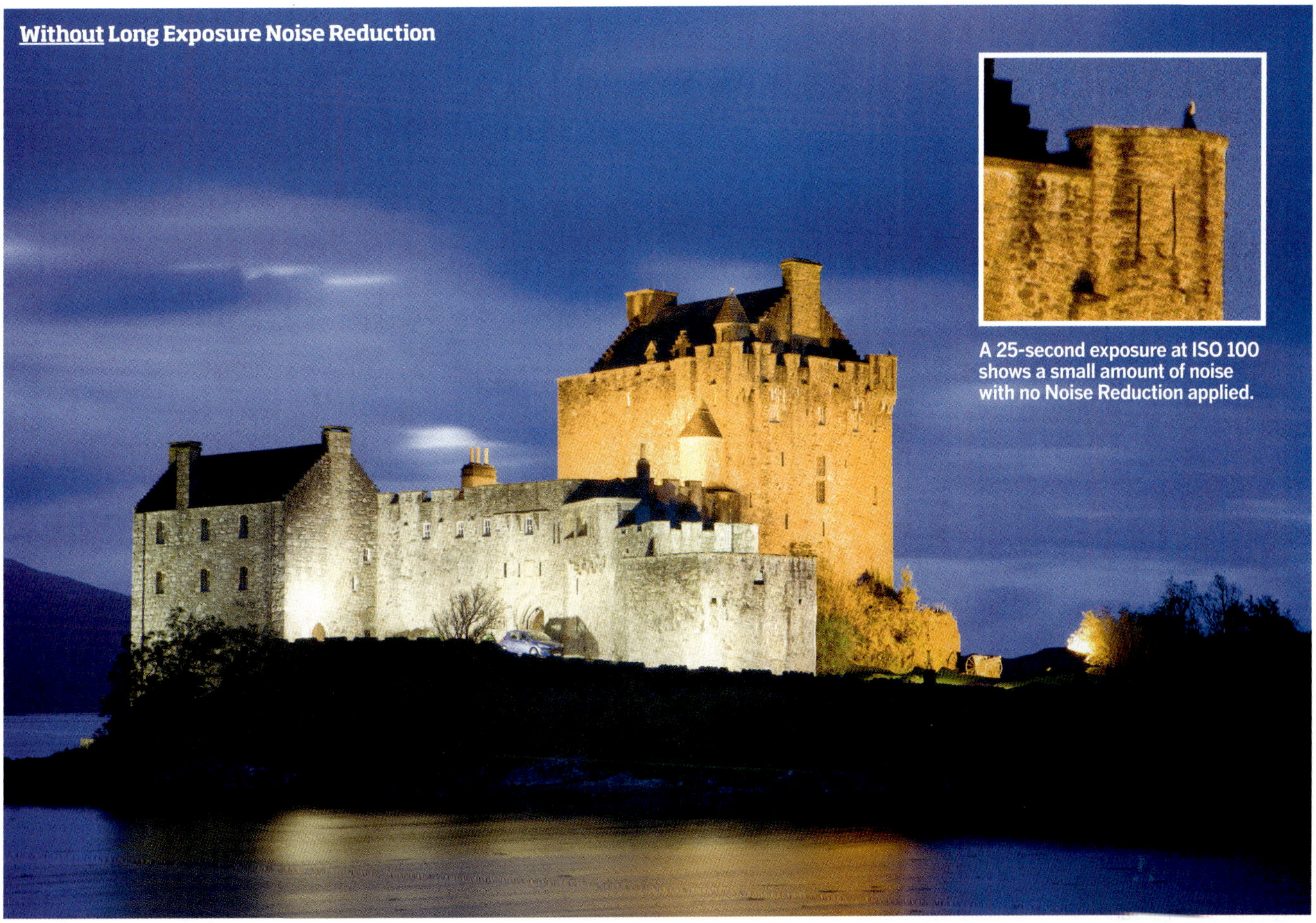

A 25-second exposure at ISO 100 shows a small amount of noise with no Noise Reduction applied.

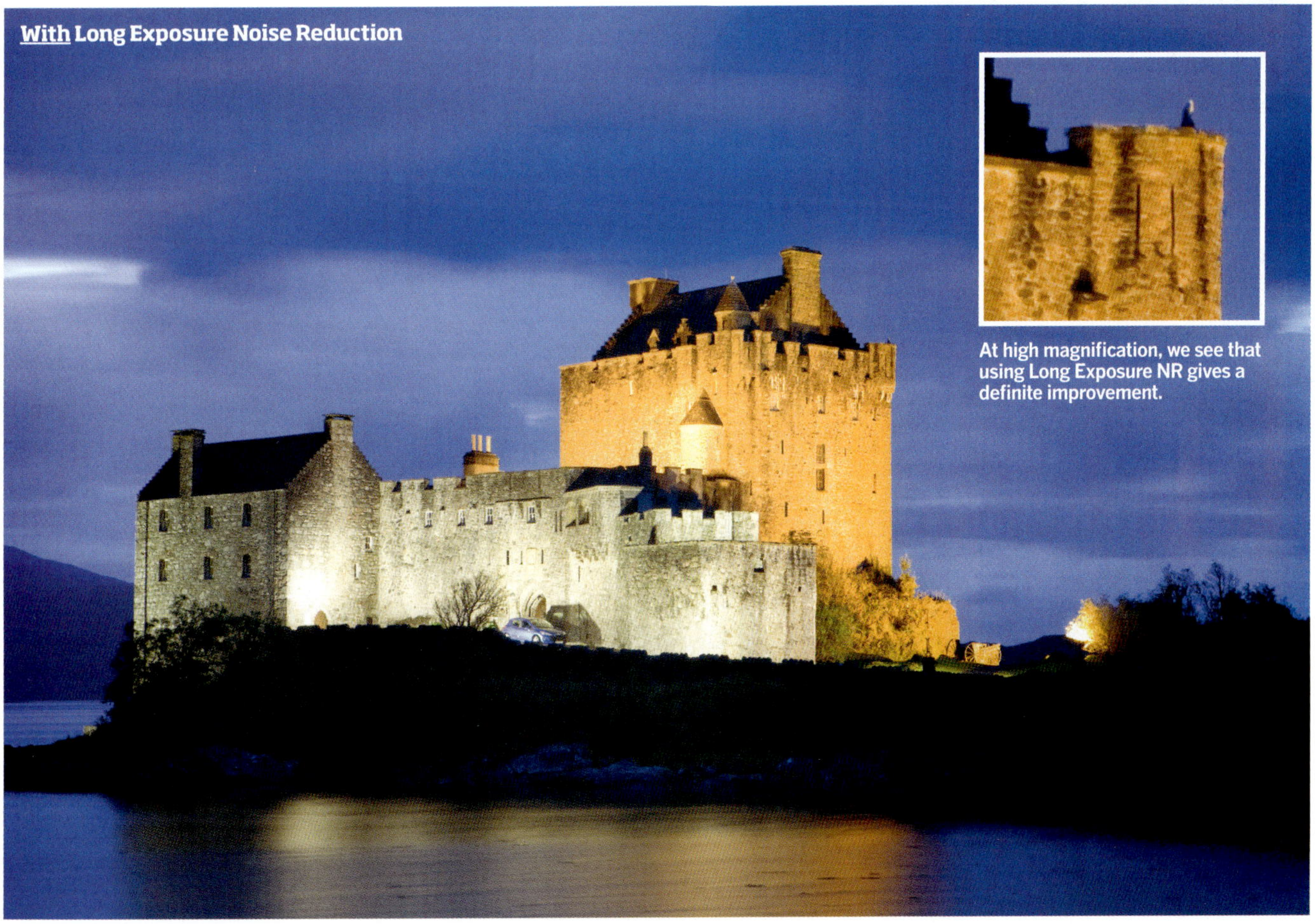

At high magnification, we see that using Long Exposure NR gives a definite improvement.

Working with Raw files

Shooting in Raw format produces superior image files and, ultimately, better photographs than JPEGs – but only if you know what to do with your Raw files once you've shot them! Here, we explain how to do just that

PHOTOGRAPHERS LIKE TO have a topic to argue about. Film, lenses, camera models: pretty much everything associated with picture-taking has been the subject of one debate or another over the decades. For the last few years, 'Raw v JPEG' has been the hot topic, with the vast majority of serious photographers insisting that Raw files are better by a mile, while a small, but vocal, minority burst blood vessels in support of JPEGs and accuse Raw fans of being lemming-like nerds who haven't got a clue. As one American JPEG devotee once said: "Shooting in Raw is like hoarding newspapers for 20 years – you know you might need the information sometime, but it sure gets in the way. And other people think you're crazy!" Whether that's true or not depends on what you shoot, how you shoot it and how much control you like to have over the final image. There are pros and cons to both formats, just as there were with negative film and slide film. Back in the days of film, photographers accepted that and used both. In this digital age, however, there seems to be a reluctance to follow suit – it's either Raw or JPEG and 'never the twain shall meet'.

It's often thought shooting in Raw is for experienced photographers and JPEGs are better suited to beginners – which is why newcomers tend to use JPEG over Raw. However, to a large extent the opposite applies, as this guide will hopefully show.

When you take a photo, data is recorded by the sensor. If you leave this data in its original form, you have a Raw file, which is a 12-14 bit uncompressed file containing all the lossless data from the sensor.

All digital cameras initially produce Raw files, but if you shoot in JPEG format, the camera's firmware (its internal software) processes the Raw file before saving it to the memory card. In doing so, it compresses the file by deleting data it doesn't think is necessary – data that can't be retrieved later – as well as adjusting colour, contrast and sharpening the image. A simple way to compare Raw files and JPEGs is by making an analogy with film. If you imagine that Raw files and JPEGs are the digital equivalent of negatives, shooting in Raw is like processing and printing your own film in that you have far more control and creative scope, but it takes longer to achieve the end result. JPEG, on the other hand, is like taking your film to a mini lab and picking up a wallet of prints an hour later – quick and convenient, but the prints have been made by a machine and aren't necessarily the best that can be achieved from those negatives.

Key benefits of Raw

- ✔ Raw files contain more data than you need to create a successful image, so they can be processed and interpreted in any number of ways – think of them as digital negatives with high dynamic range.
- ✔ You can correct exposure error without compromising image quality.
- ✔ When you process a Raw file, you still have the original in its unmolested form.
- ✔ You can return to Raw files in the future when you're more experienced and skilled and reprocess them again, achieving better results.
- ✔ Image quality is superior – Raw files are 12-14 bit uncompressed.
- ✔ A computer has far more processing power than a camera.

Software for Raw

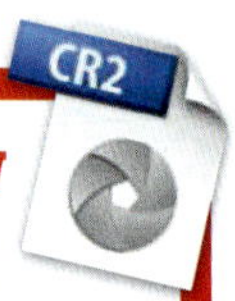

Perhaps the biggest drawback of using Raw is that, in order to work with Raw files, you need specialist software, often referred to as a Raw Converter, to open and edit Raw files before saving as a TIFF or JPEG.

Each camera brand has its own Raw format, so when you buy a camera, it's supplied with its own Raw Converter, but in truth, most photographers prefer to use a third-party converter. There are a number available, from freeware like Gimp, to the likes of Capture One and Apple Aperture (Mac only), which are both aimed at enthusiasts and pros. However, for the vast majority of us, it's Adobe Camera Raw (ACR), found in Lightroom and Photoshop, that is used, and is the one covered in detail in this guide. It works brilliantly and, for most, produces results indistinguishable from specialist Raw packages. Please note: if you upgrade your camera, you may have to wait for Photoshop's updated Raw plug-in. Worse still, if you have an older version of Photoshop (eg CS2 or CS3) and buy a new camera model, no upgraded plug-ins for your old version of Photoshop are available, meaning you need to buy a Photoshop upgrade!

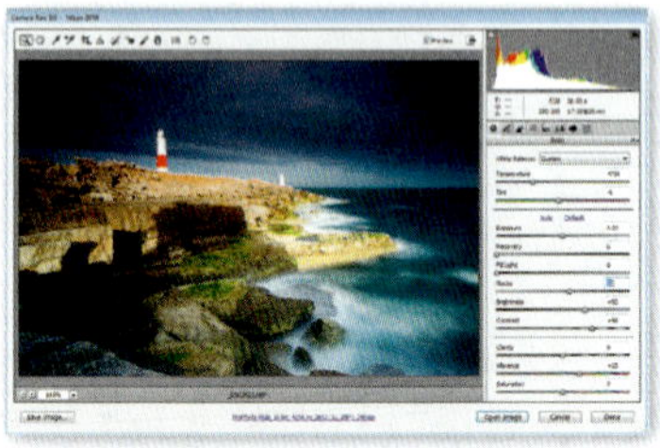

Three reasons why you should use Raw

1) White Balance (WB)

Shoot in JPEG and your camera applies the selected White Balance to the images. In Raw, you can change it later in post-production to suit your tastes or salvage images taken using the wrong WB preset.

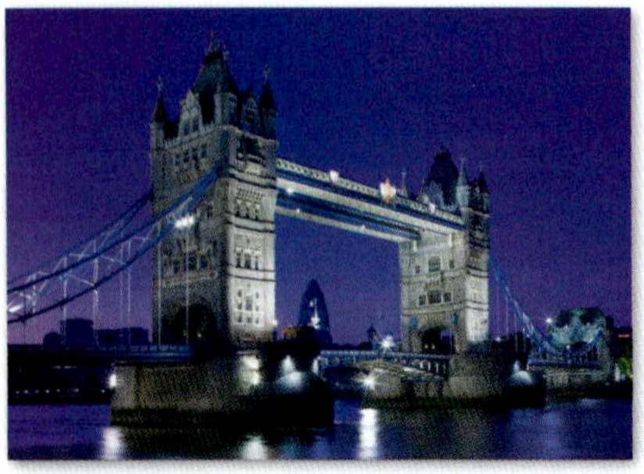

2) Exposure

While there are limits to what is possible, you can pull a lot more information from a poorly exposed Raw file than you can from a JPEG. Such versatility allows for special uses, such as HDR images.

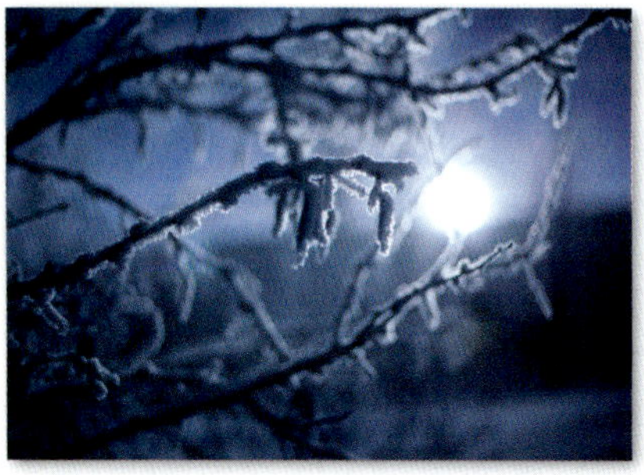

3) Image quality

JPEGs made in-camera are very good quality, but can't match a Raw file for detail. Also, while it's hard to spot unless scrutinised carefully, JPEGs from Raw are better than in-camera JPEGs.

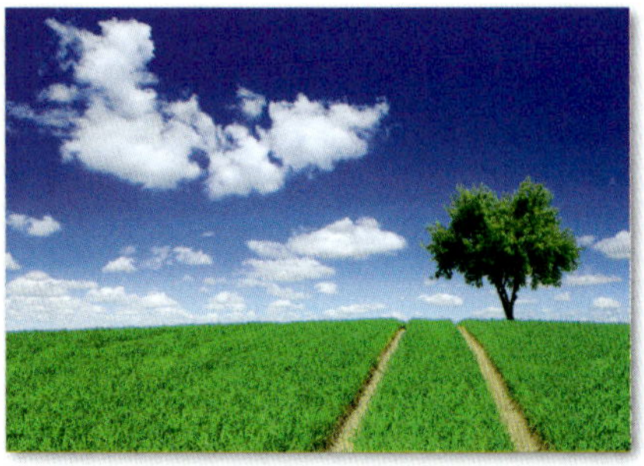

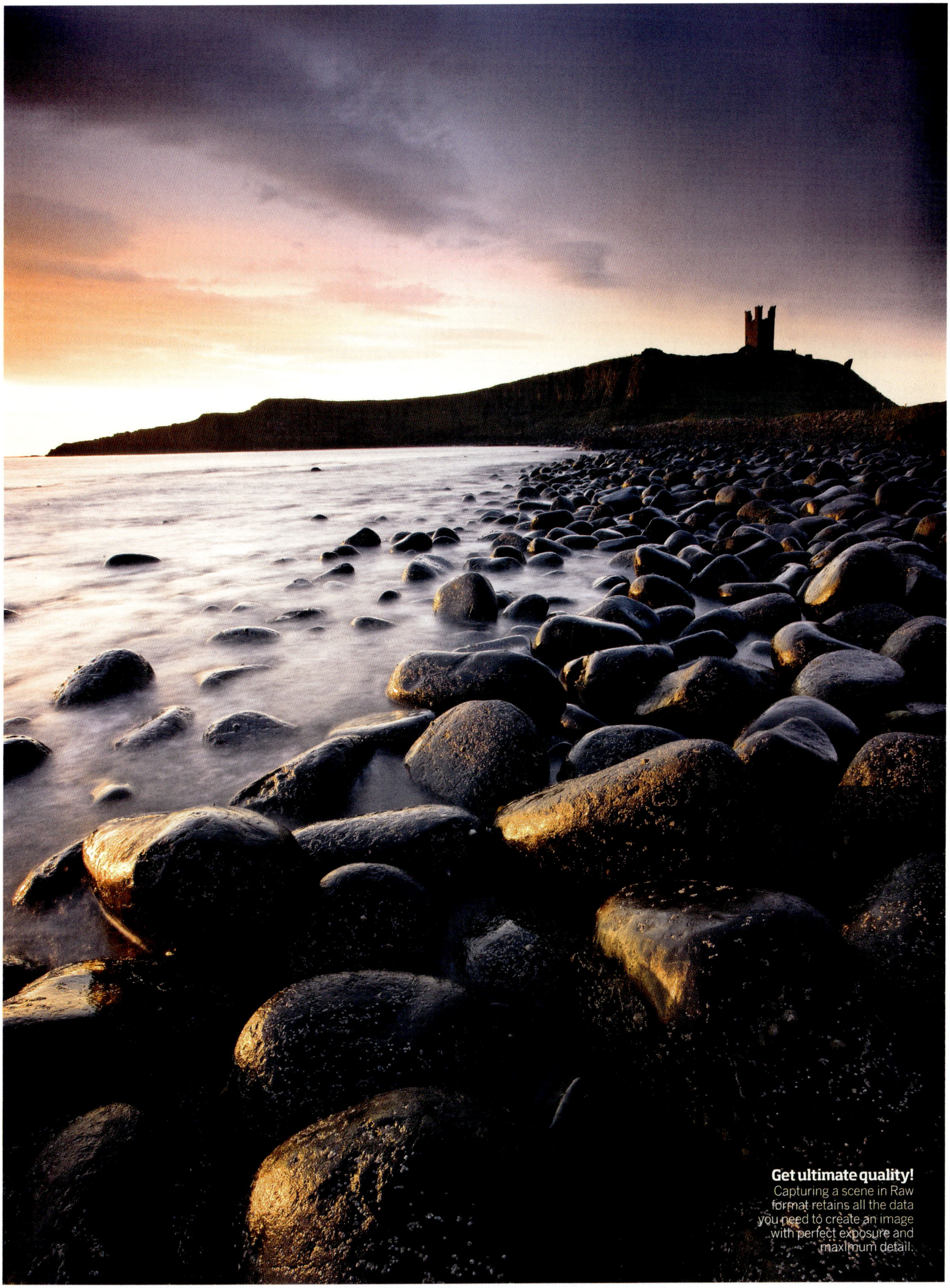

LEE FROST

Get ultimate quality! Capturing a scene in Raw format retains all the data you need to create an image with perfect exposure and maximum detail.

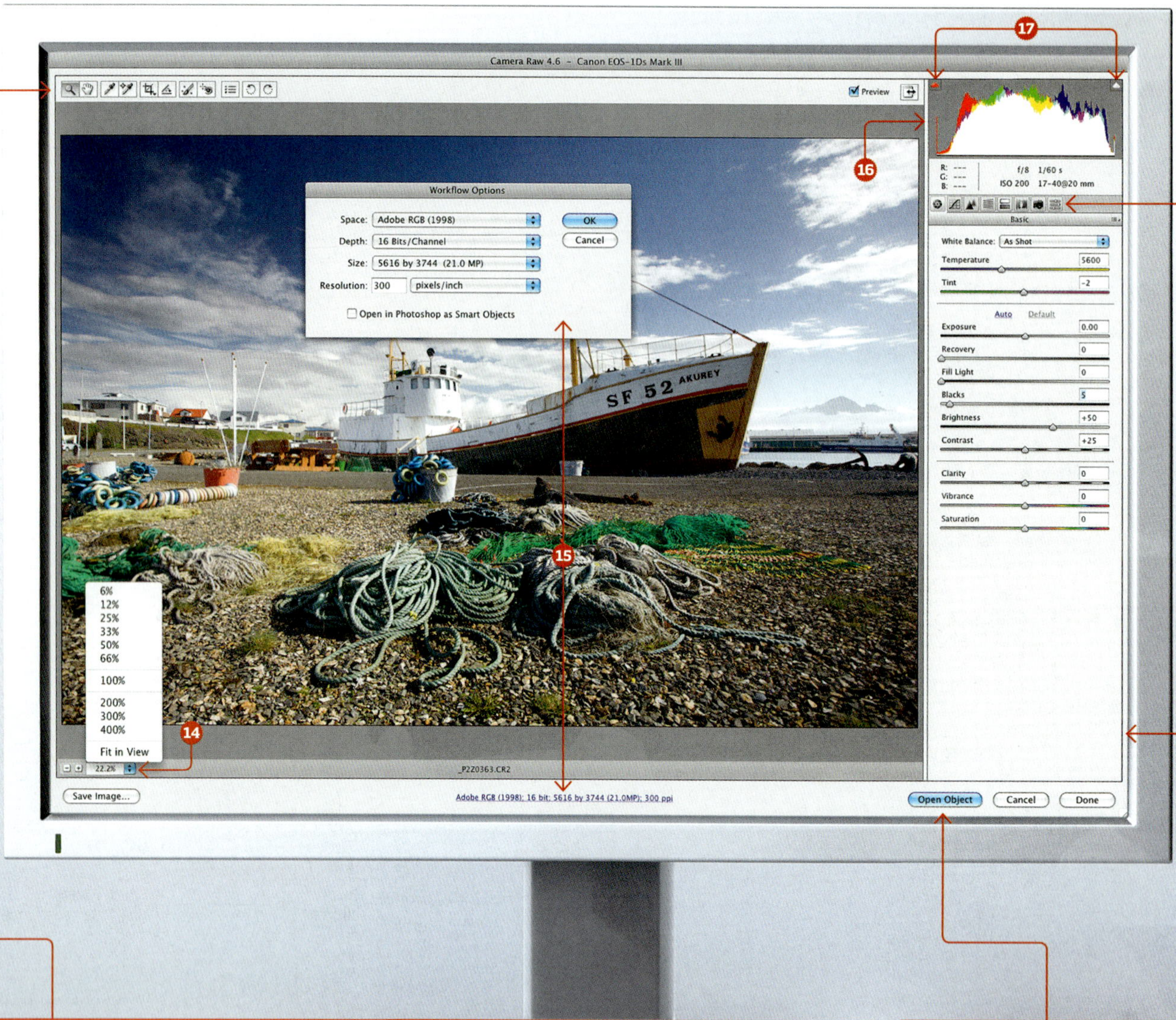

The toolbar

At the top-left corner of the interface are various symbols, each with a use to edit your pictures. CS5 has a few new additions to the CS4 arsenal, which we outline below, but the main tools you'll use for everyday Raw editing are the Zoom, Hand, Rotate and White Balance tools. Others, such as Color Sampler, Crop, Straighten and Retouch tools, work well, but unless you're editing solely in Raw, are best left to Photoshop once the Raw file is processed. Red-Eye Removal is handy if you need it, but you're unlikely to process many portraits shot in Raw that suffer from red-eye!

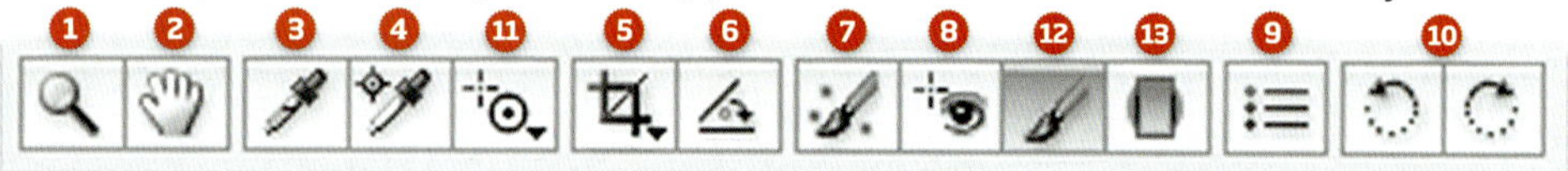

1) Zoom Tool: Magnify the image to see it in more detail.

2) Hand Tool: Navigate around the magnified image.

3) White Balance Tool: Allows you to correct and set a custom White Balance by clicking on neutral areas in the preview image, such as white.

4) Color Sampler Tool: Allows you to select a colour you want to adjust by clicking on that area of the image.

5) Crop Tool: Use this to crop your image.

6) Straighten Tool: Correct a wonky horizon or rotate.

7) Retouch Tool: Gets rid of sensor spots and other unwanted blemishes.

8) Red-Eye Removal Tool: Click on the eye to get rid of red-eye in portraits.

9) Preferences: Click here to access the Camera Raw Preferences dialogue box.

10) Rotate counterclockwise & Rotate clockwise tools: Rotate anticlockwise or clockwise by 90°.

11) Targeted Adjustment Tool: Instead of using the sliders, drag this tool on the image to make edits (CS5).

12) Adjustment Brush: Use this tool to make localised edits to the image (CS5).

13) Graduated Filter: Draw a line across your image to recreate the effect of a graduated filter. You can then adjust the Exposure, Brightness, Contrast, Saturation, Clarity, Sharpness and Color of the filter to suit your picture (CS5).

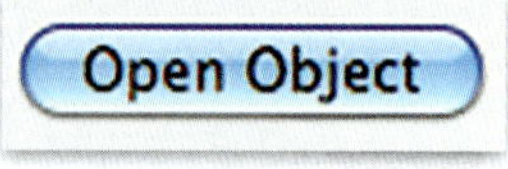

Open Object

Once you've done all your necessary Raw editing, press Shift to turn the Open button to Open Object to process your Raw file in Photoshop as a Smart Object. The benefit of a Smart Object is that you can double-click on the layer in Photoshop to reopen the Raw file and continue any Raw edits in ACR. Alternatively, hold down Alt to turn the Open button to Open Copy (so you don't work on the original Raw file in Photoshop) and the Cancel button to Reset to revert your image back to its original state.

Understand your Raw converter

To go from an original Raw file to a final image, 'process' it using a Raw converter like Adobe Camera Raw

ANY TECHNICAL PROCESS seems complicated and daunting when you try it for the first time. Remember taking your first digital photograph or 'Photoshopping' your first image? Chances are, you didn't have a clue what you were doing, but through trial and error and making lots of mistakes, you got there in the end. It's the same with processing your Raw files.

The main reason why photographers stick to shooting in JPEG is because it's quick, easy and safe: the camera does the complicated stuff and all you're left with are a few tweaks in Photoshop or Lightroom to finish the job off. Shooting in Raw, on the other hand, involves another steep learning curve because every shot you take needs to be worked on. It's the digital equivalent to going from taking your films to a high street lab for processing and printing to setting up a darkroom and doing the job yourself. Is it really worth all the hassle?

In a word, yes! To realise your full potential as a photographer, you need to take control of your photography and the only way to really do this is to shoot and process Raw files. It's important therefore to learn how to use the main controls and tools available in Photoshop's Raw converter – Adobe Camera Raw – to really make the most of your Raw files. Below is an explanation of the Basics tab, which features everything you need for a basic Raw file conversion.

The basic tools for Raw conversion

Most of Adobe's Raw controls are adjusted via sliders, making them fast and easy to use. Here are the key features located under the Basics tab:

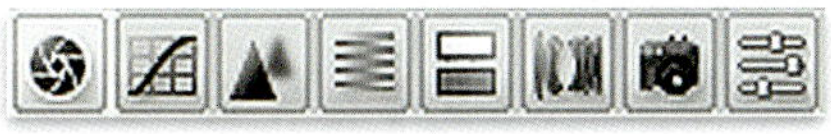

Adjustment panels: The main controls you're going to use when processing Raw files are to be found on the right side of the Raw Interface, between the histogram and the control sliders. There are eight icons covering the following set of options (from left to right): Basic, Tone Curve, Detail, HSL/Grayscale, Split Toning, Lens Corrections, Camera Calibrations and Presets.

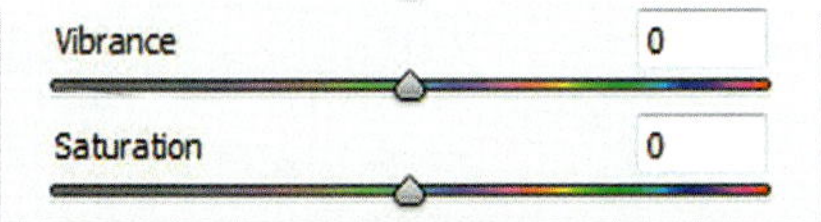

Vibrance and Saturation: This tool is an alternative to the Saturation slider, which adjusts all the colours in an image equally. The Vibrance Tool, on the other hand, affects colours that need boosting, having less effect on the colours already high in saturation.

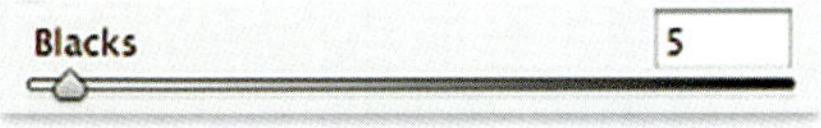

Blacks: This slider shifts the left part of the histogram even more to the left, making the blacks in the image a lot more dominant, and is a useful way of increasing the overall contrast.

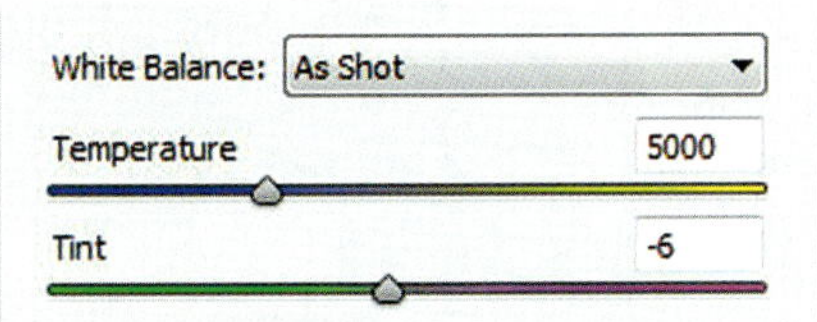

White Balance: Shooting in Raw means that you can control the White Balance in post-production, rather than having to select the right White Balance preset in-camera. Under the Basic tab, you have all the in-camera WB presets available in a drop-down menu to pick from (eg Auto, Daylight, Cloudy etc). You can also use the Temperature and Tint sliders to create your own Custom WB. Alternatively, you could use the White Balance Tool, found in the toolbar.

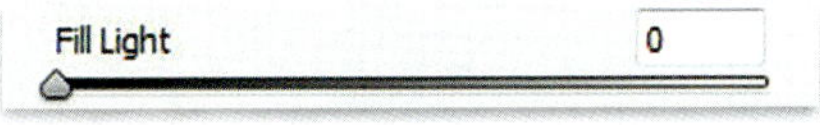

Fill Light: Fill Light attempts to recover details from shadows, without brightening any blacks. Similar to using fill-in flash, this tool will cast some light into your foreground. Use it with the Blacks slider to add more punch, but be careful not to overdo it for unnatural results.

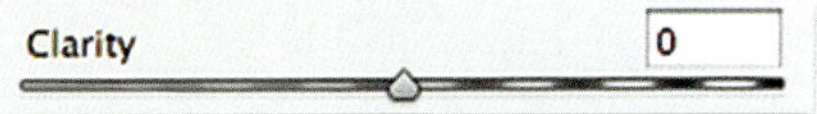

Clarity: Adds depth to an image by increasing local contrast, with the greatest effect on the mid-tones. It works similar to a large radius Unsharp Mask in Photoshop. Zoom into the image 100% to see the effects and stop when you start to see halos appear near the edges in the image.

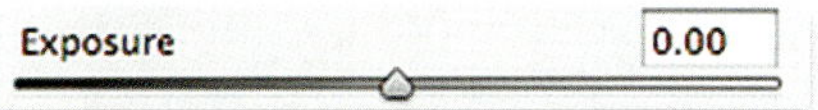

Exposure: Found at the top of the Basics tab, under White Balance, the Exposure slider adjusts the overall brightness of the image, with greater focus on the highlights. The values are in increments equivalent to f/stops. For many photographers, this tool is their saving grace as it allows them to correct their in-camera exposure. Watch out for noise and artefacts creeping in when you push the exposure too far. Use in conjunction with Recovery to reduce the highlight values.

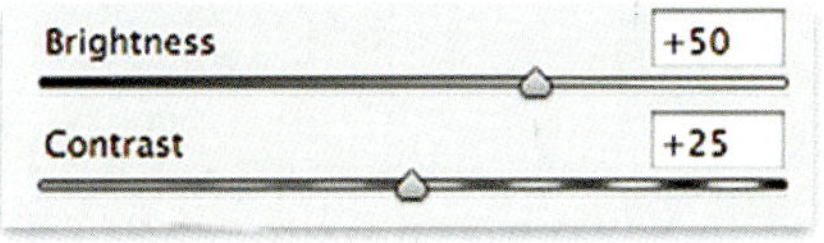

Brightness/Contrast: Brightness works in a similar way to Exposure. However, instead of clipping the highlights and shadows, it compresses and expands the information. Set the overall tonal range first using the Exposure, Recover and Blacks sliders, then adjust Brightness. The Contrast slider mainly affects mid-tones, causing them to brighten or darken to increase contrast.

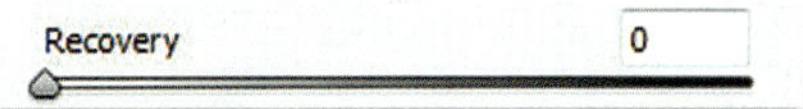

Recovery: This is an image saver for anyone who has slightly overexposed their highlights. This nifty tool should obviously not be relied upon, but is definitely one of the most invaluable features in ACR as it can recover mid-tone detail from clipped highlights. It's not a miracle worker, though: the detail has to be there to begin with.

Raw interface

When you open a Raw file in Adobe Camera Raw, you're presented with this interface. The preview image shows the Raw image in its original state.

14) Zoom: You can vary the size of the preview image and also zoom into it using the tabs in the bottom left-hand corner of the interface.

15) Workflow Option: At the bottom of the screen is the Workflow Option. If you click on this, a dialogue box opens, giving you various options. For Space (colour space), Adobe RGB (1998) is most widely used. For Depth, choose 16 Bits/Channel. For Size, go for the one that matches the pixel resolution of your camera (no point paying for those megapixels then not using them!). And for Resolution, enter 300 pixels/inch.

16) Histogram: In the top right-hand corner is the image's histogram, which shows the distribution of tones in the Red, Green and Blue channels. Where you see cyan, it indicates a crossover between the green and blue channels, yellow is the crossover between red and green channels, and magenta is the crossover between red and blue channels. White shows where all three channels crossover. Use the histogram to judge the exposure as you adjust the sliders.

17) Clipping warning: The two triangular tabs in the top left and right of the histogram tell you if there has been any clipping of the highlights or shadows. If the triangles are black, no clipping has occurred. If the tabs change colour, the colour tells you that a colour channel or a combination of channels have been clipped. If the triangle is white, all three channels are clipped. If you click on the tabs, areas in the preview images will be highlighted to show where clipping has occurred – clipped shadows show as flashing blue and clipped highlights as flashing red.

How to process Raw files to perfection

Our step-by-step provides a simple and effective way to convert a Raw file into a stunning JPEG or TIFF

PROCESSING RAW FILES is a straightforward task, though how long it takes and how many adjustments you need to make to the image depends on how close you get it to finished image in-camera. Photographers who are used to shooting film before switching to digital, tend to do more work on their images at the time they're taken because that's what they had to do with film. Old habits die hard, and that's not a bad thing in this case. If you've only ever used a digital camera there's a greater chance you'll rely more on software to sort out your mistakes, which means spending far longer at a computer than you need to.

Our step-by-step guide shows you how to process Raw files using Adobe Camera Raw (ACR) and what the different tools do to the image. We've intentionally chosen a Raw file that needed plenty of work, but ideally it shouldn't take longer than a handful minutes to open a Raw file, process it and turn it into a high-quality JPEG or TIFF file.

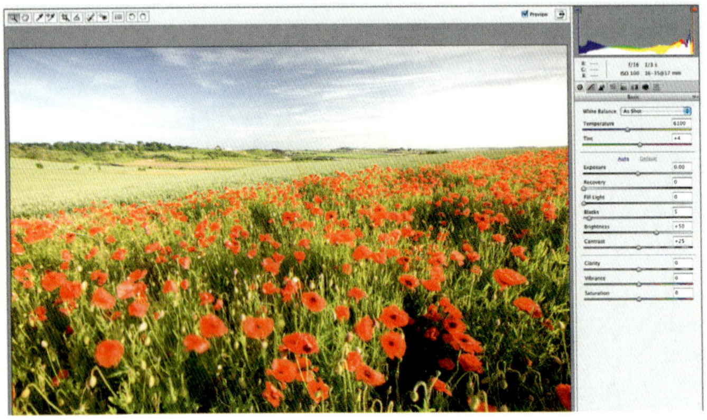

1 When you open your Raw files, you may be disappointed because they often look rather flat and washed-out. This is because you're seeing the image in an unadulterated state, whereas the preview image you see on your camera's LCD is a small JPEG of the Raw file and so tends to look better.

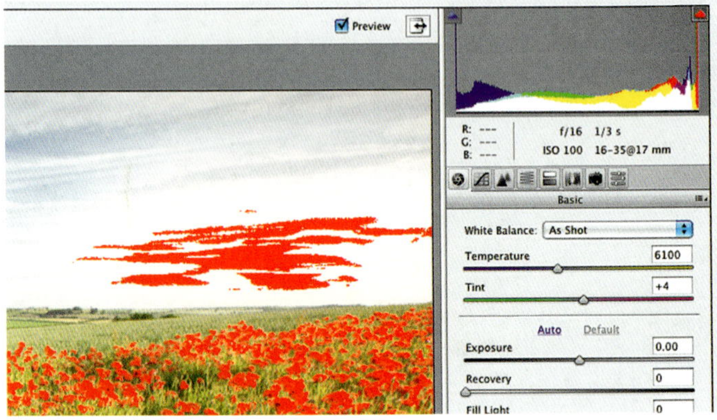

2 Raw files produce the best image when the tones are weighted to the right side of the histogram. But if they touch the right side, highlights will be 'clipped', which means some area of the image have no recorded detail. Click the red triangle above the histogram to show overexposed areas in red.

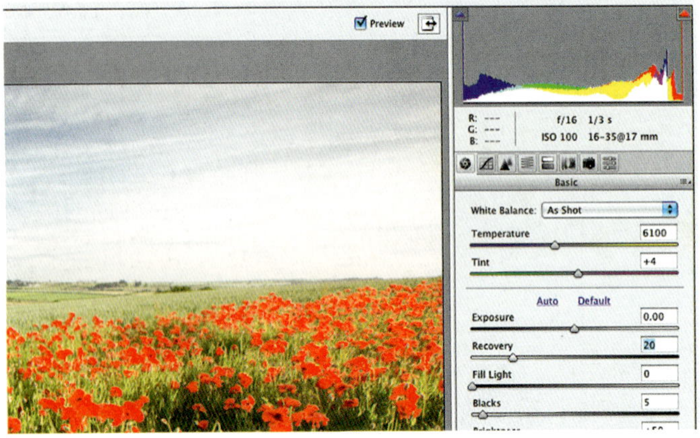

3 'Clipped' highlights mainly happen in the sky and are quite common when shooting landscapes. Overexposed highlights can be recovered, to an extent, using the Recovery slider in ACR. In this case, applying it to a level of 20 sorts out the sky. Recovery flattens contrast, so use it sparingly.

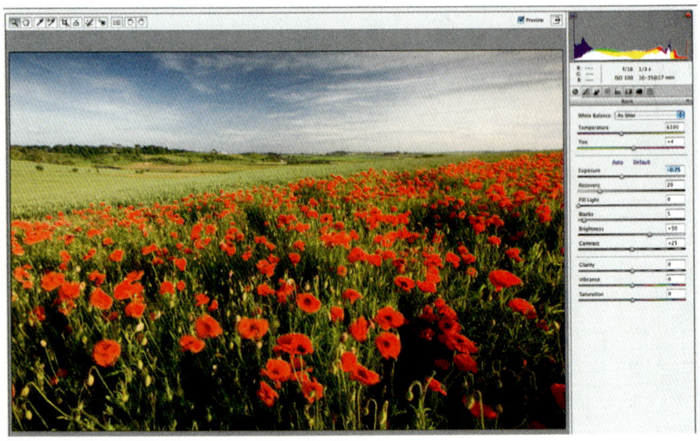

4 The next job is to tackle the exposure as the image is still looking wishy-washy. Pulling the Exposure slider to the left to -0.75 makes a noticeable difference by darkening the image, though it still looks a little flat and lifeless. Again, this is common when you shoot in Raw, but easily solved.

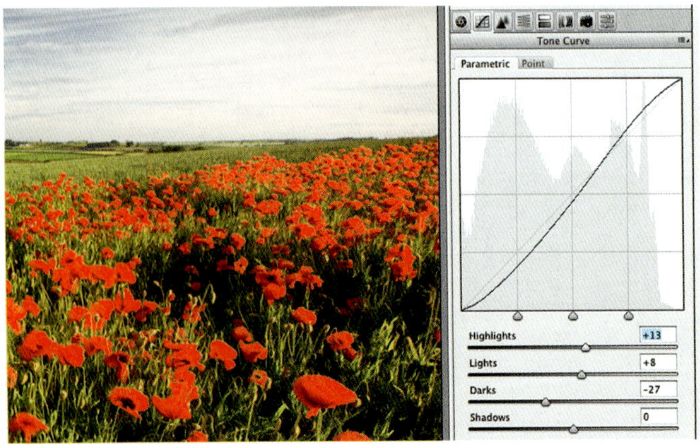

5 Clicking on the Tone Curve icon in the tool bar brings up a Curves window with sliders for Highlights, Lights, Darks and Shadows. In this case, increasing the values for the Highlights and Lights, and reducing the values for Darks and Shadows boosts contrast and brings the image to life.

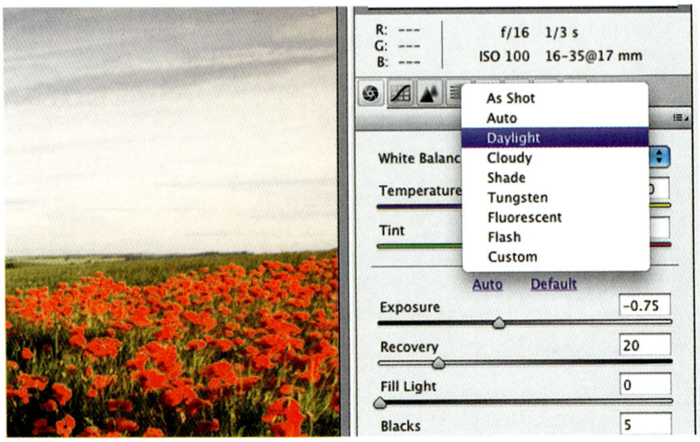

6 Check the Colour Temperature next. Our shot was taken with the camera set to Auto White Balance and has a slight warm cast. Normally, that would be a good thing, but, in this case, it gives the image a muddy look, so the colour temperature is changed to Daylight (5500K) to cool it down a little.

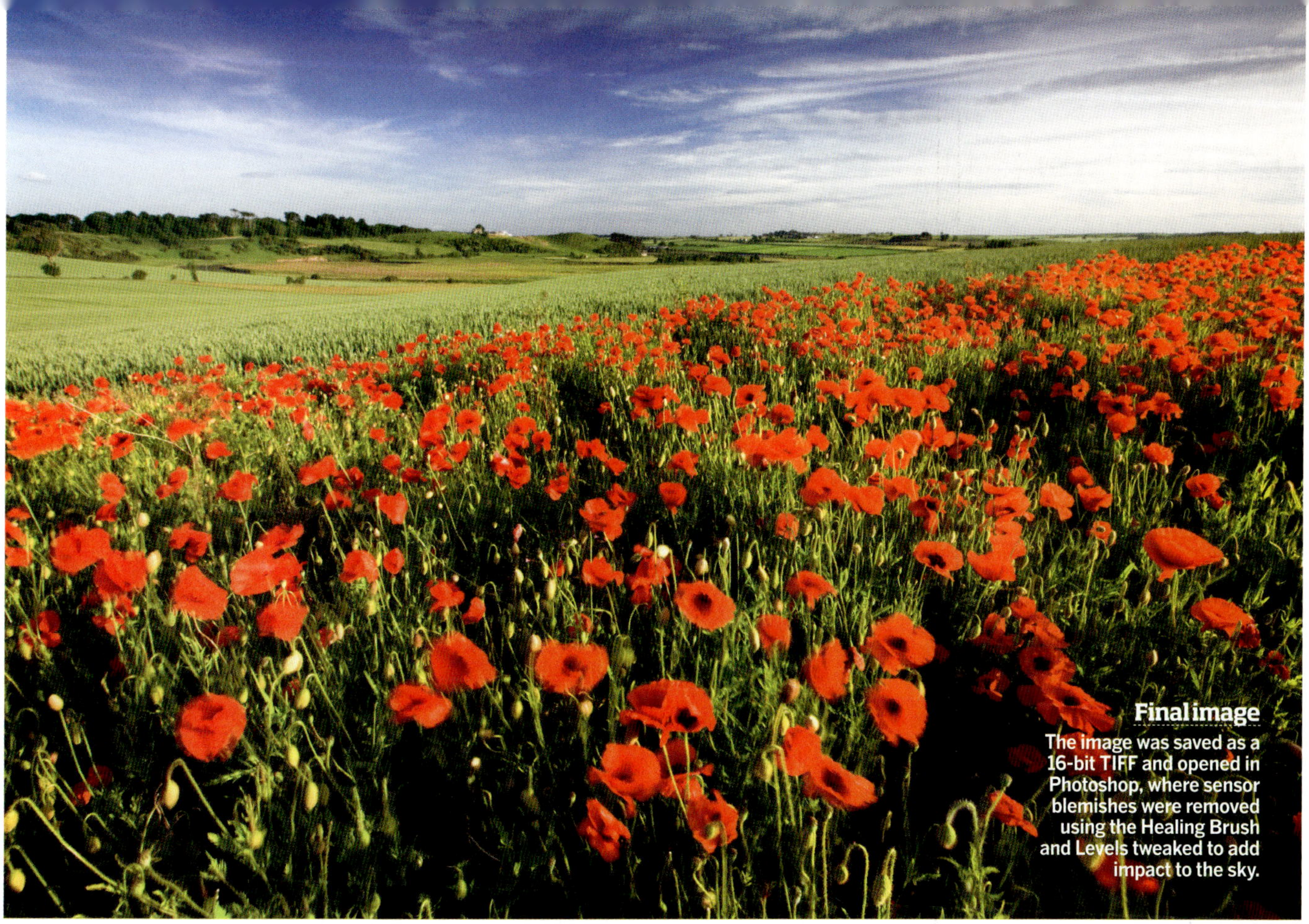

Final image

The image was saved as a 16-bit TIFF and opened in Photoshop, where sensor blemishes were removed using the Healing Brush and Levels tweaked to add impact to the sky.

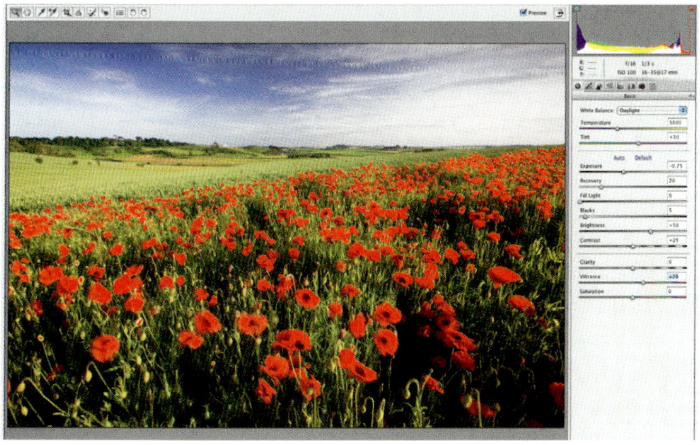

7 Now it's time to boost the colours. There are two sliders you can use in ACR – Vibrance and Saturation. Vibrance is more subtle because it affects lower-saturated colours and leaves alone those that are already deeply saturated. Here, setting Vibrance to 20 does the trick.

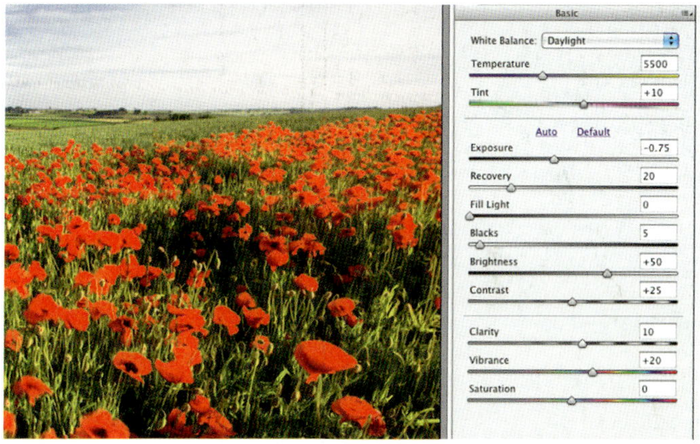

8 Another handy slider in ACR is Clarity, which adds depth to an image by increasing local contrast. Zoom in to 100% when using it, increase the level until halos appear near the edge details then reduce it slightly. Or simply apply in a low level – in this case +10 – to give the image an extra boost.

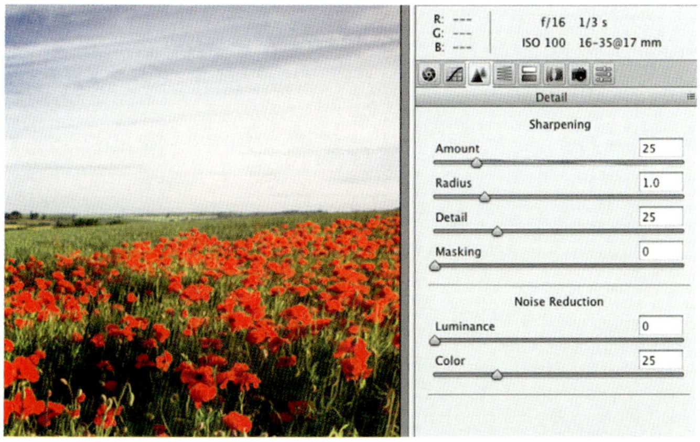

9 Raw files always need sharpening to optimise image quality. There are several ways to do this and photographers have their own favourites, but when using ACR, zoom in to the image 100% and adjust the sliders, keeping Radius at 1.0. Watch out for noise creeping in.

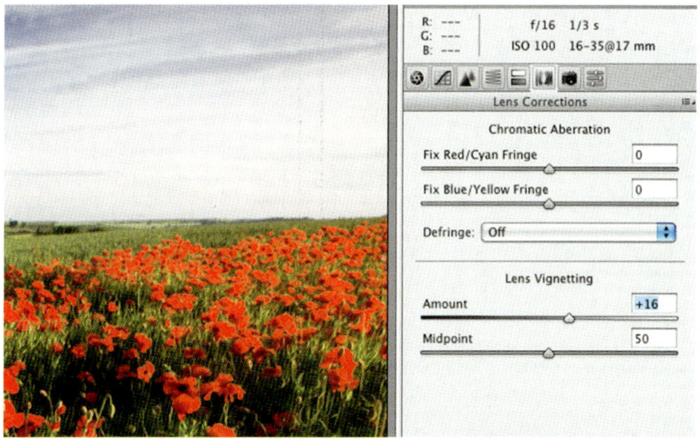

10 Images shot with ultra-wide lenses or zooms often exhibit vignetting where the corners of the image come out darker than the rest. This can be corrected in ACR using the Lens Vignetting slider in the Lens Correction window. Chromatic aberration can also be corrected.

White Balance

Your camera's sensor is very sensitive to the colour temperature of light, and it's the White Balance setting that helps with colour reproduction

EVERY LIGHT SOURCE has a varying amount of the three primary colours: red, green and blue (RGB), with the temperature of light measured in degrees of Kelvin (K). Lower temperatures have a greater percentage of red wavelengths, so appear warmer; higher temperatures have a larger proportion of blue wavelengths, so appear cooler. While our eyes naturally adjust for the light's temperature – so that we 'see' it as white or neutral – a camera's sensor needs a little help. A digital SLR or CSC's White Balance function is designed to do exactly that – correct undesired casts produced by varying temperatures of light.

In order to capture the light's colour authentically, photographers need to match the colour temperature of the light falling on the subject with the appropriate White Balance setting. The camera makes this simple by being programmed with a variety of White Balance presets to correct the most common lighting conditions, for example, Daylight, Cloud, Shade, Fluorescent, Tungsten and Flash. Match the preset with the light source and the camera biases the settings to neutralise the cast. There is even an Auto White Balance setting, where the camera looks at the overall colour of the image and sets White Balance accordingly. While not infallible, the Auto setting is often very reliable, producing good results in the majority of situations. However, as a result, it is easy to simply leave your camera's White Balance set to automatic and overlook the huge creative possibilities of this camera function.

Although White Balance is designed for correction, it can also be used creatively. By deliberately mismatching White Balance with the scene's lighting conditions, you can create strong, artificial colour casts that dramatically alter the mood, look and feel of your images. Just think of White Balance as a handy form of in-camera filtration. You can apply a vast number of different colour casts to your images by simply adjusting the WB setting – effects that, before digital, you could only create by using filters.

White Balance is an underused creative function. Presets designed to correct a low colour temperature – like Fluorescent – will cool down an image; while settings designed to compensate for a high colour temperature – like Cloudy or Shade – will create an artificially warm cast. And you don't have to rely on the camera's presets if you don't wish to – your digital SLR or CSC has a Custom White Balance feature, which allows photographers to manually set the exact colour temperature they require for the look and feel of the image. To provide you with a simple example of creative WB use, Ross Hoddinott headed to the coast to capture a tranquil scene with mood.

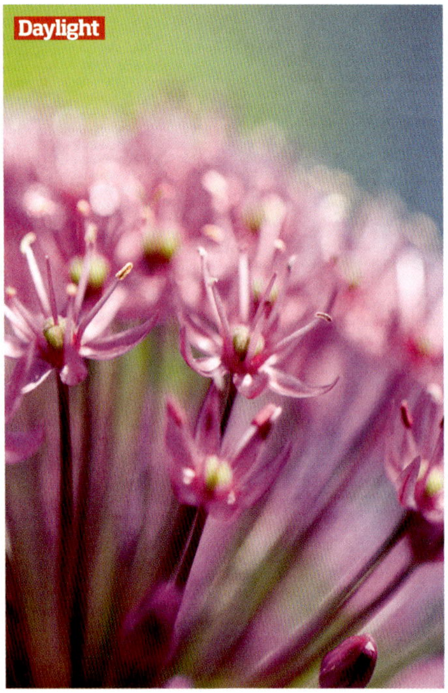

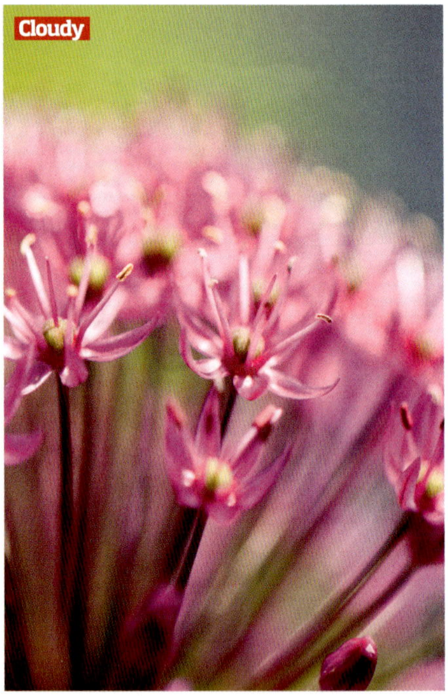

ABOVE: We shot an image in Raw on a sunny day and then converted it into five different White Balance settings to show how the colours will vary. Note that while inaccurate, the effects can be pleasing!

Raw and White Balance

If you shoot in Raw format, or Raw+JPEG, the need to get WB as you want it in-camera is less critical. Raw images are effectively unprocessed data. The shooting parameters are 'attached' to the file, rather than applied to the image at the time of capture. Therefore, settings like WB can be altered and fine-tuned for creative effect using Raw processing software like Lightroom, Aperture or the software supplied with your camera.

AWB (Auto White Balance)

The camera evaluates the scene and sets its own White Balance accordingly. It's a good choice for beginners, but you should think about setting the appropriate preset for the lighting conditions you're shooting in whenever possible, as it will give the most accurate colours. The value for fluorescent light varies because the colour temperature given off by fluorescent tubes can be different. Some cameras, in fact, have three settings to balance these different types of fluorescent light. With Custom, you set the White Balance by following your digital SLR or CSC's preset procedure – it's a good choice when shooting in mixed lighting.

White Balance bracketing

Some cameras allow you to bracket the White Balance of your exposures. This fires an image at the White Balance preset you've selected, then another frame that's slightly warmer and another that's cooler.

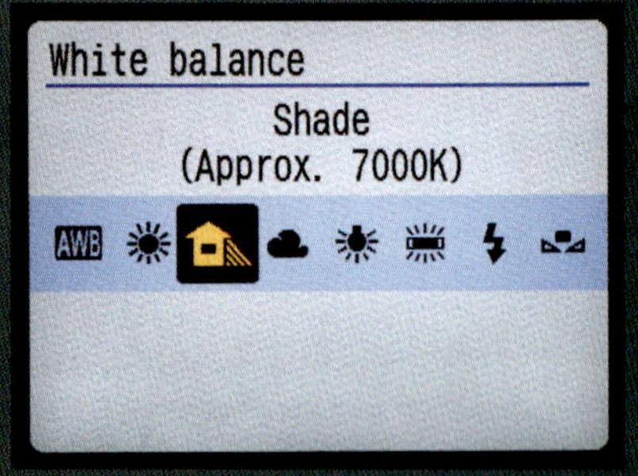

Setting WB

Selecting White Balance (WB) is easy via the camera's menu system. Typically, WB is found under the Shooting Menu. Scroll through and select the preset you require. Some cameras will allow you to fine-tune the WB value to suit your exact taste. For ultimate control, select the camera's Custom setting and dial in the value you require. Some models will allow you to save your custom WB settings to reuse later.

White Balance accessories

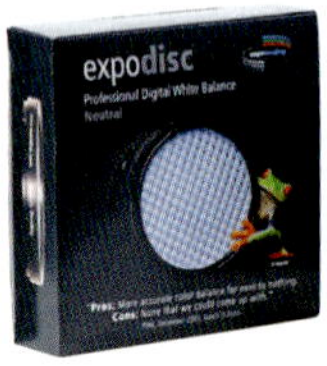

You can use the Custom preset to set an exact White Balance by using a white surface or grey card (depending on your camera) as a benchmark. An alternative is to place a custom-made disc in front of the lens to take a White Balance reading from. The advantage is that it's small enough to keep with you everywhere you go. Look at the ExpoDisc (www.flaghead.co.uk) or obtain a cheap and cheerful grey card from your local photo retailer.

BELOW: KELVIN SCALE This scale indicates colour temperatures and rates the main White Balance presets (it's worth noting that these temperatures may vary from model to model). The Kelvin scale runs from warm to cool, with the Kelvin value increasing as the light becomes cooler.

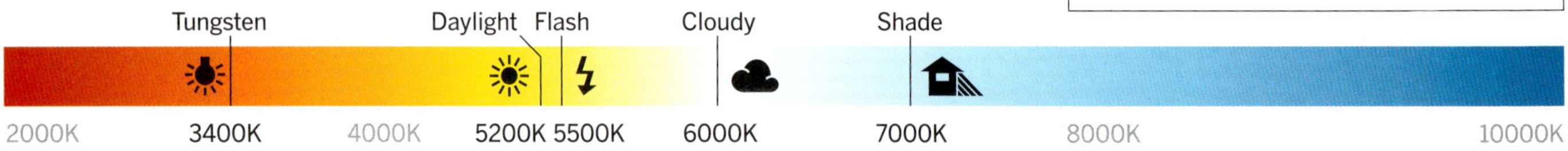

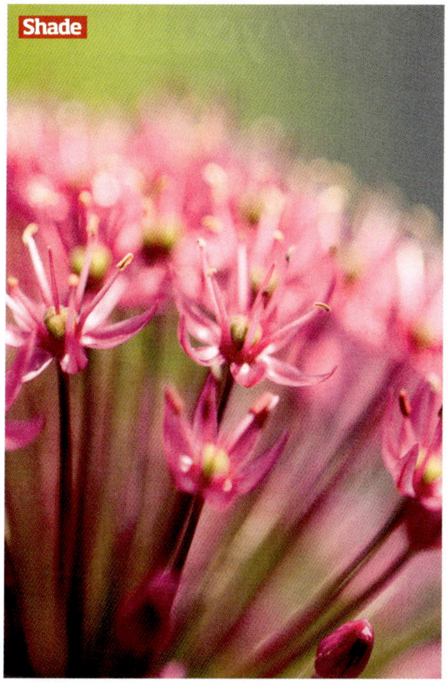

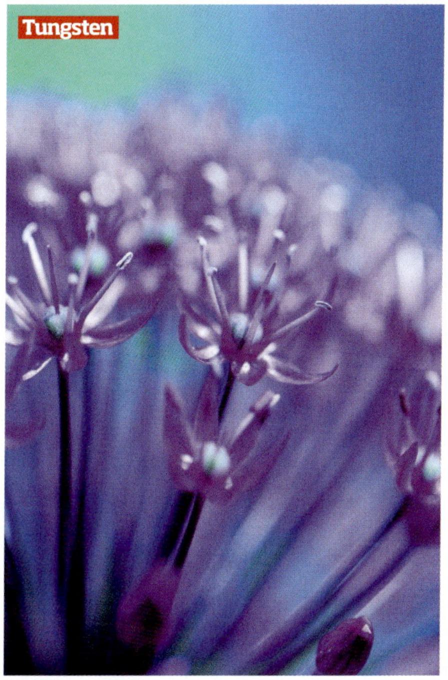

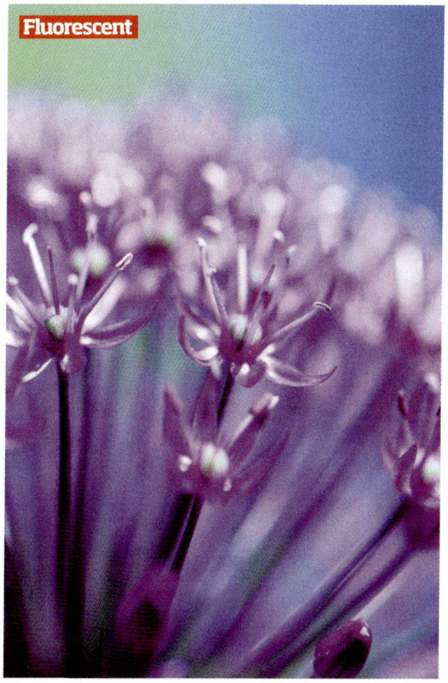

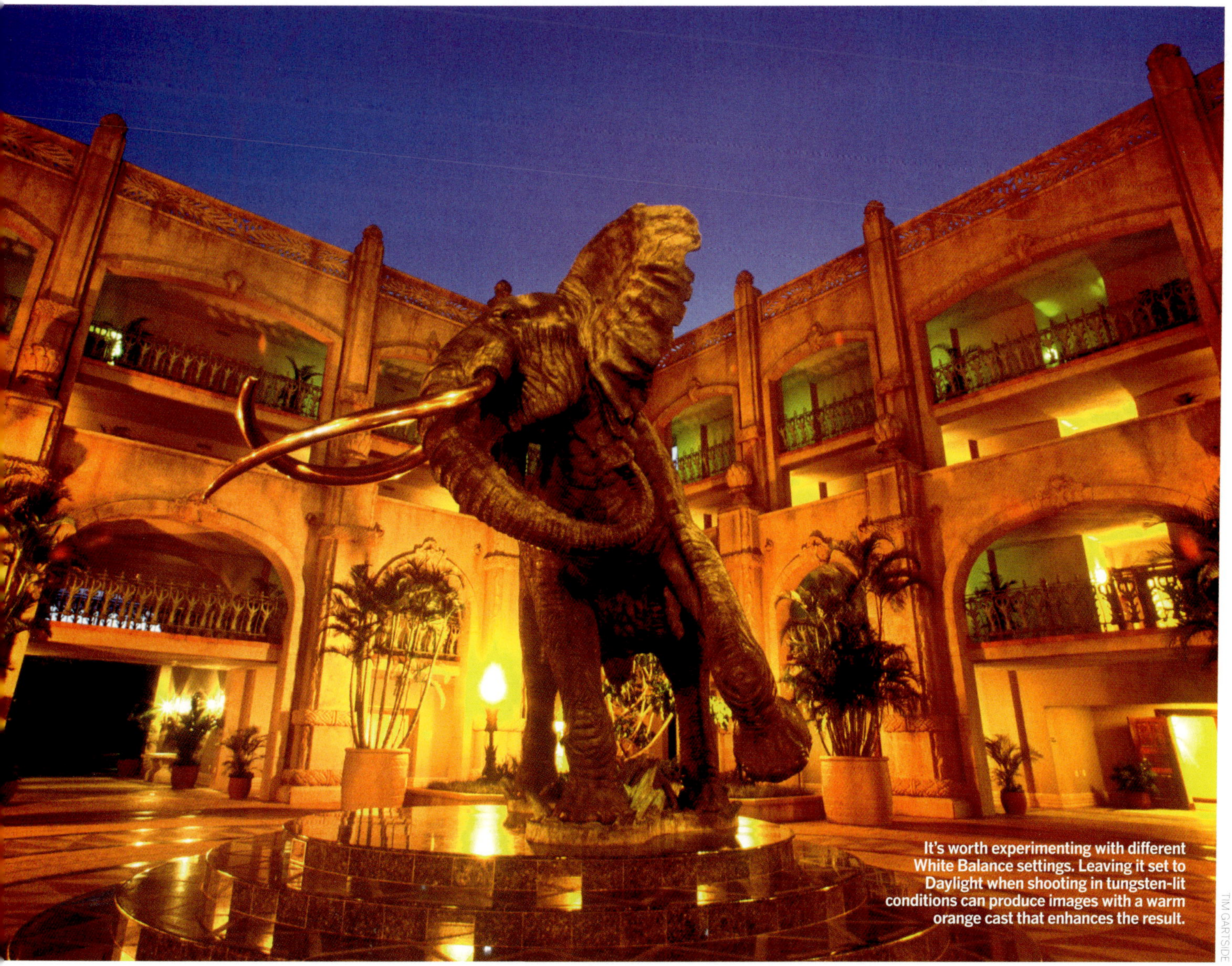

It's worth experimenting with different White Balance settings. Leaving it set to Daylight when shooting in tungsten-lit conditions can produce images with a warm orange cast that enhances the result.

TIM GARTSIDE

Set up your camera the way you like it!

In less time than it takes to drink a cup of tea, you can learn something new about your camera that will change the way you take pictures – guaranteed!

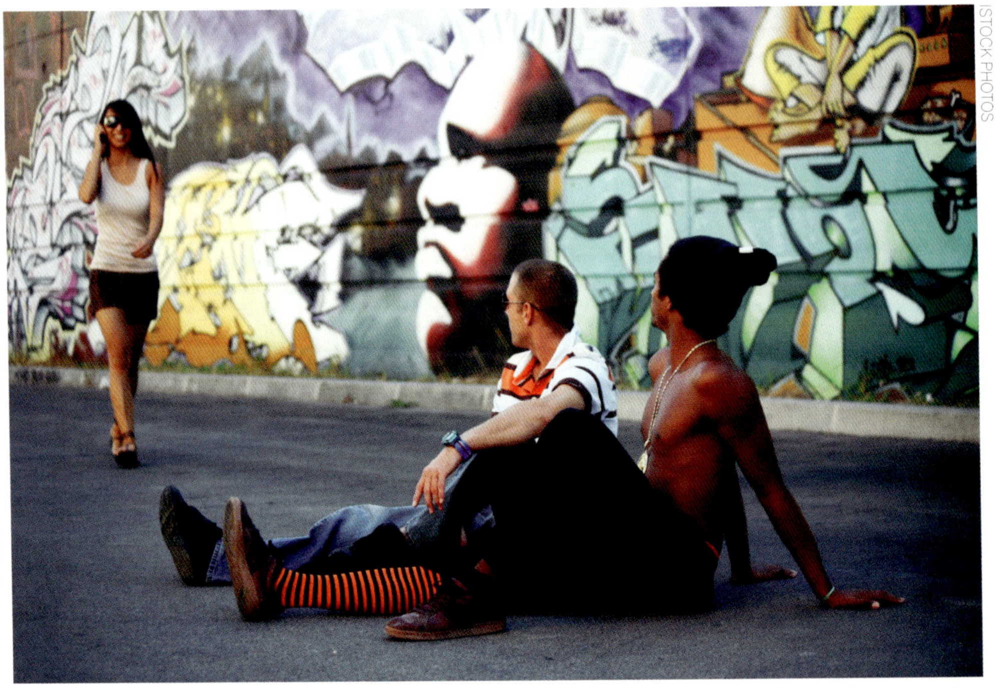

ISTOCK PHOTOS

Make your tweaks

How well do you know your camera's set-up menu and custom functions? Hidden away in these menus are settings that control virtually every aspect of your camera's behaviour. It's worth spending time customising it to work the way you want. Here are some of our favourites…

FILE NUMBERING

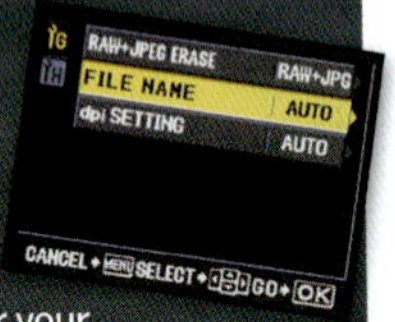

With this setting, choose whether you want to start numbering images from 0001 every time a new card is inserted, or number your shots continuously. We'd recommend the latter, otherwise you can end up with different pictures with identical file names, meaning you could accidentally copy over one image file with another. Some cameras also let you change the letters at the start of each file to your initials (for example: DPL0127.jpg).

SET UP YOUR INPUT DIALS

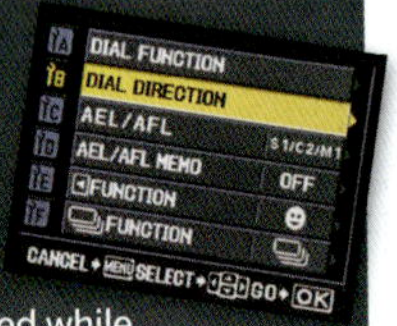

If your camera has two input dials, and it's annoying you that the thumbdial adjusts shutter speed while the front dial under your forefinger controls aperture, then it will be welcome news that some cameras allow you to swap this functionality around. You can also often specify in which direction the dial turns to increase or decrease the value. On a similar theme, some Olympus models even allow you to swap the direction in which the focus ring is turned!

AUDIBLE 'BEEP'

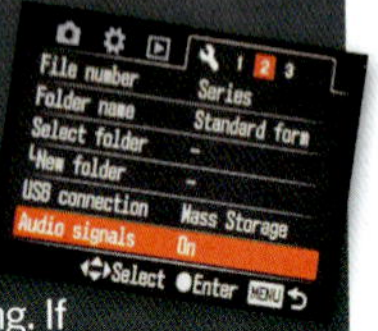

The world is divided into those who like a beep to tell them their camera has achieved proper focus, and those who find this irritating. If you're in the second of these camps, look for the setting in your camera's menu system to silence the sound.

VIEWFINDER GRID

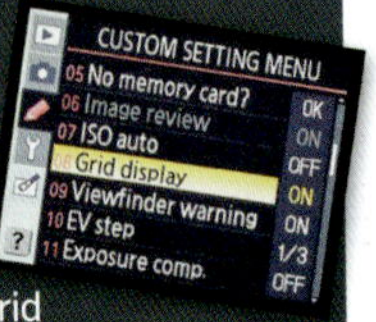

If you are one of those people who can never hold their camera level, resulting in wonky horizons, then the ability to switch on grid lines will be a bonus. Other manufacturers let you view grid lines when composing in LiveView, which proves particularly useful for architectural photography.

FUNCTION BUTTON

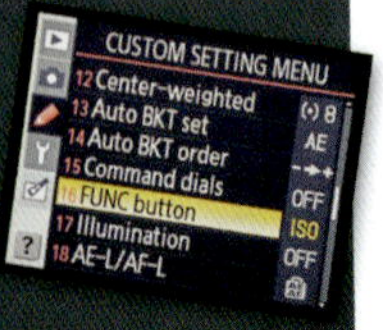

Many DSLRs and CSCs offer a 'Function' button that you can set to perform one of a number of predetermined options. These tasks can include activating LiveView, switching to RAW mode, activating a particular metering pattern or selecting a certain AF area mode.

Auto ISO mode

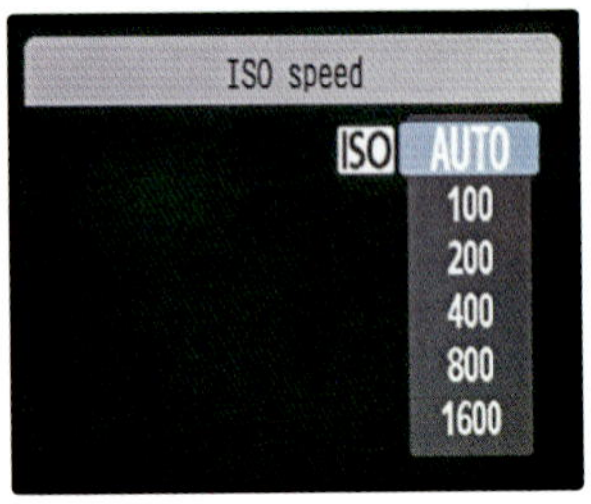

In the days of film, you picked your ISO rating and you stuck with it for the next 36 frames. In the digital world, though, ISOs have become another variable, just like apertures and shutter speeds. You can change them in halves or thirds of a stop over a range of some seven stops, depending on your camera. That's more than the aperture range in some standard zooms.

To reflect this, most DSLRs and CSCs have an Auto ISO setting where the ISO is raised automatically as light levels dim, usually in order to maintain a shutter speed for shake-free handheld shooting. Some Pentax DSLRs even go so far as to include an ISO priority mode (SAv), where the shutter speed and aperture are both locked and it is only the ISO that is changed in response to changing light.

Auto ISO is a particularly useful function for the street photographer. When light levels are changing, but you are working quickly, you don't always have chance to notice whether your shutter speed has dipped into the camera-shake territory or not, and up the ISO to compensate. Why not let your camera do this for you?

Many DSLRs and CSCs allow you to customise their Auto ISO option, specifying a minimum shutter speed after which the camera will start to change ISO instead. You'll also be able to specify the maximum ISO value here, which is crucial if this feature is going to work for you, for as the ISO climbs higher, picture quality tends to degrade, with noise becoming more apparent. Experiment with your camera to find your own ISO limit – a setting which you're happy to work at, but not beyond. If you are lucky enough to have a high-spec full-frame camera – like an EOS 5D MkII or Nikon D700 – then this could be some ISO 3200 or higher. Back in the real world, though, it's more likely to be around ISO 640-800 on a model like a Canon EOS 550D or Nikon D3100.

LiveView mode

LiveView is a feature that lets you compose a picture on the DSLR or CSC's rear monitor – as you might with a compact camera – instead of through its viewfinder. When it was first introduced, many labelled it a gimmick, but since then, more and more uses for this technology have emerged. The most obvious use for LiveView is working at different viewpoints without pulling a muscle. Shooting from down below or over heads in large crowds is much easier this way. There are other advantages, too. Some argue that it's easier to see whether a composition will work or not by using the LCD monitor and not the viewfinder – and if you set your camera to black & white mode, it's possible to preview the scene in front of you in mono. Furthermore, on some DSLR and CSCs (Canon and Pentax particularly), LiveView is carried out using the aperture set on the camera, which means you can use it to preview depth-of-field and the effect of ND grad filters.

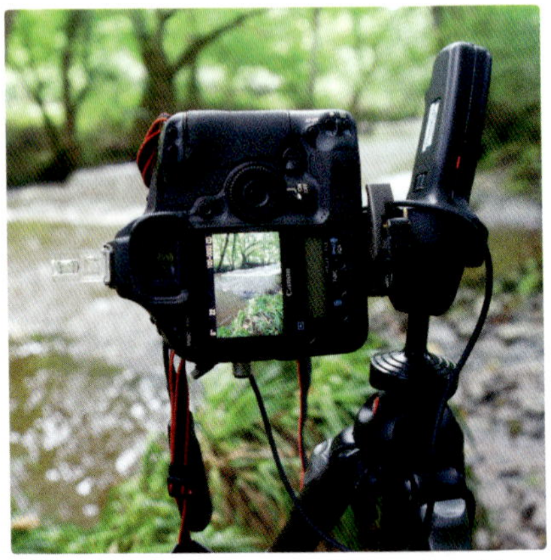

ABOVE: LiveView can be useful for composition.

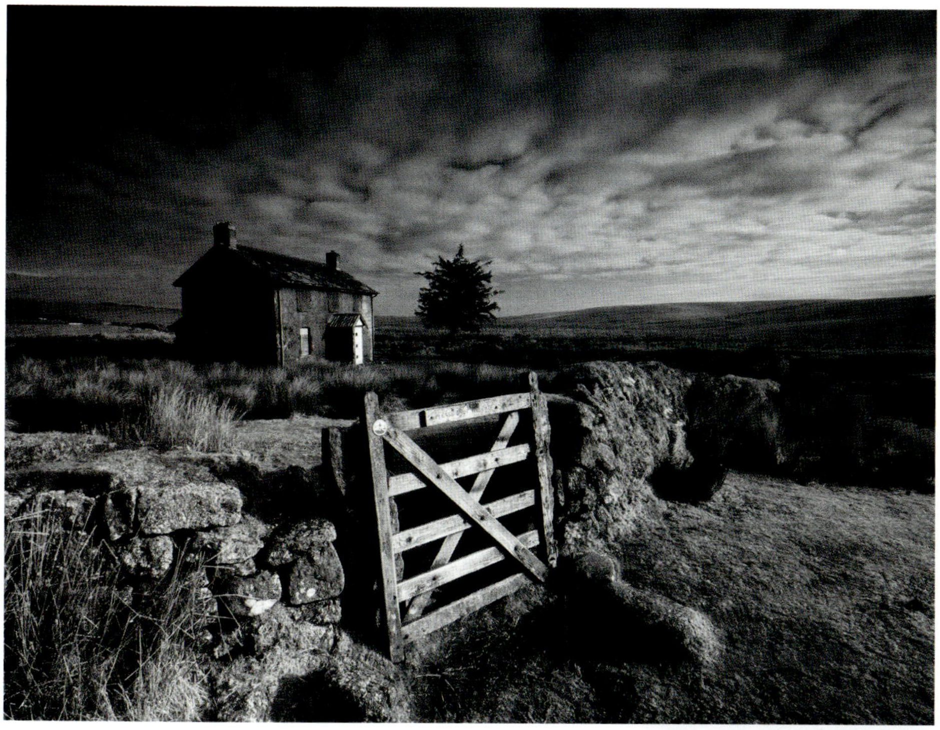

ROSS HODDINOTT

Picture styles/filter effects

The great thing about digital photography is the control you have over factors such as colour saturation, contrast and sharpness when editing pictures on your computer – but did you know you can also do this in-camera? Most DSLRs and CSCs offer the facility to tweak image settings like this. Some have predetermined picture settings, such as Landscape or Portrait, while others give more individual control over settings like brightness, contrast and saturation, letting you save these as presets. If your camera offers manual control over picture settings, here's one to get you started: try reducing the colour saturation as much as you can without making the image completely mono, and then pump up the contrast as high as it'll go. You'll get a hard, gritty look that is great for striking portraiture. Landscapers may like to try the opposite – boosting saturation and leaving contrast set to normal.

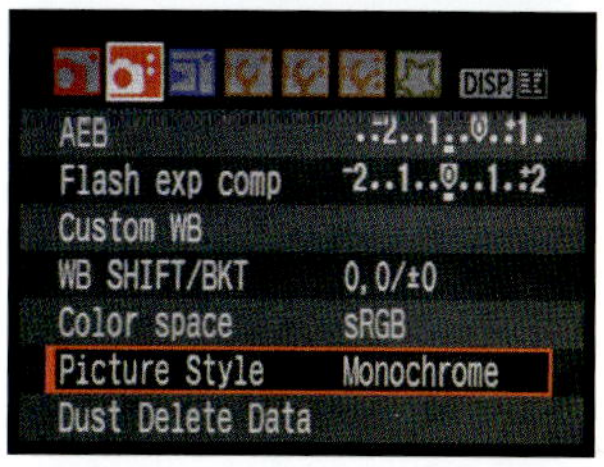

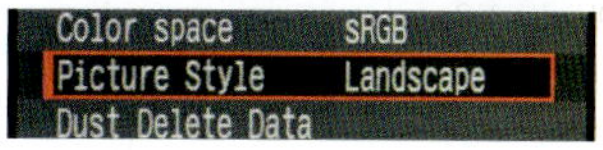

ABOVE: Select picture styles from the menu and choose from the options.

Using your histogram

Take a picture on your DSLR or CSC and we bet the first thing you do is take a good long look at the back of your camera to review the picture on the LCD monitor. Nothing wrong with that, of course – it's one of the best things about digital photography – but can you really believe what you are looking at in this preview? Well, yes and no. You can zoom in and check that the sharpness is okay, and, of course, it'll show your composition and framing, but when it comes to exposure, the humble screen doesn't always show the truth. It can be influenced particularly by ambient light – bright sunlight makes pictures appear underexposed, while dim conditions will make things look too bright. The answer is to use your camera's histogram. This is a graphic representation of how the various tones are distributed throughout the picture: on the X-axis are tones, from pure black on the left-hand side to pure white on the right. On the Y-axis is the number of pixels in the scene that have a specific tone.

Rather than interpret the histogram in terms of hard and fast numbers, it's better to look for trends and shapes. For an average, properly-exposed scene that contains a variety of tones, you'd expect to see an even distribution of tones throughout the histogram. If the scene is underexposed, though, the histogram will be skewed to the left-hand side (the black end). Likewise, if overexposed, the peak will appear on the right of the scale. This is a much more reliable indication of exposure accuracy than looking at the image itself.

This is, of course, only true for 'average' subjects. Shoot a high-key or low-key scene (ie one filled mostly with dark or light tones) and you should expect to see the histogram biased towards one end of the scale anyway. Again, once you know what to look for in a histogram, you can use it to gauge just how close you are to getting the perfect exposure. For further information on using histograms, see page 60.

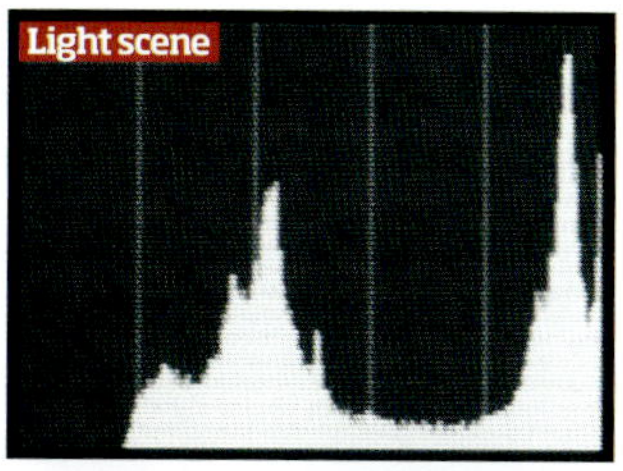

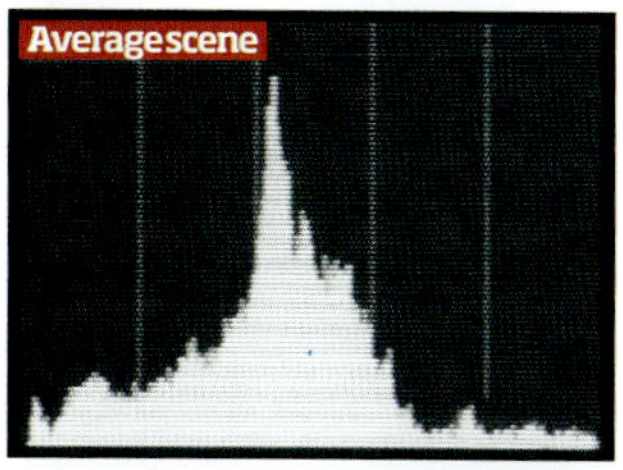

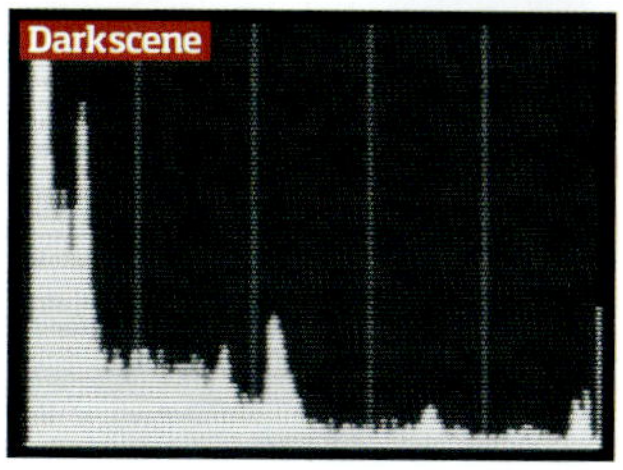

AUTO IMAGE-REVIEW OFF

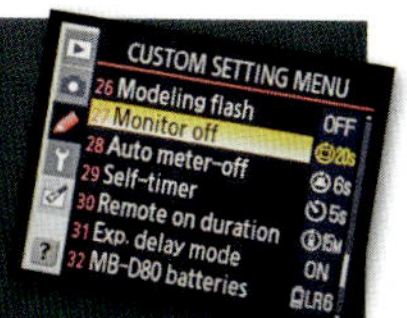

One feature that divides opinion almost as much as the audible beep is the auto-image review. This is where the image of the last frame taken appears on the LCD screen shortly after firing the shutter. Not only does this use extra battery power, it can be quite distracting when looking through the viewfinder. Some photographers switch off the instant playback for another reason, too – it's too tempting to check it straight away, and while you are looking at the screen, you could be missing out on other good photo opportunities. Some cameras also have an auto-power off function, designed to save battery power. This can usually be disabled or extended in the camera's menu system as well.

SHUTTER RELEASE W/OUT CARD

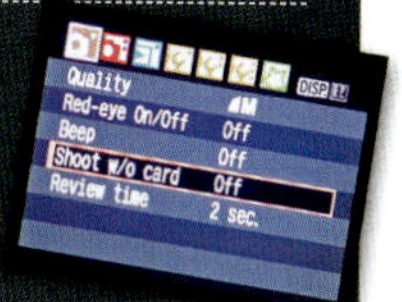

This is a setting to find, switch off and leave alone. We recommend you never have your camera set so it can fire with no memory card in it. It'll only be a matter of time before you make the ultimate mistake and take a dozen (great) shots, and fail to record any of them!

AF/AE LOCK

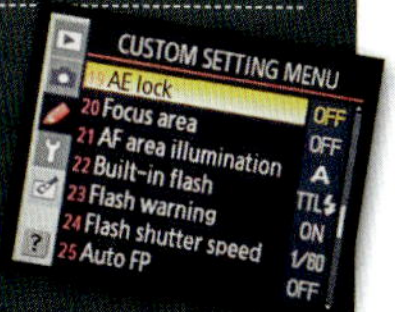

One of the most useful custom functions is that which dictates how the AF and AE locks work. Everyone has their own preferred way of working, so it's good that you can customise this control so well. For instance, when you half-press the shutter release, do you like both the exposure and focus to lock? Or just the focus? Or just the exposure? Maybe you like the exposure to lock when you hold down the AE-L button. Or maybe you want it to lock when you simply press the AE-L button once, and not unlock until it's pressed again. Whichever way you prefer to work, it's most likely your DSLR or CSC can be set up to work that way.

SCREEN BRIGHTNESS

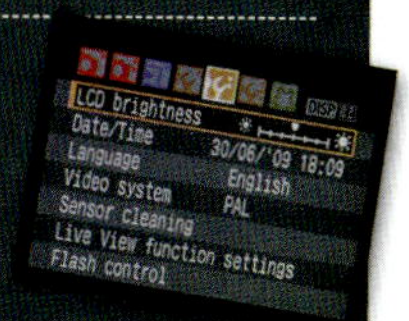

Struggling to see your screen in the bright sunlight? You can turn its brightness up in your camera's menu. Or turn it down if you want to save battery, or are working in dim conditions at night.

CREATING 'MY MENU'

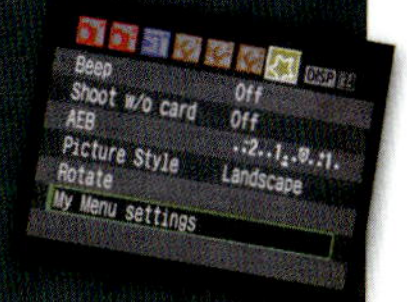

Having read this far, and discovered a few new things about your camera just by playing with it, you'll have learned a lot about how your camera works. You may also be irritated because you can't remember which menu is home to a specific function. Usefully, some DSLRs and CSCs have a custom menu (often called My Menu) that you can set-up for fast access to your favourite commands. Give it a try!

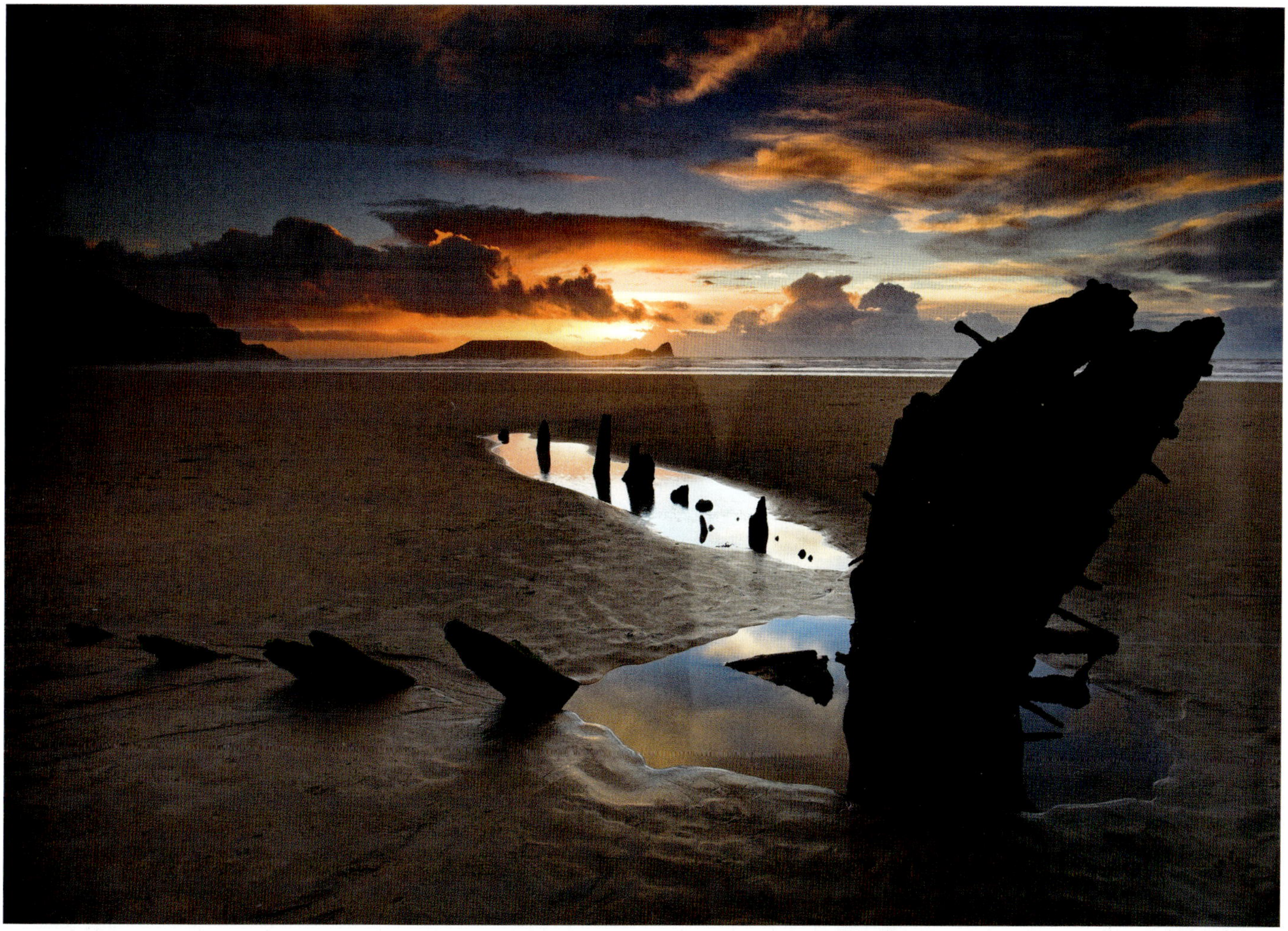

PHOTO TECHNIQUE

The essential knowledge you need to take impressive photos with your camera

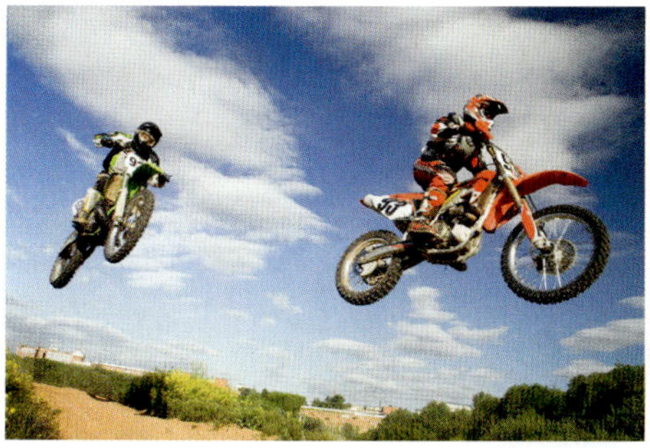

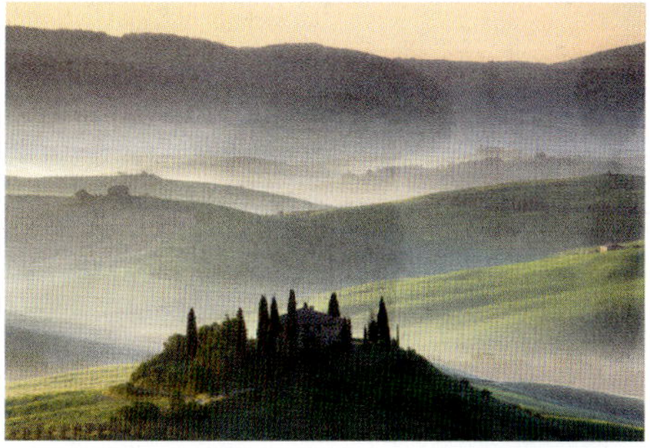

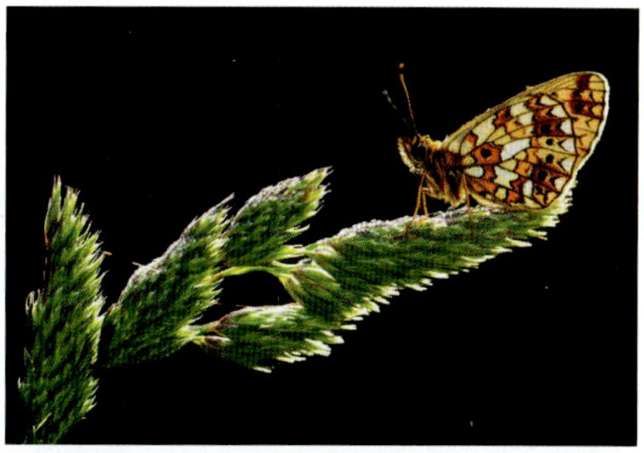

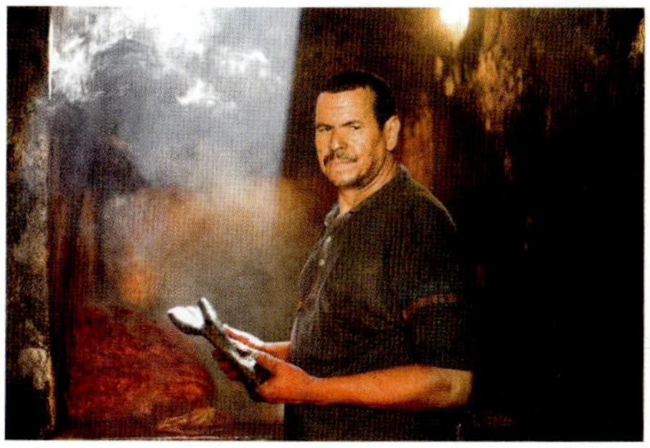

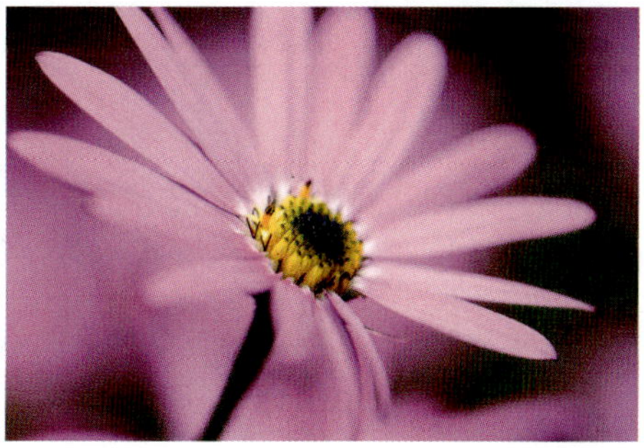

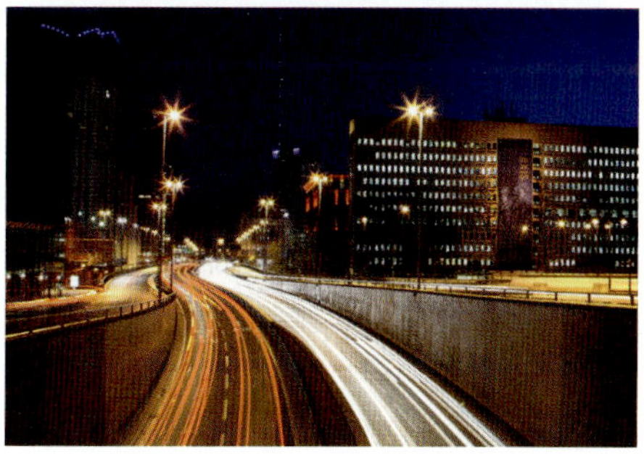

The fundamentals of composition

EVERY TIME WE raise a camera to our eye to take a photo we're 'composing', but the mistake many photographers make is failing to spend enough time deciding if what they've got in the viewfinder is actually interesting before hitting the shutter release.

Painters have a distinct advantage over photographers because they start off with an empty canvas, then set about filling it, so they can move things around a little, add things that don't exist, or omit elements that spoil the composition and detract from the overall impact. Our canvas is already full, so we have to decide what part of a scene or subject we want to capture. There are various aids and tricks available to help us do this correctly: the rule-of-thirds is a classic and effective compositional tool; natural or man-made lines can be used to lead the eye around an image, while foreground interest adds depth and scale; colour has great power, helping to highlight specific elements so they dominate the composition or influence the overall mood of the image.

Lens choice allows us to control exactly what appears in the frame and how perspective is recorded, while viewpoint changes the relationship between the elements in a scene. Ultimately, though, the most powerful tools at your disposal are your eyes, and it's only by using them and thinking about what you're doing that your compositional skills will improve. Once you've established an eye for composition, you'll find that your images take on more balance and offer stronger visual impact.

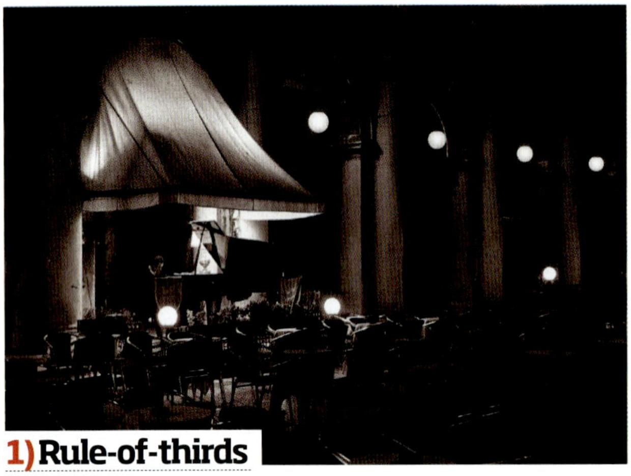

BJORN THOMASSEN

1) Rule-of-thirds

The rule-of-thirds is the most common photographic 'rule' and was first devised by artists to use when painting landscapes. It's based on the idea of dividing the image area into thirds and placing the desired focal points on the intersection of those thirds for a more balanced composition. A photographer can do this by simply dividing the viewfinder into an imaginary grid using two horizontal and two vertical lines. Use the horizontal lines to aid positioning of the horizon, the bottom line to emphasise the foreground and the top line to emphasise the sky. Use vertical lines to position features such as buildings, trees or a person. Finally, the four intersection points make ideal places to position your main focal points.

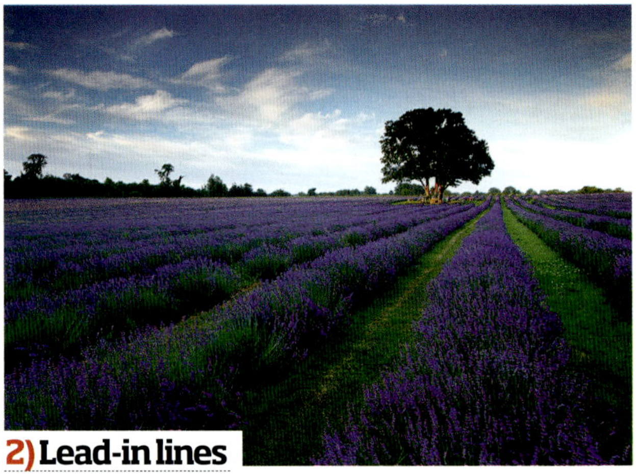

HELEN DIXON

2) Lead-in lines

Lead-in lines can make a good scenic shot great, because they provide a natural entry point into the composition and carry the viewer's eye into the scene. These could include rivers, streams, walls and hedges in landscapes, or arms and legs in portraits: any line that travels into and through the frame will work well. If the lines travel diagonally, ideally they should run from the bottom left of the composition to top right – where you will have hopefully placed your focal point according to the rule-of-thirds. Converging lines are even more powerful as they not only lead the eye into and through the scene, but they also add a strong sense of distance and depth so the composition looks three-dimensional.

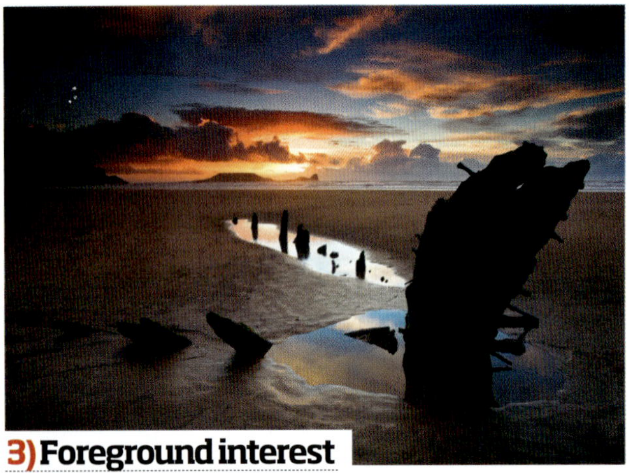

ADAM BURTON

3) Foreground interest

By placing subject matter in the foreground of a composition, you can create depth and scale. This is easiest and most effective if you use a wide-angle lens, as you can include features literally at your feet. These lenses also appear to exaggerate perspective so that subjects closer to the camera are much larger than the distant features. This illusion conveys depth because your brain knows the distant features are normally bigger, and so assumes they're further away. The landscape is full of potential foreground interest, such as rocks, driftwood and flowers. Be sure to use a small aperture (f/16 or f/22) to maximise depth-of-field, because unless everything in the composition is sharp from front-to-back, your efforts will be in vain.

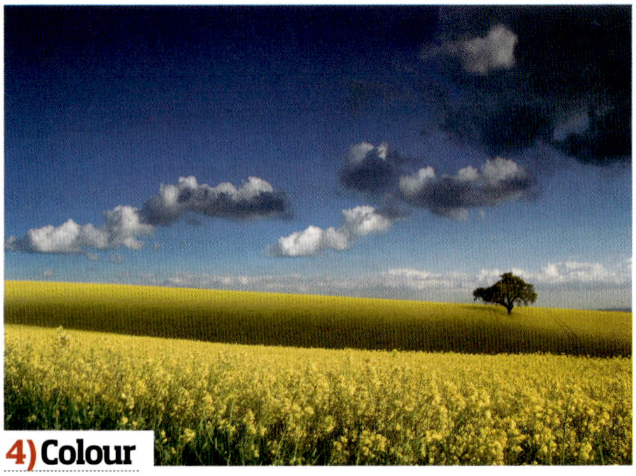

HELEN DIXON

4) Colour

Colour doesn't just make images look realistic, it can also influence the mood of a photograph. Warm colours such as yellow and orange are soothing and restful, while green is refreshing, and blue can be cold and hostile. If you include contrasting colours, such as blue and yellow or red and green, the composition will be more eye-catching, whereas colours that complement each other, such as red and yellow, are more gentle and atmospheric. Warm colours are said to advance, so they work well in the foreground on a shot, while cool colours (green and blue) recede and so they make better backgrounds. Finally, red is the most potent of all colours and will dominate a composition, even if red areas are only small in the frame.

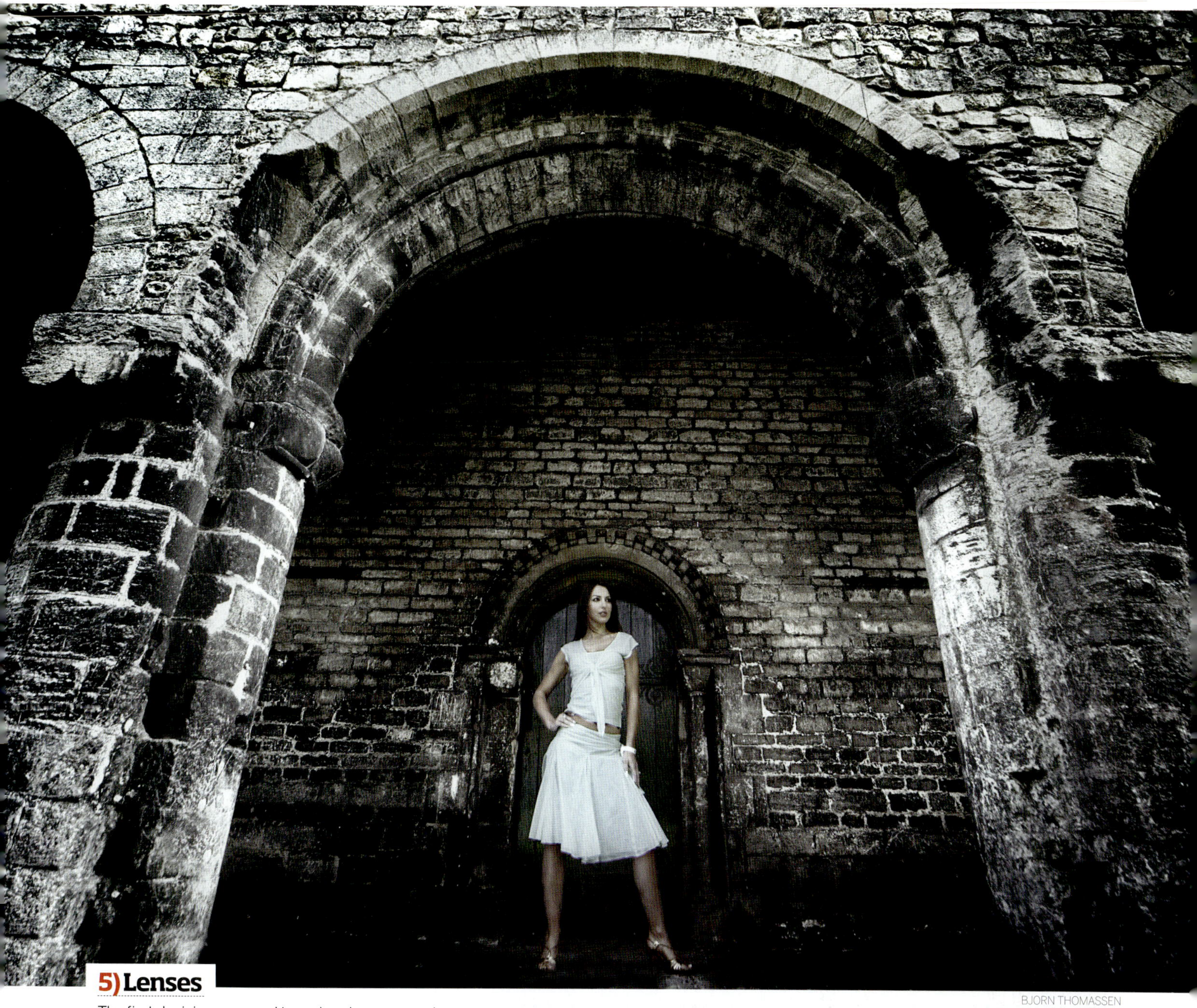

BJORN THOMASSEN

5) Lenses

The first decision you need to make when composing a photograph is deciding how much, or how little, of the scene or subject you actually want to include – this is mainly controlled by which lens you use. Wide-angle lenses obviously have a generous angle of view and can capture more than our eyes can see, whereas telephotos magnify the scene so you can be more selective about what you include in the composition. Zooms covering wide-angle and telephoto settings are ideal because you can control what you include or exclude with great precision. But lenses do more than this – they also allow you to make use of perspective and scale. Wide-angles seem to stretch perspective so the features in a scene appear spaced apart, which is great for emphasising lines and foreground interest. Telephotos, on the other hand, appear to compress perspective so the features in a scene appear more crowded together than they really are, allowing you to create dramatic images. Finally, wide-angle lenses give extensive depth-of-field, especially at small apertures, so you can achieve front-to-back sharpness. Whereas telephotos limit depth-of-field so you can throw the background and/or foreground out of focus and make specific parts of the image stand out, such as a person set against a potentially distracting background.

Using LiveView & viewfinder grid lines

LiveView allows you can use it to check the composition of a shot far more effectively than if you look through the viewfinder. By using the rear LCD monitor, you detach yourself from the scene and can make a more objective assessment. Some viewfinders allow grid lines to be superimposed on the screen, allowing you to divide up the frame and position important features using the rule-of-thirds.

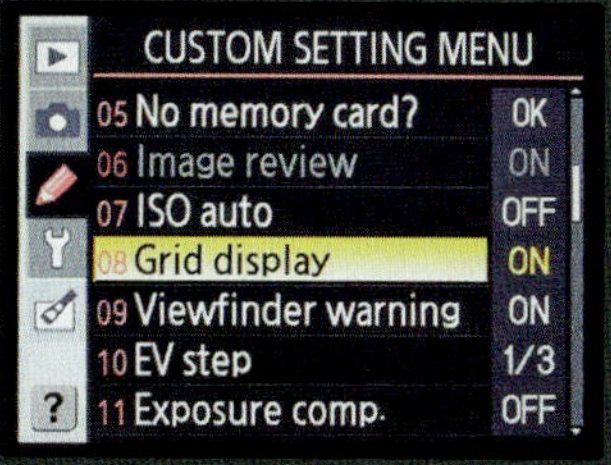

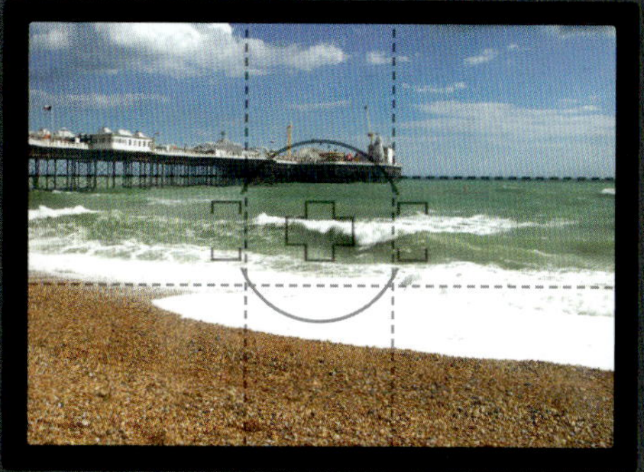

Some cameras allow grid lines to be superimposed on the viewfinder or LCD monitor via a custom function, while LiveView is another aid you can use for accurate composition.

The basics of exposure

Our jargon-free guide to the fundamentals of exposure provides everything you need to know to get to grips with apertures and shutter speeds

EVERY EXPOSURE YOU take is made up of a combination of an aperture and shutter speed that determines how much light will reach the sensor. The aperture is the iris in the lens, much like the pupil of the eye, that can widen to allow more light through or contract to restrict the amount of light that enters the lens. Use a wide aperture and more light is able to pass through during a set timespan than if you had selected a small aperture setting.

The shutter is a barrier in front of the sensor that moves out of the light's path when you press the shutter release, allowing light to reach the sensor and create an exposed image. The exposure's duration is determined by the shutter speed. There is an obvious relationship between the aperture and the shutter speed in determining the correct exposure and this is selected by the exposure mode. While the full-auto AE (Auto Exposure) mode provides point-and-shoot simplicity by automatically selecting a combination of aperture and shutter speed, and allows beginners to take great pictures with the minimum of fuss, the beauty and enjoyment of digital photography is to take control and directly determine how the picture will look.

The first major step to doing this is to take your camera off full-auto and select one of the exposure modes that allow for far more creative photography. Follow our guide and experiment with apertures and shutter speeds – after all, it's not like you'll be wasting any film! Before you know it, you'll soon be creating imaginative images rather than just shooting snaps.

Take control of the exposure mode and determine how the final image will be captured. A small aperture and slow shutter speed means the entire scene is sharp and the water's motion is beautifully blurred.

Exposure controls

Many beginners believe it's difficult to use aperture- or shutter-priority but, in fact, it's very easy to do. Once you've selected the exposure mode (1), it's simply a case of rotating the input dial (2) until the aperture or shutter speed you'd like to use appears on the top-plate (or rear) LCD panel (3). Depress the shutter button halfway and the camera works out the rest. It's as easy as that!

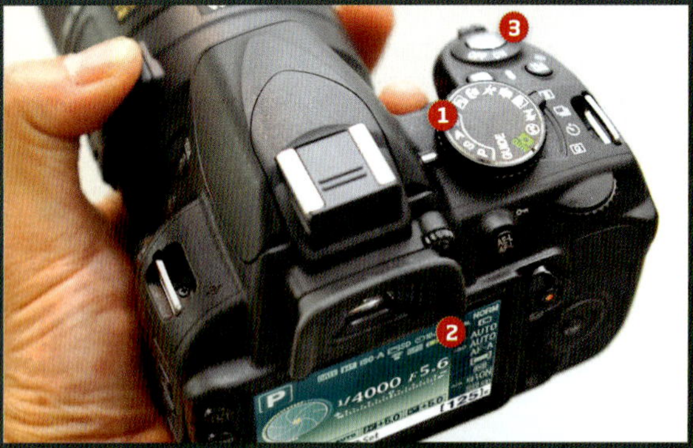

Understanding shutter speeds

Exposure settings are made by changing either the aperture or the shutter speed. The increments at which you change these settings are normally referred to as 'stops'. When you change a setting by a 'stop', you are either doubling or halving the exposure. So, for instance, changing from 1/500sec to 1/250sec doubles the duration of the exposure. As well as full stops, you can also vary exposure in ½ or ⅓ stops, depending on the camera model you use. The diagram below shows shutter speeds from one second to 1/4000sec.

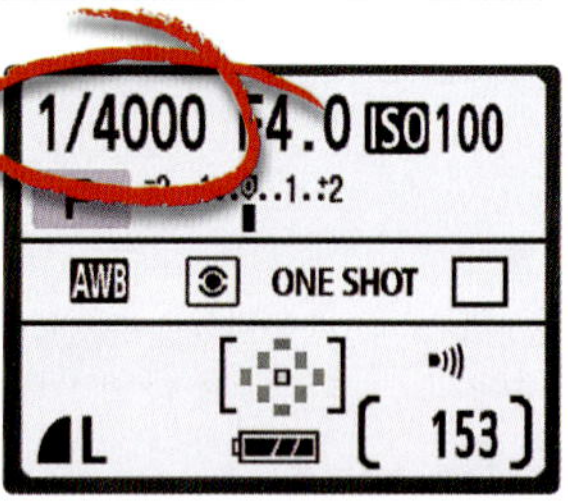

Full stops	1sec	1/2sec	1/4sec	1/8sec	1/16sec	1/30sec	1/60sec	1/125sec	1/250sec	1/500sec	1/1000sec	1/2000sec	1/4000sec
Half stops	0.7sec	1/3sec	1/6sec	1/10sec	1/20sec	1/45sec	1/90sec	1/180sec	1/350sec	1/750sec	1/1500sec	1/3000sec	

Understanding aperture settings

The illustration below shows the iris at one-stop increments, ie each step from left to right halves the amount of light passing through the lens. The maximum aperture setting refers to the iris wide open (in this instance f/2.8) and the minimum aperture is the iris at its smallest setting (f/22 in this case). An explanation of where the f/number derives from would require an extensive scientific explanation. The key to understanding apertures is to learn how f/numbers correlate with the size of the aperture.

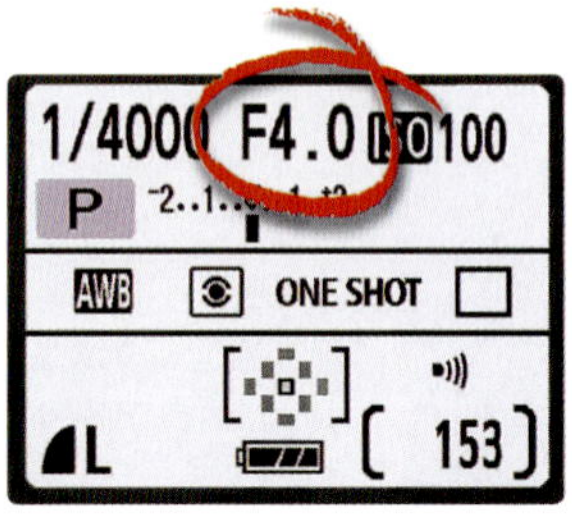

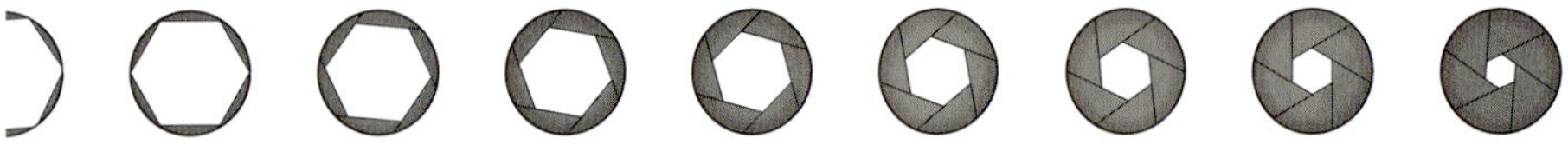

Full stops	f/2.8	f/4	f/5.6	f/8	f/11	f/16	f/22	f/32
Half stops	f/3.5	f/4.5	f/6.7	f/9.5	f/13	f/19	f/27	

The ISO rating

It's worth mentioning the ISO rating. Basically, this indicates the sensor's sensitivity to light. A low setting, such as ISO 100, indicates less sensitivity, while a higher ISO setting, for instance 800, similarly represents an increased sensitivity. We explain which ISO rating is best for certain situations on pages 36-37, but it's worth noting that the ISO you set determines the combination of apertures and shutter speeds available at particular light levels. If you're starting out, setting a low ISO rating (ISO 100-200) is best in bright conditions and a mid-setting (eg ISO 400) for general use.

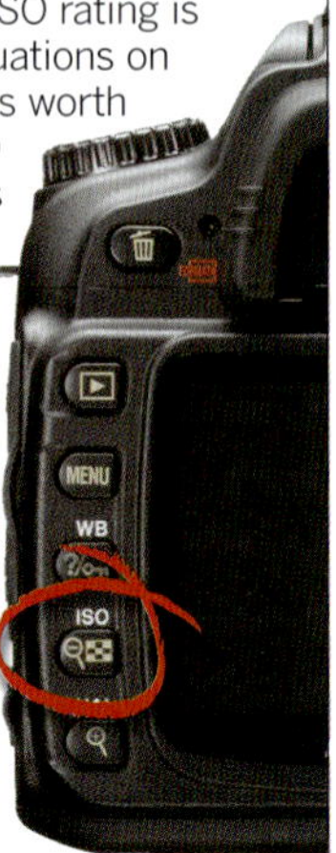

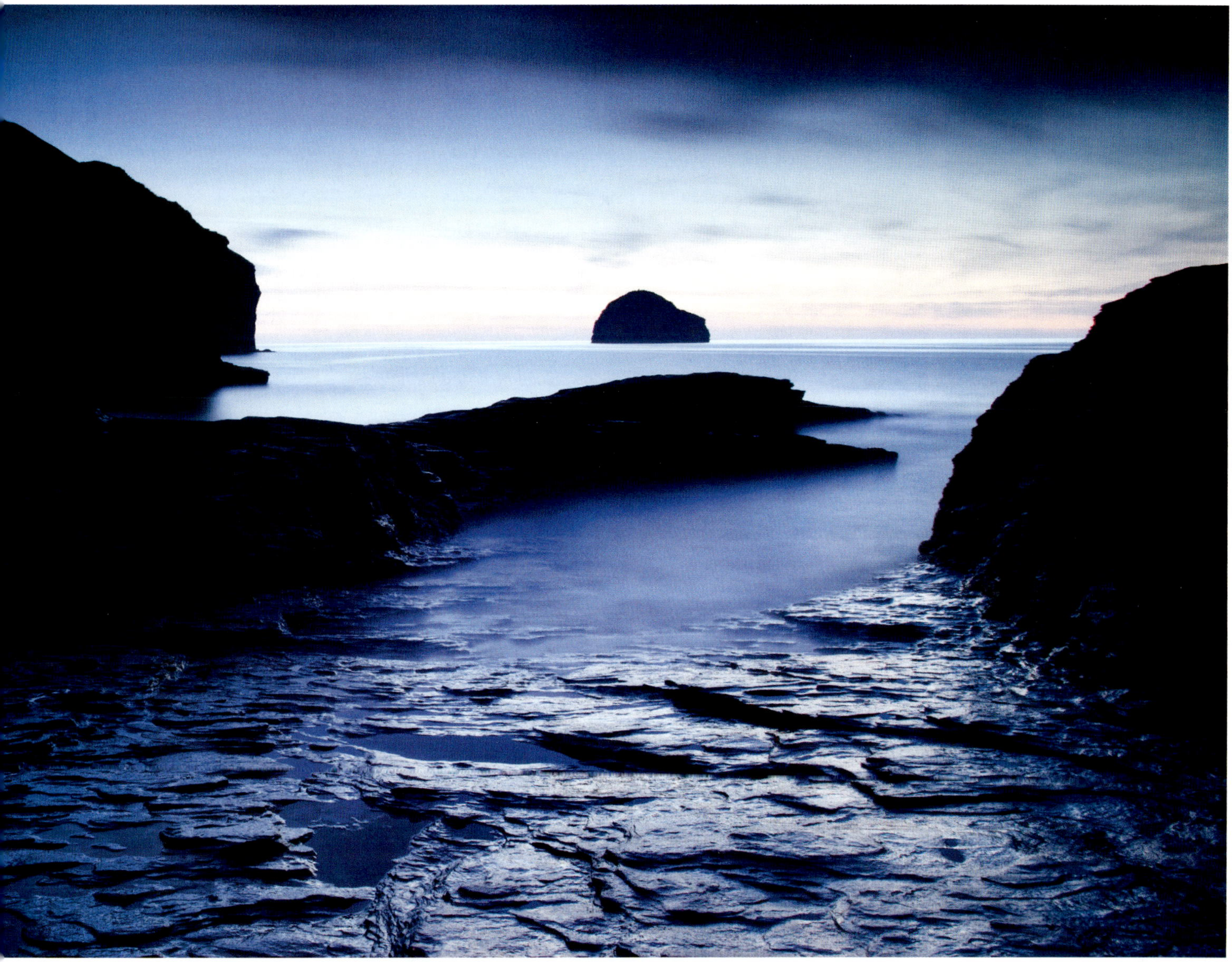

ROSS HODDINOTT

Q&A: Exposure

What's a maximum and minimum aperture?
These are the widest and smallest apertures that can be set on a lens.

Why are some zooms stated as having two maximum aperture values?
Two figures are provided for the majority of zooms to indicate that the maximum aperture changes as you zoom the lens. For instance, an 18-55mm f/3.5-4.5 zoom indicates that the lens has a maximum aperture of f/3.5 when set to 18mm, and when it has zoomed into 55mm, it becomes f/4.5.

What are reciprocal exposure settings?
There are a variety of combinations of shutter speeds and apertures that give the same exposure.

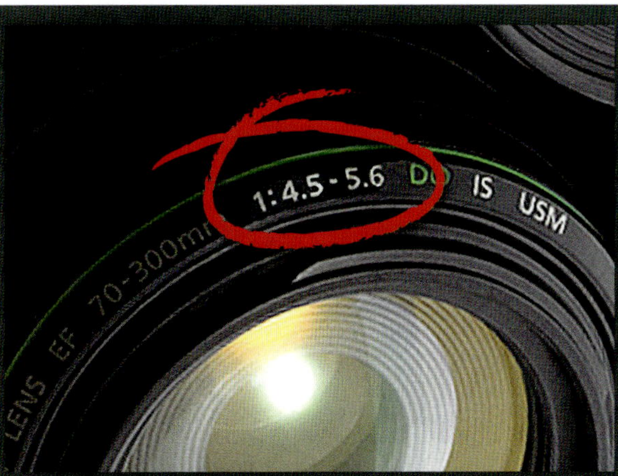

For instance, 1/250sec at f/4 would give the same exposure as 1/500sec at f/2.8 or 1/125 at f/5.6. These combinations are said to be reciprocal.

What are fast lenses?
A fast lens is one with a wider maximum aperture than the standard. For instance, a 70-200mm f/2.8 lens is described as fast because most lenses of this type have a maximum aperture of f/4.

What is exposure compensation for?
This facility allows you to alter the set exposure, which we will cover in detail later on.

Useful accessories

Make the most of exposure modes with the following accessories:

1) TRIPOD A basic tripod that provides a sturdy support will allow you to use longer shutter speeds without fear of camera shake. Look to spend £40.

2) NEUTRAL DENSITY (ND) FILTER An ND filter reduces the amount of light reaching the lens. Use it when you want to set long exposures but the light level is too high. Check out filters from brands such as Hoya and Cokin.

3) REMOTE RELEASE To avoid shake with long exposures, use a remote release to fire the shutter rather than the camera's shutter button. Your camera's instruction manual will tell you which you need. You can also help avoid shake by using the self-timer.

Master metering patterns

Your camera is equipped with different metering patterns. Learn which one to use for particular shooting situations to give you the best control over exposure

AS WE'VE MENTIONED, the job of your camera's metering system is to assess the scene you'd like to capture and work out the aperture and shutter speed settings that will result in a correct exposure. The camera assumes the average tone within the scene is a mid-tone of 18% grey and works out the exposure based on this assumption. All metering patterns use the mid-tone principle, but how each measures the scene varies from pattern to pattern. For example, the multi-zone system divides the image frame into zones, takes individual readings from each and uses sophisticated algorithms to determine the final exposure. Partial and spot metering patterns, however, take an exposure reading from a small area (usually between 3-9%) at the centre of the frame.

Why have different metering patterns? Well, the option of taking a reading from the whole frame or just small elements of it gives the photographer a tremendous amount of control for precise metering.

Of course, care must be taken when selecting your metering pattern to make sure it's suitable for the subject you are attempting to capture. For example, if you are shooting a typical landscape scene with a bright blue sky, lush green grass and a dark shaded tree, you will want to use multi-zone instead of spot metering, because if you meter for the dark shaded tree, the camera will think it's taking a reading from a mid-tone and overexpose the scene. But with multi-zone metering, the camera takes into account the variation from every zone – the sky, grass and dark tree etc – and uses this to calculate an accurate exposure.

We've covered each metering pattern below, along with how to identify it on your camera and a suggestion of situations where using this metering pattern may pay dividends, so that when you're next taking pictures, you'll know which mode will work best for you and avoid taking pictures that turn out to be poorly exposed.

Spot & partial metering

Ideal for situations when you wish to take a reading from a specific area of the frame, the spot and partial metering modes must be used with care to avoid metering mishaps. These precise modes operate by metering from a small area, usually at the centre of the frame. Most spot meters have a precise metering circle that reads off 3% of the image frame, while partial metering isn't so precise, taking readings from an area of 9% or so.

To get a correct exposure when using these patterns, the metering area must be placed over a mid-tone or the scene may be over- or underexposed. This mid-tone doesn't have to be grey, it could be any other mid-tone colour, such as green grass, brown dirt or brickwork. Most cameras offer spot metering, some have partial metering, while a few have both.

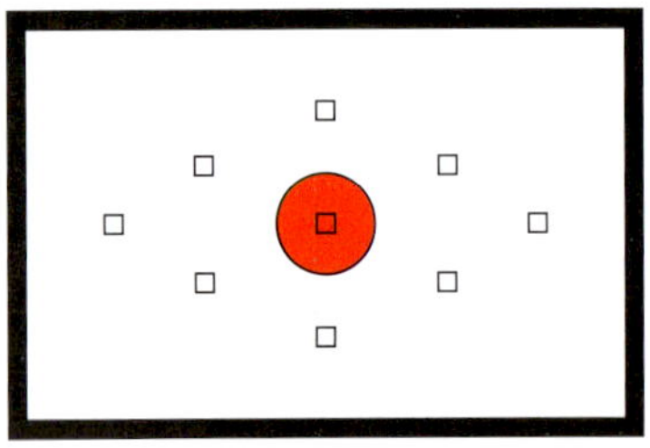

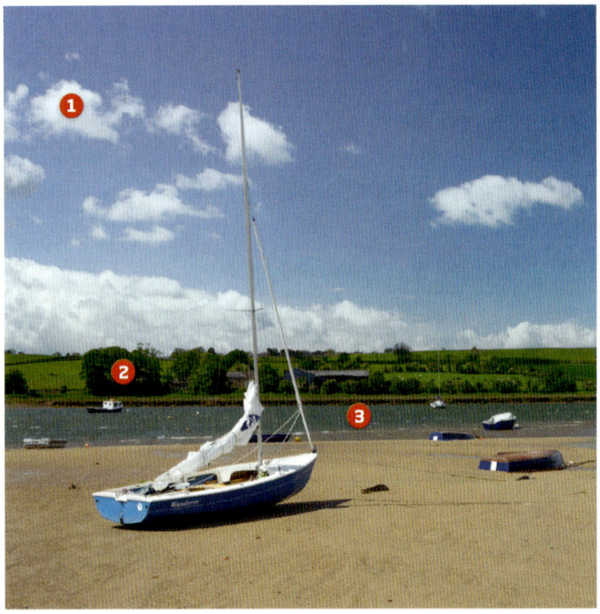

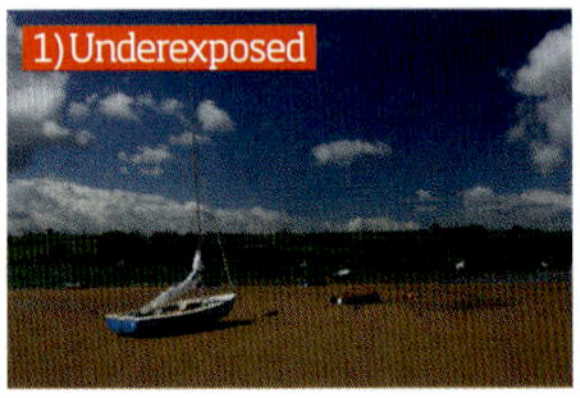

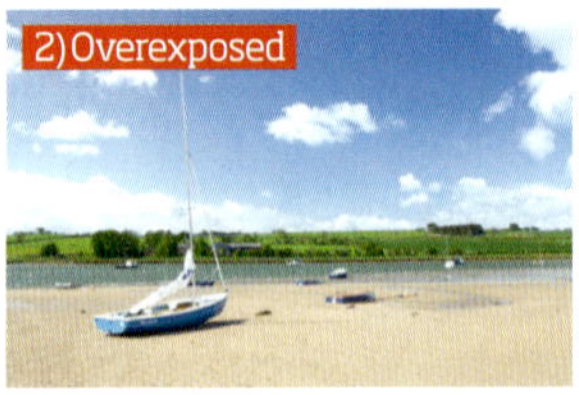

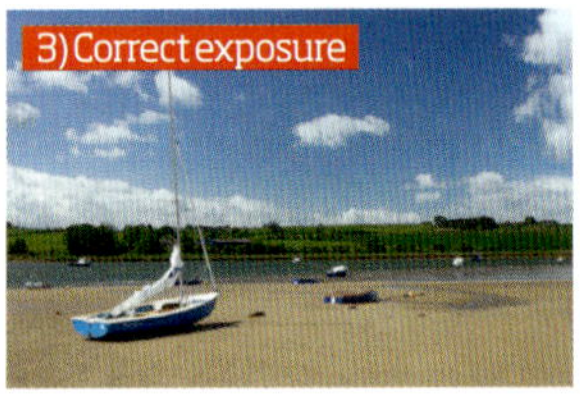

EXPOSING FROM A MID-TONE: When using spot or partial metering, it's important to remember that you must place the metering area over a mid-tone to achieve the correct exposure. In this typical scene, we took spot readings from different areas of the frame to show you how the exposure varies.

Spot & partial icons

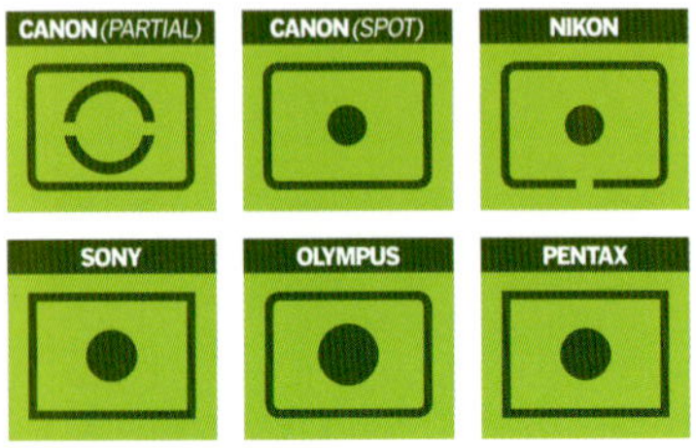

Spot & partial metering: Perfect for...

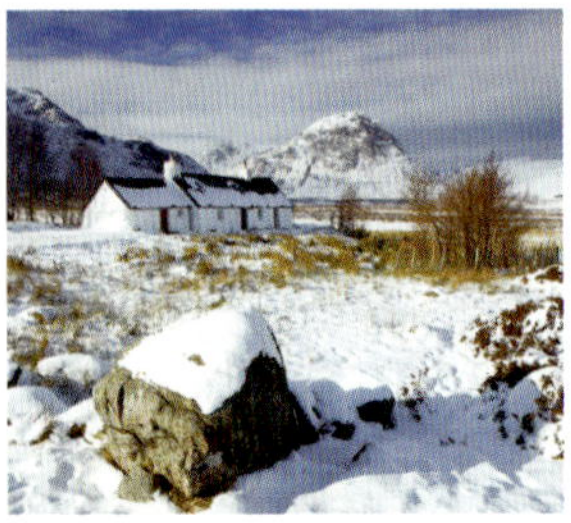

SNOWY CONDITIONS
Aim the spot meter at an area with mid-tones to prevent the snow causing underexposure.

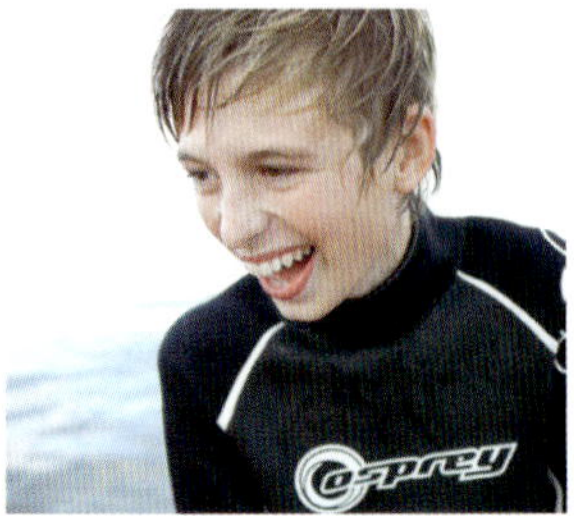

BACKLIT PORTRAITS
The intense backlight from the sky can fool multi-zone systems, so spot-meter from the face.

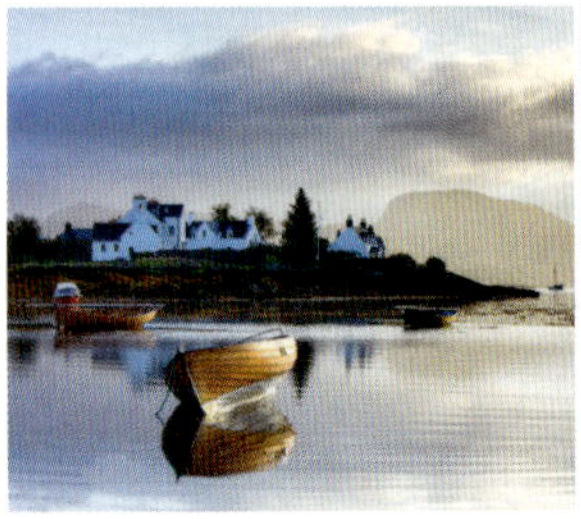

SCENES WITH HIGHLIGHTS
Meter from a mid-tone when scenes are dominated by highlights like reflections.

IMAGES: LEE FROST

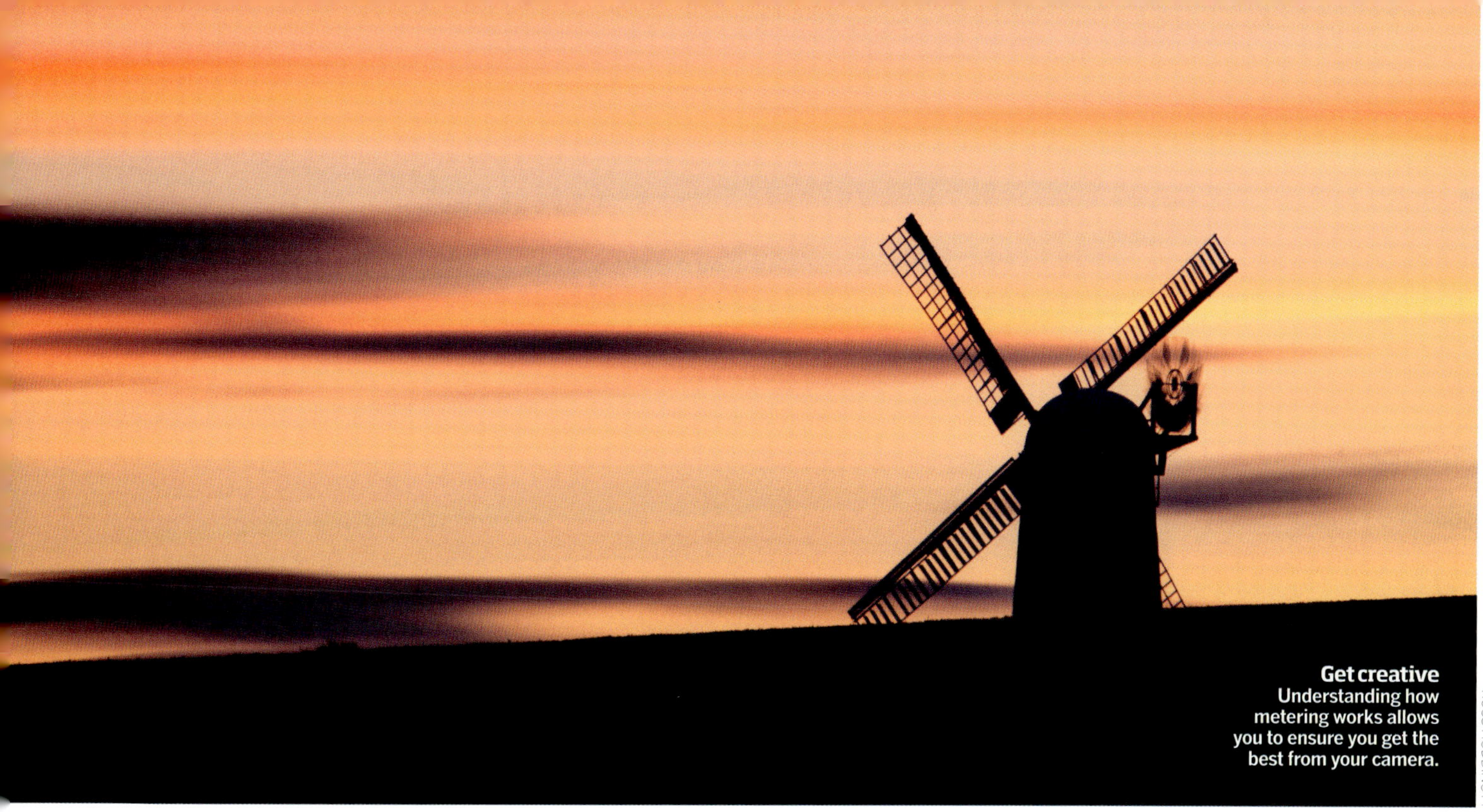

Get creative Understanding how metering works allows you to ensure you get the best from your camera.

ROSS HODDINOTT

Multi-zone metering

Multi-zone metering systems are incredibly reliable and return a correct exposure for the vast majority of scenes. The multi-zone pattern is the most sophisticated metering system available. It works by dividing the entire frame into zones, with individual meter readings taken from each zone. The data from these readings is then run through a series of algorithms, and often the data is compared to a database of images, to calculate the final exposure. The various brands have names to describe their own multi-zone mode – Nikon has Matrix, Canon calls its system Evaluative, while Pentax has multi-segment. The number of zones vary from camera to camera, and while the general rule is that the more zones a pattern has, the better its accuracy, it's not always the case.

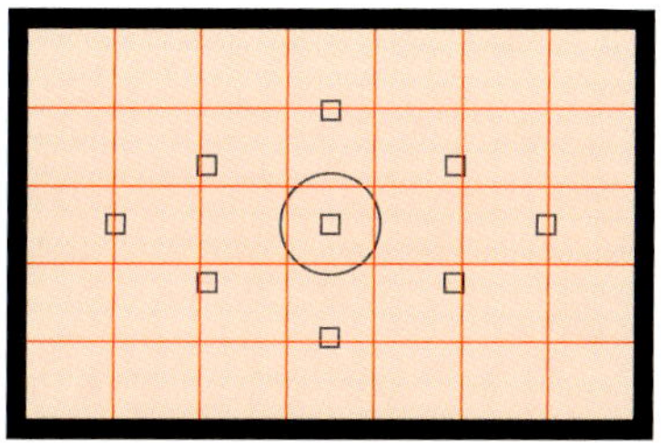

Multi-zone icons

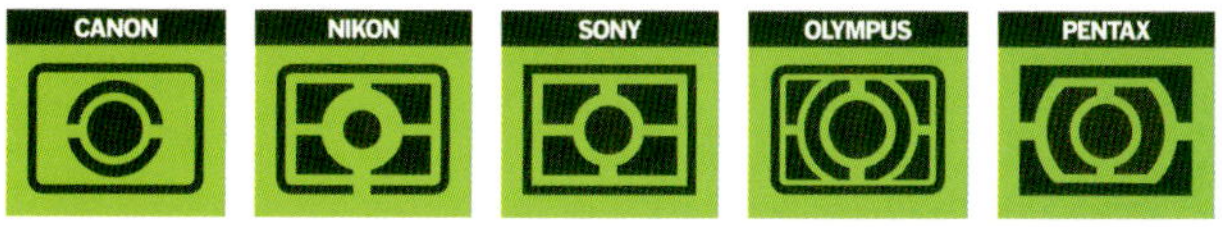

Multi-zone: Perfect for...

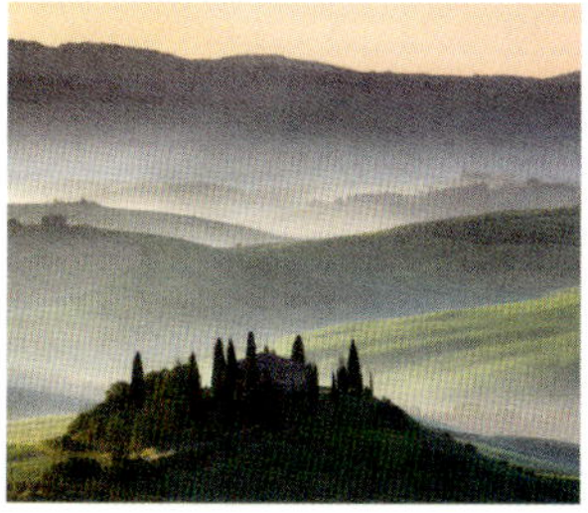

LANDSCAPES
Scenes with sky and foreground that have a variation in exposure are easily handled.

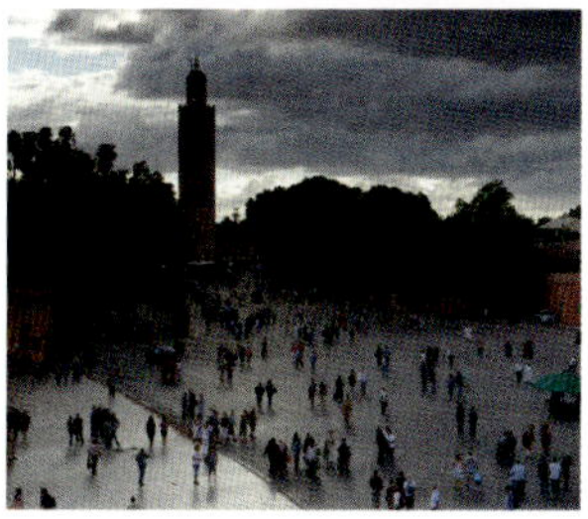

IMAGES: LEE FROST

GENERAL SCENES
Unless your scene has unusual lighting conditions, you'll have no problems with multi-zone.

Centre-weighted average

Film camera enthusiasts will recognise centre-weighted average from the darkroom days. This mode has been used for years on SLR cameras, but has been superseded by multi-zone metering. Centre-weighted average works by taking an average reading from the entire frame, giving most emphasis to the central area. Those who are familiar with this pattern are more likely to use it, and it's also the recommended choice when using AE-Lock. The bias towards the centre of the frame varies between brands, but it is 60-80% towards the centre of the frame. The main problem with this pattern is that, when shooting landscapes, the expanse of sky in bright conditions can lead it to underexpose the scene, unless you're experienced enough to know what to do (see below).

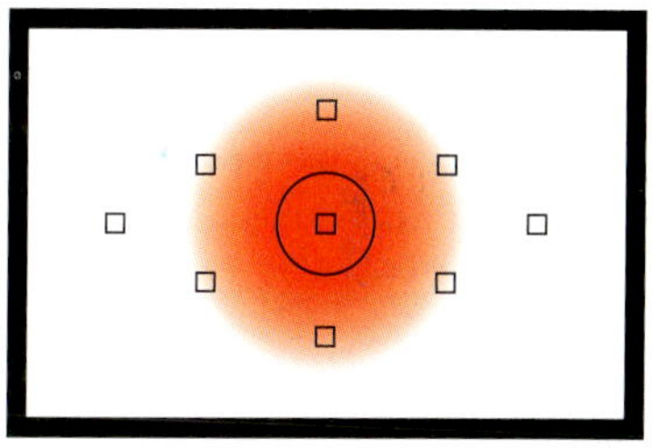

Centre-weighted average icons

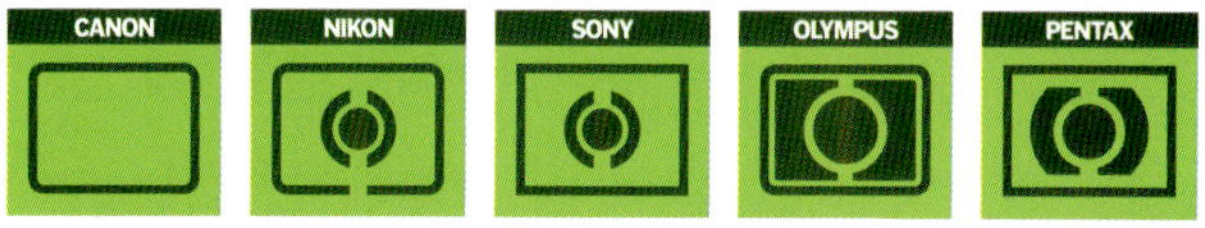

Centre-weighted average: Perfect for....

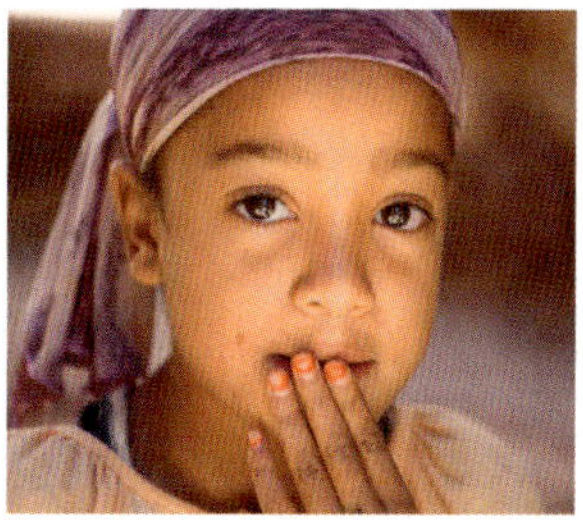

LEE FROST

GENERAL PORTRAITS
Variances between light and dark shades are well handled to ensure accurate results.

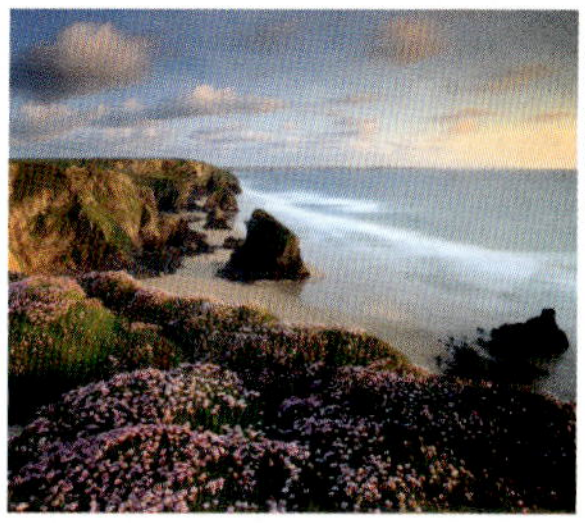

ROSS HODDINOTT

LANDSCAPES WITH AE-L
In scenes with bright sky, point the camera at the ground, use AE-L then recompose and shoot.

Exposure overrides: Taking more control

Although cameras have very sophisticated metering systems, they're not infallible and will occasionally produce incorrect exposures. Lighter or darker than average scenes, as well as tricky lighting situations, such as backlighting, are the most common situations that lead to poor results. Therefore, it is important to know how to override your camera's meter reading to ensure you can take control and ensure a perfect exposure

Exposure compensation

The most common and simplest override is exposure compensation – a feature found on every DSLR and CSC that allows the user to increase or decrease the camera's suggested exposure. Exposure compensation is very easy to use as you adjust the exposure in set increments of either 1/3 or 1/2 stops, depending on your camera. Applying a positive (+) value increases the amount of exposure, with the aim to lighten the image, while dialling in a negative (–) value will darken it. Because the compensation is applied in incremental steps that correspond with adjusting apertures and shutter speeds, it shouldn't take too long to get used to. The amount of exposure compensation is usually displayed on a scale or as a figure on the LCD or in the viewfinder. It's often stated as an EV (Exposure Value), so adding half a stop will appear as +1/2EV. How the camera applies exposure compensation depends on which exposure mode you use. In aperture-priority mode, it's the shutter speed that is changed, while in shutter-priority mode, the compensation is applied via the aperture setting. In program mode, the camera alters either variable, depending on light levels and the risk of camera shake. The general rule to remember is that if the subject or scene is dominated by a light subject, the camera may underexposure, so to avoid this, dial a positive (+) value. When photographing a very dark subject or scene, the camera is likely to overexpose it, so set a negative value (–) compensation to obtain a correct exposure.

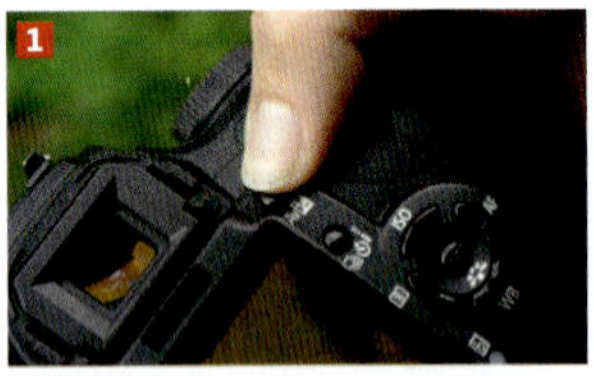

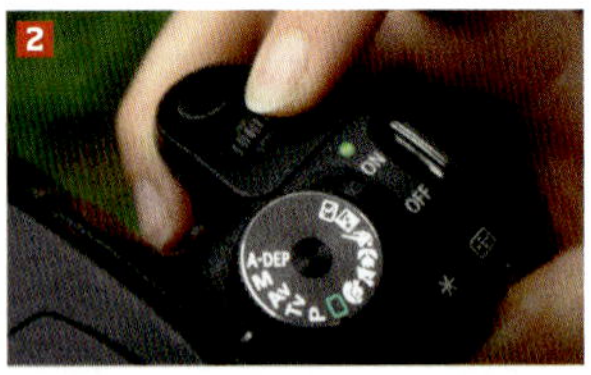

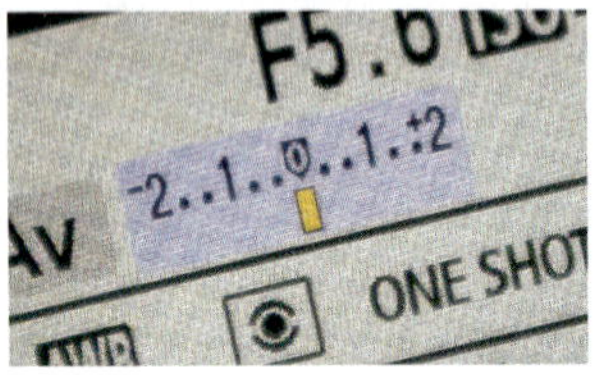

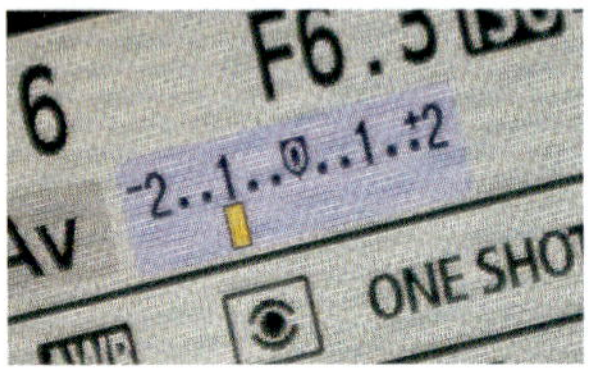

HOW TO USE EXPOSURE COMPENSATION:
1) Locate and press your DSLR or CSC's exposure compensation button (usually indicated by a +/- icon).
2) To dial in the desired amount of exposure compensation, turn the input dial in either direction. A negative input results in less exposure being applied, while a positive input increases exposure. Once you've taken a shot, check the LCD to review your results.

Exposure compensation: Perfect for...

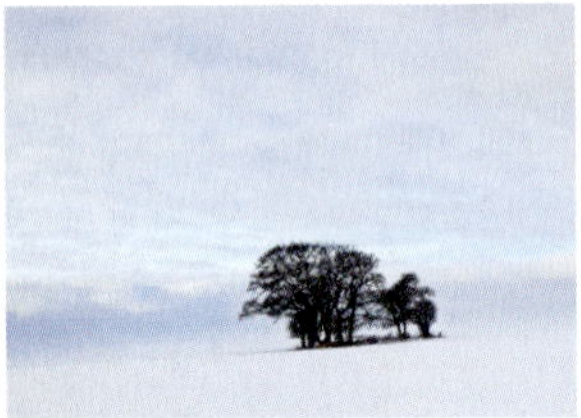
MARK BAUER

SNOWY LANDSCAPES
Adding positive compensation (between +1 to +2EV) prevents winter wonderlands turning grey.

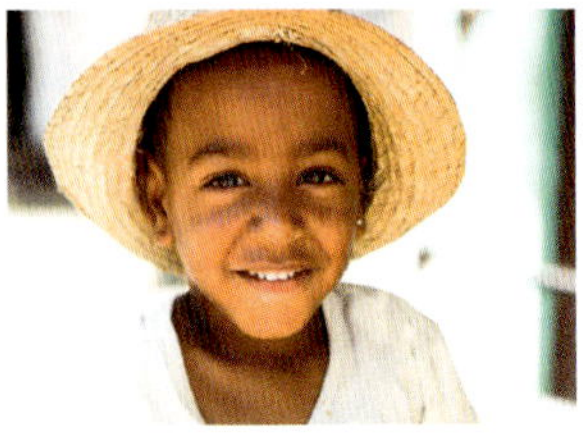
LEE FROST

MANAGING SKIN TONES
Exposure compensation can help balance the skin tones of tanned or dark-skinned subjects.

Auto Exposure Lock (AE-L)

This exposure override doesn't actually lead to an increase or decrease in the exposure, but rather allows you to specify the area from which the camera takes a reading from. It's an override that is nowhere near as popular as exposure compensation, mainly because it requires users to be more experienced and have a better understanding of what lighting situations and scenes demand its use.

As its name suggests, the AE-Lock facility allows you to lock an exposure reading, which is retained even when you recompose the scene. Normally when you take a picture, pressing the shutter button halfway engages the AF and exposure systems together, which is suitable for most scenes. However, this can lead to exposure error where the subject or scene is very bright or dark, or where there is very high contrast or unusual lighting conditions. In these conditions, taking a reading from a mid-tone and locking this with the AE-L facility can ensure perfect results.

While you can use multi-zone metering with AE-L, you are better off switching to spot or partial metering to ensure the exposure reading is taken off a mid-tone. This is relevant whether you are taking a reading off an area of grass, brickwork or a grey card. Just remember that the lighting on the area you use AE-L with should be the same as that for your main subject. For example, using AE-L to meter from an area bathed in bright sunshine, while your subject is sat in shade, will only result in a very overexposed subject.

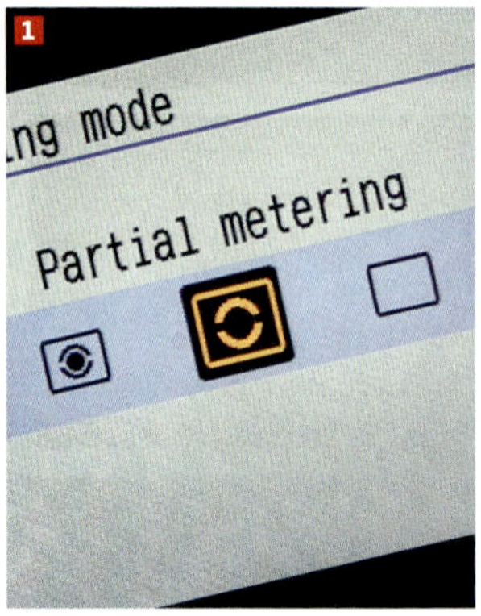

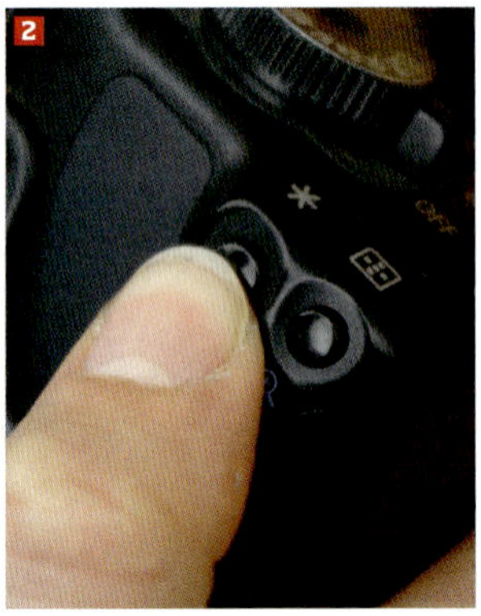

HOW TO USE AUTO EXPOSURE LOCK (AE-L):
1) Set your metering pattern to either spot or partial. Access the scene, find the area that you want to meter from and press the shutter halfway to activate the metering system.
2) Now press the AE-L button to lock in the exposure settings. Recompose your scene and, when happy, press the shutter button to capture your image, which should be perfectly exposed.

Auto exposure lock: Perfect for...

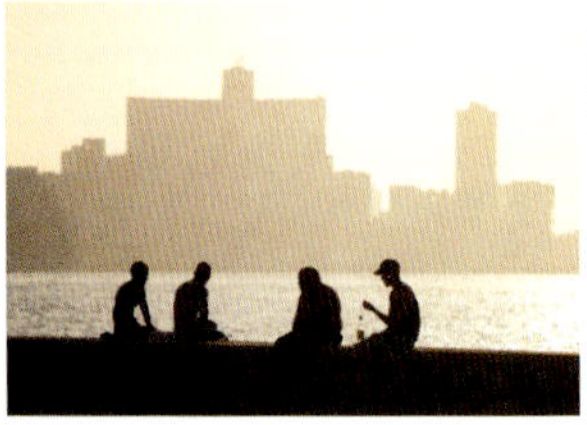
LEE FROST

SILHOUETTES AT SUNSET
Metre off the sunset and hit AE-L. Other elements in the scene will become silhouetted.

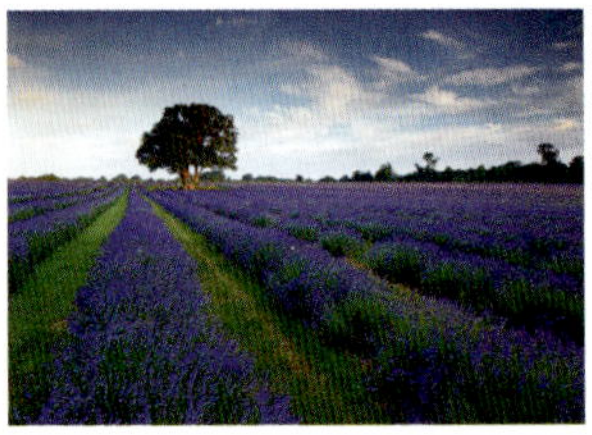
HELEN DIXON

SCENES WITH BRIGHT SKIES
Large expanses of bright sky can lead to underexposure. Use AE-L to take a reading off grass.

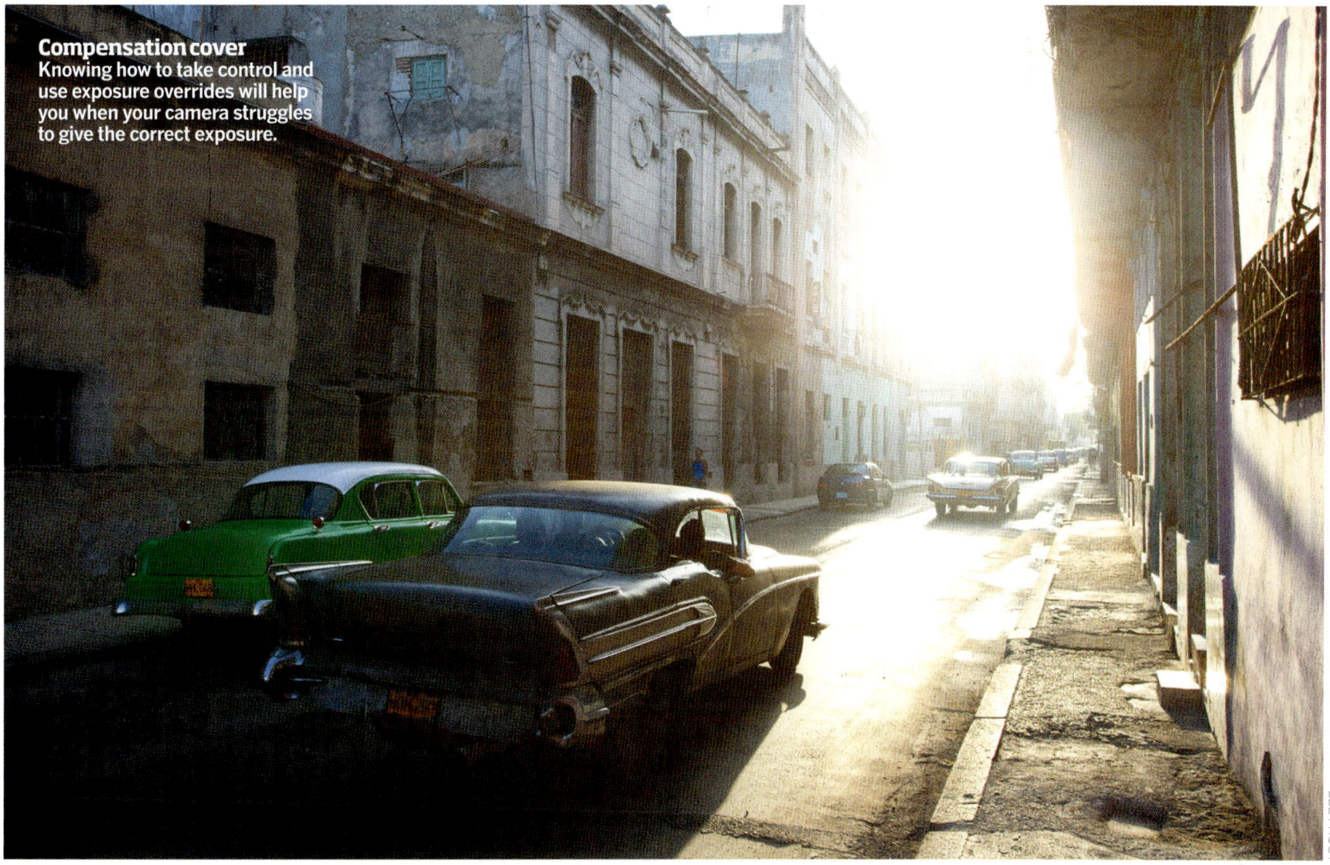

Compensation cover
Knowing how to take control and use exposure overrides will help you when your camera struggles to give the correct exposure.

LEE FROST

Auto Exposure Bracketing (AEB)

AEB

Auto Exposure Bracketing (AEB) allows the photographer to capture a series of three images at different exposures without you having to adjust any settings between each frame. Most cameras allow sequential shots at +/– three stops from the base exposure, although some cameras offer up to five stops of AEB; and the function is available in program, shutter-priority, aperture-priority and manual mode. The feature was originally introduced to allow inexperienced photographers shooting in very difficult situations to take three exposures in combination with exposure compensation to ensure one good result. How? Well imagine you're shooting a snow scene and you're unsure if you need to apply +1 or +2EV. Set +1.5EV in exposure compensation and in AEB set +/-0.5EV. When you shoot your sequence, the result is a set of three images at +1, +1.5 and +2EV.

Today, AEB is predominantly used to capture frames that are then used to produce High Dynamic Range (HDR) images, which are normally processed using Photoshop or a third-party software like Photomatix. When shooting HDR, the user needs to be very careful not to move the camera between frames, as this will render the rest of the sequence completely useless. It's also recommended that focus is achieved prior to taking the first of the AEB sequence and then switch to manual – the last thing you want is your lens hunting around for a focal point in between shots while someone walks into your frame and spoils the result. A remote release or the self-timer can be used with AEB, so you only have to press the shutter button once.

1

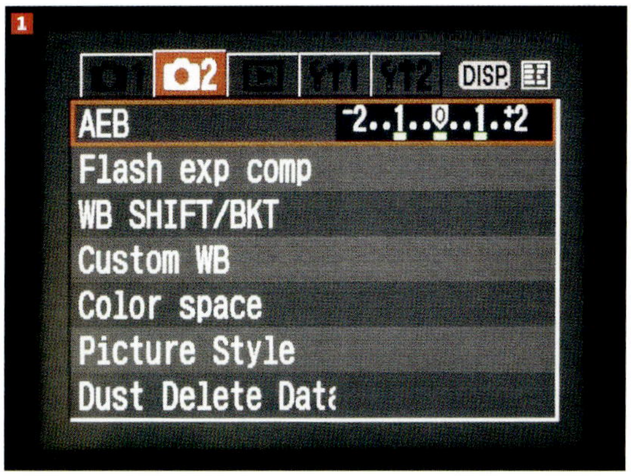

HOW TO USE AEB:
1) Access the AEB function via the menu and use the input dial to select how many stops you want to cover.
2) Half-press the shutter button to exit the menu screen.
3) Set up your shot and depress the shutter button three times (or use a remote release) to capture the bracket.

AEB: Perfect for...

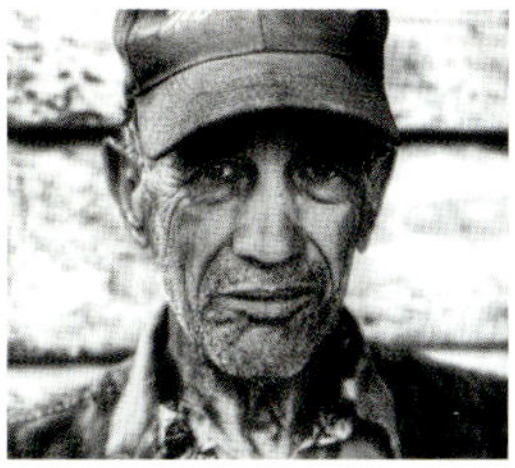

HDR IMAGES
Bring out the shadows and highlights of your scene using this popular technique.

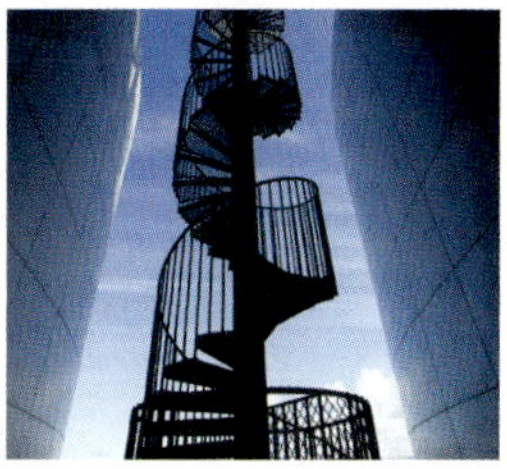

HEDGING YOUR BETS
Use AEB with exposure compensation to ensure one out of three shots is perfect.

IMAGES: LEE FROST

Flash exposure lock

Flash Exposure Lock (FEL) is an often overlooked facility, available when using flash in difficult situations. FEL isn't available on all cameras and only works with certain flashguns, so you need to check your instructions to ensure you can use it. Usually, it works by pressing the partial meter button (*) or AE-L button to fire a pre-flash, which effectively takes a spot-meter reading with flash. The information is stored for a short length of time (anything from six to 20 seconds, depending on your camera), giving the photographer time to recompose and take the shot. FEL is particularly useful in scenes where there are highly reflective surfaces, such as mirrors or glass, or scenes that include light sources like neon lights. These can fool the camera's metering system by reflecting back flash, which could lead to poorly exposed flash pictures. Using FEL helps to avoid this problem.

Exposure aids: Fine-tune your exposure!

As we've shown in this guide, your camera has a variety of modes and overrides aimed at helping you obtain correct exposures. Here, we highlight a number of other popular ways that you can ensure exposure error is a thing of the past, ranging from a variety of inexpensive exposure aids to the invaluable histogram facility. We'd recommend you consider using one or more of these options, as all will benefit your photography

Grey cards

As we've already mentioned earlier in this guide, your camera's exposure system assumes that the average tone it is metering is a mid-tone of 18% grey. Therefore, failure to meter off a mid-tone can cause havoc with how your camera reads the scene, resulting in an over- or underexposed image.

To help get around this problem, a lot of photographers choose to use a grey card: a piece of card that is printed with a shade of 18% grey. Place it in the scene you want to capture, under the same lighting as your subject, then lock an exposure reading using AE-Lock.

This should provide you with a perfect exposure. However, there are a few precautions to take. Firstly, make sure the card is evenly lit and not tipped too far forward or back, as this could lead to a false reading. Secondly, be mindful to make sure no shadows, including your own, are falling onto the card, as this could also affect your exposure. If your camera can't focus, switch to manual focus and lock a reading from the card. If the card is at a distance from you (because you're standing in very different lighting to your subject), use the spot meter to take a reading. Finally, remember your grey card is ideal for White Balance, too.

USING A GREY CARD:

1) Our before image, taken using multi-zone, is poorly exposed.

2) With the image frame filled by the grey card, an exposure reading is taken and locked using the AE-Lock facility.

3) Metering from the grey card has resulted in a perfect exposure.

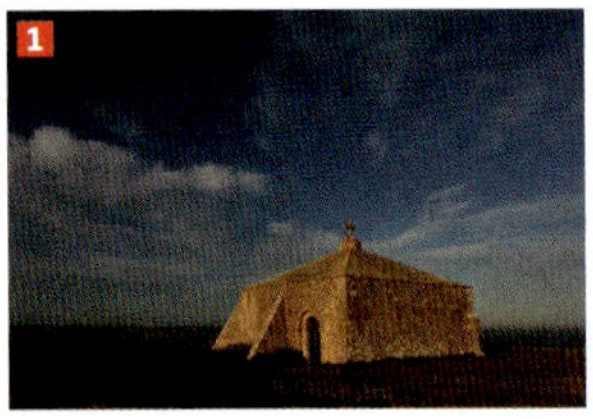
1

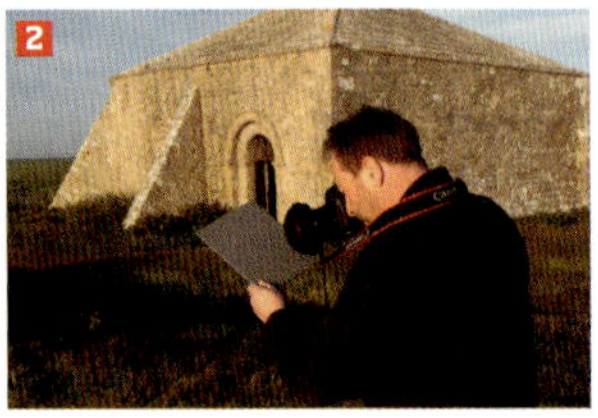
2

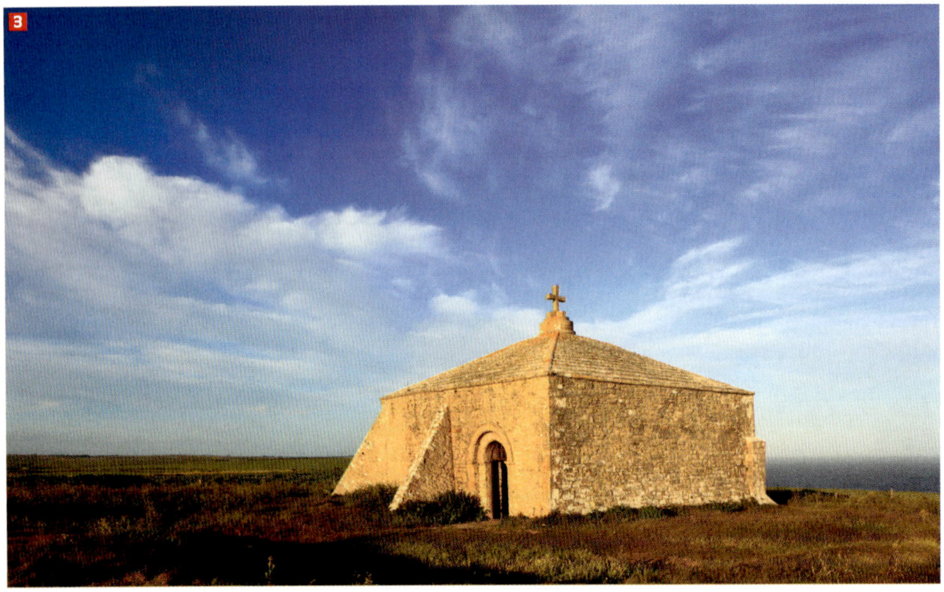
3

Perfect for...

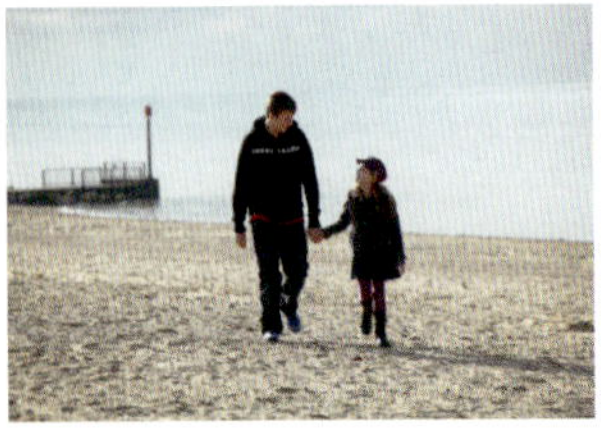

BEACH SCENES
Reflections off the sea and sand can play havoc with metering. A grey card can easily correct this.

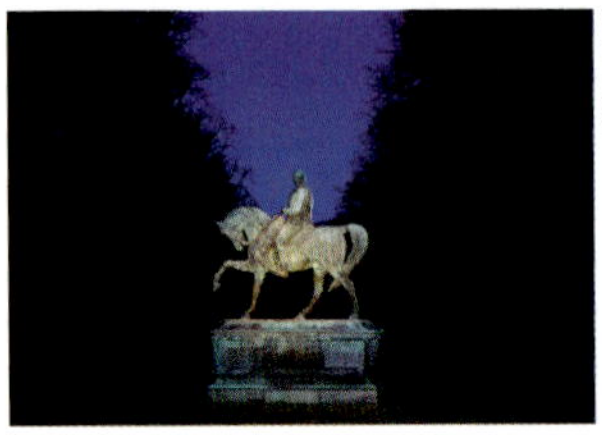
LEE FROST

SPOTLIT SUBJECT
If your subject is lit by a small pool of light, place the grey card near to it for an accurate reading.

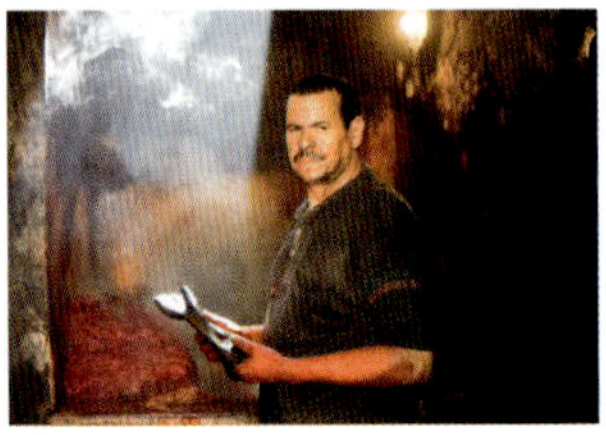
LEE FROST

MIXED LIGHTING
Use a grey card to not only work out the exposure, but to also set a custom White Balance.

Light meters

If you're serious about photography and have some money to invest in your kit, you may choose to splash out on a hand-held light meter. Although they're not the cheapest of accessories (decent models start at around £100), light meters give the most accurate exposure readings. They can be used to take an incident light reading, which is when an exposure reading is taken of the light falling on to the subject. This is far more accurate than the exposure reading taken by your camera, which measures the light reflected off your subject. The reason for this is simple: incident light readings, as opposed to reflected readings, aren't affected by the colour or tone of a subject. Place a black horse next to a white horse in the same lighting conditions and the incident light reading will be exactly the same as it measures the light falling on the subjects. Your camera's reflected light reading, however, will give very different readings for each horse, resulting in the white horse being underexposed and the black horse being overexposed. So, while they involve a little more effort, used correctly, a light meter provides perfect exposures every time. We'd recommend you check out models from Sekonic and Gossen.

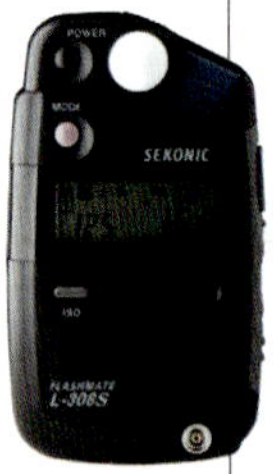

Perfect for...

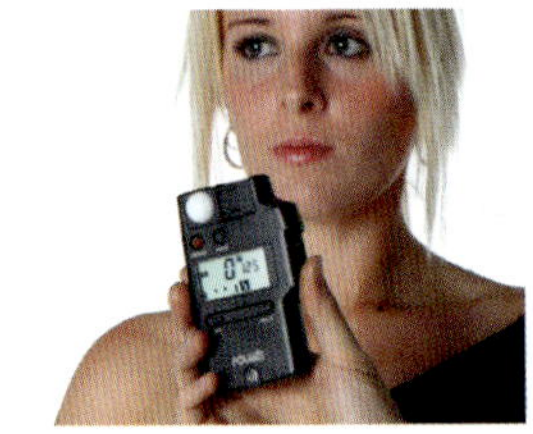

BACKLIT PORTRAITS
Place the light meter close to the face so its reading isn't affected by the backlight.

IMAGES: LEE FROST

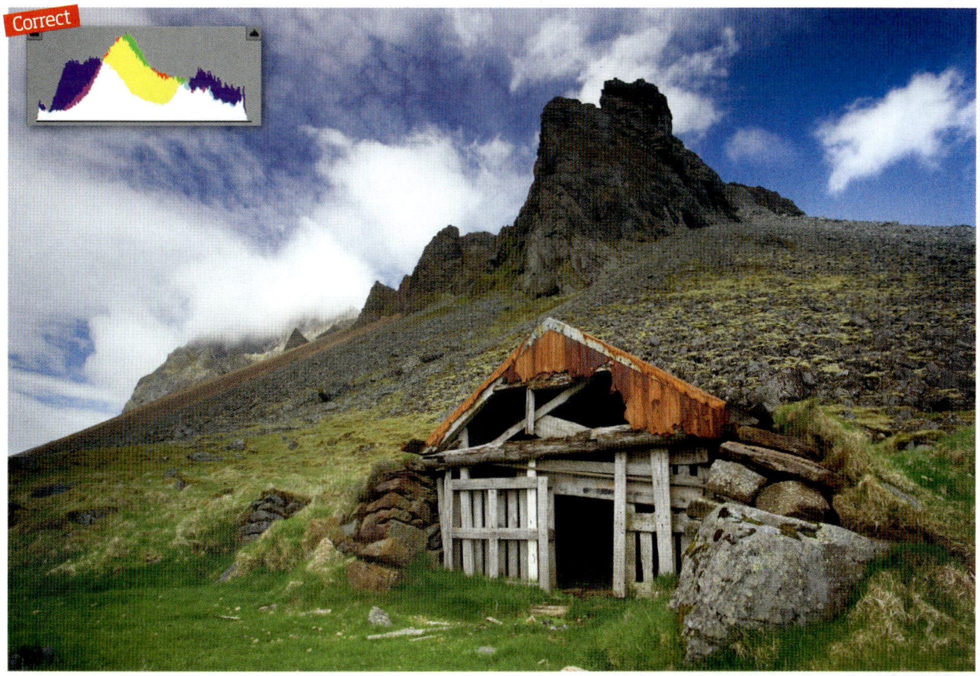

Histogram

Most of us check our photo simply by reviewing the image on the LCD monitor. However, have you ever questioned how accurate the tones and brightness really are? A simple method to improve the accuracy of your review is to use the camera's histogram function to assess the exposure. A histogram is a graph with an X and Y axis that shows the distributions of tones across your image. Shadows are on the left, mid-tones are found in the central area, while highlights are on the right side. You can work out where most of the tones are found by looking at the distribution of the peaks and troughs. The higher the peak, the more tones in this area. Understanding how to read histograms provides you with a fast and easy way to judge the scene's exposure. However, it's important that you learn how histograms vary from scene to scene.

In most average situations, like this landscape image, you should expect to see a peak towards the centre. A peak to the left indicates underexposure while an overexposed image will peak to the right. That said, the distribution of tones and the position of the peak is very different for overly dark or light scenes. As you can see in our examples, a dark scene that has been correctly exposed has peaks to the left, while a bright or snowy scene will have peaks to the right. Take time to review images and learn the characteristics of histograms for different scenes.

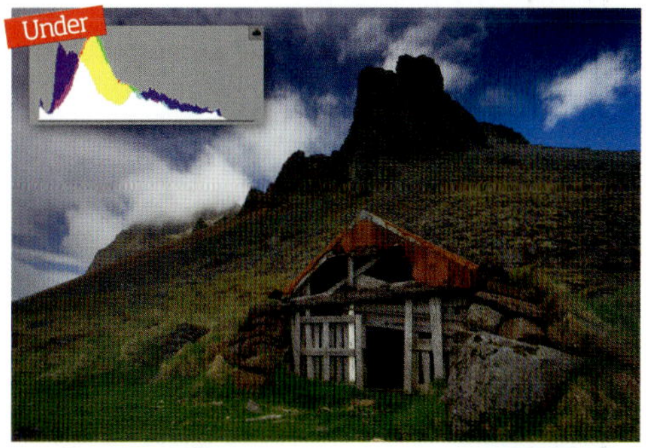

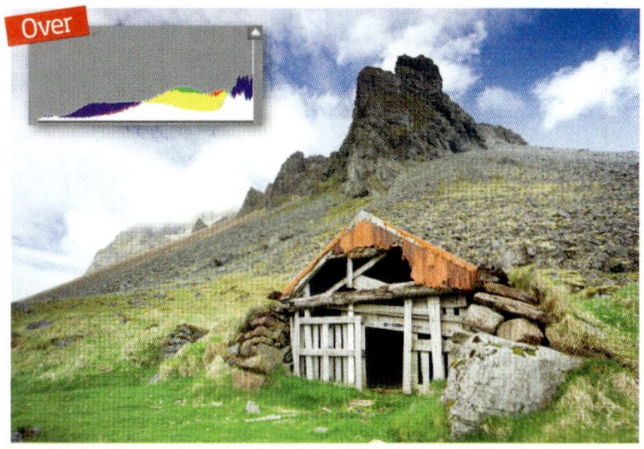

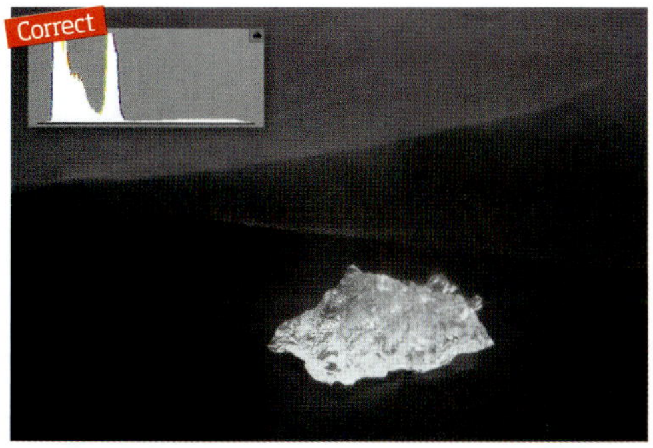

DARK SCENE: A predominantly dark scene will generally have more information to the left of the histogram.

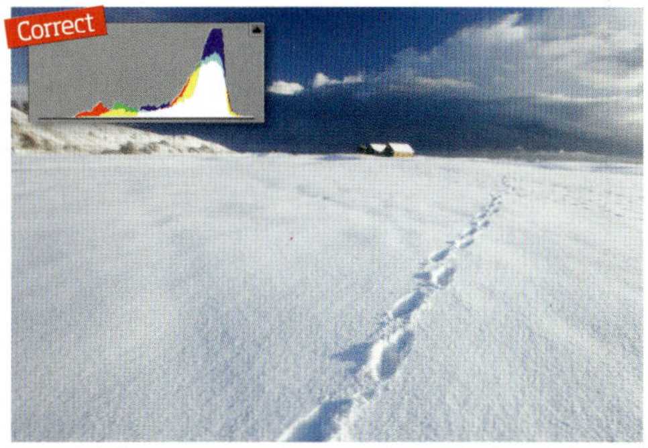

SNOW: The snow dominating this scene and the lack of shadows result in a histogram with a peak to the right.

Other useful aids

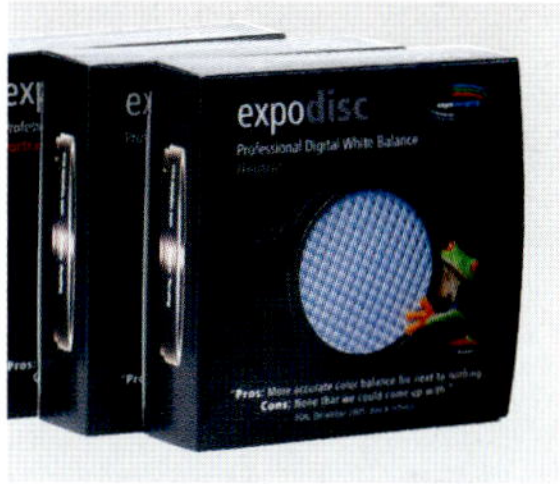

EXPODISC From £55
The Expodisc screws straight on to your lens much like a filter, and represents a fast and easy way to correctly expose for your scene, whatever the lighting.
www.flaghead.co.uk

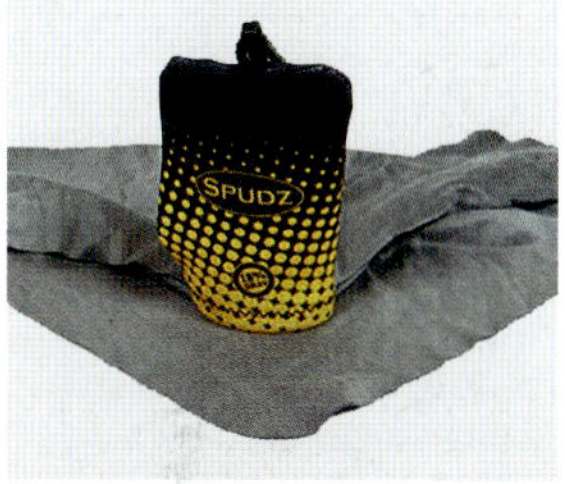

SPUDZ From £5
If space and weight is important to you, try a Spudz microfibre cloth. Not only will it clean your lens, but the cloth is 18% grey, so you can meter from it.
www.robertwhite.co.uk

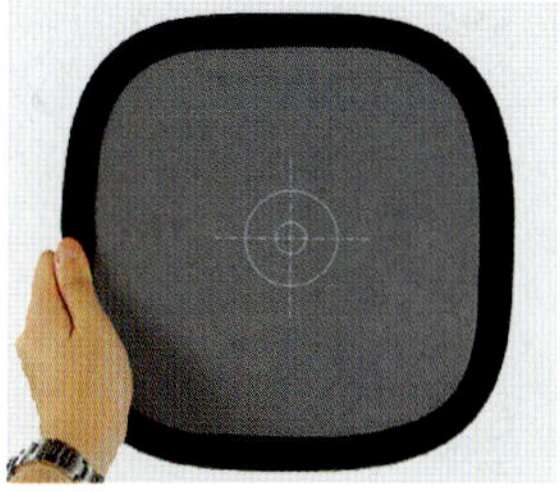

LASTOLITE 30CM EZYBALANCE £15
A handy double-sided pop-up 18% grey/white card that can be used for both exposure and colour correction. Its focusing target enables the camera to focus on the card to take necessary readings.
www.lastolite.com

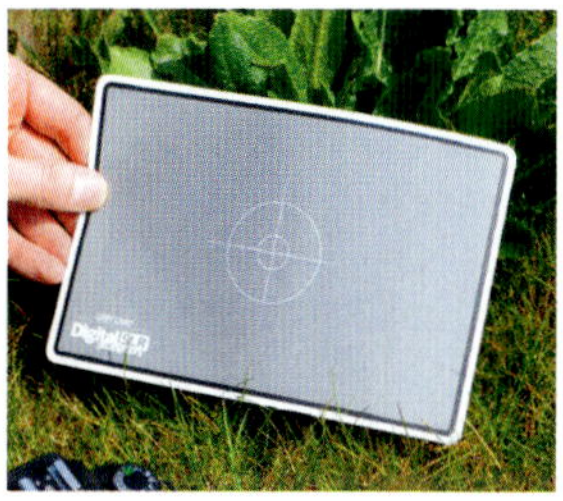

***DIGITAL SLR PHOTOGRAPHY* WHITE & GREY CARD £7.99**
Turn to the back of this guide and you'll discover a free white and grey card to help ensure accurate exposures.

Shooting a scene with lots of sky

Ross Hoddinott explains how to use ND grad filters to achieve a perfect exposure in a scene in which the sky is far brighter than the foreground

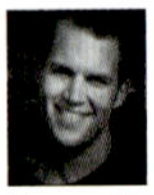

INCLUDING LOTS OF sky can add drama and impact to your landscapes, particularly in stormy conditions or when there is an amazing cloud formation. Placing the emphasis on the sky rather than the foreground can prove very effective. However, achieving a correct exposure can be tricky as, typically, the sky is brighter than the land. The difference can be negligible, or it *can* amount to several stops, which will cause exposure problems. If your multi-zone metering system biases its reading for the sky, the exposure will be shorter, underexposing the foreground, but if you correctly meter for the land, the longer exposure will blow out the sky.

When shooting a scene with more sky than foreground, multi-zone metering (such as Evaluative or Matrix) can struggle. Metering systems try to record subjects as a mid-tone, so will assess the scene and typically produce an image in which nothing is quite exposed correctly; the sky is slightly overexposed, and the land slightly underexposed. Even if you switch metering modes, problems will arise. For example, 'spot' – the most accurate form of metering – calculates exposure from a circle covering just two to three percent of the frame. By pointing the spot-metering sensor at the part of the scene you wish to base your exposure from, you'll get a very precise reading. However, in situations like this – when the scene's range of brightness exceeds the sensor's dynamic range – you will encounter problems with exposure, regardless of what you do. Spot-meter from the sky and the foreground will be underexposed. In contrast, if you take a spot-meter reading from a mid-tone in the foreground (like grass), the land will now be correctly exposed, but the sky washed out. It's a no-win situation. Different metering patterns, or using exposure compensation, will not solve the problem of shooting unevenly lit landscapes. Don't panic, though: the problem is relatively easy to correct. Firstly, you can take two identical images – one exposed for the foreground and one for the brighter sky – and merge them on your computer. However, most landscape photographers prefer to correct the problem in-camera using neutral density (ND) graduated filters. These filters are half-clear and half-coated with a transitional zone where they meet. The neutral density coating is designed to absorb light, so by positioning it in the filter holder so that the coated area covers the sky, you can balance the exposure and achieve a correct exposure throughout the scene with one frame and without the hassle of having to blend images. Graduated NDs are available in different densities to suit different lighting conditions – a 0.3ND equals a one-stop exposure reduction, 0.6ND a two-stop and 0.9ND equates to three stops. To show you how to solve the problem of shooting an unevenly lit scene, boasting a large sky, I headed out to the rugged beauty of Roughtor on Bodmin Moor with my Lee Filters' 100mm ND graduate set.

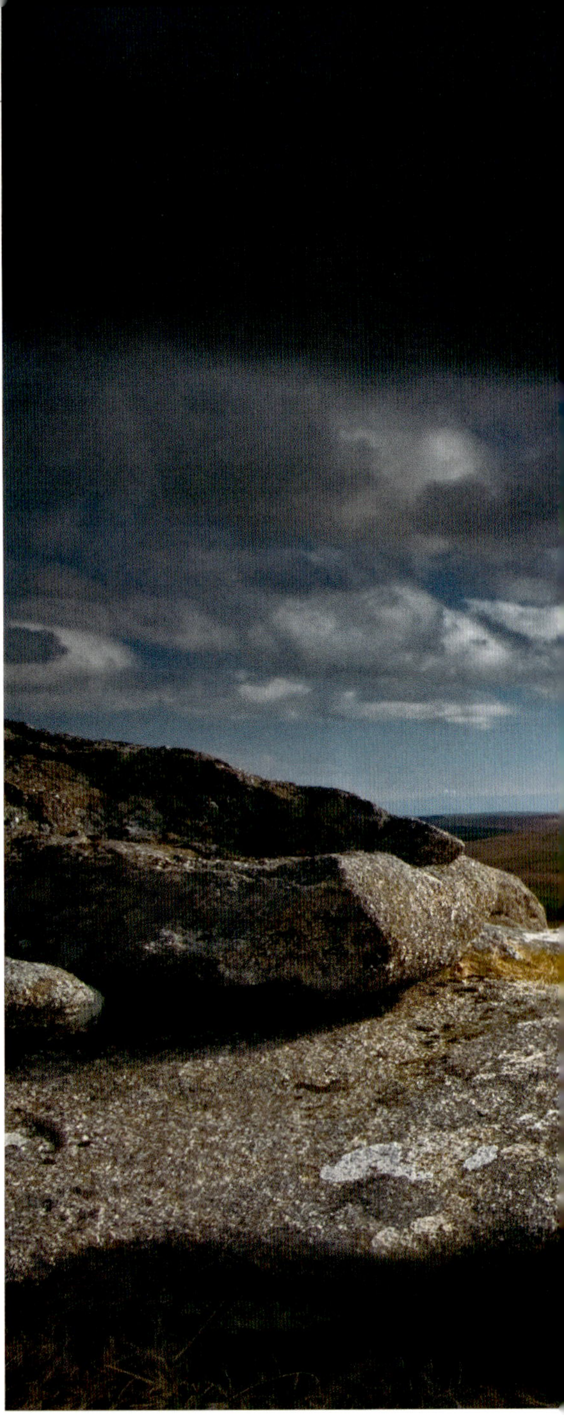

Graduated ND filters

Graduated neutral density filters (ND) are available in two types of transition: hard and soft. The soft type has a feathered edge, providing a more gentle transition suited to scenes with a broken horizon (the filter won't significantly darken objects breaking the horizon, such as a building or tree). A hard ND has a more sudden transition, ideal if the horizon is straight. This allows you to reduce the brightness of the sky with greater accuracy.

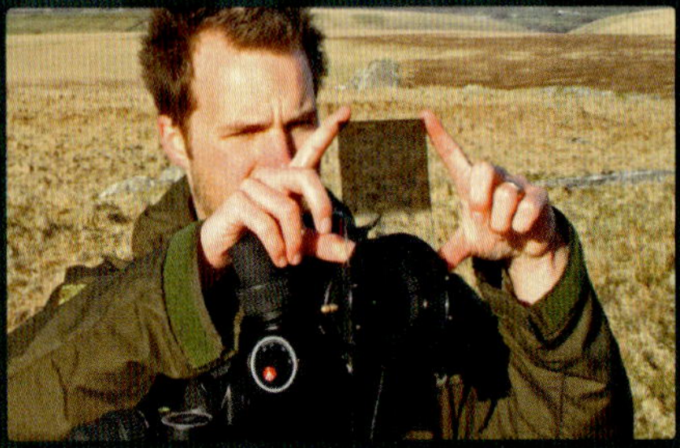

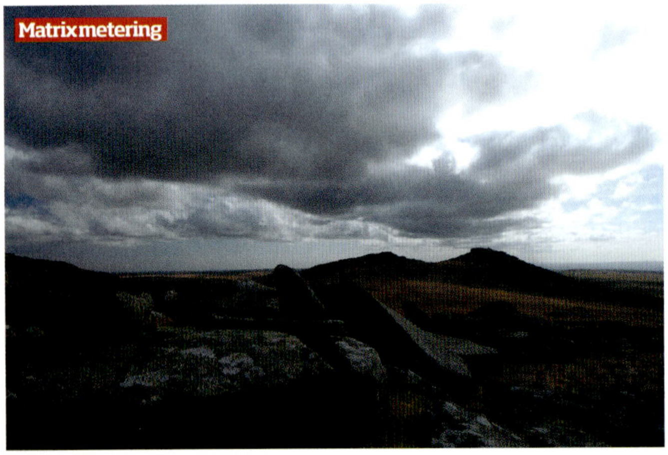

Step 1 It was a stormy evening when I visited Roughtor, so I decided to include more sky than foreground. I settled on a simple composition, using the granite outcrops as foreground interest. I set my Nikon D300 to aperture-priority, selecting an aperture of f/16 for a deep depth-of-field and the camera set to a shutter speed of 1/40sec. However, the result is poor. The foreground is underexposed and the highlights in the sky washed out.

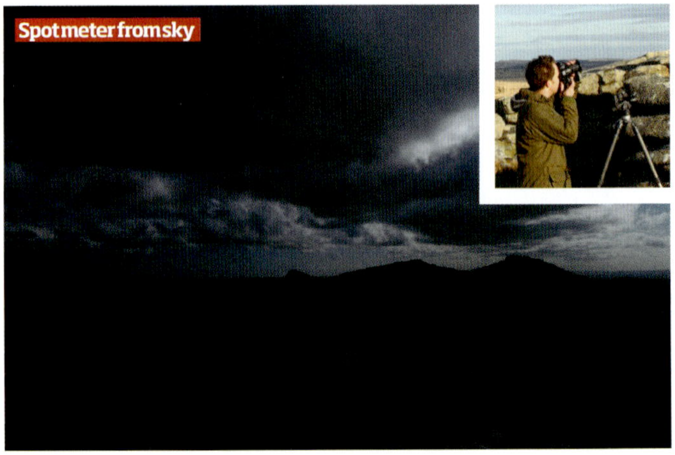

Step 2 In order to prevent highlights in the sky from burning out, I decided to take a spot-meter reading from the sky. I switched my DSLR to spot metering and took a reading from a bright region of the sky. This gave me a shutter speed of 1/80sec. I locked this setting by pressing the AE-L button, and took another shot. The bright regions of sky were now correctly exposed, but as a result of using a shorter exposure, the rest of the scene is now even darker.

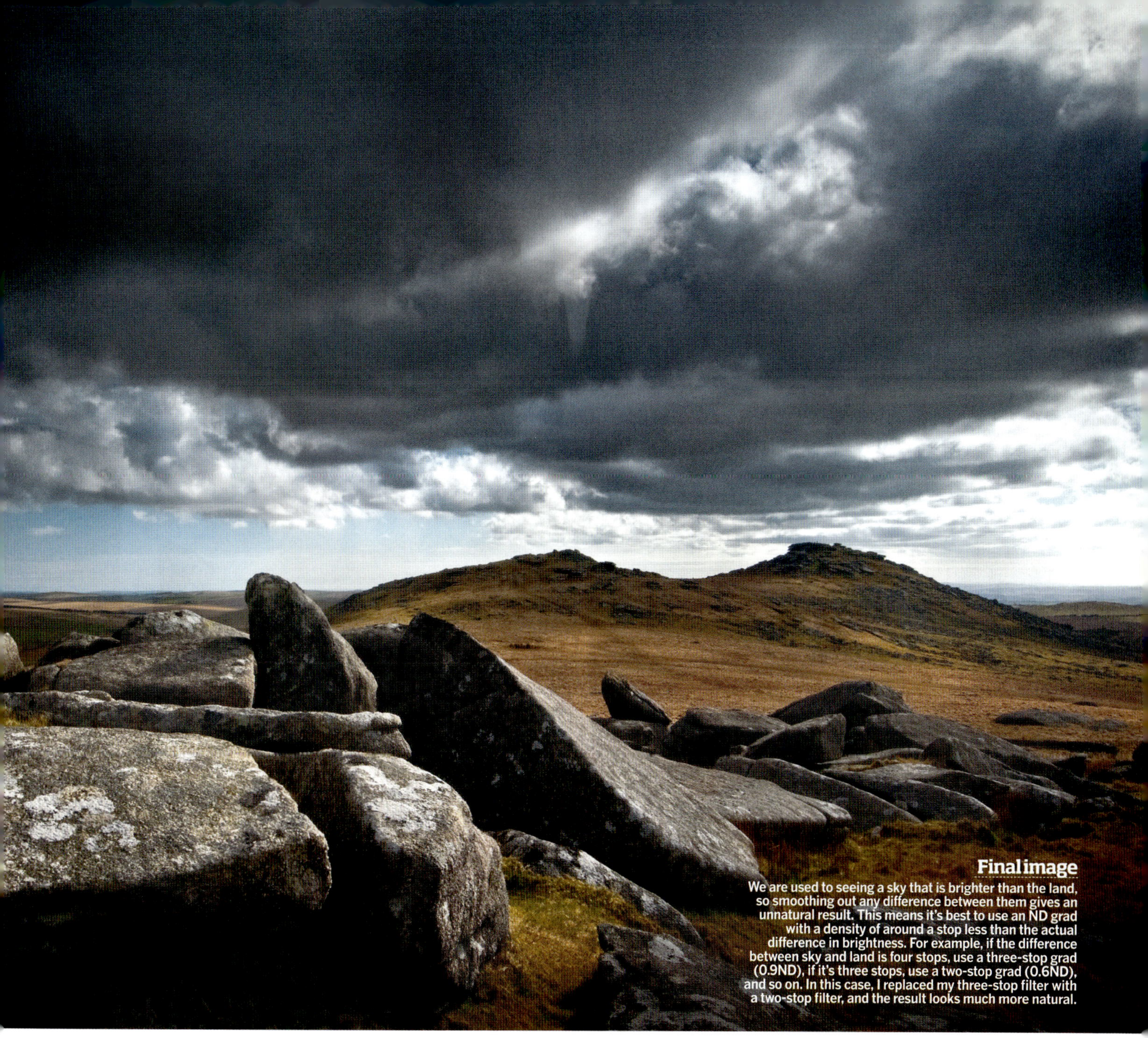

Final image

We are used to seeing a sky that is brighter than the land, so smoothing out any difference between them gives an unnatural result. This means it's best to use an ND grad with a density of around a stop less than the actual difference in brightness. For example, if the difference between sky and land is four stops, use a three-stop grad (0.9ND), if it's three stops, use a two-stop grad (0.6ND), and so on. In this case, I replaced my three-stop filter with a two-stop filter, and the result looks much more natural.

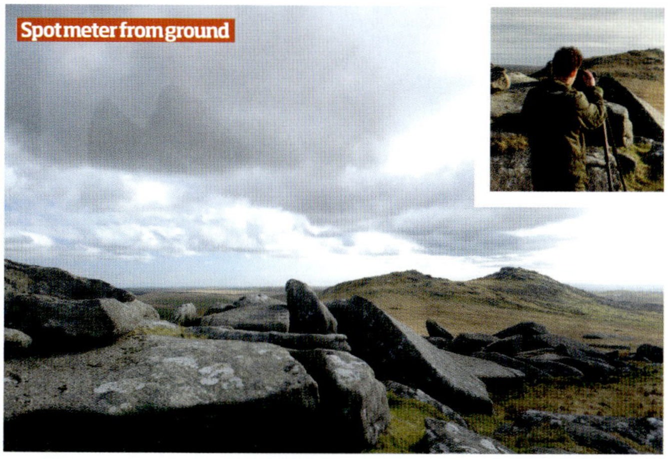

Step 3 The scene's range of brightness was too great for my DSLR's dynamic range. To show this, I took another shot, this time correctly metering for the foreground. I spot-metered from the granite, giving me an exposure time of 1/10sec – again at f/16. The detail in the rock was good, but, as anticipated, the longer exposure blew out the sky, ruining the image. I could have merged these two exposures in Photoshop, but I wanted to get a 'perfect' exposure in-camera.

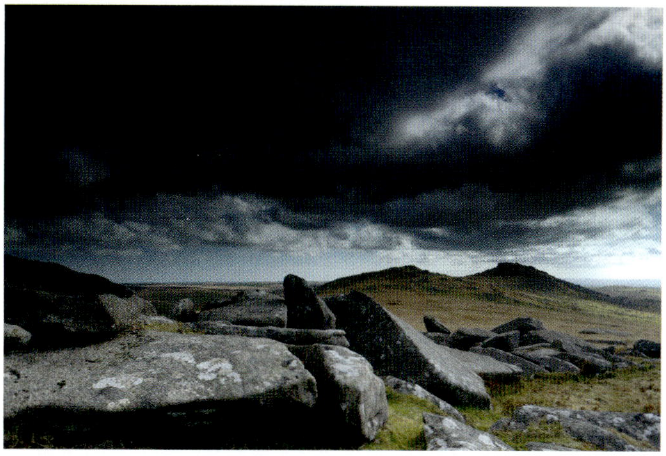

Step 4 If the sky is brighter than the land, you can balance the exposure by positioning the graduated zone of an ND grad filter over the lighter sky. In this instance, the difference in exposure between the land (1/10sec) and sky (1/80sec) amounted to three stops. So, I positioned a three-stop graduated ND filter in my camera's filter system, carefully aligning the transitional zone with the horizon. However, the result looks a little too even and unnatural.

The basic principles of apertures

What is an aperture? How do you control it? What does it actually do? All these questions and more are answered in an easy-to-follow, jargon-free style

WHAT IS AN APERTURE?

Aperture is defined by the iris within a lens that controls the amount of light allowed to pass from the front to the rear of the lens. A wide aperture allows lots of light through, while a narrow aperture restricts the amount of light. The various aperture settings appear as f/numbers, which you'll see on your LCD monitor and in the viewfinder. There's a long-winded and boring scientific explanation for f/numbers, but let's keep it simple and stick to the fact that they indicate the size of the aperture. A low f/number, such as f/4, indicates a wide aperture, while a high f/number like f/22 indicates a small aperture.

WHAT DOES THE APERTURE DO AND HOW DO I CONTROL IT?

You can compare the function of an aperture to the pupil of your eye. In low light, your pupil widens to allow more light to reach the retina, while in bright light, it constricts to limit the amount of light passing through. When left to function automatically, a DSLR or CSC works in the same way, selecting the aperture size (and corresponding shutter speed) that is required to give the correct exposure. If you're completely new to digital photography, it's understandable that you may have left the camera set to program or Full-Auto mode, leaving the camera to control the aperture selection. But if you have a little faith in what you're reading here, believe us when we say that moving the dial from P to A (or Av) and trying out aperture-priority mode will allow you to take a big step forward in your photography, and the major improvements you'll make will be far easier to achieve than you think.

Setting aperture-priority AE (A or Av) moves the camera into a semi-automatic mode. You'll decide the aperture and the camera will automatically select the shutter speed that is required. So you've no complicated calculations to make as the camera will still take care of working out the correct exposure. However, you'll have the major benefit of being able to influence how the image looks depending on your choice of the aperture. How? You'll find out soon enough! So, we can see that the principal job of an aperture is to determine how much light you allow through at any given time. And how we change the aperture is extremely easy – select A or Av on your camera and you're in control.

The important thing we now have to grasp is how the aperture we choose affects two very important aspects of the image: the exposure and the amount of depth-of-field within a scene. We'll see how shortly.

A DSLR's depth-of-field preview button

To ensure the viewfinder is at its brightest – to assist viewing and focusing – DSLRs are designed to view the image at the lens's fastest (maximum) aperture. As a result, what you see through the viewfinder isn't normally a true representation of the depth-of-field that will actually be achieved. The depth-of-field preview button works by stopping the lens down to the selected aperture (f/stop). When you do this, the scene will darken in the viewfinder. The smaller the aperture, the darker the preview, but you will be able to assess whether the selected f/number provides sufficient depth-of-field. If not, adjust the aperture accordingly. While this function can take a while to get used to, it can prove highly useful. However, it may be helpful to reduce apertures gradually, stop by stop, so that changes in depth-of-field are more obvious. It is worth noting that not all cameras have this facility. If yours doesn't, assess the depth-of-field by shooting a test shot and reviewing the image on your camera's LCD monitor instead.

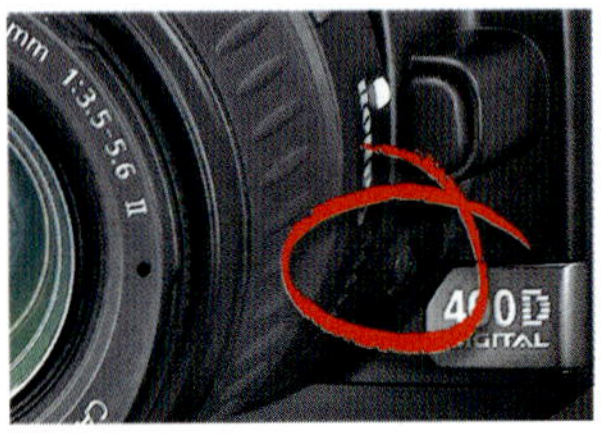

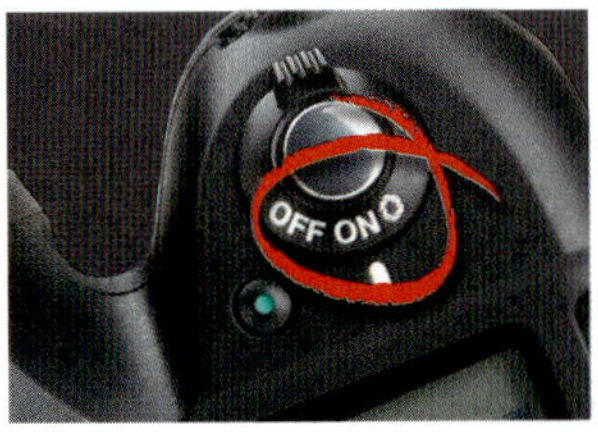

Setting apertures on your DSLR or CSC

As you'll discover, changing apertures on your digital SLR or CSC is simply a matter of selecting aperture-priority and making your choice!

CANON EOS DSLRS

(1) Set the exposure mode dial on the top-plate to Av to select aperture-priority mode

(2) Turning the input dial just behind the shutter button allows you to select the aperture value

(3) You can see the aperture setting by looking at the information display on the rear LCD or the information panel in the viewfinder display

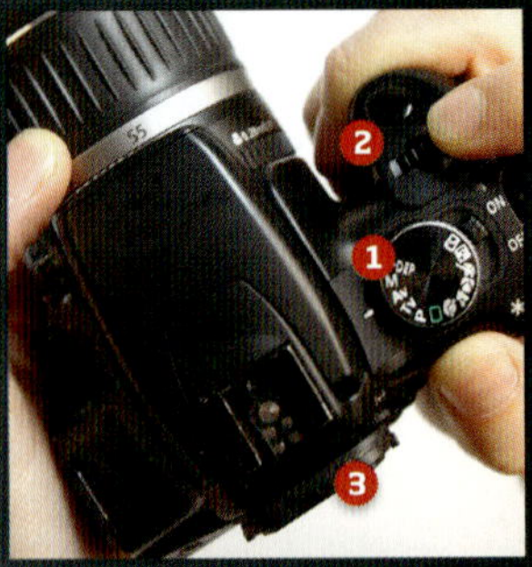

NIKON DSLRS

(1) Set the exposure mode dial on the top-plate to A to select aperture-priority mode

(2) Turning the input dial on the front of the handgrip allows you to select the aperture value

(3) You can see the aperture setting by looking at the top-plate or review LCD or the information panel in the viewfinder display

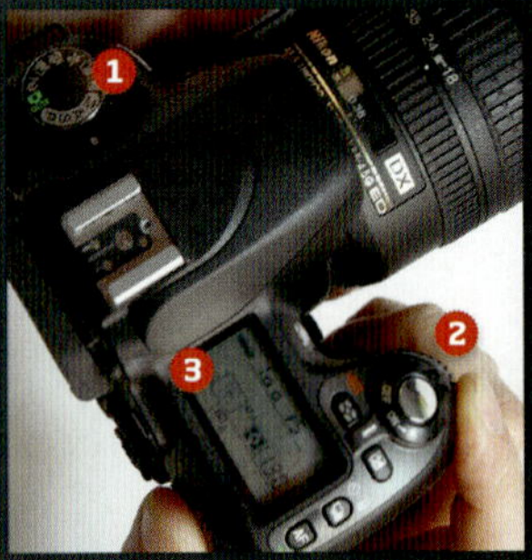

PENTAX K-SERIES DSLRS

(1) Set the exposure mode dial on the top-plate to Av to select aperture-priority mode

(2) Turning the input dial on the rear of the camera with your right thumb allows you to select the aperture value

(3) You can see the aperture setting by looking at the top-plate or rear LCD or the information panel in the viewfinder display

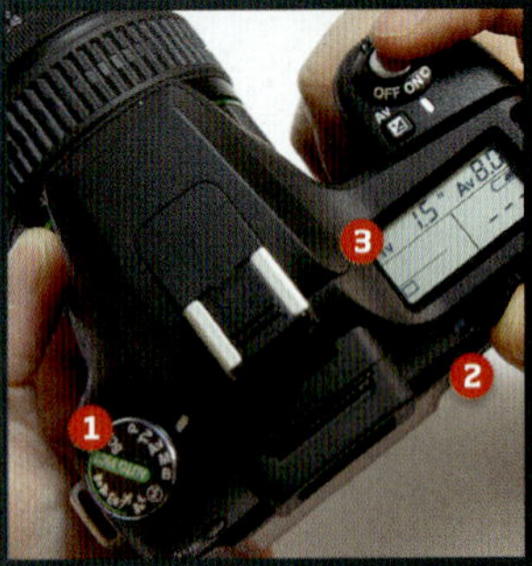

SONY ALPHA DSLRS

(1) Set the exposure mode dial on the top-plate to A to select aperture-priority mode

(2) Turning the input dial on the top of the handgrip just in front of the shutter button allows you to select the aperture value

(3) You can see the aperture setting by looking at the rear LCD monitor or information panel in the viewfinder display

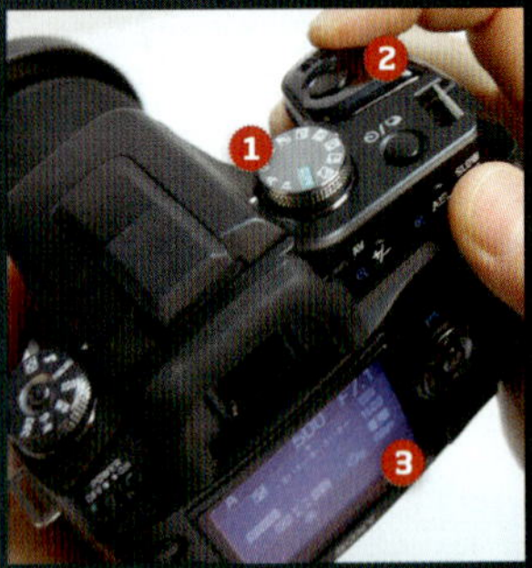

MOST COMPACT SYSTEM CAMERAS

Very few CSCs sport the exposure mode dial found on the majority of digital SLRs. However, it's still very easy to select the exposure mode. With most models all you need to do is press the Menu button or the four-way control dial to display a choice of exposure modes and rotate the wheel to A to select aperture-priority mode. With touchscreen models, simply press the A icon on the screen.

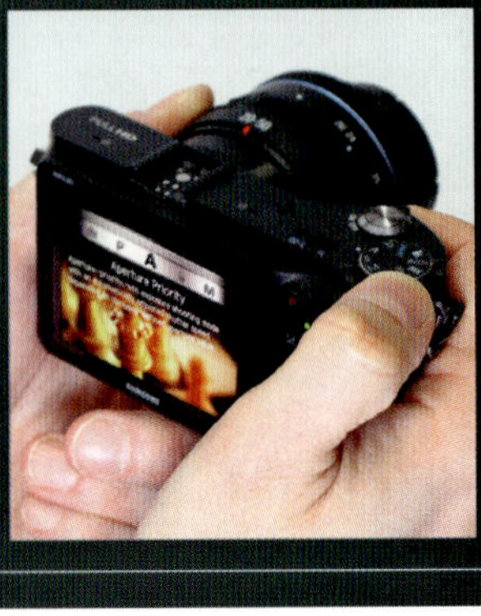

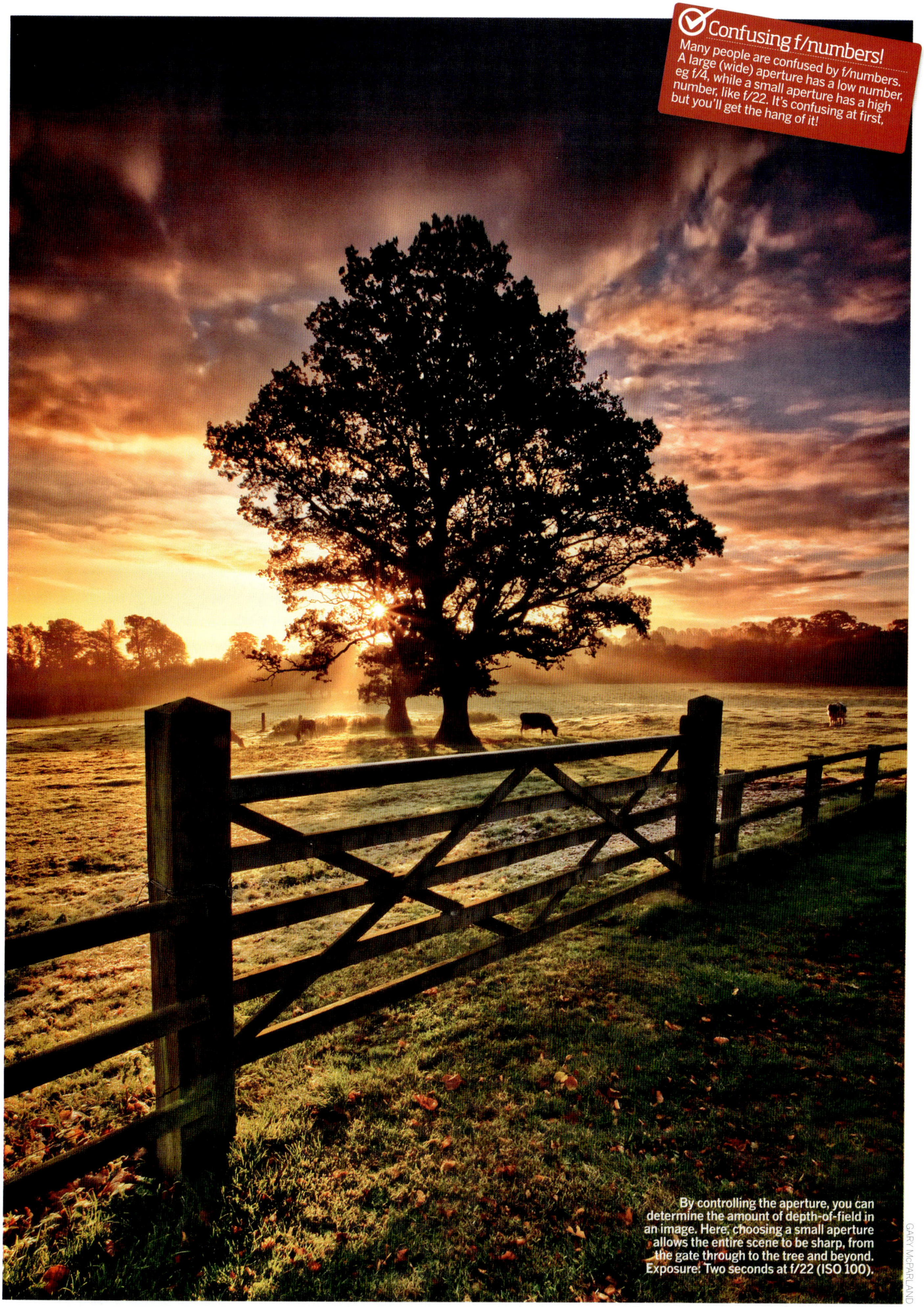

Confusing f/numbers!

Many people are confused by f/numbers. A large (wide) aperture has a low number, eg f/4, while a small aperture has a high number, like f/22. It's confusing at first, but you'll get the hang of it!

By controlling the aperture, you can determine the amount of depth-of-field in an image. Here, choosing a small aperture allows the entire scene to be sharp, from the gate through to the tree and beyond. Exposure: Two seconds at f/22 (ISO 100).

GARY McPARLAND

Apertures & exposure

Knowing how aperture settings affect the exposure is one of the first things you need to get to grips with

EVERY EXPOSURE YOU make is determined by three key variables: aperture, shutter speed and ISO rating. When you take a picture in aperture-priority mode, the ISO rating remains 'fixed' unless you change it yourself; in other words, the ISO is not influenced by the aperture setting you select. However, that's not true of the shutter speed, which automatically increases or decreases to provide the correct exposure for the aperture that you select. You can see for yourself by setting Av (or A) on your camera and rotating the input dial to change the aperture.

As you open up the aperture to a wide setting, you allow more light through, so the camera reacts by giving a faster shutter speed, while closing the aperture, so that it restricts the light and prompts the camera to set a slower shutter speed. It's important to experiment and understand this balance as it is a fundamental principle of exposure. Knowing how it works will help you shoot more creatively.

In average lighting conditions, you'll find that you can choose most apertures and take pictures without any problems. But in low or bright light, the camera's choice of shutter speed can present you with some problems. Understanding how the aperture setting controls the amount of light passing through the lens will help you overcome them.

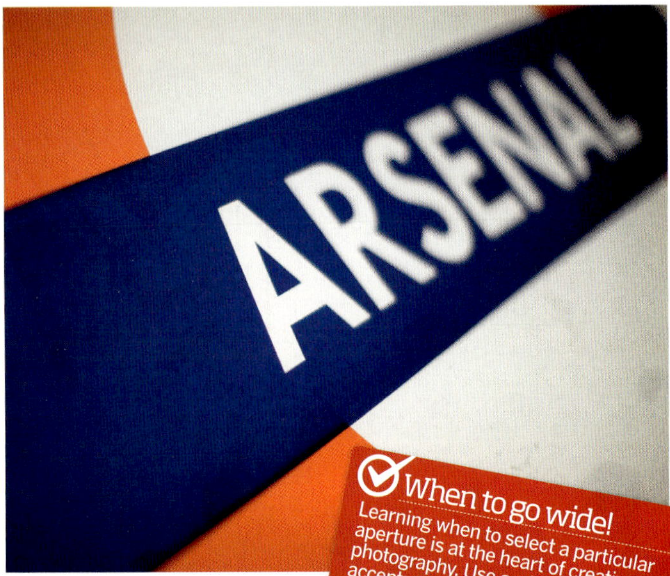

When to go wide!
Learning when to select a particular aperture is at the heart of creative photography. Use a wide aperture to accentuate focus on a certain point and use the shallow depth-of-field for effect

ISTOCK PHOTO

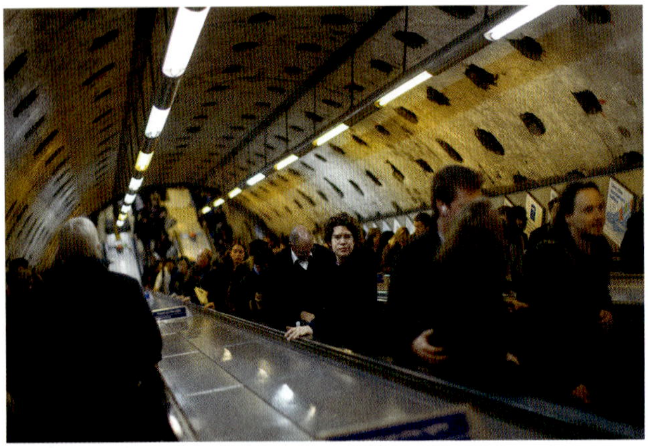

Apertures and low-light conditions

When you're shooting indoors or in low light, you will be working with a limited amount of available light and need to take the appropriate action. Assuming you're not using flash, the key thing to do is to have an exposure that doesn't suffer from camera shake. The two best ways to do this are as follows:

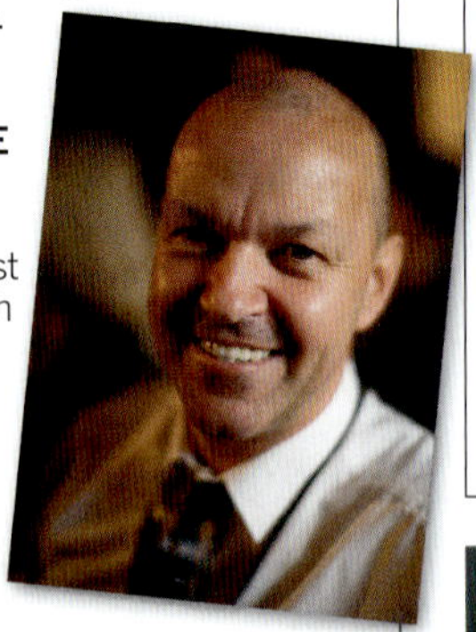

1) SET A WIDE APERTURE AND INCREASE THE ISO RATING Select the widest aperture to give the fastest possible shutter speed. If it's still too slow, increase the ISO rating until you have a fast enough shutter speed. This is the best approach if hand-holding the camera, but using the method below will give better quality results.

This portrait was taken in very dark conditions, requiring an aperture of f/1.2 at ISO 800 to give a sharp result. Note how minimal the depth-of-field is and the drop-off of sharpness.

2) USE A TRIPOD! Place your DSLR or CSC on a tripod (or other support) and you'll get far better results than the first method, because you can shoot at a lower ISO rating for optimum colour and minimum noise. Also, you're not limited to using a wide aperture, so can choose a mid-aperture setting for the best sharpness.

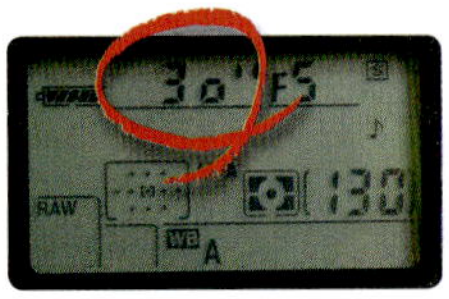

LOW-LIGHT LEVEL WARNING! You may sometimes see the shutter speed flashing in the viewfinder or on the LCD when shooting in low light. This indicates that the camera has selected the slowest shutter speed in its range but still can't give the correct exposure, because an even longer exposure than it's capable of setting is required. The two ways around this are to select a wider aperture and/or increase the ISO until the flashing stops.

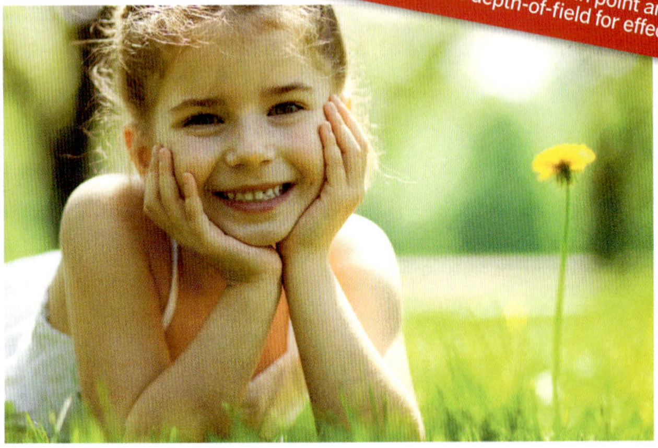

Apertures and bright conditions

Bright lighting conditions are much easier to work in than low light, as you have many more options for the aperture setting you can use. Choose an aperture that gives the results you want, but make sure the shutter speed remains fast enough to avoid camera shake.

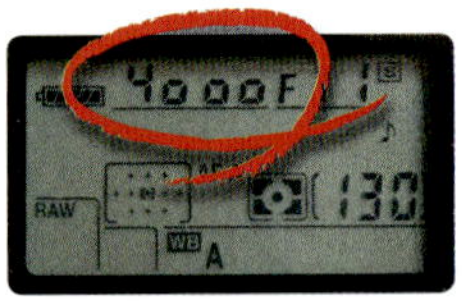

TOO BRIGHT WARNING! It's uncommon you'll ever have this happen, but you may see the shutter speed flashing when shooting in bright light. This indicates that the camera has selected the top shutter speed, but it's still not fast enough to give a correct exposure for the aperture you've chosen. This is often because you've left the ISO rating at a very high setting while shooting indoors, so lower this and/or use a smaller aperture.

Aperture terminology

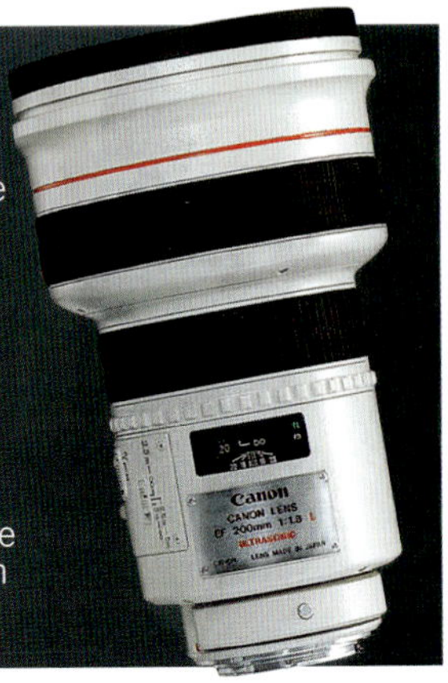

- **'Close down'** the aperture is another way of saying select a smaller aperture
- **'Open up'** the aperture is another way of saying use a wider aperture
- The **'maximum aperture'** is the widest aperture setting on a lens
- The **'minimum aperture'** is the smallest aperture setting on a lens
- A **'fast'** lens is one that has a wider than normal maximum aperture for the lens type. It usually refers to those with an f/2.8 or faster maximum aperture

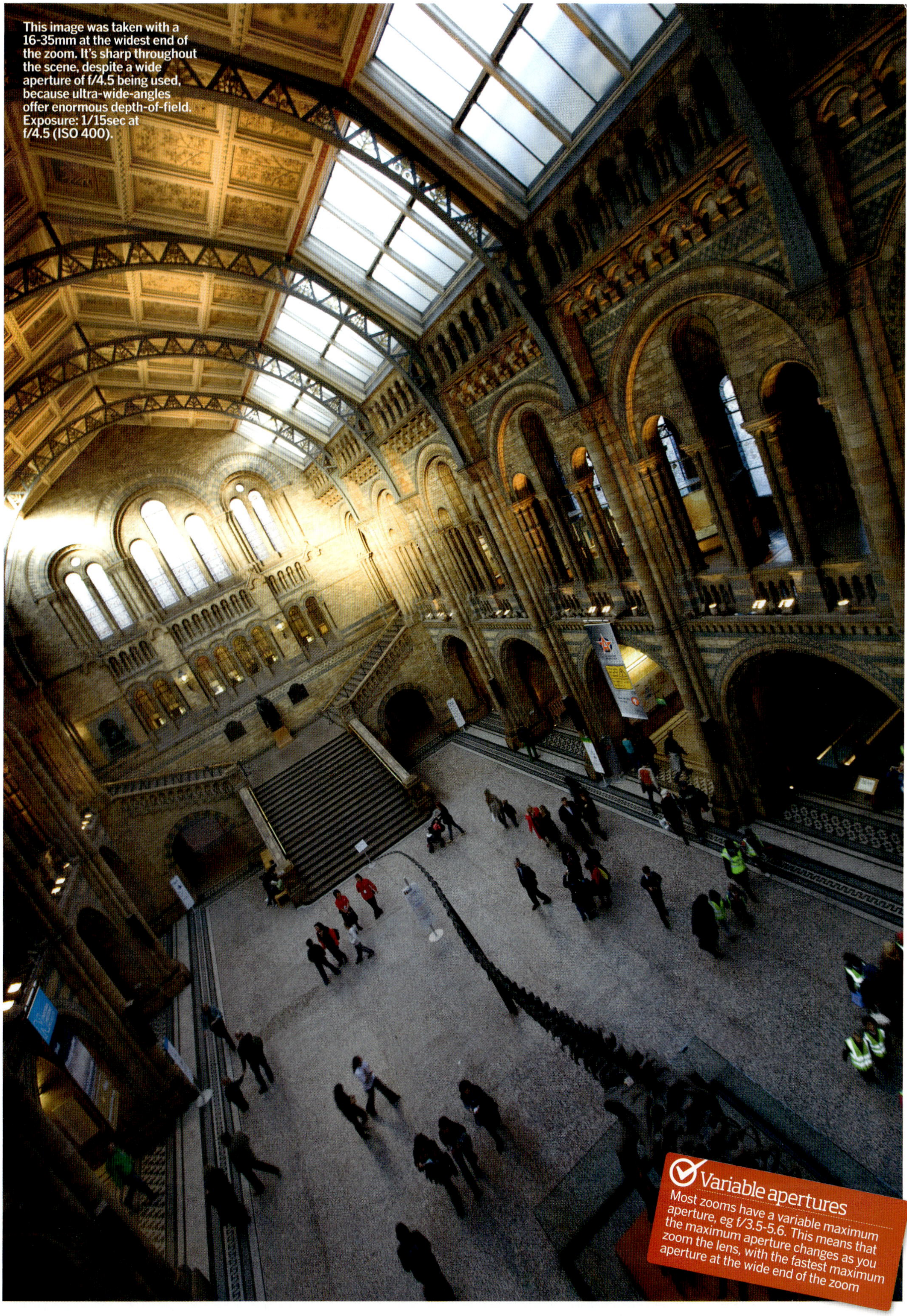

This image was taken with a 16-35mm at the widest end of the zoom. It's sharp throughout the scene, despite a wide aperture of f/4.5 being used, because ultra-wide-angles offer enormous depth-of-field. Exposure: 1/15sec at f/4.5 (ISO 400).

ALL IMAGES: DANIEL LEZANO

Variable apertures

Most zooms have a variable maximum aperture, eg f/3.5-5.6. This means that the maximum aperture changes as you zoom the lens, with the fastest maximum aperture at the wide end of the zoom

Apertures & depth-of-field

For real creative control, practise using different aperture settings and see how sharpness changes within the scene

THE RELATIONSHIP BETWEEN aperture and depth-of-field is quite possibly the most important thing for you to get to grips with in photography. Thankfully, it's very easy to understand. Here's a quick explanation: depth-of-field relates to the area in front of and behind the point of focus that appears sharp. The depth-of-field in a scene is determined by a number of factors, including the focal length of the lens you use and the distance between the subject and lens but, most importantly, by your choice of aperture. If you set the lens to the maximum aperture (ie its widest setting) you minimise the amount of depth-of-field. Setting the lens to progressively smaller apertures increases depth-of-field and adds focal sharpness throughout the frame, with the minimum (smallest) aperture giving the greatest depth-of-field.

With some images, everything from the nearest blade of grass to the distant mountains will be in focus. The lens may be set to focus on a certain point, but to provide depth-of-field and sharpness throughout a scene, you'll need to have selected a small aperture.

You can see the effect of using a wide aperture in images that have a shallow depth-of-field, where there is only a single point in the scene that's sharp and the rest of it is thrown out of focus. The choice of aperture you'll use will really depend on what you're trying to show in your images and there are no hard and fast rules, although there are some generalisations that can be made. For instance, landscape photographers often want the entire scene to appear sharp, so will usually opt for a small aperture, while portrait photographers want to isolate the subject from the background, so opt for a wide aperture, so that the subject's sharp against a blurred background.

As you can see, knowing how to use apertures can have a major effect on the way a scene is recorded, so trying out different aperture settings for different scenarios can really help to improve your creative skills. As you'll see from the images in this guide, simply by practising with different apertures, you'll increase your understanding of how some apertures suit certain subjects.

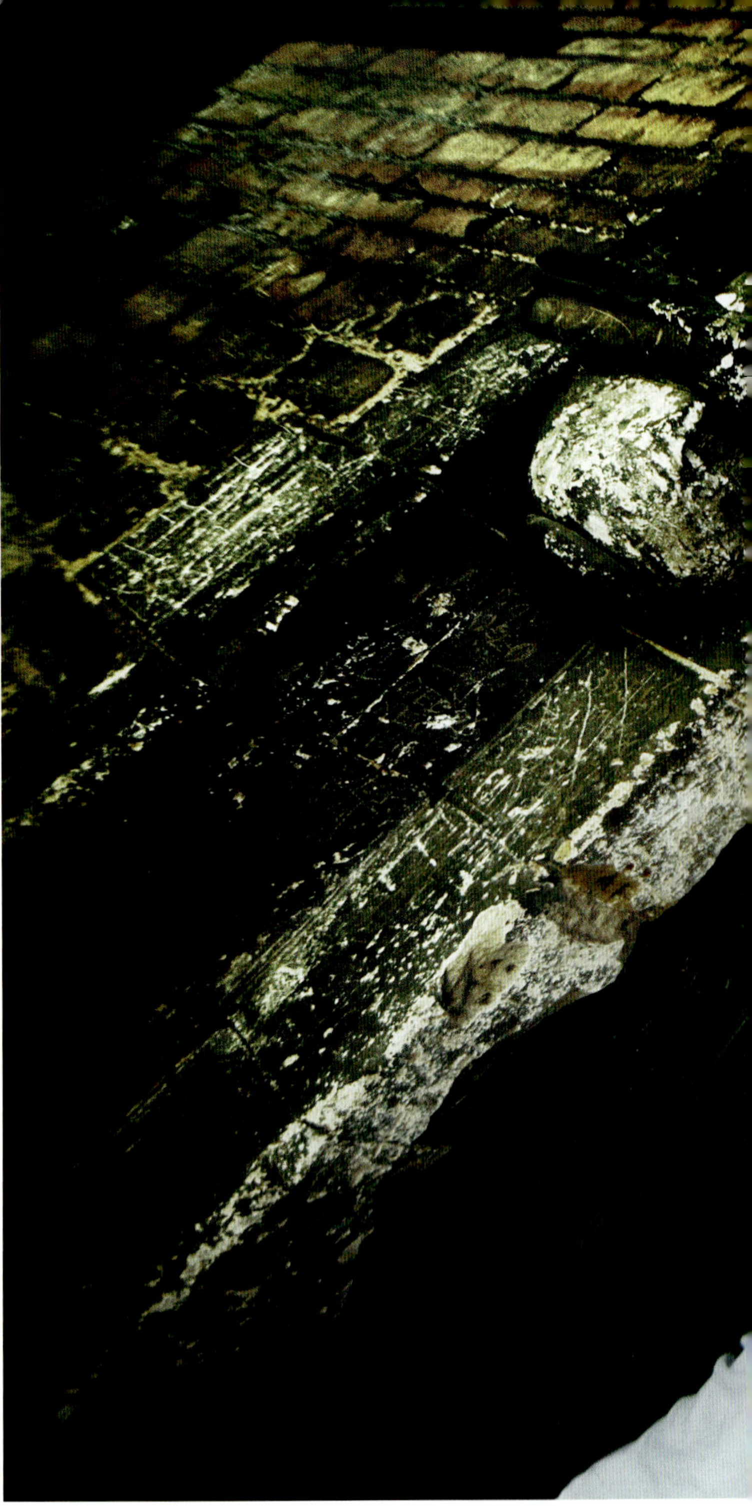

Depth-of-field

For this comparison set, the lens (28-70mm set to 70mm) was focused on the girl's face. The only thing that was changed was the aperture setting, in full stops from f/2.8 to f/22. Note how the railings behind the subject become progressively sharper as the aperture is closed down.

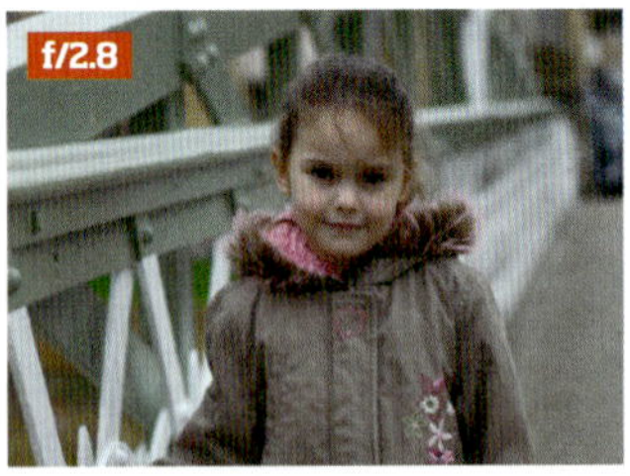

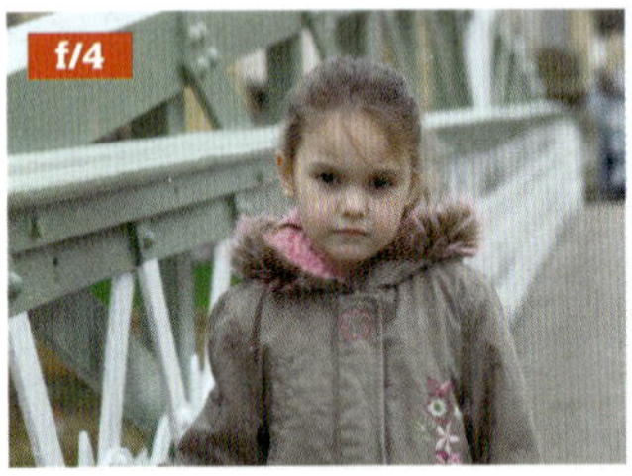

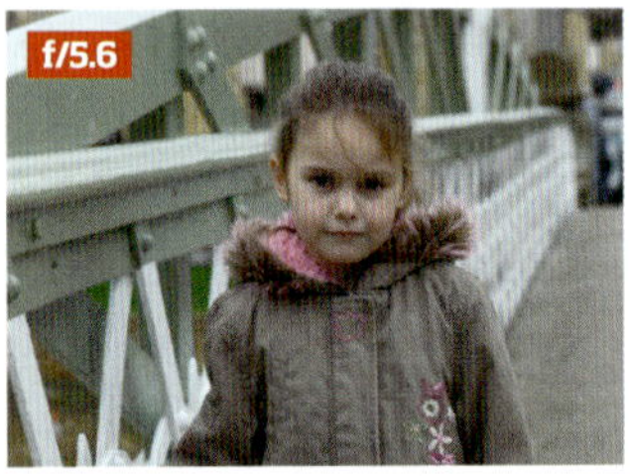

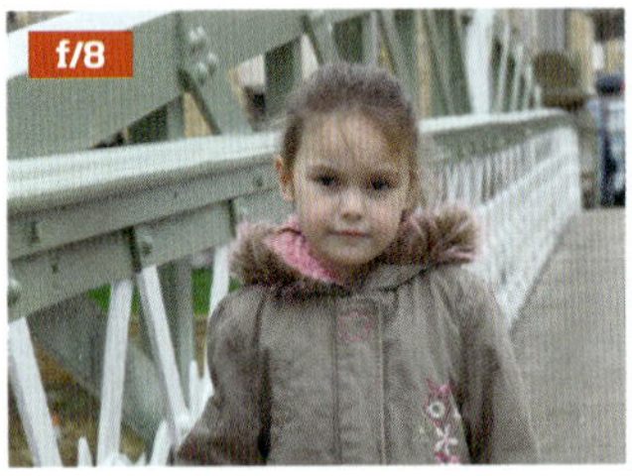

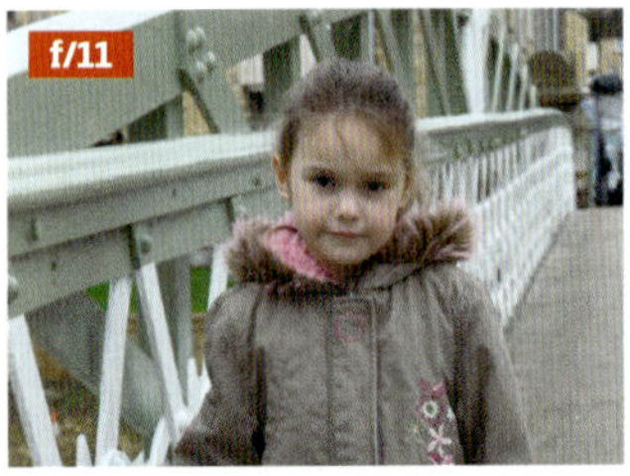

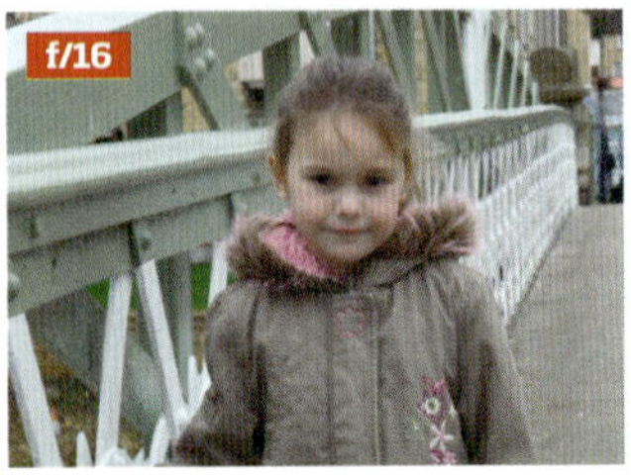

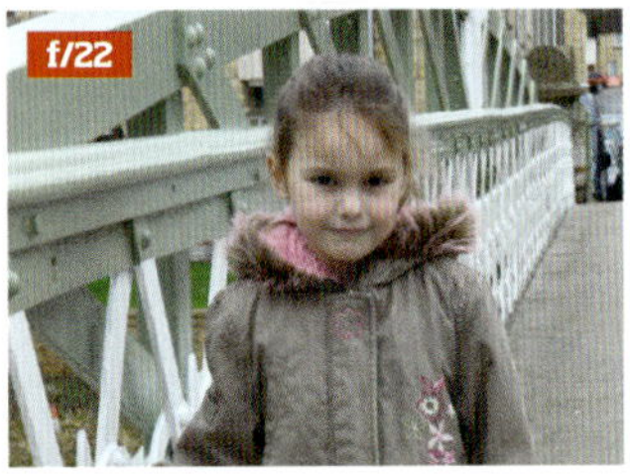

What affects depth-of-field?

For any given aperture, you'll find that both of the following factors will affect the amount of depth-of-field that appears in a scene.

LENS CHOICE Wide-angles give more perceived depth-of-field than a telephoto at the same aperture setting. So f/4 with a 28mm lens gives more depth-of-field than f/4 at 200mm!

SUBJECT-TO-CAMERA DISTANCE The closer the subject is to the camera, the less depth-of-field the image will have.

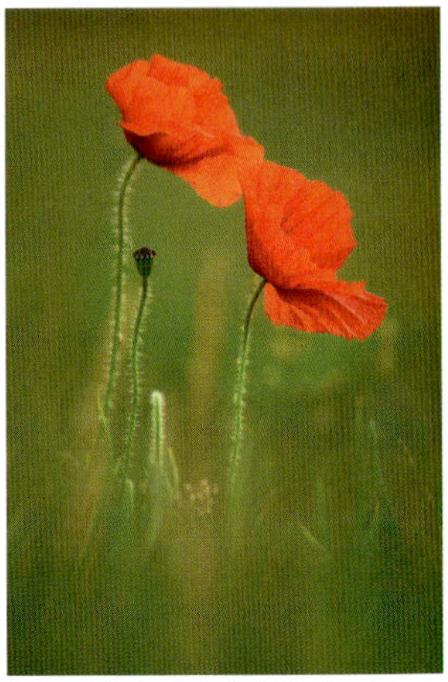

HELEN DIXON

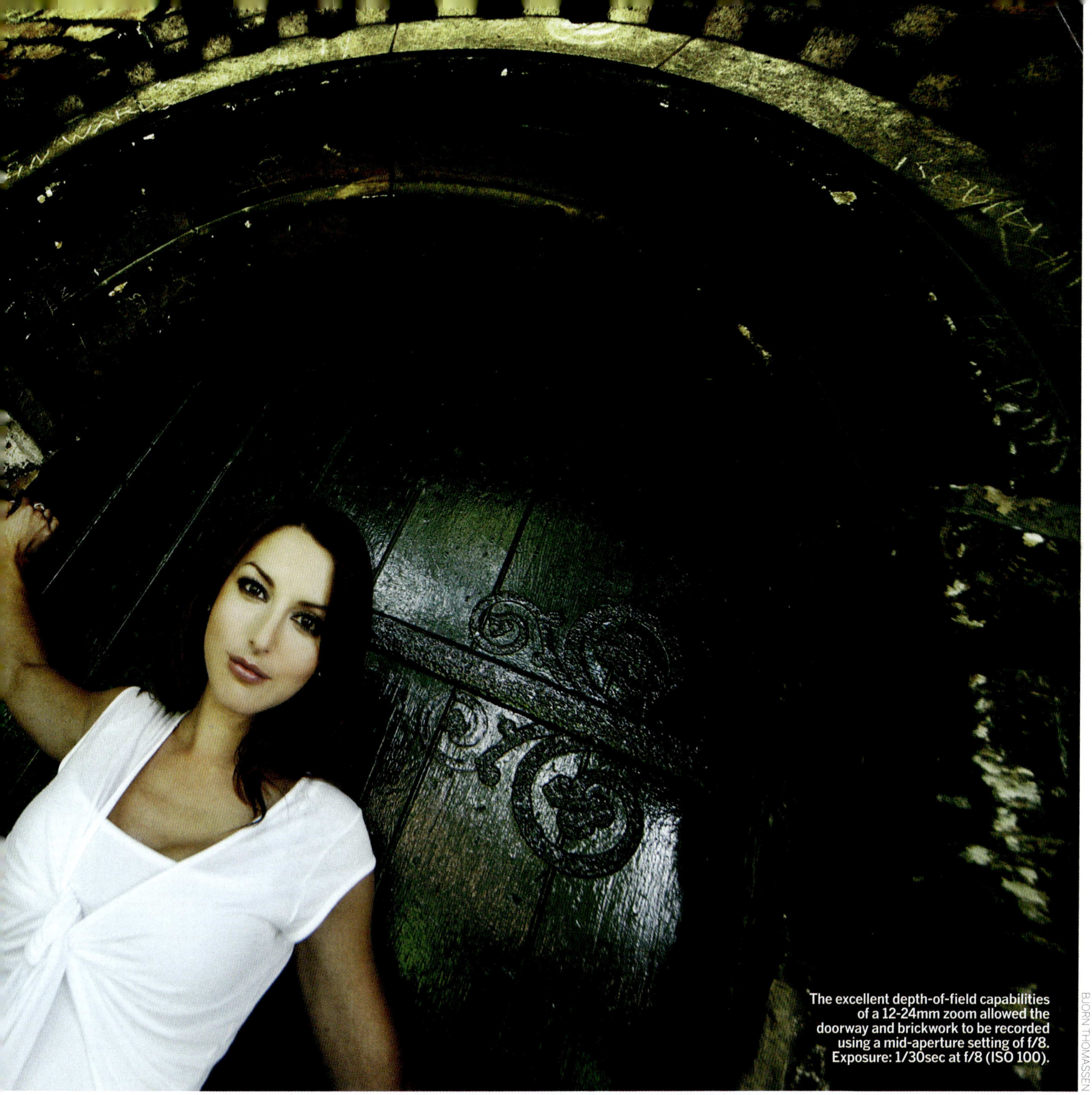

The excellent depth-of-field capabilities of a 12-24mm zoom allowed the doorway and brickwork to be recorded using a mid-aperture setting of f/8. Exposure: 1/30sec at f/8 (ISO 100).

BJORN THOMASSEN

Apertures and 'sharpness'

We've already assessed how choosing a small aperture increases depth-of-field, which boosts sharpness throughout the scene. It's also worth noting how apertures can affect sharpness in two other ways:

OPTIMUM LENS SHARPNESS
Every lens has an optimum setting to give the very sharpest results and, in the majority of instances, this is between f/8 and f/13.

DIFFRACTION While a small aperture gives more depth-of-field, at the extremes it can also betray inferior optical quality, so the benefit of one is cancelled out by the other. This usually happens when f/16 or smaller is used. The effect varies from lens to lens and is only really noticeable in very large prints.

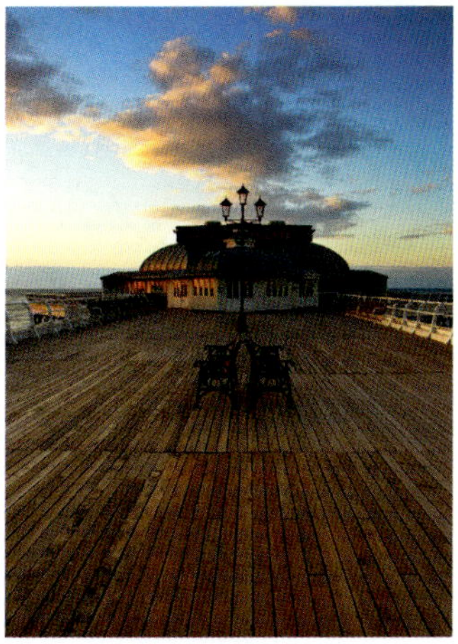

CHRIS HERRING

Apertures: Quick reference guide

There's a lot to take in about apertures, but with a little practice it should all make more sense in no time at all. However, below is a very succinct summary guide for when you need a quick reference

USE A WIDE APERTURE WHEN...
- ✔ You're shooting in low light and handholding the camera
- ✔ **You want to minimise the depth-of-field**
- ✔ You want to keep shutter speeds as fast as possible
- ✔ **You want to keep the ISO rating low to optimise quality**

USE A MID-APERTURE WHEN...
- ✔ You want to optimise quality and are not concerned so much about the amount of depth-of-field in the scene

USE A SMALL APERTURE WHEN...
- ✔ You want the maximum amount of depth-of-field

Aperture-priority & landscapes

Landscape specialist Lee Frost shows why aperture-priority is the most practical exposure mode to use when shooting scenics

ONE OF THE FUNDAMENTALS of successful landscape photography is being able to control and assess depth-of-field, to ensure that the image is sharp from front-to-back.

Aperture-priority mode helps you to achieve this, not only by forcing you to think about which aperture to set, but also by making sure that once it is set, that aperture won't change if light levels fluctuate or you attach filters to the lens. If the exposure has to be adjusted when shooting in aperture-priority mode, the camera does it by changing the shutter speed, so the aperture remains constant. This is vitally important because achieving extensive depth-of-field is not just about aperture selection, but also focusing distance, and a careful balancing act between the two is required to ensure the best possible results. You could take every picture at f/22, with the lens set to infinity, and most wide-angle shots would end up with front-to-back sharpness. Unfortunately, this simple approach doesn't always work, so you're not going to get the best results. Wide-angles and zooms tend to give their worst optical performance when at minimum aperture and their best mid-range around f/8 to f/13, so ideally you should shoot as close to these settings as you can to achieve optimum optical quality, and focus the lens at a distance that maximises depth-of-field at that aperture.

My favourite technique is based around something known as hyperfocal focusing, which involves focusing on a point known as the hyperfocal distance, where you maximise the depth-of-field available for the aperture in use. Lenses once featured a hyperfocal distance scale on the barrel, but virtually none do today. There is an equation for calculating hyperfocal distance for any lens and aperture, so in true *Blue Peter* fashion, I did just that and created a hyperfocal distance chart, which you can copy and refer to when you're on location.

The distances in metres (m) represent the hyperfocal distances for each focal length and aperture. If you focus your lens on that distance and set the corresponding aperture, depth-of-field will extend from half the hyperfocal distance to infinity. So, if you're shooting at 24mm and f/11, focus on a point 1.5m away and depth-of-field will extend from 0.75m (half the hyperfocal distance) to infinity – which is more than enough depth-of-field in most situations.

Aperture-priority & multi-zone metering

Before finally 'going digital' back in the spring of 2008, I'd spent 20 years shooting with film cameras that had no internal metering, so I used a hand-held spot meter to determine correct exposure, which then had to be manually set on the camera. Thankfully, those days are long gone. Digital SLRs and CSCs have fantastic integral metering systems, capable of producing perfectly exposed images in all but the most demanding situations, so I can't see the point in making my life more complicated than it needs to be. These days, my digital SLR is set to aperture-priority mode and multi-zone metering and generally stays that way. Combined with the feedback provided by the camera's preview image and the image histogram, I've got all I need to ensure I get perfect exposures in any shooting situation. The same applies to you.

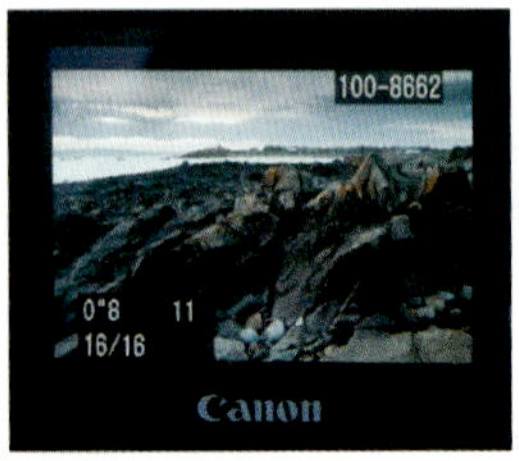

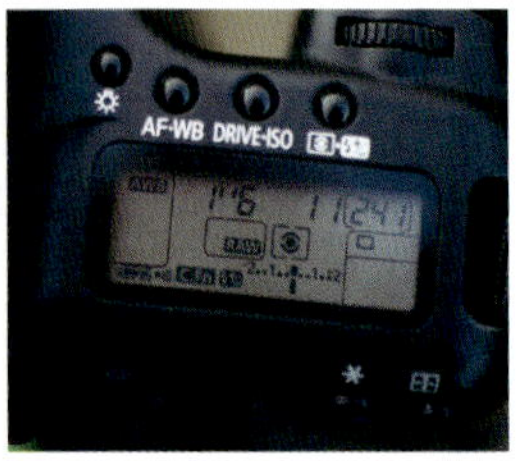

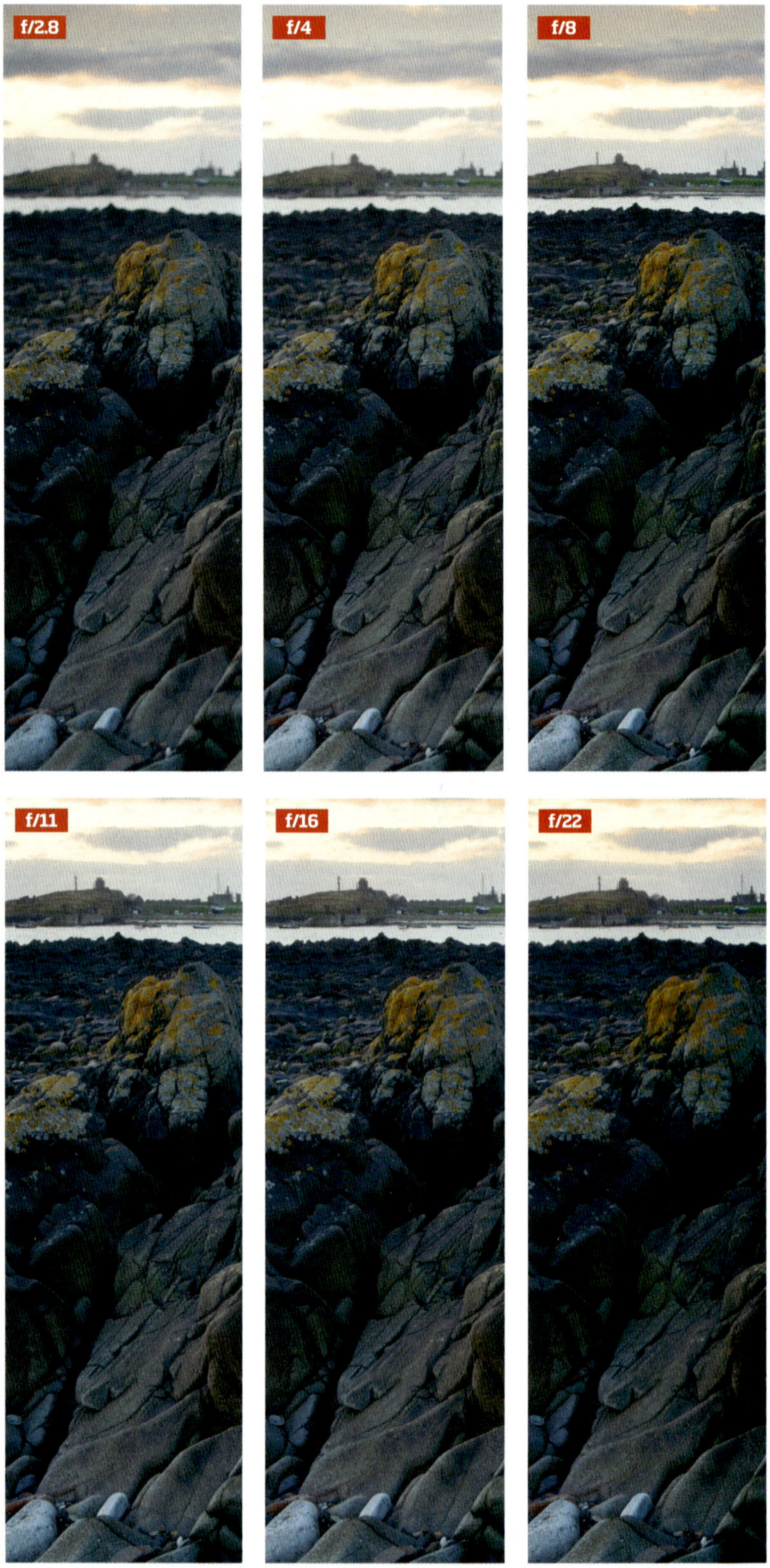

	Hyperfocal distance chart for focal lengths from 16mm to 200mm								
	16mm	20mm	24mm	28mm	35mm	50mm	70mm	100mm	200mm
f/8	1.0m	1.4m	2.0m	2.8m	4.2m	8.5m	17m	35m	140m
f/11	0.75m	1.0m	1.5m	2.0m	3.0m	6.3m	12.3m	25m	100m
f/16	0.5m	0.7m	1.0m	1.4m	2.1m	4.3m	8.5m	17.5m	70m
f/22	0.35m	0.5m	0.7m	1.0m	1.5m	3.1m	6.2m	12.5m	50m
f/32	0.25m	0.35m	0.5m	0.7m	1.0m	2.2m	4.2m	8.5m	35m

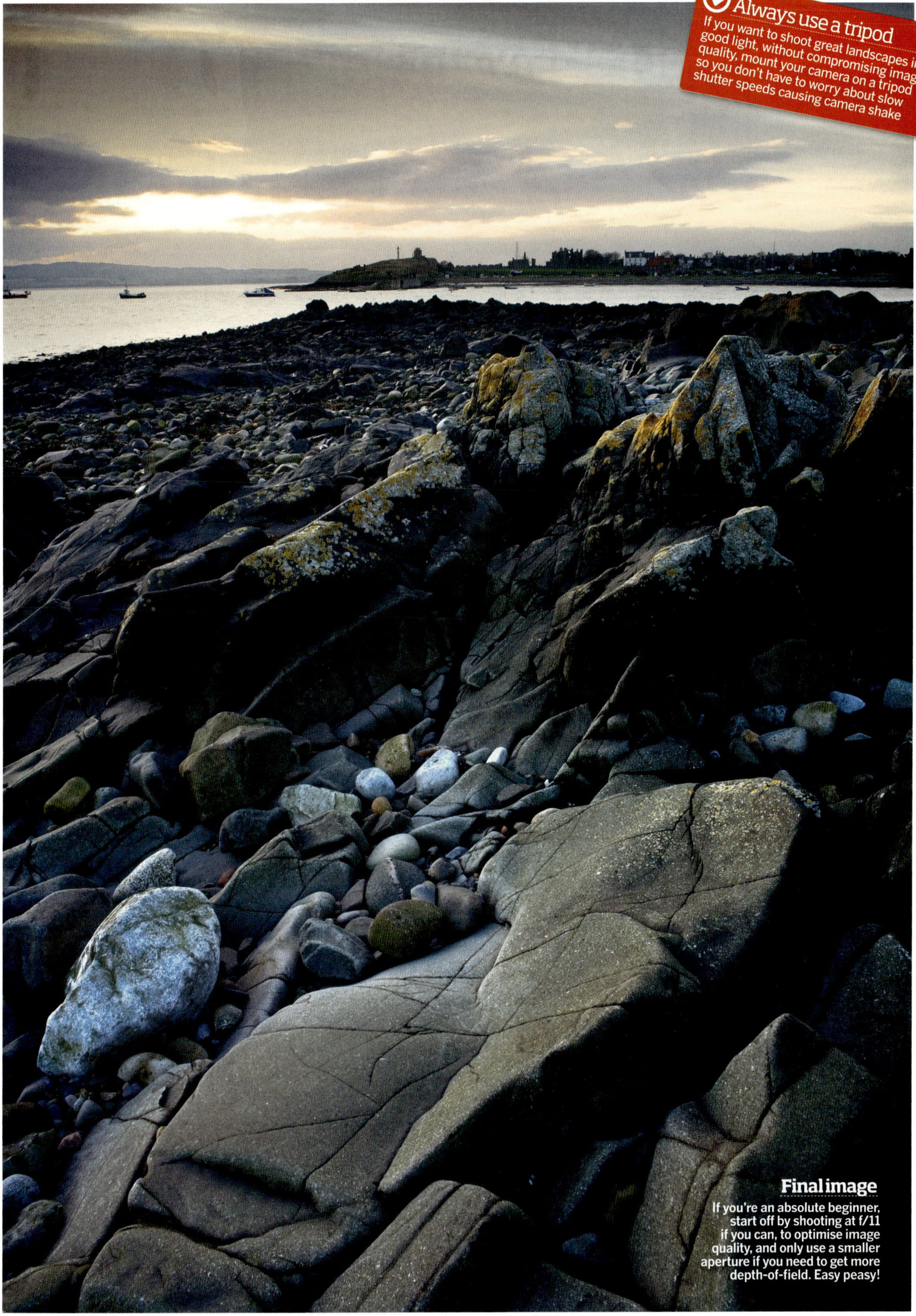

Always use a tripod

If you want to shoot great landscapes in good light, without compromising image quality, mount your camera on a tripod so you don't have to worry about slow shutter speeds causing camera shake

Final image

If you're an absolute beginner, start off by shooting at f/11 if you can, to optimise image quality, and only use a smaller aperture if you need to get more depth-of-field. Easy peasy!

Using depth-of-field in your portraits

By altering your shooting distance, being creative with how you focus and thinking about your choice of aperture, you can learn to really make your portraits stand out

THERE ARE FEW, if any, more rewarding feelings in photography than capturing a portrait that not only pleases you, but has the subject over the moon with how they look in the shot. Most people have had their picture taken, but few get the chance to have their portrait shot. There is a subtle difference between the two: one is a quick snap, with little attention given to the technical aspects of the image, except some basic composition; the other has more consideration given to how the final result should look.

It's often said that a good portrait captures a little bit of the personality of a subject, and that's true. But what it also does is record the sitter in a way that's different from other pictures that they have had taken of themselves. By using a couple of simple techniques based around depth-of-field and focusing, you can deliver really distinctive portraits, as we'll discover shortly.

The general rule for portraits is that you focus on the eyes and set a wide aperture (usually around f/5.6) to throw the background out of focus, while keeping the face sharp. This 'f/5.6 rule' is one that is used successfully by many lifestyle photographers who like to work fast, preferring to concentrate on interacting with the subject and minimise having to change settings.

If you want to include more of the environment in the scene, a smaller aperture (usually coupled with a wider lens) is required to keep the background, as well as the subject, in focus.

While ambient light is often ideal, you should also consider using a studioflash kit. As well as allowing you to control lighting direction, you can also adjust its intensity to provide the correct lighting levels to suit whichever aperture you select.

A technique that works really well is to shoot a portrait where the zone of sharpness is extremely shallow. The easiest way to do this is to follow all the 'tricks' that are required to give an image the shallowest depth-of-field possible, using a telezoom set to its maximum aperture and at a relatively short subject distance. The result of this is a tight crop of the face where, bar a small focused area, much of the frame is thrown out of focus. The result is a very 'soft' image that, with some thought given to lighting, can look romantic if lit by diffused light, or more arty and striking if strong directional light is used. When using this technique, be sure to focus on the appropriate part of the face, usually an eye, but also try the mouth, too. It's certainly worth giving it a go with a friend or family member and seeing how you get on.

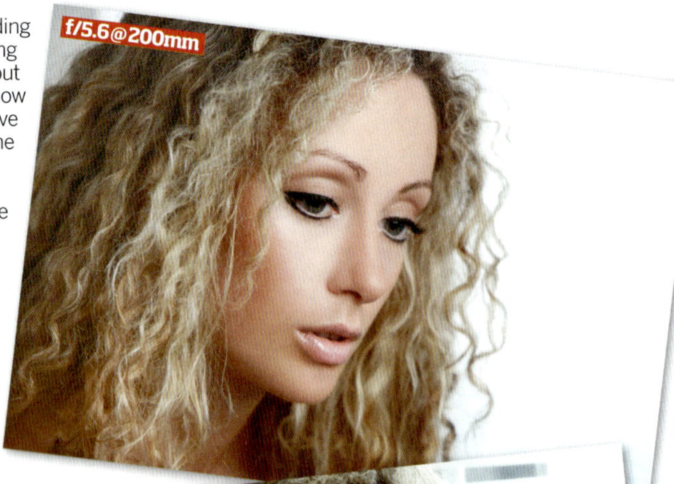

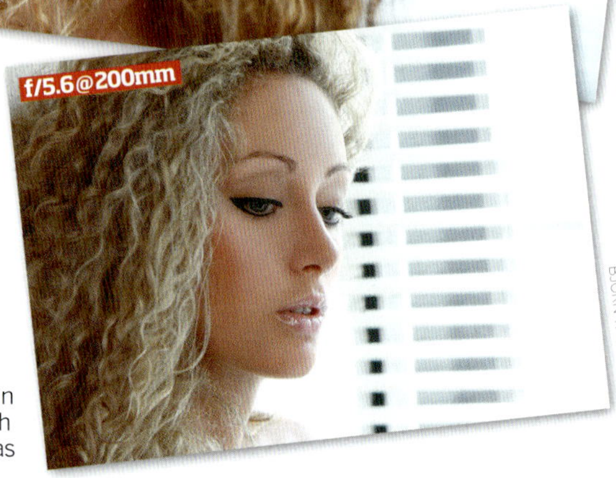

BJORN THOMASSEN

SHOOTING DISTANCE
Both shots were taken using the same lens and aperture, but depth-of-field was altered by changing the shooting distance. The shorter distance gives less depth-of-field, which blurs the window blinds.

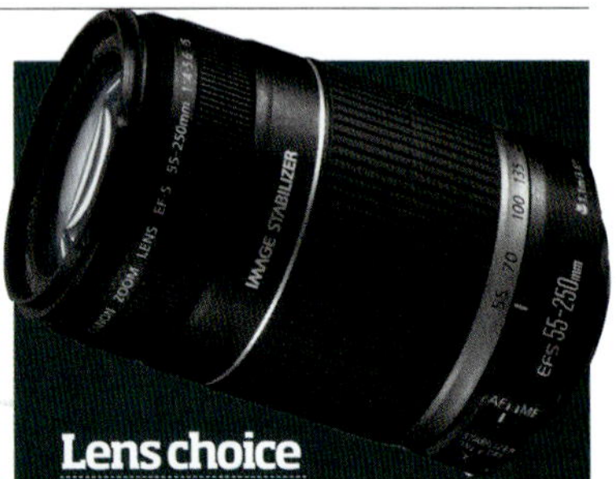

Lens choice

You can use most lenses for portraits, from the tele-end of an 18-55mm kit lens to telezooms like a 55-200mm. Using a longer focal length provides a more flattering perspective than using a wide-angle and also produces a shallower depth-of-field, making it ideal for eye-catching portraits.

Portraits checklist

1) SHOOT HAND-HELD It will mean you can move around and frame quickly or, better still, use a monopod. Using the maximum aperture provides the fastest possible shutter speed, but if it's still low, use the image stabiliser if your camera or lens has it and/or raise the ISO rating.

2) CHECK YOUR DISTANCE At very wide apertures, you have to be careful not to move forward or backward after focusing, as this can lead to unsharp results.

3) EYE CONTACT Ensure that the subject's eyes are clean and that make-up has been carefully applied. Try some shots with the subject looking into the lens and others with them looking away.

4) USE THE SHADOWS Pay attention to lighting and how shadows fall across the face – use them to add mood to the image.

5) CONSIDER MONO It's always worth converting portraits to black & white and seeing how they compare to colour images.

Differential focusing

Another popular technique when using shallow depth-of-field is differential focusing. It's simple to master, but the secret is to know when to use it. The principle of the technique is to use a very wide aperture to emphasise a particular subject within the frame, by having it pin-sharp while the rest of the scene is thrown out of focus. It's particularly effective when there is a lot of depth in the scene and an aperture is used that blurs unwanted elements in the frame, while remaining sharp enough to be recognisable. Use it to pick out a particular person in a crowd or to produce a creative portrait with a story to tell.

HIDE & SEEK: These images illustrate how differential focus can have a major effect on the result. The same exposure was used in both shots, but the focus was changed to reveal different elements in the scene.

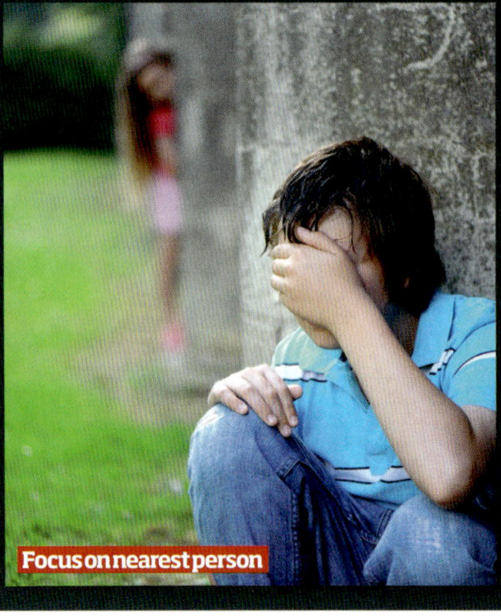

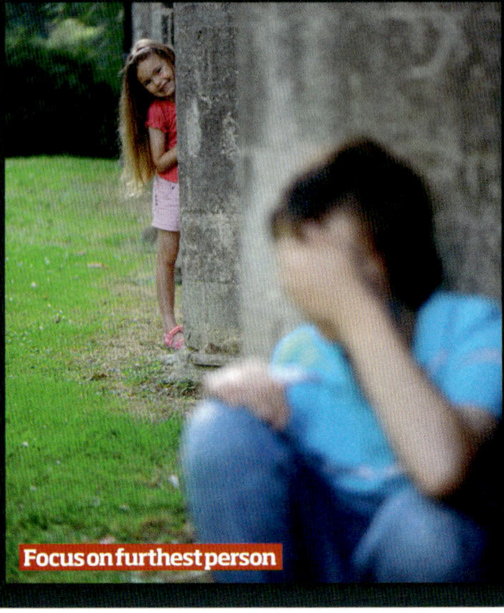

DANIEL LEZANO

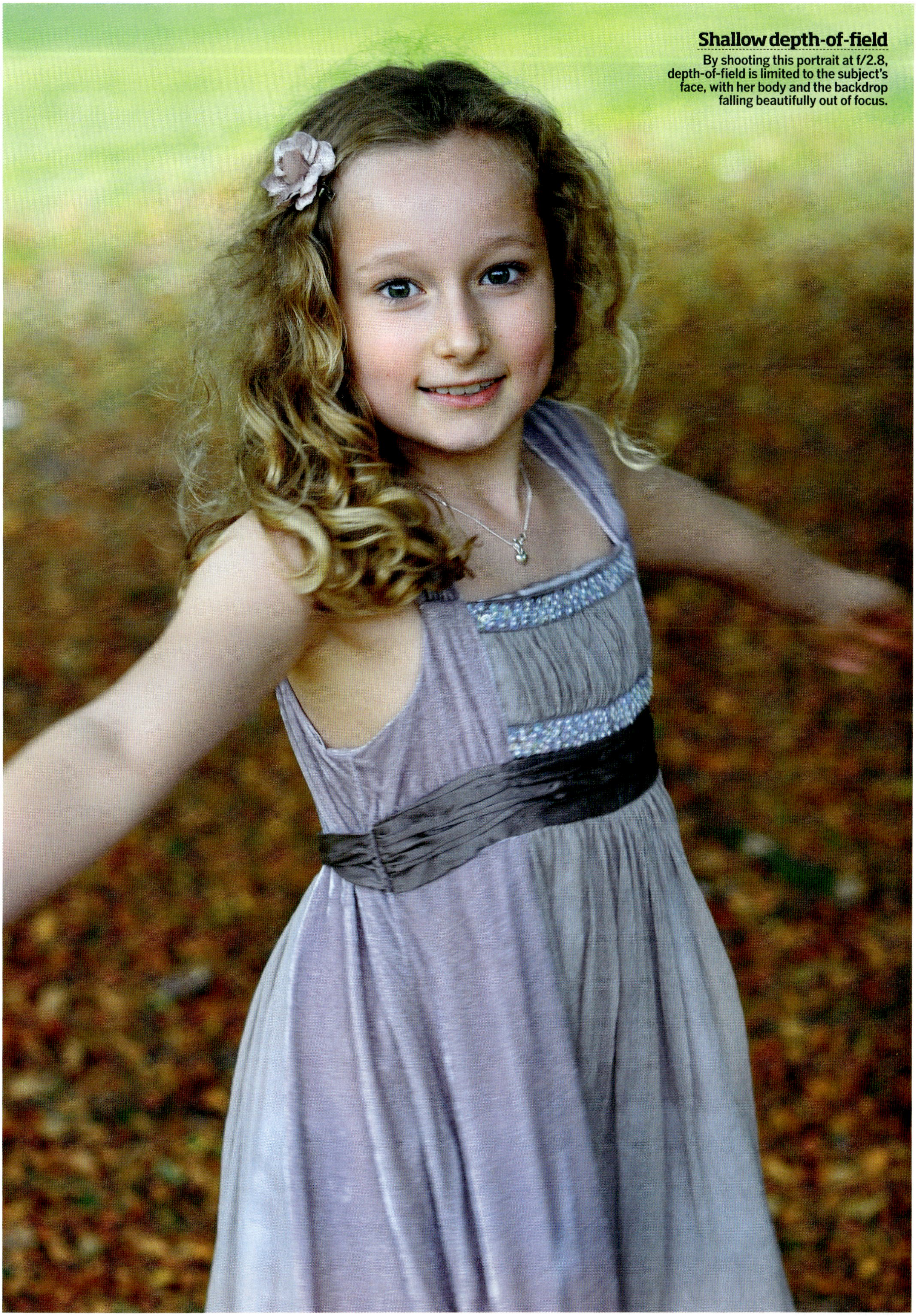

Shallow depth-of-field

By shooting this portrait at f/2.8, depth-of-field is limited to the subject's face, with her body and the backdrop falling beautifully out of focus.

DANIEL LEZANO

Control depth-of-field in close-ups

By reducing the distance between subject and camera, you increase the impact created by limited depth-of-field. Here, we give you a few key tips to better control

DEPTH-OF-FIELD is one of the most important creative elements of close-up photography. The lack of distance between the subject and the camera's sensor means the area that appears sharp will be very limited. Depending on how you set your shot up, it could be just mere millimetres, even when using a small aperture! For this reason, macro photography requires very accurate focusing; even being fractionally off with your focus could result in an unusable result. A good knowledge of apertures is the single most important factor, as the f/number you choose will have the greatest influence on the amount of depth-of-field in your image. But macro photography brings with it its own unique challenges and rules.

One notable difference between macro and other types of photography is how depth-of-field is evenly distributed in front of and behind the point of focus. In other words, the amount of the scene that appears to be sharp will be equal both in front of and behind the point of focus. In other areas of photography, the distribution is $\frac{1}{3}$ in front and $\frac{2}{3}$ behind the point of focus.

It is important to have an idea of how much depth-of-field best suits your subject. For arty, abstract close-ups, or shots in which you only want one specific point to appear in focus, such as petals on a flower, shallow depth-of-field is best, keeping only a small part of a petal or stamen in focus. For this, you would use the widest aperture available on your lens. If, however, you were shooting an insect, such as a dragonfly, and wanted to keep the whole subject sharp, you would use a small aperture, such as f/22.

The aperture is not the only way that you can influence depth-of-field: the position of your DSLR or CSC's sensor is also crucial. The focal plane runs parallel to the sensor, so if you want to keep your subject sharp, your subject must be square-on to the camera. By rotating or tilting the camera (and sensor plane) you can reduce depth-of-field further, as the subject will move out of the focused area quicker. (To line up, use the back of your camera or the ⊖ symbol on the top-plate as a guide, as it is parallel with the sensor!) Finally, the other way to have a major effect on depth-of-field is by using selective focus, as described below.

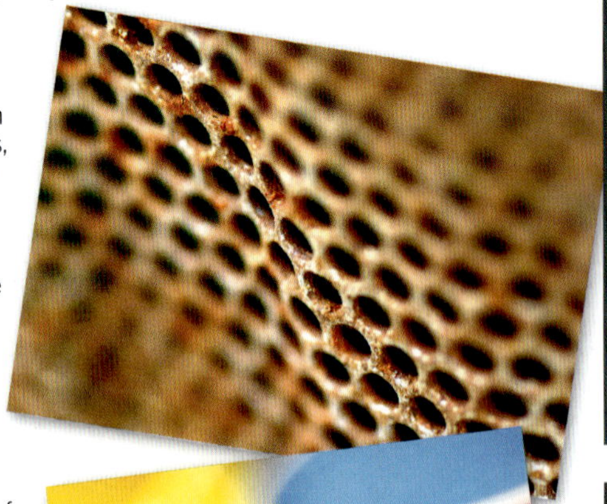

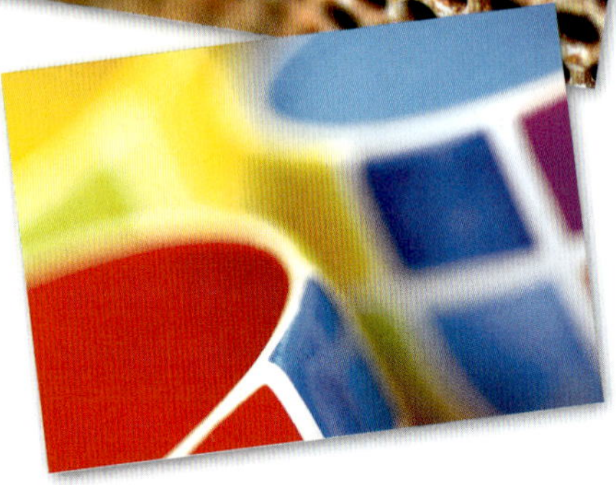

ABOVE: These shots show how the depth-of-field can be very limited when shooting at close range with a macro lens.

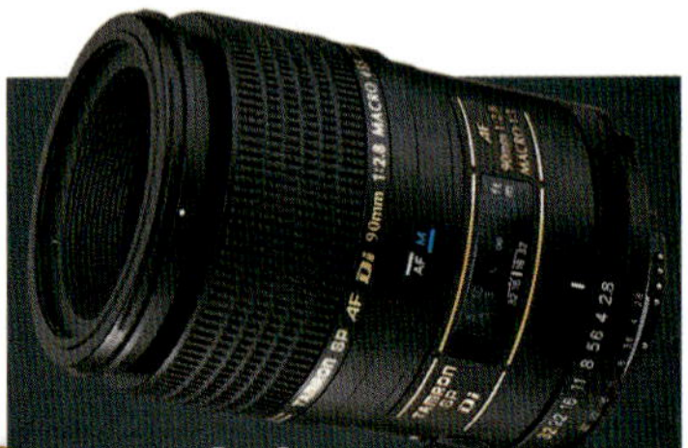

Lens choice

Macro lenses are ideal for close-up work, as they allow you to get really close to your subject, giving you a huge amount of creative control over depth-of-field. If you don't want to splash out on a macro lens, you can pick up extension tubes or close-up filters to convert your standard zoom for close-up photography.

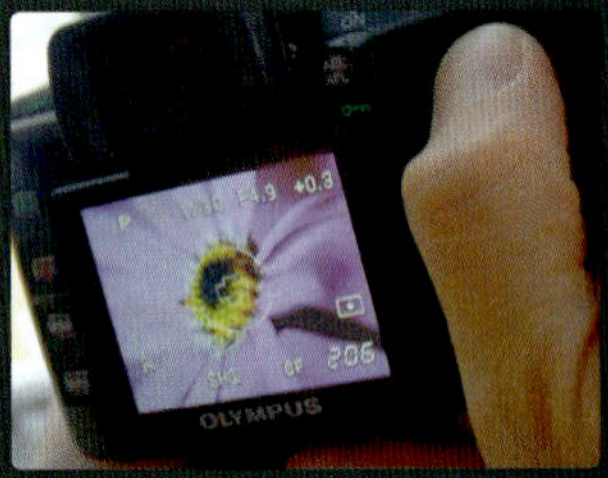

Using LiveView

Canon's LiveView system allows you to adjust the aperture setting and observe in 'real time' the changes that this has on depth-of-field, allowing you to choose your favourite setting!

Selective focusing

In close-up photography, the depth-of-field is so shallow that any slight adjustment to the focus has a huge effect on the result. This is furthered by the fact that, unlike other areas of photography, depth-of-field falls evenly both in front of and behind the focal plane. Many macro enthusiasts prefer to use manual focus; the precision of having full control of the point of focus. This can be quicker than having the lens 'hunt' during AF, so don't be afraid of switching your lens to manual focus and having a go.

FOCAL POINT These shots illustrate the dramatic difference that a slight adjustment in focus can make to a close-up shot. The closer you are to your subject, the more impact these adjustments will make.

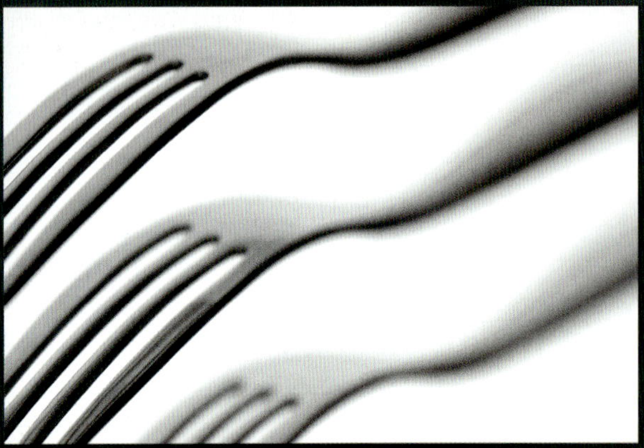

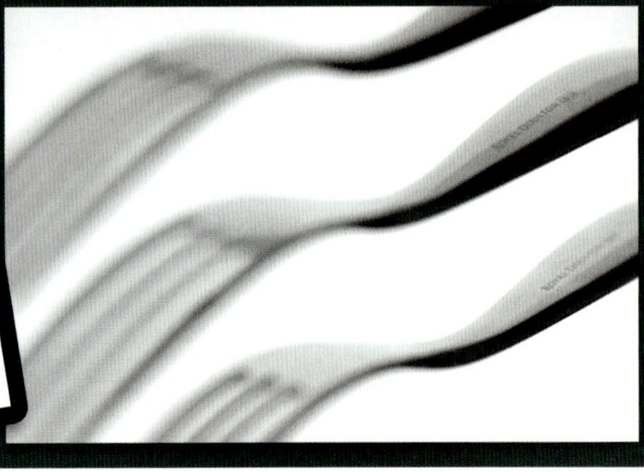

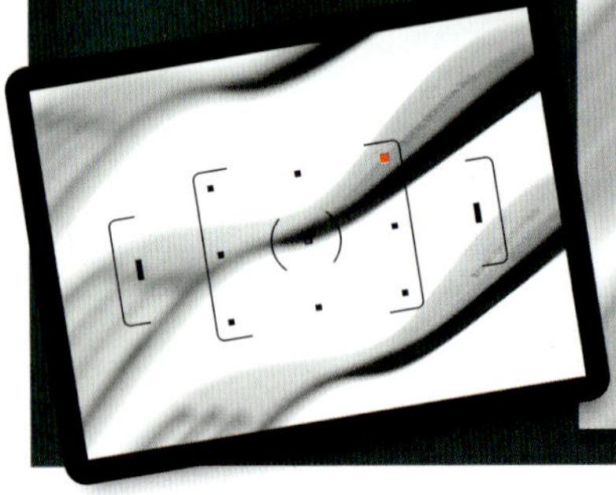

Close-up checklist

1) USE A STURDY TRIPOD It will eliminate camera shake when using small apertures and aid focus, as when hand-holding the camera, you'll find any slight body movements will throw your subject out of focus.

2) FOCUS ACCURATELY! It is essential that you get the focus right. When depth-of-field is this limited, anything that is not on the point of focus may appear unsharp. Manual focus is quite often the quickest and best option to use.

3) USE MIRROR LOCK-UP (DSLRS) To prevent blur caused by the mirror moving as the shutter is triggered, try locking the mirror and using the self-timer. A remote release is useful, too.

4) CHECK YOUR FOCUS The depth-of-field preview button is useful, but with short exposures, it can often be easier to simply take a test shot and review it on your LCD. And let's not forget the benefit of using LiveView, too.

5) CHANGE YOUR DISTANCE The depth-of-field depends greatly on your distance from the subject. Try shooting from further away to increase depth-of-field and closer up to reduce it.

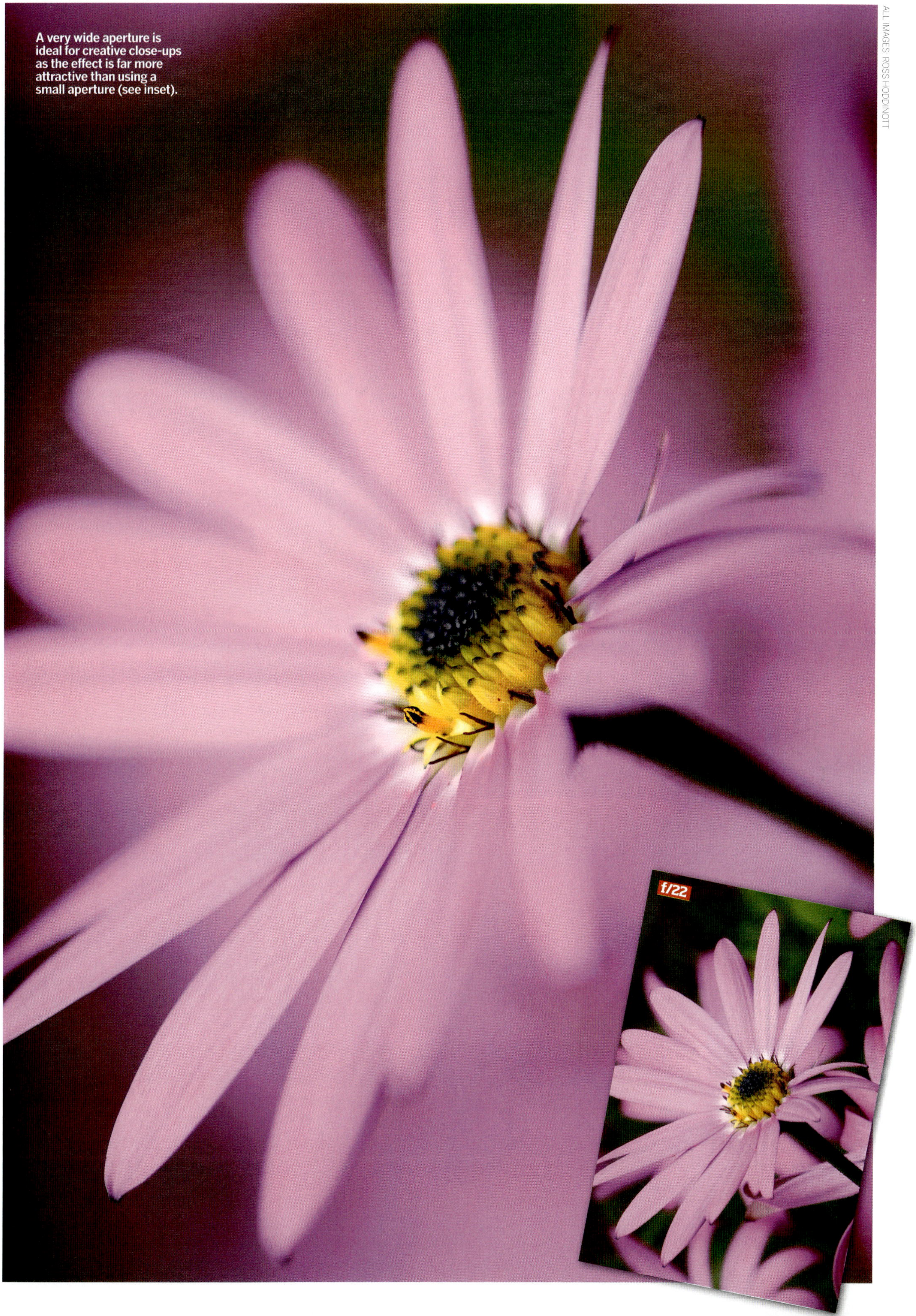

A very wide aperture is ideal for creative close-ups as the effect is far more attractive than using a small aperture (see inset).

ALL IMAGES: ROSS HODDINOTT

The basic principles of shutter speeds

So, what are shutter speeds? How are they controlled and what do they do? Read on for the answers to these and other shutter speed-related queries

WHAT ARE SHUTTER SPEEDS?

The shutter speed is the precisely-calibrated length of time that a camera's shutter remains open to enable the correct amount of light to pass through the lens to expose the sensor. The majority of images taken require speeds of just a fraction of a second, although shutter times can potentially run to seconds, minutes or, in the case of some specialised forms of photography, even hours. The shutter speed dictates how motion is recorded. A fast shutter speed will freeze subject movement – perfectly suspending action and recording fine detail. Setting a slow shutter will blur movement – helping to create a visual feeling of motion and energy.

Digital SLRs and CSCs have a wide range of shutter speeds, typically from 30 seconds to speeds of, or exceeding, a staggeringly fast 1/4000sec. Most DSLRs and CSCs also have a 'Bulb' setting, which allows the shutter to be opened for as long as you depress the shutter release button.

HOW ARE THEY CONTROLLED AND WHAT DO THEY DO?

Combined with any given lens aperture, the shutter speed is designed to allow sufficient light to reach the image sensor to produce a correctly exposed image. If the shutter speed is too fast, insufficient light will reach the sensor, so the resulting shot will be too dark, ie underexposed. In contrast, if the shutter speed is too slow, too much light will strike the sensor, resulting in an image that is too bright, ie overexposed.

If you are using your camera in one of its automated exposure modes, the shutter speed – along with the corresponding aperture – will be set automatically. While this is the easiest option, it doesn't give you any control over the way your subject is recorded. After all, while your camera may be highly sophisticated, it is not able to predict the effect you want to achieve. Therefore, if you haven't already, it is time to grasp control of your camera by selecting shutter-priority (S or Tv) mode.

Shutter-priority is a semi-automatic mode that allows you to manually select the shutter speed, while the camera sets a corresponding f/stop to achieve the correct exposure. Therefore, it really isn't as complex or daunting as you might imagine and there are no tricky calculations to make. Instead, this mode allows you to concentrate on selecting a shutter speed that will suit the subject you are about to photograph. This choice will greatly dictate the look of your final shot, influencing the appearance of the subject's motion… as we will discover over the following pages.

Choosing filters

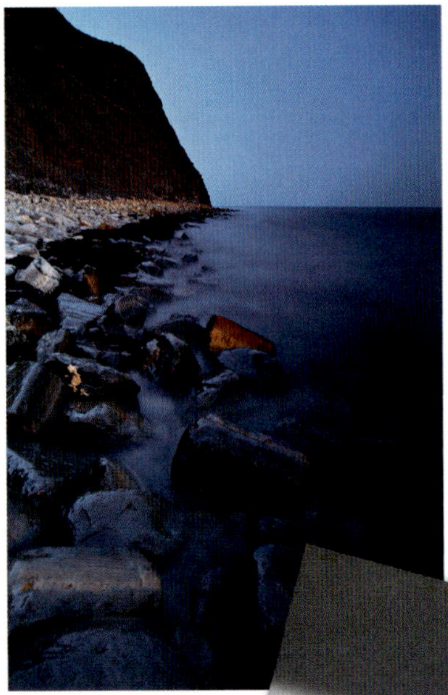

MARK BAUER

If shooting long exposures in low light, there will often be quite a difference in brightness between the foreground which, after the sun sets, will have no direct light on it, and the sky, which will be lit from below. A Graduated Neutral Density filter will ensure that this contrast stays within the dynamic range of your camera's sensor. If shooting along the coast, with cliffs to one side, angle the grad so that it doesn't cut into the cliffs too much. Another useful filter is the polariser. Not only will it reduce the glare off any wet foreground rocks, but it will cut out up to two stops of light (exactly how much depends on how much polarisation you use), enabling you to extend exposure times.

Setting shutter speeds on your DSLR or CSC

Controlling shutter speeds on your camera couldn't be easier; it is simply a matter of selecting shutter-priority mode and rotating a dial!

CANON EOS DSLRS

(1) Set the main control dial on the right-hand side of the top-plate to Tv to select shutter-priority mode

(2) Turning the input dial just behind the shutter button allows you to select the shutter speed value

(3) You can see the shutter speed setting by looking at the information display on the rear LCD monitor or the information panel in the viewfinder display

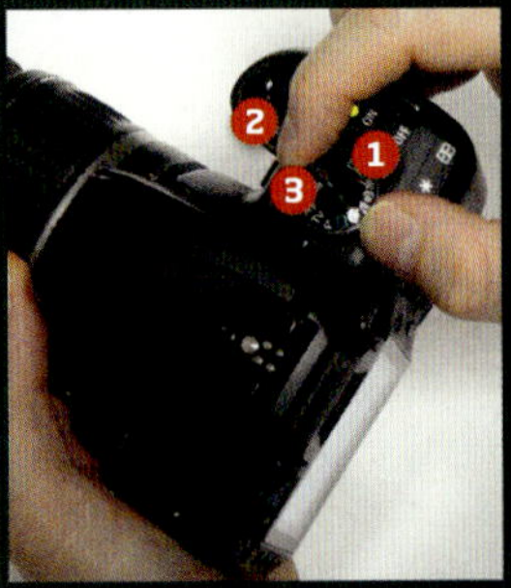

NIKON DSLRS

(1) Set the main control dial on the left-hand side of the top-plate to S to select shutter-priority mode

(2) Turning the input dial on the front of the handgrip allows you to select the shutter speed value

(3) You can see the shutter speed setting by looking at the top-plate LCD panel or the information panel in the viewfinder display

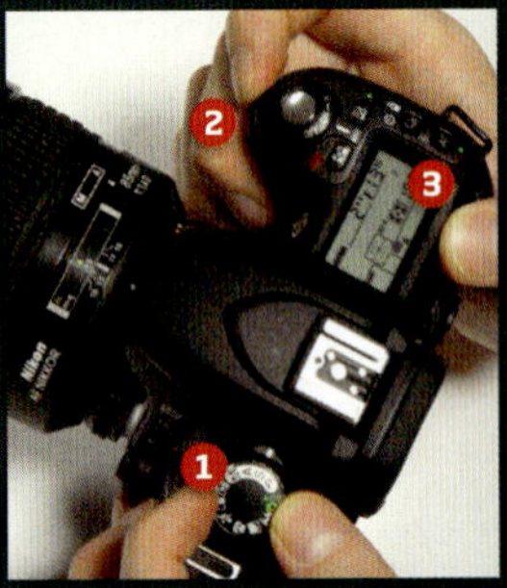

PENTAX K-SERIES DSLRS

(1) Set the main control dial on the left-hand side of the top-plate to Tv to select shutter-priority mode

(2) Turning the input dial on the rear of the camera with your right thumb allows you to select the shutter speed

(3) You can see the shutter speed setting by looking at the top-plate LCD panel or the information panel in the viewfinder display

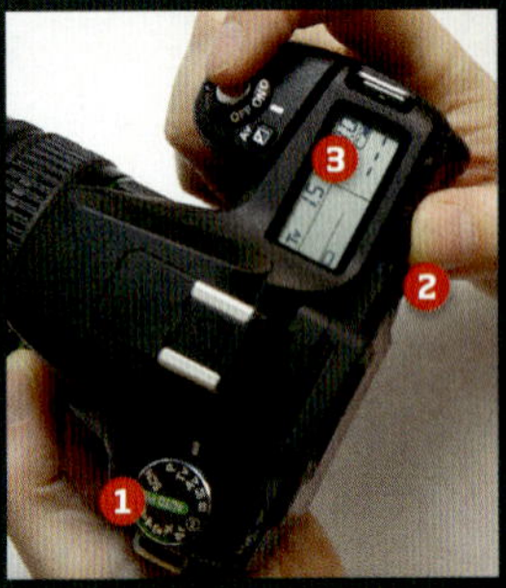

SONY ALPHA DSLRS

(1) Set the main control dial on the right-hand side of the top-plate to S to select shutter-priority mode

(2) Turning the input dial on the top of the handgrip just in front of the shutter button allows you to select the shutter speed value

(3) You can see the shutter speed by looking at the rear LCD monitor or the information panel in the viewfinder display

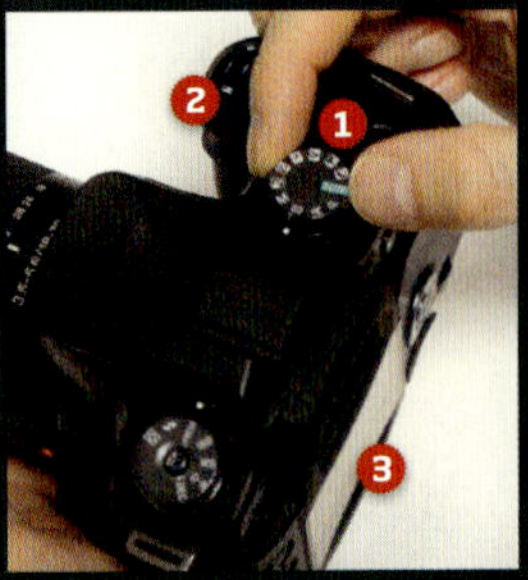

MOST COMPACT SYSTEM CAMERAS

Very few CSCs sport the exposure mode dial found on the majority of digital SLRs. However, it's still very easy to select the exposure mode. With most models all you need to do is press the Menu button or the four-way control dial to display a choice of exposure modes and rotate the wheel to S to select shutter-priority mode. With touchscreen models, simply press the S icon on the screen.

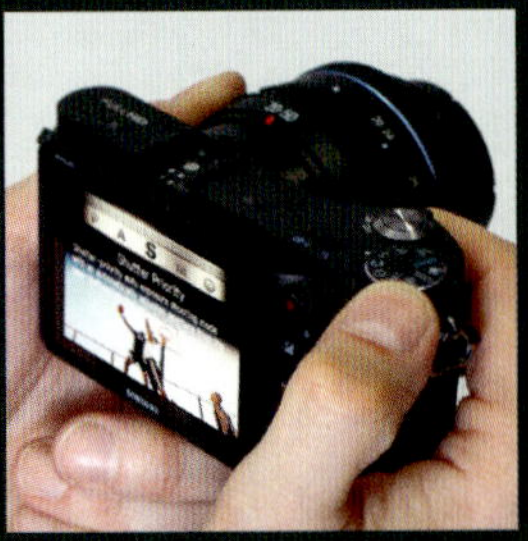

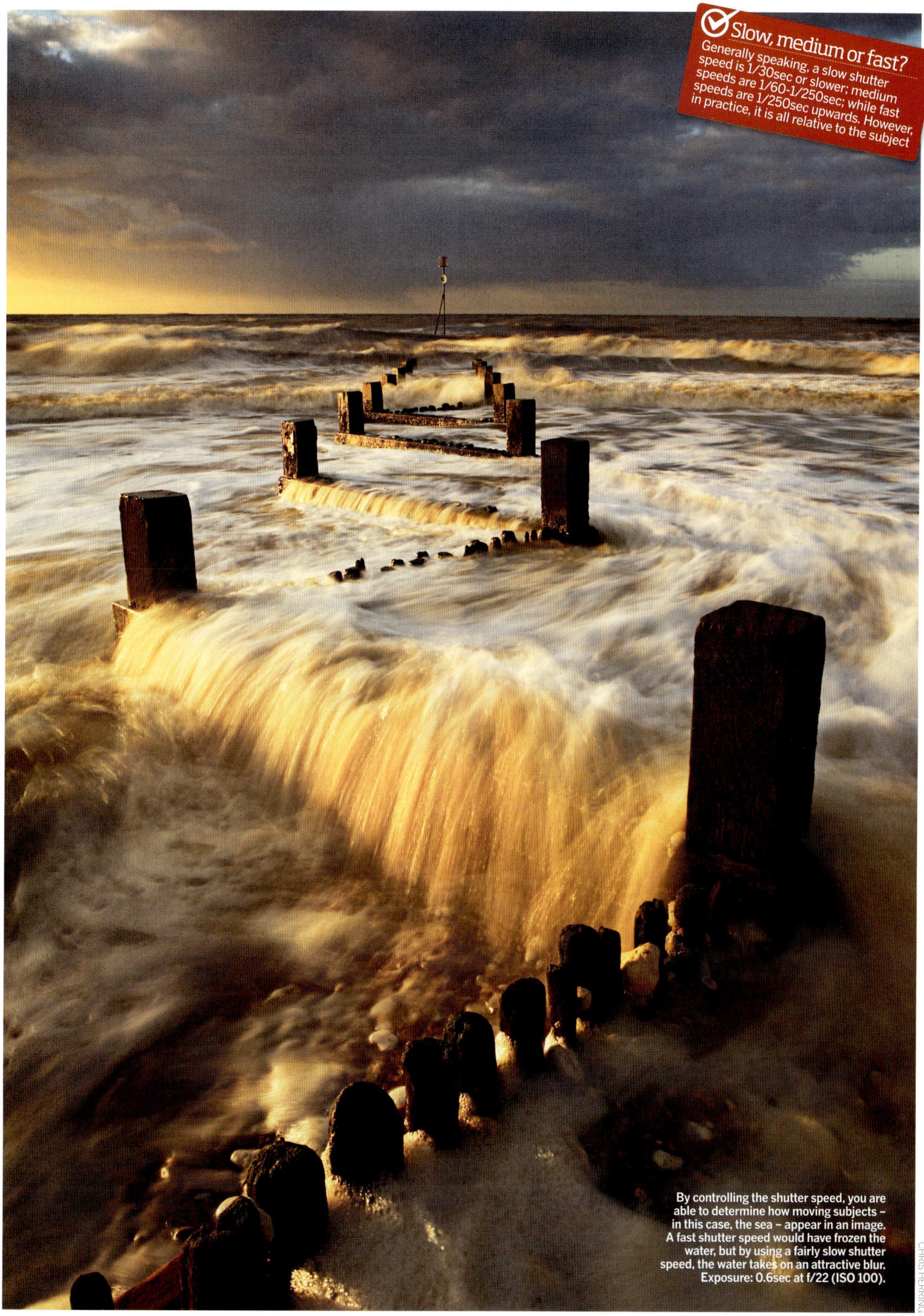

Slow, medium or fast?

Generally speaking, a slow shutter speed is 1/30sec or slower; medium speeds are 1/60-1/250sec; while fast speeds are 1/250sec upwards. However, in practice, it is all relative to the subject

By controlling the shutter speed, you are able to determine how moving subjects – in this case, the sea – appear in an image. A fast shutter speed would have frozen the water, but by using a fairly slow shutter speed, the water takes on an attractive blur. Exposure: 0.6sec at f/22 (ISO 100).

CHRIS HERRING

Shutter speeds & exposure

You've made a positive step by selecting your camera's shutter-priority exposure mode; but before you can begin setting shutter speeds with confidence, you must understand the effect it has on your exposure

EXPOSURE IS INFLUENCED by three variables: shutter speed, lens aperture and ISO sensitivity. The camera will not alter the ISO sensitivity in shutter-priority mode (S or Tv) – only you can do this, by adjusting it manually. However, the f/stop will alter, depending on the shutter speed you select. This is because shutter speeds and apertures have a reciprocal relationship – if you increase one, there must be an equal and opposite adjustment in the other to maintain the correct exposure.

To help you to understand this relationship, grab your camera, switch it to shutter-priority mode, and adjust the shutter speed by rotating the input or command dial. You will notice how the f/number changes in response to the shutter speed you select. This simple exercise will help you to appreciate the way exposure works. For example, if you set a fast shutter speed, the aperture will be larger (a low f/number, such as f/4, will be selected) to allow more light to pass through; if you select a slow shutter speed, the aperture will be smaller, so you will have a higher f/stop, such as f/16, which will restrict the light reaching the sensor.

The maximum and minimum shutter speeds you can select will be strongly dependent on ambient light. Too much or too little can limit your options, meaning that you will have to adapt or compromise. This guide will serve you as a starting block and give you a basic understanding of shutter speeds, how the exposure of your shots will be affected by them and how to overcome any difficulties you might encounter. It is not as daunting as it sounds, so be brave and give it a go! Here, we've included some advice about coping when faced with extreme lighting conditions.

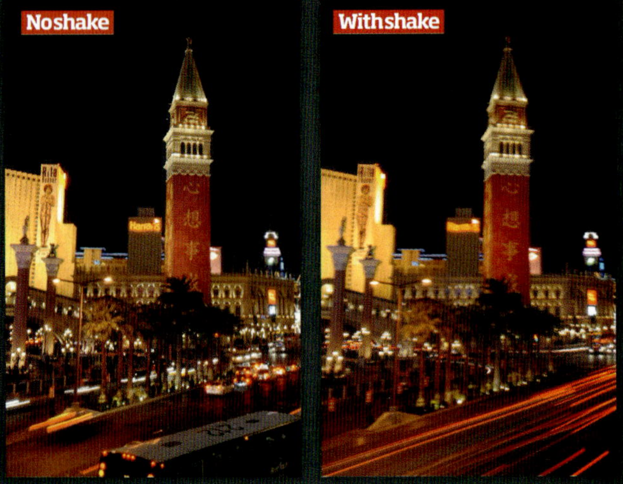

Avoiding camera shake

There are several ways to prevent camera shake from ruining your shots when a tripod isn't available. Using a fast shutter speed is the most traditional – make sure that the shutter speed matches the focal length of your lens, so if you are using a 300mm lens, make sure the shutter speed is at least 1/300sec, and so on (image stabilisation also helps with this!). Increasing the ISO rating and using wide apertures help with setting faster shutter speeds.

ISTOCK PHOTOS

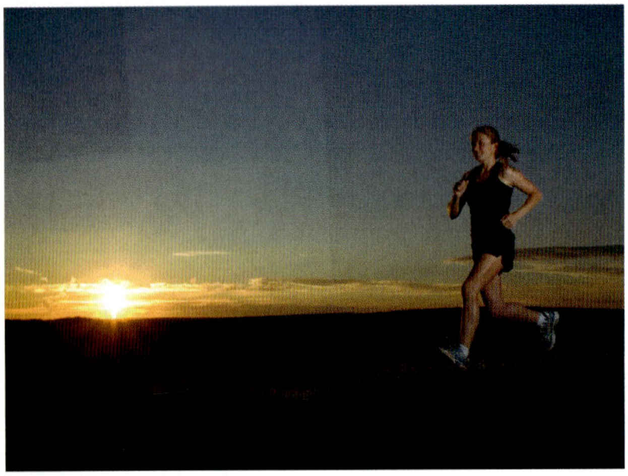

Not enough light

Whether you are shooting indoors or out, low light levels can present problems for photographers. Shutter speeds grow longer in response to the dull conditions and, if you are shooting hand-held, the risk of camera shake is greatly increased – particularly at speeds of 1/60sec and longer. So what is the solution?

You might presume that the best thing to do is select the fastest shutter speed that the light levels will allow, but this is not always the best option. By doing so, you are also effectively setting the largest aperture (smallest f/number) – remember they have a reciprocal relationship. This will result in a very shallow depth-of-field that may not be sufficient to record enough of your subject in acceptable focus. Therefore, it is often better to use a tripod to support your set-up instead, as this will allow you to employ longer shutter speeds to create a greater depth-of-field, while also eliminating the risk of shake.

However, if the subject isn't static and you wish to freeze its movement – or you have to shoot hand-held – you will indeed need to prioritise a fast shutter. Therefore, opt for the fastest shutter speed available to you. If this still isn't quick enough to freeze movement, select a higher ISO sensitivity of 400 or above. Doing so will generate a faster shutter speed – although noise will increase as a result. Alternatively, use a burst of flash (above) to provide more light.

ISTOCK PHOTOS

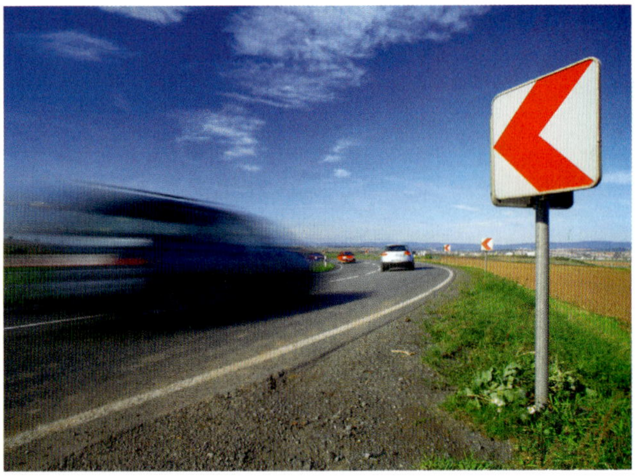

Too much light

In bright light, shutter times will be fast. Many entry-level DSLRs and CSCs have a maximum shutter speed of 1/4000sec; while more advanced models are up to 1/8000sec. To be honest, it is very unlikely you will ever need to use this speed and – unless you are using your camera at a high ISO rating of 800 or above on a very sunny day – it is rare to reach these speeds in everyday photography.

In bright conditions, photographers have more options. You can select a fast shutter speed while also enjoying a wide depth-of-field, due to the corresponding aperture being smaller than if there were less light. This is extremely useful when you wish to shoot rapid action, such as in sports and wildlife, which require a fast shutter to freeze movement. However, believe it or not, it is possible to have too much light, such as when you wish to blur a subject's movement to create a sense of motion. This isn't possible using a fast shutter speed, so you will want to reduce shutter time. In shutter-priority mode, it is quick and easy to select the slowest shutter speed available by rotating the input dial. Also, ensure the lowest ISO rating is selected – typically 100 or 200. If shutter time is still too fast to create the effect you desire, you will need to reduce the light entering the lens. The best way to do this is by using something called a Neutral Density filter, which restricts the light passing through it.

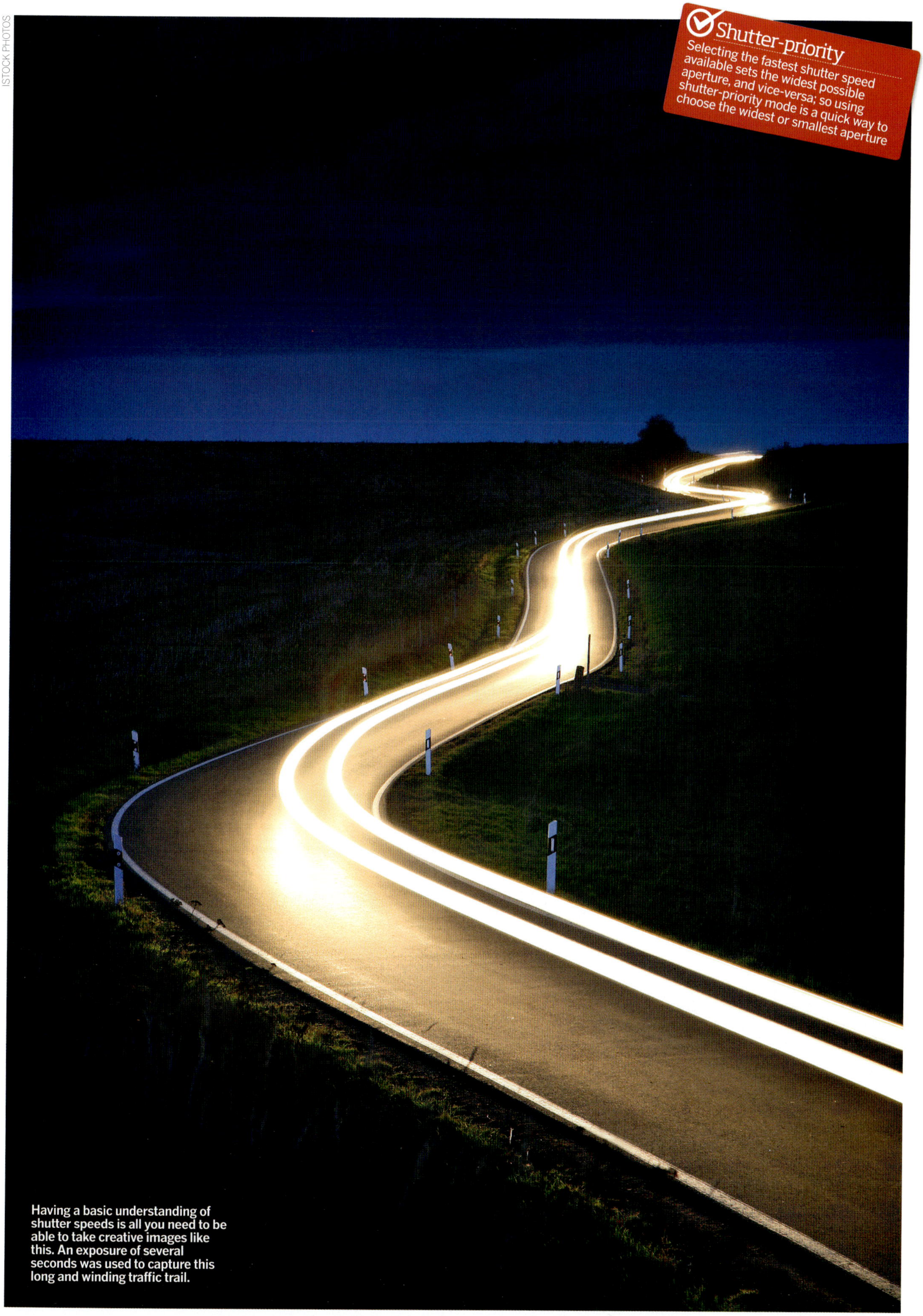

Shutter-priority
Selecting the fastest shutter speed available sets the widest possible aperture, and vice-versa; so using shutter-priority mode is a quick way to choose the widest or smallest aperture

Having a basic understanding of shutter speeds is all you need to be able to take creative images like this. An exposure of several seconds was used to capture this long and winding traffic trail.

Using fast shutter speeds

As we have already seen, shutter times play a crucial role in the making of an image. Varying the shutter speed/aperture equation can greatly affect the way the subject is recorded – particularly moving subjects

WHEN SHOOTING POPULAR subjects such as sports, action, birds and mammals, photographers will often want to suspend movement mid-action, freezing it in sharp detail. To capture this sort of image successfully, your exposure will require a fast shutter speed.

You'll find that the speed required will be relative to the subject's movement (speed and direction will each have an effect), and also the focal length of the lens being used. For example, a man running parallel with the viewfinder will be moving more slowly across the frame than, say, a travelling car. Therefore, the slowest shutter speed needed to 'freeze' the runner will be slower than that for the vehicle, but faster than if the man were simply walking. If the runner is jogging directly toward you, they will be crossing less of the sensor plane and therefore will require a slower minimum shutter speed to be rendered sharper than if they were running parallel across the frame. In other words, you need a faster shutter speed if the subject moves across the frame than if moving towards/away from you.

Using a longer focal length or a telephoto lens means that the subject fills more of the image space, and therefore moves faster within the frame than it would if you were using a shorter focal length or wide-angle lens.

The minimum shutter speed required to freeze subject movement will be greatly dictated by the factors mentioned above, so there is no hard and fast rule regarding the speed you must select. A degree of trial and error is often required to achieve the correct speed. However, in practice, a good starting point is to set a shutter speed of 1/500-1/1000sec. A speed in this region normally proves sufficient to suspend the motion of most moving subjects.

ISTOCKPHOTO

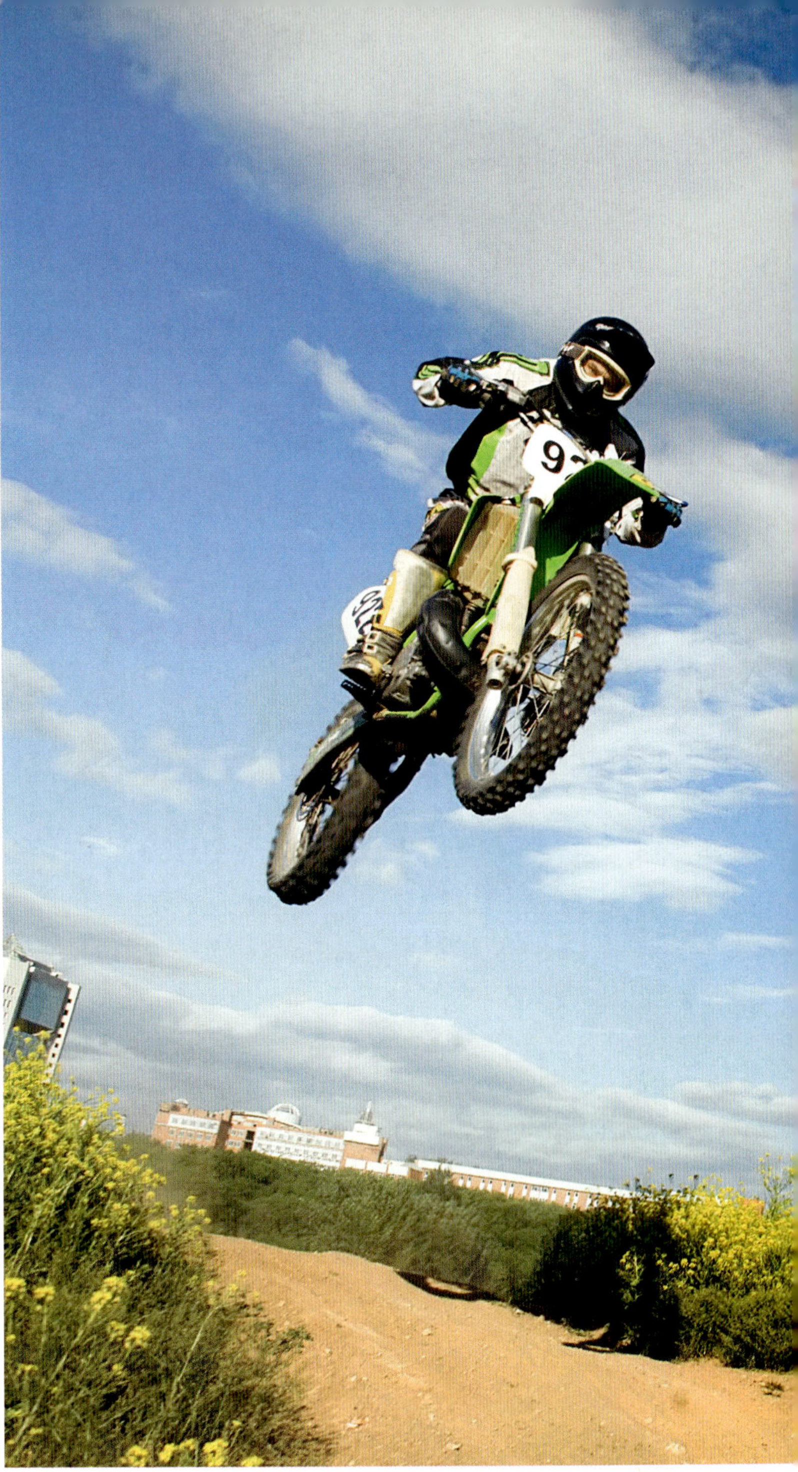

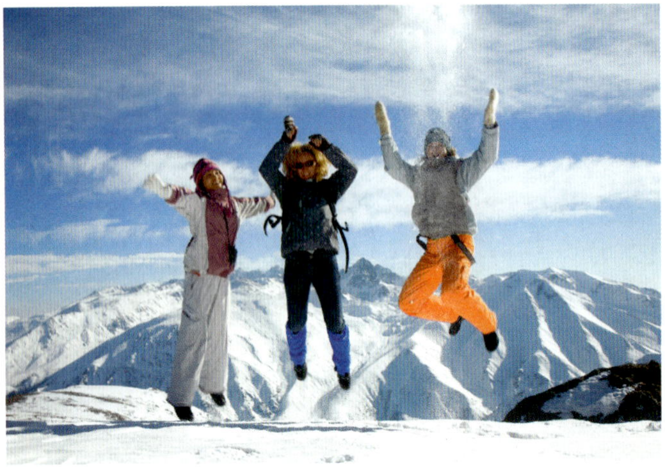

To capture a moment, such as those above and right, it is important to set a fast shutter speed to keep the subjects sharp. Using continuous shooting mode will also increase your chances of getting the best possible result.

Shutter speeds for moving subjects

This quick-reference table provides a starting point for which shutter speeds to try when shooting a number of different types of moving subjects. Try these to begin with, then experiment with other speeds, and study how different the subject appears when it has been captured with slower or faster settings.

Subject	Recommended shutter speeds	
	Subject moving towards camera	Subject moving across frame
Jogger	1/125-1/200sec	1/250-1/500sec
Sprinter	**1/250-1/500sec**	**1/250-1/500sec**
Car (30mph)	1/250-1/500sec	1/250-1/500sec
Car (70mph)	**1/250-1/500sec**	**1/500-1/1000sec**
Cyclist	1/200-1/250sec	1/250-1/500sec
Galloping horse	**1/250-1/500sec**	**1/500-1/1000sec**
Fast motorsports	1/500-1/750sec	1/1000-1/2000sec

How to go faster!

Here are two easy ways to set up your camera to give you the fast shutter speeds that freeze moving subjects.

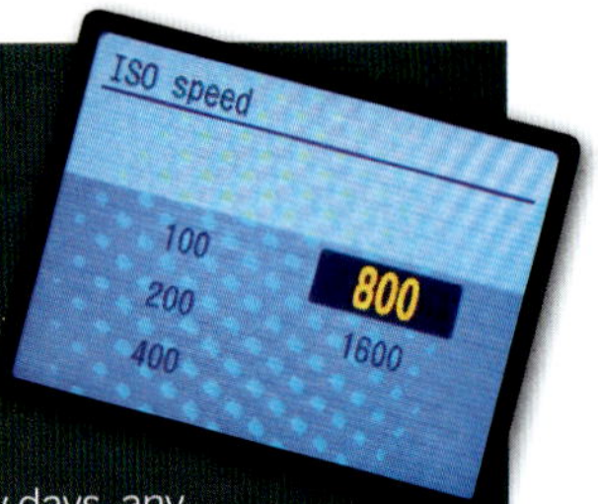

✔ **HIGH ISO** Increase the ISO rating to enable you to set faster shutter speeds: it's the equivalent of using a faster film on a 35mm SLR. In the early days, any ISO over 400 would have been too noisy for most uses, but on today's cameras, ISO 800 or even 1000 is okay to try.

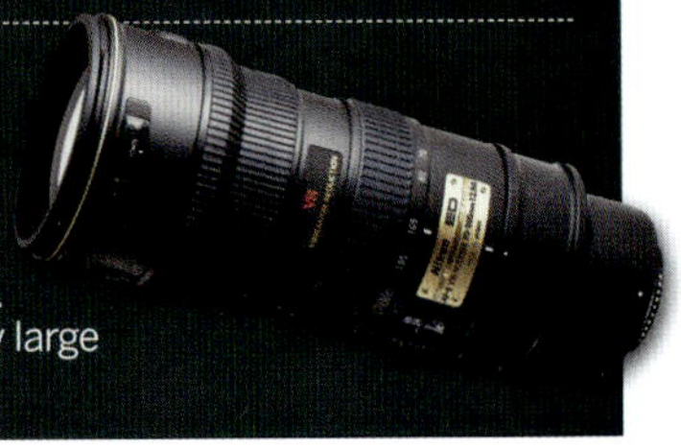

✔ **FAST LENSES** The term 'fast lens' is used to refer to lenses with a wider than average aperture. Because these allow more light through, you're able to select a faster shutter speed. Unfortunately, they're relatively large and heavy, and very expensive!

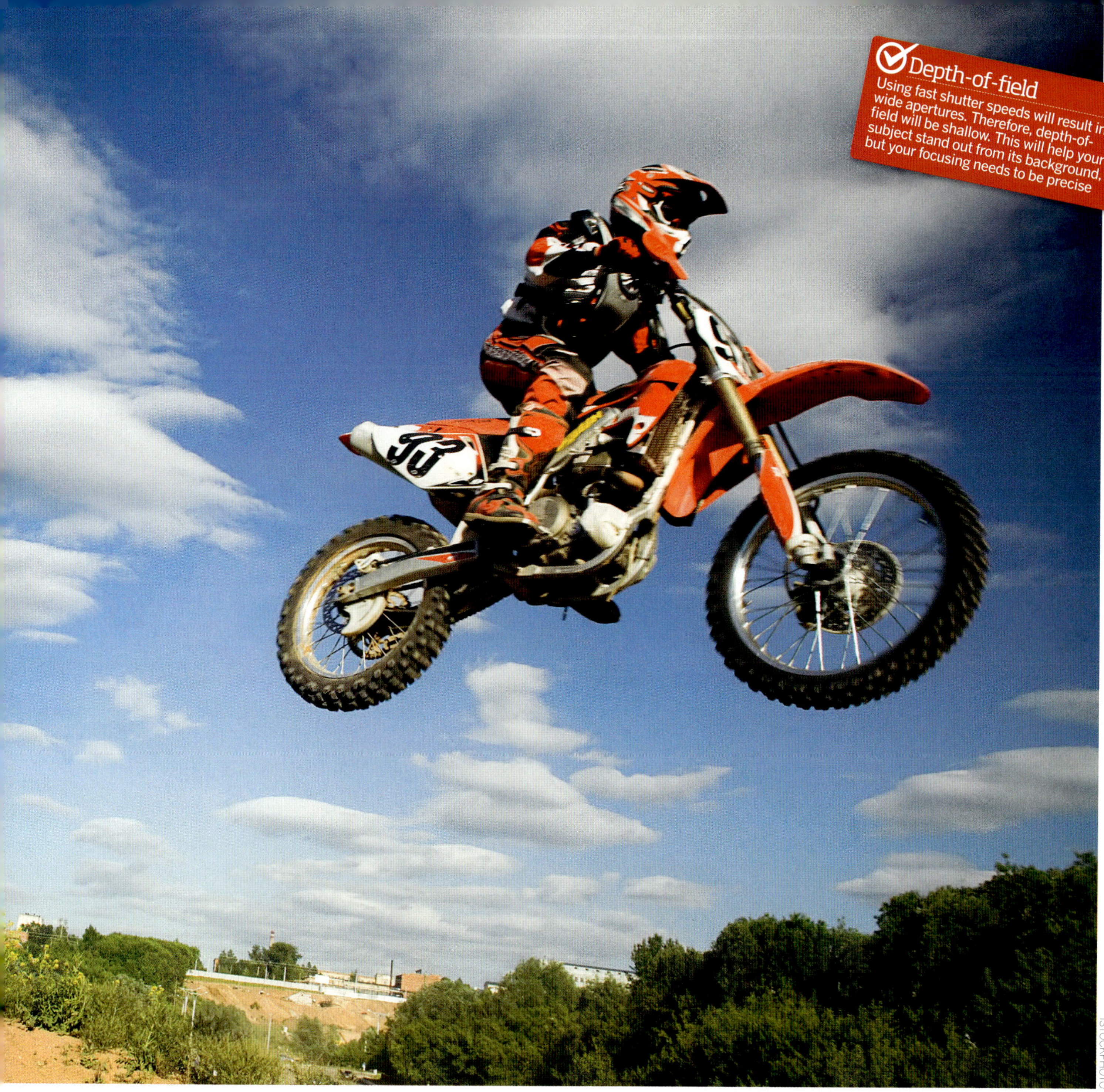

ISTOCKPHOTO

Depth-of-field

Using fast shutter speeds will result in wide apertures. Therefore, depth-of-field will be shallow. This will help your subject stand out from its background, but your focusing needs to be precise

Shutter speeds in landscapes

When shooting landscapes, you will sometimes have to decide between a long or short exposure. A fast shutter speed can freeze motion, while a longer exposure might be used to include plants in the foreground, blowing in the breeze, or to create a 'silky' effect in running water. With fast-moving subjects, a 'long' exposure might be anything slower than 1/250sec, so you should shoot a series of exposures at various shutter speeds and use the LCD monitor to review the results.

The shots on the right illustrate the effect that shutter speeds can have on a landscape shot. With moving subjects, shutter speeds can make a big difference.

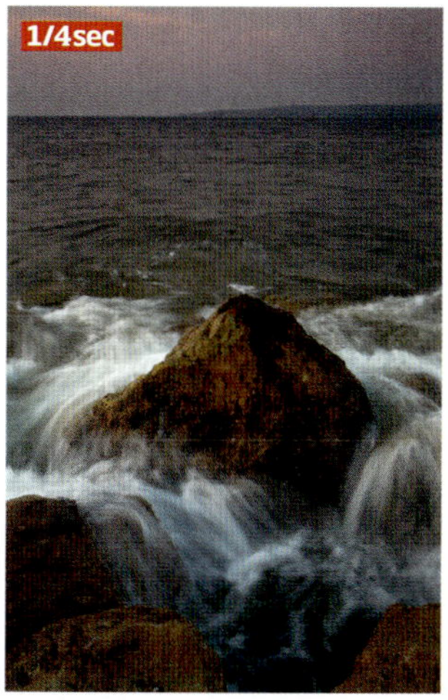

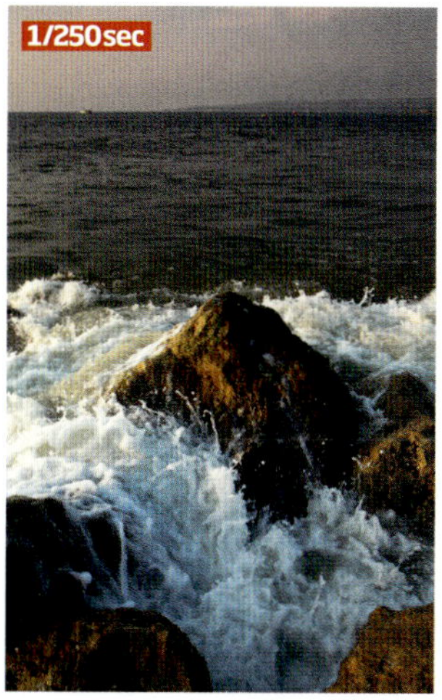

MARK BAUER

Summary: Fast shutter speeds

USE A FAST SHUTTER SPEED WHEN...

- ✔ You want to freeze the subject's movement
- ✔ **When you want to keep the corresponding aperture large to minimise depth-of-field**
- ✔ You are shooting hand-held and want to eliminate the risk of camera shake
- ✔ **You are shooting in very bright conditions, to avoid any risk of overexposure**

Using movement in landscapes

Ross Hoddinott has a closer look at how to get the best from slow shutter speeds

DO YOU EVER feel that your landscape images sometimes appear static and lifeless? It is a common complaint, but one that is easily remedied by taking creative control over exposure. While landscape photographers are often taught to prioritise front-to-back image sharpness, as we have mentioned before, a degree of subject blur within the scene can prove a powerful visual tool. It can create a genuine sense of motion that, when combined with a suitable scene, can be very attractive. Landscapes are probably one of the best subjects to use if you want to experiment with, and explore, the potential of slow shutter speeds. The range of material to shoot is endless and the wind can enhance any movement you try to capture. So, instead of attempting to freeze the movement of a crop of golden barley, swaying buttercups or wind-blown trees, why not go to the opposite extreme and shoot to capture their movement? The results can be stunning. However, creating just the right effect can be tricky. Too much motion, and detail can grow indistinguishable; too little, and it will not look intentional. It is a fine balancing act. There are no set rules regarding the shutter speed you should select; it will vary depending on the landscape, the strength of the wind and the effect you wish to achieve. Experimentation is important. Bracket exposures by one-stop increments and check images on your LCD monitor to help discover the best effect.

Use a polariser

If you don't own a Neutral Density filter, then use a polariser instead. While not all polarising filters are totally neutral, they have a 'filter factor' of two stops – equivalent to a 0.6ND. Therefore, they can be used as a makeshift ND with the added benefit that reflective glare will also be reduced. This will saturate colour and give your shot more impact.

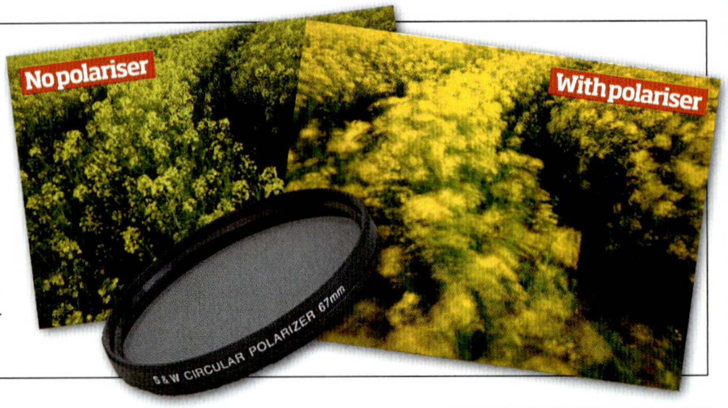

Noise Reduction (NR)

Noise – randomly-spaced, coloured pixels – is more obvious in images captured using a long exposure. It is for this reason that the majority of cameras are designed with a long exposure Noise Reduction (NR) facility. This can normally be accessed via one of the camera's set-up menus and is designed for when shutter speeds exceed four seconds. When switched on, images will be processed in-camera to reduce the image-degrading effects of noise. Although continuous burst speed, and the number of images that can be stored in the camera's buffer, will be reduced as a result, NR is a handy feature to use with very long exposures.

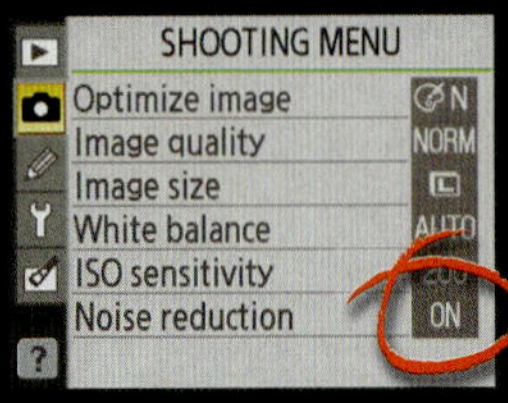

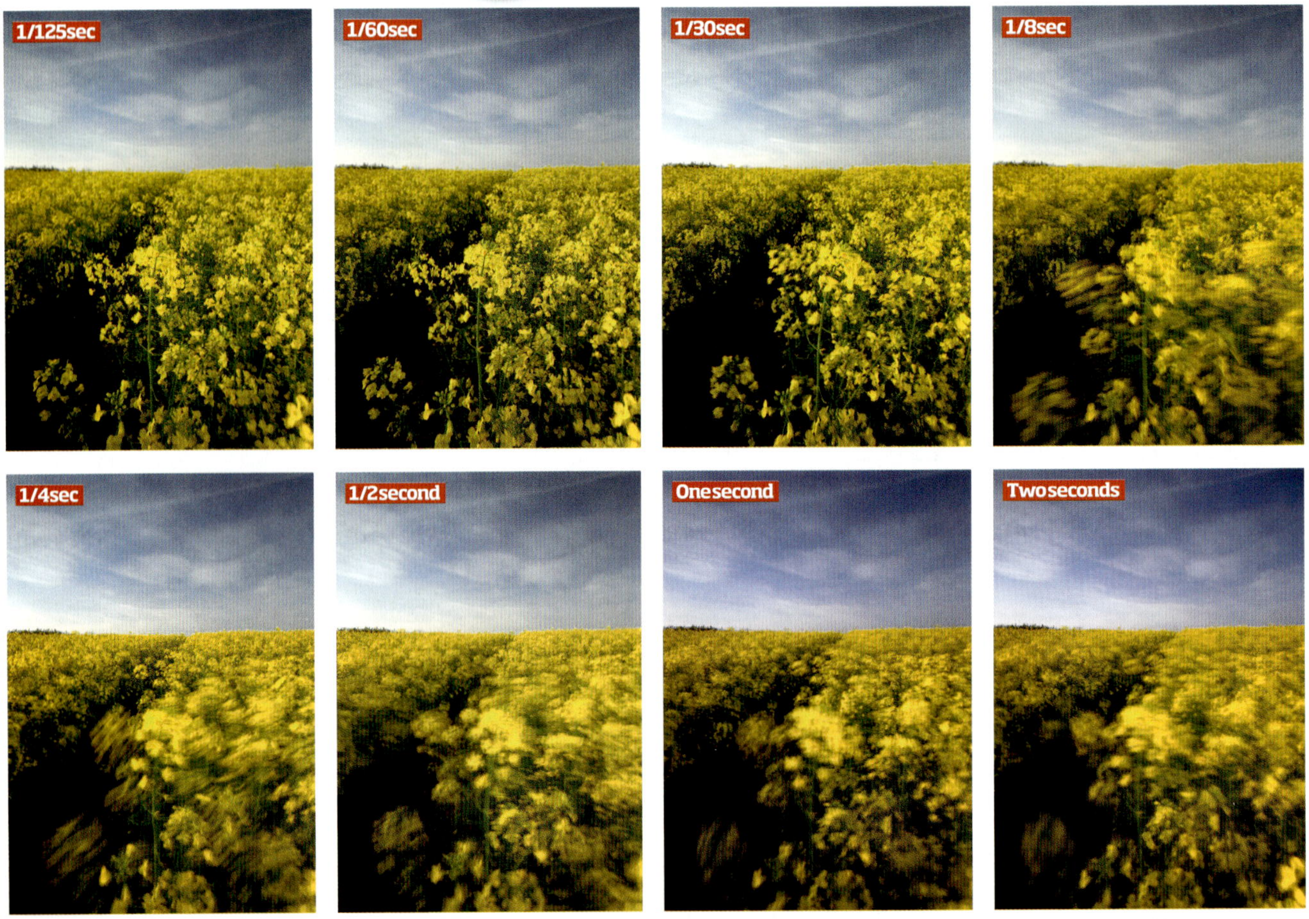

ABOVE & OPPOSITE: This field of oilseed rape made a bright and colourful landscape. I composed my shot and then took a sequence of images employing progressively longer shutter speeds. The first image, shot at 1/250sec, has perfectly frozen the movement of the flowers in the summer breeze. Subsequent images, at 1/125sec and 1/60sec, look very similar. However, once exposure time lengthens beyond 1/30sec, subject movement grows increasingly noticeable and at shutter speeds of one second and more, the flowers are rendered as a yellow haze. While the effect isn't unpleasant, in this instance, I prefer the result achieved using a shutter speed of ½ second.

It's not heavy!

Most tripods are made to be lightweight, so they can move slightly during long exposures. Try hanging your gadget bag off your tripod for extra stability and use a remote to trigger the shutter release

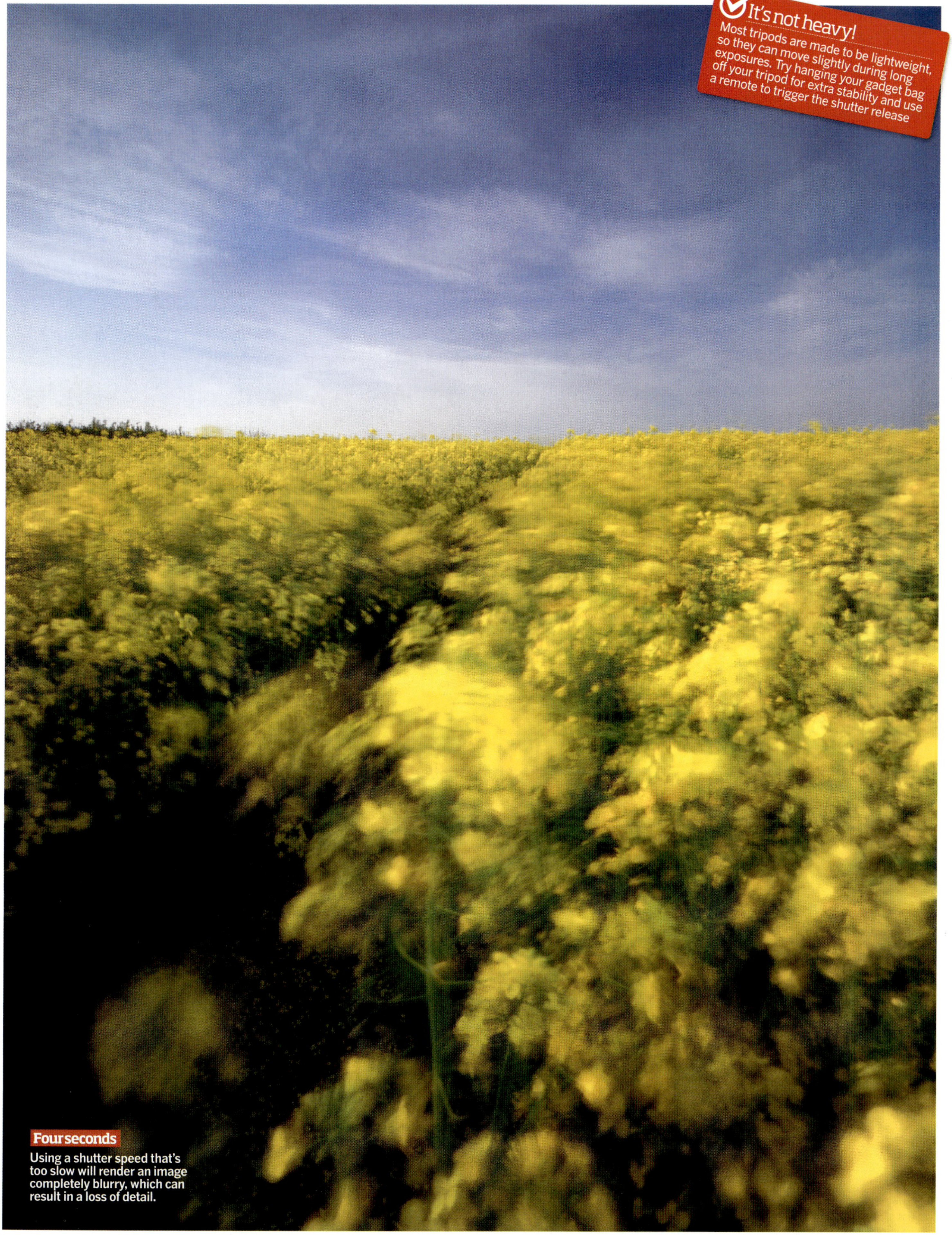

Four seconds

Using a shutter speed that's too slow will render an image completely blurry, which can result in a loss of detail.

Traffic trails in low light

Professional photographer Paul Ward explains how to avoid getting yourself in a jam while shooting traffic trails in an urban scene

One of the most stunning techniques on which to practise your low-light photography skills is the capturing of traffic trails. Not only are there an abundance of vehicles on the road, but on dark evenings from late autumn through to springtime, you can venture out just after *EastEnders* to give this technique a go, rather than waiting until the dead of night.

Images of traffic trails work by combining a long shutter speed with the fast-moving lights caused by cars passing through the frame. Because of the low light and long exposure, the cars are invisible, leaving only the streaks of their headlights in the shot. The technique requires the smallest amount of kit, which makes it even more appealing. All you need is a DSLR or CSC and a tripod, although a remote release will make the process a lot easier.

Ready to give this technique a go, I grabbed my gear and headed out into the dark, taking a position on an overpass of a busy Birmingham road. I recommend always arriving at your location at least ten minutes before the sun goes down so you can take your time and find the best angle to shoot from, and also to take advantage of the sky's blue tint that's visible directly after the sun goes down.

Because you're shooting at night, it's worth remembering a few important safety precautions. Always have permission to photograph if you are snapping from privately owned land. Remember to be as discreet as possible – you don't want to advertise that expensive camera body to thieves. Finally, because you will be shooting in the vicinity of moving traffic – it may be an obvious one to consider – be aware of the cars around you. It may be a wise decision to wear a fluorescent bib, which can be bought from cycling shops such as Halfords.

White Balance

If you shoot in Raw, you can alter the White Balance when you upload your images on to your computer. However, if you want to try different White Balances while taking your shot, there are a couple of ways this can be achieved. Either take a test shot, changing the WB in the menu as you go, or switch to LiveView and use the LCD monitor to judge how the White Balance presets affect your image. We cover WB in more detail on p46.

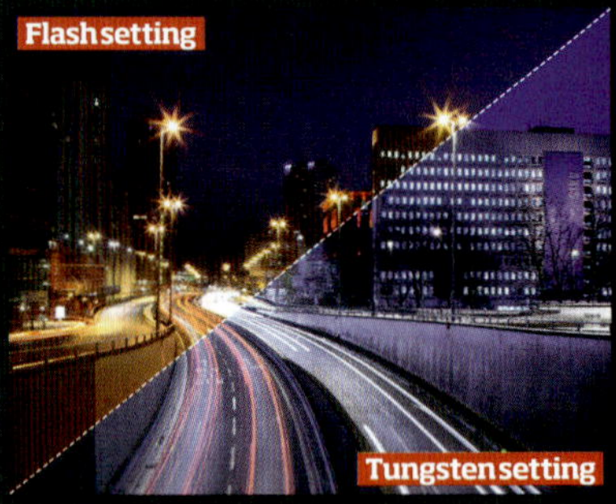

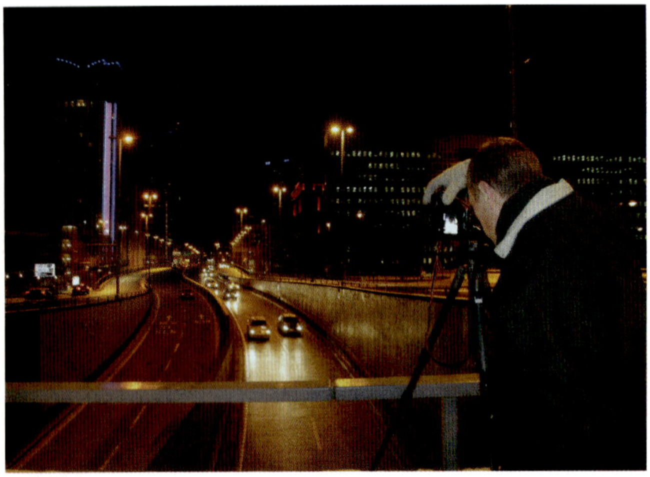

Step 1 I set up my tripod to take a few quick test shots at a high ISO, to see how the angles and lights look, before returning the ISO to 100 and placing the camera on the tripod. I choose to shoot the image in portrait format to emphasise the long winding streaks caused by the headlights, and also to include the tall buildings bordering the road.

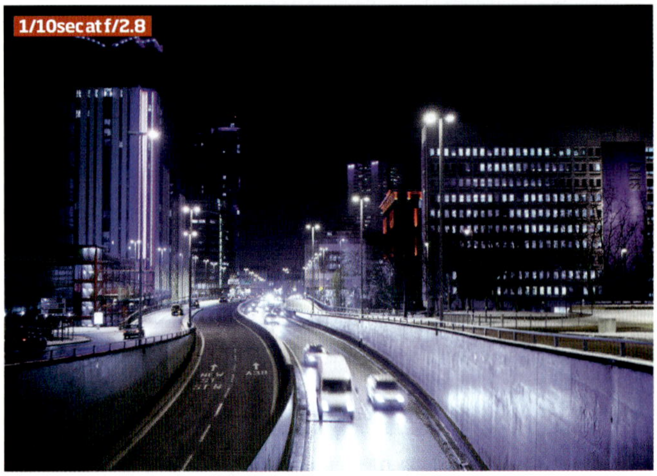

Step 2 I set the camera mode to manual. You can use aperture-priority mode, but the streetlights can trick the camera's metering system. My exposure of 1/10sec at f/2.8 (ISO 100) isn't long enough to create any traffic trails. Also, the wide aperture makes the streetlights look bland – using a smaller aperture will give the lights a pleasant starburst effect.

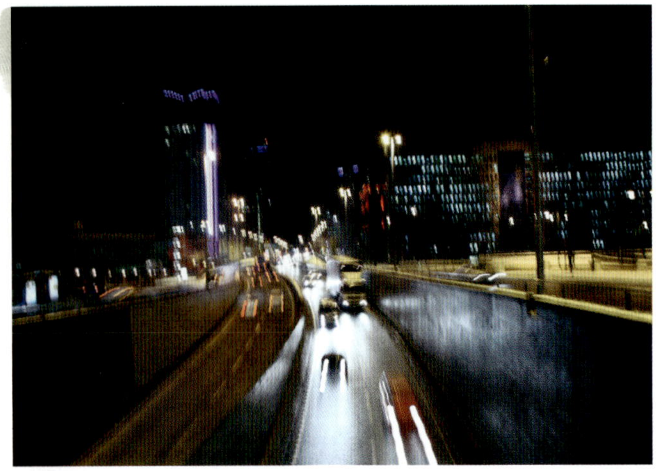

Step 3 I attempt to take another shot with a longer shutter speed. However, as I trigger the shutter button, my hand causes some vibration to the camera, blurring the image. To get around this problem, I attach my remote release, although if you don't have one, you can simply set your camera's self-timer. Remember not to knock the tripod during the exposure.

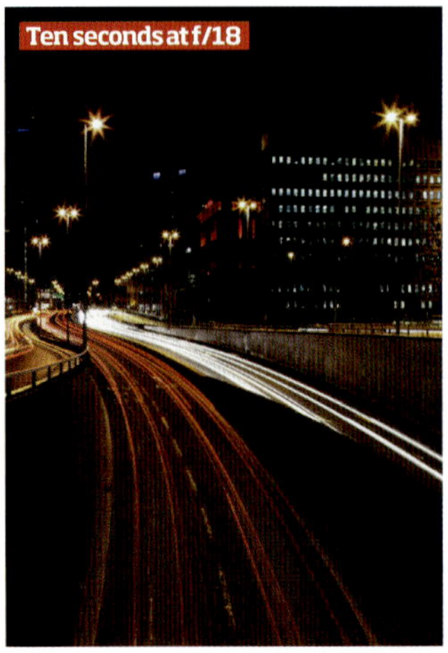

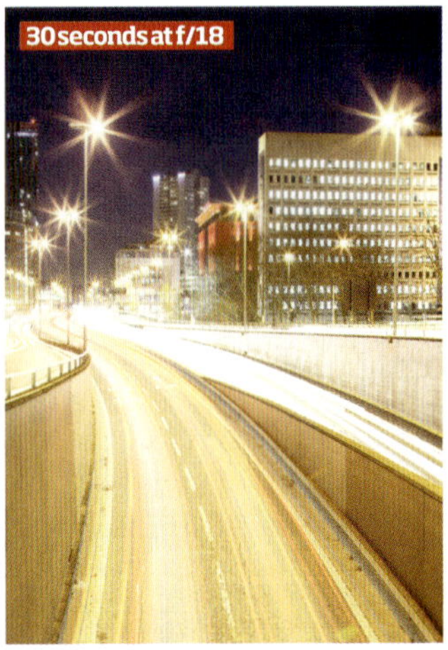

Step 4 I play around with some different shutter speeds to see how they affect the image. At ten seconds the image is too dark, losing detail in the road. However, at 16 seconds the image is too light, with the light trails burning out. A shutter speed between these two points should give me the correct exposure. You should experiment with your shutter speeds, too.

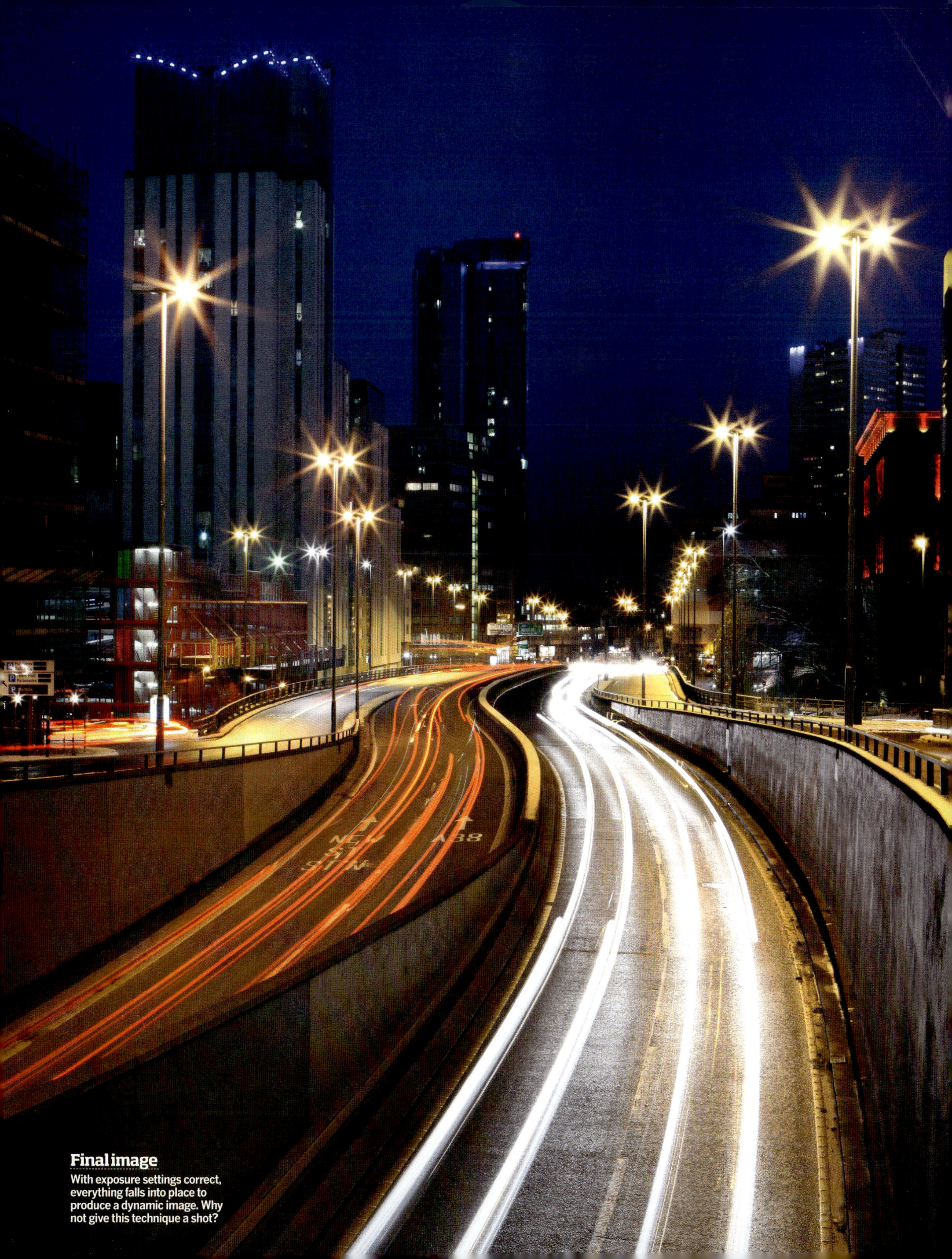

Final image
With exposure settings correct, everything falls into place to produce a dynamic image. Why not give this technique a shot?

Shoot daylight portraits

The creative scope for composition and the use of daylight is vast. But while there are no rules, we offer some guidelines that are sure to improve your portraits

PORTRAITURE IS ONE of the most popular subjects for photographers but also one that newcomers to digital photography struggle with. That's understandable, as not only do you have to take control of all your camera's settings, you also need to be able to work with your subject and know how to manipulate the lighting. In this section of the guide, Daniel Lezano covers all the basics you need to know to help you develop your portrait photography skills, using nothing more than ambient daylight as your source of illumination. We'll also be showing you the best camera settings to use and recommending essential gear to ensure that, no matter what the conditions, you'll be able to create stunning portraits with ease.

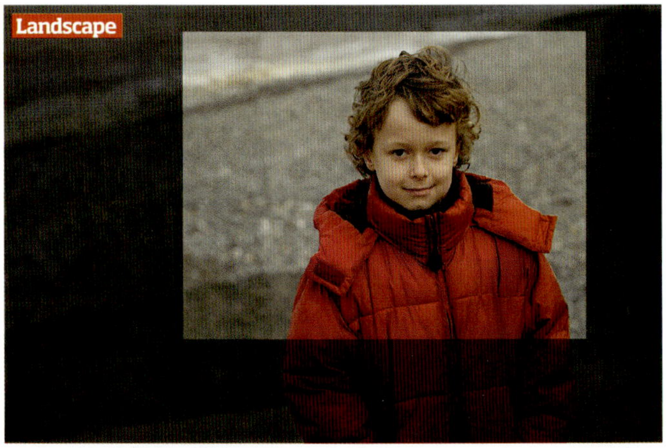

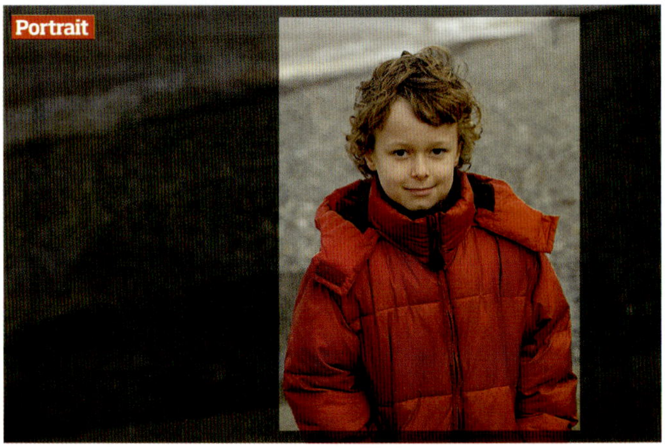

Landscape or upright format?

It's natural to tilt the camera on its edge when you're shooting a portrait as it allows you to fill the frame with the subject's head and shoulders or entire body. It's also a good format to adopt when you're trying to exclude as much of the background as possible to concentrate attention on the subject. Because this orientation is used so often when shooting people, the upright format is often termed the portrait format. Shooting portraits with the camera held horizontal to produce a landscape-format shot often allows for more creative compositions. For one, it allows you to place the subject off-centre to include some of the backdrop in the frame. It also allows you to crop tightly into the face, which can add drama and impact to the scene. Both options are worth trying while looking through the viewfinder to see which works best. If in doubt, shoot both ways!

We cropped the same image into a landscape and portrait format. Which do you prefer? Choosing the orientation of your picture is a key decision you need to make each time you compose, as it can make or break your shot.

Viewpoint

It's natural when taking a picture to stand and shoot from your normal eye-level height. However, while there is nothing wrong with this, shooting from a normal viewpoint is a little unimaginative. It's not the most flattering angle either. You'll find that by shooting from slightly above your subject's eye level, you'll create a more dynamic image. Experiment by shooting from a much higher or lower viewpoint to your subject and see how the results turn out.

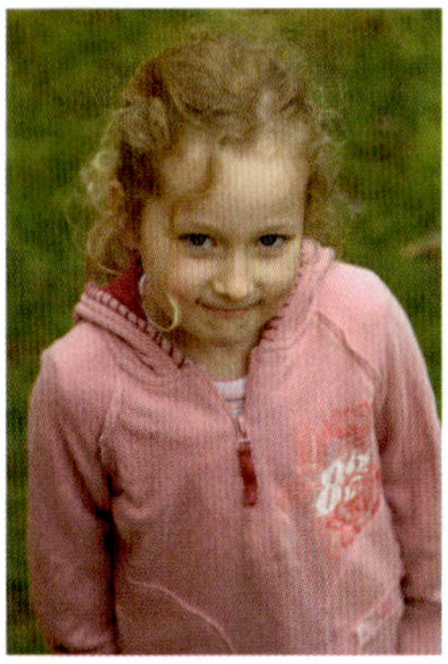

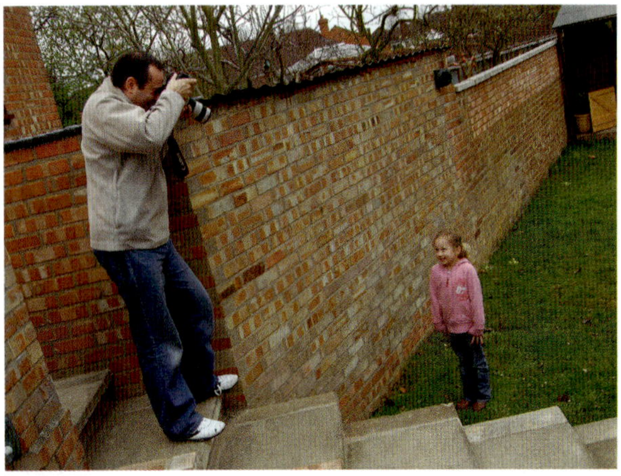

Shooting a subject from halfway up some steps provides a very high viewpoint and an unusual and quirky result. Give it a go!

Breaking the rules: New angles to try

USE A WIDE-ANGLE

Set your standard zoom to wide-angle (or use an ultra wide-angle zoom) and shoot portraits with a difference. Because they completely distort perspective, it's possible to shoot very unusual portrait images, where the part of the subject closest to the lens appears much larger than the parts of the body that are further away.

EYE CONTACT

We harp on about you making sure both eyes are in focus with the subject looking at the camera, yet there are many stunning examples where the subject's looking away or their eyes are obscured. A lack of eye contact can add intrigue to your portrait or give it a candid feel, so don't be afraid of having your subject look away from the camera.

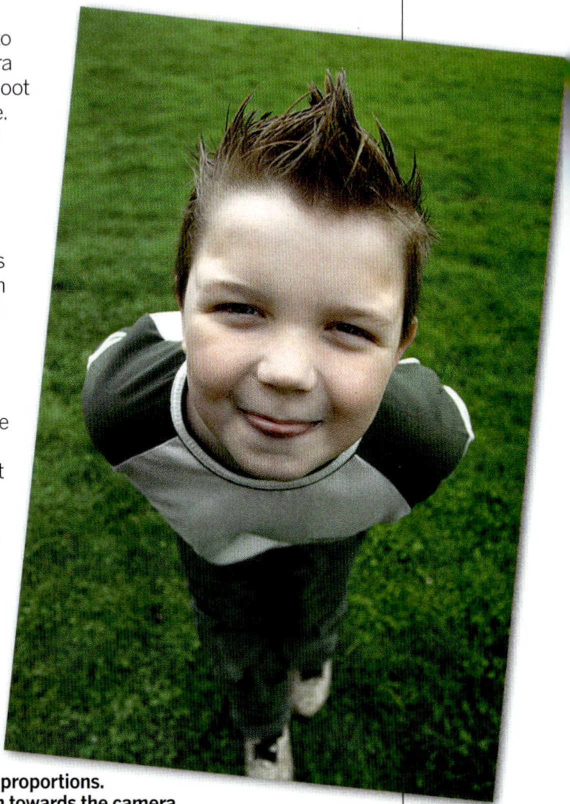

A wide-angle lens distorts proportions. Try having a subject lean in towards the camera for a more interesting, fun take on a portrait shot.

Controlling daylight situations

If you're developing your skills as a portrait photographer, then you'll need a good understanding of how to control daylight. Over the next few pages, we'll show you some basic techniques that can make major improvements to your daylight portraits, whether shooting in sunlight, shade or overcast conditions

A COMMON MISCONCEPTION for many newcomers to photography is that bright sunshine is the best light to take portraits in. The truth is that it's actually one of the worst. It's potentially a very unflattering light to work with, unless you know how to control it. If your subject's facing into the sun, it's likely that they are heavily squinting, which won't look great in the photos! Also, the directional light won't be making the most of their features, with strong highlights and deep shadows. However, if you know how to manipulate and control sunlight, it opens up the options for you to shoot in virtually any outdoor location in the knowledge that you'll capture great results.

Use a diffuser

Stick a diffuser between the sun and your subject and you'll instantly cut off the direct light and get better results. Diffusers play their part when shooting in strong, directional light, such as bright sunshine. They're basically a large sheet of diffusing material fitted to a frame (normally lightweight aluminium tubing). Placing the diffuser between the light source and the subject cuts down the light's intensity, while also diffusing it to give a softer, more pleasing effect. They're usually quite large and come in various diffusion strengths, with Lastolite and California Sunbounce being two of the more popular brands. The diffusing material can be replaced and comes in different thicknesses, which determines the extent of the diffusion.

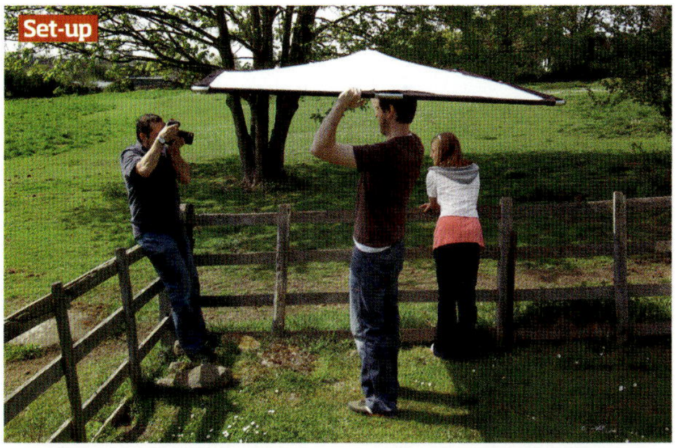

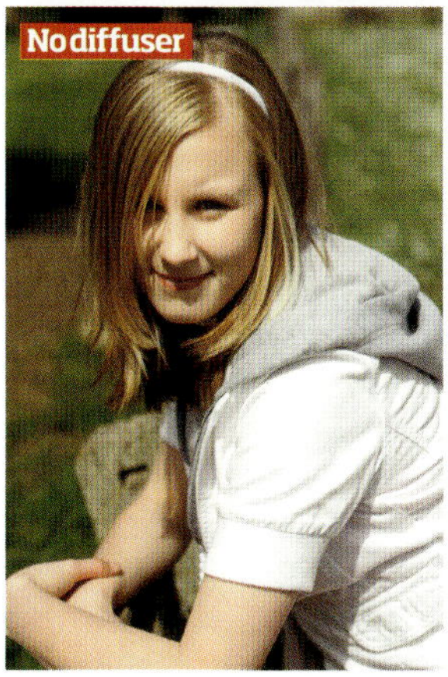

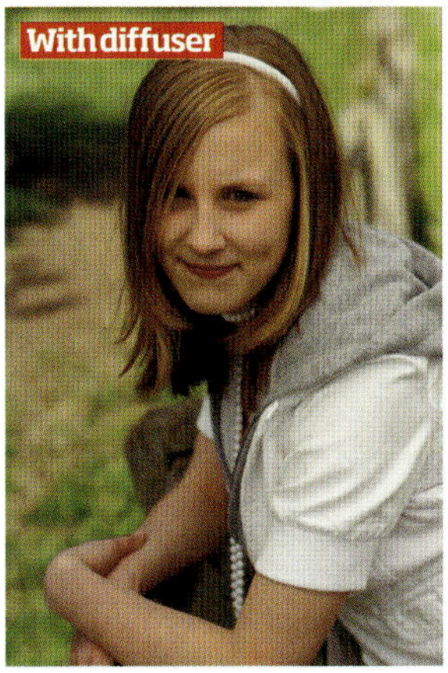

Direct sunlight is a very harsh type of light and extremely unflattering for portraits. As our set of examples show, the simple use of a diffuser reduces the harsh contrast, making an immediate improvement.

Essential accessories

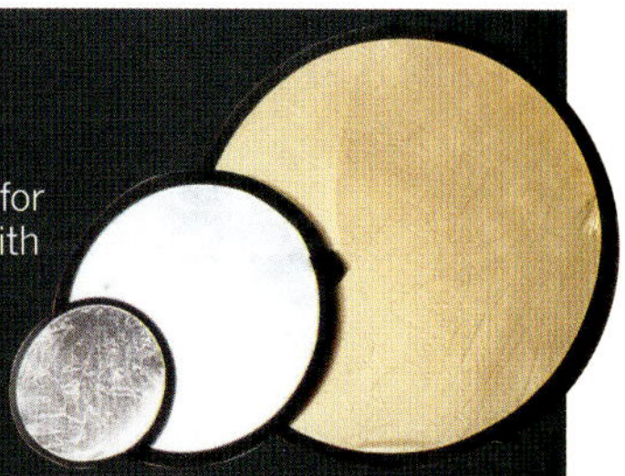

REFLECTORS: One of the best accessories that you can invest in for shooting portraits is a reflector. With good, collapsible hand-held reflectors starting at around £20, these inexpensive items will make a major difference to your photographs. Reflectors can be used in virtually any situation to bounce light on to your subject to help shape the light on their face, fill in shadows etc. Reflectors come in various shapes, sizes and colour finishes which affect the intensity and colour of the light being reflected back on to your subject. White produces medium-intensity and quite soft light, while silver and gold are far more efficient, delivering a stronger result. Most reflectors come with a different colour surface on each side – we'd recommend silver/white as a good first choice.

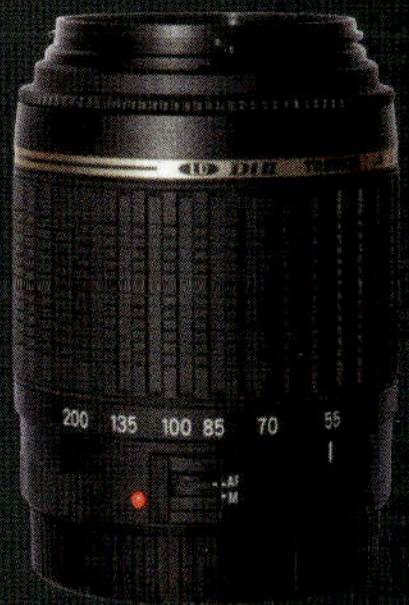

LENSES: A short telephoto provides the most flattering focal length. Lenses that cover focal lengths of around 50-130mm (35mm equivalent: 75-200mm) are ideal for portraits as they flatten perspective. So you can happily use the tele-end of your standard zoom (18-55mm) or, even better, a telezoom like a 55-200mm. Unless you're looking to purposely exaggerate perspective and produce wacky effects, we'd suggest you steer clear of using wide-angles to begin with.

Face away from the sun

If you haven't got a diffuser, then try facing the subject away from the sun. This way, their face will be in shade, and often the sun captures attractive highlights in the hair. If your subject has long hair, use it to provide a light shield to prevent sunlight hitting their face, as we've done here.

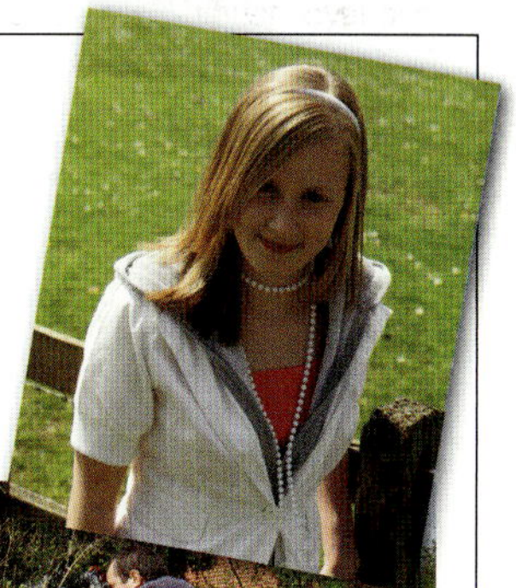

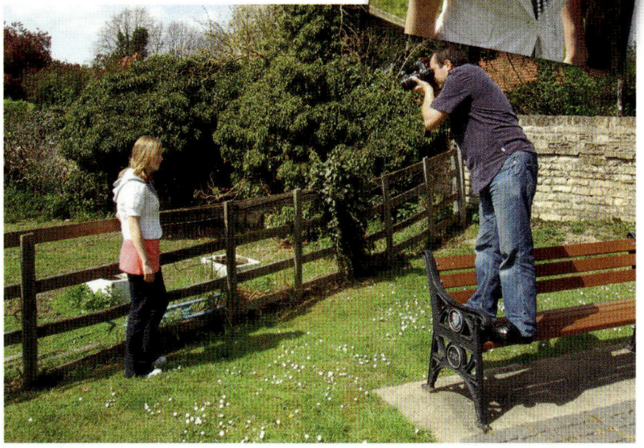

If a diffuser is unavailable, then have your subject face away from the sun. Adopting a higher viewpoint and having the subject tilt her head down slightly helps make the most of the sunlight on her hair.

Cloudy conditions

Dull days can sometimes be the best for portrait photography. We show you how to make the most of minimal light using a reflector and a dash of creativity

IF YOU WERE planning to shoot landscapes and looked out of the window to find the sky filled with grey cloud cover, you'd not be happy. However, for the portrait photographer, a grey blanket of cloud is viewed as Mother Nature's own diffuser. Overcast conditions take away much of the pain of shooting outdoors, as there is no need to worry about strong sunlight. However, that's not to say that, because there's no direct light, there is no way for you to manipulate light. Even on the dullest of days, using a white or metallic reflector can bounce light back on to the subject. And because you have no directional light to contend with, you have almost total freedom to position your subject where you like, as there's no sun to deal with. Bear in mind that, because the light source is diffused light from above, you'll find it better to keep the reflector below the subject and angled to point upwards. Move the reflector towards and away from the subject to achieve the intensity of reflectance that you require. Also, change its position and angle to help 'shape' the light that bathes your subject's face.

The following step-by-step was taken on a day when the sky was totally covered by a blanket of grey cloud. We photographed Ruby in her garden, sitting in front of a brown playhouse which provided a dark, neutral backdrop for minimal distractions. She wore a light pink top that added colour into the scene without being overpowering.

Environmental reflectors

Keep your eye out for objects in the location that can act as a reflector. White walls are ideal not only as a backdrop, but also to provide reflected light. You'll also find the light that bounces from standard house bricks works well, too. Bear in mind that coloured walls will reflect coloured light, so avoid strong coloured walls like red, blue or green.

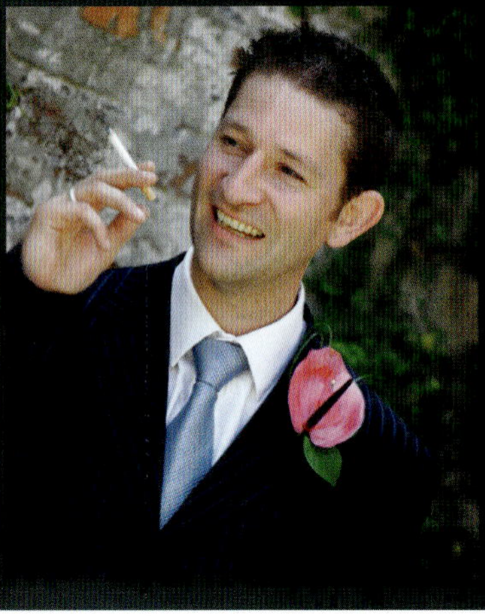

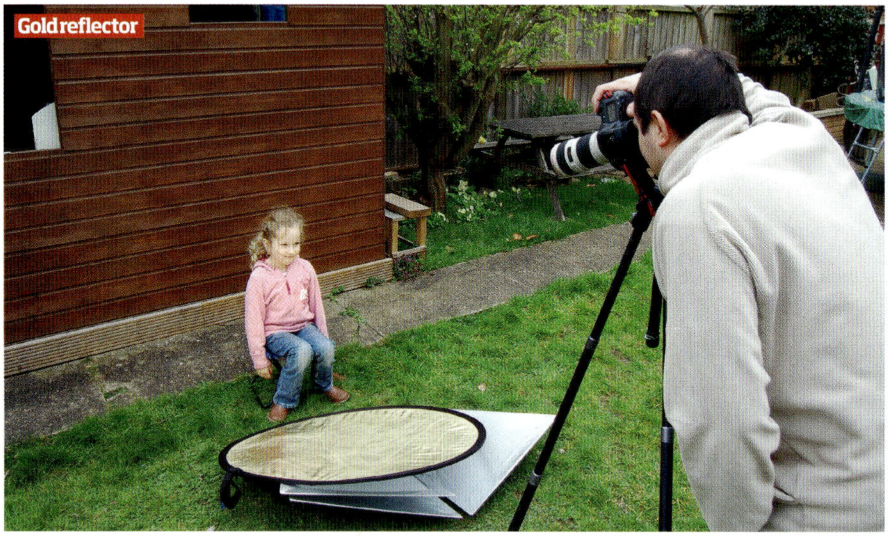

Gold reflector

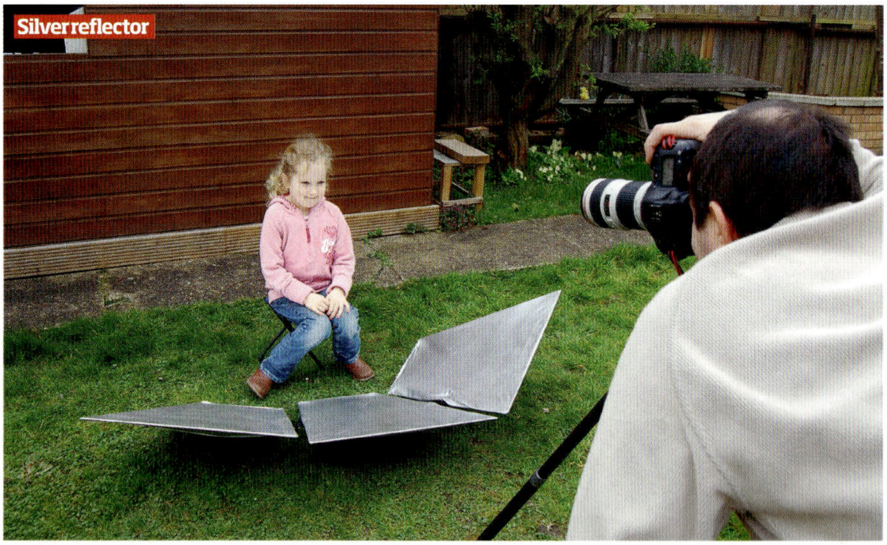

Silver reflector

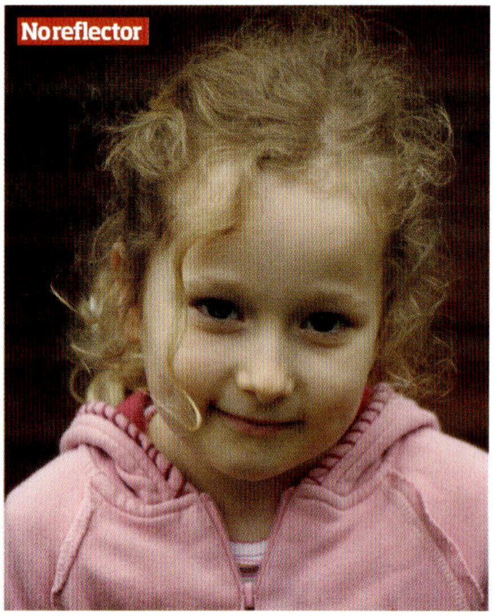

No reflector

1 This is Ruby photographed without any form of lighting control used. The shot's okay, but shadows under the eyes and on the lower parts of her cheeks and chin aren't particularly attractive. Tilting her head up would remove many of them but then the pose would be quite awkward. We'll aim to get around the problem by using reflectors. We try a white reflector but the dull light means it has minimal effect.

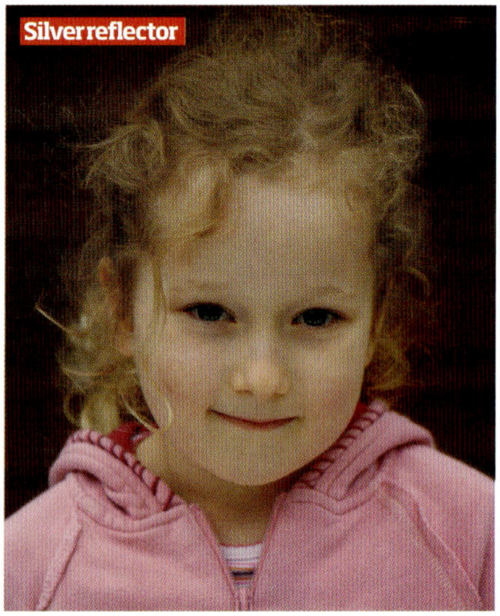

Silver reflector

2 Instead we opt for the use of a silver reflector. The Lastolite Triflector is a versatile accessory that uses three separate panels so that you can control the angle of reflection. It's placed on the ground, quite close to Ruby and below my eye level, so that I'm shooting over the top of it. As you can see, its effect is obvious – shadows are removed and the effect is more flattering than before.

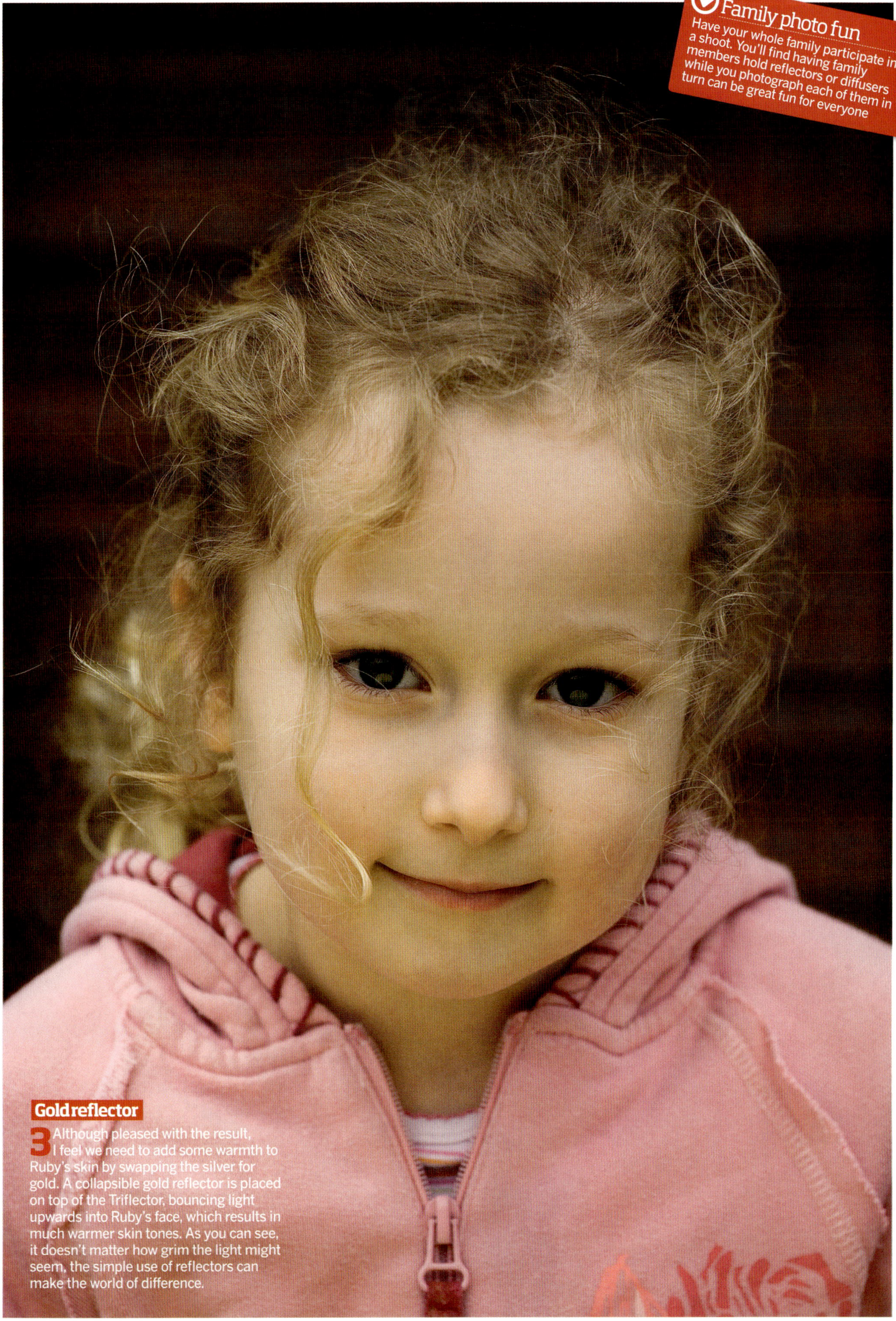

Family photo fun

Have your whole family participate in a shoot. You'll find having family members hold reflectors or diffusers while you photograph each of them in turn can be great fun for everyone

Gold reflector

3 Although pleased with the result, I feel we need to add some warmth to Ruby's skin by swapping the silver for gold. A collapsible gold reflector is placed on top of the Triflector, bouncing light upwards into Ruby's face, which results in much warmer skin tones. As you can see, it doesn't matter how grim the light might seem, the simple use of reflectors can make the world of difference.

Shooting in shade

Like clouds, shady places are a natural diffuser and will make shooting portraits a whole lot easier

WHILE SHADY CONDITIONS are associated with flat, cool light, the opposite is often true and taking portraits in shade offers great opportunities for portrait photography. The lack of direct light means that you've not got any harsh highlights or deep shadows to contend with. Instead, the subject is usually bathed in a very soft light that flatters their features – in many ways much like in overcast conditions.

One thing you may not realise is that you can manipulate the light to quite an extent in shade. The key thing to remember is that the light reaching your subject is determined by the reflective surfaces in the scene around him or her. So have a look at different locations and see how your subject looks when close to white surfaces, brick walls, metal shutters etc. Bear in mind that dark or black surfaces can also be used – you'll find that rather than bounce light onto your subject's skin, they absorb light, and that can help reveal the shape and contours of your subject's face. You'll find that all surfaces produce their own type of effect and that moving the subject closer or further away varies its intensity.

On days when the sun is shining, in particular, you'll not only have the advantage of making the most of shade's non-directional and flattering light, you'll also have the option of bouncing light from sunlit areas into the scene. So look for locations where you can position the subject in shade but close to areas in direct sunlight. You can then think about using reflectors to bounce light in to add extra illumination.

You should also consider how your subject is positioned against the backdrop. On a sunny day, if you place your subject with their back to the sunlight, because you're exposing for the shaded subject, the brighter background will be grossly overexposed, resulting in a clean, bright backdrop. The other major advantage of shooting in shade on a sunny day is that, compared to overcast conditions, light levels are higher, which allow for more control and manipulation. We headed for a favourite portrait location that offers excellent potential for shooting in shade on a sunny day. An old priory offered the perfect setting for our shoot, providing an interesting and attractive backdrop. We asked Hayley to wear a bright, summery outfit in keeping with the bright, warm conditions and placed her in the shade of the priory's side.

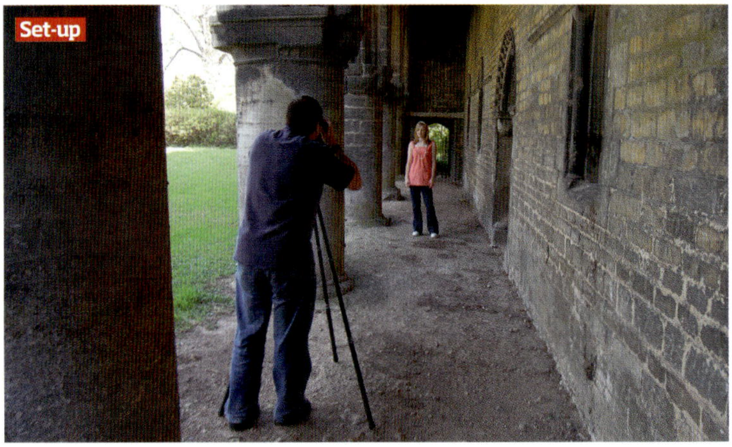

Bouncing sunlight into shade

An advantage of taking pictures in shade on a sunny day is that you can bounce sunlight back into the frame. This allows you to add stronger side-lighting or to lift the brightness level of your subject to make them stand out against the background. What you have to take care with is that you don't bounce too much sunlight into the scene and create too harsh a side-light, as is often the case when using metallic reflectors.

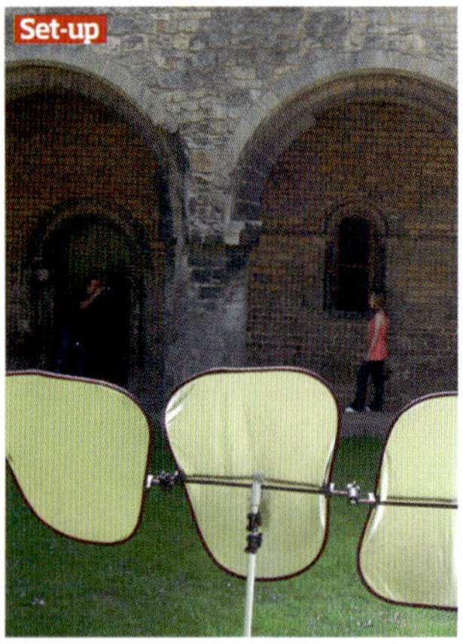

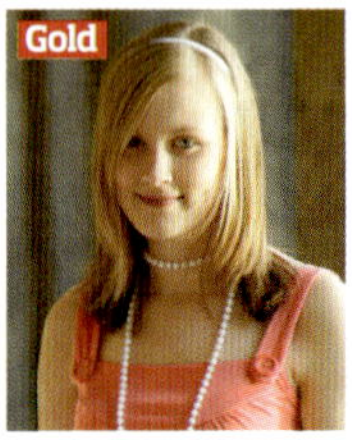

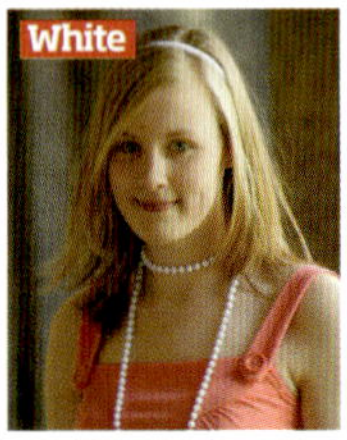

We asked Hayley to stand quite close to the edge of the shaded area and used the gold reflector to bounce light towards her. As you can see, she receives a very strong side-light that is harsh and unflattering. We swap the gold reflector for a white one and there is an instant improvement. The light from this reflector is softer and more diffuse, so gives a far better result.

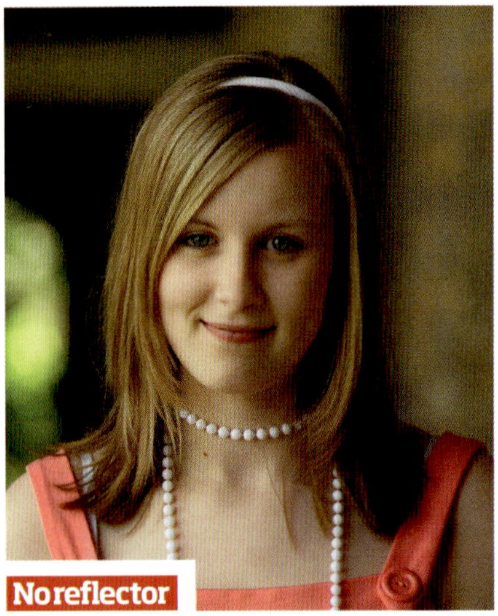

1 Our first shot was taken without any form of lighting control. As you can see, she receives quite a strong side-light from sunlight being bounced into the area by natural reflectors in the scene (in particular, a brick wall around 30 feet away). It produces a pleasant enough result that many people would be happy with.

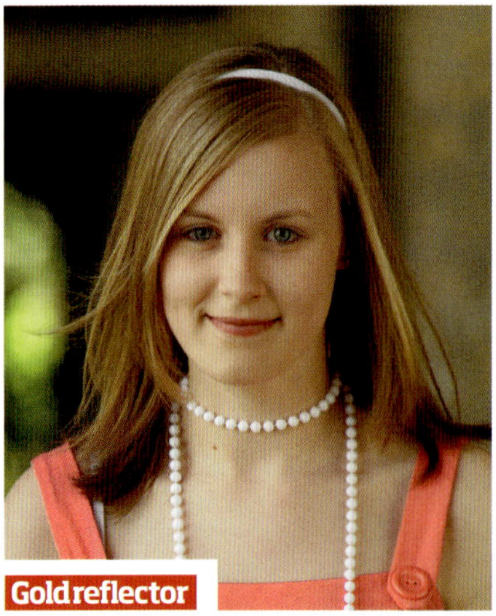

2 We place a gold reflector to Hayley's left and the effect is instantly apparent. Her face receives warmth from the reflected gold light, which fills in shadows on the left side of her face. But the reflector is too close to her (the building's wall prevents us moving it further away), so its effect doesn't extend to her shoulders and arms.

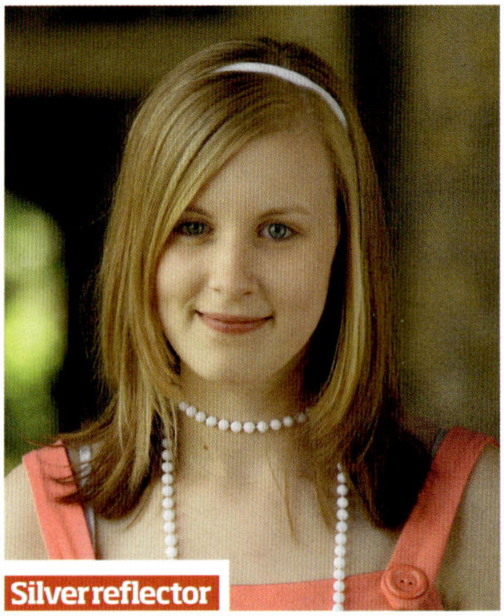

3 We swap the gold reflector for a silver one and the result is better – the shadows are filled in and Hayley's skin tones look better without the gold effect. However, the tones on Hayley's face remain quite even, which doesn't reveal the shape of her face as much as we'd like to. It's time to swap the silver for the white…

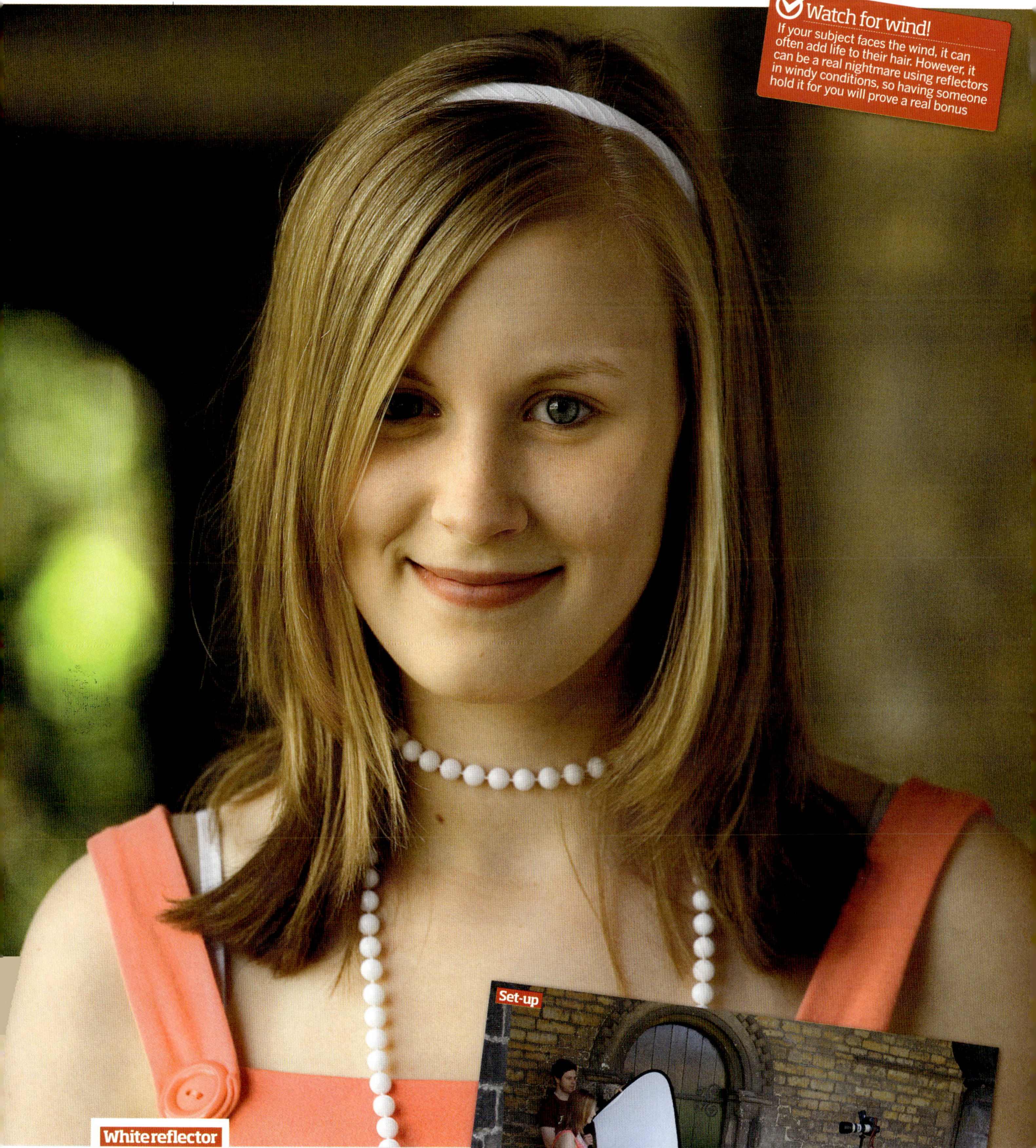

Watch for wind!

If your subject faces the wind, it can often add life to their hair. However, it can be a real nightmare using reflectors in windy conditions, so having someone hold it for you will prove a real bonus

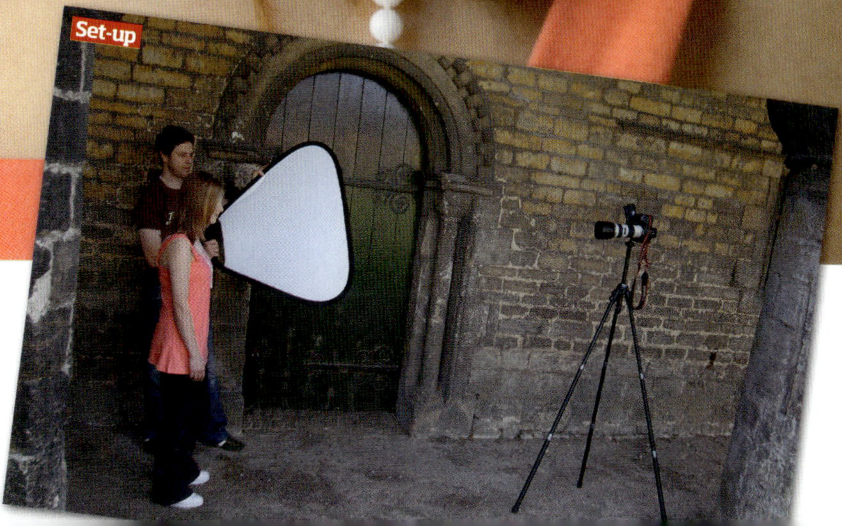

Set-up

White reflector

4 This yields the best result so far. The white reflector lacks the efficiency of the silver and gold; in other words, it reflects less light. While this isn't always preferable, in this situation, with the reflector literally just out of frame, it's perfect. While the shadows have been filled in on the left side of Hayley's face, the brightness difference compared to the right side helps accentuate her contours and reveal her natural beauty.

Stay simple with daylight

Daniel Lezano shows how – with a few little tricks to make the most of the daylight – you can create fantastic lifestyle shots in your own home…

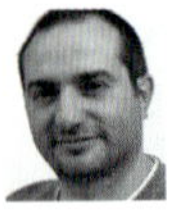

Many leading lifestyle portrait photographers use nothing more than ambient daylight for the vast majority of their portrait shoots. So, when we have the benefits of bright, sunny days at our disposal, we should use it to capture some simple yet effective portraits of family and friends. The best thing about shooting lifestyle portraits is that you can do it with the minimum amount of equipment – your DSLR or CSC with a kit lens is enough – although I'm using my favourite optic, the humble (and cheap!) 50mm f/1.8 lens. Due to the unpredictable nature of daylight, lighting aids such as a reflector and a diffuser can come in handy, too, but aren't essential. The key thing to remember is that you want to capture a 'clean' image: in other words, try to keep the subject and the setting as simple as possible. I've opted for the classic combination of having my subject, Bethany, wear a white top and jeans, and shot her lying on my dining room's laminate flooring.

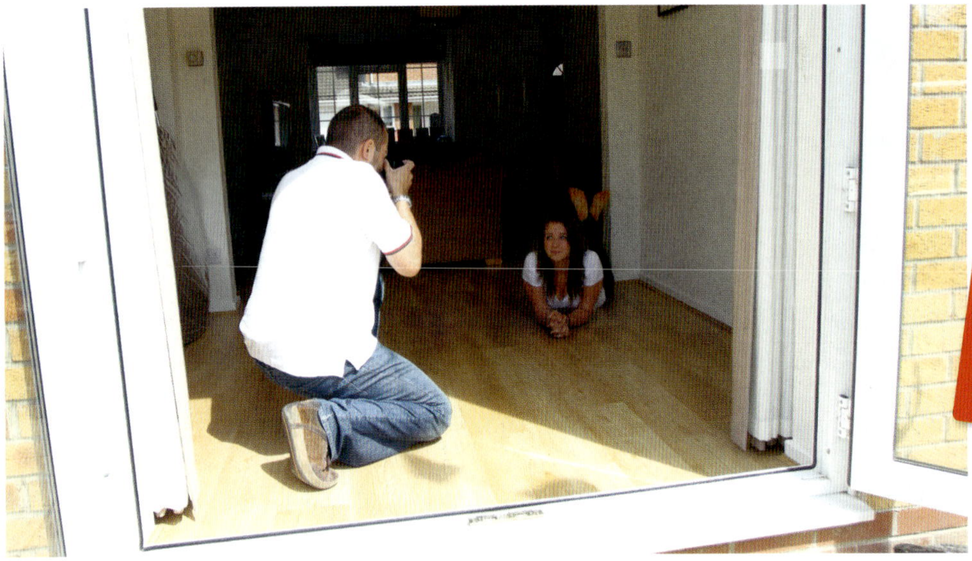

My dining room is quite small, so I've had to clear it completely of furniture. As my subject will be lying on the floor, I vacuum it to ensure it's as clean as possible. Due to the cramped space, I open the patio doors in case I need to shoot from the patio. However, I'll start by shooting from within the room and use the white walls as a neutral backdrop. Using a wide aperture to give a shallow depth-of-field is ideal for this type of shot and I'll be trying out my 50mm's maximum aperture of f/1.8, although I'll take most of the images at f/2.5-3.5 as it will improve sharpness.

Shoot at a slant

One compositional trick that most lifestyle photographers apply to their images is to slant the camera so that the images are captured with an uneven horizon. This simple technique adds a little energy into the image and is very effective – just take care not to tilt the camera too far.

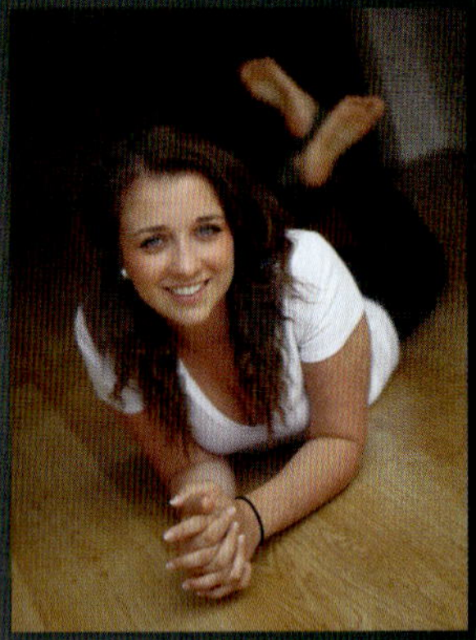

Take care with focus!

You need to ensure your focusing is precise, as using a wide aperture – which gives limited depth-of-field – leaves little margin for error. Select single-point AF, lock the focus on the eye and recompose

Diffused daylight

For flattering portraits, the light should be as diffused as possible to avoid your model squinting in direct sunlight or having the light on their face too harsh. In this instance, try to reposition them so they're in the shade or use a diffuser to shade the scene (inset right). If neither of these work, you may need to wait until the sun's position changes or shoot when the sky is more overcast. A silver reflector is handy, even when shooting in non-directional light, to fill in shadows.

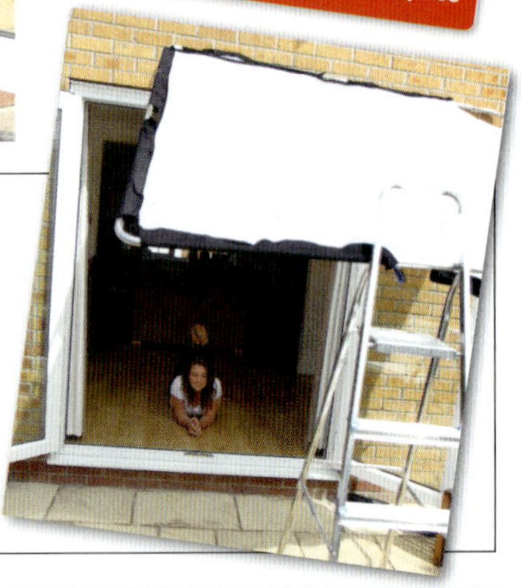

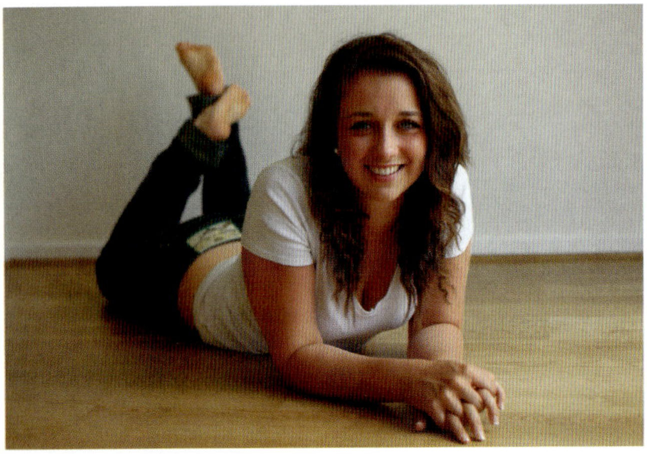

Step 1 My first shot is just a tester for composition and exposure. I've a pretty clear idea in my head of the type of shot I'm looking for, with Bethany lying down with her lower legs and feet bent back towards her head. This shot isn't bad, but the side-lighting causes her right side to be too dark.

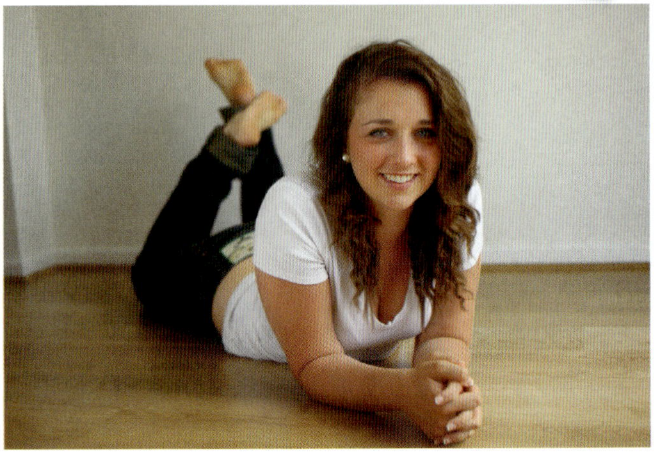

Step 2 I place a silver reflector to Bethany's right, just out of frame, and it makes a noticeable difference, bouncing back enough light to even out the lighting on the face. The lighting's better, but the wall behind, while plain, causes the whole scene to appear a little too cramped for my liking.

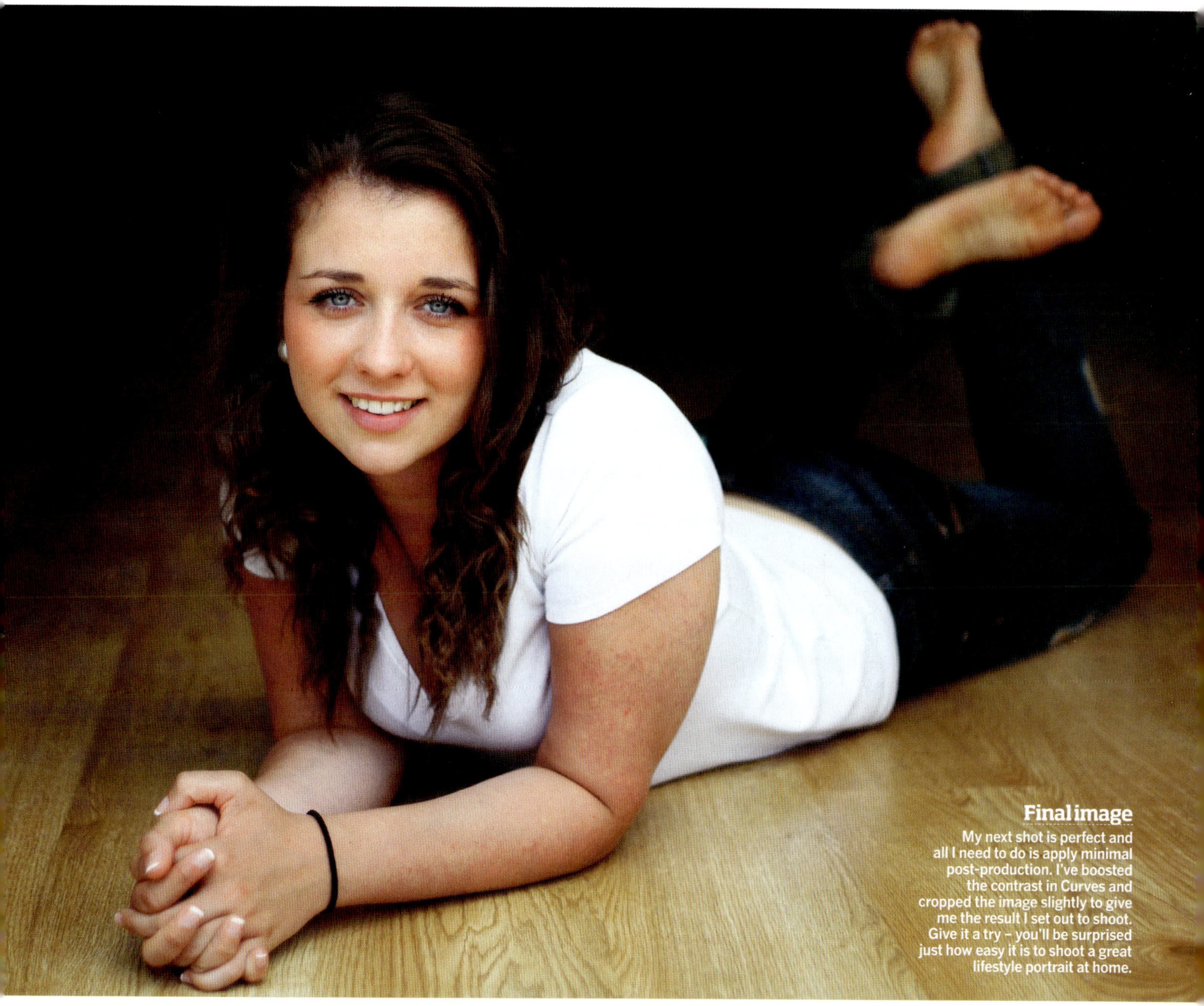

Final image

My next shot is perfect and all I need to do is apply minimal post-production. I've boosted the contrast in Curves and cropped the image slightly to give me the result I set out to shoot. Give it a try – you'll be surprised just how easy it is to shoot a great lifestyle portrait at home.

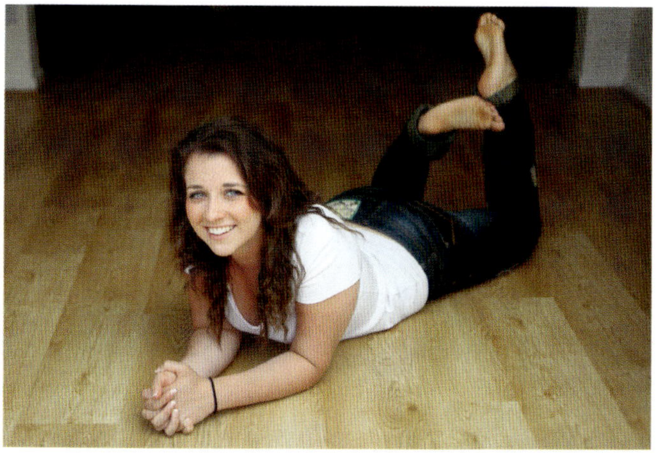

Step 3 I shift Bethany and my position so that I'm now shooting into the room from the patio rather than from the side. I close the blinds in the backdrop to darken the background. The empty space created behind her is an improvement over the original set-up, but my viewpoint is too high.

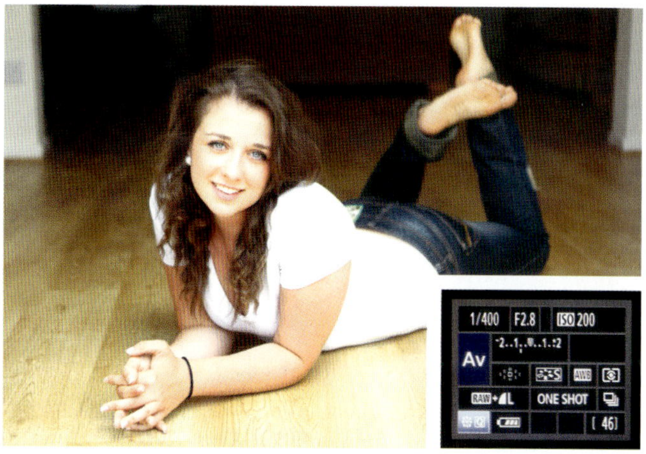

Step 4 I crouch down and the lower viewpoint is far better. However, the multi-zone meter has bleached out Bethany's face due to the dark background causing it to overexpose the scene. This is easily taken care of by dialling in some negative exposure compensation. I find -2/3EV is ideal.

Add flare to outdoor portraits

Pro photographer Paul Ward shows how deliberately letting the sun encroach in the frame to add a touch of flare can work with portraits

NOTHING DIVIDES OPINION like lens flare. Some photographers love it, while others abhor it, going to great lengths to avoid it. Lens flare is caused by direct light travelling through a lens and bouncing off its glass elements, usually having one of two effects: bleaching colours with a white haze, reducing contrast, and creating rings of colour (known as artefacts) that dart across the frame from the sun. Using a lens hood or shooting with your back to the sun helps avoid it, but lens manufacturers have developed such effective lens multi-coatings that it's difficult to create flare with some lenses. If you struggle, try an older uncoated lens: good quality secondhand manual focus lenses can be picked up for just a few quid. Artefacts vary depending on the type of lens, too: flare from a zoom will look very different from that of a prime lens, so experiment a little.

When using aperture-priority mode, you'll find that every time you change position, your exposure will change. You can avoid this by working in manual mode, but for the time being, pro photographer Paul Ward will show you how to achieve the stylised look with your camera set to aperture-priority mode. Take a test shot with the aperture set between f/3.5-f/5.6 to give a shallow depth-of-field. The trick is to position the model in front of the sun. Depending on how high the sun is, you might need to kneel and shoot from a lower than normal perspective. Winter, or early morning and evening are perfect, as the sun is never that high in the sky. Nearly every lens produces flare if it's aimed in the general direction of the sun, but it takes the right kind of lens to give artefacts, which gives fashion and portrait photographers that stylised finish they like.

Old lenses can create flare

Often older lenses create better flare because they lack anti-flare multi-coatings. If you're lucky enough to have only new kit that's not proving very effective, have a look on eBay for a lens adapter so you can buy an old lens to fit to your camera. Paul Ward bought an 'M42 for Canon' adaptor and a 28mm Vivitar lens for £15 each. Car boot sales and secondhand stores are also good places to pick up a bargain lens.

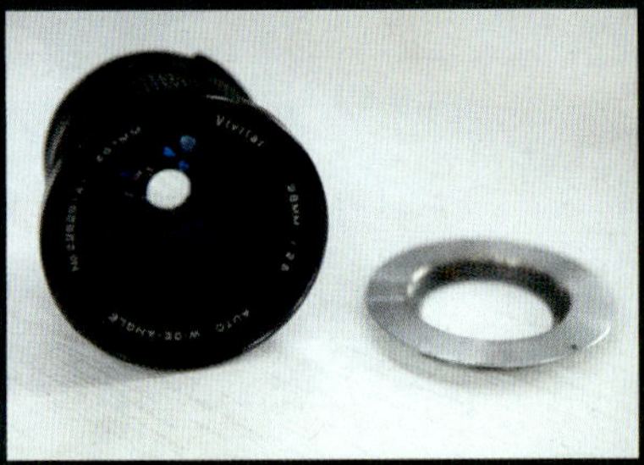

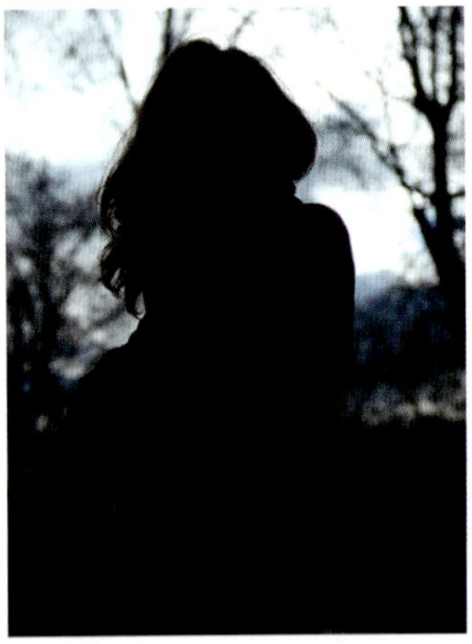

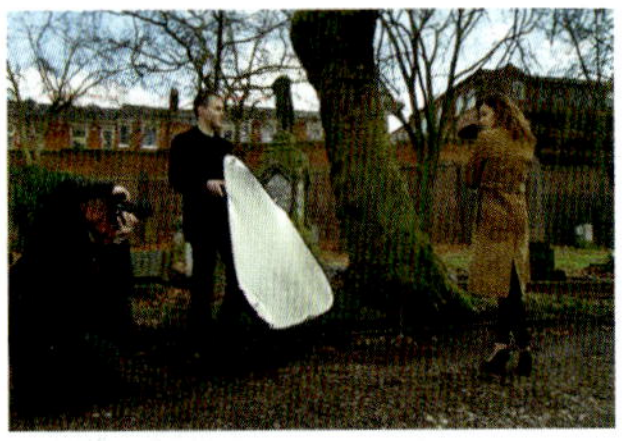

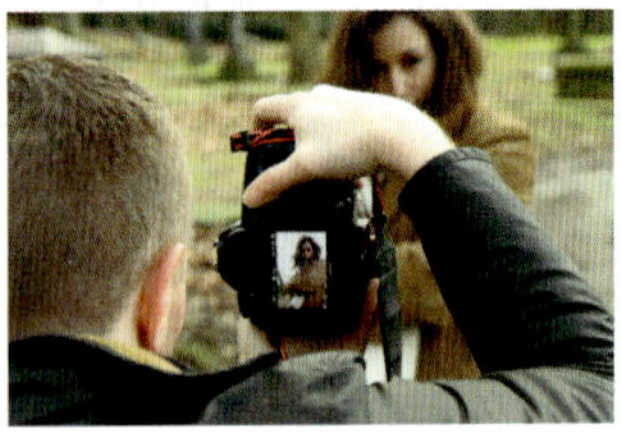

Step 1 As the subject is backlit, you can expect the multi-zone metering of of your camera to produce an underexposed result. You could add positive exposure compensation, but there is another option. Using a reflector is a really easy and effective way to bounce the sun's rays back on to the subject's face. A gold reflector gives a warmer light than a silver or white reflector, which suits this technique. If the model squints, have them close their eyes and then open them moments before you take the shot.

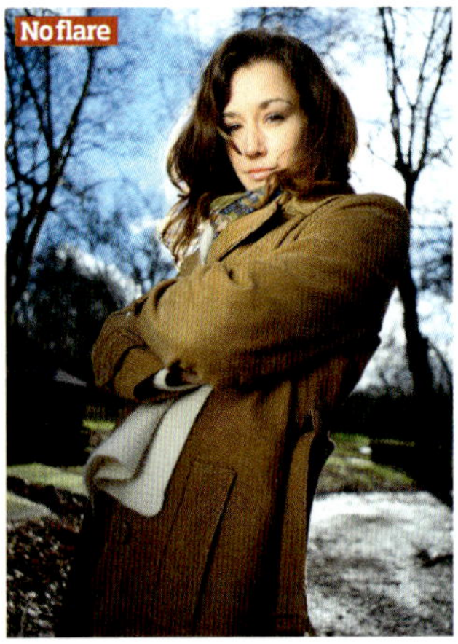

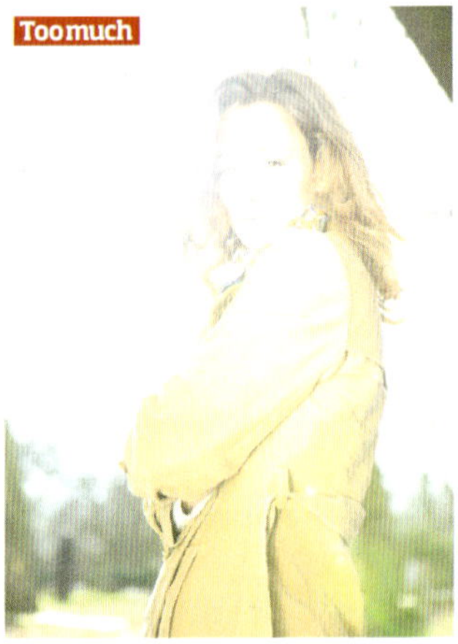

Step 2 It can be tricky to autofocus on a subject when the sun is in the frame, as it causes a lack of contrast. To get around this, use the subject to block the sun and focus, keep the shutter button half-depressed to lock focus, and then move slightly to the side so the sun enters the frame. This can mess around with your exposure, so it takes a little trial and error. Depending on where you put the sun in the frame, it may cause too much flare, leading to blown-out highlights, so be patient and keep trying.

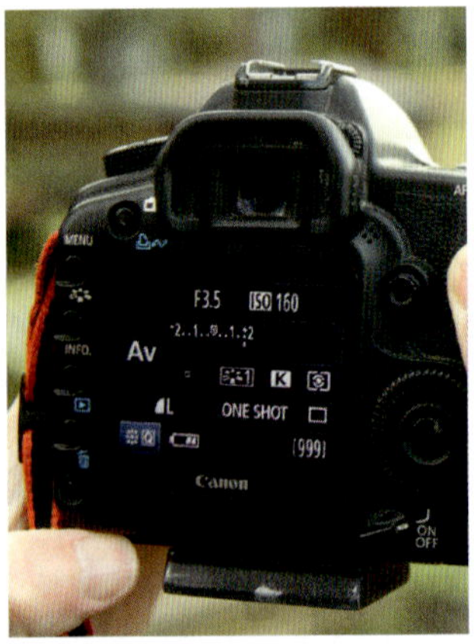

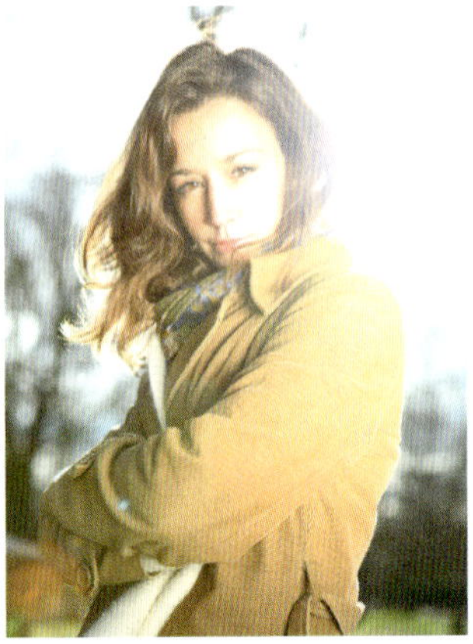

Step 3 If the shots look too bright, dial in a couple of stops of negative exposure compensation or don't let as much sun encroach into the frame. If the shots are too dark, but the sun is as much in the frame as you want it to be, dial in a couple of stops of positive exposure compensation. For this image, as the sun is just peeping past her head, I used two stops of positive exposure compensation to overexpose, but it's slightly too much. For the next shots, I try to replicate the position of the sun and use one stop of positive exposure compensation.

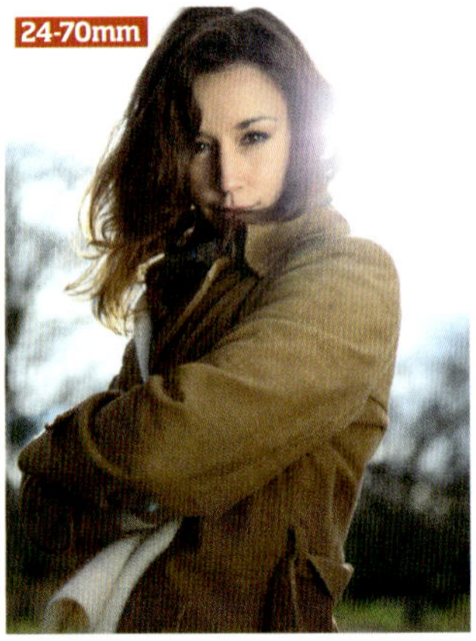

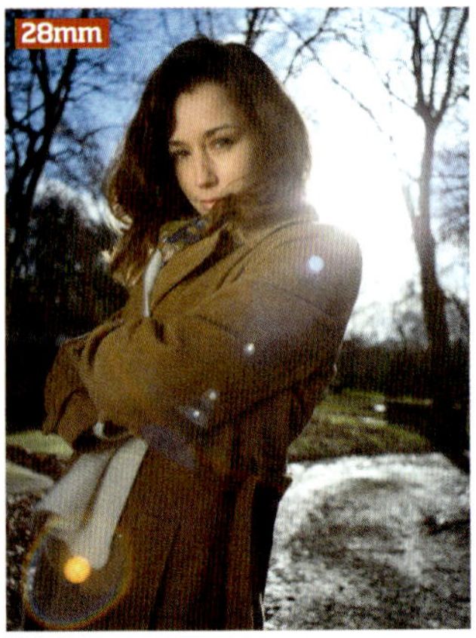

Step 4 The Canon EF 24-70mm f/2.8L USM lens I've been using is so efficient at blocking flare that I'm struggling to get any artefacts in the picture, and am only getting the haze. The more I overexpose the shot, the more streaks of white flare expand across the subject's face, which is not the effect I want. I switch to my new, 20-year-old 28mm Vivitar lens (not anti-flare coated) to see if it does a better job. With the model in the same position, I take another shot that produces some excellent artefacts running across the picture, giving me the stylised effect I'm looking for.

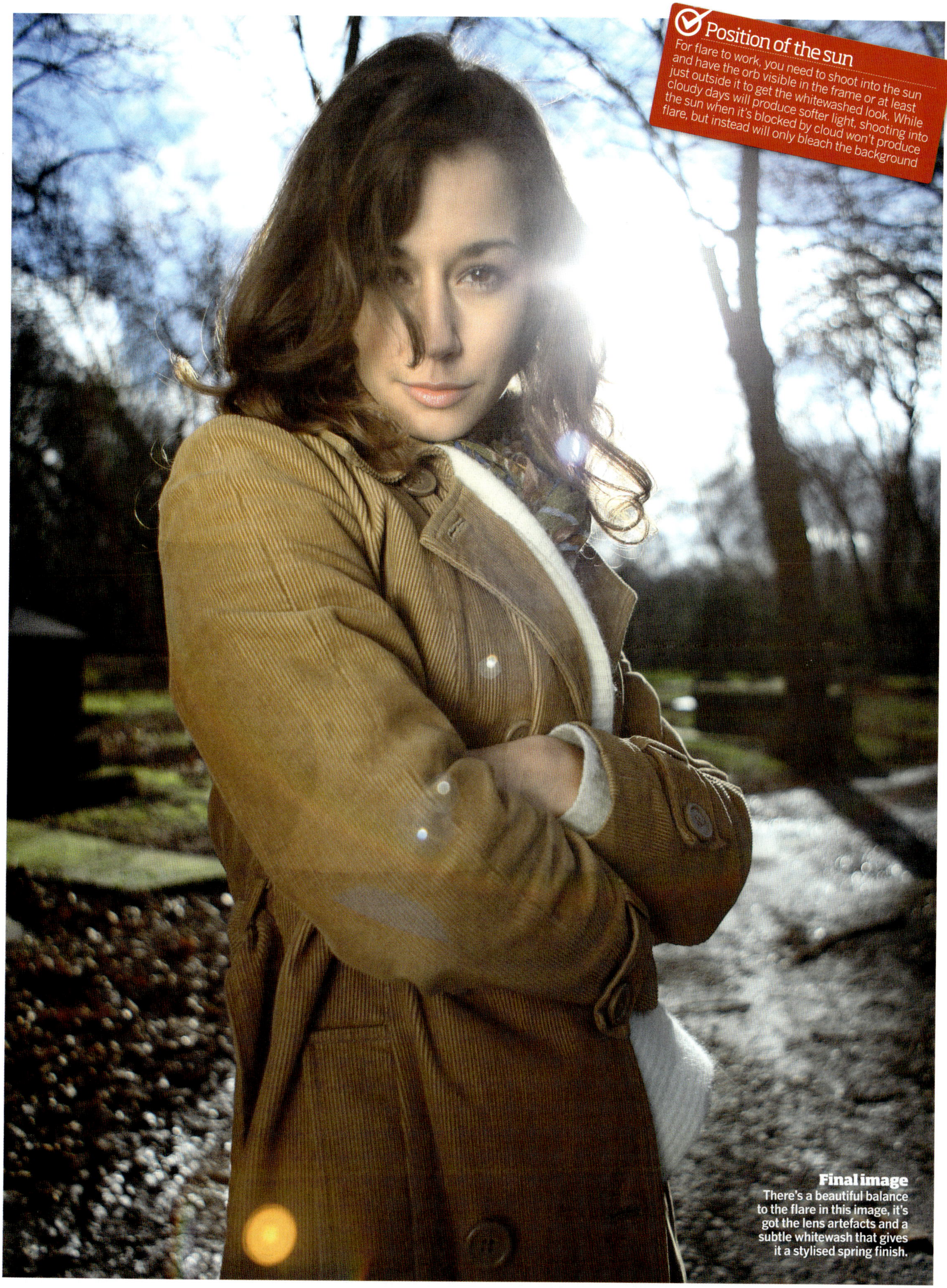

Position of the sun

For flare to work, you need to shoot into the sun and have the orb visible in the frame or at least just outside it to get the whitewashed look. While cloudy days will produce softer light, shooting into the sun when it's blocked by cloud won't produce flare, but instead will only bleach the background

Final image
There's a beautiful balance to the flare in this image, it's got the lens artefacts and a subtle whitewash that gives it a stylised spring finish.

Have a ball at the beach

The beach is a fantastic location for shooting striking silhouettes – Ross Hoddinott shows you how to capture them with ease…

THERE'S NO BETTER place to spend a warm, summer's evening than the seaside. Maybe you like to surf, paddle or play – or simply relax, by reading a book or topping up your tan. However, if you are heading to the beach with the family this month, whatever you do, don't forget your camera as there are endless photo opportunities at the beach. Colourful skies are highly seductive and you'll find that sunsets are particularly photogenic by the sea. With the sun so low in the sky, anything between you and the sun will be cast in silhouette. Personally, I love the simplicity of silhouetted subjects. They are the most extreme form of backlighting, where the subject is rendered without colour or detail. Therefore, bold, easily recognisable shapes and outlines work best.

People are particularly photogenic silhouetted at sunset. The warm, evening light can create a romantic mood, so think about photographing a couple kissing with the sun setting behind. Children also make great subjects – holding hands with a parent, or just playing and having fun. You could try shooting candids on the beach, but ask permission first – particularly if photographing minors. However, you can apply far more control over the look of your results by photographing a family member or someone you know. Using a willing 'model' gives you the opportunity to experiment more, perfect your exposure and try again if your first attempts are unsuccessful.

With this in mind, I asked my sister if I could borrow my eight-year-old nephew for the evening. She enthusiastically agreed and while she poured herself a glass of wine and relaxed for an hour or two, Tom and I headed to the local beach with the promise of a large ice cream if he would happily let me photograph him having fun…

Exposure compensation

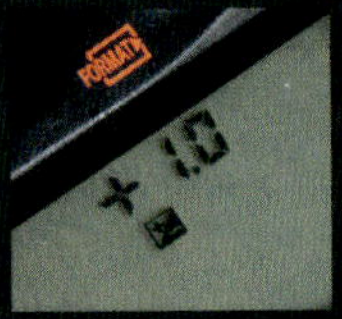

TTL metering systems are highly sophisticated and reliable. However, that doesn't mean that they don't make mistakes. In awkward lighting conditions – for example, backlighting – they can easily be deceived. By regularly viewing the histogram, any exposure error is easy to spot, as there will be a spike of data at one end of the graph. Correcting under- or overexposure is easy using your camera's exposure compensation button. If your images are too light, dial in negative (–) compensation; this will make the image darker. If your images are too dark, dial in positive (+) compensation to lighten results. You do this by pressing the +/– (exposure compensation) button and rotating the command dial until you have set the desired level of compensation. However, the way you select compensation will vary from camera to camera. Most cameras allow you to set compensation at up to three or five stops in ⅓ or ½-stop increments. Note: it doesn't automatically reset itself to 0 when you switch the camera off. Therefore, remember to reset compensation after you have finished shooting. Fail to do so and you will apply the compensation to future images, too.

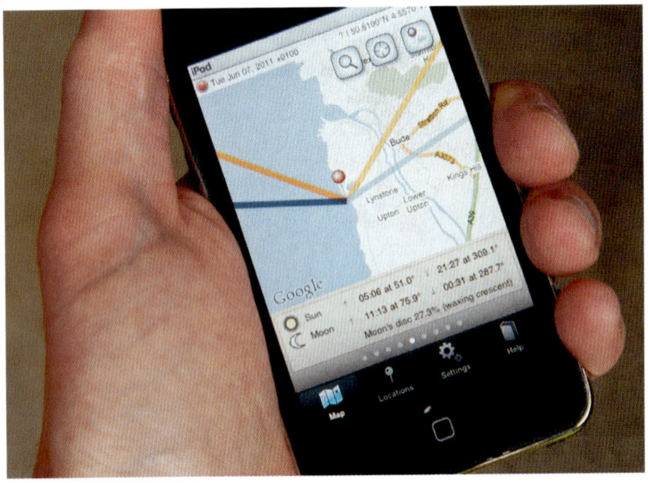

1 If you are visiting the beach to shoot silhouetted portraits, then plan carefully. Check the time of sunset, and its position, by visiting www.photoephemeris.com (or download the app The Photographer's Ephemeris). For safety, also check the time of high tide. Arrive an hour before sunset to give yourself time to set up before the best light and colour appears.

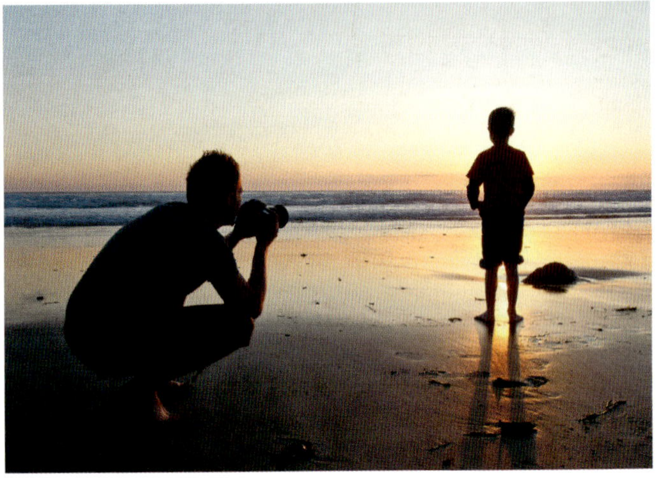

2 Use a standard zoom as it's very versatile. I use a Nikon 24-70mm as its fast maximum aperture of f/2.8 provides a bright viewfinder image, aiding focusing and composition – perfect for low-light photography. Using aperture-priority, I set f/8 and opt for a low ISO of 200. With this image, shooting hand-held allows you more creative freedom than using a tripod.

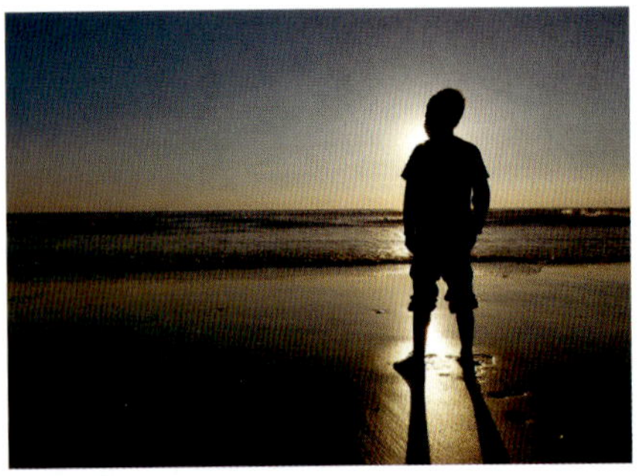

3 By adopting a low angle and carefully aligning your model with the sun, you will be able to use your subject to obscure the sun's intensity and create an inky black silhouette. However, with Tom standing on the wet, reflective sand and looking out to sea, the result looks too static and posed. Overall, the shot is too dark, being at least a stop underexposed.

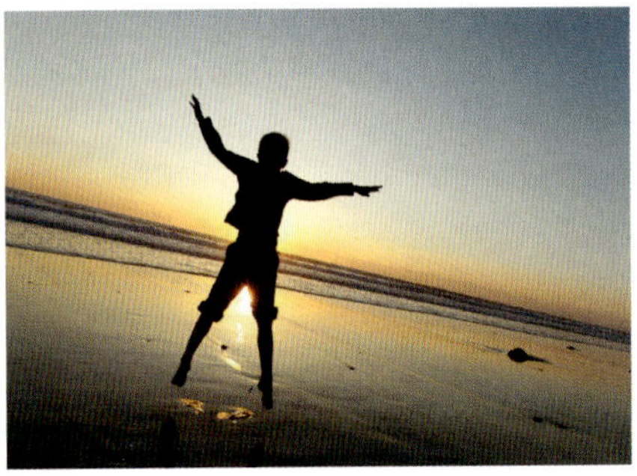

4 When shooting backlit subjects, the sun's intensity can fool multi-zone metering patterns into believing the scene is brighter than it is. As a result, the camera selects a faster shutter speed than required, resulting in underexposure. To compensate, I dialled in a stop of positive (+) exposure compensation. I also asked Tom to jump to add motion to the image.

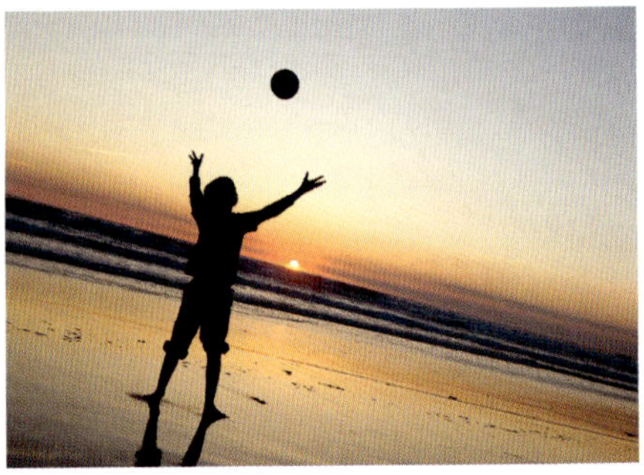

5 Use trial and error or your camera's histogram to fine-tune the amount of exposure compensation needed. Once you're happy, turn your attention to composition. Props work well when photographing kids and help them to relax in front of the camera. I asked Tom to play catch with a ball, tilting the camera at a slight angle to add energy to the composition.

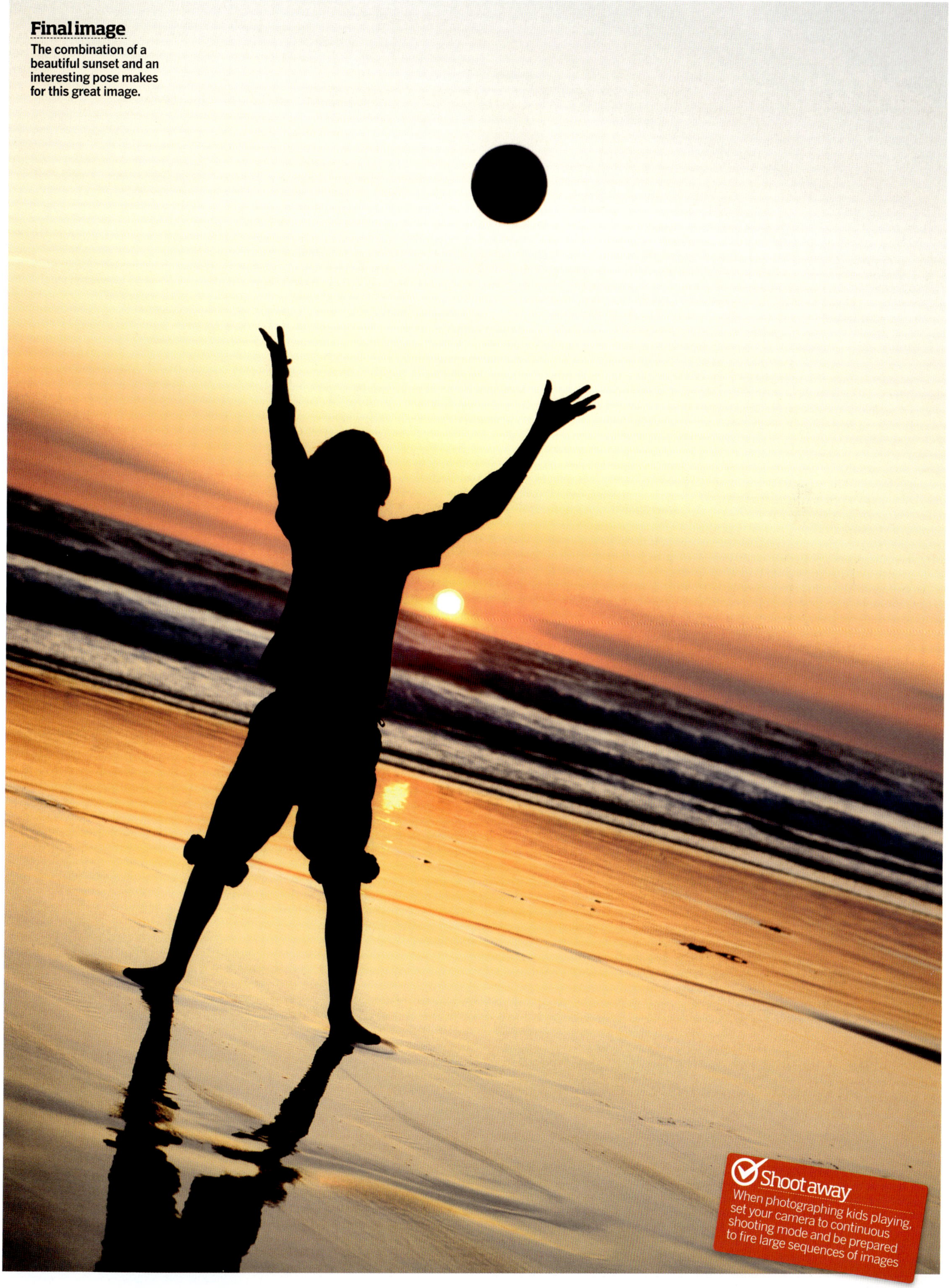

Final image

The combination of a beautiful sunset and an interesting pose makes for this great image.

Shoot away

When photographing kids playing, set your camera to continuous shooting mode and be prepared to fire large sequences of images

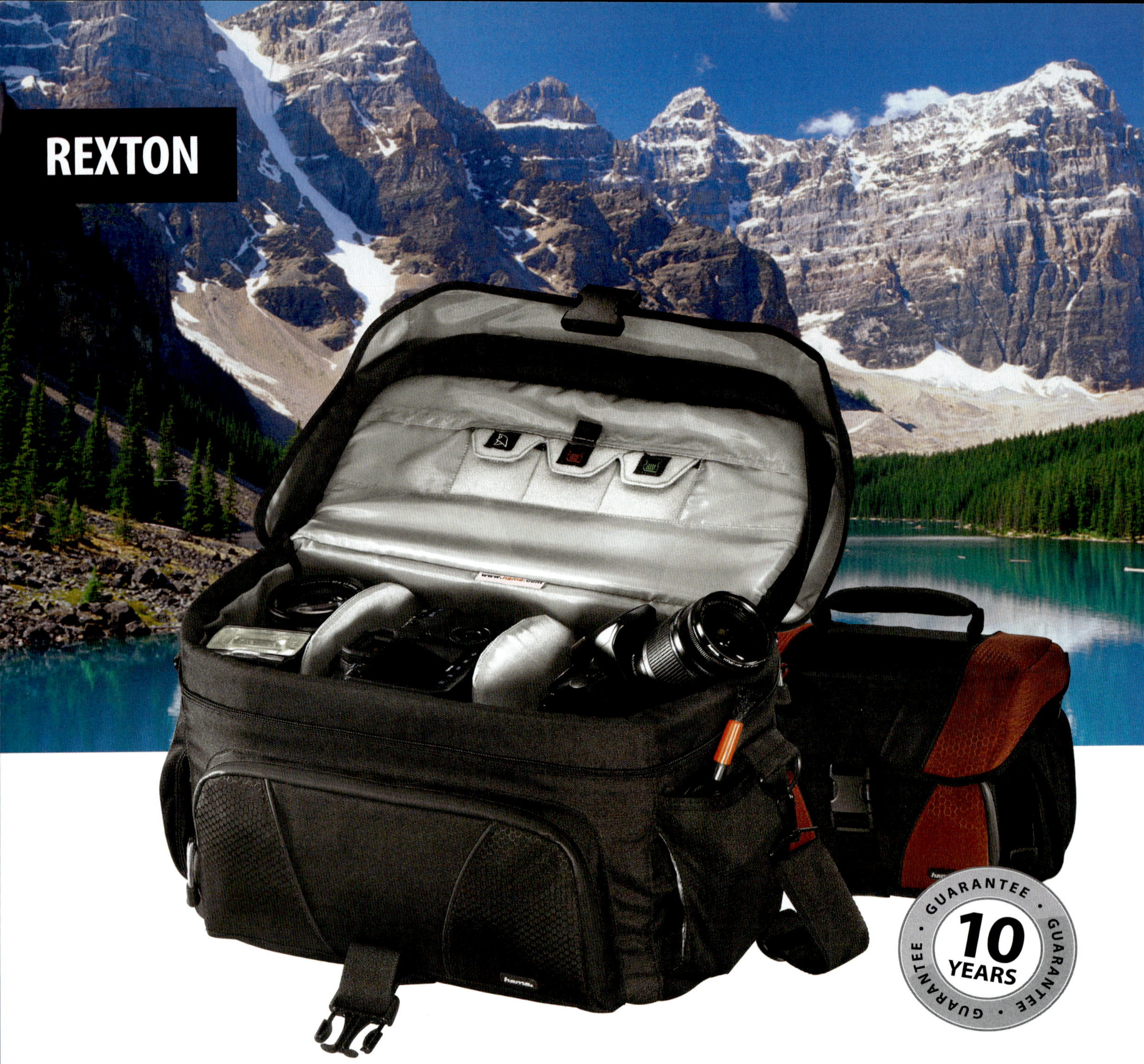
REXTON
GUARANTEE
10 YEARS

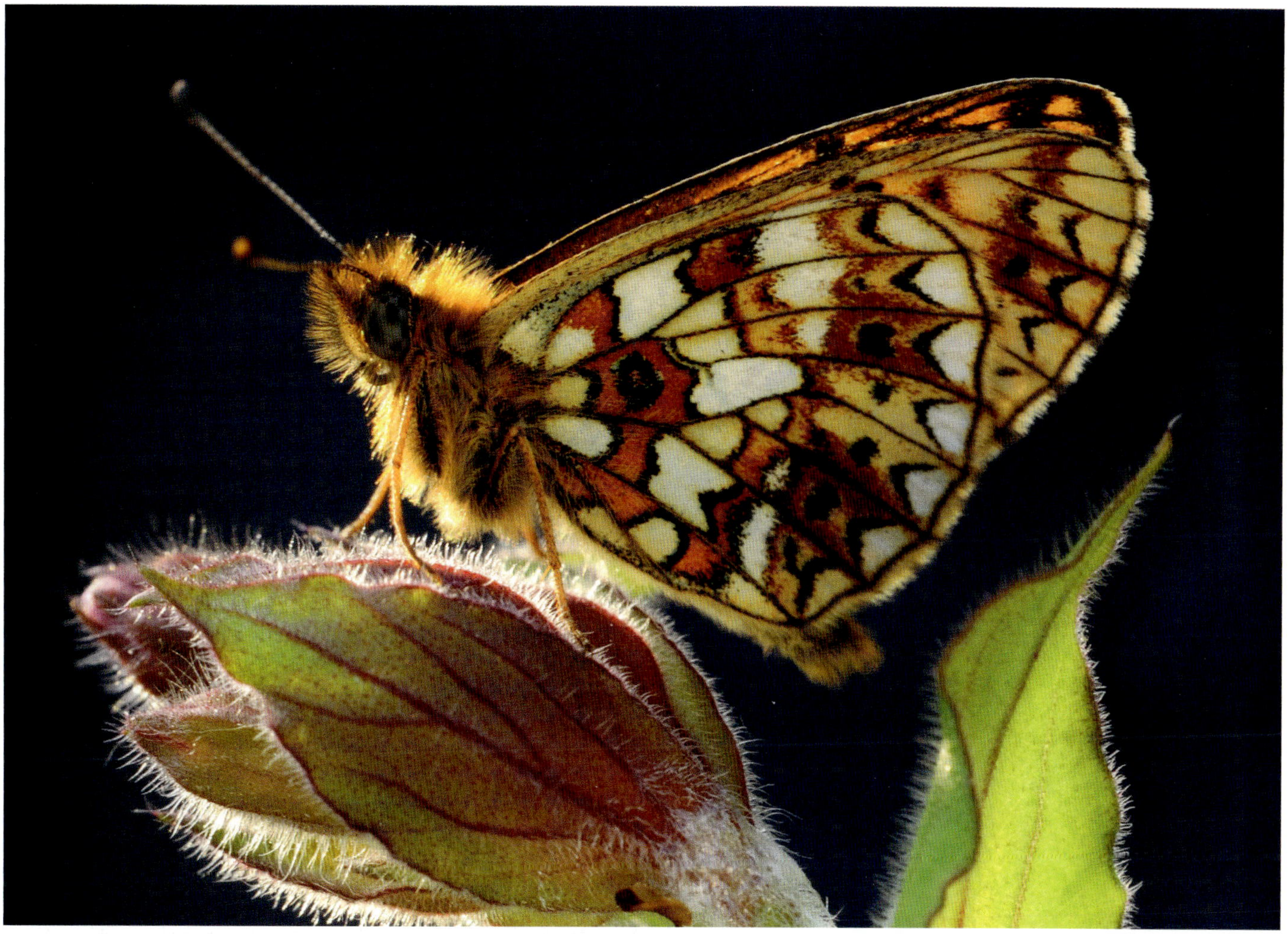

ESSENTIAL CAMERA KIT

Expert advice on choosing and using the best kit for your DSLR or CSC

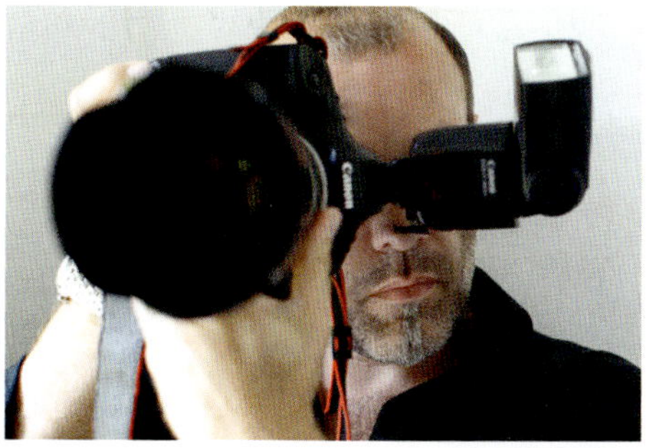

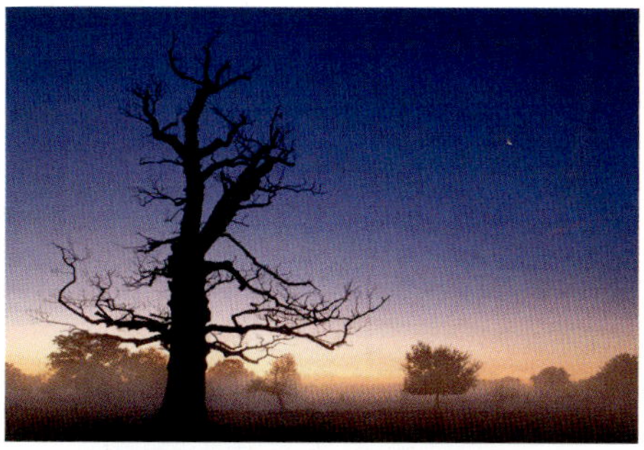

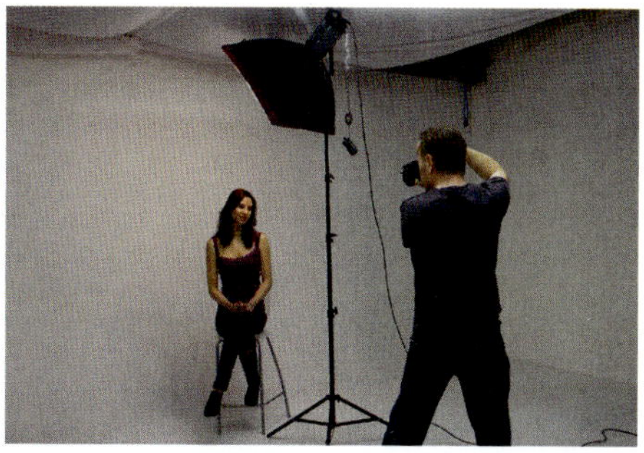

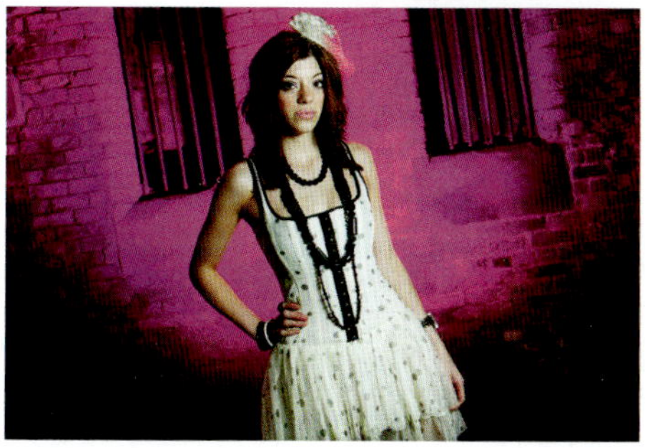

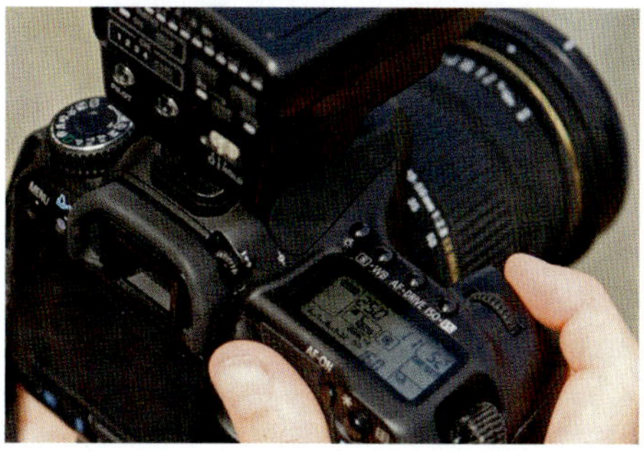

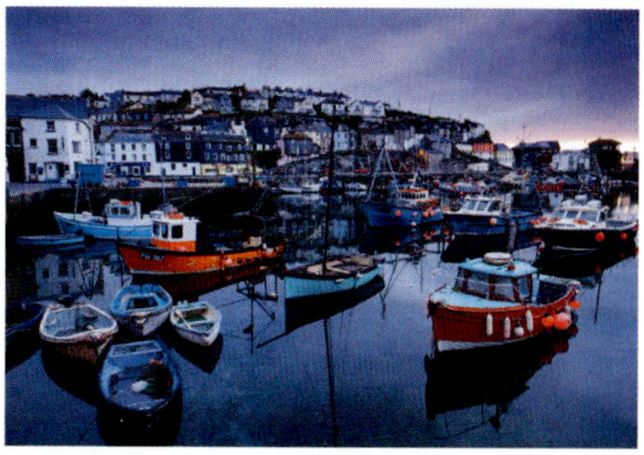

Fundamentals of lenses

Follow our essential advice to choosing the right lens for your needs

THE KEY WITH choosing lenses is to put together a system that serves all your needs. What those needs are will depend on the subjects you tend to shoot – specialist subjects, such as sport, nature and close-ups, have specific optical requirements. However, most of us like to try a bit of everything, so a more general selection will be required. In terms of focal lengths, if you have lenses covering 17-300mm on a full-frame DSLR (12-200mm for cameras with APS-C sensors), you'll be equipped for just about any situation. The wider focal lengths are ideal for scenic photography – landscapes, architecture, street scenes, travel – the mid-range focal lengths are great for portraiture, details and general use, while telephotos suit sport, candids and nature. Saying that, you can take brilliant landscapes with a telephoto and amazing nature shots with an ultra-wide, so use your imagination and make the most of all your lenses.

In this digital age, lens quality is more important than ever. High-resolution sensors are so good that they can easily out-resolve inferior lenses, so any flaws in optical design will be highlighted. These problems are at their worst in ultra wide-angle zooms, where chromatic aberration, diffraction, vignetting, distortion and loss of sharpness at the image corners are all common problems – and the less you pay for the lens, the more it's likely to suffer; though not in all cases. Telezooms tend to suffer less from all of the above because their optical design isn't as extreme, but they don't escape completely and the more pixels your camera has, the more your images will highlight any problems.

Optical flaws can be corrected, to an extent, during post-production, but it's preferable if they don't exist in the first place, or are at least minimised. The best way to ensure that is by buying the best lenses you can afford. Don't necessarily take the price of a lens as the only indicator of quality, as certain lenses from certain manufacturers have reputations, both good and bad. Instead, read reviews and ask the opinion of other photographers. Whether you buy prime (fixed focal length) or zoom lenses is down to you and your budget. Primes tend to have the edge in terms of image quality, but zooms are more versatile and you'd be hard-pressed to tell the difference between a shot taken using a £500 zoom and another shot with a £1,000 prime lens. Lenses from independent manufacturers, such as Sigma and Tamron, should be considered alongside the likes of Canon and Nikon – optically, they're often as good, but at more attractive prices. Whichever lenses you buy, to get the best optical performance from them, always use a mid-range aperture of f/8 or f/11 whenever you can. Image quality is at its lowest at the widest and smallest apertures, especially with wide-angle zooms, and at its sharpest at mid-apertures.

Lens choice: Prime v Zoom

A prime lens has a fixed focal length while a zoom's is variable. Both have advantages and disadvantages. In general, primes offer higher image quality, faster maximum apertures and are more compact and lightweight, but buying several proves costly. A zoom is more versatile and saves money as it covers a range of focal lengths. Quality isn't as high (but comes close) and the maximum aperture is slower, but its convenience makes it more popular.

Main types of lenses for digital photography

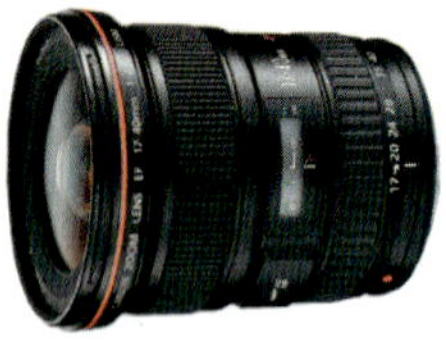

1) Wide-angle

With a wider field-of-view than the human eye can see, wide-angle lenses allow you to include more of the scene in the image frame, making it the ideal choice when shooting scenics, taking pictures indoors or when space is tight. There's an extensive choice of primes and zooms available, so you're not short of options. Wide-angles allow you to exaggerate perspective, which can lead to creative results. However, you do need to be aware of its tendency to distort, which can be used to your advantage, but can also ruin images if you go too far. See page 104 for more details on wide-angles.

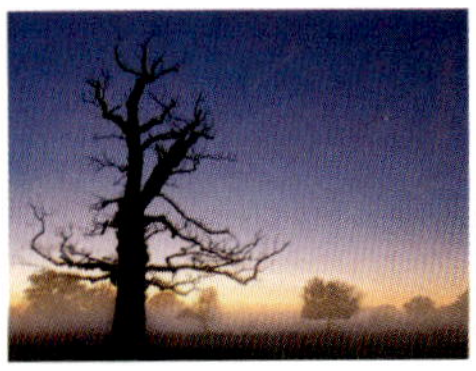

HELEN DIXON

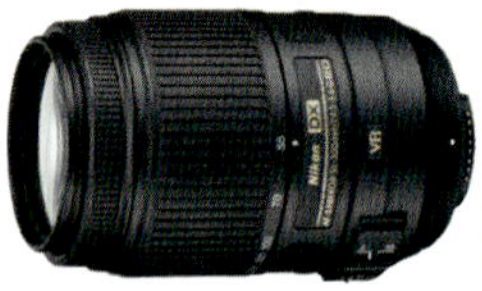

2) Telephoto

A telephoto zoom is often the first lens a DSLR or CSC photographer will add to their outfit. The extra pulling power a telephoto gives is ideal for filling the frame with relatively small or distant subjects. It's also ideal when you're trying to take pictures of a subject without it being aware, such as wildlife or when shooting candids. Its flattering perspective also makes it perfect for portraits. The 50-200mm and 70-300mm telezooms are popular choices, but need to be used with care to avoid the problem of camera shake. See page 106 for more details on telephoto lenses.

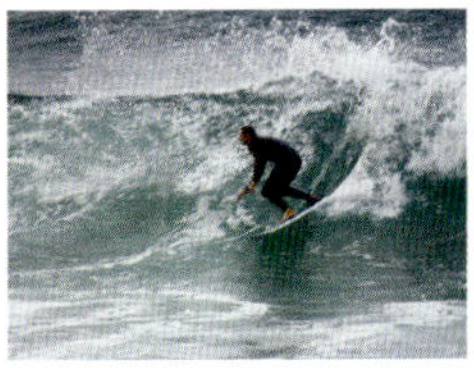

HELEN DIXON

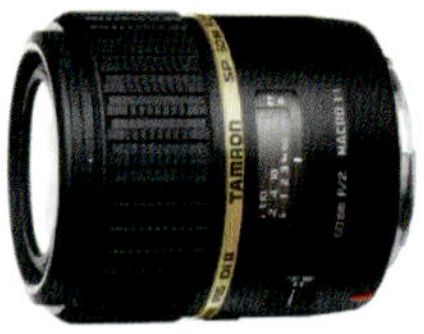

3) Macro

Physically, macro lenses look just like a normal lens, but the major difference is that they can focus much closer, allowing you to fill the frame with tiny subjects, such as insects and butterflies. They're also specially designed for use at close focusing distances, so optical quality is superb. The focal length tends to be either 50/55mm or 90/105mm. Both are useful and the vast majority offer 1:1 (life-size) reproduction, but the longer focal lengths are more suited to nature photography because they have a longer working distance, making them less likely to frighten away subjects.

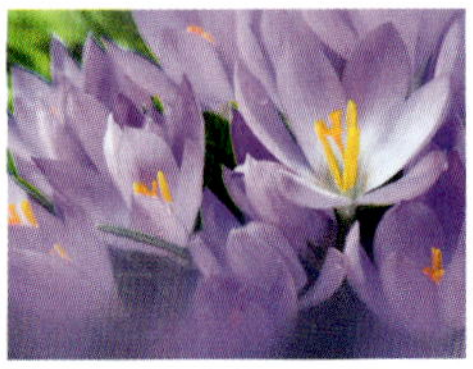

HELEN DIXON

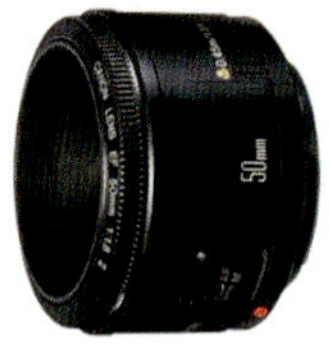

4) Standard

Once upon a time, SLRs were sold with a 50mm 'standard' lens, so every keen photographer had one. Today you get a standard zoom instead. However, it's worth investing in a 50mm prime, because for little outlay you get a compact and lightweight lens that's pin-sharp, focuses down to just a few inches, has a super-fast maximum aperture of f/1.8 and is perfect for hand-held, low-light photography. Use with an APS-C sensor and you have a brilliant 75-80mm portrait lens which, used at its widest aperture, will give minimal depth-of-field and produce superb images.

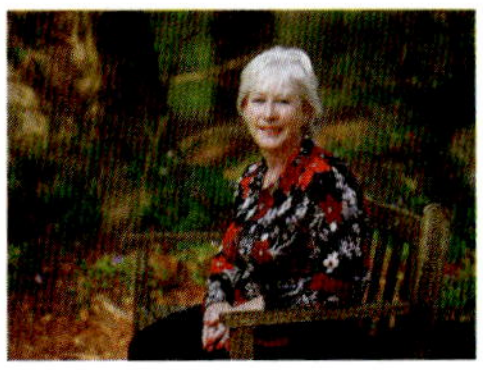

BJORN THOMASSEN

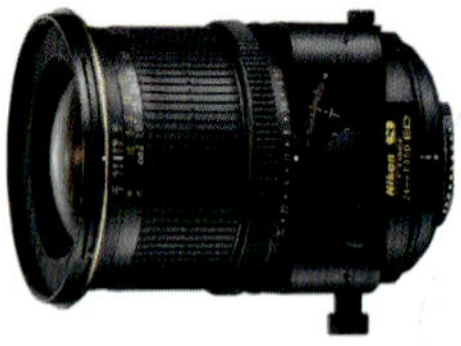

5) Tilt and shift

These expensive lenses serve two purposes. First, they prevent converging verticals when shooting architecture – instead of leaning back to include the top of a building, you shift the front of the lens up but keep the camera back parallel to the subject building. Second, the 'tilt' facility lets you tilt the front section of the lens down so the plane of focus is more in line with the plane of the camera's sensor. Doing this increases depth-of-field without having to set a smaller aperture. By tilting the other way, it reduces depth-of-field to almost nothing, achieving unusual effects.

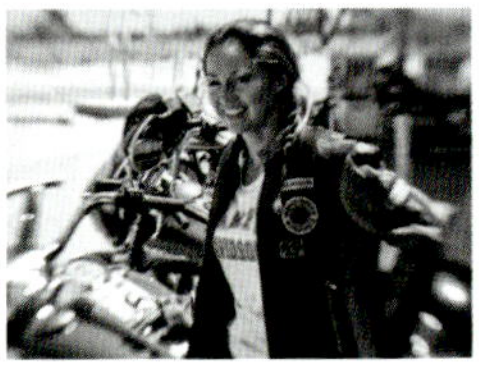

BENEDICT CAMPBELL

Understanding effective focal length

Most lenses available for use on your digital camera were designed for 35mm film SLRs or full-frame digital SLRs that have a sensor the same size as a 35mm film frame (24x36mm). However, only a handful of digital SLRs at present actually have a full-frame sensor, while the vast majority use an APS-C sized sensor that's smaller than full frame 35mm. This means that the focal length of 'normal' lenses is increased, to what is usually termed the effective focal length. The amount of increase can be calculated using a magnification factor (MF) and this is governed by the size of the sensor in the camera. Most cameras have an MF of 1.5x, although for Canon it is 1.6x and for Four Thirds cameras, 2x.

For landscape and other subjects where wide-angle lenses are mainly used, this focal length increase is a disadvantage. For example, an ultra-wide 17-40mm zoom will effectively work like a 25-60mm standard zoom on a digital camera with a MF of 1.5x. To get the same effect as a 17-40mm zoom, you would therefore need something like a 10-20mm or 12-24mm zoom. For sport, nature and other subjects requiring telephoto lenses, the focal length increase is more beneficial because it makes modest lenses more powerful.

A 70-300mm zoom effectively becomes a 105-450mm zoom on a camera with a MF of 1.5x, for example, so you can fill the frame with more distant or smaller subjects.

Another factor to consider is that lenses are at their sharpest in the centre and at their softest towards the edges. Cameras with an APS-C sensor therefore get the best from full-frame lenses as they use the sharper central area of the lens's image circle and exclude the outer limits of the image circle where image quality is lower. Understanding focal length can be confusing, but our tables below should help you understand it better.

Camera brand/models	Multiplication factor
Canon	
All EOS models (except those below)	1.6x
EOS-1D MkI to MkIV	1.3x
EOS 5D & EOS-1DS series	1x
Fujifilm	
All S-series models	1.5x
Nikon	
All D-series (except those below)	1.5x
D700 and D3 series	1x
Olympus & Panasonic	
All digital SLRs and CSCs	2x
Pentax	
All *ist and K-series models	1.5x
Samsung	
All GX and NX series models	1.5x
Sigma	
All SD models	1.7x
Sony	
All Alpha & NEX (except those below)	1.5x
Alpha 850 and 900	1x

EFFECTIVE FOCAL LENGTH The table above shows the effective focal length increase on the majority of popular brands of DSLR and CSC cameras. Use this magnification factor with the table on the right to work out the effective focal length of popular prime and zoom lenses.

SENSOR SIZES These images were all taken with a 35mm lens from the same spot and show the effect of the magnification factor.

Focal length on lens	Sensor size: Full frame	APS-H	APS-C	APS-C (Canon)	Four Thirds & Micro Four Thirds
	1x	1.3x	1.5x	1.6x	2x
14mm	14mm	18mm	21mm	22mm	28mm
15mm	15mm	19mm	22mm	23mm	30mm
20mm	20mm	26mm	30mm	32mm	40mm
24mm	24mm	31mm	36mm	38mm	48mm
28mm	28mm	36mm	42mm	45mm	56mm
50mm	50mm	65mm	75mm	80mm	100mm
85mm	85mm	110mm	127mm	136mm	170mm
100mm	100mm	135mm	150mm	160mm	200mm
10-17mm	10-17mm	13-22mm	15-25mm	16-27mm	20-34mm
10-20mm	10-20mm	13-26mm	15-30mm	16-32mm	20-40mm
10-22mm	10-22mm	13-29mm	15-33mm	16-35mm	20-44mm
11-18mm	11-18mm	14-23mm	16-27mm	18-29mm	22-36mm
12-24mm	12-24mm	16-31mm	18-36mm	19-38mm	24-48mm
16-35mm	16-35mm	21-45mm	24-53mm	26-56mm	32-70mm
17-35mm	17-35mm	22-45mm	25-53mm	27-56mm	34-70mm
17-40mm	17-40mm	22-52mm	25-60mm	27-56mm	34-80mm
18-55mm	18-55mm	23-71mm	27-82mm	29-88mm	36-110mm
18-200mm	18-200mm	23-260mm	27-300mm	29-320mm	36-400mm
18-270mm	18-270mm	23-351mm	27-405mm	29-432mm	36-540mm
24-105mm	24-105mm	31-136mm	36-157mm	38-168mm	48-210mm
28-70mm	28-70mm	36-91mm	42-105mm	45-112mm	56-140mm
28-300mm	28-300mm	36-390mm	42-450mm	45-480mm	56-600mm
55-200mm	55-200mm	71-260mm	82-300mm	88-320mm	110-400mm
70-300mm	70-300mm	91-390mm	105-450mm	112-480mm	140-600mm
100-400mm	100-400mm	130-520mm	150-600mm	160-600mm	200-800mm

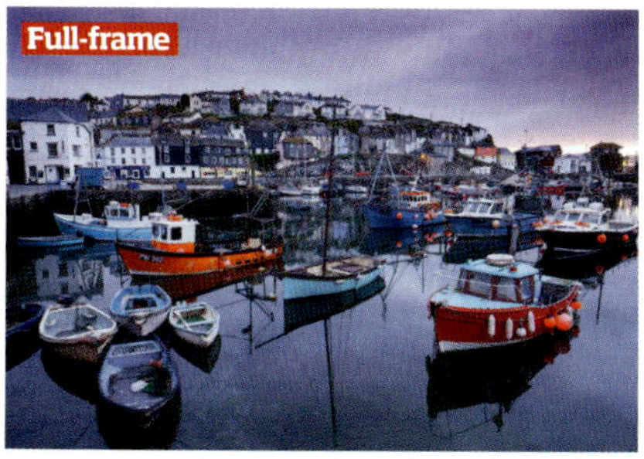
Full-frame

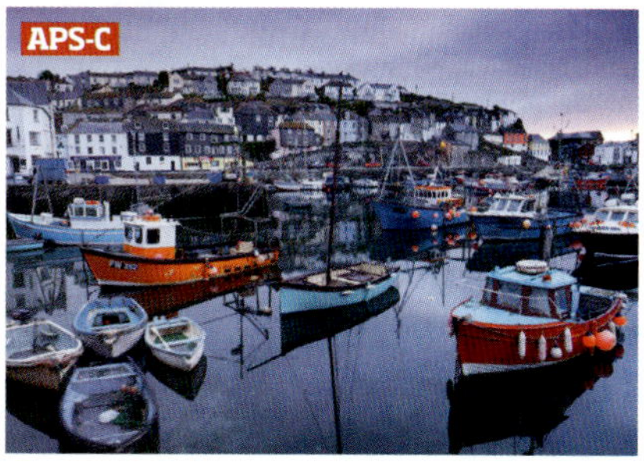
APS-C

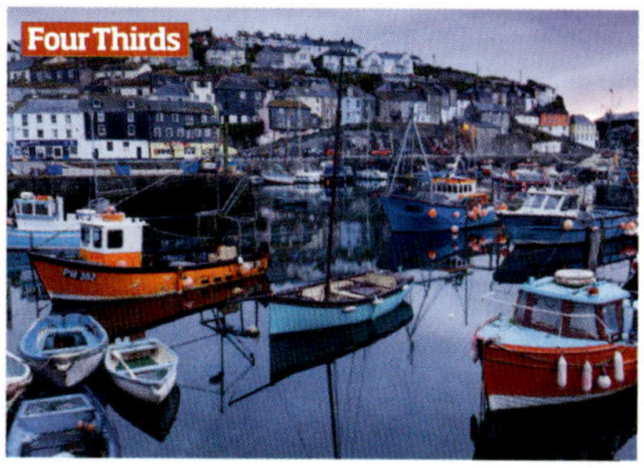
Four Thirds

ADAM BURTON

How different lenses record a scene

Your choice of lens determines how the scene is captured, so you need to be clear which is best to use for every shooting situation. Our comparison sets show how lenses affect field-of-view and perspective

The angle-of-view

This term, measured in degrees, refers to how much a lens actually 'sees' and is generally related to focal length. A 50mm standard lens (33mm in APS-C) is generally regarded as having the closest field-of-view to the human eye. Wide-angle lenses have a greater angle-of-view than the 50mm 'standard' and therefore include much more in a picture than you can see with your own eyes. The shorter the focal length (smaller the number), the wider the lens and the greater the angle-of-view. Normal wide-angle lenses have a focal length of 24mm or less (on a full-frame DSLR). Any wider than that – such as 20mm or 17mm – is classed as 'ultra wide'.

Telephoto lenses have a tighter angle-of-view than a standard lens and magnify the subject so it appears bigger in the frame. The longer the focal length (bigger the number), the narrower the angle-of-view and therefore the less you can include in a picture.

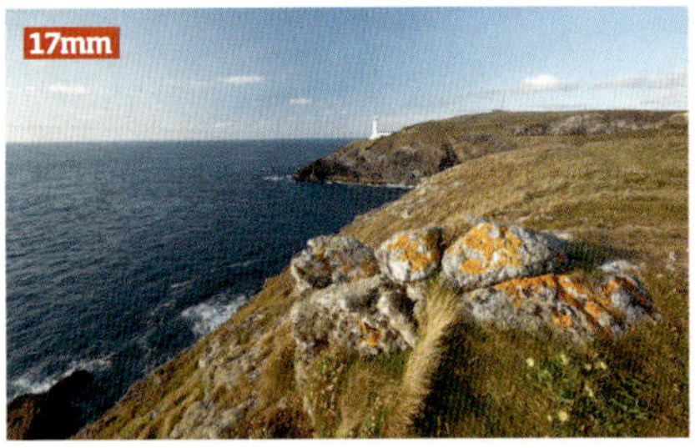

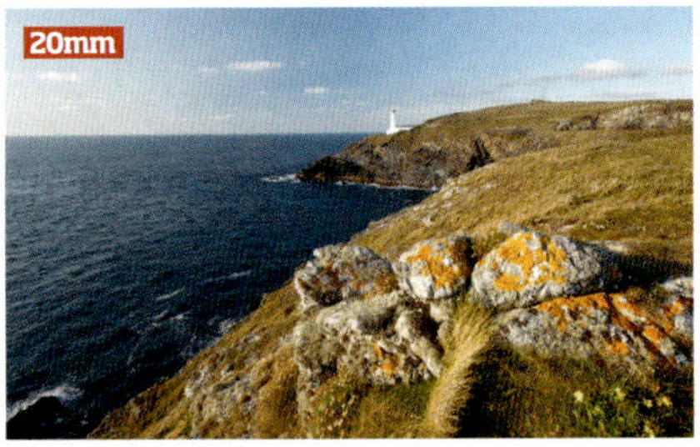

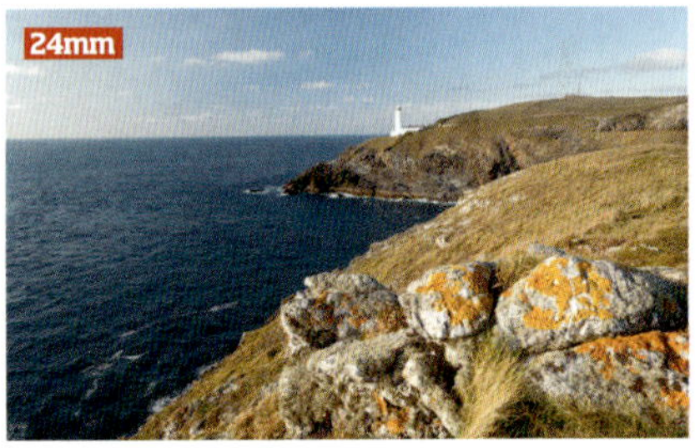

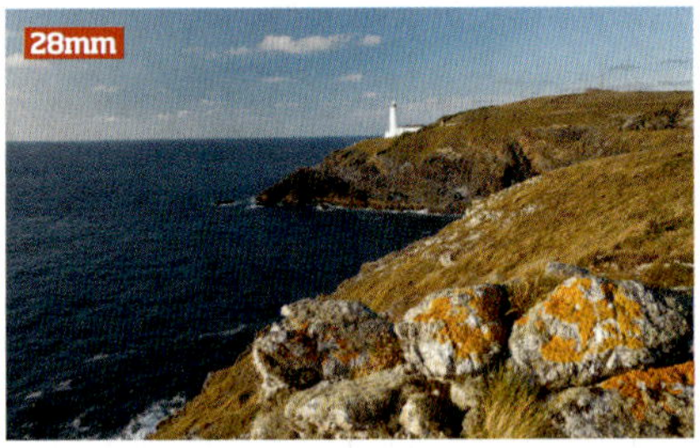

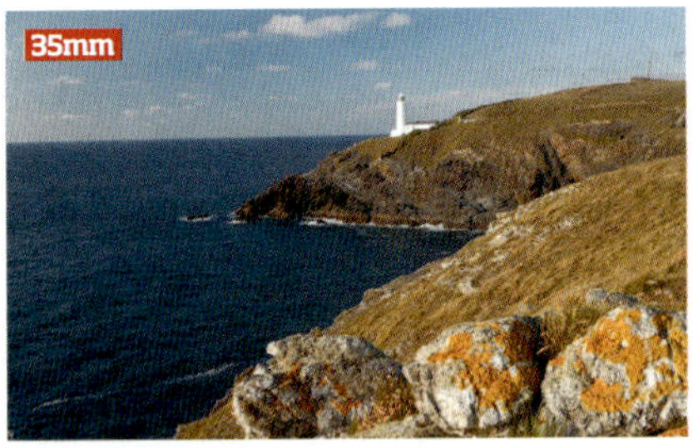

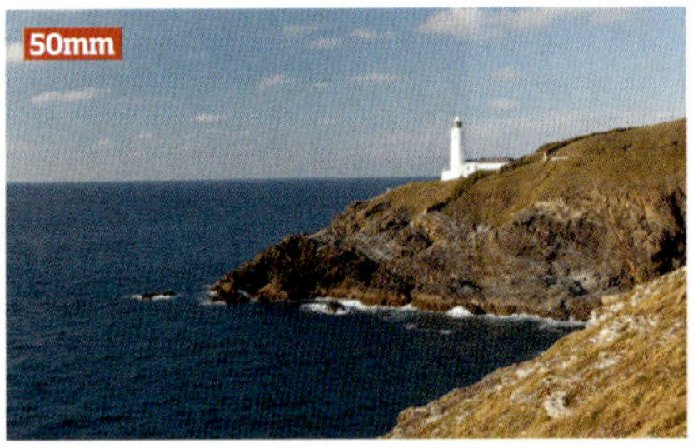

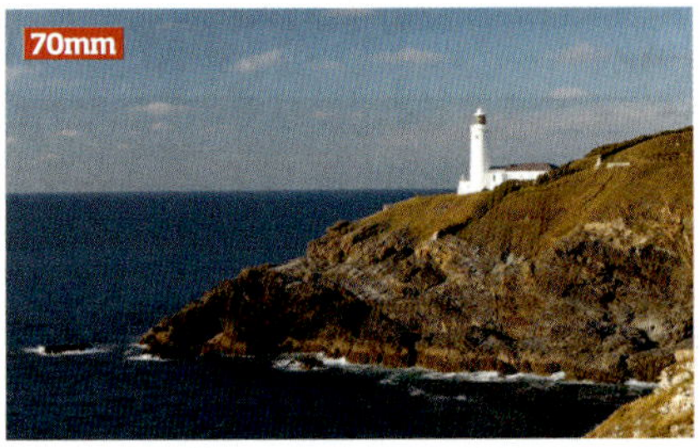

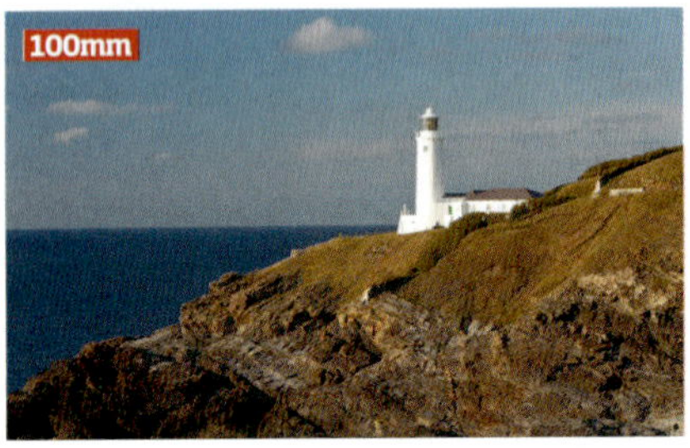

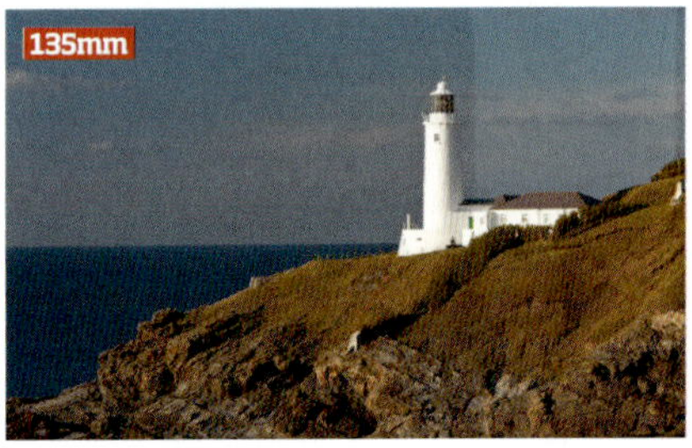

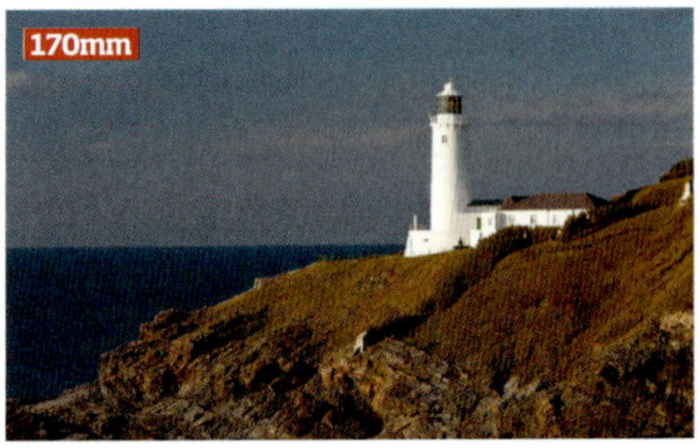

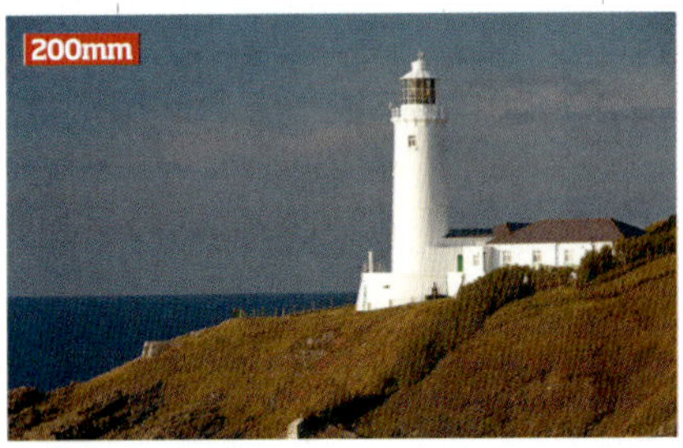

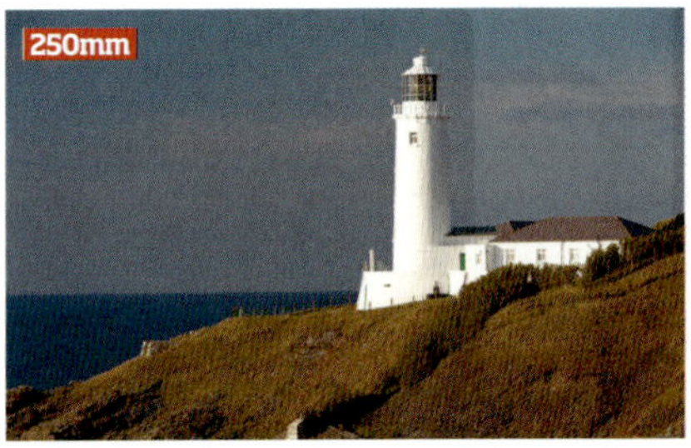

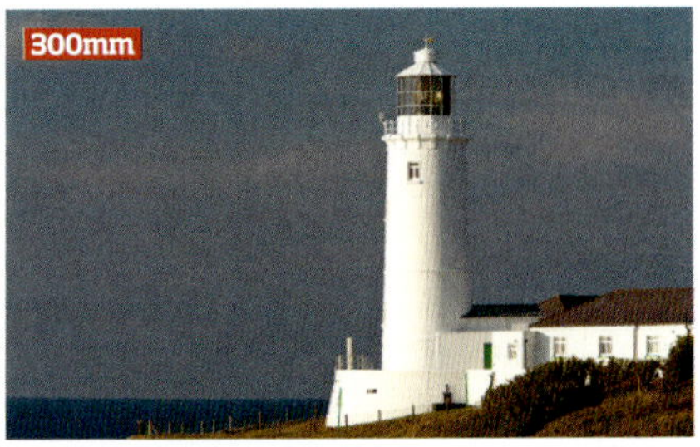

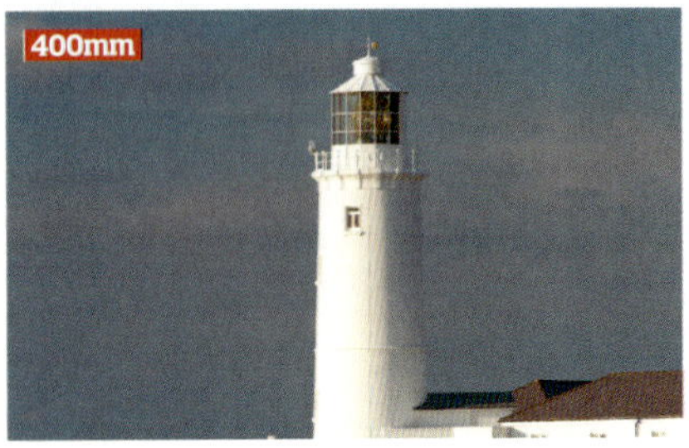

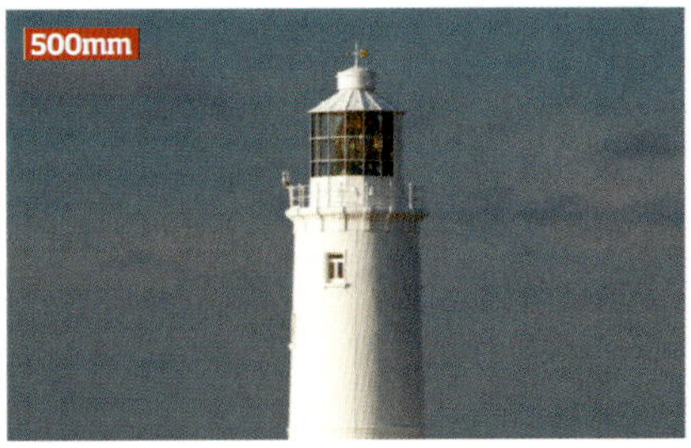

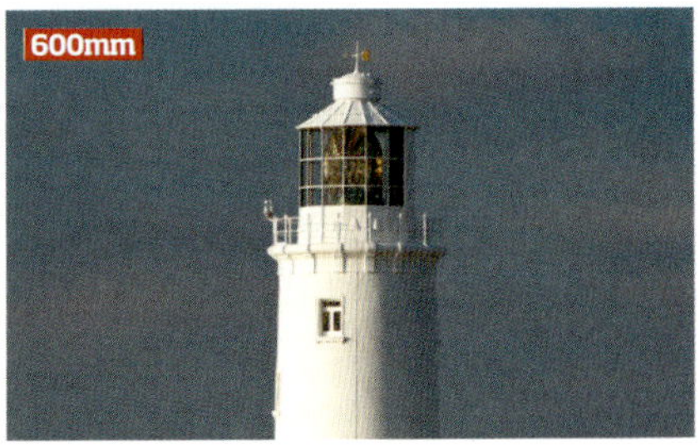

IMAGES: ROSS HODDINOTT

Perspective

What many photographers don't realise is your choice of lens can have a drastic effect on perspective. When shooting a subject, how you relate it to the background can be radically altered by the type of lens you use. Take an image with a wide-angle and you increase the depth of the scene and strengthen perspective. Use a telephoto and perspective is reduced; the scene is compressed so that it has far less depth.

To show changes in perspective, we shot a series of images at focal lengths from 10mm to 400mm, ensuring that the main subject appeared at a constant size in each image. This was achieved by adjusting the camera-to-subject distance – shooting from close-up with a wide-angle and moving further away as the telephoto setting increased. As you can see, the difference in perspective is enormous – bear this in mind when placing subjects against a backdrop.

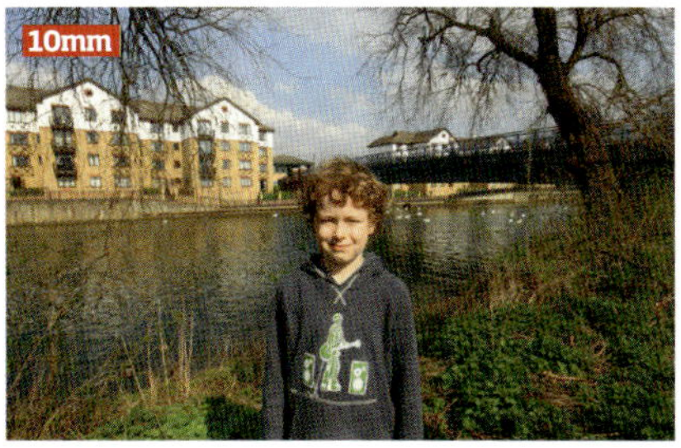

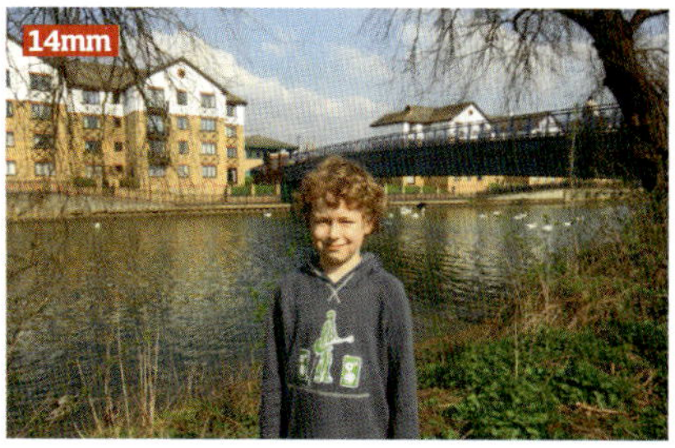

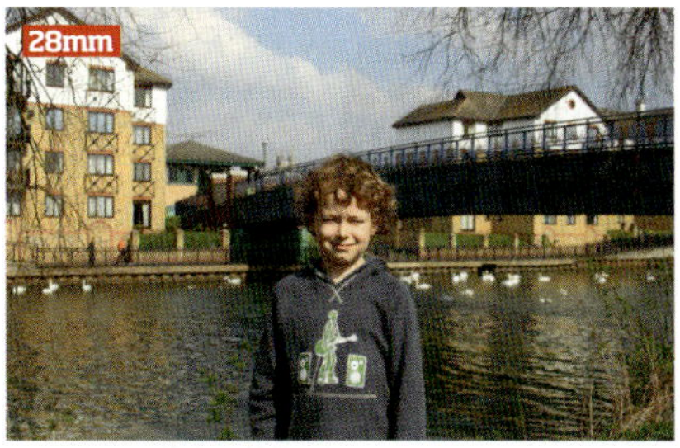

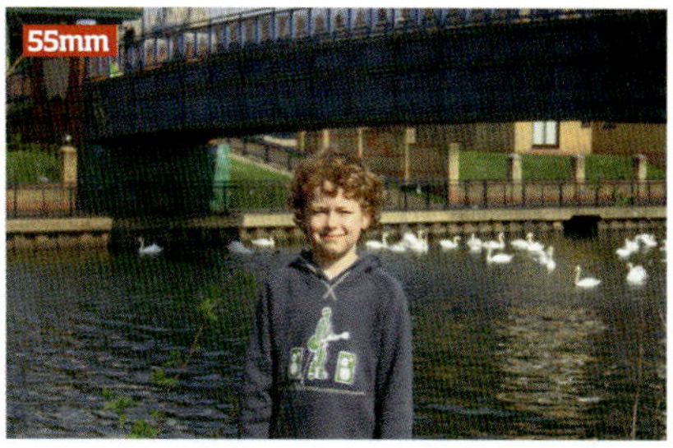

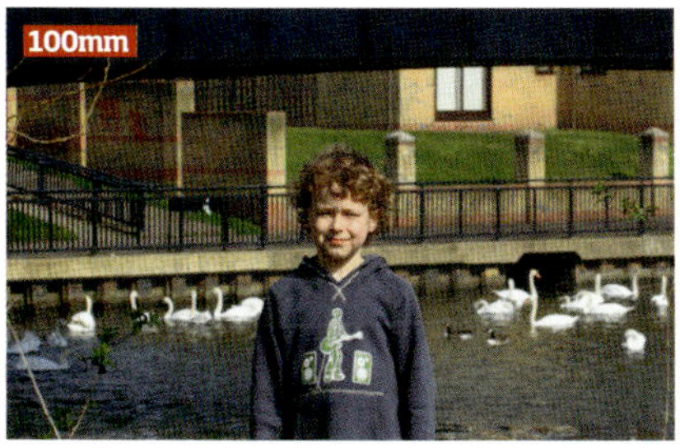

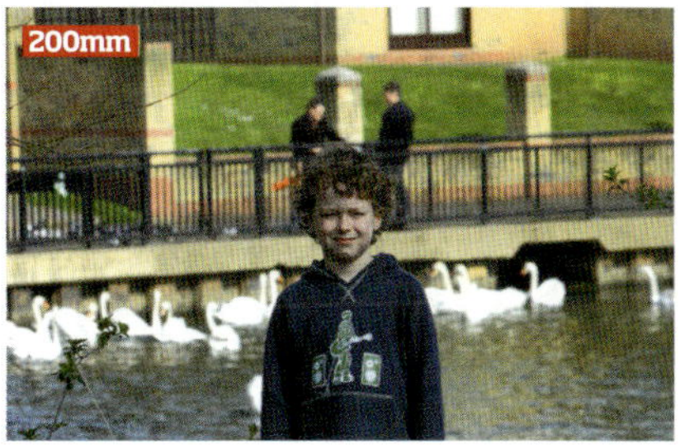

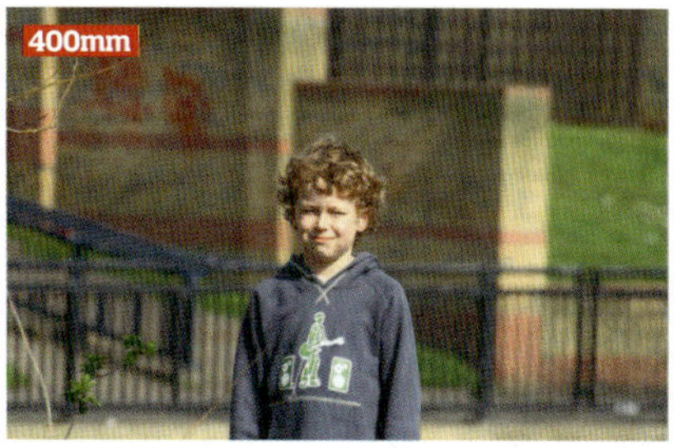

Depth-of-field

When you focus on a subject, an area in front and behind the focused point also appears sharp and this area is termed depth-of-field. The choice of aperture has a major effect on depth-of-field, with large apertures providing a shallow depth-of-field and small apertures allowing far more of the scene to be recorded in sharp focus. However, two other factors affect depth-of-field – the camera-to-subject distance and the focal length of the lens in use. As you'll discover when you use a variety of lenses, you get far more depth-of-field with wide-angles than with telephotos. So with an 18-200mm zoom set to f/8, the depth-of-field at 18mm far exceeds that at 200mm. Therefore, as well as considering how focal length affects perspective, you should also consider how you can use it to limit or increase depth-of-field. The shots below were all taken at f/8 from the same spot. Note how depth-of-field appears to reduce as you zoom in.

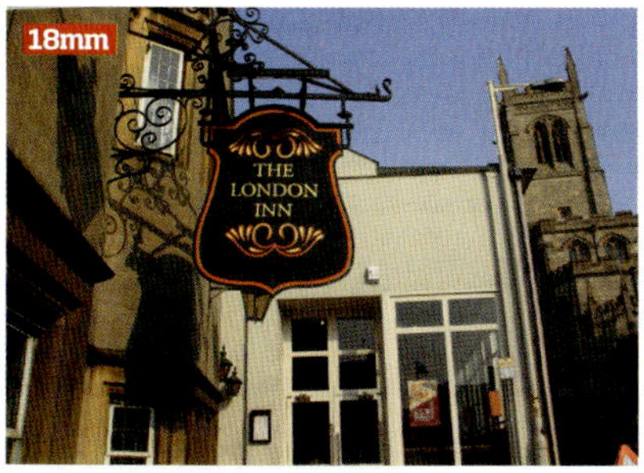

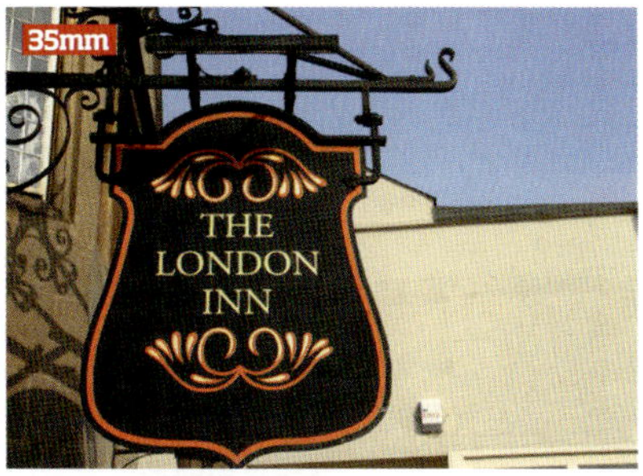

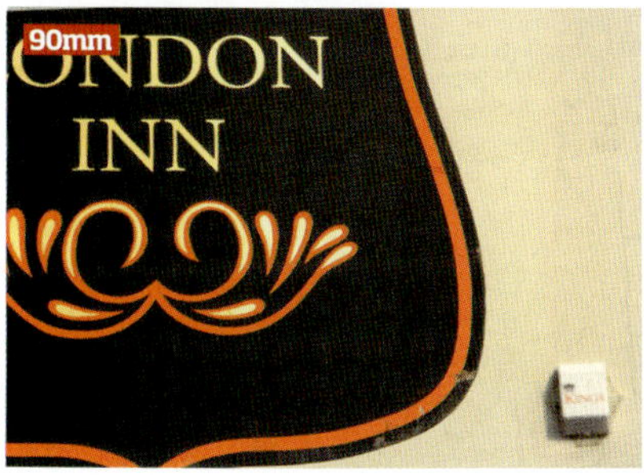

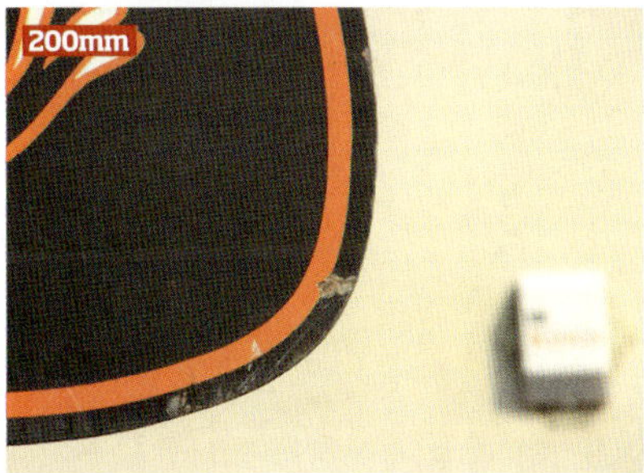

Lens problems

There are a number of problems to watch out for with lenses:

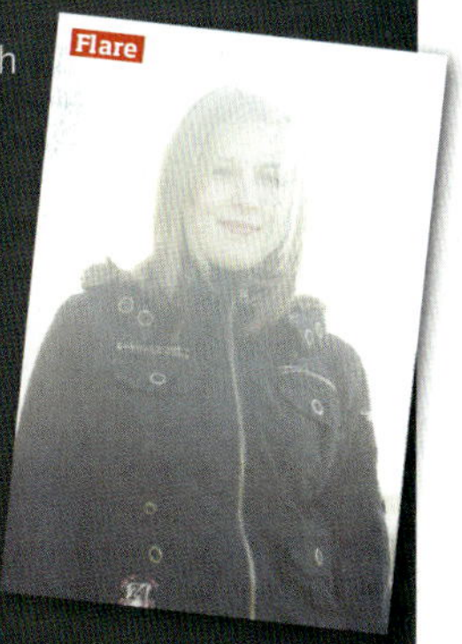

✗ FLARE Stray light from the sun, or any bright light source, can result in flare, which can reduce image contrast and result in hotspots in the image. It's easily avoided by using a lens hood or shading the lens with your hand or a bit of card.

✗ DISTORTION This is the phenomenon where straight lines appear curved in an image. Barrel distortion makes the centre of a line bow towards the frame edge, while with pincushion distortion, the opposite happens. Barrel distortion is most prominent in wide-angle shots, while pincushion distortion can appear at telephoto settings. This particularly affects cheaper lenses and zooms with a wide range. Lenses boasting aspherical lens elements minimise problems with distortion. It can also be rectified to a lesser or greater extent using Photoshop.

✗ CHROMATIC ABERRATION This technical term refers to how different wavelengths of light passing through a lens focus at various points. The result is usually a colour fringing; a thin but marked colour band that runs along the edge of contrasty image subjects. It is a lens problem that is controlled by the use of apochromatic lens elements.

Types of wide-angles

There are three main types of wide-angle lenses available, each offering its own pros and cons. Here, we explain the virtues of each...

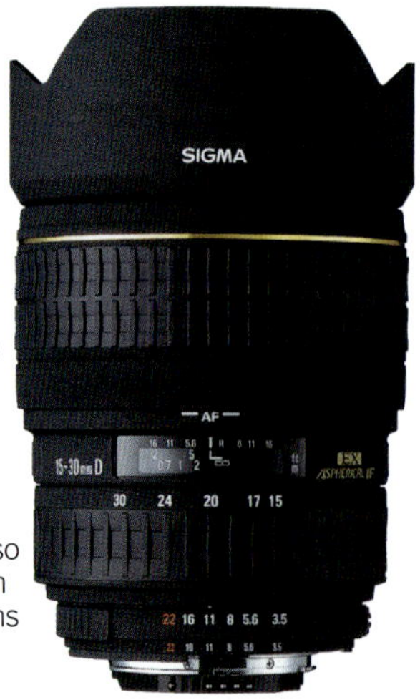

Ultra wide-angle zooms

This group of lenses has become increasingly popular. That's no surprise as the range they cover offers incredible versatility in such a small and inexpensive lens. In fact, the ultra wide-angle zoom is arguably one of the best value lenses you could own. There are a variety of focal lengths available, with those around 11-22mm being the most suitable for cameras with an APS-C sized sensor. In truth, all cover a very similar range, although there are one or two exceptions to note. The Pentax 10-17mm fisheye offers a 180° angle of view at its widest end, so, in a sense, you're getting a fisheye and ultra-wide zoom rolled into one. It's also worth noting that, unlike most ultra-wide zooms, the Sigma 12-24mm can be used on full-frame and APS-C cameras. Finally, while the 16-35mm lens is popular with film and full-frame camera users, the 24-53mm range it covers with APS-C sensors is quite limited, so we'd suggest you avoid it.

Fixed wide-angles

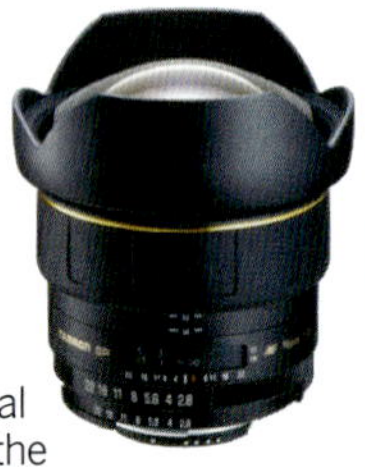

Small, lightweight and compact, with high quality optics, these are very desirable lenses that are available in various focal lengths and have been designed to offer the ultimate in wide-angles for digital photographers. They start with the ultra wide-angle 14mm, which is particularly suited to architectural photography, when trying to fill the frame with a building from a short distance. Wide-angles from 20mm to 28mm are ideal for landscape photography and are also used by travel photographers. However, their use with cameras sporting an APS-C sensor is limited, especially as a standard kit lens covers this range.

Fisheye lenses

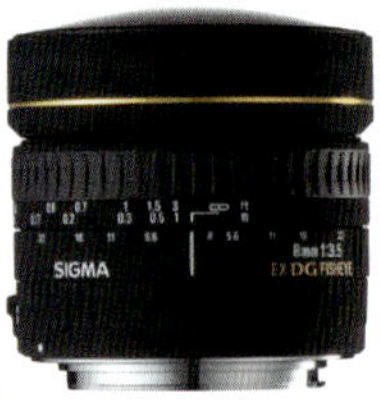

The fisheye offers the most extreme field-of-view. There are two types – the circular and the full-frame fisheye, both producing very different results. Circular fisheye lenses, when used on a full-frame camera, provide round images with a 180° angle of view. They distort perspective, especially when the subject is close and, with close-focusing capabilities, are perfect for comical portraits. The full-frame fisheye (also known as a diagonal fisheye) offers a 180° field of view and can capture incredibly wide vistas. They're very specialist, very expensive and have limited use, so hire one from a pro dealer before you buy.

Why use a wide-angle?

Ever wanted to photograph a subject or a scene and found that you can't fit it all in the frame? Then you need a wide-angle lens. With a field-of-view that extends far wider than the human eye, it's the perfect optic for capturing wide vistas or cramming large objects in the frame. Using such a lens comes at the price of characteristics like exaggerated perspective and distortion, but knowing what to expect and how to use it creatively allows you to take shots that aren't possible with any other type of lens.

Understanding focal lengths: Wide-angles

The focal length stated on a lens is usally related to cameras using 35mm film or full-frame sensors. If your camera has an APS-C-sized sensor, then you're effectively cropping the image and so giving the effect of a longer focal length lens on a full-frame sensor. The chart below shows popular wide-angles and how the effective focal length changes when used with digital cameras.

Focal length on lens	Cameras				
	Full-frame	APS-H	APS-C	APS-C (Canon)	Four-Thirds
	1x	**1.3x**	**1.5x**	**1.6x**	**2x**
8mm	8mm	10mm	12mm	13mm	16mm
14mm	14mm	18mm	21mm	22mm	28mm
15mm	15mm	19mm	22mm	23mm	30mm
20mm	20mm	26mm	30mm	32mm	40mm
24mm	24mm	31mm	36mm	38mm	48mm
28mm	28mm	36mm	42mm	45mm	56mm
10-17mm	10-17mm	13-22mm	15-25mm	16-27mm	20-34mm
10-20mm	10-20mm	13-26mm	15-30mm	16-32mm	20-40mm
10-22mm	10-22mm	13-29mm	15-33mm	16-35mm	20-44mm
11-18mm	11-18mm	14-23mm	16-27mm	18-29mm	22-36mm
12-24mm	12-24mm	16-31mm	18-36mm	19-38mm	24-48mm
16-35mm	16-35mm	21-45mm	24-53mm	26-56mm	32-70mm
17-35mm	17-35mm	22-45mm	25-53mm	27-56mm	34-70mm
17-40mm	17-40mm	22-52mm	25-60mm	27-56mm	34-80mm

Anatomy of a wide-angle zoom

1) Petal hood Ultra wide-angles come supplied with a dedicated hood to avoid vignetting and flare.

2) Large, concave front element The front element normally has a prominent curve, leaving it exposed to dust and scratches, so take care to keep it covered in transit.

3) Manual focus ring Normally towards the front of the lens and reasonably wide. You'll rarely need to use it, as wide-angle lenses have excellent autofocus.

4) Zoom ring This is normally found towards the back of the barrel. Most are wide with a grooved surface to allow you to grip it easily.

5) Focus distance Many lenses have the focus distance scale marked on the barrel, while some of the more upmarket models have a focus distance window.

6) Hyperfocal scale (see inset) This scale allows you to estimate how much of the scene will appear sharp at your choice of aperture.

7) Internal focusing system If you're planning to use filters, lenses with an internal focusing system offer the benefit that the front of the lens doesn't rotate when focusing, so you don't have to keep readjusting them.

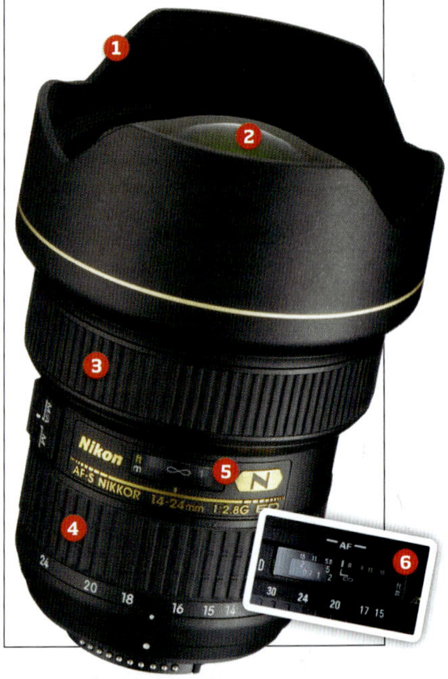

Digital-only lenses

When you're choosing a lens, check if it's for use film/full-frame digital SLRs, or for DSLRs with APS-C/FourThirds sensors only. Those made for film and digital are usually more expensive; those designed for digital-only are optimised only for sensors. If you're using a DSLR with an APS-C or smaller sensor and never plan to buy a full-frame DSLR, go for a digital-only lens, such as the Canon EF-S range or Nikon's DX.

Watch your feet!

The 180° angle of view for a fisheye lens means that you have to take great care not to include your feet! Lean slightly forward when using one to prevent feet appearing in the bottom of the frame

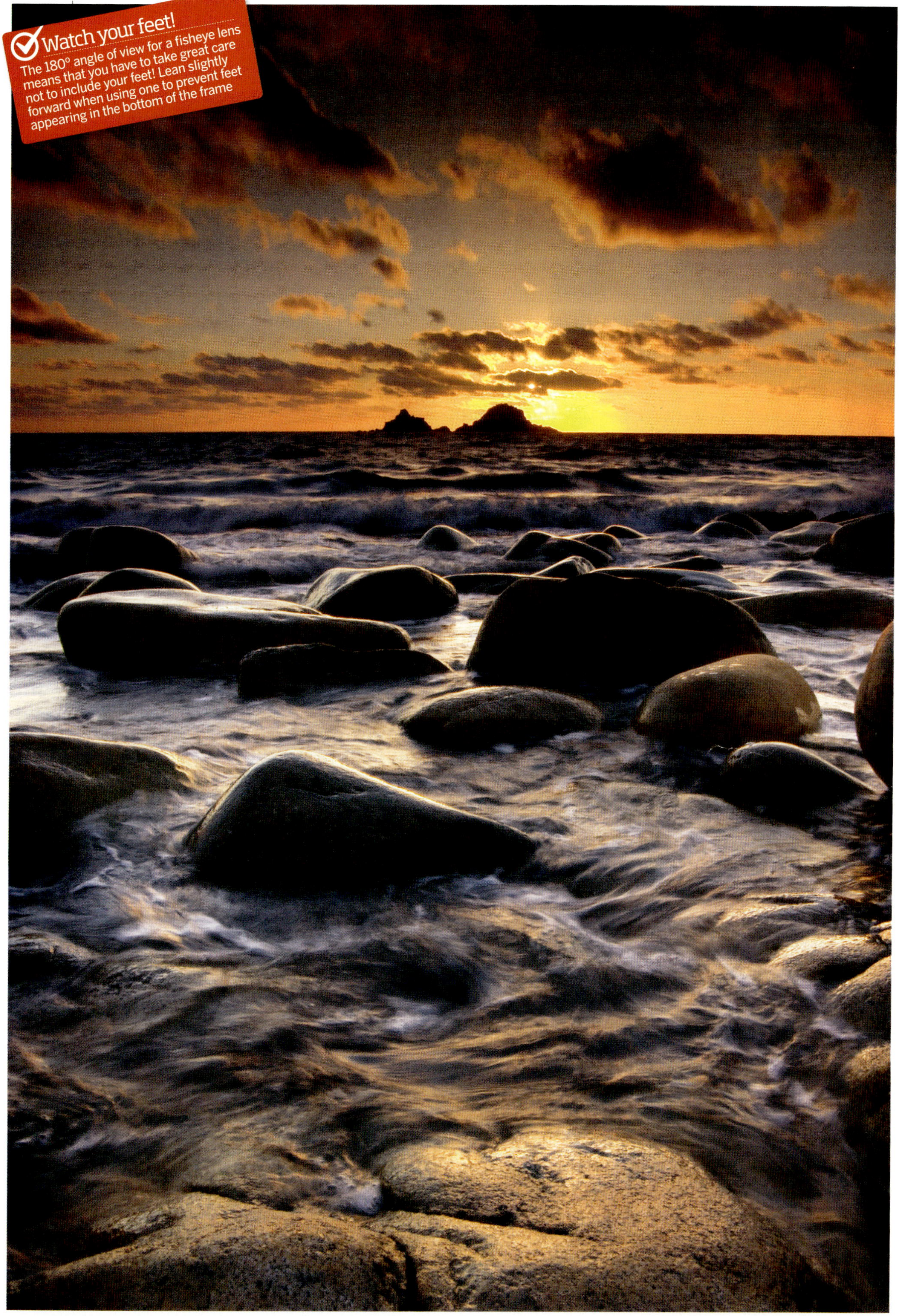

MATT WHORLOW

Types of telephoto lenses

A telephoto lens is a wise investment and a good addition to your gadget bag. However, there are a number of different types of 'tele' available, each with their own advantages, drawbacks and, of course, price tags!

Why use a telephoto/telezoom? Have you ever found yourself too far away from a subject to take a good frame-filling picture? It is often frustrating, but the solution may be as simple as using a lens with a longer focal length. Telephoto lenses are designed to magnify distant subjects, bringing them within photographic range without the need for you to get physically closer to the subject. This is ideal in situations where it is impractical to get nearer to the subject – for example, timid or dangerous wildlife or sporting events. However, while the effect can be considered similar to moving closer to the subject, it is not the same. Perspective and depth-of-field are altered through the use of long focal lengths, but providing you know how this will affect the scene or subject you are shooting, this can be used to your advantage.

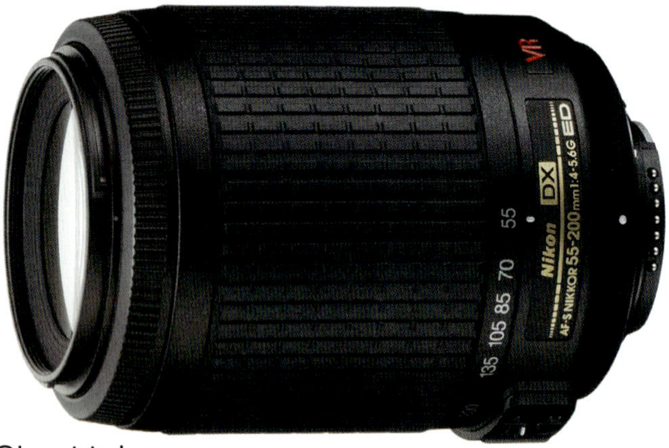

Short telezoom

A fixed lens simply can't match the versatility of a zoom. Short telezooms have focal lengths of around 50-200mm. They are available in a variety of different ranges: for example, 50-150mm, 55-200mm and 70-200mm. They allow you to choose from a wide variety of focal lengths at a fraction of the cost of buying individual 'primes' covering the same range. They allow for precise framing without the need to alter shooting position. However, a zoom's image quality isn't generally as high as that of a fixed lens and budget telezooms tend to be slow. Many have a variable maximum aperture (eg f/4-5.6), the lens being a stop (or more) slower at the long end of the zoom's range. Although budget models tend to suffer from some lens aberrations, modern zooms offer increasingly good image quality and the best short telezooms are good enough for use by pros. A short telezoom is well suited to a wide variety of subjects, including candids, nature, scenics, action and still-lifes. In fact, it is one of the most useful focal ranges available.

WHICH SHORT TELEZOOM? There is a huge number of lenses to choose from in this zoom category. However, if you are on a limited budget, consider the Sigma 55-200mm f/4-5.6 DC or Tamron 55-200mm f/4-5.6Di II, as both offer excellent value at around £130.

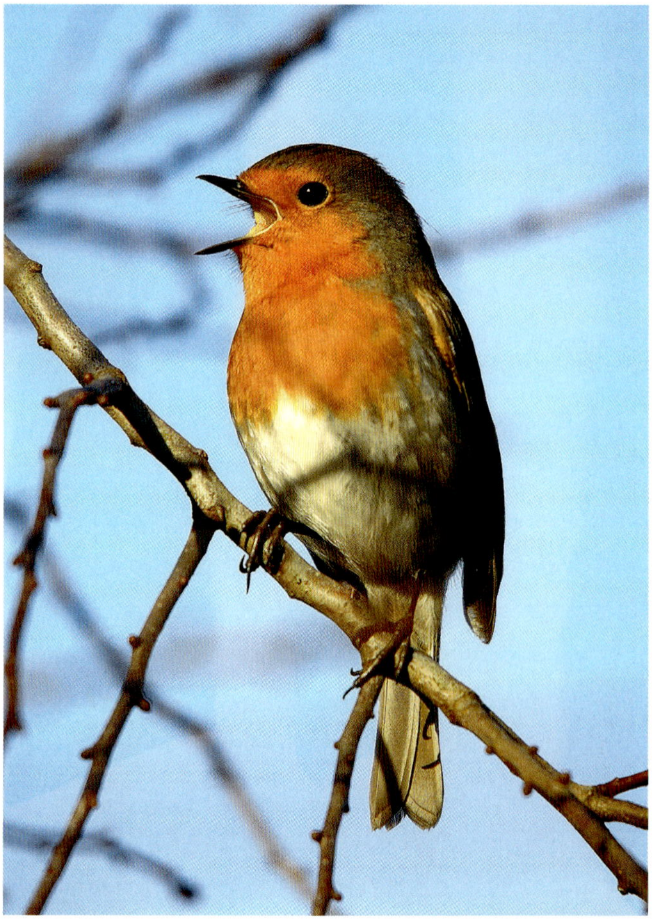

ROSS HODDINOTT

Super-telezooms

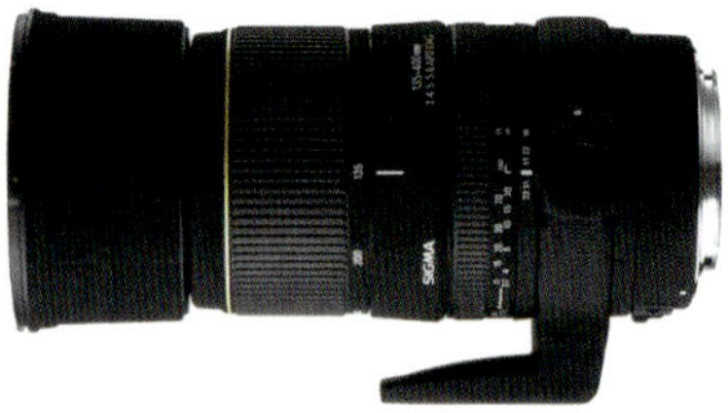

For an even greater magnification, try a super-telezoom; 70-300mm and 80-400mm are the most popular super-telezoom focal ranges, but they are available with an even more powerful range. For example, Sigma offers both a 170-500mm and 300-800mm telezoom. However, this degree of magnification is only required by a very small percentage of photographers – often those who shoot wildlife or sports. For the majority, a 70-300mm zoom will be more than adequate as, on a camera with an APS-C size sensor, this is equal to a full-frame 105-450mm lens.

Super-telezooms are ideally suited to shooting birds and mammals and for taking frame-filling sports shots from a distance. Do bear in mind that many super-telezooms have a relatively slow maximum aperture of f/5.6 at their longest end, which can be restrictive when shooting in low light. Also, be aware that autofocus can prove a little slow and noisy on budget models. However, when you consider that you can buy a 70-300mm for as little as £130, a super-telezoom is a great investment if you want to try your hand at action photography.

WHICH SUPER TELEZOOM? The £200 Sigma 70-300mm f/4-5.6 APO macro DG is a good lens, with a good close-focusing facility. The £350 Tamron 70-300mm f/4-5.6 Di VC USD offers image stabilisation too.

Fixed telephoto

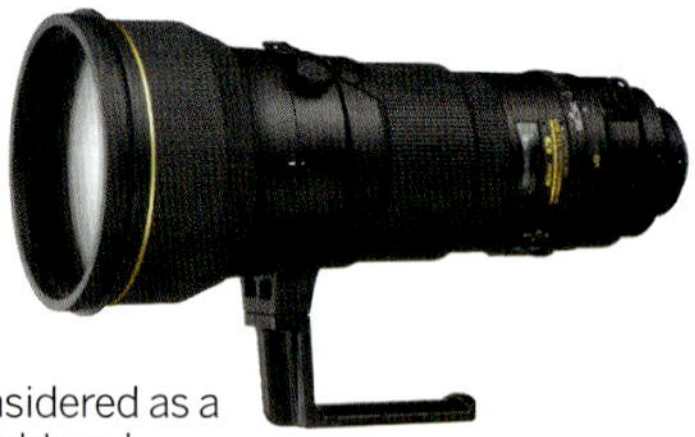

Prime telephoto lenses have a fixed focal length. While some might consider this a drawback, they are often favoured by professional photographers as they are optically superior to a zoom. A lens under 200mm is considered as a 'short' telephoto and is normally light and compact, so can be used hand-held. Also, most boast a small filter thread size, making it cheaper to buy lens attachments for them. Short telephotos in the region of 85mm to 135mm are ideal for portraiture, allowing photographers to work from a distance that isn't uncomfortably close to the sitter. This focal length is also suited to isolating details in scenics. Focal lengths upwards of 200mm are deemed 'long' telephoto and these lenses are generally big and heavy, making the use of a tripod almost essential. Long telephotos other than pro models also have a slower maximum aperture. While those with fast maximum apertures of f/2.8 or f/4 are best, they can cost thousands; so only pros and those with deep pockets can justify the price. Fast prime telephotos are bulky and heavy, but for wildlife and action photographers, their quality can't be surpassed.

WHICH PRIME LENS? For general day-to-day photography, a 200mm is a good, versatile focal length. Consider the Canon EF 200mm f/2.8L USM or Nikon 180mm f/2.8 D IF ED, both priced at around £650.

Anatomy of a telephoto

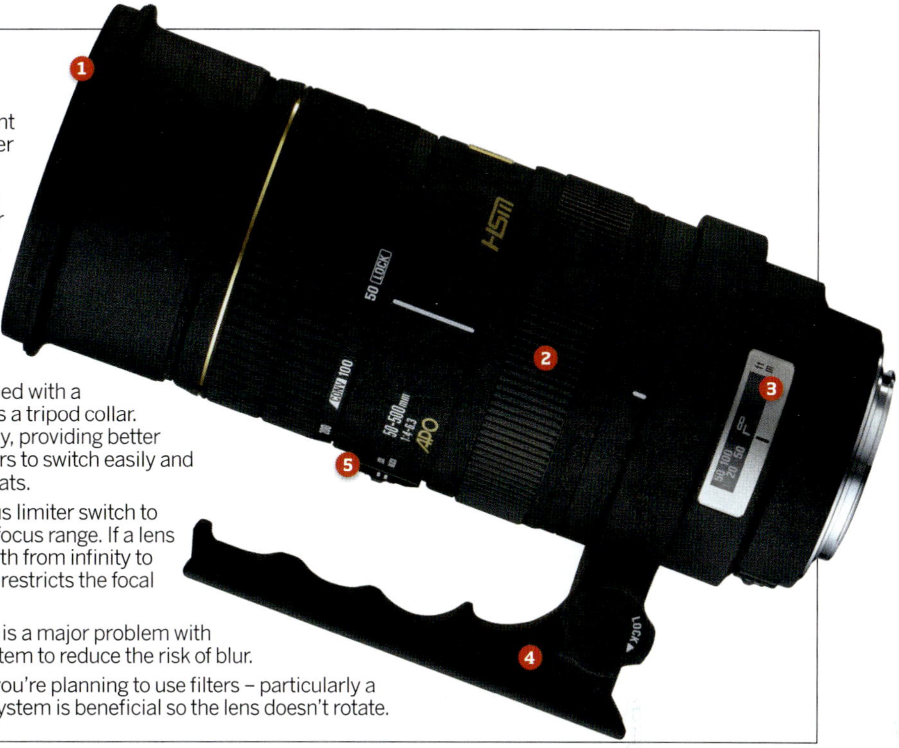

1) FRONT ELEMENT Fast telephotos will have a large diameter front element and filter thread size. To prevent scratches and dirt, consider using a UV or Skylight filter for added protection.

2) MANUAL FOCUS RING These are normally towards the front of the lens and are quite wide and grooved for grip. It is well worth focusing manually when you want added precision.

3) FOCUS DISTANCE Many lenses have the focusing distance scale marked on the lens's barrel, while some of the higher-spec models have a focusing distance window.

4) TRIPOD COLLAR Many 'long' telephotos are designed with a mount that features a tripod bush at its base, known as a tripod collar. This allows the lens to be attached to the tripod directly, providing better balance and stability. Many are rotatable, allowing users to switch easily and quickly between horizontal and vertical shooting formats.

5) FOCUS LIMITER Some telephoto lenses have a focus limiter switch to prevent the lens from focus 'hunting' across its entire focus range. If a lens is struggling to focus, it will 'hunt' – going back and forth from infinity to the minimum focus. To prevent this, the limiter switch restricts the focal range that the autofocus system will use.

6) IMAGE STABILISATION *(not shown)* Camera shake is a major problem with telezooms, so many boast an integral stabilisation system to reduce the risk of blur.

7) INTERNAL FOCUSING (IF) SYSTEM *(not shown)* If you're planning to use filters – particularly a polariser – a telephoto boasting an internal focusing system is beneficial so the lens doesn't rotate.

Understanding focal lengths: Telephotos

The focal length of a lens – referred to in mm – relates to a 35mm film SLR or digital camera employing a full-frame image sensor. Therefore, if your camera has an APS-C sized sensor, then you are effectively cropping the image and increasing the focal length of the lens. Our table lists below the most popular telephotos and how the effective focal lengths change with different sensor sizes.

Focal length on lens	Cameras				
	Full-frame	APS-H	APS-C	APS-C (Canon)	Four-Thirds
	1x	**1.3x**	**1.5x**	**1.6x**	**2x**
50mm	50mm	65mm	75mm	13mm	16mm
100mm	100mm	130mm	150mm	160mm	200mm
200mm	200mm	260mm	300mm	320mm	400mm
300mm	300mm	390mm	450mm	480mm	600mm
400mm	400mm	520mm	600mm	640mm	800mm
500mm	500mm	650mm	750mm	800mm	1000mm
55-200mm	55-200mm	72-260mm	83-300mm	88-320mm	110-400mm
70-300mm	70-300mm	91-390mm	105-450mm	112-480mm	140-600mm
100-300mm	100-300mm	130-390mm	150-450mm	160-320mm	200-600mm
80-400mm	80-400mm	104-520mm	120-600mm	128-640mm	160-800mm

Teleconverters

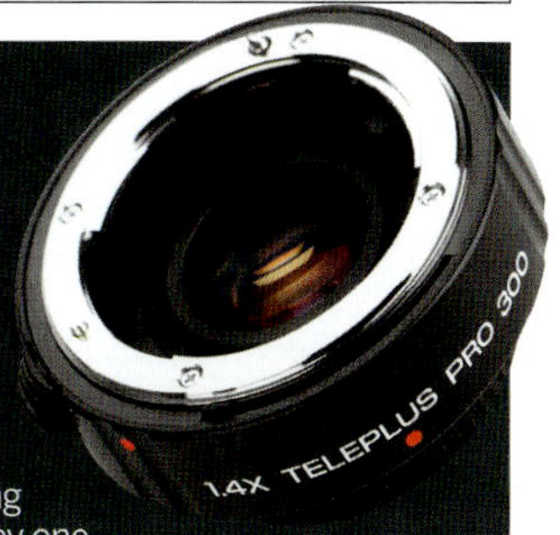

A teleconverter is an optical component that fits between camera and lens and increases the focal length without altering the minimum focusing distance. They are most commonly made in 1.4x and 2x versions – although 1.7x and 3x versions are also produced. Therefore, a 200mm telephoto combined with a 1.4x converter would be equivalent to 280mm, while the same lens coupled with a 2x multiplier would be transformed into a 400mm lens. Converters are relatively inexpensive, light and compact, so are a convenient and economical way to expand the overall flexibility of your kit. However, there are disadvantages to using converters. Firstly, they reduce the amount of light entering the camera by one stop (1.4x) or two stops (2x) respectively. This can prove a problem in low light, when the risk of camera shake is increased, and when photographing fast action, when subject blur is more likely due to the resulting slower shutter speed. The other drawback of attaching one is that image quality is slightly degraded, with zoom lenses being affected more than fixed focal lengths. Generally speaking, though, the benefits of using one outweigh the disadvantages. For best quality, opt for one with more elements in the construction. Nikon, Canon and Sigma are among the camera manufacturers which boast converters within their range, but don't overlook independent brands either, like Tokina, Tamron and Kenko. Due to their design, some optics are incompatible with teleconverters, so check your lens instruction manual or ask before buying.

Prime or telezoom lens?

It is the age-old question – why buy a fixed lens, with only one focal length, when a zoom is much more versatile? Here we have listed the 'pros and cons' to both lens types to help you decide which suits your photography best.

PRIME TELEPHOTO LENS:

✔ Simpler optical design means sharper results with better contrast

✔ More robust, compact construction

✔ The faster maximum aperture provides a brighter viewfinder and better low-light capabilities

✔ Will often boast a closer focusing distance than a zoom

✘ **Restricted to just the one focal length**

✘ **Cost – prime lenses are typically more expensive than zoom lenses**

TELEZOOM LENS

✔ Covers a range of focal lengths, so provides greater versatility

✔ Replaces the need to carry several different fixed lenses, meaning that there is less for you to lug about

✔ Lots of flexibility at a very good price

✘ **Not as good optically as a fixed lens, particularly towards the edges of the frame**

✘ **Maximum aperture slower than a fixed lens**

✘ **Paradoxically, zooms can offer too much choice – complicating framing and composition**

The perfect 'general use' lens

The standard kit zoom supplied with your camera is a good general purpose lens that is capable of decent results, but we'd recommend you consider buying an inexpensive standard lens for better optical quality

CSC 'standard' lenses

A 'standard' lens is available for most CSC brands. Micro Four-Thirds have the Panasonic G 20mm f/1.7 lens, Samsung the 30mm f/2 lens and Sony NEX the 50mm f/1.8 lens

The 'standard' 50mm f/1.8

In the days of 35mm film SLRs, you'd invariably find a 50mm f/1.8 prime lens attached to the front of virtually every SLR. It was the first lens that virtually everyone with an SLR used and remained popular until the late eighties. It was around this time that standard zooms started to appear. With variable focal lengths ranging from wide-angle to short-telephoto, the 28-70mm (and similar) lens represented a step forward in terms of flexibility and sadly it led to the demise of the 50mm as the standard lens of choice. However, its popularity has recently seen a resurgence for a number of reasons.

The first is that it's a very inexpensive lens to get hold of. With 50mm lenses from the likes of Canon, Nikon and Sony costing just over £100 new, and used versions available for a little over half that, they're an affordable choice for most of us. To add further credence to the value-for-money argument, consider this fact. The lens of choice for many portrait pros has long been the 85mm telephoto, which for an f/1.8 version will set you back around £300. If your DSLR uses an APS-C sensor, as most do, a 50mm that costs you £100 equates to a 75mm f/1.8 (or 80mm f/1.8 if you use Canon) – but with an effective saving of around £200!

Also, if you don't mind buying a used manual focus lens, you can pick one up for around £25. So for the price of a decent memory card, you can get a high-quality piece of glass that may be a few decades old and lack AF, but won't leave you wanting in the optical department. So, there's no denying a 50mm lens is affordable, but what else does it offer? Well, the biggest selling point must surely be its maximum aperture of f/1.8. Having a lens with such a fast maximum aperture offers stacks of potential. With your average 18-55mm having a maximum aperture of f/3.5-5.6, the 50mm is two to three stops faster, giving a brighter viewfinder image and allowing you to shoot handheld in low light, while using lower ISO ratings than you would normally get away with.

The main benefit of the wide maximum aperture is the extremely shallow depth-of-field when you shoot wide open, which helps isolate the main subject from its surroundings. This single feature provides significant creative opportunities, especially in the field of portraiture. The 50mm also scores better than virtually any lens in the size and weight department. Weighing around 150 grams and measuring about 5cm in length, it's the perfect optic to keep with you, especially when you're travelling and storage is at a premium.

The final benefit is possibly the most important – image quality. As with the majority of prime lenses, the optical quality from the humble 50mm lens is arguably better than all but the high-end zooms and in terms of sharpness, is far superior to a standard zoom. In terms of sharpness, distortion, light fall-off and contrast and even when used wide open, you'll have little to complain about. So, there you have it, a small, lightweight and highly affordable lens with a super-fast aperture and razor-sharp optics. Is it not time you bought one?

Current AF 50mm f/1.8 lenses

You'll find that brands with full-frame DSLRs in their range have retained 50mm lenses in their line-up. If you're on a budget, avoid the faster f/1.4 and f/1.2 variants aimed at pros, as they're larger and cost far more. The Canon and Nikon lenses have been around for years, so look for mint-condition used lenses!

Canon EF 50mm f/1.8II

Guide Price: £130
Street Price: £100
Size (WxL): 68.2x41mm
Weight: 130g

The MkII lens is virtually identical to the original – both are well worth buying.

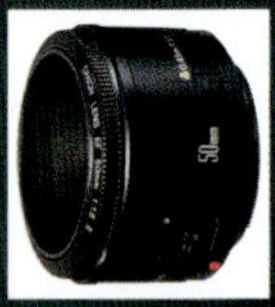

Nikon 50mm f/1.8D

Guide Price: £135
Street Price: £110
Size (WxL): 63x39mm
Weight: 160g

Small, light and very sharp. Look for the 'D' tag to avoid buying an older series lens.

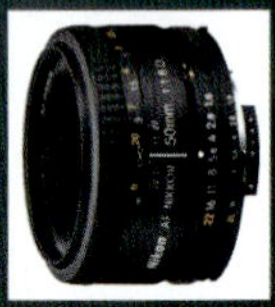

Sony DT 50mm f/1.8 SAM

Guide Price: £160
Street Price: £150
Size (WxL): 70x45mm
Weight: 170g

A great lens but not so easy to find. Remember, Minolta Dynax lenses fit too!

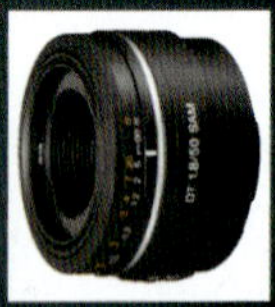

What's the big deal about the 50mm's f/1.8 aperture?

You have to experience a lens as fast as the 50mm to really understand and appreciate its benefits but, trust us, once you've tried you'll be hooked. The 50mm's f/1.8 aperture enables you to throw the background completely out of focus and isolate the main subject from its setting. This set of images shows the changes in depth-of-field at various apertures from f/1.8 to f/22.

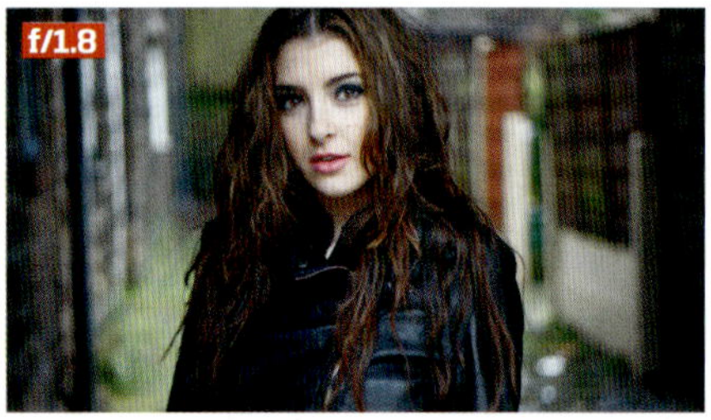
f/1.8

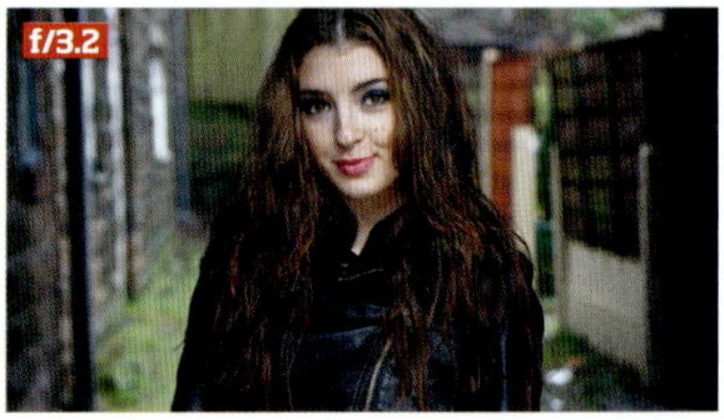
f/3.2

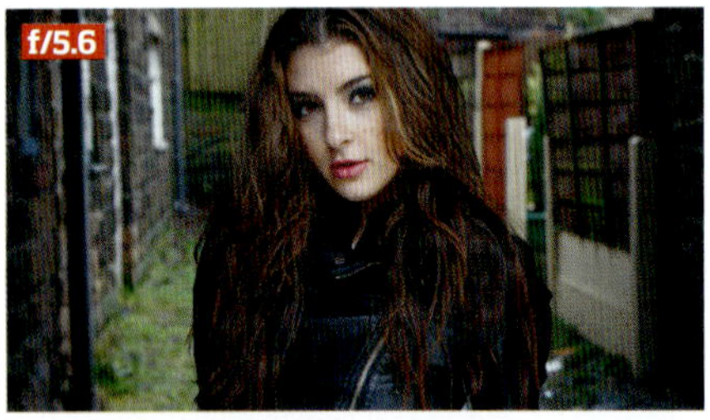
f/5.6

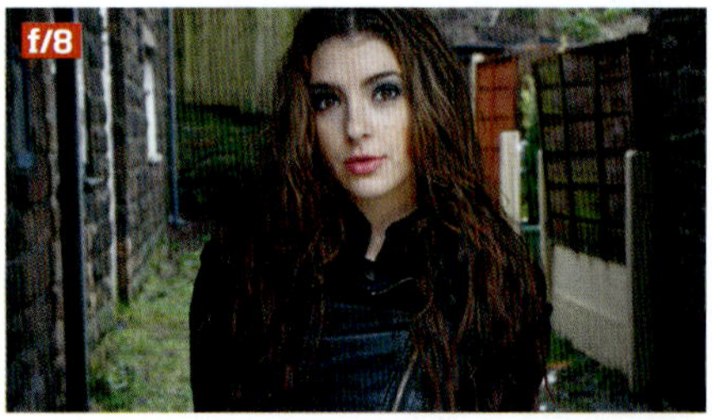
f/8

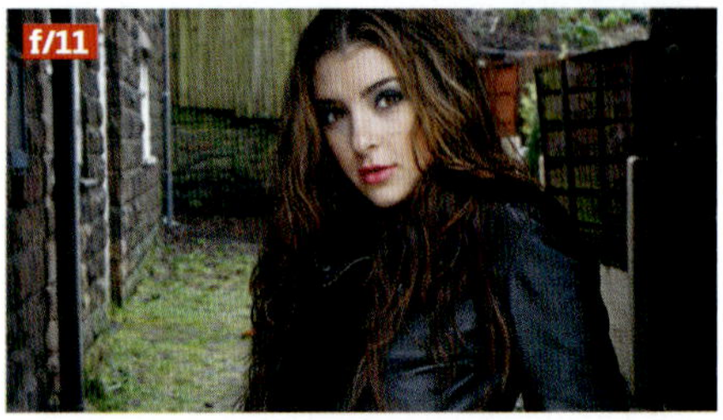
f/11

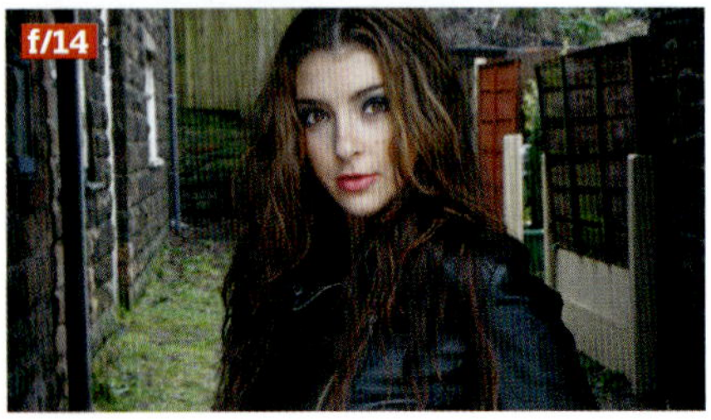
f/14

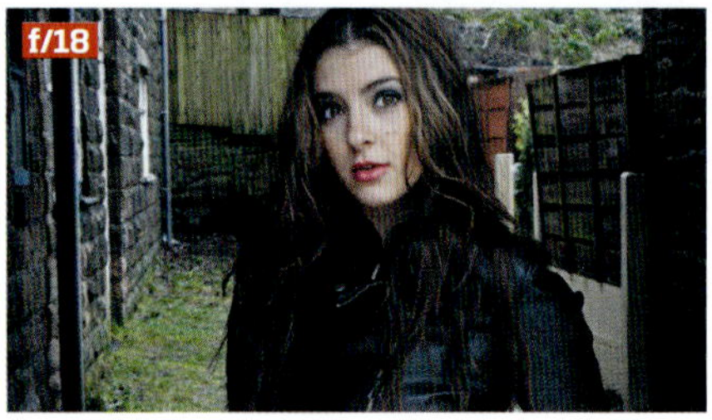
f/18

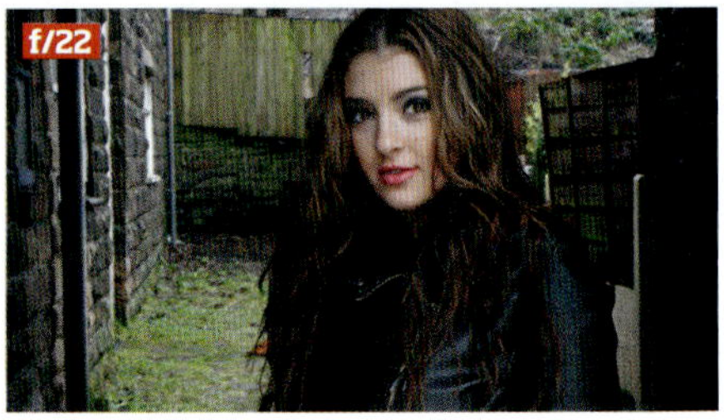
f/22

Our selection of great value lenses

We've tested many lenses over the years, so we have selected a few we think are worth considering. We've focused on a selection of six lenses from independent brands that offer great value and high-quality optics

Sigma 10-20mm f/4-5.6 EX DC HSM

www.sigma-imaging-uk.com

Guide price: £550
Street price: £430

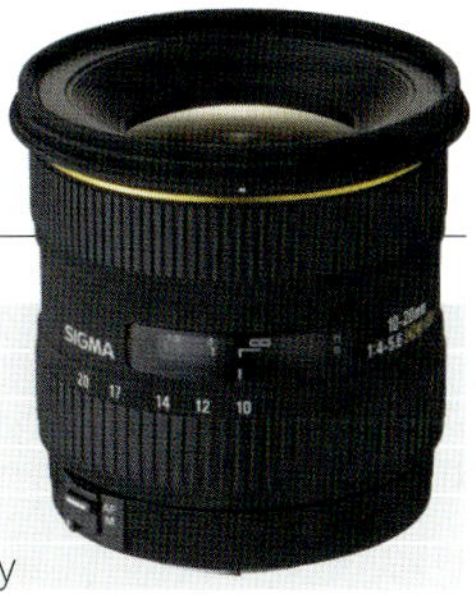

MAIN SPECIFICATIONS
- **Lens construction:** 14 elements in ten groups
- **Aperture range:** f/4-5.6 to f/22
- **Filter thread:** 77mm
- **Dimensions:** 83.5 x 81mm
- **Weight:** 470g
- **Fittings:** Canon, Nikon, Pentax, Sigma and Sony

This ultra-wide zoom is a real favourite with landscape snappers, thanks to its compact design and sharp optics. Like all Sigma EX lenses, it's well constructed and it feels solid. The barrel sports a manual focus ring and the optics deliver high sharpness throughout the range, with slight evidence of chromatic aberration.

Tamron 10-24mm f/3.5-4.5 Di II LD

www.intro2020.co.uk

Guide price: £500
Street price: £380

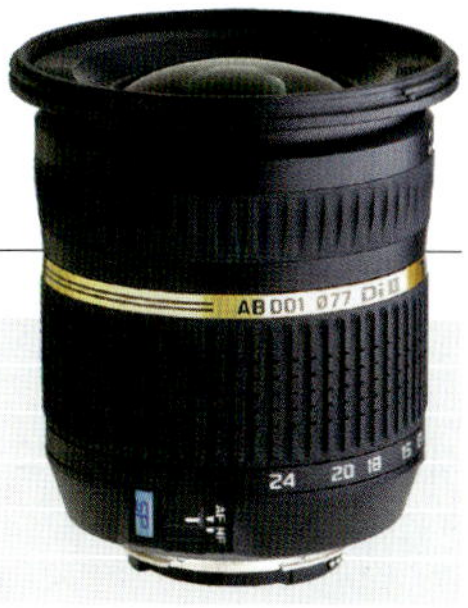

MAIN SPECIFICATIONS
- **Lens construction:** 12 elements in nine groups
- **Aperture range:** f/3.5-4.5 to f/22
- **Filter thread:** 77mm
- **Dimensions:** 83.2 x 86.5mm
- **Weight:** 406g
- **Fittings:** Canon, Nikon, Pentax and Sony

Tamron's 11-18mm has proved popular for years, but this addition, with its very wide focal length range, is even more versatile. It's compact and lightweight with good handling and an internal focusing system that will please filter users. Optical quality is good, thanks to the inclusion of aspherical and low-dispersion elements.

Tamron AF 55-200mm f/4-5.6 LD Di II

www.intro2020.co.uk

Guide price: £160
Street price: £130

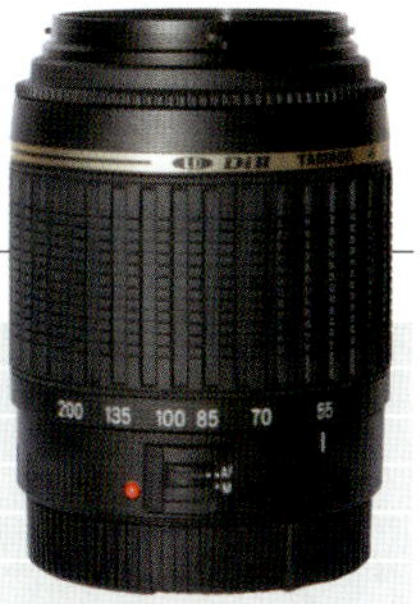

MAIN SPECIFICATIONS
- **Lens construction:** 13 elements in nine groups
- **Aperture range:** f/4-5.6 to f/32
- **Filter thread:** 52mm
- **Dimensions:** 71.6x83mm
- **Weight:** 300g
- **Fittings:** Canon and Nikon

Normally sharpness falls off as you zoom through the focal lengths, but this lens retains good sharpness throughout. Its wide zoom ring is very easy to use. The autofocus turns in a good performance – it's not the quickest or quietest, but is accurate and performs well in low light. It's light and compact and is a great budget telezoom.

Tamron 18-270mm f/3.5-6.3 Di II VC PZD

www.intro2020.co.uk

Guide price: £650
Street price: £500

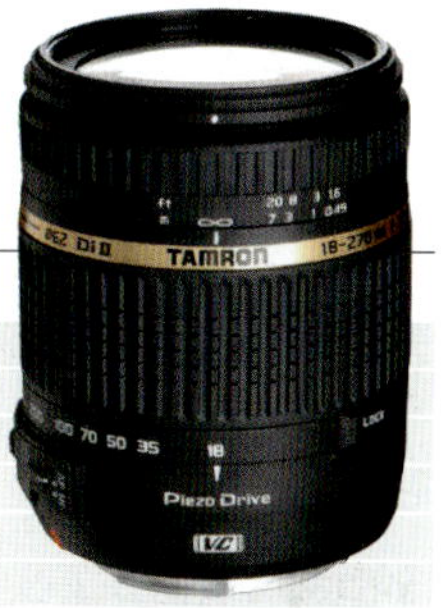

MAIN SPECIFICATIONS
- **Lens construction:** 16 elements in 13 groups
- **Aperture range:** f/3.5-6.3 to f/22
- **Filter thread:** 62mm
- **Dimensions:** 74.4x88mm
- **Weight:** 450g
- **Fittings:** Canon, Nikon and Sony

The Tamron 18-270mm boasts an incredible 15x zoom range, giving an effective focal length of 28-419mm, making this suitable for almost every type of subject. The addition of image stabilisation gives it a four-stop benefit, so it can be used hand-held in low-light conditions, while the Piezo Ultrasonic Motor provides fast, quiet AF.

Tamron SP AF 60mm f/2 Di II LD Macro

www.intro2020.co.uk

Guide price: £450
Street price: £380

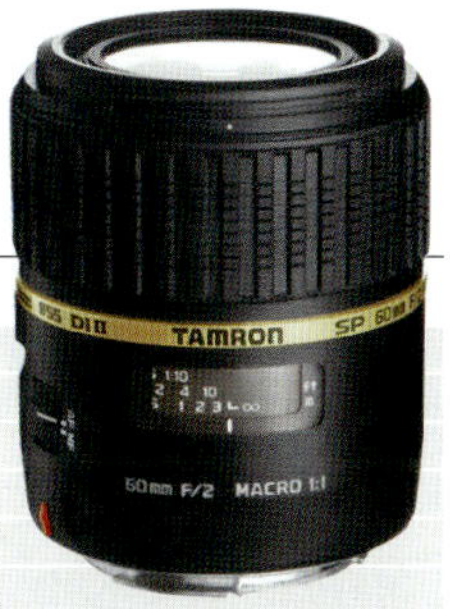

MAIN SPECIFICATIONS
- **Lens construction:** 14 elements in ten groups
- **Aperture range:** f/2 to f/22
- **Filter thread:** 55mm
- **Dimensions:** 73X80mm
- **Weight:** 400g
- **Fittings:** Canon, Nikon and Sony

Designed for exclusive use with cameras with APS-C sensors, this lightweight lens holds an ace card in the form of its maximum aperture of f/2, which gives a couple of big advantages over its rivals. As well as a brighter viewfinder image, it creates a very shallow depth-of-field – highly desired by macro photographers.

Sigma 120-400mm f/4.5-5.6 DG OS HSM

www.sigma-imaging-uk.com

Guide price: £900
Street price: £760

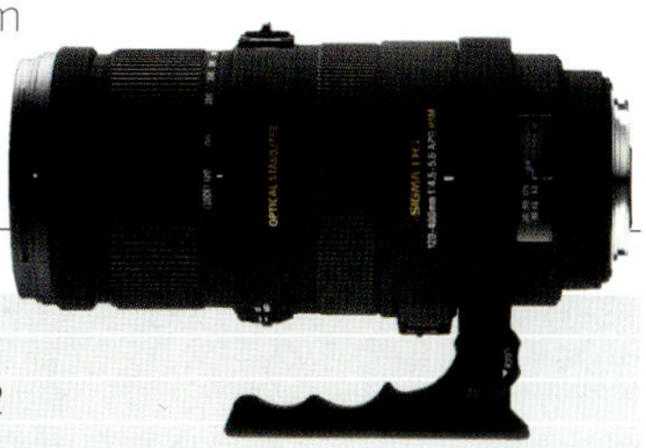

MAIN SPECIFICATIONS
- **Lens construction:** 21 elements in 15 groups
- **Aperture range:** f/4.5-5.6 to f/32
- **Filter thread:** 77mm
- **Dimensions:** 92x203mm • **Weight:** 1,640g
- **Fittings:** Canon, Nikon, Pentax, Sigma and Sony

Despite its focal length, this high-ratio zoom is relatively compact and includes an Optical Stabiliser (OS), a rear focusing system and HyperSonic Motor (HSM) for quiet, high-speed focusing. Its minimum focusing distance is 150cm with a magnification of 1:4.2 – something that is sure to appeal to nature photographers.

Equipment for close-ups

Many standard zooms boast a useful reproduction ratio of around 1:4 – quarter life-size. This is ideal to get you started, but if you want to get even nearer to your subjects, you may need to invest in a close-up attachment or dedicated macro lens. Here, we look at the most popular and widely used options and cover the merits of each...

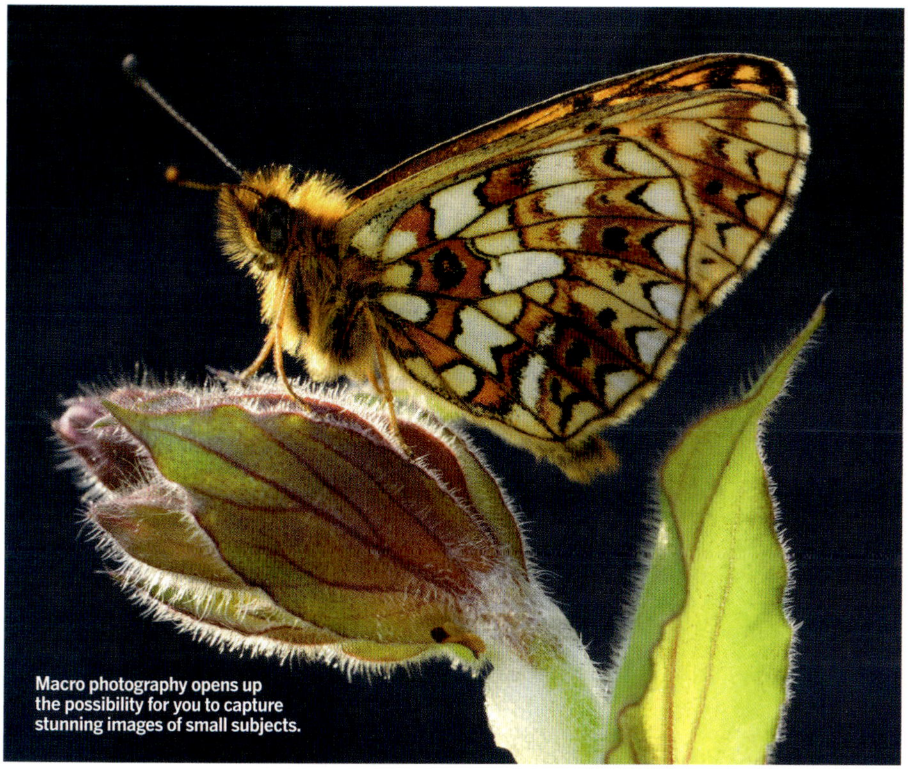

ROSS HODDINOTT

Macro photography opens up the possibility for you to capture stunning images of small subjects.

Useful close-up accessories

TRIPOD At high magnification, the effect of camera movement is exaggerated. A tripod is the best form of support. A flexible design is best suited to shooting close-ups, as it lets you get low.

REFLECTOR Small, collapsible reflectors can be angled to bounce light accurately onto your subject. The intensity of the light can be adjusted by moving the reflector closer or further away.

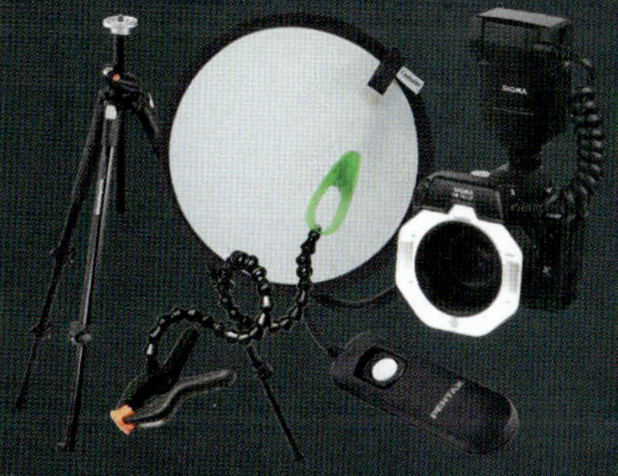

PLAMP The Plamp is an articulated arm with a clamp fixed at either end. One end can be attached to a tripod leg, while the other can be used to hold a reflector.

RING-FLASH A ring-flash is designed specifically for close-up work. It attaches directly to the front of the lens, so the burst can illuminate close-up subjects. Twin flash units work in a similar way.

REMOTE RELEASE Depressing the shutter release button while using at high magnification, and a slow shutter speed, can cause slight camera vibration. A remote release allows you to trigger the shutter without any fear of camera shake.

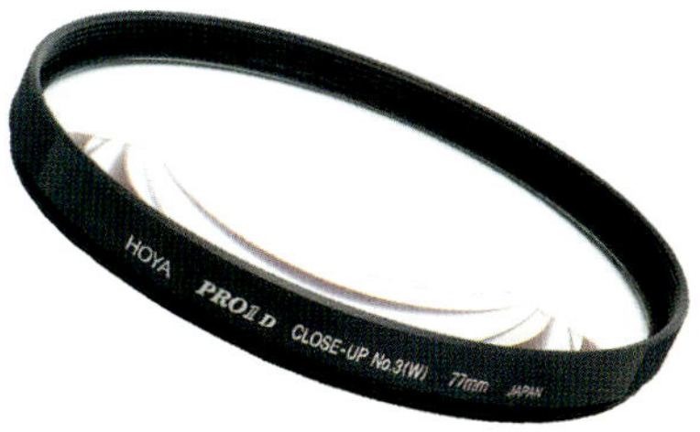

Close-up filters

Close-up filters screw to the filter thread of your lens and work like a magnifying glass. Depending on the brand and size, they can cost as little as £10. They are normally of a single element construction and available in progressive strengths, stated in dioptres. +1, +2, +3 and +4 are the most popular, although a two-element +10 dioptre is also available. The higher the number, the nearer the lens can focus and the higher the magnification. Although they can be used in combination, image quality will degrade if you attach more than two at one time. Close-up filters do not affect normal camera functions, so are easy to use and well suited to giving beginners a taste of close-up photography. Despite their modest price, they can produce excellent results and, being so small and lightweight, can easily be used hand-held without affecting stability.

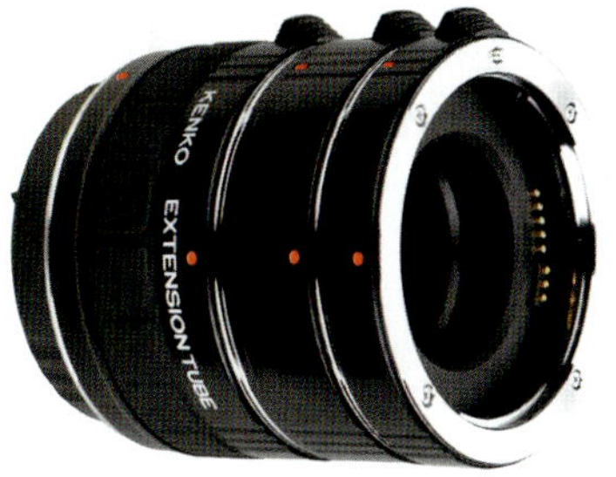

Extension tubes

Extension tubes are hollow rings that fit between the camera and lens. They work by increasing the distance between the sensor and lens, allowing the camera to focus closer than normal and increase magnification. They lack any optics and so do not affect the image quality of the lens they're coupled with, making the image quality superior to close-up filters. They can be purchased individually or in a set of three lengths: 12mm, 25mm and 36mm. Their level of magnification is calculated by dividing the amount of extension by the focal length of the lens being used. For example, 25mm of extension used with a 50mm standard lens results in a 1:2 reproduction – or half life-size. To achieve 1:1 life-size, the extension would need to equal the focal length of the lens attached. Therefore, they are most effective when combined with relatively short focal lengths.

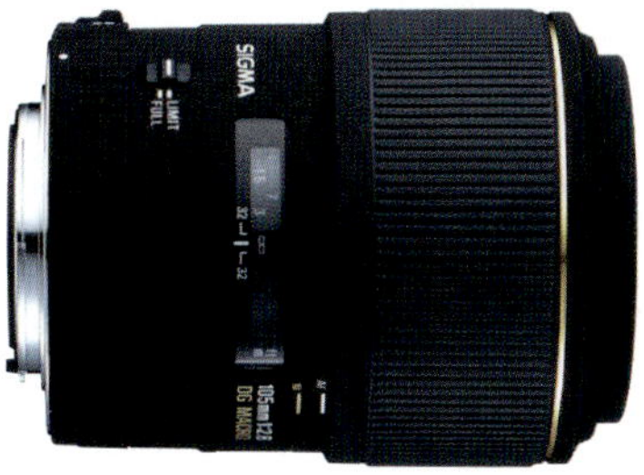

Macro lens

A macro lens is optimised for close focusing. While they are highly corrected to give their best results at close range, they can also be for general use and are popular among portrait photographers. At its minimum focusing distance, a dedicated macro lens will normally produce 1:1 reproduction. They are available in a range of focal lengths: short macro lenses, in the region of 50mm to 70mm, are lightweight and compact, making them easy to use hand-held. However, at their maximum magnification, they don't have a generous working distance. Therefore, this focal length is not the best if you wish to photograph subjects which are easily disturbed, such as butterflies. Generally speaking, focal lengths upwards of 90mm are a better choice. They provide a greater subject-to-camera distance and make it easier to isolate your subject.

Introduction to flash

Using flash isn't as difficult as you might think. It's just a matter of knowing what to do, when to do it, and how

WE'VE ALL BEEN disappointed, when using a flash, that we have failed to capture the ambience of a scene. This usually happens when we shoot in auto mode with no real thought as to what we are doing or why. What we hope you'll discover in this section of the guide is that the secret to good flash photography lies in using the full range of your camera's exposure modes, and thinking carefully about how light from the flash – and from other sources – affects the final result.

The result of a flash-lit picture will depend on whether you are using aperture-priority or program exposure mode, or whether you have auto or slow-sync flash set, for example. This is because, by changing modes, you are altering settings such as shutter speed, which in turn affects the amount of ambient light that reaches the sensor. Additionally, flash modes can command the flash to fire at the beginning or end of the exposure. Either option changes how moving objects will appear in the final photograph.

While all this may seem complicated, it isn't. The beauty of digital SLR photography is that you are free to experiment (and learn from your mistakes), and we recommend you do this while following our advice.
Take inspiration, try it out yourself, and adapt it with your own ideas.
Before long you'll be using flash as an everyday part of your photography – rather than being afraid of it – no matter what your subject matter.

Common flash modes you'll find on DSLRs

The way your DSLR and flash work together is governed by the flash mode that you use. Here are the most common flash modes that you'll find on your digital SLR and dedicated hotshoe-mounted flashguns.

Auto: When light levels fall, your DSLR will activate the built-in flash. It calculates aperture via TTL metering, but sets a high shutter speed to avoid camera shake. Convenient, but not very creative.

Slow-sync: It uses a slower shutter speed to record ambient light properly. Good for night-time portraits where the mood needs to be recorded too, but watch for camera shake.

Rear/second-curtain sync: Works the same as slow-sync mode, except that the flash is fired at the end of the exposure, rather than at the start. Great for leaving a trail of light behind moving subjects.

Anti red-eye: Aims to prevent or reduce so-called red-eye in flash portraits by using a series of pre-flashes to make a subject's pupil contract before the exposure is taken.

Flash-off: Stops a camera from automatically engaging the built-in flash. More useful than you'd think, especially when trying to shoot low-light scenes on a tripod.

Flash exposure compensation: Your DSLR automatically calculates the amount of flash needed for an exposure. Use this feature to increase or decrease the amount of flash output to your liking.

Jargon buster

GUIDE NUMBER A numerical measure of a flashgun's power. The higher the number, the greater the power. In manual flash mode, divide the Guide Number by the camera-to-subject distance in meters to calculate the required aperture for a good exposure.

HIGH-SPEED FLASH The ability to use your flash at faster shutter speeds than the camera's standard sync speed. Very useful when trying to work with fill-in flash outdoors in sunny, high-contrast conditions.

PAINTING WITH FLASH The practice of locking open your camera's shutter on a long exposure, in darkness, and then firing an off-camera flash at your subject multiple times from different angles.

TTL Through the lens metering, known as TTL, is the way in which a flashgun and camera work together to properly expose a scene. The camera measures flashgun output coming through the lens and tells it when to stop.

WIRELESS FLASH Firing an external flashgun without cables, using an infrared transmitter or integral flash instead. This can be very useful when you're skilled enough to use multiple-flash set-ups.

FLASH COVERAGE This refers to the area covered by the flashgun's output. You'll normally find focal lengths up to 18mm provide an even flash coverage. Wider than this and the edges start to darken off. It's worth checking what your flash coverage is if you often shoot group portraits indoors. Some hotshoe-mounted flashguns boast a built-in diffuser panel that widens coverage.

How to set flash modes on your camera

Choosing which flash mode to use is easy. Most cameras have a flash mode button on the four-way control that allows you to access and change the flash mode. If your camera lacks a flash button, press the Menu button to access the flash mode. With most cameras, the selection you make will affect the integral flash or any flashgun mounted on the hotshoe.

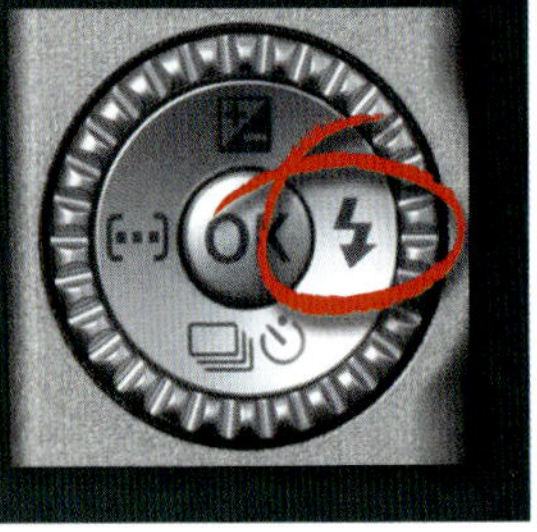

Try these creative flash techniques...

The best way to use flash is often to balance the flash exposure with ambient light. That way, the flash ensures the subject is well lit, while the background is exposed by ambient light. The way to do this is simple – expose for the scene as normal, but pop up the integral flash (or attach a flashgun) and let the camera handle the flash exposure. This method is often termed slow-sync flash.

Slow-sync flash: This mode involves using flash with a shutter speed/aperture combination that correctly exposes the general scene. The flash takes care of the main subject and the longer exposure time allows ambient light to reveal background detail. How you set slow-sync mode depends on the camera you use. With Canon, use aperture-priority (Av), with Pentax select shutter-priority (Tv); with Nikon and Olympus, press the flash mode button, select slow-sync and use it with aperture-priority (A) or shutter-priority (S). You'll find many cameras employ slow-sync when you set Night-Portrait mode. The slow shutter speed means a tripod (or other support) is recommended.

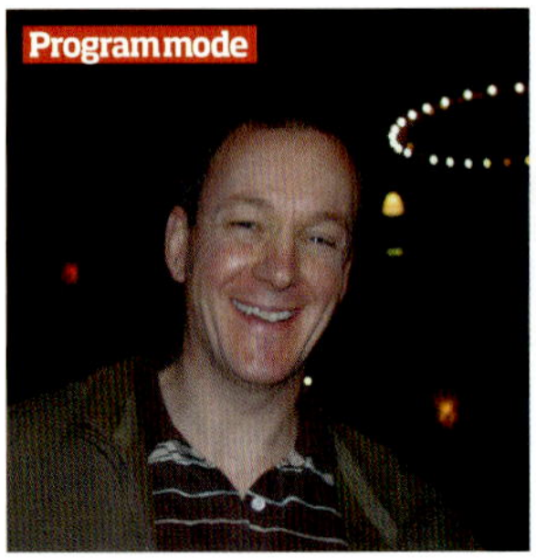

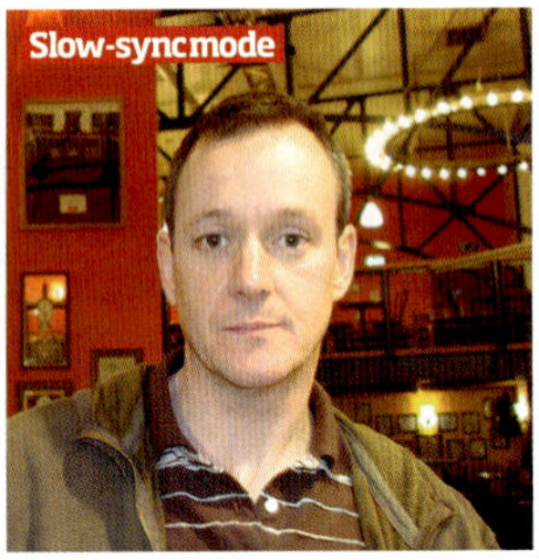

As this comparison set shows, Program flash exposes the subject well but the background is dark. Slow-sync mode balances the flash with ambient light for a much nicer effect.

Rear-curtain sync: Rear-curtain sync is also known as second-curtain synchronisation and it's well worth noting what it does. Normally, when you take a shot using flash, the flashgun fires right at the start of the exposure (known as first-curtain sync) and this is fine for most uses. However, if you're shooting a moving subject, especially with a slow shutter speed, you'll find that first-curtain sync isn't always the best choice. That is because the flash freezes the subject at the start of the exposure and their movement after the flash has fired may be recorded by ambient light as an unusual streak ahead of their starting position. However, by using rear-curtain sync, this streak is behind the subject, which appears far more natural.

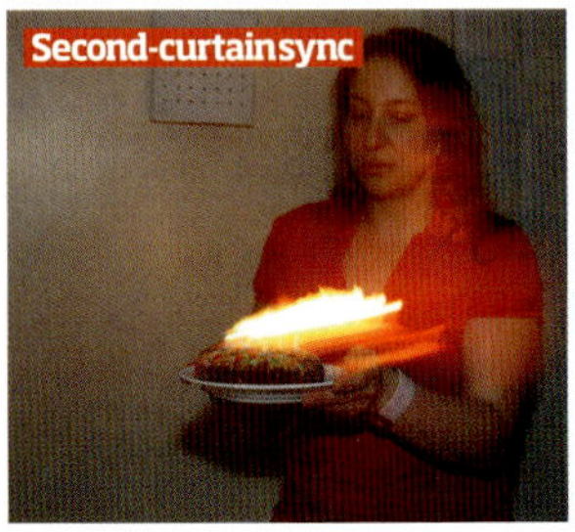

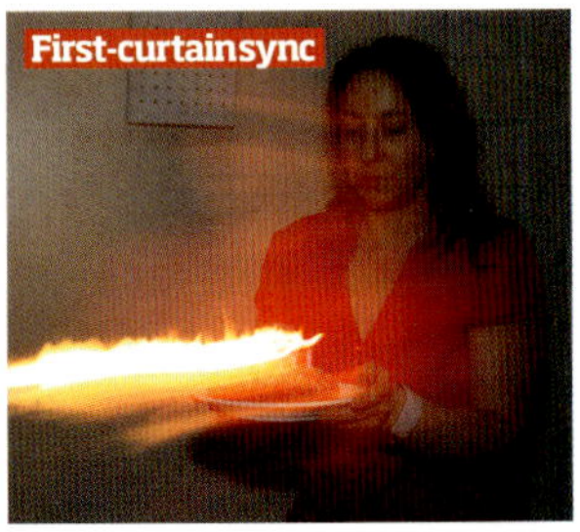

The difference between first- and second-curtain synchronisation is most obvious looking at the light trails of the candles.

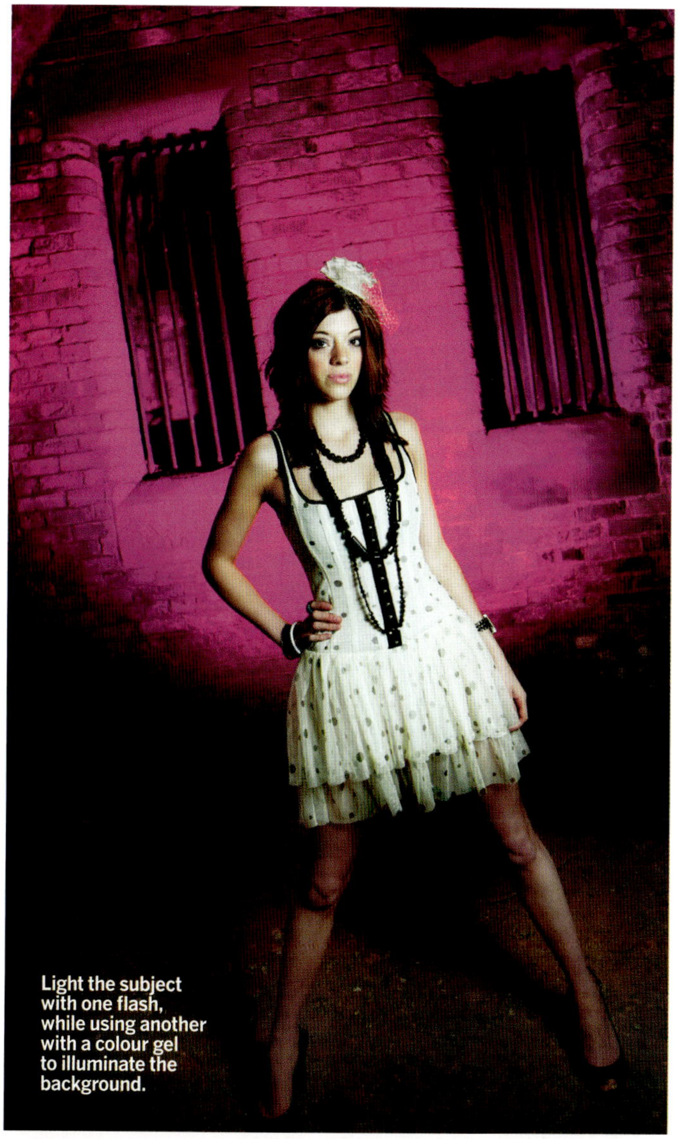

BRETT HARKNESS

Light the subject with one flash, while using another with a colour gel to illuminate the background.

Anatomy of a flashgun

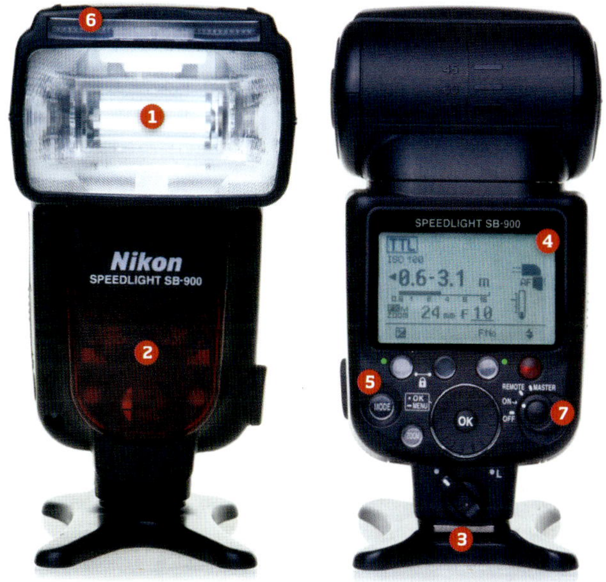

1) FLASH HEAD Can be rotated or flipped to bounce light off walls and ceilings. Most zoom to match light coverage to the focal length.

2) AF ASSIST Projects an infrared beam to help focus in dim light.

3) HOTSHOE The connection between camera and flash. Used to trigger the flash and communicate data for TTL light metering.

4) LCD SCREEN Shows the status of the flashgun. In this case the metering mode, range, zoom setting and f/stop are all visible. Here, we can see that the unit is set to TTL exposure mode for an aperture of f/10 and a 24mm lens, giving a range of between 0.6 to 3.1m.

5) BUTTONS AND CONTROL WHEEL Used to set advanced features, like flash exposure control, metering mode etc.

6) FOLD-AWAY REFLECTOR AND DIFFUSER The reflector can be used with the gun in bounce mode to direct a small amount of light towards the subject. The diffuser is used to disperse light over a wider area when shooting with ultra wide-angle lenses.

7) POWER AND MODE SWITCH Turns on power to the flashgun and, in this case, dictates how the unit behaves when used off-camera in wireless TTL mode.

Exposure modes and flash

How exposure modes and overrides affect flash for different brands of DSLRs*

BRAND	CANON	NIKON	PENTAX	OLYMPUS	SONY
PROGRAM MODE	Camera sets shutter speed and aperture, but raises shutter speed to avoid camera shake. Background may be dark.	Camera sets exposure, but raises shutter speed to avoid camera shake, unless slow-sync mode is set. Background may be dark.	Camera sets exposure, but raises shutter speed to avoid camera shake, unless slow-sync mode is set. Background may be dark.	Camera sets exposure, but raises shutter speed to avoid camera shake, unless slow-sync mode is set. Background may be dark.	Camera sets exposure, but raises shutter speed to avoid camera shake, unless slow-sync mode is set. Background may be dark.
APERTURE-PRIORITY	User picks aperture; camera calculates flash exposure accordingly. Shutter speed is picked to render ambient light correctly. Be aware of camera shake.	User picks the aperture and the camera selects flash exposure accordingly. Shutter speed is limited to prevent camera shake, unless slow-sync mode is selected.	User sets aperture and camera sets shutter speed to correctly expose background, up to the maximum sync speed. Risk of camera shake in low light.	User picks aperture and camera selects flash exposure accordingly. Shutter speed limited to prevent camera shake, unless slow-sync mode is also selected.	User picks aperture and camera selects flash exposure accordingly. Shutter speed limited to prevent camera shake, unless slow-sync mode is also selected.
SHUTTER-PRIORITY	User picks shutter speed and camera picks corresponding aperture for ambient light, then calculates flash output according to this aperture.	User picks shutter speed and camera picks corresponding aperture to expose ambient light correctly, then calculates flash output according to this aperture.	User picks shutter speed and camera picks corresponding aperture to expose ambient light properly, then calculates flash output according to this aperture.	User picks shutter speed and camera picks corresponding aperture to expose ambient light correctly, then calculates flash output according to this aperture.	User picks shutter speed and camera picks corresponding aperture to expose ambient light correctly, then calculates flash output according to this aperture.
EXPOSURE COMPENSATION	Affects ambient light exposure only.	Affects both ambient and flash exposure.	Affects both ambient and flash exposure.	Affects ambient light exposure only.	Affects both ambient and flash exposure.
FLASH EXPOSURE COMPENSATION	Affects flash exposure only.	Affects flash exposure only.	Affects flash exposure only.	Affects flash exposure only.	Affects flash exposure only.

* Please note that the stated information relates to most general shooting conditions. However, in certain situations, the camera and flash will operate differently.

Add colour with flash gels

Try out our inexpensive and simple wireless flash technique

Getting to use just one flashgun proves a daunting prospect for many, so how does the thought of using two grab you? This technique deals with showing you how to light a subject with one flashgun, while a second flash is used to illuminate the background. This technique is useful when you want to highlight detail in the scene or, as shown here, you want to use flash gels to light it in a completely different colour.

While the technique may sound incredibly difficult, it's actually quite easy to achieve. You need to use your camera's integral flash (or a hotshoe-mounted flashgun) to illuminate your subject, which is pretty straightforward as the exposure is taken care of automatically by the camera thanks to the wonders of TTL flash. A second flashgun is triggered automatically by the main flash to illuminate the background, so you've little to do other than ensure that the remote flash is set up correctly, which, as the panel on the right reveals, is pretty easy to do. And, if you think this sounds expensive, it's not, all you need is a remote trigger or, if you're using non-dedicated flashguns, a slave cell, to trigger your off-camera flash.

Flash gels are essentially small sheets of coloured plastic that are placed over the flash head to colour the flash output. The flash gel is held in place over the head via Velcro or an elastic band and with a number of kits available with a choice of colours, it's an inexpensive and easy way to add creative flash effects to your images. Incidentally, larger flash gel kits are available that can be used with studioflash heads, too, and, in fact, the technique we've used here can easily be applied to studioflash set-ups as well as flashguns.

Using flash gels to illuminate a background is equally suited to both indoor and outdoor locations. Plain backdrops as well as textured surfaces are suitable, although the latter does provide additional visual interest. It's also worth bearing in mind that you can use more than one flashgun for the background, so feel free to mix colour gels. The key is to experiment as much as possible, as this is when creative photos present themselves.

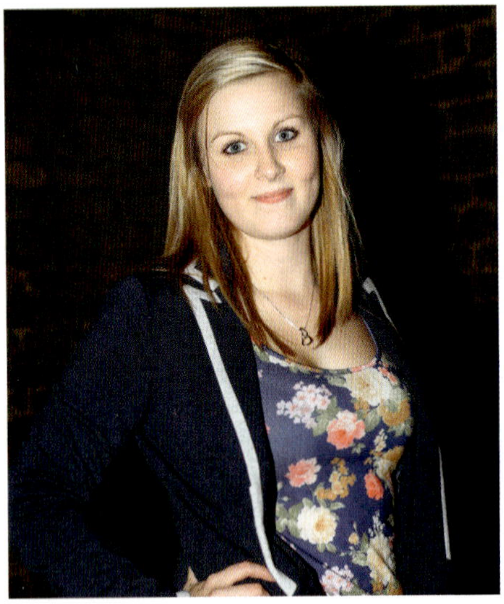

1 Here's our subject photographed using only our hotshoe-mounted flashgun. She's well exposed but the background is drab and dark.

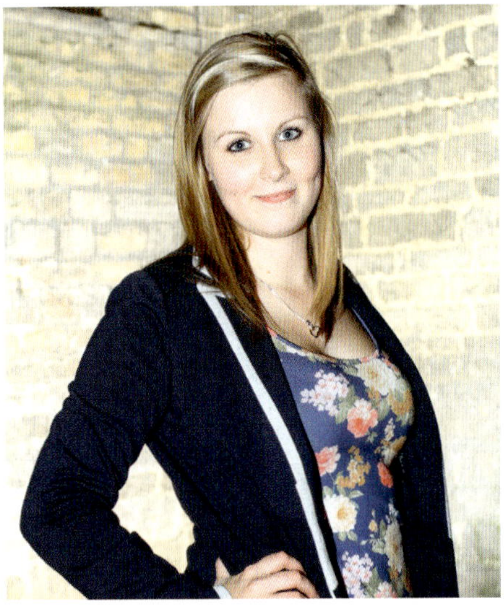

2 We've set up a remote flashgun behind her, which fires to light the wall in the background, but the effect isn't particularly attractive.

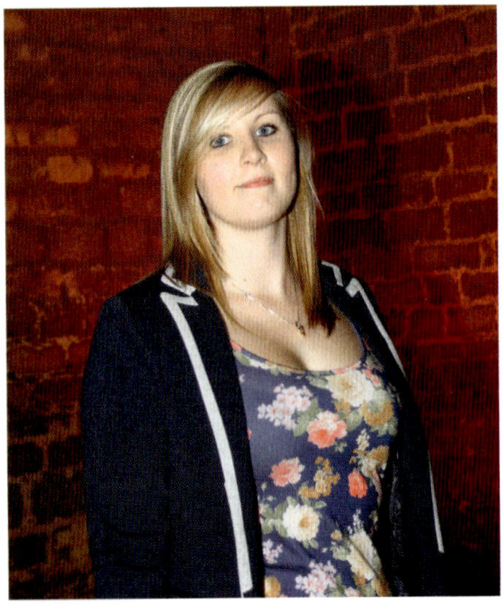

3 We've fitted a Lumiquest red gel and the colour adds interest, but, with the remote flash set to TTL, its output isn't as strong as we'd like.

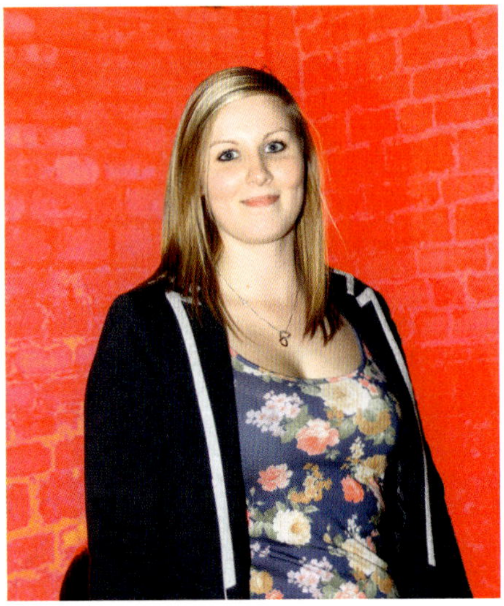

4 Setting the remote flash to manual power provides a far stronger output, although the full-power 1/1 setting is far too strong.

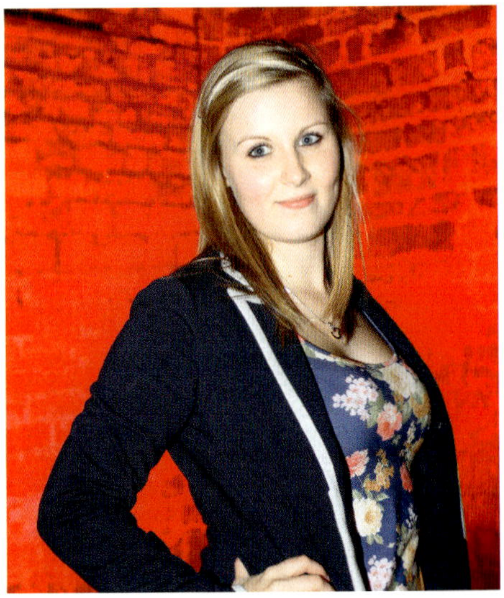

5 We try various manual power settings to see which provides the best result and find that, for this set-up, half-power works best.

Remote flashgun set-up

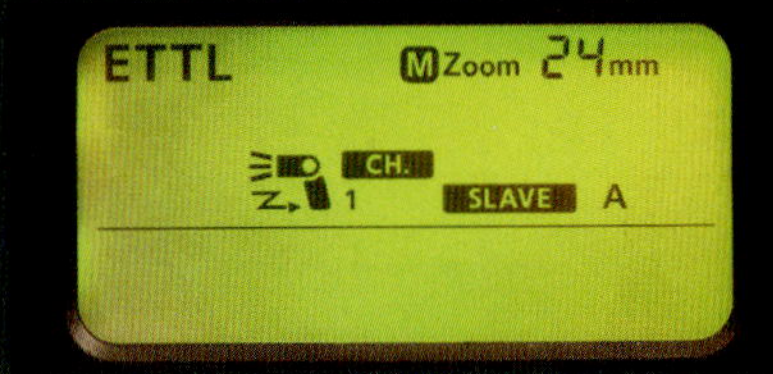

WAYS TO TRIGGER A REMOTE FLASHGUN: Depending on the types of flashgun and accessories you are using, there are a number of ways of triggering your remote 'gelled' flash. If you have a dedicated flashgun with a slave function, you can use the Master/Slave facility to trigger it when you release the shutter. You'll need to refer to your camera/flashgun instructions, as this varies according to the camera/flash brand and mode. Alternatively, you can fit a slave cell to the bottom of any flashgun, which is then triggered by the output from the camera's built-in or hotshoe-mounted flashgun (depending on which you are using).

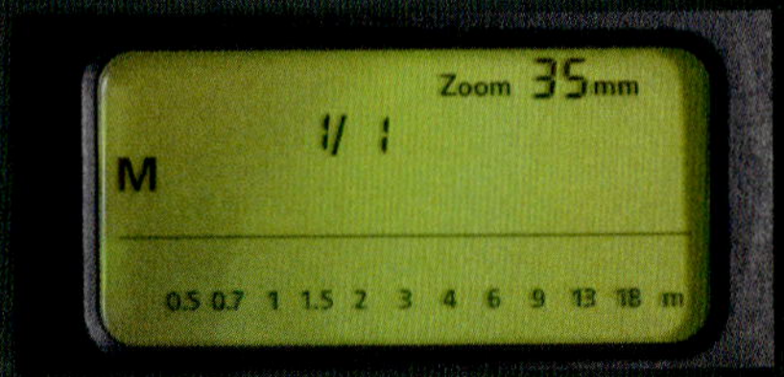

SETTING UP THE EXPOSURE ON THE REMOTE FLASHGUN: If you're using a dedicated Master/Slave flash system to trigger the off-camera flashgun, then you can either set up its output to be based on a TTL exposure or manual power setting. While selecting TTL is normally the best choice, we'd actually recommend you set the flash to manual for this technique, as the results will be more consistent. If you are using a slave flash, you should set the flashgun to manual to allow you to set a specific power setting. With the flash in manual, you can set the remote flash to fire at fixed power settings such as full power (1/1), half power (1/2), quarter power (1/4) and so on. Take some test shots and adjust the power settings to suit the scene. Adjust power if you want a stronger or weaker effect or if you switch colour gels, as some absorb more light than others.

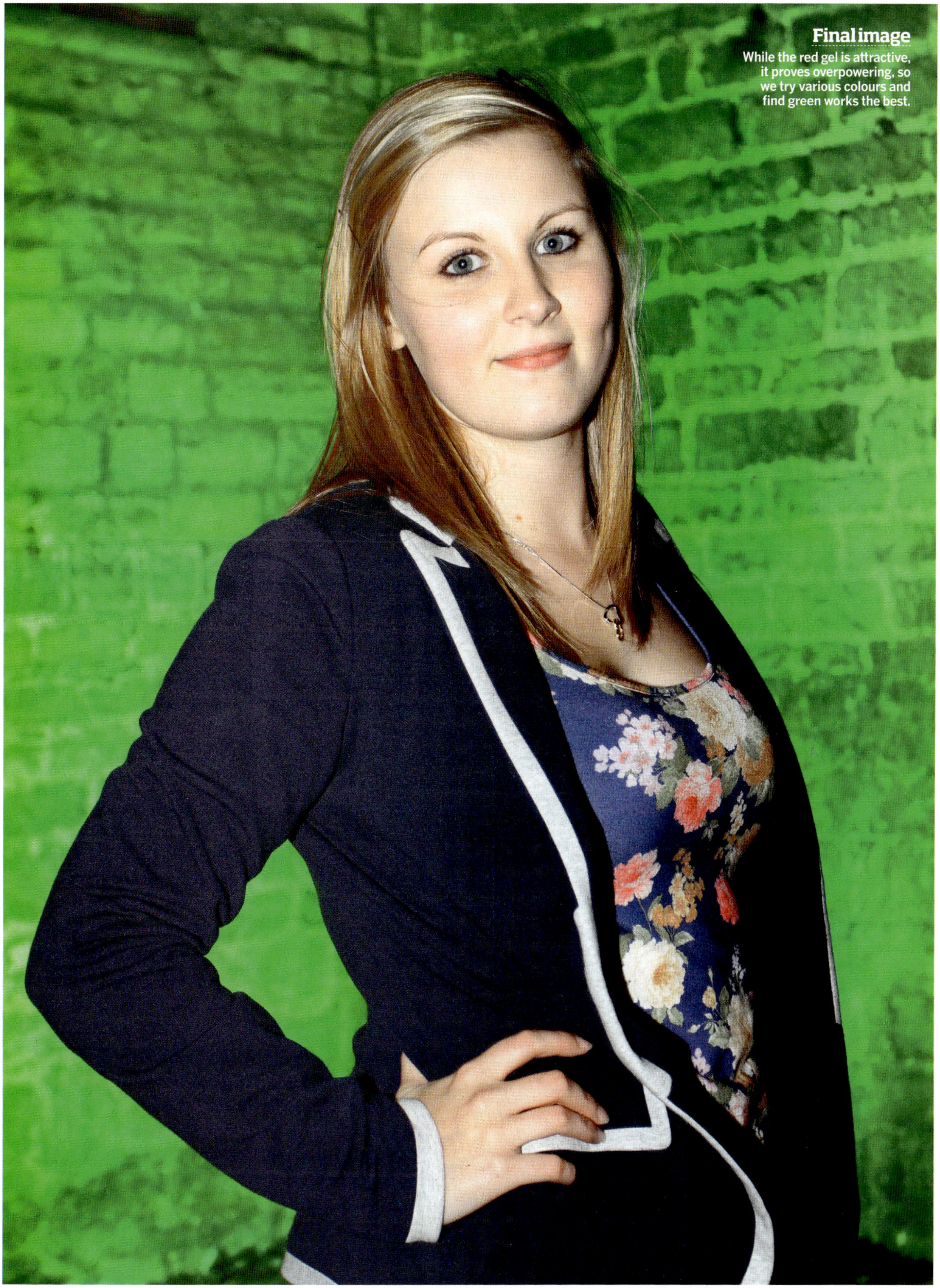

Final image
While the red gel is attractive, it proves overpowering, so we try various colours and find green works the best.

Simulate evening sun with flash

Learn how to use off-camera flash to create attractive hairlight

WHEN USING FLASH to light a portrait, the first thing most photographers do is point it at the subject's face, but by placing it behind the model's head, you can create attractive hairlight – adding a different dimension to the image. It's a great creative technique to try in the winter months, too, when you don't fancy going outdoors, but want to simulate the look of a low evening sun from the warmth of your home.

To get the best results, the subject should ideally have curly or wavy hair and be placed in front of a dark background to accentuate the light. You'll also need to experiment with your flash's power to find a balance between overpowering the ambient light and getting the right spread through the hair. For instance, if you're doing a full-body portrait, a burst of flash at $\frac{1}{2}$ power would work best, while a head shot might require only $\frac{1}{4}$ power. It's worth playing with the distance of your flash to your subject's head as well, but make sure the flash is completely hidden so it diffuses through the hair. Also consider your aperture: minimal depth-of-field will soften the spread of light, while a narrow aperture will produce a star-like effect from the flash.

Professional lifestyle photographer Brett Harkness frequently uses his off-camera flash behind his subjects, whether to create a dramatic burst of light behind a full-body portrait or to add a subtle, attractive hairlight to a head shot. He shows us how…

Reflectors

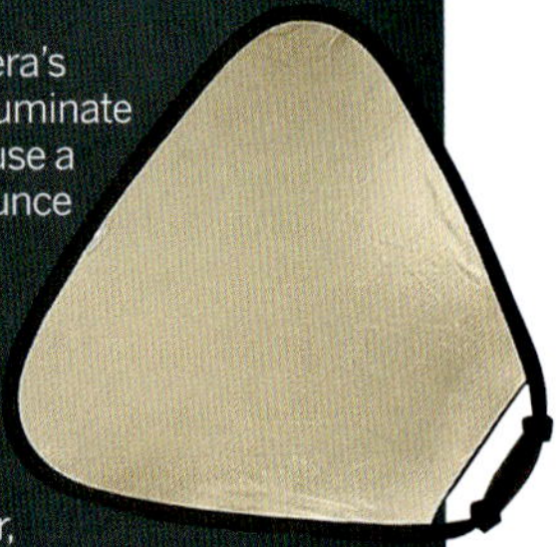

You can use your camera's integral flash unit to illuminate the face, or you could use a reflector instead to bounce some light on to the subject's face. You can control the tone of the light by the choice of your reflector, too. If you want a cool tone, opt for a silver reflector, or, for a warm cast, try a gold reflector. Alternatively, why not try Lastolite's TriGrip Sunfire or Sunlite reflector, like we've used in this step-by-step, as it has strips of silver and gold for a more natural cast. If you only have a silver or gold reflector, you could always experiment with your image's White Balance in-camera or Adobe Camera Raw to warm it up or cool the tone down.

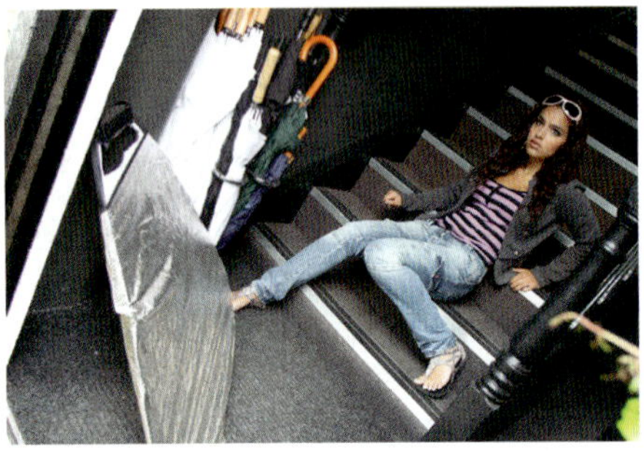

1 (Above) To start with, we position Emma in a doorway so we can use natural light to fill in the shadows on her face. During the winter months, however, when light levels are low, you may need to use a reflector or a second flash to light her face, held approximately three or four feet away so as not to overpower the backlight. With the camera and flash set to manual, I dial in f/5.6 and ISO 500, because of the relatively low light, and place the flashgun on the step behind Emma.

2 (Right) I take a test shot of Emma at f/5.6 with the flash behind her set to $\frac{1}{8}$ power and no reflector. As you can see, the flash isn't strong enough to have any effect and her face is underexposed. So I set the flash to $\frac{1}{4}$ power and ask my assistant to hold a reflector a few feet away from Emma's face to fill in the shadows.

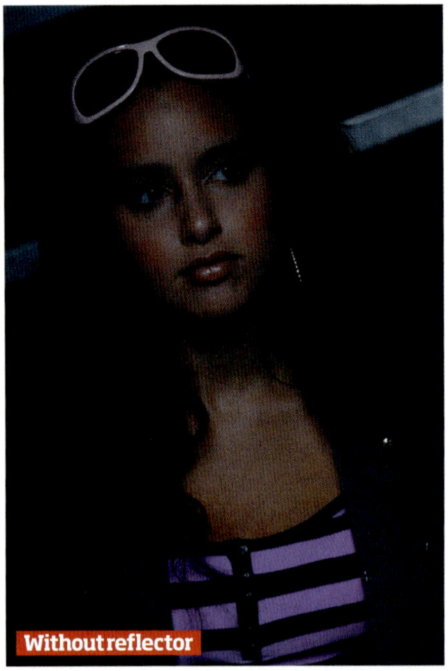

Without reflector

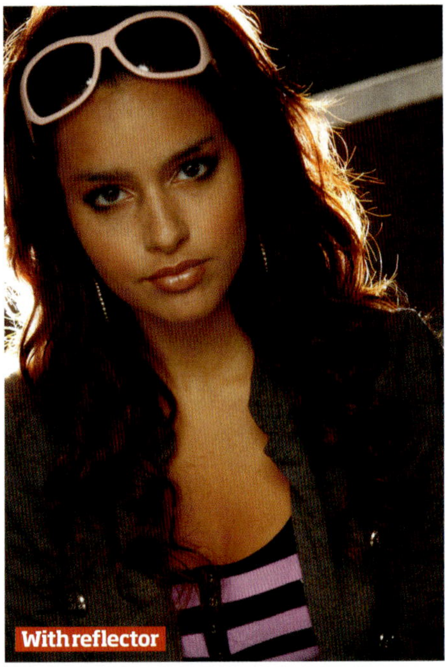

With reflector

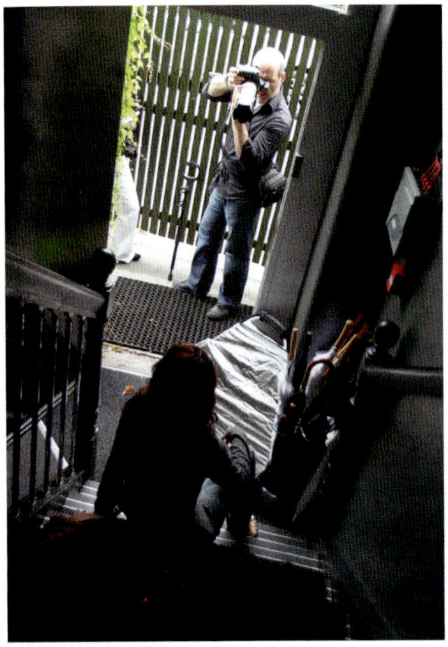

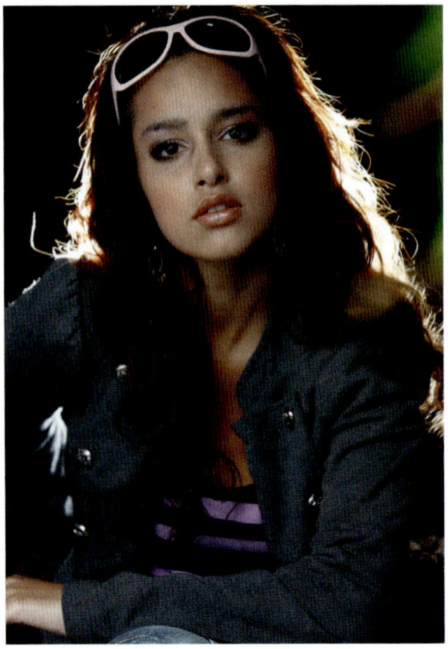

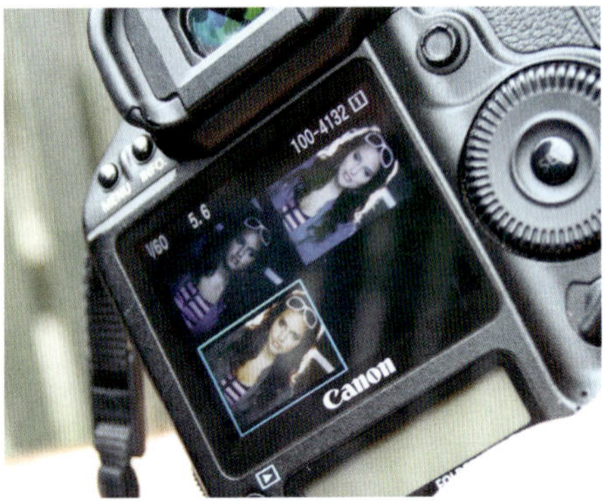

3 (Left) As I can see the stairs in the background of the pictures, I add a blanket over the steps to get rid of the white line and darken the background to enhance the backlight.

4 (Above) You may also want to try playing with your camera's White Balance settings to see what effect it has on the picture. Normally, if you're working with flash, you would set Flash or Custom WB, but why not try Daylight or Tungsten to alter the tone of the image? Alternatively, you could shoot in Raw and play with the WB in post-production.

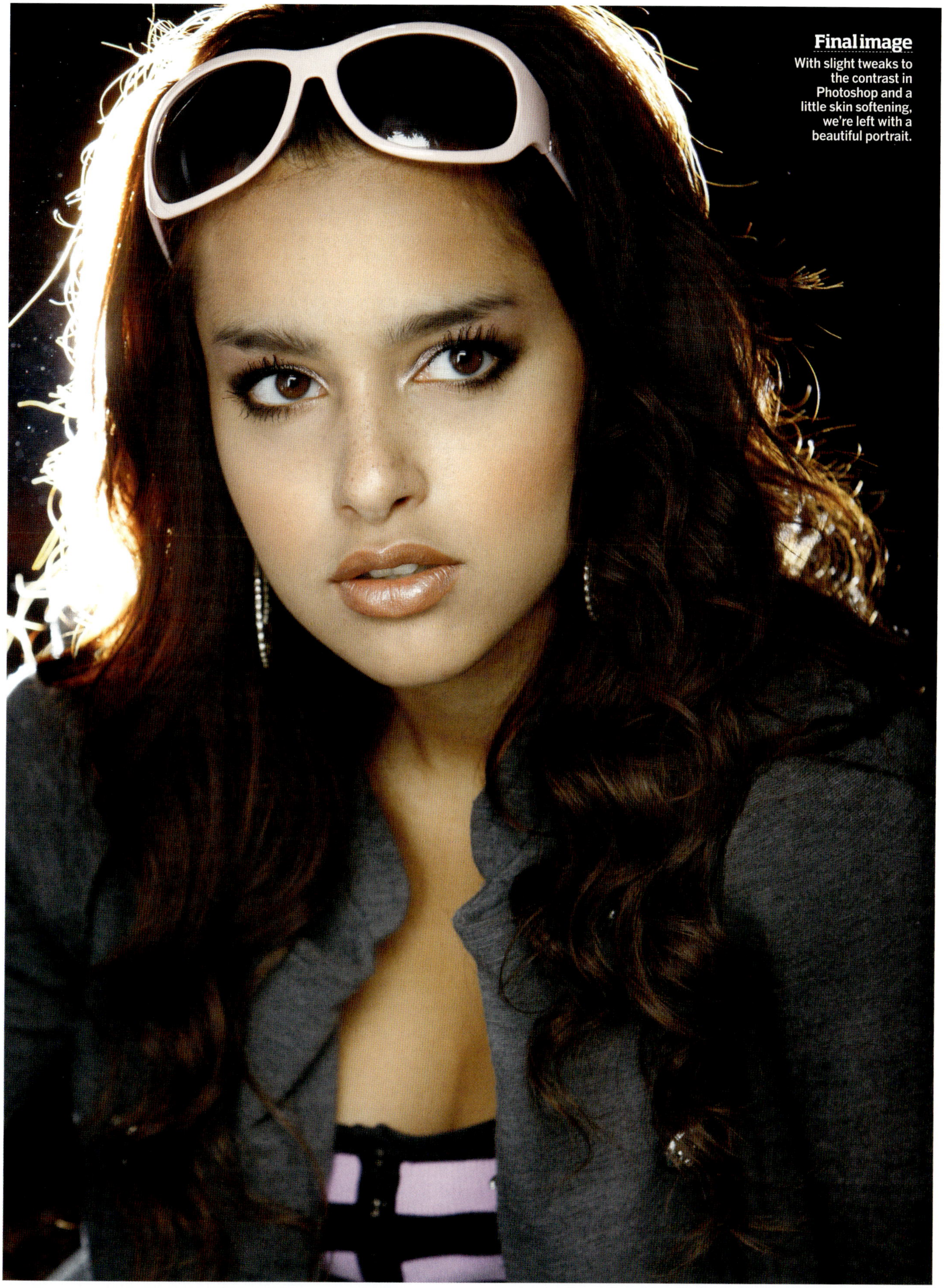
Final image
With slight tweaks to the contrast in Photoshop and a little skin softening, we're left with a beautiful portrait.

Painting with flash

PAINTING WITH FLASH is the practice of locking a camera's shutter open for a long exposure while someone selectively illuminates parts of the scene by repeatedly firing a hand-held (hotshoe) flashgun using the Test button. It's a technique that ideally suits shooting buildings at night.

Painting with flash is a very flexible and creative technique. You can fire the flash as many times as you like, from any angle. Coloured gels or filters can also be attached to the flashgun, to change the colour of the projected light to add more interest. Night scenes of church graveyards are popular subjects for this technique, with the photographer lighting the church and headstones with different-coloured gels over a long exposure, resulting in an unusual, multi-coloured image.

It's worth arriving at the scene at dusk and getting set up while there is still enough light to allow you to pre-focus on your subject and see what you're doing. You'll need to mount your camera on a sturdy tripod and fire each exposure using a remote release or your camera's self-timer. The former has the advantage of reducing the risk of camera shake, while also giving you time to get into position with your flashgun. Use aperture-priority or manual mode and choose an exposure of at least ten seconds to begin with. Depending on your initial results, you may want to increase the exposure time. If you can, take a friend along, too, to help fire the shutter or to run around during the exposure, firing the flashgun! The key thing to remember is that you must not point the flash head towards the camera. If you do, a hotspot will be recorded on the image, potentially ruining it. It's also important to keep moving when in front of the lens, or you'll be recorded as a ghostly figure. Ensure you take plenty of spare batteries, too, as the power will soon start to deplete due to the high number of flash bursts you'll fire.

There is lots of trial and error involved with this technique, but it's worth setting the flash to manual at ½, ¼ or ⅛ power, to allow you to fire off more bursts in different positions around the scene. Leave it at full power and you'll get fewer flash bursts, due to longer recycling times. The one thing about painting with flash is that it is very hit and miss, and no two exposures will ever be the same. With practice, you'll be able to work out the exposure time you should set and the approximate number of flashes to fire for each frame. Daniel Lezano headed down to Rutland Water to paint with flash using a Canon EOS 40D and Canon Speedlite 430EX II.

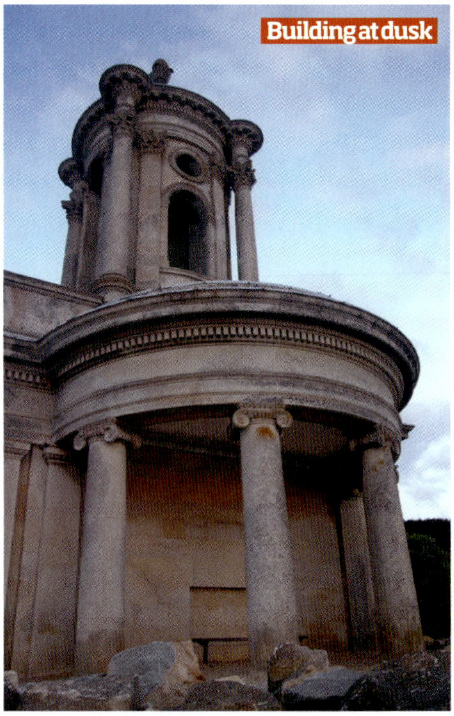
Building at dusk

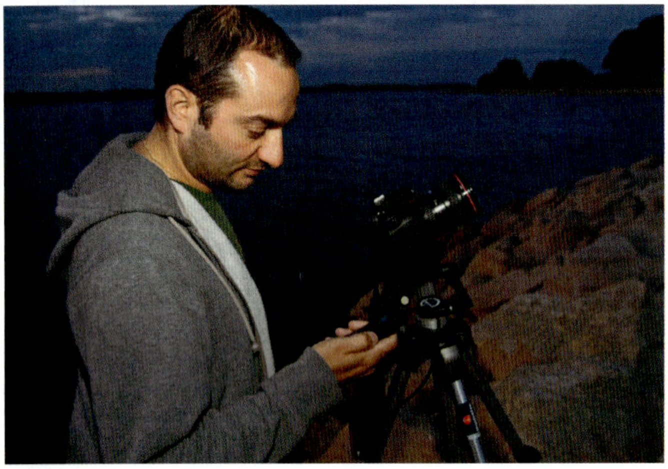

Step 1 I'm using aperture-priority mode and setting the aperture to f/16, which gives an exposure time of 15 seconds. I set a delay of 20 seconds via a remote release to give me time to get in position with my flashgun.

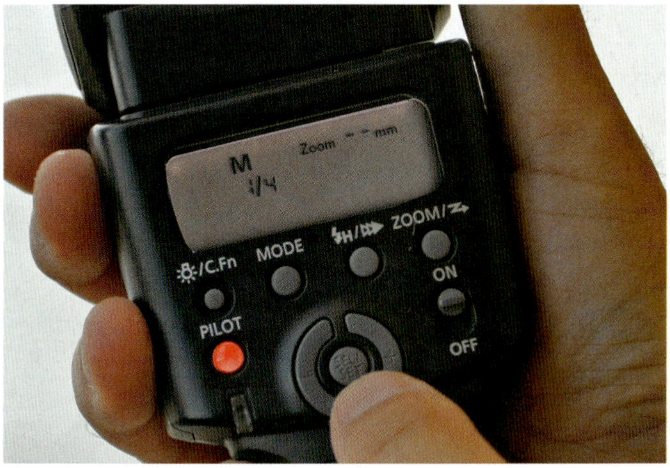

Step 2 I've already set the flashgun to manual and selected ¼ power. This reduces the recycling time, allowing me to move around and fire more flash bursts than I could if the flashgun was set to full power.

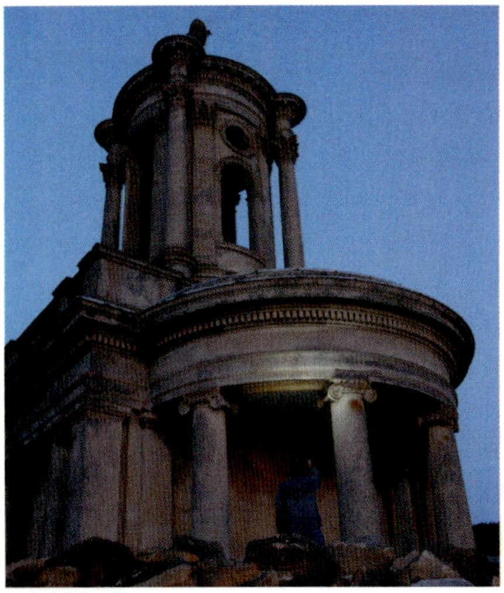

Step 3 Here, you can see me firing the flash. If you don't move around during the exposure, you can expect to see yourself appear as a ghostly blur within the scene.

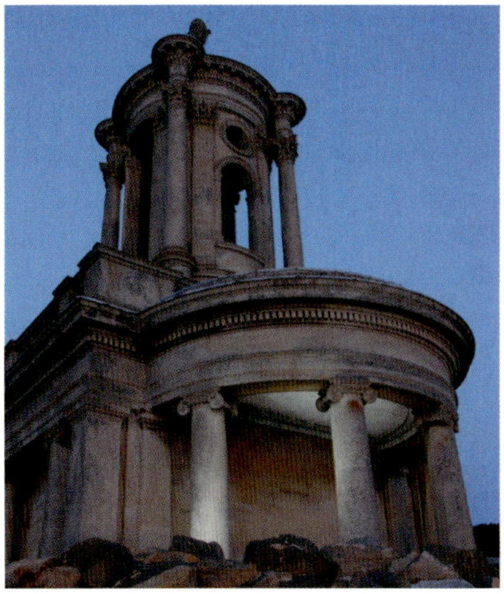

Step 4 By moving around during the exposure, I'm no longer visible. I focus most of my flash bursts toward the ceiling of the semi-circular area at the front of the building.

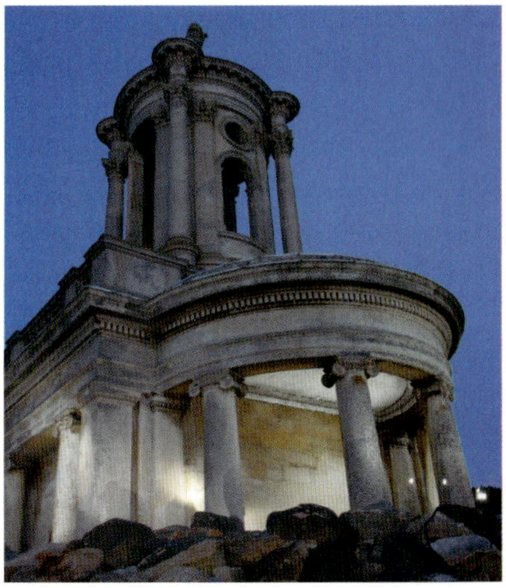

Step 5 A longer exposure of 20 seconds means more time and more flash bursts to illuminate a wider area of the building. But I'm careless with my aim, resulting in flash hotspots.

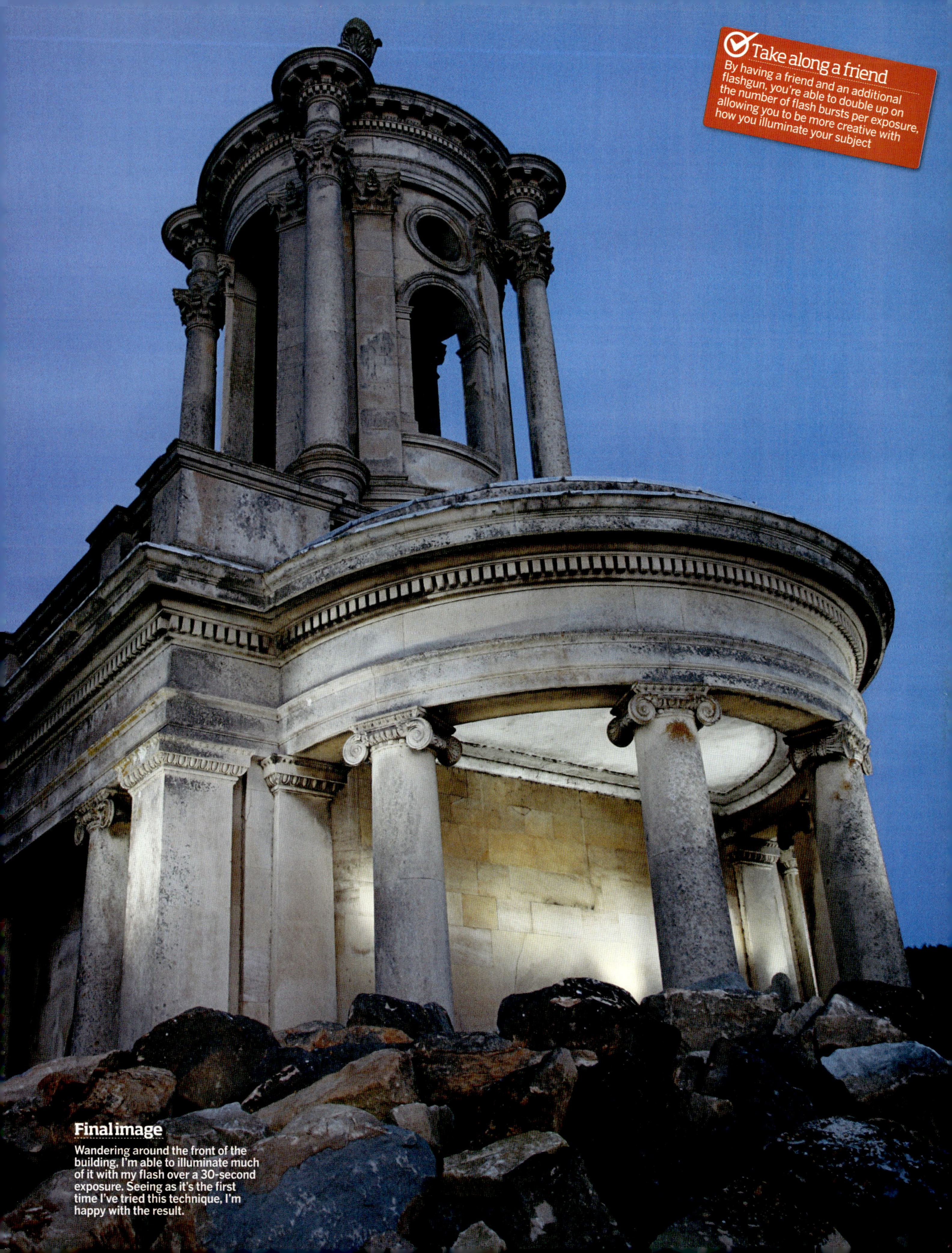

Take along a friend

By having a friend and an additional flashgun, you're able to double up on the number of flash bursts per exposure, allowing you to be more creative with how you illuminate your subject

Final image

Wandering around the front of the building, I'm able to illuminate much of it with my flash over a 30-second exposure. Seeing as it's the first time I've tried this technique, I'm happy with the result.

How to use bounce flash

THE MAIN PROBLEM with using your camera's built-in flash (apart from its relatively low power) is that it fires its output directly at the subject, so you are always going to get a portrait illuminated by relatively harsh light, which is not flattering at all! There are ways around this, though, such as using a flash diffuser, but the best solution is to use a hotshoe-mounted flashgun and to bounce the flash off a wall or ceiling. Most flashguns offer this option, with some rotating side to side, as well as flipping up and down. Exposure control is automatic, too, making the whole process very easy. Nevertheless, there are a few tips to ensure you use this technique well.

It's best to pick a surface to bounce off that is neutral in colour – white is the most reflective surface (and also the most common ceiling colour), but you'll find a cream wall or ceiling can illuminate your subject with a warmer cast. Also, remember that you don't always have to bounce light upwards onto the ceiling. If you are shooting portraits, a sideways bounce means that your subject will be lit from the side, which can produce flattering results by casting soft shadows across the face.

Shadows aren't always a good thing, though. Portraits taken with ceiling-bounced flash can often exhibit shadows under the eyes – which is not a good look! To get around this, check if your flashgun has a built-in reflector that bounces some of the light towards the subject while allowing the majority of it to bounce off the ceiling. If it hasn't, you can take the DIY approach and build a makeshift reflector. To do this, stick a small piece of white card in place to do the same job.

Bounce flash with built-in reflector

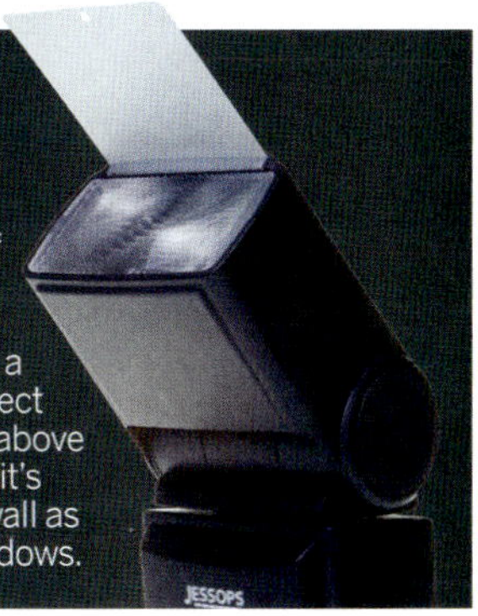

Many flashguns now have a built-in reflector, which directs a small amount of light towards the subject, while letting the majority bounce off the ceiling. In turn, this helps reduce red-eye and offers a softer, more even light compared with direct flash. Be aware that a bounce flash from above can produce shadows under the eyes, so it's worth pointing the head to bounce off a wall as this can create softer, more flattering shadows.

1) Direct flash

The camera's TTL flash metering has done a good job with the flash exposure, but the quality of the light from the direct flash is too harsh, which is not a flattering look for our subject.

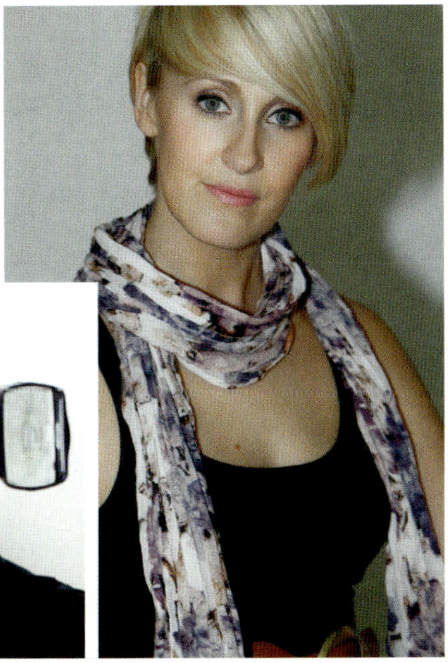

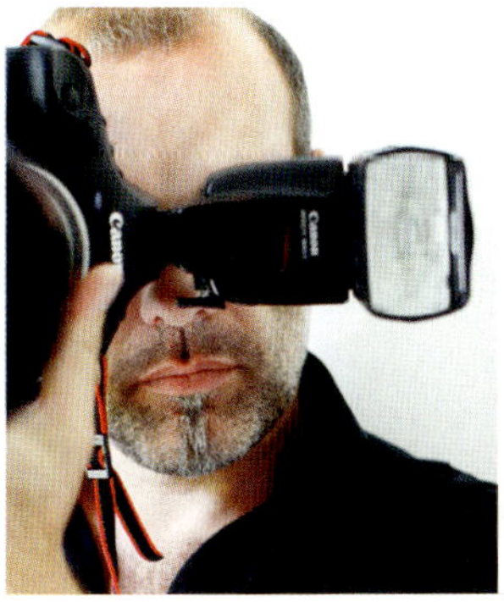

2) Bounce flash

A much better result. With the light being bounced off the ceiling, the flash is more diffused. The result is a softer effect that is far better than the harsh result produced by direct flash.

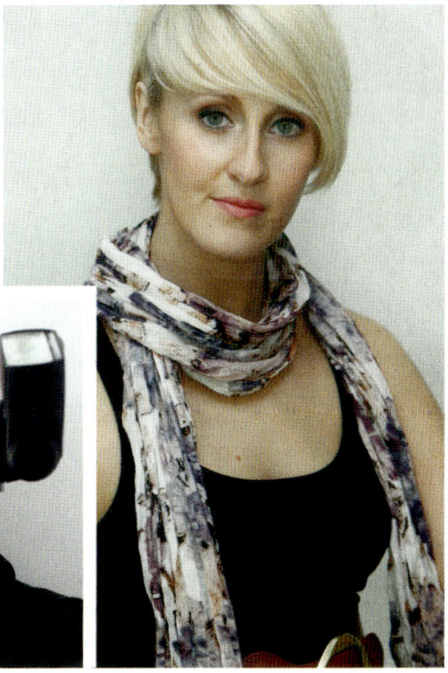

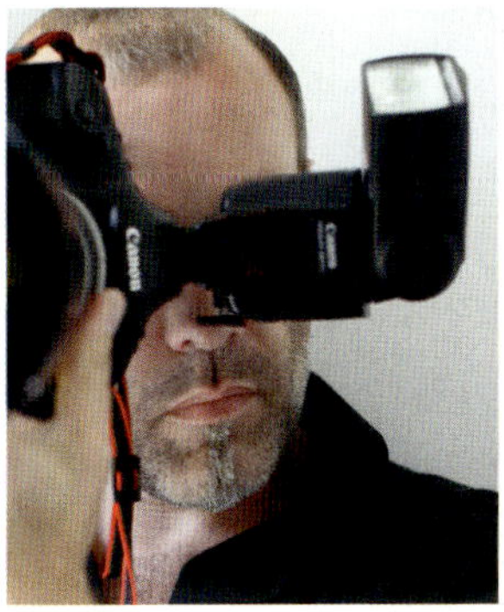

3) Bounce flash with reflector

The flashgun's built-in reflector sends some of the light directly towards the subject, while letting the majority of the flash bounce off the ceiling. The technique gives the best of both worlds.

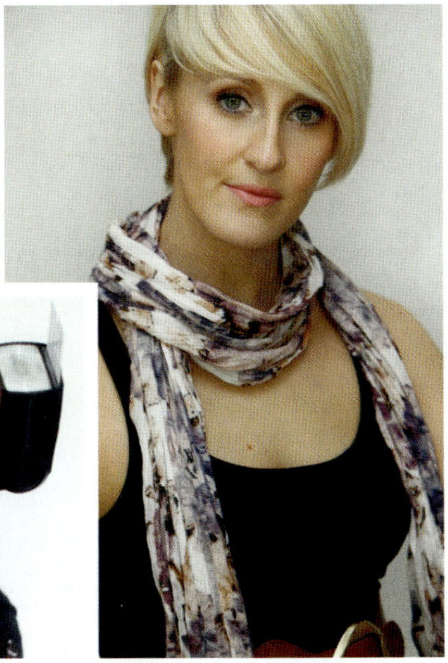

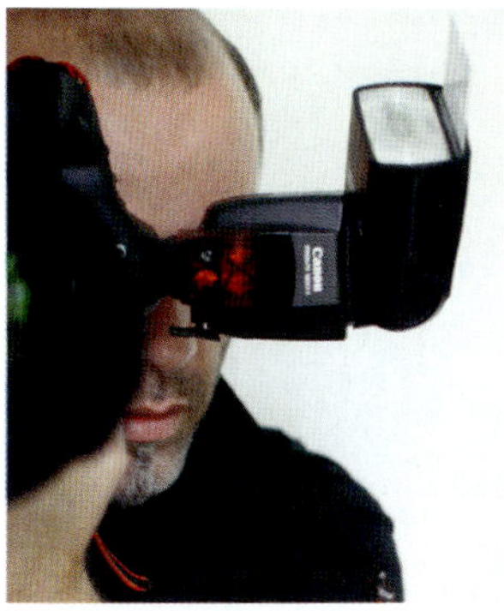

4) Bounce flash off a colour surface

Always try to use a white (or cream) surface when bouncing flash, as the light picks up the tone of a coloured wall and will result in pictures with a horrible cast.

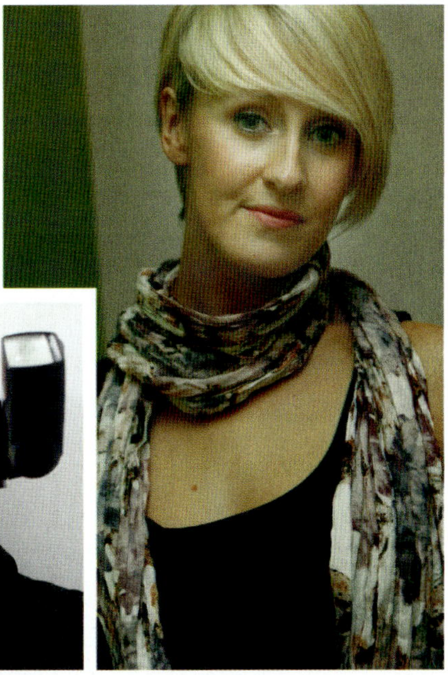

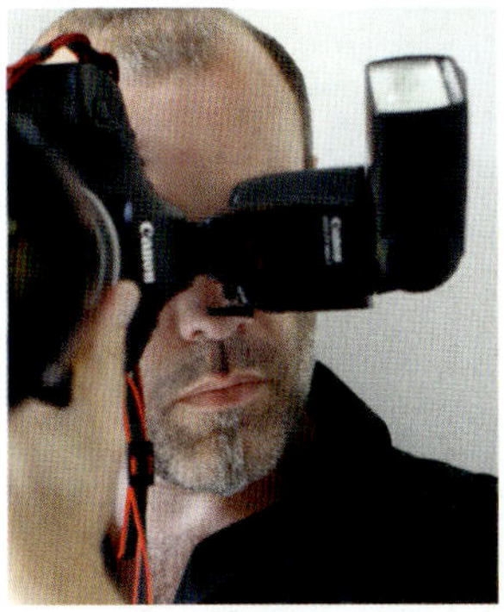

Top picks: Flashguns and studioflash kits

Photography is simply the manipulation of light. But, sometimes, natural light just doesn't provide the effect you want, so we've selected our two top flashguns and studio kits to help shed some light on products which offer great value

Nissin Speedlite Di622 II

www.kenro.co.uk; 01793 615836

Guide price: £150
Street price: £130

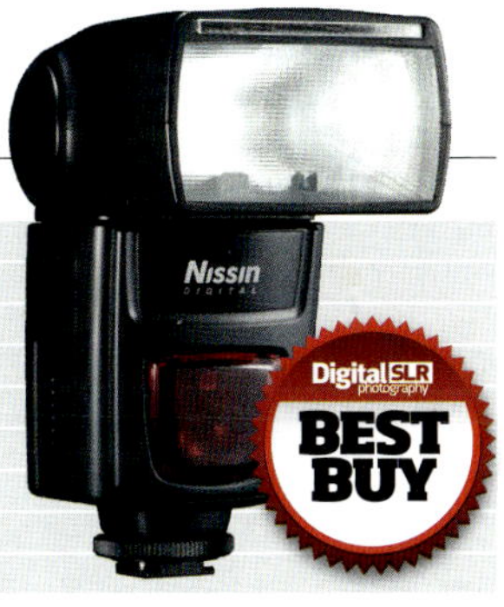

MAIN SPECIFICATIONS
- **Guide Number:** 44-62 (ISO 100, m)
- **Flash coverage:** 16-70mm (24-105mm)
- **Recycling time:** four to six seconds
- **Bounce facility:** Yes (0 to 90°)
- **Swivel facility:** Yes (0 to 270°)
- **TTL:** Yes
- **AF assist beam:** Yes
- **Strobe flash:** No
- **Wireless flash:** Yes

The Nissin Di622 has excellent build quality for a flash unit costing under £150; it's as good as models costing twice its price. This flashgun also has some rewarding features that set it apart from many other flashguns at this price range. These include second-curtain sync, slave flash and a standby mode that kicks in after two minutes of non-use to save your battery power. It also includes a flash stand, a diffuser for coverage as wide as 16mm and a fill-in reflector. There is no LCD panel on the rear; instead, a series of LEDs indicate power and a single button handles the modes. The Nissin Di622 MkII flashgun is available for Canon, Nikon and Sony DSLRs and considering the quality of features and the reasonable price, offers a decent cut-price alternative to branded models.

Sigma EF-530 DG Super

www.sigma-imaging-uk.com; 01707 329999

Guide price: £250
Street price: £150

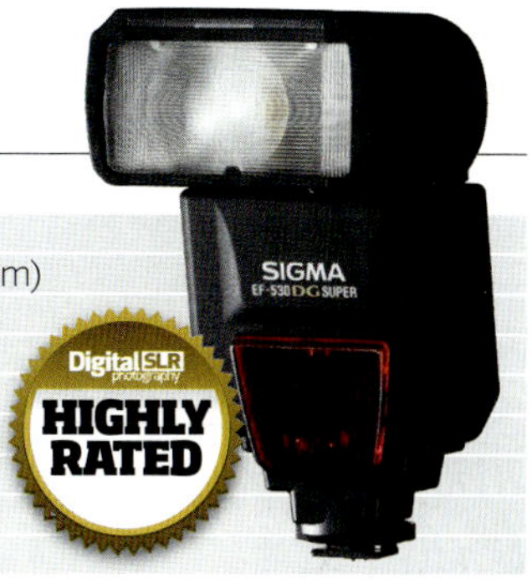

MAIN SPECIFICATIONS
- **Guide Number:** 28-53 (ISO 100, m)
- **Flash coverage:** 16-70mm (24-105mm)
- **Recycling time:** four to six seconds
- **Bounce facility:** Yes (0-90°)
- **Swivel facility:** Yes (0-270°)
- **TTL:** Yes
- **AF assist beam:** Yes
- **Strobe flash:** Yes
- **Wireless flash:** Yes

Sigma not only makes great value lenses, it also boasts a couple of excellent flashguns, with this being its top model. The EF-530 is available in Canon, Nikon, Pentax, Sigma and Sony versions, and is packed with stacks of features. In fact, it will take you quite a while to read the EF-530's instruction manual to get to grips with them all! One interesting feature is the High Speed Sync, which allows you to fire the unit at shutter speeds above your camera's usual flash sync speed. The unit can also be used as a master or a slave unit, and offers a wide-angle flash diffuser panel. The unit is also easy to use with the buttons spaced out, and a bright and clear LCD monitor. The battery compartment slider, however, could be a potential weak spot after sustained use. An excellent flashgun.

Interfit EX150 MKII outfit

www.interfitphotographic.com

Guide price: £250
Street price: £220

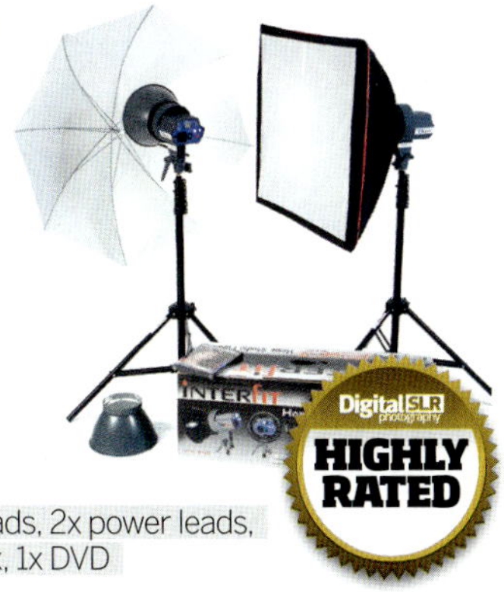

MAIN SPECIFICATIONS
- **No. of heads:** 2x 150Ws
- **Power:** 19-150Ws
- **Guide number (ISO 100, m):** 22
- **Modelling lamp:** Full (100W)/Off
- **Fitting:** EX type
- **Trigger Voltage:** 5v

KIT INCLUDES
2x flash heads, 2x stands, 2x sync leads, 2x power leads, 1x white brolly, 2x spill kills, 1x softbox, 1x DVD

Replacing the successful EX150 kit, the Mark II version has some impressive new features. The heads are a decent size, with a strong polycarbonate build, and are compatible with the full Interfit range of accessories. Though there is no storage bag with this kit, the box it comes in is sturdy and adequate for holding it. The modelling lamps give a useful amount of light and the flash power (1/8 to full-power) is very respectable and, when channelled by the spill kills, can add 50% to the Guide Number. Light temperature is a little on the cool side, so using RAW or a manual WB setting is advised. This is a great kit for the money and a good choice for the amateur. It may not be as extensive as some, but the build quality of the equipment more than makes up for it.

Elinchrom D-Lite 4 IT outfit

www.flashcentre.com; 0207 8375649

Guide price: £730
Street price: £550

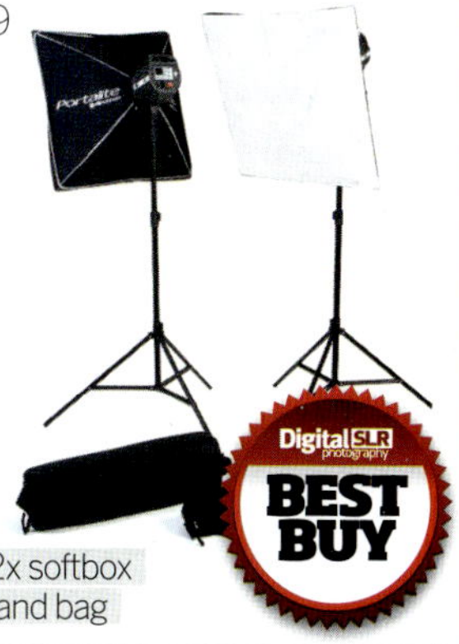

MAIN SPECIFICATIONS
- **No. of heads:** 2x 400Ws
- **Power:** 25-400Ws
- **Modelling lamp:** Full (100W)/ proportional/Low/Off
- **Fitting:** EX type
- **Trigger Voltage:** 5v

STUDIO 2 GO OUTFIT INCLUDES
2x flash heads, 2x stands, 2x power leads, 2x softbox (one medium, one small), 1x light bag, 1x stand bag

This update of the original D-Lite is one of the best kits for beginners. The heads are compact but sturdy, and feature an integral Skyport wireless trigger. The heads are available in 200 and 400-Watt versions (D-Lite 2 IT & D-Lite 4 IT respectively) and if possible, we recommend you buy the 400-Watt heads as the extra power is very useful. The control panel couldn't be easier to use. An LED shows the current power setting with two large buttons beneath allowing it to be changed. Other controls allow you to set the modelling light to be on at minimum or full power, off, or proportional to the power setting, which is set in 1/10th increments. There is also a button to switch the audible ready 'beep' on or off. The D-Lite kit has everything you need to get started.

Studioflash outfits

While newcomers may find studioflash intimidating, the truth is, using it isn't as difficult as you may think

ALTHOUGH THERE ARE various studioflash kits available, ranging in price from under £200 to thousands, most of them have very similar features and all follow basic principles of operation. A studioflash head is designed to fire a burst of flash at a given power setting – the extra functions and accessories are all geared to allow the photographer more control of the flash output. Truly mastering a studioflash system can take years but, thankfully, getting to grips with the essentials is relatively easy. Much like using ambient light, the key factor behind success is learning how to control the flash output so your subject is lit the way you'd like it to be. The big difference between studio and ambient light is the level of control you have – you are able to fine-tune the lighting's intensity and direction, as well as the nature of the light falling on the subject, far more accurately than you could ever achieve with natural light. This makes it an incredibly versatile form of lighting but, obviously, one that does take time to learn to use accurately. Here, we cover the basic workings of a studioflash system and how the various attachments, such as softboxes and brollies, can be used to control how your subject is lit.

Anatomy of a studioflash head

This illustration is of the rear of an Interfit head, but most brands will have a similar layout, with easy-to-use and well labelled controls.

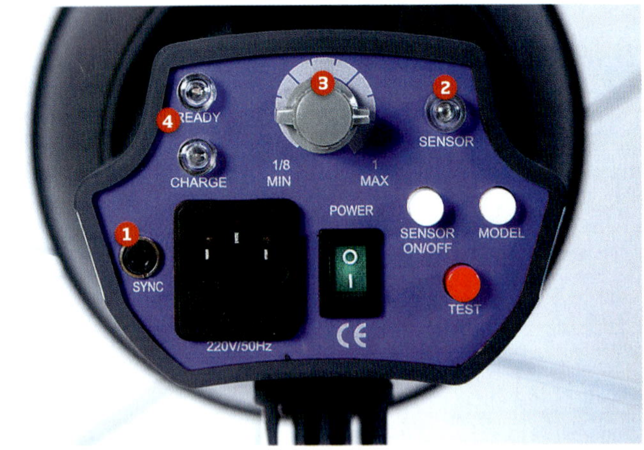

Rear of light

You'll normally find controls on the rear of the head, but some models have them on the side, too.

1) SYNC SOCKET Most studioflash outfits are supplied with a sync lead, which connects your camera to your flash head, to allow the flash to fire when you press the shutter button.

2) SLAVE CELL This sensor detects any flash output, so if your camera is connected to one light in a multiple set-up, its output will trigger the slave cell on other lights, making them fire together.

3) POWER SETTINGS A key function of studioflash heads is being able to adjust the power output. Basic heads have fixed settings, eg ¼ power, ½ power and so on, while most advanced heads have stepless variable settings.

4) STATUS LIGHTS/BEEPS Many heads have lights that indicate when the head has sufficient charge to fire.

Too hot to handle!

Flash heads heat up quickly, so take care not to burn yourself when swapping attachments. The metal mount, as well as the bulb, can get hot, especially when the modelling lamp is turned on

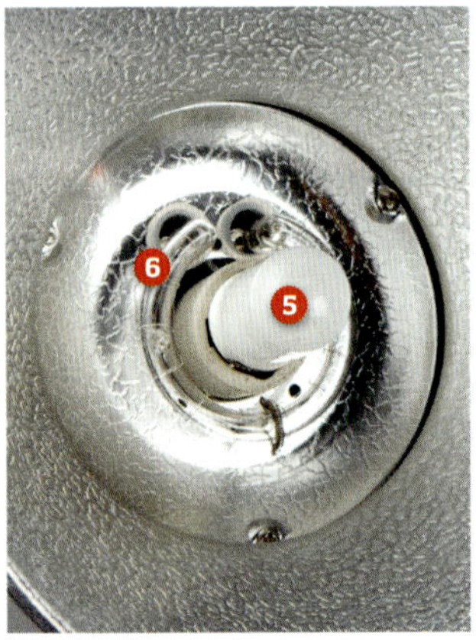

Front of light

Removing the lighting attachment will usually reveal two bulbs, each with different uses.

5) MODELLING LAMP This tungsten bulb remains switched on, to allow you to compose the image, focus on the subject and predict the flash effect.

6) FLASH BULB These provide the powerful flash output. Most brands have specialised bulbs to fit certain heads or studioflash series. They're very fragile, so handle them with utmost care.

Setting up your camera for using studioflash

Set the camera to manual and set the correct flash sync speed. Then fit a PC adaptor to your hotshoe to connect to the flash sync lead

CANON EOS DSLRS

(1) Set the main control dial to M to select manual mode

(2) Turn the input dial behind the shutter button and set the flash sync speed

(3) Once you've taken a flashmeter reading, press and hold down the +/- button, then turn the input dial to set the aperture you require

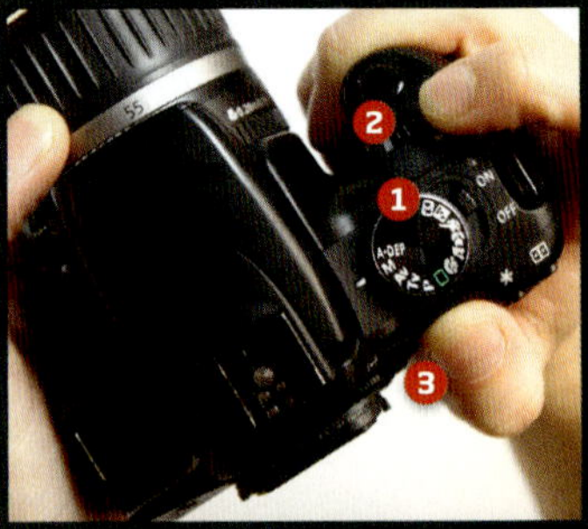

MOST NIKON DSLRS

(1) Set the main control dial to M to select manual mode

(2) Turn the input dial behind the shutter button and set the flash sync speed

(3) Once you've taken a flashmeter reading, turn the input dial on the front of the handgrip to set the aperture

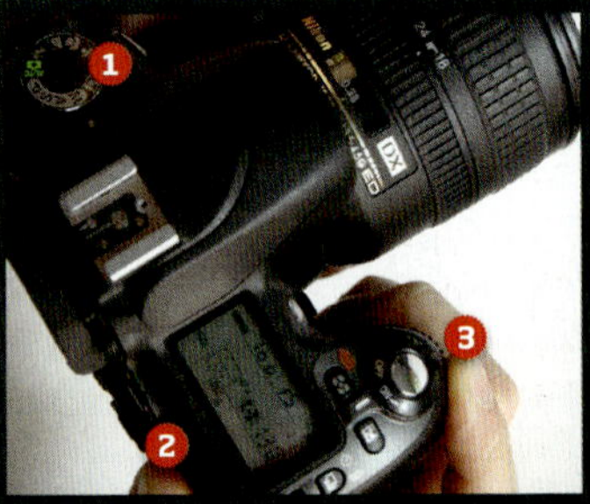

PENTAX K-SERIES DSLRS

(1) Set the main control dial on the top-plate to M to select manual mode

(2) Turn the input dial behind the shutter button and set the flash sync speed

(3) Once you've taken a flashmeter reading, press and hold down the +/- button, then turn the input dial to set the aperture you require

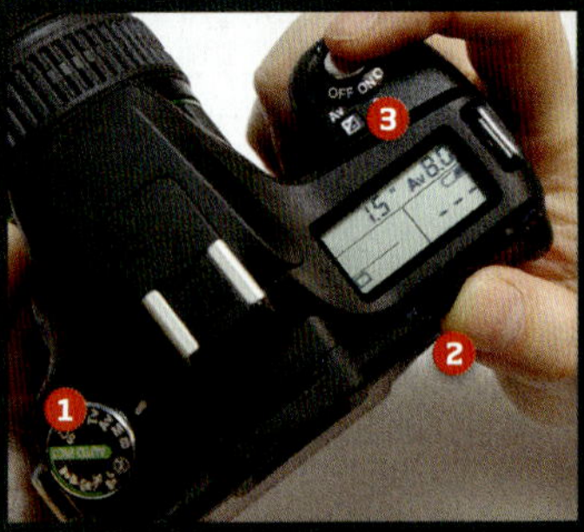

SONY ALPHA DSLRS

(1) Set the main control dial on the top-plate to Tv to select shutter-priority mode

(2) Turn the input dial in front of the shutter button and set the flash sync speed

(3) Once you've taken a flashmeter reading, press and hold down the +/- button, then turn the input dial to set the aperture you require

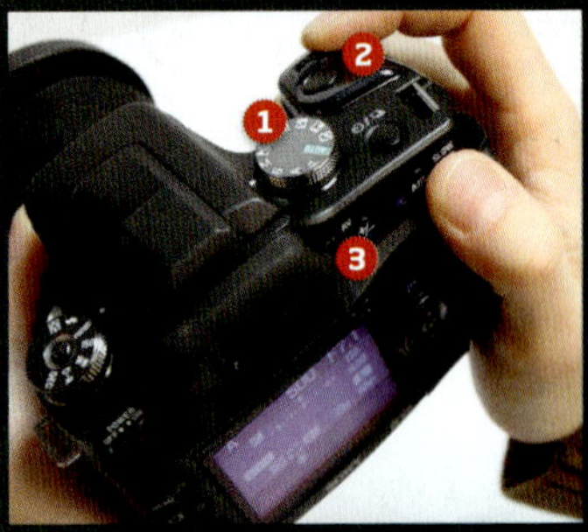

COMPACT SYSTEM CAMERAS

Very few CSCs sport the exposure mode dial found on the majority of digital SLRs, but it's still very easy to select the exposure mode. With most models all you need to do is press the Menu button or the four-way control dial to display the exposure modes and rotate the wheel to M to select Manual mode. With touchscreen models, simply press the M icon on the screen.

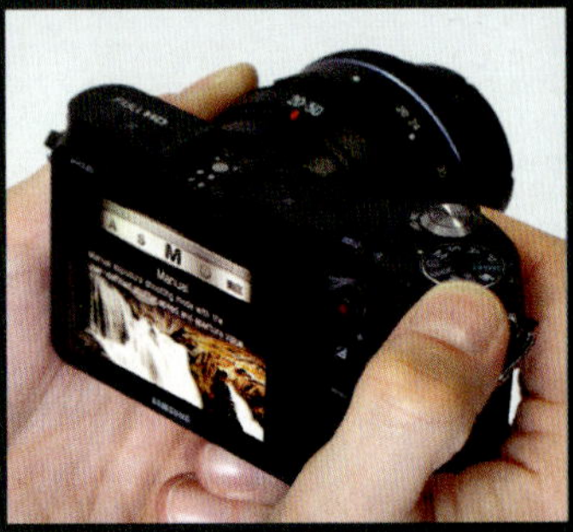

Lighting accessories

Your studioflash system is only as good as the lighting attachments and accessories

FLASH HEADS ARE designed to produce a high-power burst of light, but it's the lighting attachment that you have fitted to it that dictates the effect of the light reaching the subject. If you've ever looked into buying a studioflash system, you'll no doubt have seen various types of attachments available, each having their own way of affecting the intensity and nature of light. While most basic kits are often supplied with a brolly or two and 'spills', there are a huge number of optional accessories available and getting to know which are best suited to your needs is important. In our comprehensive comparison set below, we have used the most typical types of attachments available for most studio kits to give you an idea of how each affects the light.

As well as lighting attachments, other accessories can play a big part in the quality of your final results, or just make the process a lot easier. For instance, a flashmeter is useful to identify the correct aperture you need to set your camera to for a perfect exposure, and a remote trigger is also handy. Which background you use also affects the final image: there are a variety available, from plain to coloured patterns, to paper rolls that fit on frames and collapsible backdrops. A reflector should not be overlooked either; it bounces light back onto the subject or background as an alternative to using an additional light. Silver is the most efficient, white provides a softer and more natural effect, while a black reflector can accentuate cheekbones!

Flashmeter readings

When using studioflash, make sure the white dome (invercone) on your flashmeter is set over the sensor, so that it takes incident light readings, which will prove to be the most accurate

Umbrella (brolly)

Available in white, silver and translucent, a brolly is one of the cheapest accessories available. Silver is very efficient at bouncing light, white gives a soft, natural effect, while translucent brollies provide the most diffused light.

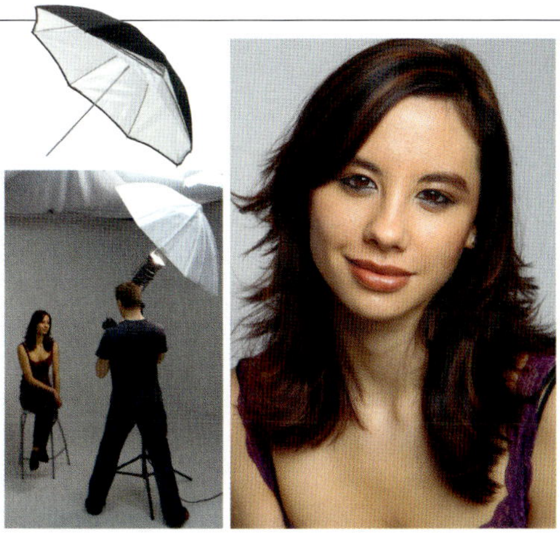

Softbox

A real favourite, as it provides a very diffused effect that's ideal for flattering portraits. The larger the softbox, the softer the light it produces. The majority are square, but some are rectangular and thin (also called strip lights).

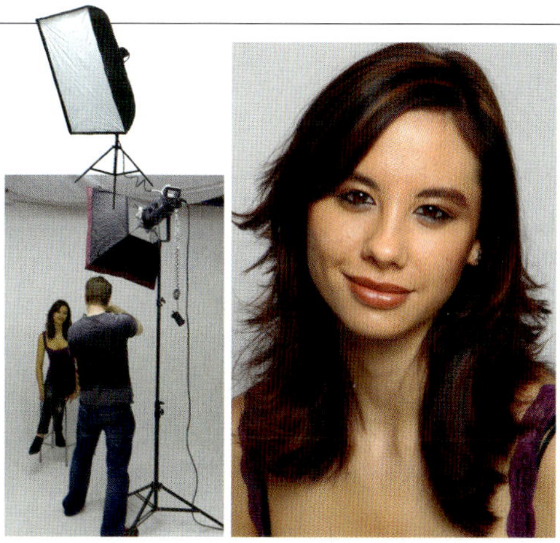

Beauty dish

Beauty dishes are often used, as you may expect, for close-up 'beauty' and make-up shots. They give off a very harsh light in the centre, which enhances make-up, but also highlights flaws on a subject's skin.

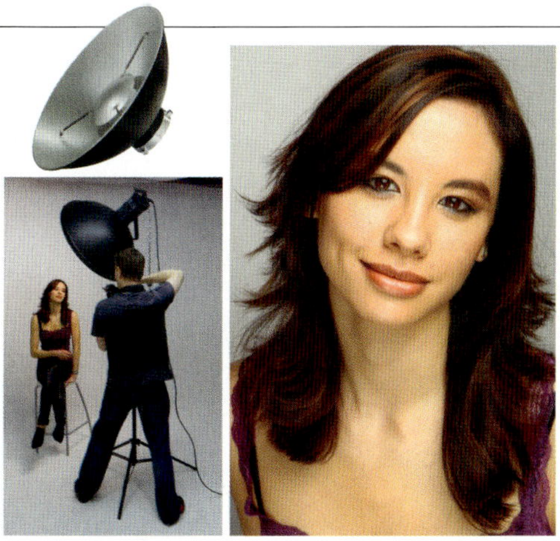

Spill (spill kill)

Often supplied with the flash head, they help direct light in a concentrated beam. With portraits, they're useful for lighting backgrounds, but quite harsh when aimed at a subject's face.

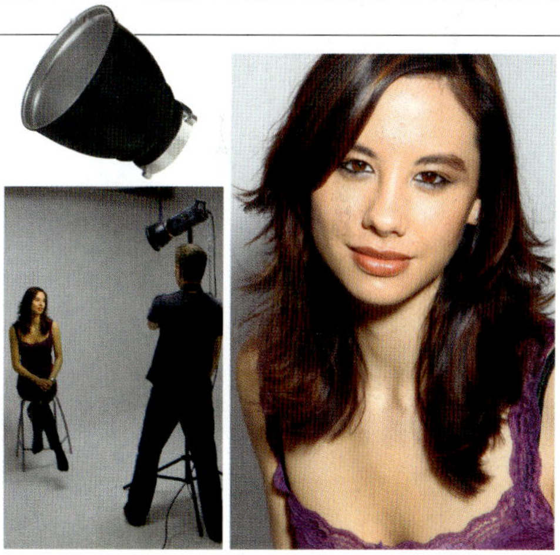

Snoot

This conical attachment provides a hard-edge and a directional beam of light that's better suited for backlighting or as a hairlight than providing the key lighting for portraits.

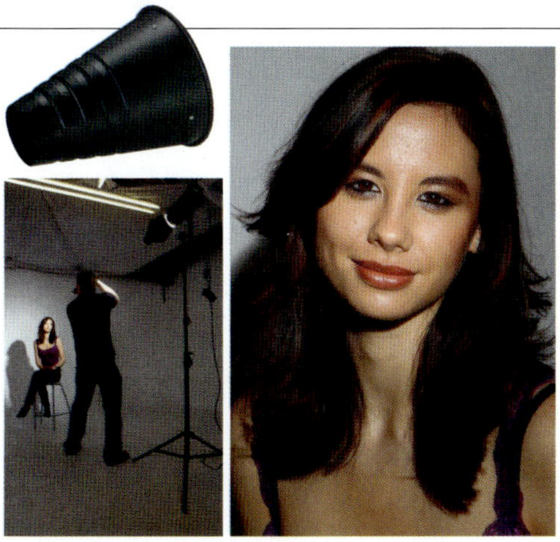

Honeycomb grid

These provide a soft-edged circle of light and are a popular alternative to a snoot. They act in a similar way to a spotlight, but provide a wider angle spot effect. Honeycombs are available with various sizes of grids.

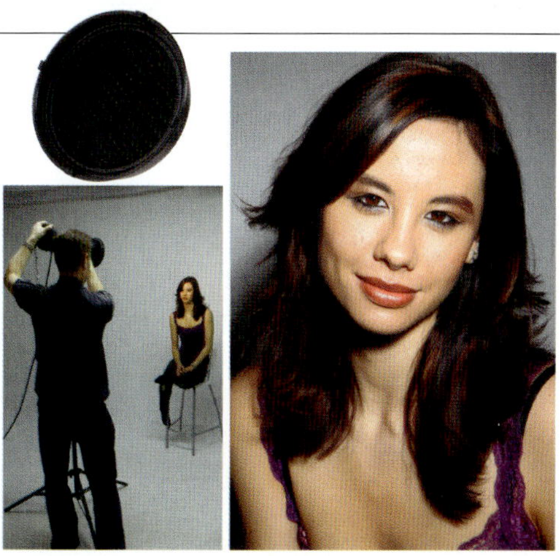

Studio set-up: one light

To get to grips with studio lighting, try a simple set-up with one light; here are five techniques to get you started

If you want to learn how to control your lighting, you're best off starting with just one light. One light is more than sufficient to produce some stunning results and many great photographers still use a single head for their work. After all, outdoors we only have a single light source – the sun. This set-up is very easy to control and the smallest adjustment to the light on your subject has a clear effect. This forces you to fine-tune the light's angle and diffusion method. And while you'll only have one source of illumination, you can also use reflectors in your set-up to bounce light and fill in any shadows.

The set of images below shows what happens when you position your single light at different heights and angles – as you can see, it's crucial that you learn the dos and don'ts of how to set up your single studioflash head to avoid some of the unflattering results shown below.

As mentioned earlier, you need to set your camera to manual mode and set it to its flash sync speed (if you don't know it, use 1/125sec as a safe bet or refer to the user's manual). The aperture is determined by the meter reading you take, which is easy to do with a one-light set-up. With the sync lead from the light attached, hold the meter in front of the subject's face and press the button to fire the flash and take a reading. By adjusting the power setting on the flash head, you can effectively change the aperture you work with, too. Add power to set a smaller aperture and reduce power to use a wider aperture.

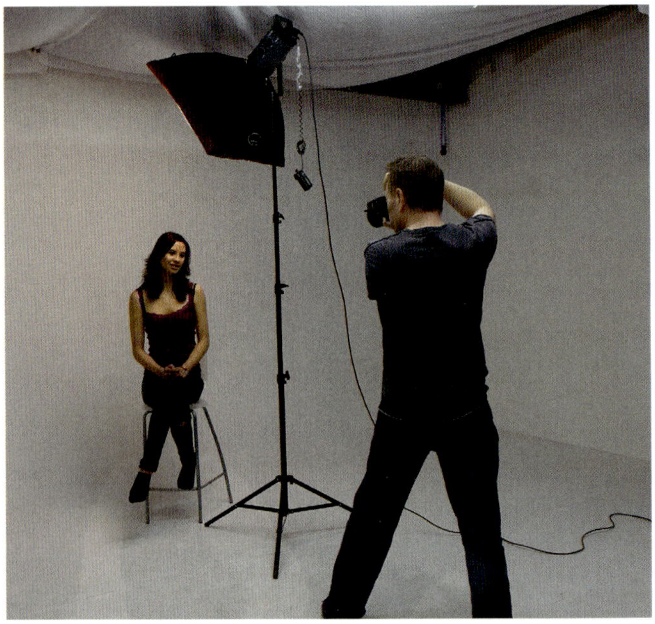

ONE LIGHT All you need to get started is your camera and a single flash head. With a bit of practice, you will soon find yourself getting great results!

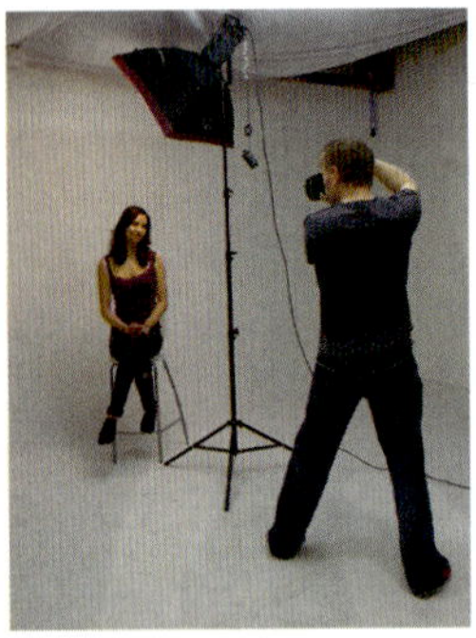

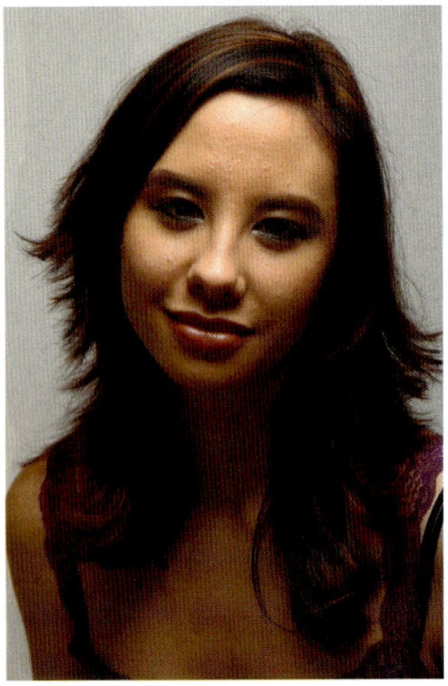

1) Lit from above With the light positioned high above the model's head, you get a natural-looking light, although shadows can become harsh under the nose and chin. For the best results, get the model to look towards the light. You could also ask her to hold a reflector to fill the shadows.

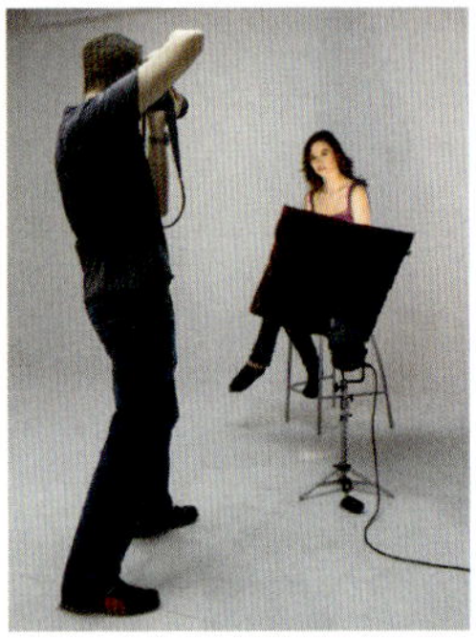

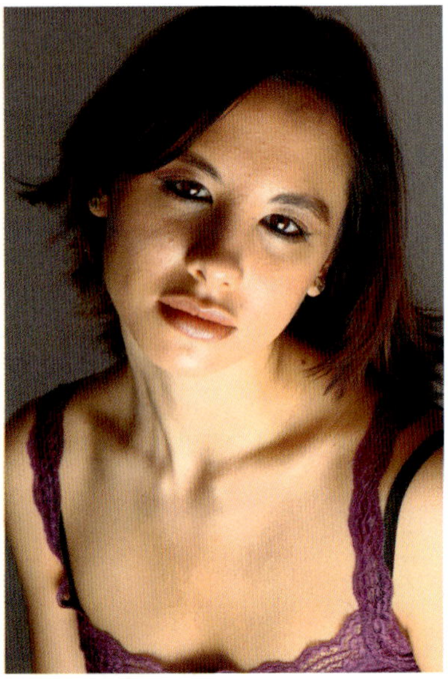

2) Lit from below Placing the light lower than the model's head, pointing upwards will eradicate any unsightly shadows under the nose and chin. For best results, get the model to look down towards the light, which, as you can see, also makes catchlights appear in the subject's eyes.

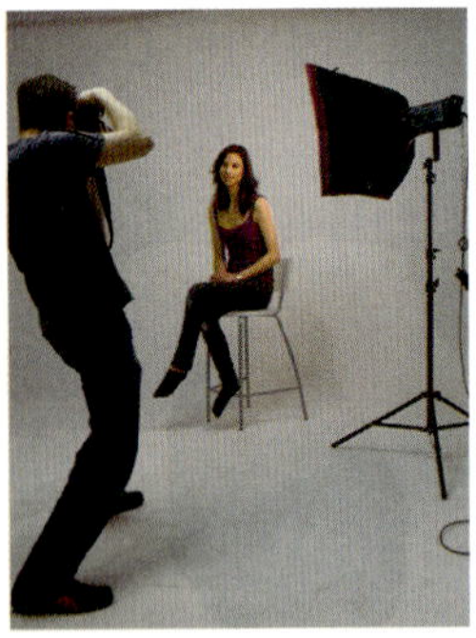

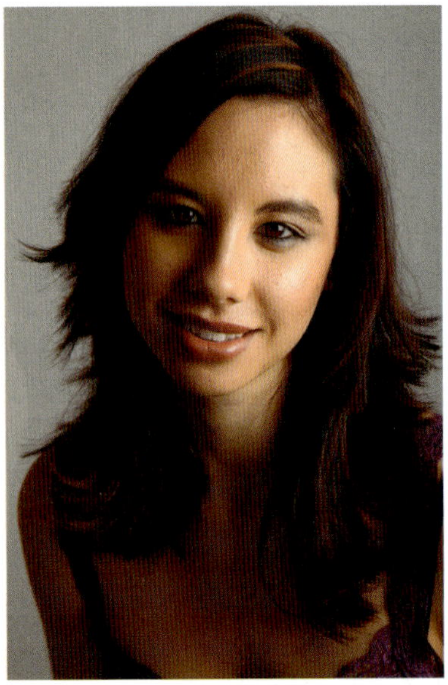

3) Lit from the side Place the light to either the left or right side of your model's face for a strong, directional light, which will keep half of the face in shadow. To increase your chances of capturing the catchlights in your subject's eyes, it is important to make sure the light is far enough forward.

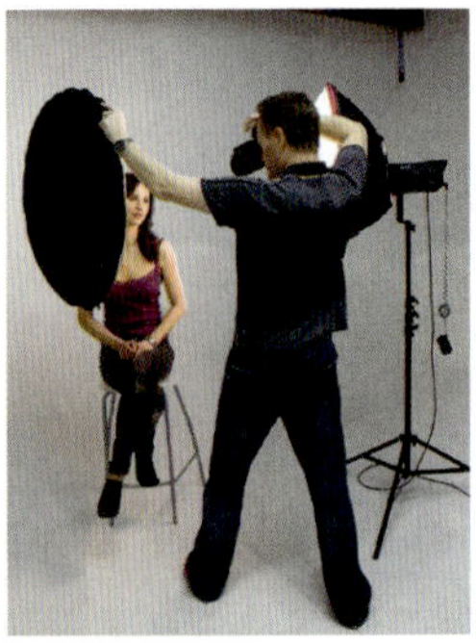

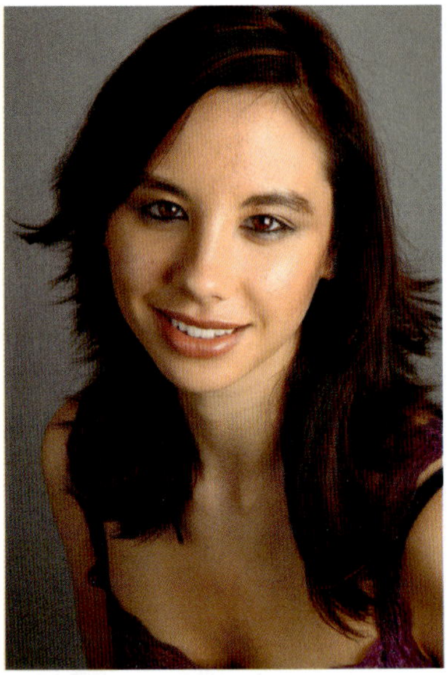

4) One light & reflector By holding a reflector close in to the face, on the opposite side from the light, you will be able to even up any harsh shadows, much like using a second head. The closer you place it to the model, the stronger the reflection will be (though it helps to have an assistant!)

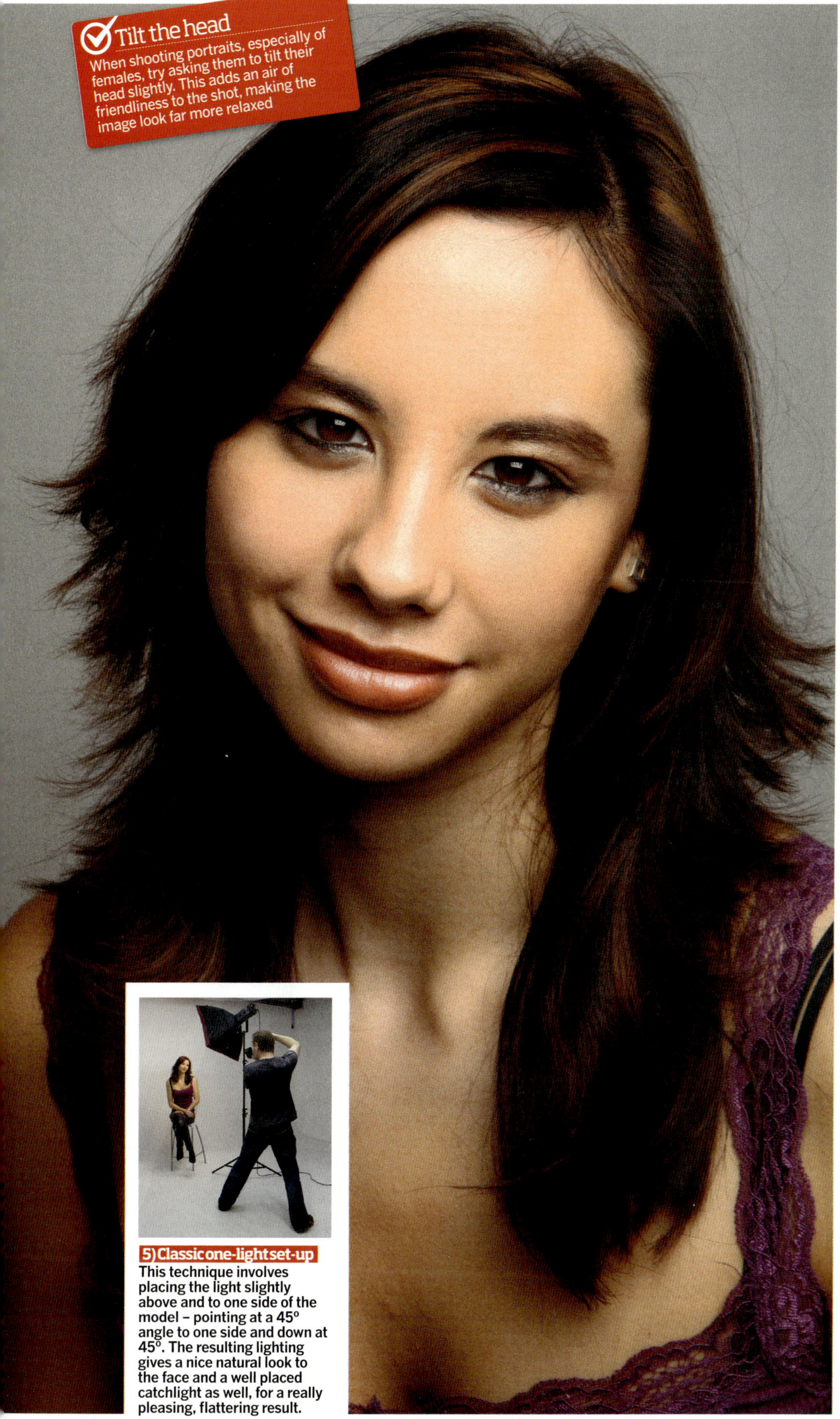

Tilt the head

When shooting portraits, especially of females, try asking them to tilt their head slightly. This adds an air of friendliness to the shot, making the image look far more relaxed

5) Classic one-light set-up

This technique involves placing the light slightly above and to one side of the model – pointing at a 45° angle to one side and down at 45°. The resulting lighting gives a nice natural look to the face and a well placed catchlight as well, for a really pleasing, flattering result.

Q&A: Studioflash

How much should I spend on a studioflash system?

We'd recommend you start with a two-head system, with a softbox and umbrella. Tests by *Digital SLR Photography* found several to be excellent, including the Interfit EX150 MkII and the Elinchrom D-Lite 4 IT Studio 2 Go outfit.

What advantages do more expensive outfits offer?

General build quality (and reliability) will be better, but the key benefits are power, features and performance. More power is useful as you can set the lights up further away from your subject, while relative light loss from attachments like softboxes is reduced. You'll find that more expensive heads allow more control over flash output and faster flash recycling times.

Are attachments from different systems compatible?

In general, different brands have their own fittings so aren't compatible. However, Chimera makes speedrings for its softboxes which are compatible with just about any system. Visit: www.chimeralighting.com

How should I set up my camera to use studioflash?

You will need to set it to manual mode, as the metering system will not work with studioflash. Set the shutter speed to the flash sync speed and aperture to the flashmeter reading.

How do I take an exposure reading with studioflash?

Use a flashmeter connected to a light via a sync lead. Once you've set up the lights, hold the meter in front of the subject's face, take a reading and set the meter's recommended aperture on the camera. Don't forget that the flashmeter and camera both need to be set to the same ISO rating!

How do I connect my camera to my studioflash system?

The plug at the end of the studioflash sync lead connects to your camera's PC socket. If your camera hasn't got a socket, buy an adaptor (around £10) that slots on your camera's hotshoe and connect the lead to this. A more expensive option is a wireless trigger that sits on your hotshoe and triggers a receiver on the flash head.

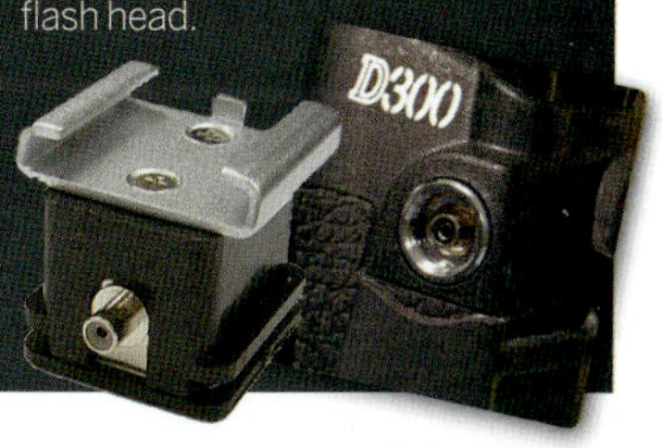

General camera accessories

As you develop your photography skills, you'll need to add to your basic camera outfit. Here we provide our recommended choices in the four main types of accessories: bags, tripods, remotes and light meters

Sekonic Flashmate L-308S

Price: £150

www.johnsons-photopia.co.uk

Ambient and flash handheld meter

Most photographers are happy with the performance of their camera's metering system, so why would anyone consider splashing out more than a hundred pounds on a handheld meter when it could be spent on a lens, tripod or another useful accessory? Well, in truth, the argument for owning a handheld meter isn't anywhere near as strong as in the days of film, but there are still some valid reasons. For starters, it can be used to measure flash readings (cordless or via a flash sync lead) as well as ambient light, so it's as useful in the studio as it is outdoors. Another benefit is that, by sliding the white dome over the sensor, it can take incident light readings (light falling on the subject), which are more accurate than reflected readings (light bouncing off the subject) – the system used by all cameras. You can set it to meter in 1/3, 1/2 or full-stop increments, to match how your DSLR works and taking a reading couldn't be easier. Choose the mode (ambient or flash), set the ISO to match your DSLR and then place the meter in front of your subject, facing the camera and press the measuring button. If measuring ambient light, you specify the shutter speed and the meter selects the corresponding aperture. This isn't ideal if you're working in aperture-priority as you need to use the up and down buttons to get to the aperture you want to use and then read off what is the correct shutter speed. The wide LCD on the front has large digits making it easier to read, although there's no backlit function to illuminate it in low light. Out in the field, and in the studio, Sekonic to be extremely accurate and consistent. But with DSLRs offering instant review and histograms, it's no surprise that its appeal is limited. However, if you regularly mix ambient and flash light, you'll find it extremely useful.

Whether you really need one or not depends on how happy you are with the exposures delivered by your camera and if you plan to regularly shoot flash as well as ambient exposures. If you are considering a light meter, this one is worth a look.

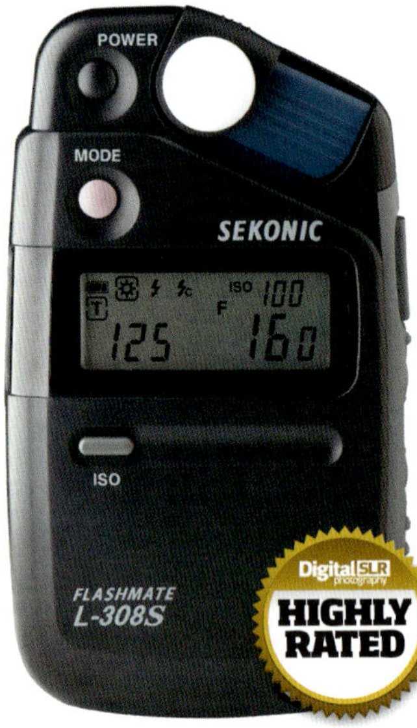

Specifications

Measuring methods: Incident and reflected
Measuring modes: Ambient and flash (corded & cordless)
ISO: 3-8000
Shutter speeds (ambient): 60 seconds to 1/8000sec
Shutter speeds (flash): One second to 1/500sec
Apertures: f/0.5 to f/90.9
EV range: 0 to EV19.9
Power Source: 1x AA battery
Size (WHD): 63x110x22mm
Weight: 95g (including battery)
Supplied accessories: Soft case, strap and Lumidisc

Verdict

Compact, light and a very versatile meter that is the ideal low-cost option for studio and outdoor work.

Build	★★★★☆
Features	★★★★☆
Performance	★★★★☆
Value for Money	★★★★☆
OVERALL	★★★★☆

Giottos MTL9351B & MH5011 head

Price: £115

Length (closed): 64cm
Number of leg sections: 3
Height (legs extended): 159cm
Type of Head: Three-way pan and tilt
Weight: 2.1kg
Website: www.daymen.co.uk

The Giottos has very solid aluminium legs with foam insulators, to keep' hands from freezing to them on cold days. The nuts and locks are a combination of plastic and die-cast aluminium, and are as solid as could be hoped for at this price. The three-way head is easily controllable and features three spirit levels in addition to the one on the legs, so there's no excuse for wonky horizons! It has a lockable rotational central column, which can be removed and re-inserted horizontally or inverted for macro or copy work. The tripod is very sturdy for the price, and comes with its own tool kit in case you need to make any adjustments. There is also a hidden bag hook underneath the central column. The MTL9351B had absolutely no problems coping with our test camera (Nikon D80) and would provide a very suitable platform on which the amateur landscaper could mount his DSLR.

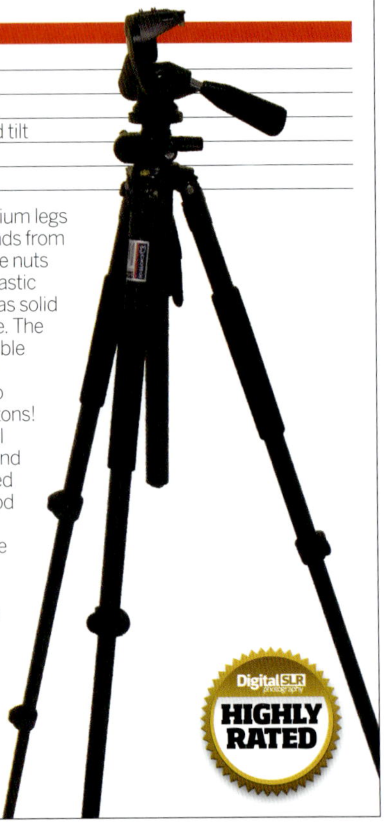

Manfrotto 190XPROB & 460MG head

Price: £170

Length (closed): 57cm
Height (legs extended): 146cm
Number of leg sections: 3
Maximum load: 5kg
Weight: 2.25kg
Website: www.manfrotto.com

This aluminium tripod from Manfrotto is one of the lightest in this price category. The legs are very sturdy and supports the camera perfectly well in all positions. The flip locks are easy to open and close and very secure, and there are vari-position locks to keep the legs secure at different settings. Perhaps the most interesting feature of the legs, is that the central column can be switched to horizontal position, for macro shots, without removing it from the legs. This is an excellent feature, as it makes the process very easy and fast to carry out. The head is very versatile, as it can pan, tilt and swivel in just about any direction, and is very easy to operate. The lack of panning handles may not be to everyone's taste, but the head is so versatile that it more than makes up for it. Spirit levels can be found on the head and central column brace, and a bag hook is located on the legs.

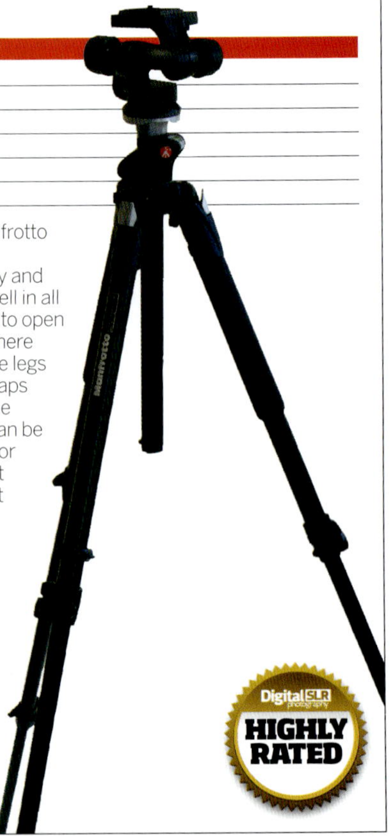

Tamrac Adventure Messenger 5

Price: £50
Dimensions: 37x30x22cm
Weight: 1.07kg
Warranty: Five years
Contact: 01628 674411
Website: www.intro2020.co.uk

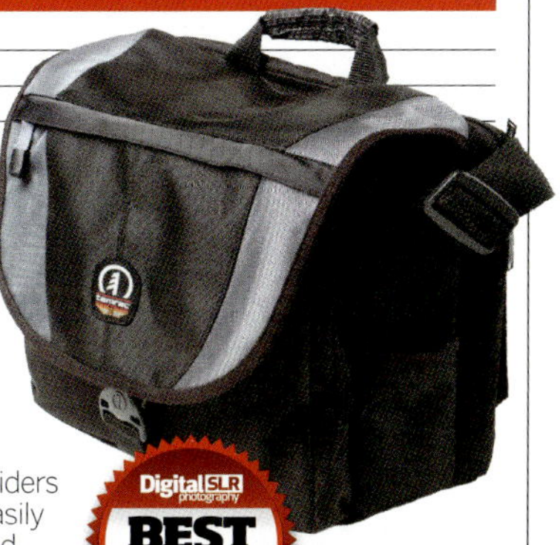

If you want to carry a laptop with you, then this is a good budget choice, as it has a well-padded, laptop compartment at the rear. There is lots of internal space and comfortably holds a large DSLR, like a Nikon D700 with 24-70mm lens attached, a 70-200mm f/2.8 zoom lens and flashgun. There are four dividers to change the layout, so you could easily keep a smaller body, extra lenses, and other accessories in there too. It's not short on features either, with a padded non-slip strap, a carry handle and slots to add on components from the Tamrac Strap Accessory System. A large pocket at the front has sections for pens, stationery or note pads, a pocket in the lid for smaller items and a dedicated mobile phone pocket. If you have a medium or large DSLR, extra lenses and a laptop, this is a great buy.

Digital SLR photography BEST BUY

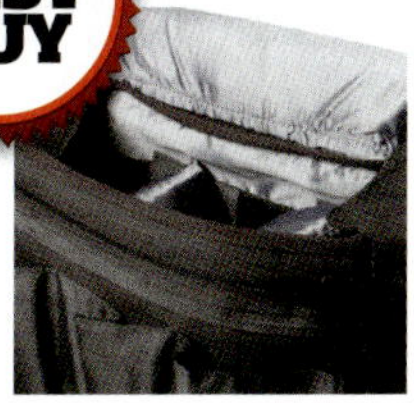

Lowepro Fastpack 250

Price: £60
Dimensions: 31.5x24x46cm
Weight: 1.6kg
Warranty: Lifetime
Contact: 01902 864646
Website: www.daymen.co.uk

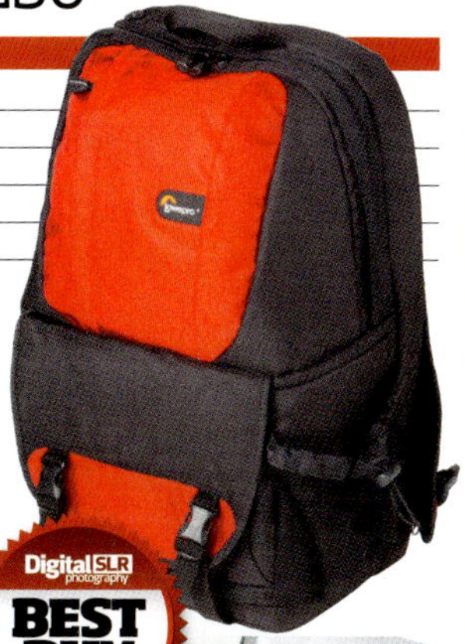

Available in black, blue or red trim, the Fastpack 250 features two compartments and is ideal for travelling light. The camera compartment is well padded, holds a large DSLR with zoom attached, along with one or two small lenses and flash. There's no room for a second body or larger lenses though, but the rear padded pocket does hold a 15in laptop. The side entry compartment helps you get at your gear quickly, but you do need to take it off to get gear out safely. The top compartment isn't as well padded, so is not designed for camera gear, but it does include two pockets for memory cards and pens. Thanks to the generous padding on the shoulder straps and back, the Fastpack 250 is comfortable to carry, the sternum and back support straps hold it nicely in place and there's a carry handle to boot.

Digital SLR photography BEST BUY

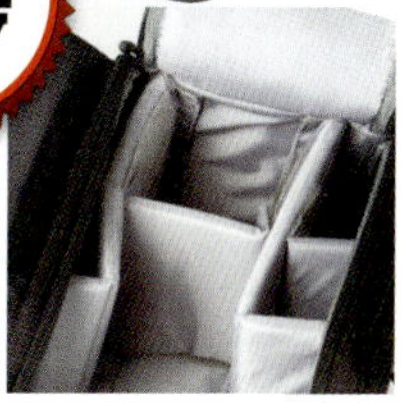

Lowepro Classified 250 AW

Price: £120
Dimensions (outer): 46.5x28x35.5cm
Weight: 1.9kg
Warranty: Lifetime
Contact: 01902 864646
Website: www.daymen.co.uk

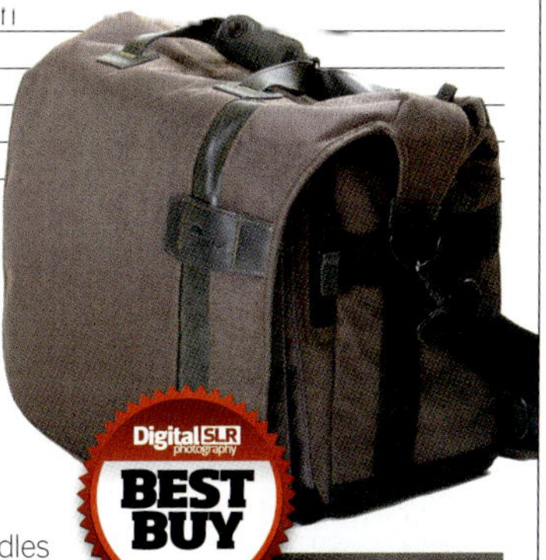

A discreet camera bag with room for lots of camera gear as well as a laptop. The interior of the bag is very deep, so you can double-up on storage by stacking items on top of each other. The bag's depth also makes it very suitable for cameras with long lenses. A padded section provides storage for a 15in laptop. Leather is used to good effect throughout the bag and the grab handles and shoulder strap are very well designed. Entry into the main section of the bag is through a clever roof zip that is easy to access on the move and is protected by the handle buckling over it. You'll be able to fit at least two DSLRs with an additional two or three lenses in the spacious main section. A luggage sleeve means that you can attach this bag to the handles of a wheelie case. The bag is hand-luggage friendly too.

Digital SLR photography BEST BUY

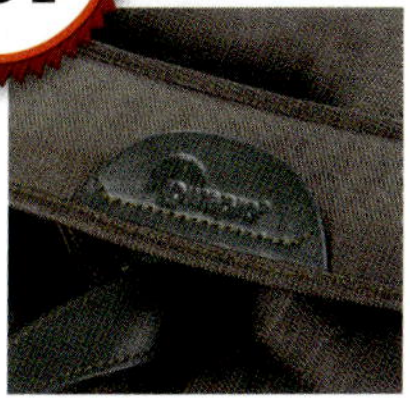

Hama Defender 170 Pro

Price: £100
Dimensions: 40x26x45cm
Weight: 2.8kg
Warranty: 30 years
Contact: 0845 2304262
Website: www.hama.co.uk

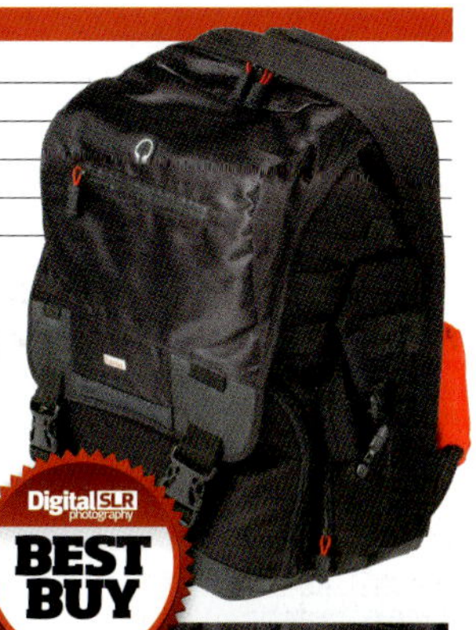

This large backpack has two compartments, both of which feature generous space. The lower compartment fits a large DSLR with 24-70mm f/2.8 attached, a long zoom, flashgun, two small primes and even a second body. The flexible dividers make it versatile too, as the whole padded section can also be removed, and there's a large 17in laptop compartment. The construction is robust with Ultra Dobby Nylon, protected zips, tough belts, strong metal hooks and a rubber base that covers the bottom, so no problems leaving it on wet ground. The shoulder straps are adjustable, but not very well padded, and there's a waist belt, lumber support and padding on the rear for improved comfort. Features are good too, with a detachable microfibre cloth, memory card wallet, rain cover and several pockets.

Digital SLR photography BEST BUY

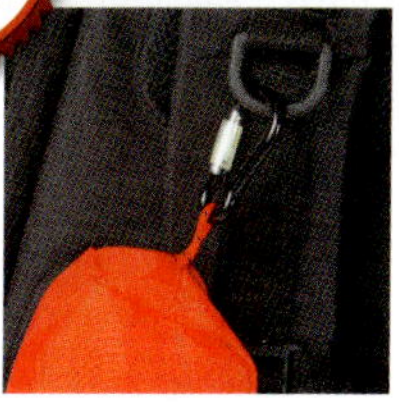

Hama Remote Control 5348

Price: £34
www.hama.co.uk

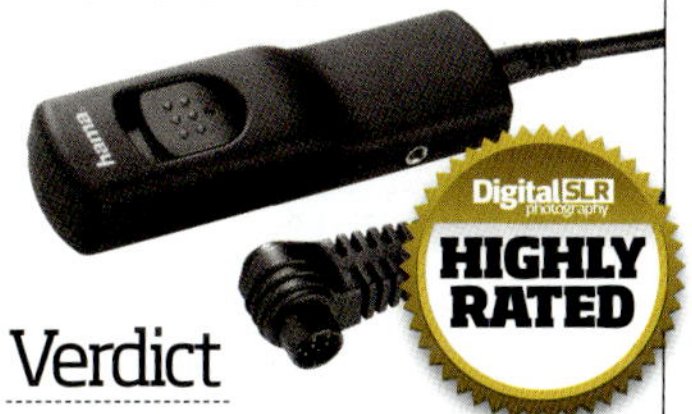

Similar in specification to Nikon's MC-30, the Hama is half the price. It's small, the plastic shell is light at 34g, while its 80cm cord is a good length. The pimpled button has a two-stage action and by sliding it forward it locks into place, with a red strip acting as a visual indicator. It's a no-frills remote that does its job well. It's very affordable compared to marque brands, but faces stiff competition from the Hähnel and Seculine remotes.

Digital SLR photography HIGHLY RATED

Verdict

A reliable, low-cost option.

Build quality	★★★☆☆
Performance	★★★★☆
Value for Money	★★★☆☆
OVERALL	★★★★☆

Hähnel Remote Shutter Release

Price: £20
www.hahnel.ie

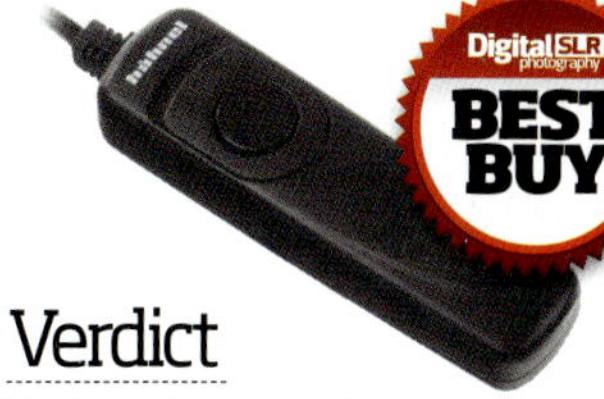

Digital SLR photography BEST BUY

The Hähnel is larger than the Hama, but this makes it easier to handle, and while its nearly double the weight at around 60g, it's still incredibly lightweight. The two-stage button has a far more positive action and the sliding lock facility is better. The 80cm cord is a useful length but the inclusion of the extension lead is a real bonus. Best of all are the pair of interchangeable connections that allow it to be used with a variety of cameras. A brilliant budget buy.

Verdict

Perfect choice as a first remote.

Build quality	★★★★☆
Performance	★★★★★
Value for Money	★★★★☆
OVERALL	★★★★★

BJORN THOMASSEN

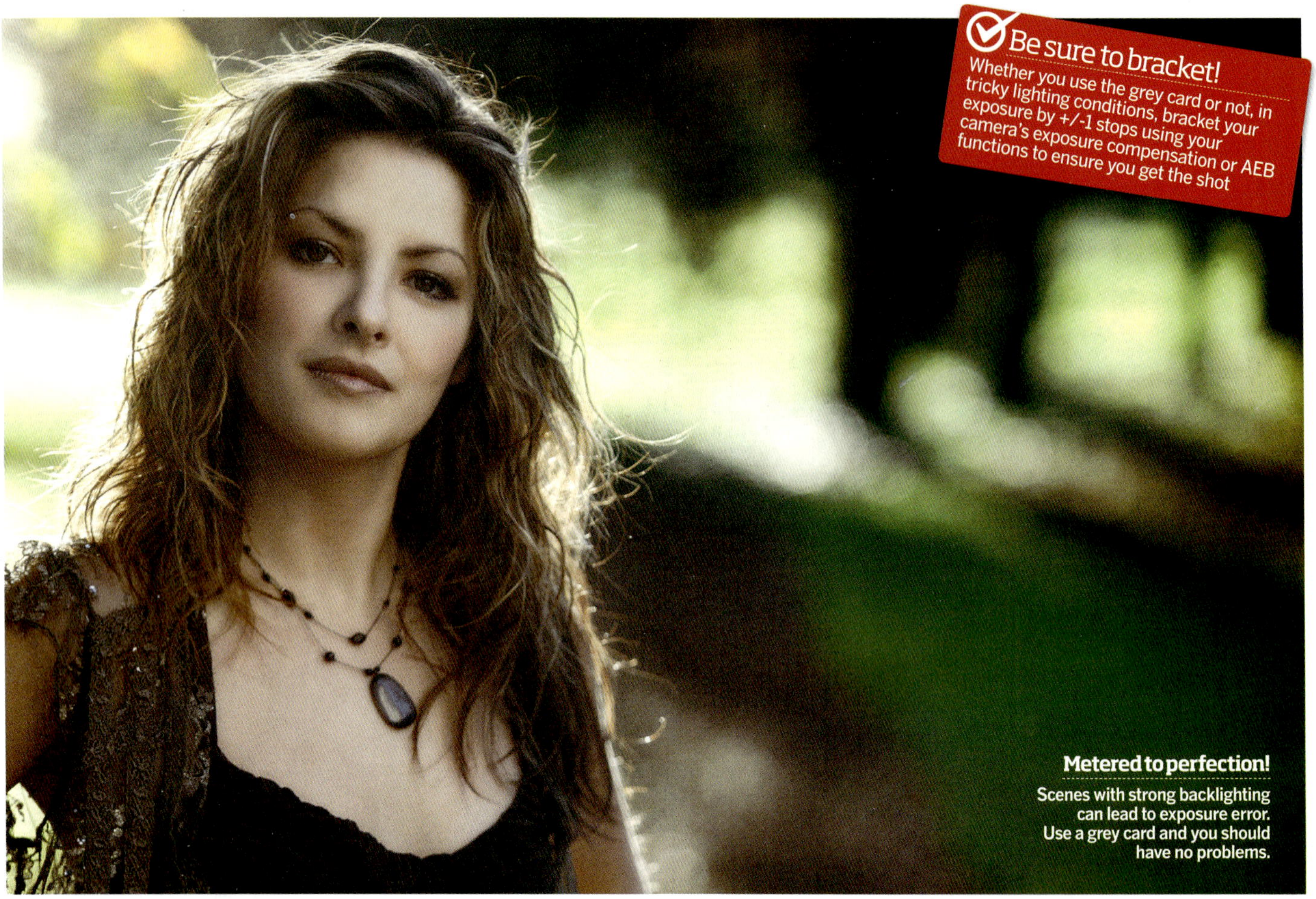

Be sure to bracket!

Whether you use the grey card or not, in tricky lighting conditions, bracket your exposure by +/-1 stops using your camera's exposure compensation or AEB functions to ensure you get the shot

Metered to perfection!
Scenes with strong backlighting can lead to exposure error. Use a grey card and you should have no problems.

How to use your free metering & White Balance cards

The 18% grey card can be used to ensure perfect exposures when shooting in tricky lighting conditions. Both reference cards can also be used to set a custom White Balance, but how you take a reading off the cards depends on your camera (refer to your camera's manual). In the meantime, here is a brief explanation to get you started

DIGITAL SLRS AND CSCS USE sophisticated exposure systems with a choice of metering patterns to suit different lighting situations. The systems work on the assumption that the area of the scene being metered is a mid-tone, or 18% grey to be precise; the average if all dark, light and mid-tones were mixed together. It's the basis of all metering patterns and works surprisingly well, but can render incorrect exposures when the overall scene or subject is considerably lighter or darker than 18% grey. For example, very dark areas or subjects can fool the metering system into overexposing the image, while very light areas can fool the camera into underexposure, as the lightmeter will take a reading that renders it as a mid-tone.

As a camera is trying to render an image 'grey', it's your job to ensure you compensate to keep the tones true to life. You can do this by either using one of your camera's exposure override facilities, such as exposure compensation, the AE-Lock button or by metering from an area of the scene that has a mid-tone. And that's where our grey card comes in. Using it is very simple, as our step-by-step guide below illustrates.

The key thing to remember is that you need to place the grey card in similar lighting to your subject: for instance, don't place it in a shaded area if your subject is bathed in sunlight. Also, make sure that the card fills the metering area – we would recommend you use spot or partial metering as the card won't need to fill the entire image area, but any is suitable. You can either lock the exposure using your camera's AE-Lock facility or note the aperture and shutter speed, then switch to manual mode and dial in these settings. This latter method isn't suitable on days where lighting is variable. The card has AF reference lines to help your camera's autofocus lock on to it. However, you don't necessarily need it to be in focus to work correctly. The grey card (as well as the white card) can also be used to take a custom White Balance reading from, too.

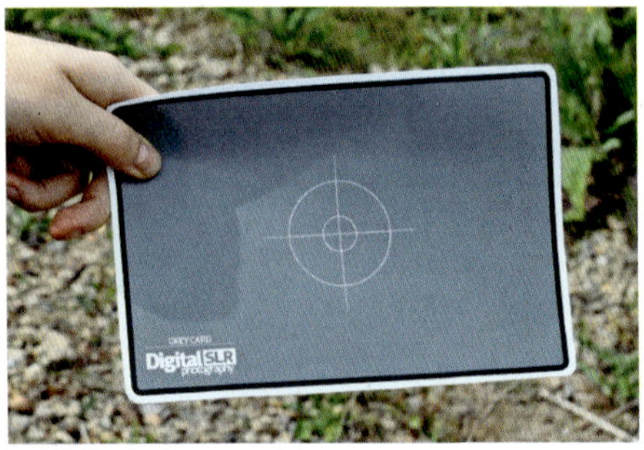

1 GETTING STARTED If you're shooting portraits in difficult lighting conditions, such as backlighting, give your subject the grey card and ask them to hold it angled towards you.

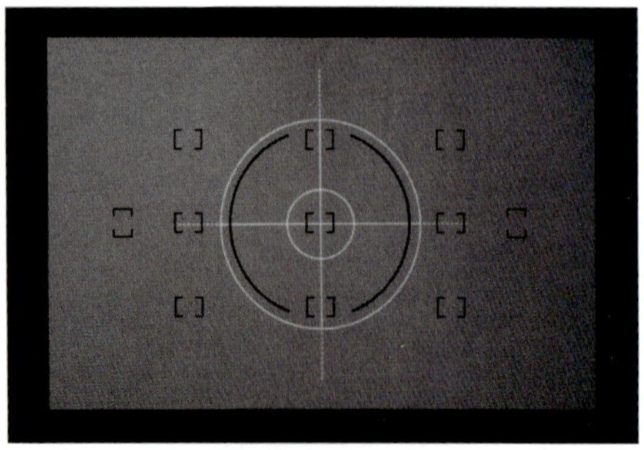

2 TAKE A METER READING Ensure that the entire metering area is filled by the grey card (in this instance, we're using spot metering) and lock the exposure with the AE-Lock button.

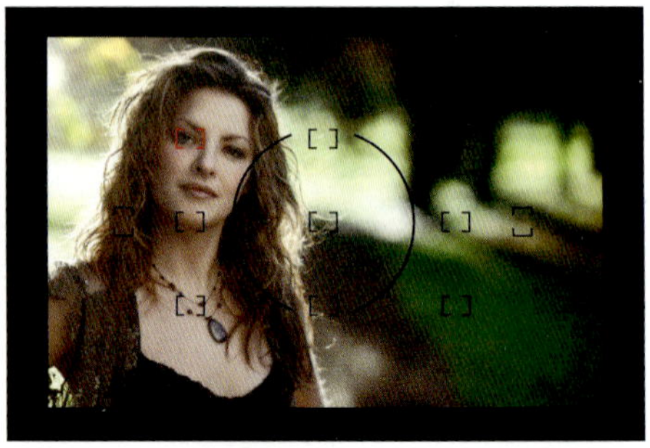

3 COMPOSE & SHOOT With this exposure locked, you can compose your scene and take your shots. When you check it on your LCD monitor, the exposure should be perfect.